CAMBRIDGE

righter Thinking

D1427324

A Level Mathematics for OCR A

Student Book 1 (AS/Year 1)

Vesna Kadelburg, Ben Woolley, Paul Fannon and Stephen Ward

CAMBRIDGE
UNIVERSITY PRESS

University Printing House, Cambridge CB2 8BS, United Kingdom

One Liberty Plaza, 20th Floor, New York, NY 10006, USA

477 Williamstown Road, Port Melbourne, VIC 3207, Australia

314–321, 3rd Floor, Plot 3, Splendor Forum, Jasola District Centre, New Delhi – 110025, India

79 Anson Road, #06–04/06, Singapore 079906

Cambridge University Press is part of the University of Cambridge.

It furthers the University's mission by disseminating knowledge in the pursuit of education, learning and research at the highest international levels of excellence.

www.cambridge.org
Information on this title: www.cambridge.org/9781316644287 (Paperback)
www.cambridge.org/9781316644652 (Paperback with Cambridge Elevate edition)

© Cambridge University Press 2017

This publication is in copyright. Subject to statutory exception
and to the provisions of relevant collective licensing agreements,
no reproduction of any part may take place without the written
permission of Cambridge University Press.

First published 2017

20 19 18 17 16 15 14 13 12 11 10 9 8 7 6 5 4 3

Printed in the United Kingdom by Latimer Trend

A catalogue record for this publication is available from the British Library

ISBN 978-1-316-64428-7 Paperback
ISBN 978-1-316-64465-2 Paperback with Cambridge Elevate edition

Additional resources for this publication at www.cambridge.org/education

Cambridge University Press has no responsibility for the persistence or accuracy
of URLs for external or third-party internet websites referred to in this publication,
and does not guarantee that any content on such websites is, or will remain,
accurate or appropriate.

....

NOTICE TO TEACHERS IN THE UK

It is illegal to reproduce any part of this work in material form (including
photocopying and electronic storage) except under the following circumstances:
(i)   where you are abiding by a licence granted to your school or institution by
      the Copyright Licensing Agency;
(ii) where no such licence exists, or where you wish to exceed the terms of a licence,
      and you have gained the written permission of Cambridge University Press;
(iii) where you are allowed to reproduce without permission under the provisions
      of Chapter 3 of the Copyright, Designs and Patents Act 1988, which covers, for
      example, the reproduction of short passages within certain types of educational
      anthology and reproduction for the purposes of setting examination questions.

....

This resource is endorsed by OCR for use with specification AS Mathematics A (H230)
and specification A Level Mathematics A (H240). In order to gain OCR endorsement, this
resource has undergone an independent quality check. Any references to assessment
and/or assessment preparation are the publisher's interpretation of the specification
requirements and are not endorsed by OCR. OCR recommends that a range of teaching
and learning resources are used in preparing learners for assessment. OCR has not paid for
the production of this resource, nor does OCR receive any royalties from its sale. For more
information about the endorsement process, please visit the OCR website, **www.ocr.org.uk.**

Contents

Introduction

You have probably been told that mathematics is very useful, yet it can often seem like a lot of techniques that just have to be learnt to answer examination questions. You are now getting to the point where you will start to see how some of these techniques can be applied in solving real problems. However, as well as seeing how maths can be useful we hope that anyone working through this book will realise that it can also be incredibly frustrating, surprising and ultimately beautiful.

The book is woven around three key themes from the new curriculum.

Proof

Maths is valued because it trains you to think logically and communicate precisely. At a high level, maths is far less concerned about answers and more about the clear communication of ideas. It is not about being neat – although that might help! It is about creating a coherent argument that other people can easily follow but find difficult to refute. Have you ever tried looking at your own work? If you cannot follow it yourself it is unlikely anybody else will be able to understand it. In maths we communicate using a variety of means – feel free to use combinations of diagrams, words and algebra to aid your argument. And once you have attempted a proof, try presenting it to your peers. Look critically (but positively) at some other people's attempts. It is only through having your own attempts evaluated and trying to find flaws in other proofs that you will develop sophisticated mathematical thinking. This is why we have included lots of common errors in our 'work it out' boxes – just in case your friends don't make any mistakes!

Problem solving

Maths is valued because it trains you to look at situations in unusual, creative ways, to persevere and to evaluate solutions along the way. We have been heavily influenced by a great mathematician and maths educator George Polya, who believed that students were not just born with problem solving skills – they were developed by seeing problems being solved and reflecting on their solutions before trying similar problems. You may not realise it but good mathematicians spend most of their time being stuck.

You need to spend some time on problems you can't do, trying out different possibilities. If after a while you have not cracked it then look at the solution and try a similar problem. Don't be disheartened if you cannot get it immediately – in fact, the longer you spend puzzling over a problem the more you will learn from the solution. You may never need to integrate a rational function in future, but we firmly believe that the problem-solving skills you will develop by trying it can be applied to many other situations.

Modelling

Maths is valued because it helps us solve real-world problems. However maths describes ideal situations and the real world is messy! Modelling is about deciding on the important features needed to describe the essence of a situation and turning that into a mathematical form, then using it to make predictions, compare to reality and possibly improve the model. In many situations the technical maths is actually the easy part – especially with modern technology. Deciding which features of reality to include or ignore and anticipating the consequences of these decisions is the hard part. Yet it is amazing how some fairly drastic assumptions – such as pretending a car is a single point or that people's votes are independent – can result in models which are surprisingly accurate.

More than anything else, this book is about making links. Links between the different chapters, the topics covered and the themes above, links to other subjects and links to the real world. We hope that you will grow to see maths as one great complex but beautiful web of interlinking ideas.

Maths is about so much more than examinations, but we hope that if you take on board these ideas (and do plenty of practice!) you will find maths examinations a much more approachable and possibly even enjoyable experience. However, always remember that the result of what you write down in a few hours by yourself in silence under exam conditions is not the only measure you should consider when judging your mathematical ability – it is only one variable in a much more complicated mathematical model!

How to use this book

Throughout this book you will notice particular features that are designed to aid your learning. This section provides a brief overview of these features.

In this chapter you will learn how to:

- use terms such as identity and equation to describe mathematical objects
- disprove a mathematical idea using a counter example
- use deduction and exhaustion to prove a mathematical idea.

Before you start...				
GCSE	You should know how to use the definition of the square root function.	1	What is $\sqrt{9}$?
GCSE	You should know how to manipulate	2	Factorise $4x^2 - 1$.

Learning objectives
A short summary of the content that you will learn in each chapter.

Before you start
Points you should know from your previous learning and questions to check that you're ready to start the chapter.

WORKED EXAMPLE

The left-hand side shows you how to set out your working. The right-hand side explains the more difficult steps and helps you understand why a particular method was chosen.

Key point

A summary of the most important methods, facts and formulae.

PROOF

Step-by-step walkthroughs of standard proofs and methods of proof.

Explore

Ideas for activities and investigations to extend your understanding of the topic.

WORK IT OUT

Can you identify the correct solution and find the mistakes in the two incorrect solutions?

Tip

Useful guidance, including on ways of calculating or checking and use of technology.

Each chapter ends with a **Checklist of learning and understanding** and a **Mixed practice exercise**, which includes **past paper questions** marked with the icon .

In between chapters, you will find extra sections that bring together topics in a more synoptic way.

Focus on ...

Unique sections relating to the preceding chapters that develop your skills in proof, problem solving and modelling.

CROSS-TOPIC REVIEW EXERCISE

Questions covering topics from across the preceding chapters, testing your ability to apply what you have learnt.

You will find **Paper 1 and Paper 2 practice questions** towards the end of the book, as well as a glossary of key terms (picked out in colour within the chapters), and **answers** to all questions. Full **worked solutions** can be found on the Cambridge Elevate digital platform, along with a **digital version** of this Student Book.

Maths is all about making links, which is why throughout this book you will find signposts emphasising connections between different topics, applications and suggestions for further research.

⏮ Rewind

Reminders of where to find useful information from earlier in your study.

📷 Focus on ...

Links to problem solving, modelling or proof exercises that relate to the topic currently being studied.

⏭ Fast forward

Links to topics that you may cover in greater detail later in your study.

ⓘ Did you know?

Interesting or historical information and links with other subjects to improve your awareness about how mathematics contributes to society.

Some of the links point to the material available only through the **Cambridge Elevate** digital platform.

⬇ Elevate

A support sheet for each chapter contains further worked examples and exercises on the most common question types. Extension sheets provide further challenge for the more ambitious.

✔ Gateway to A Level

GCSE transition material that provides a summary of facts and methods you need to know before you start a new topic, with worked examples and practice questions.

Colour-coding of exercises

The questions in the exercises are designed to provide careful progression, ranging from basic fluency to practice questions. They are uniquely colour-coded, as shown here.

1 By factorising, solve the following equations:

  a   **i** $3x^2 + 2x = x^2 + 3x + 6$ **ii** $2x^2 + 3 = 17x - 7 - x^2$

  b   **i** $9x^2 = 24x - 16$ **ii** $18x^2 = 2x^2 - 40x - 25$

  c   **i** $(x - 3)(x + 2) = 14$ **ii** $(2x + 3)(x - 1) = 12$

9 Do two lines that never meet have to be parallel?

3 Use an appropriate substitution to solve $x^2 + \dfrac{9}{x^2} = 10$.

8 The gradient of the graph of $y = e^{ax}$ at the point where $y = 4.6$ equals -1.2. Find the value of x at the point where the gradient is -5.

9   **a**   Find the value of k so that $8^x = e^{kx}$.

      b   Hence find the gradient of the graph of $y = 8^x$ at the point where $x = -0.5$.

Black – drill questions. These come in several parts, each with subparts **i** and **ii.** You only need attempt subpart **i** at first; subpart **ii** is essentially the same question, which you can use for further practice if you got part **i** wrong, for homework, or when you revisit the exercise during revision.

Green – practice questions at a basic level.

Yellow – designed to encourage reflection and discussion.

Blue – practice questions at an intermediate level.

Red – practice questions at an advanced level.

A – indicates content that is for A Level students only

AS – indicates content that is for AS Level students only

Working with the large data set

As part of your course you are expected to work with the large data set covering different methods of transport and age distributions in different parts of the country and in different years. This large data set is an opportunity to explore statistics in real life. As well as supporting the ideas introduced in Chapters 16 and 18 we shall be using the large data set to guide you through four key themes. All of these themes will be explored with examples and questions in the large data set section in the Cambridge Elevate edition. You will not have to work with the full data set in the final examination, but familiarity with it will help you as many examination questions will be set in the context of this data set.

Practical difficulties with data

Unlike most textbook or examination problems, the real world is messy. Often there are difficulties with being overwhelmed by too much data, or perhaps there are errors, missing items or labels which are ambiguous. For example, how do you deal with the fact that in 2001 Cornwall was made up of separate districts that were later combined into a single unitary authority, if you want to compare areas over time? If you are grouping data for a histogram, how big a difference does it make where you choose to put the class boundaries?

Using technology

Modern statistics is heavily based on familiarity with technology. We will be encouraging you to use spreadsheets and graphing packages, looking at the common tools available to help simplify calculations and present data effectively.

One important technique we can employ with modern technology is simulation. We will try to gain a better understanding of hypothesis testing by using the data set to simulate the effect of sampling on making inferences about the population.

Thinking critically about statistics

Why might someone want to use a pie chart rather than a histogram? Whenever statistics are calculated or data sets are represented graphically, some information is lost and some information is highlighted. An important part of modern statistics is to ask critical questions about the way evidence provided by statistics is used to support arguments.

One important part of this is the idea of validating statistics. For example, with the information presented it is not clear which category or categories a person would be included in if they travel to work by bicycle on some days and take the bus on others. We will look at ways in which we can interrogate the data to try to understand it more.

Statistical problem solving

Technology can often do calculations for us. However the art of modern statistics is deciding what calculations to do on what data. One of the big difficulties is that we rarely have exactly the data we want, so we have to make indirect inferences from the data we have. For example, you will probably not see newspaper headlines saying 'the correlation coefficient between median age and percentage of people cycling to work is 0.64', but you might see something saying 'Pensioners promote pedalling!' Deciding on an appropriate statistical technique to determine whether older people are more likely to use a bicycle and then interpreting results is the type of thing which is hard to examine but very valuable in real-world statistics.

There are lots of decisions to be made. Should you use the total number of cyclists in an area? Or the percentage of people who cycle? Or the percentage of people who travel to work who cycle? We shall see how the answer to your main question depends on decisions like these.

1 Proof and mathematical communication

In this chapter you will learn how to:

- use terms such as identity and equation to describe mathematical objects
- disprove a mathematical idea using a counter example
- use deduction and exhaustion to prove a mathematical idea.

Before you start...

GCSE	You should know how to use the definition of the square root function.	1	What is $\sqrt{9}$?
GCSE	You should know how to manipulate algebraic expressions.	2	Factorise $4x^2 - 1$.
GCSE	You should know basic angle facts.	3	a What is the sum of the angles in a triangle? b What is the sum of the exterior angles of any polygon?
GCSE	You should be able to define rational and irrational numbers.	4	Which of these numbers are irrational? $\pi, 0.\dot{3}, 0.5, \sqrt{2}$
GCSE	You should be able to work with function notation.	5	If $f(x) = 2x^2 - 3$ find $f(3)$.

Why is proof important?

One thing for which mathematicians are valued is their ability to communicate their ideas precisely and to make very convincing arguments, called proofs. In this chapter we will look at the language used by mathematicians and some of the ways they prove their ideas.

Section 1: Mathematical structures and arguments

We can represent mathematical ideas in many different ways such as tables, diagrams, graphs or words. One of the most fundamental representations is an **equation**: a mathematical statement involving an '=' sign. For example:

$$x^2 - 1 = 8$$

An equation is only true for some values of x (or perhaps none); in this case it is true for $x = \pm 3$.

Another similar mathematical structure is called an **identity**. An identity is a relation which is true for **all** values of the unknown. It is given the $\equiv$ symbol.

 Did you know?

The first recorded use of the equals sign occurs in Robert Recorde's 1557 book *The Whetstone of Witte*. He explains that he used two parallel lines 'because no two things can be more equal'.

For example, $x^2 - 1 \equiv (x-1)(x+1)$.

Two statements connected by the identity symbol are called **congruent expressions**. They are equal for **all** values of the variable(s).

There are some rules which only apply to identities. For example, if two polynomials are identically equal then their coefficients must be the same.

 Tip

A **polynomial** is a function that is a sum of terms containing non-negative (positive or zero) integer powers of x.

A **coefficient** is the constant in front of (multiplying) a variable. For example, in the quadratic $2x^2 - 3x$, 2 is the coefficient of x^2 and -3 is the coefficient of x.

The word **integer** just means 'whole number'.

 Tip

Whenever you are simplifying an expression, technically you should use an identity symbol ($\equiv$). However, it is common in mathematics to use an equals sign ($=$) instead.

 Fast forward

In Chapter 3 you will see that you often have to write quadratics in the form shown here.

WORKED EXAMPLE 1.1

$2x^2 + 12x - 3 \equiv a(x+p)^2 + q$

Find the value of a, p and q.

$2x^2 + 12x - 3 \equiv a(x+p)^2 + q$ .... Multiply out the brackets to allow coefficients to be compared.

$\equiv a(x^2 + 2px + p^2) + q$

$\equiv ax^2 + 2apx + ap^2 + q$

Coefficient of x^2: $2 = a$ .... Compare coefficients. The two expressions are equal for all values of x, so all the coefficients must be equal.

Coefficient of x: $12 = 2ap$

Constant term: $-3 = ap^2 + q$

$4p = 12$ .... Substitute $a = 2$ into the second equation.

$p = 3$

$2 \times 3^2 + q = -3$ .... Substitute $a = 2$, $p = 3$ into the third equation.

$q = -21$

Another common structure in mathematics is called a **function**. This is just a rule for changing an input into an output.

For example, if you have a function called f that transforms the number x into $\sqrt{x^2 + 9}$ you would write that as $f(x) = \sqrt{x^2 + 9}$.

So $f(4) = \sqrt{4^2 + 9} = \sqrt{25} = 5$ and $f(y) = \sqrt{y^2 + 9}$.

 Gateway to A Level

See Gateway to A Level section A for a reminder of expanding brackets.

Implication and equivalence

You can manipulate both equations and inequalities by doing the same thing to both sides. You often structure your solution by writing lines of working underneath each other. In more formal work, you can emphasise the logic of the argument by using special symbols.

Key point 1.1

- The symbol $\Rightarrow$ means that a subsequent equation follows from the previous one.

    $P \Rightarrow Q$ means 'P implies Q' or 'if P is true then Q is true' or 'P is sufficient for Q'.

- The symbol $\Leftarrow$ means that the previous statement follows from the subsequent statement.

    $P \Leftarrow Q$ means 'P is implied by Q' or 'if Q is true then P is true' or 'P is necessary for Q'

- The symbol $\Leftrightarrow$ means that a subsequent equation is equivalent to the previous one.

    $P \Leftrightarrow Q$ means 'P is equivalent to Q' or 'Q is true if and only if P is true'.

    This can also be written in the shorthand 'Q iff P'.

You will also sometimes see the symbol $\therefore$ for 'therefore,' which means we are drawing a conclusion from previous lines of working.

WORKED EXAMPLE 1.2

Insert either a $\Rightarrow$ or a $\Leftrightarrow$ symbol on each line of working:

a $2x + 1 = 9$
$\quad 2x = 8$
$\quad\quad x = 4$

b $\quad x = 4$
$\quad x^2 = 16$

a $2x + 1 = 9$	
$\Leftrightarrow 2x = 8$	These statements are equivalent: the logic flows both ways.
$\Leftrightarrow x = 4$	Again $2x = 8$ and $x = 4$ are equivalent.
b $x = 4$	$x = 4$ implies that $x^2 = 16$ but the reverse is not true as
$\Rightarrow x^2 = 16$	$x^2 = 16$ implies $x = \pm 4$ (not just $x = 4$).

When solving equations, it is important to know whether or not each line of working is equivalent to the previous one. If it is, then you can be sure that you have found the complete set of solutions. For example:

$$x^2 - x = 2$$
$$\Leftrightarrow x^2 - x - 2 = 0$$
$$\Leftrightarrow (x - 2)(x + 1) = 0$$
$$\Leftrightarrow x = 2 \text{ or } -1$$

From this chain of equivalences you can be certain that both 2 and −1 are solutions of the equation, and that there are no others.

However, if some of the lines are only connected by implications, it is possible to find 'solutions' which don't actually work, or to miss some of the solutions.

✓ **Gateway to A Level**

See Gateway to A Level sections B and C for a reminder of solving quadratic equations by factorising.

WORKED EXAMPLE 1.3

A student is attempting to solve the equation $\sqrt{x+6}=x$.

a Find the error with the following:

$\sqrt{x+6}=x$

$x+6=x^2$

$x^2-x-6=0$

$(x-3)(x+2)=0$

$x=3$ or $x=-2$

b Solve the equation correctly.

a $\sqrt{x+6}=x$
$\Rightarrow x+6=x^2$

Look at each line in turn to see whether a $\Leftrightarrow$ symbol is valid.

They are not equivalent since:

$x+6=x^2$
$\Rightarrow \pm\sqrt{x+6}=x$

The first line implies the second, but the second does not imply the first, so they are not equivalent.

This leads to one incorrect solution, coming from $-\sqrt{x+6}=x$.

All subsequent lines are equivalent, so one of the solutions is correct.

b Check both "solutions":
$x=3$: $\sqrt{(3+6)}=3$, so this is a solution.

$x=-2$: $\sqrt{(-2+6)}=2 \neq -2$, so this is not a solution.

$\therefore$ The correct solution is $x=3$.

You need to check both solutions: substitute the x values into the LHS and the RHS and check whether they are equal.

💡 **Tip**

Squaring an equation is a common way of introducing incorrect solutions since it prevents lines of working being equivalent.

💡 **Tip**

LHS and RHS are standard abbreviations for the left-hand side and right-hand side of an equation.

In practice it is often easier not to worry about whether every line is equivalent, but to be aware that the 'solutions' you get need to be checked by substituting them back into the original equation. Any that are not correct can then just be deleted.

Dividing by zero can remove solutions in the same way that squaring can introduce them.

⏩ **Fast forward**

You will also see this problem arise when you solve equations involving logarithms in Chapter 7.

WORKED EXAMPLE 1.4

Insert an appropriate $\Rightarrow$, $\Leftarrow$ or a $\Leftrightarrow$ symbol in the space marked $\square$. Hence explain why the solution is incomplete.

$$x^2 = 6x$$

Dividing by x:

$$\square\, x = 6$$

$\square$ is a $\Leftarrow$ .... If $x = 6$ then $x^2 = 6x$, but the reverse is not always true...

So $x = 6$ may not be the only solution –
in this case there is also the possibility
that $x = 0$.

EXERCISE 1A

1 If $f(x) = x^2 + 1$, find and simplify where possible:

a **i** $f(2)$ **ii** $f(3)$

b **i** $2f(1) + f(4)$ **ii** $f(5) - f(3)$

c **i** $f(x)$ **ii** $f(y)$

d **i** $f(2x)$ **ii** $f(3y)$

e **i** $f(x + 1)$ **ii** $f(x - 2)$

> **▶▶I) Fast forward**
>
> **A** You will learn more about functions in Student Book 2, Chapter 5.

2 Where appropriate insert a $\Rightarrow$, $\Leftarrow$ or a $\Leftrightarrow$ symbol in the space marked $\square$.

a **i** Shape P is a rectangle. $\square$ Shape P is a square.

    ii Shape Q is a quadrilateral. $\square$ Shape Q is a rhombus.

b **i** n is even. $\square$ n is a whole number.

    ii n is a prime number. $\square$ n is a whole number.

c **i** A triangle has two equal sides. $\square$ A triangle has two equal angles.

    ii Two circles have the same area $\square$ Two circles have the same radius.

d **i** $x^2 - 2x - 3 = 0$ $\square$ $x = 3$

    ii $x^2 - 2x + 1 = 0$ $\square$ $x = 1$

e **i** Sam can do 10 press-ups. $\square$ Sam can do 100 press-ups.

    ii Niamh is over 21. $\square$ Niamh is over 18.

f **i** Neither A nor B is true. $\square$ A is false and B is false.

    ii A and B are not both true. $\square$ A and B are both not true.

g **i** Chris is a boy. ☐ Chris is a footballer.

ii Shape X is a right-angled triangle. ☐ Shape X is an isosceles triangle.

3 $x^3 - 4x^2 - 3x + 18 = (x + a)(x - b)^2$ for all x. Find the values of a and b.

4 $x^4 + 8x^3 + 2x + 16 = (x^3 + a)(x + b)$ for all x. Find the values of a and b.

5 What is the flaw in the following working?

Question: For $x = 4$, find the value of $2x + 2$

Working: $2 \times 4 = 8 + 2 = 10$

6 Where is the flaw in the following argument?

Suppose $1 = 3$

Subtract 2: $-1 = 1$

Square: $1 = 1$

Therefore the first line is true.

7 Consider the equation $\sqrt{x^2 + 9} = 3x - 7$.

a Add appropriate symbols ($\Leftrightarrow$ or $\Rightarrow$) to each line of working in the solution shown.

$\sqrt{x^2 + 9} = 3x - 7$

Square: $x^2 + 9 = 9x^2 - 42x + 49$

Subtract $x^2 + 9$: $0 = 8x^2 - 42x + 40$

Divide by 2: $0 = 4x^2 - 21x + 20$

Factorise: $0 = (4x - 5)(x - 4)$

$x = \dfrac{5}{4}$ or $x = 4$

b Hence explain the flaw in the solution shown.

8 **a** Insert appropriate symbols ($\Rightarrow$, $\Leftarrow$ or $\Leftrightarrow$) in the spaces marked ☐.

$\dfrac{1}{x^2} = \dfrac{2}{x}$

☐ $x = 2x^2$

☐ $0 = 2x^2 - x$

☐ $0 = x(2x - 1)$

☐ $x = 0$ or $x = \dfrac{1}{2}$

b Hence explain the error in the working.

9 **a** Insert appropriate symbols ($\Rightarrow$, $\Leftarrow$ or $\Leftarrow$) in the spaces marked ☐.

$x^2 + 3x = 4x + 12$

☐ $x(x + 3) = 4(x + 3)$

☐ $x = 4$

b Hence explain the error in the working.

---

i **Did you know?**

In all of these examples, we are assuming that each statement is either true or false. The study of this type of logic is called Boolean algebra.

10 Do you agree with the following statement?

Either A or B is true $\Leftrightarrow$ A and B are not both true.

11 Where is the flaw in the following argument?

Suppose two numbers a and b are equal.

$$a = b$$

Multiply by a: $\qquad a^2 = ab$

Subtract b^2: $\qquad a^2 - b^2 = ab - b^2$

Factorise: $\qquad (a - b)(a + b) = b(a - b)$

Cancel $(a - b)$: $\qquad (a + b) = b$

Use the fact that $a = b$: $\quad 2b = b$

Divide by b: $\qquad 2 = 1$

i) Did you know?

The word 'or' can be ambiguous. In formal logical we use the terms OR and XOR to have two different meanings.

Section 2: Inequality notation

You know from your previous study that solving a linear inequality is just like solving an equation, as long as you don't multiply or divide by a negative number. Your answer is written as an inequality.

For example:

$$2x - 5 \geqslant 9$$

$$\Leftrightarrow 2x \geqslant 14$$

$$\Leftrightarrow x \geqslant 7$$

This solution can be written in **set notation**: $\{x : x \geqslant 7\}$.

This is read as 'x such that x is greater than or equal to 7'.

It can also be written in **interval notation**: $[7, \infty)$. This means that the solution lies in the interval from 7 (included) to infinity (not included).

It is assumed that x is a real number ($x \in \mathbb{R}$) unless stated otherwise. So the interval $[7, \infty)$ includes all the real numbers greater than or equal to 7, and the interval $(-\infty, 7)$ all the real numbers smaller than 7. Note that infinity (∞) is not a real number, so can never be included in the interval.

✓ Gateway to A Level

For a reminder and more practice of solving linear inequalities, see Gateway to A Level section D.

💡 Tip

The $\in$ symbol in set notation means 'is in the set...' or 'belongs to the set...'

🔑 Key point 1.2

- $x \in (a, b)$ means $a < x < b$
- $x \in [a, b]$ means $a \leqslant x \leqslant b$
- $x \in [a, b)$ means $a \leqslant x < b$
- $x \in (a, b]$ means $a < x \leqslant b$

Two different intervals can be combined using notation taken from set theory:

Key point 1.3

$x \in A \cup B$ means that x can be in either A or B (or both). $A \cup B$ is called the **union** of A and B.

$x \in A \cap B$ means that x is in both A and B. $A \cap B$ is called the **intersection** of A and B.

If there are no solutions to the inequality we can write $x \in \varnothing$, where $\varnothing$ is the symbol for the **empty set**.

WORKED EXAMPLE 1.5

Write the following in set notation:

a $1 \leqslant x < 7$
b $x > 1$ or $x < -2$
c $x < 2$ and $x > 4$

a $\{x : x \geqslant 1\} \cap \{x : x < 7\}$

x is **both** greater than or equal to 1, **and** less than 7 so you need the intersection.

b $\{x : x > 1\} \cup \{x : x < -2\}$

x is greater than 1 **or** less than -2 so you need the union.

c $x \in \varnothing$.

No values of x are both smaller than 2 and greater than 4.

EXERCISE 1B

1 Write the following inequalities in set notation and interval notation.

    a **i** $x > 7$ **ii** $x < 6$

    b **i** $x \leqslant 10$ **ii** $x \geqslant 5$

    c **i** $0 < x \leqslant 1$ **ii** $5 < x < 7$

    d **i** $x > 5$ or $x \leqslant 0$ **ii** $x \geqslant 10$ or $x < 2$

2 Write the following statements as inequalities in x.

    a **i** $x \in [1, 4)$ **ii** $x \in (2, 8]$

    b **i** $x \in [1, 3]$ **ii** $x \in (2, 4)$

    c **i** $x \in (-\infty, 5)$ **ii** $x \in [12, \infty)$

    d **i** $\{x : 0 < x < 10\} \cap \{x : x \geqslant 8\}$ **ii** $\{x : 1 < x < 4\} \cap \{x : x \geqslant 3\}$

3 Represent the following intervals on a number line.

   a   **i** $(1, 5]$ **ii** $[-2, 1]$

   b   **i** $(-\infty, 4) \cap (-2, \infty)$ **ii** $(-\infty, 0) \cap [-5, \infty)$

   c   **i** $(-\infty, 3] \cap (0, 3)$ **ii** $[-2, 5] \cap (2, 5)$

   d   **i** $[2, 5) \cup (7, \infty)$ **ii** $(-\infty, -3] \cup (0, 5]$

4 Write the following statements using intervals combined using set notation. Rewrite each as a single interval if possible.

   a   **i** $1 \leqslant x \leqslant 3$ and $x > 2$ **b**   **ii** $x \leqslant -1$ and $1 < x < 3$

   c   **i** $x \leqslant -2$ or $x \geqslant 2$ **d**   **ii** $1 \leqslant x < 5$ or $x \geqslant 7$

5 Solve the following inequalities and express your solution using interval notation.

   a   **i** $\dfrac{x}{2} + 1 \leqslant \dfrac{3x}{5}$ **ii** $2x - 1 > \dfrac{4x}{3} + 3$

   b   **i** $-5 \leqslant \dfrac{x}{3} - 1 < 3$ **ii** $4 < \dfrac{3x}{2} - 2 \leqslant 7$

   c   **i** $\dfrac{3x - 2}{5} > \dfrac{x + 1}{2}$ **ii** $\dfrac{x - 3}{7} \geqslant \dfrac{2x + 1}{3}$

Section 3: Disproof by counter example

It is usually not possible to prove that something is always true by looking at examples. However, it is possible to use examples to prove that something is **not** always true. This is called a **counter example**.

WORKED EXAMPLE 1.6

Disprove by counter example that $(x + 1)^2 = x^2 + 1$ for all x.

When $x = 2$:

LHS: $(2 + 1)^2 = 9$

RHS: $2^2 + 1 = 5$

So $x = 2$ is a counter example.

> When searching for a counter example, try different types of numbers.

EXERCISE 1C

1   Disprove the statement $\sqrt{x^2 + 9} \equiv x + 3$.

2   Use a counter example to prove that $2x \not\equiv 2 \sin x$.

3   Use a counter example to prove that $\sqrt{x^2}$ is not always x.

4   Prove that the product of two prime numbers is not always odd.

 Gateway to A Level

For a reminder of rational and irrational numbers, see Gateway to A Level section E.

5 Prove that the number of factors of a number is not always even.

6 Prove that the sum of two irrational numbers is not always irrational.

7 Use a counter example to disprove the following statement:

$$x < 3 \Rightarrow x^2 < 9$$

8 A student claims that $n^2 + n + 41$ takes prime values for all positive integers. Use a counter example to disprove this claim.

9 Do two lines that never meet have to be parallel?

Section 4: Proof by deduction

Proving a result is usually much harder than disproving it. You need to start with what is given in the question and form a series of logical steps to reach the required conclusion.

Algebra is a useful tool that allows you to express ideas in general terms. You will often need to use algebraic expressions for even and odd numbers. For example, it is common to express:

- an even number as $2n$, for some integer n
- an odd number as $2n + 1$, for some integer n.

Focus on …

The Focus on … sections in this book show you proofs of some important results you will meet in this course.

WORKED EXAMPLE 1.7

Prove that the product of an even and an odd number is always even.

Let the even number be $2n$, for some integer n.	Define a general even number.
Let the odd number be $2m + 1$, for some integer m.	And define a general odd number. Note that you mustn't use $2n + 1$ as that would be the next integer up from $2n$, which would be a specific odd number, not a general one.
$2n(2m + 1) = 2(2mn + n)$ $\qquad\qquad = 2k$ for some integer k.	Aim to write the product in the form $2k$ to show that it is even.
So this is even.	Make a conclusion.

WORKED EXAMPLE 1.8

Prove that the difference between the squares of consecutive odd numbers is always a multiple of 8.

Let the smaller odd number be $2n - 1$

Let the larger odd number be $2n + 1$

Define two consecutive odd numbers. This time you **do** want n in both, as the two numbers are related.

$(2n + 1)^2 - (2n - 1)^2 = (4n^2 + 4n + 1) -$
$(4n^2 - 4n + 1)$
$= 4n + 4n$
$= 8n$

Square each, and subtract the smaller from the larger.

So this is a multiple of 8.

Make a conclusion.

EXERCISE 1D

1 Prove that if n is odd then n^2 is also odd.

2 Prove that the sum of an even number and an odd number is odd.

3 Prove that the sum of any three consecutive integers is always a multiple of three.

4 Prove that:

  a the sum of two consecutive multiples of 5 is always odd

  b the product of two consecutive multiples of 5 is always even.

5 Prove that the height, h, in the following diagram is given by $h = \dfrac{ab}{\sqrt{a^2 + b^2}}$.

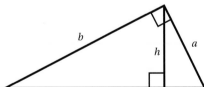

6 Prove that the sum of the interior angles of a hexagon is 720°.

7 Prove that if a number leaves a remainder 2 when it is divided by 3 then its square leaves a remainder 1 when divided by 3.

8 **a** Expand $(x + 2)^2$.

  b Prove the statement: $y = x^2 + 4x + 10 \Rightarrow y > 0$.

9 Prove that an exterior angle in a triangle is the sum of the two opposite angles.

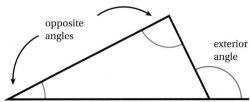

> **Elevate**
>
> For a further example on algebraic proof and more practice questions, see Support sheet 1.

10 Prove that $n^2 + 3n + 2$ is never prime if n is a positive integer.

11 **a** Let n be a four-digit whole number '*abcd*'. Explain why $n = 1000a + 100b + 10c + d$.

    b Prove that n is divisible by 9 if and only if $a + b + c + d$ is a multiple of 9.

    c Prove that n is divisible by 11 if and only if $a - b + c - d$ is divisible by 11.

12 By considering $\left(\sqrt{2}^{\sqrt{2}}\right)^{\sqrt{2}}$, prove that an irrational number raised to an irrational power can be rational.

Section 5: Proof by exhaustion

You should be aware that simply considering some examples does not constitute a mathematical proof. However, in some situations it is possible to check **all** possibilities and this can lead to a valid proof. This is called **proof by exhaustion**.

WORKED EXAMPLE 1.9

Prove that 89 is a prime number.

We only need to check prime numbers smaller than the square root of 89, since any factor above this would have to be paired with a factor below the square root.

> A prime number does not have any prime factors smaller than itself.

89 is not divisible by 2, 3, 5 or 7. Therefore it must be a prime number.

WORKED EXAMPLE 1.10

A whole number is squared and divided by 3. Prove that the remainder can only be 0 or 1.

> You cannot check all whole numbers, but you can split them into three groups when considering division by 3: those that give no remainder, those that give remainder 1 and those that give remainder 2. You can then check what squaring does to numbers from each group.

Let n be a whole number.

> Now use algebra to write each type of number.

Then n is either a multiple of 3 ($n = 3k$)

or one more than a multiple of 3 ($n = 3k + 1$)

or two more than a multiple of 3 ($n = 3k + 2$)

Continues on next page ...

If $n = 3k$ then $n^2 = (3k)^2 = 9k^2$ .... Now check what happens when you square each type of number.

which is a multiple of 3.

If $n = 3k + 1$ then

$n^2 = (3k+1)^2 = 9k^2 + 6k + 1$

$= 3(3k^2 + 2k) + 1$

which is one more than a multiple of 3.

If $n = 3k + 2$ then

$n^2 = (3k+2)^2 = 9k^2 + 12k + 4$

$= 3(3k^2 + 4k + 1) + 1$

which is one more than a multiple of 3.

So there is either no .... You have now checked each possible whole
remainder or the remainder is 1. number, so you can write the conclusion.

🔍 Explore

Proof by exhaustion can only be used when there is a relatively small number of possibilities to check. The use of computers has made it possible to apply this method to a wider variety of problems (although some mathematicians question whether we can always trust a computer check). Find out about the Four Colour Theorem – one of the most famous problems that has been solved in this way.

EXERCISE 1E

1 Prove that 11 is a prime number.

2 Prove that 83 is a prime number.

3 Prove that all regular polygons with fewer than 7 sides have angles with a whole number of degrees.

4 Prove that no square number less than 100 ends in a 7.

5 Let $f(x)$ be the function that gives the number of factors of x. For example, $f(10) = 4$ because it has factors 1, 2, 5 and 10.

Prove that for any single digit positive number $f(n) \leqslant n$.

6 Prove that $n^2 + 2$ is not divisible by 4 for integers between 1 and 5 inclusive.

✔ **Gateway to A Level**

See Gateway to A Level section F for a reminder of function notation.

7   Prove that $n^2 + n$ is always even if $n \in \mathbb{Z}$.

8   Prove that when the square of a whole number is divided by 5, the remainder is either 0, 1 or 4.

9   Prove that $2x^3 + 3x^2 + x$ is always divisible by 6 if x is an integer.

10   The modulus function, $|x|$, is defined as x if x is positive and $-x$ if x is negative so, for example, $|-2| = 2$ and $|5| = 5$. $|0|$ is defined to be 0.

Prove the triangle inequality: $|a + b| \leqslant |a| + |b|$.

 **Fast forward**

You will learn more about the modulus function in Student Book 2.

✎ Checklist of learning and understanding

- You can express mathematical ideas using descriptions such as diagrams, equations and identities.
- You can communicate a mathematical argument using a series of equations or identities put together in a logical order.

  These can be connected using implication symbols: $\Rightarrow$ or $\Leftrightarrow$.

  - The symbol $\Rightarrow$ means that a subsequent statement follows from the previous one.

  - The symbol $\Leftrightarrow$ means that a subsequent statement is equivalent to the previous one.

- An identity is a relation that is true for **all** values of the unknown. It is given the $\equiv$ symbol.
- You can represent solutions of inequalities using set notation or interval notation.

  - In interval notation, the square bracket [or] means that the endpoint is included, and the round bracket (or) means that the endpoint is **not** included.

- One counter example is sufficient to prove that a statement is not always true.
- An algebraic proof is often required to show that a statement is always true.
- Proof by exhaustion involves checking all possibilities. This can only be done if there is a small number of options, or the options can be split up into a small number of cases.

Mixed practice 1

1 Prove that the product of any two odd numbers is always odd.

2 Prove that if n is even then n^2 is divisible by 4.

3 Prove that if $\dfrac{a}{b} = \dfrac{c}{d}$ it does not follow that $a = c$ and $b = d$.

4 Prove the following statement or disprove it with a counter example:

'The sum of two numbers is always larger than their difference.'

5 Prove that the product of two rational numbers is always rational.

6 Prove that the sum of the interior angles in an n-sided shape is $(180n - 360)°$.

7 Given that $x^3 + y^3 \equiv (x + y)(ax^2 + bxy + cy^2)$ find the values of a, b and c.

8 Prove the following statement:

n is odd $\Rightarrow n^2 + 4n + 3$ is a multiple of 4

9 Prove that the angle from a chord to the centre of a circle is twice the angle to a point on the circumference in the major sector.

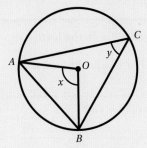

10 Prove that all cube numbers are either multiples of 9 or within one of a multiple of 9.

11 Prove the following statements, or disprove them with a counter example:

a ab is an integer $\Leftrightarrow$ a is an integer and b is an integer

b a is irrational and b is irrational $\Leftrightarrow$ ab is irrational.

12 Prove that the product of any three consecutive positive integers is a multiple of 6.

13 Prove that the difference between the squares of any two odd numbers is a multiple of 8.

14 **a** Prove that $n^2 - 79n + 1601$ is not always prime when n is a positive whole number.

b Prove that $n^2 - 1$ is never prime when n is a whole number greater than 2.

15 $x = a^2 - b^2$ where a and b are both whole numbers. Prove that x is either odd or a multiple of 4.

 Elevate

For questions on another principle used in proof, see Extension sheet 1.

2 Indices and surds

In this chapter you will learn how to:

- use laws of indices
- work with expressions involving square roots (called surds).

Before you start…

GCSE	You should know how to evaluate expressions involving powers, including working with the order of operations.	1	Evaluate 3×2^3.
GCSE	You should know how to evaluate expressions involving roots.	2	Evaluate $\sqrt[3]{27}$.
GCSE	You should know how to work with negative, fractional and zero indices.	3	a Write $\dfrac{2x^0}{x^3}$ in the form ax^b. b Write $\dfrac{1}{\sqrt[3]{x^2}}$ in the form x^d.
GCSE	You should know how to multiply out two brackets.	4	Expand $(1+x)(2-y)$.
GCSE	You should be able to recognise the difference of two squares.	5	Expand and simplify $(2a+b)(2a-b)$.

Why study indices and surds?

Powers and roots are needed to write equations describing many situations, both within pure mathematics and in applications. For example, the volume of a sphere is proportional to the cube of its radius; the magnitude of the gravitational force between two objects is inversely proportional to the square of the distance between them; and standard deviation (a measure of the spread of data in statistics) is the square root of the average square deviation from the mean.

In this chapter you will review algebraic rules for working with powers and roots and use them to simplify more complex expressions.

Section 1: Using the laws of indices

From your previous study you should know the following laws of indices:

 Gateway to A Level

For a reminder and more practice of the laws of indices, see Gateway to A Level section G.

🔑 Key point 2.1

- $a^m \times a^n = a^{m+n}$
- $a^m \div a^n = a^{m-n}$
- $(a^m)^n = a^{m \times n}$
- $a^0 = 1$
- $a^{-n} = \dfrac{1}{a^n}$
- $a^{\frac{m}{n}} = \left(\sqrt[n]{a}\right)^m = \sqrt[n]{a^m}$

You can use these rules to evaluate negative and fractional powers of numbers. For example:

$$8^{\frac{2}{3}} = \left(8^{\frac{1}{3}}\right)^2 = \left(\sqrt[3]{8}\right)^2 = 2^2 = 4.$$

The rules of indices must be combined accurately with the other rules of algebra you already know.

💡 Tip

Make sure that you can actively use these rules in **both** directions – i.e. if you see 2^6 you can rewrite it as $(2^3)^2$ and if you see $(2^3)^2$ you can rewrite it as 2^6. Both ways will be important!

⏩ Fast forward

To formally prove these rules requires a method called **mathematical induction**, which you will meet if you study Further Mathematics, in Pure Core Student Book 1.

WORKED EXAMPLE 2.1

Simplify $3xy \times 8xy^{-2}$.

$3xy \times 8xy^{-2} = 3 \times 8 \times x \times x \times y \times y^{-2}$

> You can rearrange multiplication into any convenient order.

$= 24x^2y^{-1}$

> Apply $a^m \times a^n = a^{m+n}$ (Key point 2.1) to x and y.

WORKED EXAMPLE 2.2

Simplify $\dfrac{12ab^{-2} - 16a}{8ab}$.

$\dfrac{12ab^{-2} - 16a}{8ab} = \dfrac{12ab^{-2}}{8ab} - \dfrac{16a}{8ab}$

> You can split a fraction up if the top is a sum or a difference.

$= \dfrac{12}{8} \times \dfrac{a}{a} \times \dfrac{b^{-2}}{b} - \dfrac{16}{8} \times \dfrac{a}{a} \times \dfrac{1}{b}$

> Turn each fraction into a convenient product.

$= \dfrac{3}{2}b^{-3} - 2b^{-1}$

> Then use $a^m \div a^n = a^{m-n}$ (Key point 2.1).

WORKED EXAMPLE 2.3

Write $\dfrac{\sqrt{x}}{5\sqrt[3]{x}}$ in the form kx^p.

$\dfrac{\sqrt{x}}{5\sqrt[3]{x}} = \dfrac{1}{5} \times x^{\frac{1}{2}} \div x^{\frac{1}{3}}$ .... | Dividing by 5 is the same as multiplying by $\dfrac{1}{5}$.

Re-write the roots using $a^{\frac{m}{n}} = \sqrt[n]{a^m}$ (Key point 2.1).

$= \dfrac{1}{5} x^{\frac{1}{6}}$ .... | Now use $a^m \div a^n = a^{m-n}$ (Key point 2.1).

You also need to be able to manipulate indices to solve equations.

WORKED EXAMPLE 2.4

Solve $x^{\frac{4}{3}} = \dfrac{1}{81}$.

$x^{\frac{4}{3}} = \dfrac{1}{81}$

$\left(x^{\frac{4}{3}}\right)^{\frac{3}{4}} = \left(\dfrac{1}{81}\right)^{\frac{3}{4}}$ .... | Using $(a^m)^n = a^{m \times n}$ (Key point 2.1), $\left(x^{\frac{4}{3}}\right)^{\frac{3}{4}} = x^{\frac{4}{3} \times \frac{3}{4}} = x^1 = x$ so raise both sides of the equation to the power $\dfrac{3}{4}$.

$x = \dfrac{1}{27}$

WORKED EXAMPLE 2.5

Solve $2^x \times 8^{x-1} = \dfrac{1}{4^{2x}}$.

$2^x \times 8^{x-1} = \dfrac{1}{4^{2x}}$

$2^x \times \left(2^3\right)^{x-1} = \dfrac{1}{\left(2^2\right)^{2x}}$ .... | Express each term in the same base (2 is easiest) so that the laws of indices can be applied.

$2^x \times 2^{3x-3} = \dfrac{1}{2^{4x}}$ .... | Use $(a^m)^n = a^{m \times n}$ (Key point 2.1).

$2^{4x-3} = 2^{-4x}$ .... | And then $a^m \times a^n = a^{m+n}$ on the LHS and $a^{-n} = \dfrac{1}{a^n}$ on the RHS.

$4x - 3 = -4x$

$8x = 3$ .... | Equate the powers and solve.

$x = \dfrac{3}{8}$

An equation like this with the unknown (x) in the power is called an **exponential equation**. In Chapter 7 you will see how to solve more complicated examples using logarithms.

Be careful when you are combining expressions with different bases by multiplication or division. Just remembering 'multiplication means add the exponents together' is too simplistic because it is **only** true when the **bases are the same**. There is another rule that works when the bases are different, but then the exponents have to be the same. Consider the following:

$$3^2 \times 5^2 = 3 \times 3 \times 5 \times 5 = 3 \times 5 \times 3 \times 5 = 15 \times 15 = 15^2$$

This suggests the following rules:

Key point 2.2

- $a^n \times b^n = (ab)^n$
- $a^n \div b^n = \left(\dfrac{a}{b}\right)^n$

WORKED EXAMPLE 2.6

Simplify $\left(\dfrac{x^6}{8}\right)^{\frac{1}{3}}$.

$$\left(\frac{x^6}{8}\right)^{\frac{1}{3}} = \frac{\left(x^6\right)^{\frac{1}{3}}}{8^{\frac{1}{3}}}$$

Use $a^n \div b^n = \left(\dfrac{a}{b}\right)^n$ (Key point 2.2) to apply the power to each part of the fraction.

$$= \frac{x^2}{2}$$

Use $(a^m)^n = a^{m \times n}$ (Key point 2.1) on the top of the fraction and recognise the cube root of 8 on the bottom.

WORKED EXAMPLE 2.7

Simplify $\dfrac{\left(16a^2b^8\right)^{\frac{1}{2}}}{ab^3}$.

$$\frac{\left(16a^2b^8\right)^{\frac{1}{2}}}{ab^3} = \frac{16^{\frac{1}{2}}\left(a^2\right)^{\frac{1}{2}}\left(b^8\right)^{\frac{1}{2}}}{ab^3}$$

Use $a^n \times b^n = (ab)^n$ (Key point 2.2).

$$= \frac{4ab^4}{ab^3}$$

$$= 4b$$

Apply $a^m \div a^n = a^{m-n}$ (Key point 2.1) to the a's and b's.

WORK IT OUT 2.1

Simplify $(16x^2 + 16y^2)^{\frac{1}{2}}$.

Which is the correct solution? Can you identify the errors made in the incorrect solutions?

Solution 1	Solution 2	Solution 3
$\left(16x^2 + 16y^2\right)^{\frac{1}{2}} = 16^{\frac{1}{2}}\left(x^2 + y^2\right)^{\frac{1}{2}}$ $= 4\left(x^2 + y^2\right)^{\frac{1}{2}}$	$\left(16x^2 + 16y^2\right)^{\frac{1}{2}} = 16^{\frac{1}{2}}\left(x^2 + y^2\right)^{\frac{1}{2}}$ $= 8\sqrt{x^2 + y^2}$	$\left(16x^2 + 16y^2\right)^{\frac{1}{2}} = \left(16x^2\right)^{\frac{1}{2}} + \left(16y^2\right)^{\frac{1}{2}}$ $= 4x + 4y$

EXERCISE 2A

1 Evaluate without a calculator:

a **i** $16^{\frac{1}{2}}$ **ii** $27^{\frac{1}{3}}$

b **i** 2^{-3} **ii** 5^{-2}

c **i** $\left(\frac{2}{3}\right)^{-2}$ **ii** $\left(\frac{1}{4}\right)^{-3}$

d **i** $27^{\frac{2}{3}}$ **ii** $9^{\frac{3}{2}}$

e **i** $125^{-\frac{2}{3}}$ **ii** $16^{-\frac{3}{4}}$

f **i** $\left(\frac{4}{9}\right)^{-\frac{3}{2}}$ **ii** $\left(\frac{27}{8}\right)^{-\frac{2}{3}}$

g **i** $0.25^{\frac{1}{2}}$ **ii** 0.5^{-2}

h **i** $32^{0.2}$ **ii** $81^{-0.25}$

> ✔ **Gateway to A Level**
>
> For more practice with indices, see Gateway to A Level section G.

2 Write the following in the form 4^p:

a **i** $\sqrt{4}$ **ii** $\sqrt[3]{4}$

b **i** 16 **ii** 1

c **i** 2 **ii** $\frac{1}{2}$

d **i** 0.25 **ii** 0.5

e **i** 8 **ii** 32

f **i** $4\sqrt[3]{4}$ **ii** $2\sqrt[5]{4}$

g **i** $\sqrt{2}$ **ii** $\sqrt{8}$

3 Simplify the following:

a **i** $\left(x^6\right)^{\frac{1}{2}}$ **ii** $\left(x^9\right)^{\frac{4}{3}}$

b **i** $\left(4x^{10}\right)^{0.5}$ **ii** $\left(8x^{12}\right)^{-\frac{1}{3}}$

c **i** $\left(\frac{27x^9}{64}\right)^{\frac{1}{3}}$ **ii** $\left(\frac{x^4}{y^8}\right)^{-1.5}$

4 Solve the following:

a **i** $x^{-\frac{5}{2}} = 32$ **ii** $x^{\frac{3}{2}} = \frac{8}{27}$

b **i** $2^{x-1} = \frac{4^x}{8}$ **ii** $27^x = \sqrt{3} \times 9^{x+2}$

5 Write in the form ax^p:

a **i** $3\sqrt{x}$ **ii** $5\sqrt[3]{x}$

b **i** $x\sqrt[3]{x}$ **ii** $x^2\sqrt{x}$

c **i** $\dfrac{3}{\sqrt{x}}$ **ii** $\dfrac{5}{\sqrt[3]{x}}$

d **i** $\dfrac{1}{(2x^2)}$ **ii** $\dfrac{1}{(3x^2)}$

e **i** $\dfrac{2}{3\sqrt{x}}$ **ii** $\dfrac{5}{2\sqrt[3]{x}}$

6 Write in the form $ax^p + bx^q$:

a **i** $\dfrac{(3+2x)}{\sqrt{x}}$ **ii** $\dfrac{\left(4-3\sqrt{x}\right)}{x}$

b **i** $\dfrac{(x^2-3)}{(2x)}$ **ii** $\dfrac{(4x-3)}{(2x^2)}$

c **i** $\dfrac{(2x^2+1)}{4\sqrt{x}}$ **ii** $\dfrac{\left(2-9\sqrt{x}\right)}{(3x)}$

7 Simplify $\left(100x^4\right)^{-\frac{1}{2}}$.

8 Simplify $\dfrac{x^{\frac{2}{3}}\times x^{\frac{1}{2}}}{x^{\frac{1}{6}}}$.

9 Simplify $\dfrac{\sqrt[3]{64p^6q^4}}{2q}$.

10 Write $\dfrac{1-x^3}{\sqrt[3]{x}}$ in the form $x^a - x^b$.

11 An elementary computer program is known to be able to sort n input values in $k \times n^{1.5}$ microseconds. Observations show that it sorts a million values in half a second. Find the value of k.

12 The volume and surface area of a family of regular solid shapes are related by the formula $V = kA^{1.5}$ where V is given in cubic units and A in square units.

a For one such shape, $A = 81$ and $V = 243$. Find k.

b Hence determine the surface area of a shape with volume $\dfrac{64}{3}$ cm³.

13 A square-ended cuboid has volume xy^2, where x and y are lengths. A cuboid for which $x = 2y$ has volume 128 cm³. Find x.

14 Simplify $\left(3x^9 + \dfrac{3}{8}x^9\right)^{-\frac{1}{3}}$.

15 If $\sqrt{3^{2a+b}} = \dfrac{27^a}{3^b}$ express a in terms of b.

16 Express $\left(3x^{\frac{3}{4}} - x^{-\frac{3}{4}}\right)^2$ in the form $ax^n + \dfrac{b}{x^n} + c$ where a, b, c and n are to be found.

17 Make x the subject of the equation $4^{ax} = b \times 8^x$ where a and b are constants. Leave your answer in a simplified form.

18 Anything raised to the power of zero is 1, but zero raised to any power is zero, so what is the value of 0^0?

19 What is the value of 2^{2^2}?

Gateway to A Level

For a reminder of basic manipulations with surds, see Gateway to A Level section H.

Hint

You can solve this equation using logs, which are introduced in chapter 7.

Section 2: Working with surds

A **surd** is any number that can only be expressed using roots. You need to be able to work with surd expressions, for example:

$$2+3\sqrt{5}, \ \sqrt{3}-\sqrt{7}, \ \sqrt[3]{2}+\sqrt{2}$$

The most important thing to know when working with surds is that square rooting is just another way of writing 'raise to the power of a half' so all the rules for indices apply to surds.

▶▶❙ Fast forward

A In Student Book 2, Chapter 1, you will see a method for proving that surds **cannot** be written as rational numbers.

WORKED EXAMPLE 2.8

Write $\sqrt{8}+\sqrt{2}$ in the form $\sqrt{a}$.

$\sqrt{8}=\sqrt{4\times2}$

$\quad=\sqrt{4}\times\sqrt{2}$

$\quad=2\sqrt{2}$

Square root is equivalent to the power $\frac{1}{2}$. You can apply $(ab)^{\frac{1}{2}}=a^{\frac{1}{2}}\times b^{\frac{1}{2}}$ (Key point 2.2) to $\sqrt{8}$ to split it up into a product. Choose to split 8 into a square number and something else.

$\sqrt{8}+\sqrt{2}=2\sqrt{2}+\sqrt{2}$

$\quad=3\sqrt{2}$

$2\sqrt{2}$ plus another $\sqrt{2}$ is just 3 lots of $\sqrt{2}$.

$\quad=\sqrt{9}\sqrt{2}$

$\quad=\sqrt{18}$

If you want to put it all under one square root, you can use Key point 2.2 again. However, you need to write 3 as the square root of another number.

WORKED EXAMPLE 2.9

Simplify $\left(1+\sqrt{2}\right)^{2}$.

$\left(1+\sqrt{2}\right)^{2}=\left(1+\sqrt{2}\right)\left(1+\sqrt{2}\right)$

$\quad=1+\sqrt{2}+\sqrt{2}+\sqrt{2}\times\sqrt{2}$

Expand the brackets as normal.

$\quad=1+2\sqrt{2}+2$

$\quad=3+2\sqrt{2}$

Note that $\sqrt{2}\times\sqrt{2}=(\sqrt{2})^{2}=\left(2^{\frac{1}{2}}\right)^{2}=2^{1}=2$.

One important method used when dealing with surds in fractions is called **rationalising the denominator**. This is the process when surds are removed from the denominator.

WORKED EXAMPLE 2.10

Rationalise the denominator of $\dfrac{2}{\sqrt{3}}$.

$\dfrac{2}{\sqrt{3}}=\dfrac{2\times\sqrt{3}}{\sqrt{3}\times\sqrt{3}}$

$\quad=\dfrac{2\sqrt{3}}{3}$

One obvious thing that would make the bottom rational is to multiply it by $\sqrt{3}$. If you do this you have to multiply the top by $\sqrt{3}$ also.

It is also possible to rationalise the denominator of more complicated expressions. The trick to do this uses the difference of two squares:

$$a^2 - b^2 = (a - b)(a + b)$$

If you have an expression such as $5 + \sqrt{3}$ you know that by multiplying it by $5 - \sqrt{3}$ the result will be $5^2 - \left(\sqrt{3}\right)^2 = 22$. Importantly, this product is a rational number.

 Gateway to A Level

For revision of the difference of two squares factorisation, see Gateway to A Level section B.

 Key point 2.3

To rationalise the denominator of a fraction, multiply top and bottom by the appropriate expression to create a 'difference of two squares'.

WORKED EXAMPLE 2.11

Rationalise the denominator of $\dfrac{3}{8 - 2\sqrt{3}}$.

$\dfrac{3}{8 - 2\sqrt{3}} = \dfrac{3 \times (8 + 2\sqrt{3})}{(8 - 2\sqrt{3}) \times (8 + 2\sqrt{3})}$

The appropriate term to multiply top and bottom by is $8 + 2\sqrt{3}$

$= \dfrac{24 + 6\sqrt{3}}{64 - 4 \times 3}$

You do not need to multiply the bottom out. You can use the difference of two squares identity.

$= \dfrac{24 + 6\sqrt{3}}{52}$

There is a factor of 2 on top and bottom.

$= \dfrac{12 + 3\sqrt{3}}{26}$

WORK IT OUT 2.2

Rationalise the denominator of $\dfrac{1}{\sqrt{5} - \sqrt{2}}$.

Which is the correct solution? Can you identify the errors made in the incorrect solutions?

Solution 1	Solution 2	Solution 3
$\dfrac{1}{\sqrt{5} - \sqrt{2}} = \dfrac{1}{\sqrt{3}}$ $= \dfrac{\sqrt{3}}{3}$	$\dfrac{1}{\sqrt{5} - \sqrt{2}} = \dfrac{1 \times \left(\sqrt{5} + \sqrt{2}\right)}{\left(\sqrt{5} - \sqrt{2}\right) \times \left(\sqrt{5} + \sqrt{2}\right)}$ $= \dfrac{\sqrt{5} + \sqrt{2}}{3}$	$\dfrac{1}{\sqrt{5} - \sqrt{2}} = \dfrac{1}{\sqrt{5}} - \dfrac{1}{\sqrt{2}}$ $= \dfrac{\sqrt{5}}{5} - \dfrac{\sqrt{2}}{2}$ $= \dfrac{2\sqrt{5} - 5\sqrt{2}}{10}$

EXERCISE 2B

1 Write the following in the form $k\sqrt{5}$.

  a i $\sqrt{125}$ **ii** $\sqrt{20}$

  b i $7\sqrt{5} - 2\sqrt{5}$ **ii** $\sqrt{5} + 9\sqrt{5} - 3\sqrt{5}$

  c i $3\sqrt{80} - 5\sqrt{20}$ **ii** $\sqrt{125} + 7\sqrt{45}$

2 Write the following in the form $\sqrt{a}$.

  a i $4\sqrt{2}$ **ii** $10\sqrt{3}$

  b i $\sqrt{7} + 2\sqrt{7}$ **ii** $3\sqrt{5} + \sqrt{5}$

  c i $\sqrt{3} + \sqrt{75}$ **ii** $\sqrt{32} + \sqrt{8}$

3 Write in the form $a + b\sqrt{3}$.

  a i $2(3 - \sqrt{3}) - 3(1 - \sqrt{3})$ **ii** $(1 + \sqrt{3}) - (1 - \sqrt{3})$

  b i $(1 + 2\sqrt{3})(2 - \sqrt{3})$ **ii** $(1 + \sqrt{3})(2 + \sqrt{3})$

  c i $(1 + \sqrt{3})^2$ **ii** $(2 - \sqrt{3})^2$

> ✔ **Gateway to A Level**
>
> For a reminder and more practice of questions like this, see Gateway to A Level section I.

4 Rationalise the denominator of:

  a i $\dfrac{7}{\sqrt{7}}$ **ii** $\dfrac{2}{\sqrt{5}}$

  b i $\dfrac{3 - \sqrt{6}}{\sqrt{6}}$ **ii** $\dfrac{\sqrt{2} + \sqrt{6}}{\sqrt{3}}$

  c i $\dfrac{1}{\sqrt{2} - 1}$ **ii** $\dfrac{1 + \sqrt{5}}{1 + \sqrt{7}}$

5 Simplify $\dfrac{1}{1 + \sqrt{n}} + \dfrac{1}{1 - \sqrt{n}}$.

6 Show that $\dfrac{4}{\sqrt{20} - \sqrt{12}}$ can be written in the form $\sqrt{a} + \sqrt{b}$ where a and b are whole numbers.

7 Show that $\dfrac{5 + \sqrt{2}}{3 - 2\sqrt{2}}$ can be written in the form $a + b\sqrt{2}$ where a and b are constants to be found.

8 Explain without using decimal approximations why $3\sqrt{2}$ is larger than $2\sqrt{3}$.

9 Solve the equation $x\sqrt{27} = 5x\sqrt{3} + 2\sqrt{48}$.

10 Rationalise the denominator of $\dfrac{1}{2\sqrt{n} - 3}$.

> ⬇ **Elevate**
>
> For more practice at solving equations involving surds, see Support sheet 2.

11 If n is a positive whole number write $\left(n\sqrt{15} - \sqrt{5}\right)^2$ in the form $a + b\sqrt{3}$.

12 A rectangle has length $a + b\sqrt{2}$ and width $b - a\sqrt{2}$.

    a Find the area of the rectangle in the form $m + n\sqrt{2}$.

    b Find and simplify an expression for the length of the diagonal of the rectangle.

13 **a** Write $\sqrt{27} + \sqrt{3}$ in the form $\sqrt{a}$.

    b Explain without using decimal approximations whether $\sqrt{27} - \sqrt{20}$ is bigger or smaller than $\sqrt{5} - \sqrt{3}$.

14 **a** Find and simplify an expression for $(a + b\sqrt{2})^2$.

    b By considering $(1 - \sqrt{2})^4$ prove that $\sqrt{2} < \dfrac{17}{12}$.

15 **a** Show that $a^3 - b^3 = (a - b)(a^2 + ab + b^2)$.

    b Hence rationalise the denominator of $\dfrac{1}{\sqrt[3]{3} - \sqrt[3]{2}}$.

16 Is it always true that $\sqrt{x^2}$ equals x?

✎ Checklist of learning and understanding

- You need to learn these laws of indices:

  - $a^m \times a^n = a^{m+n}$
  - $a^{\frac{m}{n}} = (\sqrt[n]{a})^m = \sqrt[n]{a^m}$
  - $a^0 = 1$

  - $a^{\frac{1}{n}} = \sqrt[n]{a}$
  - $(a^m)^n = a^{m \times n}$
  - $a^n \div b^n = \left(\dfrac{a}{b}\right)^n$

  - $a^m \div a^n = a^{m-n}$
  - $a^n \times b^n = (ab)^n$
  - $a^{-n} = \dfrac{1}{a^n}$

- The second point above means that you can write roots as powers; in particular, $\sqrt{x} = x^{\frac{1}{2}}$ and $\sqrt[3]{x} = x^{\frac{1}{3}}$.

- Surds are numbers that can only be expressed using roots. To rationalise the denominator of a fraction you can multiply top and bottom by the appropriate expression to create a 'difference of two squares'.

Mixed practice 2

1 Express $\left(n+\sqrt{5}\right)^2$ in the form $a+b\sqrt{5}$.

2 If $z = xy^2$ and $y = 3x$ express z in terms of x only.

3 Show that $\dfrac{10}{\sqrt{28}-\sqrt{8}}$ can be written in the form $\sqrt{a}+\sqrt{b}$.

4 If $y = \dfrac{2}{\sqrt{x}}$, write y^{-4} in the form kx^a.

5 If $3x\sqrt{8} = x\sqrt{2} + \sqrt{32}$, find x.

6 Simplify

 i $\left(\sqrt[3]{x}\right)^6$,

 ii $\dfrac{3y^4 \times (10y)^3}{2y^5}$.

   © OCR, AS GCE Mathematics, Paper 4721, January 2009

7 Express each of the following in the form 3^n:

 i $\dfrac{1}{9}$,

 ii $\sqrt[3]{3}$,

 iii $3^{10} \times 9^{135}$.

   © OCR, AS GCE Mathematics, Paper 4721, June 2009

8 Simplify $\left(x^4 + 7x^3 \times \dfrac{x}{9}\right)^{-\frac{1}{2}}$.

9 Rationalise the denominator of $\dfrac{\sqrt{n}+1}{\sqrt{n}-1}$.

10 **a** Find and simplify an expression for $(a+b\sqrt{5})^2$.

 b By considering $(2-\sqrt{5})^4$ show that $\sqrt{5} < \dfrac{161}{72}$.

 c By considering $(2-\sqrt{5})^3$ show that $\sqrt{5} > \dfrac{38}{17}$.

 d **i** Explain why considering $(3-\sqrt{5})^3$ gives a worse upper bound on $\sqrt{5}$ than found in part **b**.

   ii Explain why considering $(4-\sqrt{5})^4$ would not give as good an upper bound on $\sqrt{5}$ as found in part **b**.

Elevate

For more challenging questions on indices and surds, see Extension sheet 2.

3 Quadratic functions

In this chapter you will learn how to:

- recognise the shape and main features of graphs of quadratic functions
- complete the square
- solve quadratic inequalities
- identify the number of solutions of a quadratic equation
- solve disguised quadratic equations.

Before you start...

GCSE	You should know how to multiply out brackets.	1	Expand $(3x+1)(2x-3)$.
GCSE	You should know how to solve quadratics by factorising.	2	Solve: a $\quad x^2 + x - 20 = 0$ b $\quad 2x^2 + 15x - 8 = 0$ c $\quad 5x^2 - 3x = 0$ d $\quad 4x^2 - 9 = 0$
GCSE	You should know how to solve quadratics using the formula.	3	Solve: a $\quad x^2 - 4x + 2 = 0$ b $\quad 2x^2 - 10x - 5 = 0$
GCSE	You should know how to solve linear inequalities.	4	Solve $5x - 1 > 2x + 5$.

Quadratic phenomena

Many problems in applications of mathematics involve maximising or minimising a certain quantity. They are common in economics and business (minimising costs and maximising profits), biology (finding the maximum possible size of a population) and physics (electrons move to the lowest energy state).

The quadratic function is the simplest function with maximum or minimum points, so it is often used to model such situations. It also arises in many natural phenomena, such as the motion of a projectile or the dependence of power on voltage in an electric circuit.

Section 1: Review of quadratic equations

A quadratic function is one of the form $f(x) = ax^2 + bx + c$ where a, b and c are constants and $a \neq 0$.

You should be familiar with two methods for solving quadratic equations:

- factorising
- the quadratic formula.

Many calculators have an equation solver that just lets you type in the coefficients a, b and c to generate the solutions, but you need to be able to apply these methods as well, particularly factorising.

Remember that you may first have to rearrange the equation to get it in the form $ax^2 + bx + c = 0$.

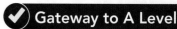

✓ Gateway to A Level

For a revision of factorising and using the quadratic formula, see Gateway to A Level sections B and C.

WORKED EXAMPLE 3.1

Find the values of x for which $(2x - 3)^2 = x + 6$.

$(2x - 3)^2 = x + 6$ $4x^2 - 12x + 9 = x + 6$	Expand the brackets. Remember: $(2x - 3)^2 = (2x - 3)(2x - 3)$.
$4x^2 - 13x + 3 = 0$	Move everything to one side: $f(x) = 0$.
$(4x - 1)(x - 3) = 0$ $x = \dfrac{1}{4}$ or 3	Factorise and solve.

WORKED EXAMPLE 3.2

Find the values of x for which $x = 2 + 8x^{-1}$.

$x = 2 + 8x^{-1}$ $x = 2 + \dfrac{8}{x}$	This might not look like a quadratic at first, but whether or not you spot that it is, it is always a good idea to start by replacing x^{-a} with $\dfrac{1}{x^a}$.
$x^2 = 2x + 8$	Now multiply through by x to remove the denominator.
$x^2 - 2x - 8 = 0$	Move everything to one side: $f(x) = 0$.
$(x - 4)(x + 2) = 0$ $x = 4$ or -2	Factorise and solve.

The quadratic formula

Sometimes you can't see how to factorise the equation, for example if the solutions are not whole numbers or simple fractions. In that case you can use the quadratic formula to solve the equation.

Key point 3.1

The solutions of $ax^2 + bx + c = 0$ are given by the quadratic formula:
$$x = \frac{-b \pm \sqrt{b^2 - 4ac}}{2a}$$

When using the quadratic formula, you may need to use your knowledge of surds to simplify the answer.

WORKED EXAMPLE 3.3

Solve the equation $x^2 + 3x = 7x + 3$.

Give your solutions in exact form.

$x^2 + 3x = 7x + 3$	Move everything to one side: $f(x) = 0$.
$x^2 - 4x - 3 = 0$	
$x = \dfrac{-(-4) \pm \sqrt{(-4)^2 - 4 \times 1 \times (-3)}}{2 \times 1}$	If you can't see how to factorise it, use the formula:
$= \dfrac{4 \pm \sqrt{28}}{2}$	$a = 1, b = -4, c = -3$
$= \dfrac{4 \pm 2\sqrt{7}}{2}$	Simplify the surd: $\sqrt{28} = 2\sqrt{7}$
$= 2 \pm \sqrt{7}$	

> **Tip**
>
> The quadratic formula is **not** given on the formula sheet.

> ▶▶ **Fast forward**
>
> The other alternative is to solve the equation by completing the square. You will see in Section 3 that this is where the quadratic formula actually comes from.

> **Tip**
>
> If you are told to give your solutions to a certain number of decimal places or significant figures, or to give exact solutions, it usually means the quadratic won't factorise easily.

> ◀◀ **Rewind**
>
> You learnt to simplify surds in Chapter 2, Section 2.

WORKED EXAMPLE 3.4

Solve the equation $\sqrt{3}x^2 - 6x - 2\sqrt{3} = 0$, giving your answer in simplified surd form.

$x = \dfrac{6 \pm \sqrt{36 - 4\sqrt{3}(-2\sqrt{3})}}{2\sqrt{3}}$	The answers are not going to be whole numbers, so use the quadratic formula.
$= \dfrac{6 \pm \sqrt{36 + 24}}{2\sqrt{3}}$	Use $\sqrt{3} \times \sqrt{3} = 3$.
$= \dfrac{6 \pm \sqrt{60}}{2\sqrt{3}}$	
$= \dfrac{6 \pm 2\sqrt{15}}{2\sqrt{3}}$	Use $\sqrt{60} = \sqrt{4 \times 15} = 2\sqrt{15}$.
$= \dfrac{3 \pm \sqrt{15}}{\sqrt{3}}$	
$= \sqrt{3} \pm \sqrt{5}$	Use $\dfrac{3}{\sqrt{3}} = \sqrt{3}$ and $\dfrac{\sqrt{15}}{\sqrt{3}} = \sqrt{5}$.

EXERCISE 3A

1 By factorising, solve the following equations:

a i $3x^2 + 2x = x^2 + 3x + 6$ **ii** $2x^2 + 3 = 17x - 7 - x^2$

b i $9x^2 = 24x - 16$ **ii** $18x^2 = 2x^2 - 40x - 25$

c i $(x - 3)(x + 2) = 14$ **ii** $(2x + 3)(x - 1) = 12$

d i $2x = 11 + \dfrac{6}{x}$ **ii** $3x + \dfrac{4}{x} = 7$

2 Use the quadratic formula to find the exact solutions of the following equations:

a i $2x^2 + x = x^2 + 4x - 1$ **ii** $x^2 - 3x + 5 = 6 - 2x$

b i $3x^2 - 4x + 1 = 5x^2 + 2x$ **ii** $9x - 2 = 5x^2 + 1$

c i $(x + 1)(x + 3) = 5$ **ii** $(3x + 2)(x - 1) = 2$

d i $2x + \dfrac{1}{x} = 6$ **ii** $x = 4 + \dfrac{3}{x}$

3 Solve the equation $8x - 9 = (3x - 1)(x + 3)$.

4 Solve the equation $6x = 5 + 4x^{-1}$.

5 Find the exact solutions to the equation $x + x^{-1} = 3$.

6 Solve the equation $x^2 + 8k^2 = 6kx$, giving your answer in terms of k.

7 Solve the equation $2\sqrt{5}x^2 + 3x - \sqrt{5} = 0$, giving your answers in simplified surd form.

8 Find the exact solutions of the equation $x^2\sqrt{2} + 2x\sqrt{5} - 3\sqrt{2} = 0$.

9 Rearrange $y = ax^2 + bx + c$ to find x in terms of y.

10 The positive difference between the solutions of the quadratic equation $x^2 + kx + 3 = 0$ is $\sqrt{69}$. Find the possible values of k.

Section 2: Graphs of quadratic functions

All quadratic graphs are one of two possible shapes. The graph $y = ax^2 + bx + c$ is called a **parabola**. Its shape depends on the coefficient a.

Key point 3.2

- If $a > 0$ the parabola is a **positive** quadratic.

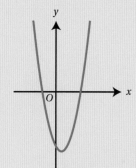

- If $a < 0$ the parabola is a **negative** quadratic.

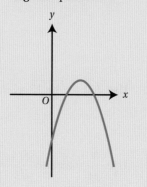

When sketching a graph, you should show the point(s) where it crosses the coordinate axes.

Tip

A quadratic curve may not cross the x-axis at all. Try sketching this for yourself to see.

Key point 3.3

The graph $y = ax^2 + bx + c$ crosses the:

- y-axis at the point $(0, c)$
- x-axis at the root(s) of the equation $ax^2 + bx + c = 0$ (if it crosses the x-axis at all).

Tip

A root of an equation is a solution.

WORKED EXAMPLE 3.5

Match each equation to the corresponding graph, explaining your reasons.

a $y = 3x^2 - 4x - 1$

b $y = -2x^2 - 4x$

c $y = -x^2 - 4x + 2$

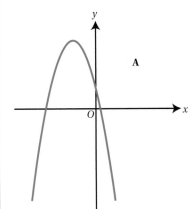
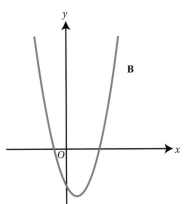
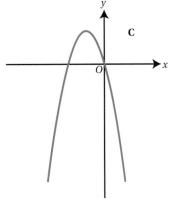

Graph B shows a positive quadratic, so graph B corresponds to equation **a**.

Graph B is the only positive quadratic.

Graph A has a positive y-intercept, so graph A corresponds to equation **c**.

You can distinguish between the other two graphs based on their y-intercepts.

Graph C corresponds to equation **b**.

WORKED EXAMPLE 3.6

Sketch the graph of $y = 3x^2 + 2x - 8$.

This is a positive quadratic as $a > 0$.

When $x = 0$, $y = -8$ .... Find the y-intercept.

When $y = 0$, $3x^2 + 2x - 8 = 0$ .... Find the x-intercepts. To do this, solve the equation $y = 0$.

$(3x - 4)(x + 2) = 0$ .... This factorises.

$x = \dfrac{4}{3}$ or -2

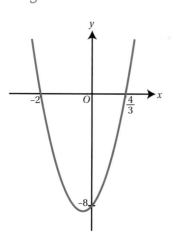

Sketch the graph. It does not have to be to scale but it should show all relevant features, and axis intercepts should be labelled.

WORKED EXAMPLE 3.7

Find the equation of this graph, giving your answer in the form $y = ax^2 + bx + c$.

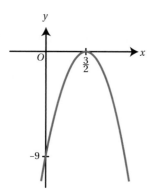

Repeated root at $x = \dfrac{3}{2} \Rightarrow (2x - 3)^2$ is a factor. .... The x-intercepts tell us about the factors.

Continues on next page ...

$y = k(2x - 3)^2$ .... Write in factorised form. The factor $(2x - 3)^2$ could be multiplied by **any** constant, so we will label this unknown constant k.

$-9 = k(0 - 3)^2$ .... To find the value of k, use the fact that when $x = 0$, $y = -9$.
$-9 = 9k$
$k = -1$

So the equation is
$y = -(2x - 3)^2$ .... Expand to give the equation in the form required.
$= -(4x^2 - 12x + 9)$
$= -4x^2 + 12x - 9$

EXERCISE 3B

1 Match the equations and the corresponding graphs.

a **i** $y = -x^2 - 3x + 6$ **ii** $y = 2x^2 - 3x + 3$ **iii** $y = x^2 - 3x + 6$

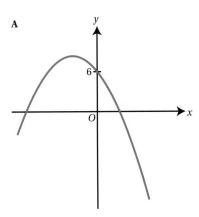
A

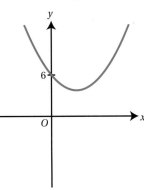
B

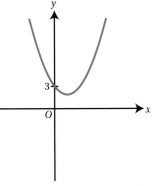
C

b **i** $y = -x^2 + 2x - 3$ **ii** $y = -x^2 + 2x + 3$ **iii** $y = x^2 + 2x + 3$

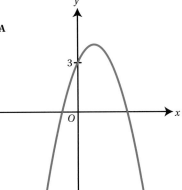
A

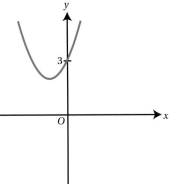
B

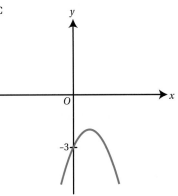
C

33

2 Sketch the following graphs, labelling all axis intercepts.

a i $y = x^2 - 3x - 10$ ii $y = 2x^2 + 11x + 12$

b i $y = -3x^2 + 14x - 8$ ii $y = 6 - 5x - x^2$

c i $y = 3x^2 + 6x$ ii $y = 4x - x^2$

d i $y = -4x^2 - 20x - 25$ ii $y = 4x^2 - 4x + 1$

3 Find the equation of each graph in the form $y = ax^2 + bx + c$.

a i

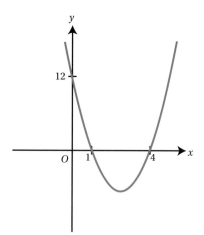

ii

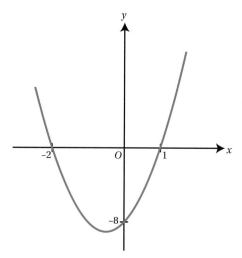

b i

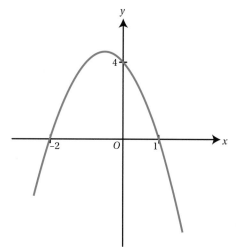

ii

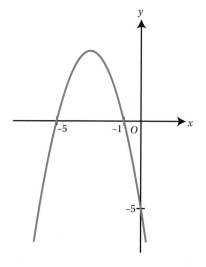

Section 3: Completing the square

It can be useful to rewrite quadratic functions in terms of a bracket squared for two main reasons:

- To solve a quadratic equation
- to find the coordinates of the vertex of a parabola.

Sometimes this just means factorising:

$$x^2 + 10x + 25 = (x + 5)^2$$

But even if this isn't possible, it is only a case of adjusting the constant at the end:

$$x^2 + 10x = (x + 5)^2 - 25$$

The important things to note here are that:

- the number in the bracket is always half the coefficient of x: $\frac{10}{2} = 5$
- the constant to be subtracted at the end is always the number in the bracket squared: $5^2 = 25$.

This process, called completing the square, allows you to write any quadratic in the form $a(x + p)^2 + q$ and is illustrated in the next few worked examples.

 Rewind

You are probably already familiar with this method from GCSE, but perhaps not in the more tricky cases shown in Worked examples 3.8 and 3.9. If you don't like this method you can use the method of comparing coefficients from Worked example 1.1.

WORKED EXAMPLE 3.8

Express $x^2 - 8x + 3$ in the form $(x + p)^2 + q$, stating the values of p and q.

$x^2 - 8x + 3 = (x - 4)^2 - (-4)^2 + 3$

Halve the coefficient of x.

Subtract $(-4)^2$.

The constant term $+3$ is still there.

$= (x - 4)^2 - 16 + 3$

Simplify.

$= (x - 4)^2 - 13$

$\therefore p = -4, q = -13$

WORKED EXAMPLE 3.9

Express $x^2 + 5x + 7$ in the form $(x + p)^2 + q$, stating the values of p and q.

$x^2 + 5x + 7 = \left(x + \dfrac{5}{2}\right)^2 - \left(\dfrac{5}{2}\right)^2 + 7$

Halve the coefficient of x.

Subtract $\left(\dfrac{5}{2}\right)^2$.

The constant term $+7$ is still there.

$= \left(x + \dfrac{5}{2}\right)^2 - \dfrac{25}{4} + 7$

Simplify.

$= \left(x + \dfrac{5}{2}\right)^2 + \dfrac{3}{4}$

$\therefore p = -\dfrac{5}{2}, q = \dfrac{3}{4}$

If the coefficient of x^2 isn't 1, you will need to factorise the expression before completing the square.

WORKED EXAMPLE 3.10

$2x^2 - 6x + 2 = a(x+p)^2 + q$

a Find the constants a, p and q.

b Hence solve the equation $2x^2 - 6x + 2 = 0$.

a $2x^2 - 6x + 2 = 2\{x^2 - 3x\} + 2$

Factorise 2 from the first two terms.

$= 2\left\{\left(x - \dfrac{3}{2}\right)^2 - \left(\dfrac{3}{2}\right)^2\right\} + 2$

Now complete the square on the terms in the bracket.

$= 2\left\{\left(x - \dfrac{3}{2}\right)^2 - \dfrac{9}{4}\right\} + 2$

$= 2\left(x - \dfrac{3}{2}\right)^2 - \dfrac{9}{2} + 2$

Multiply the 2 back in.

$= 2\left(x - \dfrac{3}{2}\right)^2 - \dfrac{5}{2}$

Simplify.

$\therefore a = 2, p = -\dfrac{3}{2}, q = -\dfrac{5}{2}$

b $2x^2 - 6x + 2 = 0$

$2\left(x - \dfrac{3}{2}\right)^2 - \dfrac{5}{2} = 0$

'Hence' means that we must use the result of part **a**.

$2\left(x - \dfrac{3}{2}\right)^2 = \dfrac{5}{2}$

Now just rearrange to make x the subject.

$\left(x - \dfrac{3}{2}\right)^2 = \dfrac{5}{4}$

$x - \dfrac{3}{2} = \pm\sqrt{\dfrac{5}{4}}$

Remember the $\pm$ when square rooting.

$x - \dfrac{3}{2} = \pm\dfrac{\sqrt{5}}{2}$

$x = \dfrac{3}{2} \pm \dfrac{\sqrt{5}}{2}$

$= \dfrac{3 \pm \sqrt{5}}{2}$

You might think that the answer ends up looking exactly like the sort of answer you get from using the quadratic formula. And you'd be right!

You can use exactly the same method for solving the equation in the previous example on the general quadratic equation $ax^2 + bx + c = 0$ to establish the quadratic formula.

 Tip

In part **a** of Worked example 3.10 you could not simply divide both sides by 2, as you would then have a different expression. However, when solving the equation in part **b**, you could have started by dividing **both sides** by 2 first.

PROOF 1

Show that if $ax^2 + bx + c = 0$ then $x = \dfrac{-b \pm \sqrt{b^2 - 4ac}}{2a}$.

$ax^2 + bx + c = 0$

$x^2 + \dfrac{b}{a}x + \dfrac{c}{a} = 0$ .... First divide by a to make the quadratic easier to complete the square.

$\left(x + \dfrac{b}{2a}\right)^2 - \dfrac{b^2}{4a^2} + \dfrac{c}{a} = 0$ .... Complete the square: halving $\dfrac{b}{a}$ gives $\dfrac{b}{2a}$.

$\left(x + \dfrac{b}{2a}\right)^2 = \dfrac{b^2}{4a^2} - \dfrac{c}{a}$ .... Now rearrange as before to make x the subject.

$\qquad = \dfrac{b^2 - 4ac}{4a^2}$

$x + \dfrac{b}{2a} = \pm\sqrt{\dfrac{b^2 - 4ac}{4a^2}}$ .... Square root both sides, remembering the $\pm$.

$\qquad = \pm\dfrac{\sqrt{b^2 - 4ac}}{2a}$

$x = -\dfrac{b}{2a} \pm \dfrac{\sqrt{b^2 - 4ac}}{2a}$

$\qquad = \dfrac{-b \pm \sqrt{b^2 - 4ac}}{2a}$

WORK IT OUT 3.1

Express $-x^2 + 10x - 7$ in the form $a(x + p)^2 + q$.

Which is the correct solution? Can you identify the errors made in the incorrect solutions?

Solution 1	Solution 2	Solution 3
$-x^2 + 10x - 7 = -(x - 5)^2 - 25 - 7$ $= -(x-5)^2 - 32$	$-x^2 + 10x - 7 = -\left[x^2 - 10x\right] - 7$ $= -\left[(x-5)^2 - 25\right] - 7$ $= -(x-5)^2 + 25 - 7$ $= -(x-5)^2 + 18$	Multiplying by -1: $x^2 - 10x + 7$ Completing the square: $(x-5)^2 - 25 + 7$ $= (x-5)^2 - 18$

As well as enabling you to find roots of a quadratic equation, completing the square also gives you a way of finding the coordinates of the maximum or minimum point of a quadratic function:

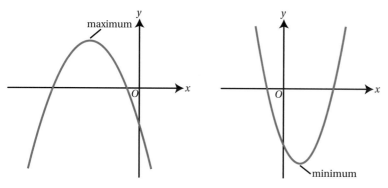

⏩ Fast forward

You will learn about turning points of other functions in Chapter 14.

This may also be referred to as the **vertex** of the quadratic, or as the **turning point** – both are general terms to cover both maximum and minimum points.

From Worked example 3.8 you know that $x^2 - 8x + 3 = (x-4)^2 - 13$.

Since $(x-4)^2 \geqslant 0$ for all x, $(x-4)^2 - 13 \geqslant -13$ for all x.

In other words, the smallest value the function can ever take is -13.

This will occur when $(x-4)^2 = 0$, i.e. when $x = 4$.

So the minimum point of $y = (x-4)^2 - 13$ is $(4, -13)$.

Quadratic functions have a vertical line of symmetry through their turning point.

🔑 Key point 3.4

The quadratic $y = (x+p)^2 + q$ has a turning point at $(-p, q)$ and the line of symmetry $x = -p$.

WORKED EXAMPLE 3.11

State the coordinates of the turning points of the functions in Worked examples 3.9 and 3.10.

a $y = x^2 + 5x + 7$

b $y = 2x^2 - 6x + 2$

a From Worked example 3.9:

$$x^2 + 5x + 7 = \left(x + \frac{5}{2}\right)^2 + \frac{3}{4}$$

Use the completed square form.

$\therefore$ coordinates of turning point: $\left(-\frac{5}{2}, \frac{3}{4}\right)$

$y = (x+p)^2 + q$ has a turning point at $(-p, q)$.

Continues on next page ...

b From Worked example 3.10:

$$2x^2 - 6x + 2 = 2\left(x - \frac{3}{2}\right)^2 - \frac{5}{2}$$ Use the completed square form.

$\therefore$ coordinates of turning point: $\left(\frac{3}{2}, -\frac{5}{2}\right)$ The factor of 2 outside the square bracket does not have any effect.

 Tip

When a parabola crosses the x-axis, the x-coordinate of the vertex (and the line of symmetry) is halfway between the roots. However, when the parabola does not cross the x-axis, you need to use completing the square to find the vertex.

 Fast forward

In Section 5, you will meet another way of deciding how many solutions a quadratic equation has.

You can use the coordinates of the vertex to say whether a quadratic graph crosses the x-axis, that is, whether the corresponding quadratic equation has solutions.

WORKED EXAMPLE 3.12

a Complete the square for $-5x^2 + 6x - 2$.
b Hence explain why the equation $-5x^2 + 6x - 2 = 0$ has no real solutions.

a $-5x^2 + 6x - 2 = -5\left(x^2 - \frac{6}{5}x\right) - 2$ Factorise -5 out of the first two terms.

$$= -5\left\{\left(x - \frac{3}{5}\right)^2 - \left(\frac{3}{5}\right)^2\right\} - 2$$ Complete the square inside the bracket.

$$= -5\left(x - \frac{3}{5}\right)^2 + \frac{9}{5} - 2$$ Multiply the -5 back in.

$$= -5\left(x - \frac{3}{5}\right)^2 - \frac{1}{5}$$

b $\left(x - \frac{3}{5}\right)^2$ is always a non-negative number.

Hence $-5\left(x - \frac{3}{5}\right)^2 \leqslant 0$ Use the fact that squares cannot be negative.

and so $-5\left(x - \frac{3}{5}\right)^2 - \frac{1}{5} \leqslant -\frac{1}{5}$

Therefore $-5x^2 + 6x - 2$ can never equal zero, so the equation has no solutions.

You can also use the completed square form to find the equation of the graph when the coordinates of the vertex are given.

WORKED EXAMPLE 3.13

Find the equation of the following quadratic graph:

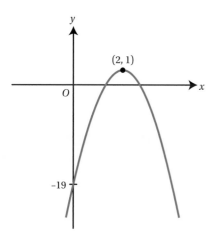

Turning point is at $(2, 1)$ so the function must be of the form $y = a(x - 2)^2 + 1$

> Since you are given the coordinates of the turning point, use the completed square form.

When $x = 0$, $y = -19$:

$-19 = a(0 - 2)^2 + 1$

> Use the other given point, $(0, -19)$ to find a.

$-19 = 4a + 1$

$a = -5$

So the equation is $y = -5(x - 2)^2 + 1$

> Give the equation. There's no need to express it in the form $y = ax^2 + bx + c$ here.

EXERCISE 3C

1 Write down the coordinates of the vertex of these quadratic functions:

a i $y = (x - 3)^2 + 4$ **ii** $y = (x - 5)^2 + 1$

b i $y = 2(x - 7)^2 - 1$ **ii** $y = 3(x - 1)^2 - 5$

c i $y = (x + 1)^2 + 3$ **ii** $y = (x + 7)^2 - 3$

d i $y = -5(x + 2)^2 - 4$ **ii** $y = -(x + 1)^2 + 5$

2 Write the following expressions in the form $a(x - k)^2 + h$.

a i $x^2 - 6x + 4$ **ii** $x^2 - 10x + 21$

b i $x^2 + 4x + 1$ **ii** $x^2 + 6x - 3$

c i $2x^2 - 12x + 5$ **ii** $3x^2 + 6x + 10$

d i $-x^2 + 2x - 5$ **ii** $-x^2 - 4x + 1$

e i $x^2 + 3x + 1$ **ii** $x^2 - 5x + 10$

f i $2x^2 + 6x + 15$ **ii** $2x^2 - 5x - 1$

3 Find the equation of each graph in the form $y = a(x - k)^2 + h$.

a **i**

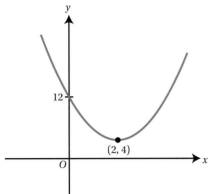

ii

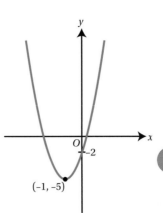

> **Hint**
>
> Question **3b ii** has already been done for you in the previous Worked example, but you should ensure that you can follow it fully.

b **i**

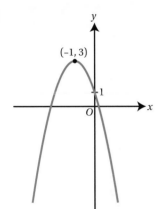

ii

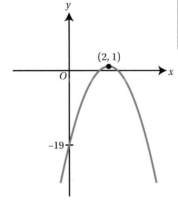

4 $y = x^2 - 6x + 11$

a Write y in the form $(x - a)^2 + b$.

b Find the minimum value of y.

5 The curve $y = a(x + b)^2 + c$ has a minimum point at $(3, 6)$ and passes through the point $(1, 14)$.

a Write down the value of b and c.

b Find the value of a.

6 **a** Express $y = 8x - x^2 - 21$ in the form $a - (x + b)^2$ where a and b are integers to be found.

b Write down the coordinates of the turning point of the graph.

c Hence explain why the equation $8x - x^2 - 21 = 0$ has no real roots.

7 **a** Write $2x^2 + 4x - 1$ in the form $a(x - p)^2 + q$.

b Hence find the exact solutions of the equation $2x^2 + 4x - 1 = 0$.

c Sketch the graph of $y = 2x^2 + 4x - 1$ clearly giving the coordinates of all axis intercepts and of the minimum point.

d Write down the equation of the axis of symmetry of this curve.

8 **a** Write $x^2 + 6x$ in the form $(x + k)^2 + h$.

b Hence find the range of values of p for which $x^2 + 6x = p$ has at least one real solution.

9 Let $f(x) = 3x^2 + 2x + 1$.

    a Complete the square for $f(x)$.

    b Hence explain why the equation $f(x) = 0$ has no real solutions.

    c Write down the equation of the line of symmetry of the graph of $y = f(x)$.

10 By writing the left-hand side in the form $a(x + p)^2 + q$, show that the equation $-2x^2 + 8x - 13 = 0$ has no real roots.

Section 4: Quadratic inequalities

As well as quadratic equations, you can also have quadratic inequalities, for example $x^2 < 144$ or $x^2 - 6x - 7 > 0$.

 Gateway to A Level

For a reminder of linear inequalities, see Gateway to A Level section D.

🔑 **Key point 3.5**

To help solve quadratic inequalities always sketch the graph.

WORKED EXAMPLE 3.14

Solve the inequality $x^2 - 6x - 7 > 0$.

$x^2 - 6x - 7 > 0$

$(x - 7)(x + 1) = 0$

$x = 7 \text{ or } -1$

To sketch the graph you need the roots of the equation.

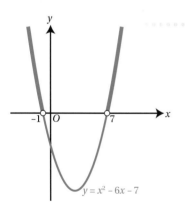

Sketch $y = x^2 - 6x - 7$.
You want the part where the graph is positive ($y > 0$).

$\therefore x < -1 \text{ or } x > 7$

There are two parts of the graph that give the required values of x, so you need to write two inequalities.

As with quadratic equations, you might need to rearrange the inequality first.

WORKED EXAMPLE 3.15

Solve the inequality $5 + 3x - 2x^2 > 1 - 4x$.

$5 + 3x - 2x^2 > 1 - 4x$ .... Rearrange: it is easiest to make the coefficient of x^2 positive.

$0 > 2x^2 - 7x - 4$

$2x^2 - 7x - 4 < 0$ .... Swap sides so that the expression is on the left.

$2x^2 - 7x - 4 = 0$ .... To find the intercepts of the graph, we need to find where the expression on the left equals zero.

$(2x + 1)(x - 4) = 0$

$x = -\dfrac{1}{2}$ or 4

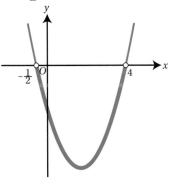

Sketch $y = 2x^2 - 7x - 4$.
You want the part where the graph is negative $(y < 0)$.

$\therefore -\dfrac{1}{2} < x < 4$ .... There is just one part of the graph that gives the required values of x, so write one inequality.

You can illustrate these inequalities on a number line. This is particularly useful if there is more than one inequality.

WORKED EXAMPLE 3.16

Solve simultaneously $x^2 < 16$ and $x^2 \geqslant 9$.

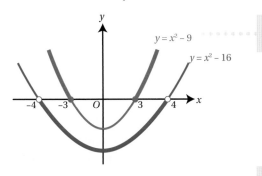

Sketch $y = x^2 - 16$ and $y = x^2 - 9$.

$\therefore -4 < x < 4$
and
$x \leqslant -3$ or $x \geqslant 3$ .... Give the solutions of each.

Continues on next page ...

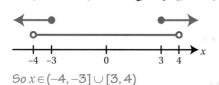

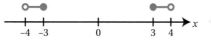

The solution to the simultaneous inequalities is the region covered by both the red and the green line.

So $x \in (-4, -3] \cup [3, 4)$

Look for the sections of the number line covered by both solutions.

You may need to look back at Chapter 1 for a reminder about interval notation.

EXERCISE 3D

1 Solve the following quadratic inequalities:

  a **i** $x^2 \leqslant 8$ **ii** $x^2 < 5$

  b **i** $x^2 > 6$ **ii** $x^2 \geqslant 12$

  c **i** $(x-4)(x+1) > 0$ **ii** $(2x-5)(3x+2) < 0$

  d **i** $(3-x)(x+1) < 0$ **ii** $(4-x)(x-2) > 0$

  e **i** $(3-x)(12-x) > 0$ **ii** $(2-x)(-2-x) < 0$

2 Solve the following inequalities. Write your answers using interval notation.

  a **i** $x^2 - 5x + 6 < 0$ **ii** $x^2 + x - 6 < 0$

  b **i** $x^2 - 4x - 12 \geqslant 0$ **ii** $x^2 + 7x + 6 \geqslant 0$

  c **i** $2x^2 + x > 6$ **ii** $3x^2 - x > 10$

  d **i** $2x^2 + 3x - 5 \leqslant 0$ **ii** $5x^2 + 6x + 1 \leqslant 0$

3 Solve the inequality $2x^2 > 6 - x$.

4 Find the set of values of x for which $2x^2 + 3x + 1 \leqslant 11 + 4x - x^2$.

5 A ball is thrown upwards and its height h m, at time t s, is given by $h = 7t - 4.9\,t^2$. How long does the ball spend more than 1.5 m above ground?

6 **a** Solve the following inequalities:

    i $7x - 5 < 3x + 5$

    ii $2x^2 - 7x < 4x - 5$

  b Hence find the set of value of x for which both $7x - 5 < 3x + 5$ and $2x^2 - 7x < 4x - 5$.

7 Solve simultaneously $x^2 + 6 > 5x$ and $x^2 \geqslant 1$.

8 Find the range of values of x for which both $2x^2 \geqslant 4x$ and $5x^2 - 13x - 6 \leqslant 0$.

9 The cost of producing n items is £$(950 + 63n)$. The items can be sold for £$(280 - 5n)$ **per item**. How many items can be produced and sold in order to make a profit? Give your answer in the form $M \leqslant n \leqslant N$ where M and N are both integers.

Section 5: The discriminant

If you try to apply the quadratic formula to find solutions of $x^2 - 3x + 3 = 0$, you get the following result:

$$x = \frac{3 \pm \sqrt{(-3)^2 - 4 \times 1 \times 3}}{2} = \frac{3 \pm \sqrt{-3}}{2}$$

As the square root of a negative number is not a real number, it follows that the expression has no real roots.

This will clearly happen whenever the expression inside the square root, $b^2 - 4ac$, is negative.

Similarly, if $b^2 - 4ac = 0$, then the quadratic formula becomes

$$x = \frac{-b \pm \sqrt{0}}{2a} = \frac{-b}{2a}$$

and there is just the one root at $x = -\dfrac{b}{2a}$.

In all other cases there will be two real roots.

The expression $b^2 - 4ac$ is called the **discriminant** of the quadratic (often symbolised by the Greek letter Δ, which is capital delta).

These graphs are examples of the three possible situations.

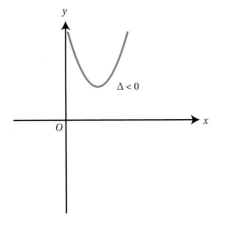

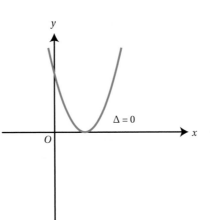

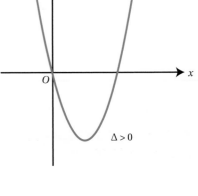

> ⏭ **Fast forward**
>
> If you study Further Mathematics, in Pure Core Student Book 1 you will meet a new type of number, called an imaginary number, which makes it possible to find roots of functions like this.

Key point 3.6:

For the quadratic equation $ax^2 + bx + c = 0$:

- if $\Delta < 0$ the equation has no real roots
- if $\Delta = 0$ the equation has one (repeated) root
- if $\Delta > 0$ the equation has two distinct real roots

where $\Delta = b^2 - 4ac$ is the discriminant.

Tip

Repeated roots can also be referred to as equal roots.

Tip

Questions of this type often lead to a quadratic equation or inequality for k.

WORKED EXAMPLE 3.17

Find the exact values of k for which the quadratic equation $kx^2 - (k+2)x + 3 = 0$ has a repeated root.

$b^2 - 4ac = 0$	Repeated root means that $b^2 - 4ac = 0$
$(k+2)^2 - 4(k)(3) = 0$	$a = k, b = -(k+2), c = 3$
$k^2 + 4k + 4 - 12k = 0$	This is a quadratic equation in k.
$k^2 - 8k + 4 = 0$	
$k = \dfrac{8 \pm \sqrt{8^2 - 4 \times 4}}{2}$	If you can't factorise it use the quadratic formula.
$\quad = \dfrac{8 \pm \sqrt{48}}{2}$	
$\quad = \dfrac{8 \pm 4\sqrt{3}}{2}$	
$\quad = 4 \pm 2\sqrt{3}$	

WORKED EXAMPLE 3.18

Find the set of values of k for which the equation $2x^2 - (k+1)x + 5 - k = 0$ has two distinct real solutions.

$b^2 - 4ac > 0$	Two distinct real root $\Rightarrow b^2 - 4ac > 0$.
$(k+1)^2 - 4(2)(5-k) > 0$	$a = 2, b = -(k+1), c = 5 - k$
$k^2 + 2k + 1 - 40 + 8k > 0$	
$k^2 + 10k - 39 > 0$	This is a quadratic inequality in k.

Continues on next page ...

$k^2 + 10k - 39 = 0$

$(k + 13)(k - 3) = 0$

$k = -13, 3$

·················· Solve the equation $k^2 + 10k - 39 = 0$.

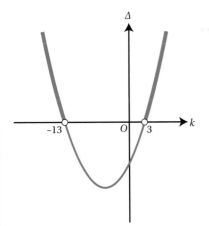

············ You want the region where $\Delta > 0$.

$\therefore k < -13 \text{ or } k > 3$ ··················· State the range of values of k as required.

💡 Tip

Note that the graph drawn in Worked example 3.18 here isn't the graph of the original quadratic expression (in the variable x) – it's the graph of a quadratic in k. You haven't solved the original equation, you've solved a quadratic inequality for k that ensures there are two distinct solutions for x in the original equation.

When $\Delta < 0$, the graph does not intersect the x-axis, so it is either entirely above or entirely below it. The two cases are distinguished by the value of a.

🔑 Key point 3.7

For a quadratic function with $\Delta < 0$:

- if $a > 0$ then $y > 0$ for all x
- if $a < 0$ then $y < 0$ for all x.

WORKED EXAMPLE 3.19

$y = -3x^2 + kx - 12$

Find the values of k for which $y < 0$ for all x.

No real roots, $\therefore \Delta < 0$ ·················· y is a negative quadratic. $y < 0$ means that the graph is entirely below the x-axis. This will happen when $f(x) = 0$ has no real roots.

Continues on next page ...

$b^2 - 4ac < 0$

$k^2 - 4(-3)(-12) < 0$ .... $a = -3,\ b = k,\ c = -12.$

$k^2 - 144 < 0$ .... This is a quadratic inequality in k.

$k^2 - 144 = 0$ .... Solve the equation $k^2 - 144 = 0$.

$(k - 12)(k + 12) = 0$

$k = -12,\ 12$

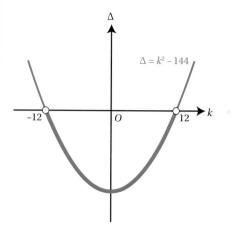

You want the region where $\Delta < 0$.

$\therefore\ -12 < k < 12$ .... State the range of values of k as required.

EXERCISE 3E

1 Evaluate the discriminant of the following quadratic equations:

   a **i** $x^2 + 4x - 5 = 0$ **ii** $x^2 - 6x - 8 = 0$

   b **i** $2x^2 + x + 6 = 0$ **ii** $3x^2 - x + 10 = 0$

   c **i** $3x^2 - 6x + 3 = 0$ **ii** $9x^2 - 6x + 1 = 0$

   d **i** $12 - x - x^2 = 0$ **ii** $-x^2 - 3x + 10 = 0$

2 State the number of solutions for each equation from question 1.

3 Find the set of values of k for which:

   a **i** the equation $2x^2 - x + 3k = 0$ has two distinct real roots

       ii the equation $3x^2 + 5x - k = 0$ has two distinct real roots

   b **i** the equation $5x^2 - 2x + (2k - 1) = 0$ has equal roots

       ii the equation $2x^2 + 3x - (3k + 1) = 0$ has equal roots

   c **i** the equation $-x^2 + 3x + (k + 1) = 0$ has real roots

       ii the equation $-2x^2 + 3x - (2k + 1) = 0$ has real roots

   d **i**   the equation $3kx^2 - 3x + 2 = 0$ has no real solutions

      ii   the equation $-kx^2 + 5x + 3 = 0$ has no real solutions

   e **i**   the quadratic expression $(k-2)x^2 + 3x + 1$ has a repeated root

      ii   the quadratic expression $-4x^2 + 5x + (2k-5)$ has a repeated root

   f **i**   the graph of $y = x^2 - 4x + (3k+1)$ is tangent to the x-axis

      ii   the graph of $y = -2kx^2 + x - 4$ is tangent to the x-axis

   g **i**   the expression $-3x^2 + 5k$ has no real roots

      ii   the expression $2kx^2 - 3$ has no real roots

4   Find the values of parameter m for which the quadratic equation $mx^2 - 4x + 2m = 0$ has equal roots.

5   Find the exact values of k such that the equation $-3x^2 + (2k+1)x - 4k = 0$ has a repeated root.

6   Find the range of values of the parameter c such that $2x^2 - 3x + (2c+1) \geqslant 0$ for all x.

7   Find the set of values of k for which the equation $x^2 - 2kx + 6k = 0$ has no real solutions.

8   Find the range of values of k for which the quadratic equation $kx^2 - (k+3)x - 1 = 0$ has no real roots.

9   Find the range of values of m for which the equation $mx^2 + mx - 2 = 0$ has one or two real roots.

10   Find the possible values of m such that $mx^2 + 3x - 4 < 0$ for all x.

Elevate

For a further example of this type and more practice questions, see Support sheet 3.

Section 6: Disguised quadratics

You will often meet equations that can be turned into quadratics by making a substitution.

WORKED EXAMPLE 3.20

Solve the equation $x^4 - 3x^2 - 4 = 0$.

Let $y = x^2$

A substitution $y = x^2$ turns this into a quadratic equation since $x^4 = y^2$.

$y^2 - 3y - 4 = 0$

$(y+1)(y-4) = 0$

This is now a standard quadratic equation.

$y = -1$ or $y = 4$

$x^2 = -1$ (reject)

Use the substitution to find x.

or $x^2 = 4$

$x = 2$ or -2

Note that some values of y will not lead to a corresponding value of x, since square numbers must be positive.

Other substitutions may not be so clear. In particular, it is quite common to be given an **exponential equation**, an equation with the 'unknown' variable in the power, which needs a substitution. Look out for an a^x and an a^{2x}.

WORKED EXAMPLE 3.21

Solve the equation $4^x - 10 \times 2^x + 16 = 0$.

$4^x - 10 \times 2^x + 16 = 0$

$4^x = (2^2)^x = 2^{2x}$

$2^{2x} - 10 \times 2^x + 16 = 0$

Let $y = 2^x$

A substitution $y = 2^x$ turns this into a quadratic equation since $2^{2x} = (2^x)^2$.

$y^2 - 10y + 16 = 0$

This is now a standard quadratic equation.

$(y - 2)(y - 8) = 0$

$y = 2$ or 8

$2^x = 2$

Use the substitution to find x.

$x = 1$

or

$2^x = 8$

$x = 3$

▶▶ Fast forward

You will see how to solve more complicated exponential equations in Chapter 7.

EXERCISE 3F

In this exercise, you must show detailed reasoning.

> **Tip**
>
> 'Detailed reasoning' means that your solution must involve algebraic rearrangement and not, for example, the solver feature on your calculator.

1 Solve the following equations, giving your answers in an exact form.

    a   **i** $a^4 - 10a^2 + 21 = 0$ **ii** $x^4 - 7x^2 + 12 = 0$

    b   **i** $2x^6 + 7x^3 = 15$ **ii** $a^6 + 7a^3 = 8$

    c   **i** $x^2 - 4 = \dfrac{2}{x^2}$ **ii** $x^2 + \dfrac{36}{x^2} = 12$

    d   **i** $x - 6\sqrt{x} + 8 = 0$ **ii** $x - 10\sqrt{x} + 24 = 0$

    e   **i** $3^{2x} - 12 \times 3^x + 27 = 0$ **ii** $2^{2x} - 17 \times 2^x + 16 = 0$

2 By letting $y = \sqrt{x}$, solve the equation $x - \sqrt{x} - 6 = 0$.

3 Use an appropriate substitution to solve $x^2 + \dfrac{9}{x^2} = 10$.

4 Use a suitable substitution to solve the equation $\dfrac{1}{(3x+1)^2} + 5 = \dfrac{6}{3x+1}$.

5 Use an appropriate substitution to solve $x^3 - 9x^{1.5} + 8 = 0$.

6 Solve the equation $9(1 + 9^{x-1}) = 10 \times 3^x$.

7 Solve the equation $5^x = 6 - 5^{1-x}$.

8 Solve the equation $\dfrac{3}{(x-1)^2} - \dfrac{5}{x-1} = 2$.

9 **a** Write $x^4 - 4x^3 - 7x^2$ in the form $(x^2 - px)^2 - qx^2$.

   b Hence use a substitution of the form $y = x^2 - px$ to solve the equation $x^4 - 4x^3 - 7x^2 + 22x + 24 = 0$.

10 Solve the equation $4^{x+0.5} - 17 \times 2^x + 8 = 0$.

11 Solve $x = \sqrt{x} + 12$.

Checklist of learning and understanding

- Quadratic functions have the general form $f(x) = ax^2 + bx + c$. The main features are summarised in this table:

Feature	What to look at	Conclusion
Overall shape	The sign of a.	$a > 0$　　　　$a < 0$
y-intercept	The value of c.	y-intercept $(0, c)$
Turning point	Completed square form: $y = a(x + p)^2 + q$	Turning point $(-p, q)$
Line of symmetry	Completed square form: $a(x + p)^2 + q$ OR x-intercepts x_1, x_2	Line of symmetry $x = -p = \dfrac{x_1 + x_2}{2}$
x-intercepts	Factorise $f(x) = 0$ or use the quadratic formula: $x = \dfrac{-b \pm \sqrt{b^2 - 4ac}}{2a}$	Roots x_1 and x_2. x-intercepts $(x_1, 0)$ and $(x_2, 0)$
The number of real roots	Discriminant: $\Delta = b^2 - 4ac$	Two distinct roots: $\Delta > 0$ One root (equal roots, repeated root): $\Delta = 0$ No real roots: $\Delta < 0$

- To solve quadratic inequalities, rearrange to make one side zero and sketch the graph.
- A substitution can transform an equation into a quadratic equation.

Mixed practice 3

In this exercise, you must show detailed reasoning.

1. A quadratic function passes through the points $(k, 0)$ and $(k + 4, 0)$. Find the x-coordinate of the vertex of the graph of the function.

2. Solve algebraically:

$$(2x - 3)(x - 5) = (x - 3)^2$$

3. Solve $x^4 - 5x^2 + 4 = 0$.

4. The quadratic function $y = (x - a)^2 + b$ has a turning point at $(3, 7)$.

   a State whether this turning point is a maximum or a minimum point.

   b State the values of a and b.

5. The quadratic function $y = a(x - b)^2 + c$ passes through the points $(-2, 0)$ and $(6, 0)$. Its maximum y value is 48. Find the values of a, b and c.

6. The diagram represents the graph of the function $f(x) = (x + p)(x - q)$.

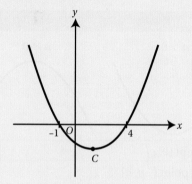

   a Write down the values of p and q if they are both positive.

   b The function has a minimum value at the point C. Find the x-coordinate of C.

7. i Find the discriminant of $kx^2 - 4x + k$ in terms of k.

   ii The quadratic equation $kx^2 - 4x + k = 0$ has equal roots. Find the possible values of k.

   © OCR, AS GCE Mathematics, Paper 4721, June 2007

8. Solve simultaneously $x^2 - 2x > 0$ and $x^2 - 4x + 3 \geqslant 0$.

 Tip

This means that your solution must involve algebraic rearrangement and not, for example, the solver feature on your calculator.

9 The diagram shows the graph of the function $y = ax^2 + bx + c$.

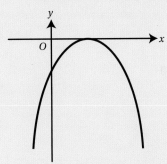

Copy and complete this table to show whether each expression is positive, negative or zero.

Expression	Positive	Negative	Zero
a			
c			
$b^2 - 4ac$			
b			

10 **a** Write $x^2 - 10x + 35$ in the form $(x - p)^2 + q$.

   b Hence, or otherwise, find the maximum value of
$$\frac{1}{\left(x^2 - 10x + 35\right)^3}.$$

11 Find the exact values of k for which the equation $2kx^2 + (k+1)x + 1 = 0$ has no real roots.

12 Solve the equation: $x^{\frac{1}{4}} + 2x^{-\frac{1}{4}} = 3$.

13 Solve the equation $\dfrac{49}{\left(5x+2\right)^2} - \dfrac{14}{5x+2} + 1 = 0$.

14 **a** Express $2x^2 - 6x + 9$ in the form $p(x + q)^2 + r$.

   b State the coordinates of the vertex of the curve $y = 2x^2 - 6x + 9$.

   c State the number of real roots of the equation $2x^2 - 6x + 9 = 0$.

15 A lawn is to be made in the shape shown. The units are metres.

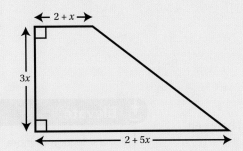

   i The perimeter of the lawn is P m. Find P in terms of x.

   ii Show that the area, A m², of the lawn is given by $A = 9x^2 + 6x$.

The perimeter of the lawn must be at least 39 m and the area of the lawn must be less than 99 m².

iii By writing down and solving appropriate inequalities, determine the set of possible values of x.

© **OCR, AS GCE Mathematics, Paper 4721, January 2010**

16 Alexia and Michaela were both trying to solve a quadratic equation of the form $x^2 + bx + c = 0$.

Unfortunately Alexia misread the value of b and found that the solutions were 6 and 1.

Michaela misread the value of c and found that the solutions were 4 and 1.

What were the correct solutions?

17 Find the values of k for which the line $y = 2x - k$ is tangent to the curve with equation $x^2 + y^2 = 5$.

18 Let α and β denote the roots of the quadratic equation $x^2 - kx + (k-1) = 0$.

a Express α and β in terms of the real parameter k.

b Given that $\alpha^2 + \beta^2 = 17$, find the possible values of k.

19 Let $q(x) = kx^2 + (k-2)x - 2$. Show that the equation $q(x) = 0$ has real roots for all values of k.

20 Two cars are travelling along two straight roads that are perpendicular to each other and meet at the point O, as shown in the diagram. The first car starts 50 km west of O and travels east at the constant speed of 20 km/h. At the same time, the second car starts 30 km south of O and travels north at the constant speed of 15 km/h.

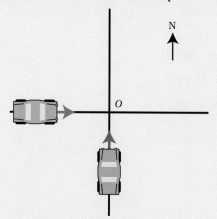

a Show that at time t (hours) the distance d (km) between the two cars satisfies
$$d^2 = 625t^2 - 2900t + 3400.$$

b Hence find the closest distance between the two cars.

> 💡 **Tip**
>
> α and β are Greek letters pronounced alpha, and beta, respectively. These are the lowercase forms of the letters.

> ⬇️ **Elevate**
>
> For a selection of more challenging problems, see Extension sheet 3.

4 Polynomials

In this chapter you will learn how to:

- define a polynomial
- find the product of two polynomials
- find the quotient of two polynomials
- quickly find factors of a polynomial
- sketch polynomials.

Before you start...

Chapter 2	You should know how to work with indices.	1 Simplify $x^2 \times x^4$.
GCSE	You should know how to multiply out brackets and collect like terms.	2 Expand and simplify $(2x+1)(x-3)$.
GCSE	You should know how to factorise quadratic expressions.	3 Factorise $x^2 - 8x + 15$.
GCSE	You should know how to solve quadratic equations using the quadratic formula.	4 Solve $x^2 + 4x + 2 = 0$.

Why study polynomials?

In Chapter 3 you were introduced to various properties of quadratic functions. As well as their mathematical interest, quadratic functions are used to model many real-world situations, such as the path of a projectile. To include more real-world situations you can extend quadratics to include terms in x^3, x^4 and so on. For example, the relationship between height and mass may be modelled using a cubic equation. This group of functions, called polynomials, turns out to be remarkably powerful.

(i) Did you know?

Polynomial functions can be used to predict the mass of an animal from its length.

▶▶ Fast forward

A It turns out that many other functions, such as $\sin x$ or e^x, can be approximated by (their graphs can closely match to) particular polynomials, as you will learn if you study Further Mathematics, in Pure Core Student Book 2.

Section 1: Working with polynomials

A polynomial is a function made up of a sum of terms containing non-negative (positive or zero) integer powers of an unknown, such as x. Polynomial functions are classified according to the highest power of the unknown (x) occurring in the function. This is called the **degree** of the polynomial.

> ### 🔑 Key point 4.1
>
> | General form of the function | Degree | Name | Example |
> | --- | --- | --- | --- |
> | $f(x) = a$ | 0 | constant function | $y = 5$ |
> | $f(x) = ax + b$ | 1 | linear function | $y = x + 7$ |
> | $f(x) = ax^2 + bx + c$ | 2 | quadratic function | $y = 3x^2 + 4x - 1$ |
> | $f(x) = ax^3 + bx^2 + cx + d$ | 3 | cubic function | $y = 2x^3 + 7x$ |
> | $f(x) = ax^4 + bx^3 + cx^2 + dx + e$ | 4 | quartic function | $y = x^4 - x^3 + 2x + \frac{1}{2}$ |

> ### ℹ️ Did you know?
>
>
>
> The Greeks had methods to solve quadratic equations, and the formulae for solving cubic and quartic equations were developed in 16th-century Italy. For over three hundred years, nobody was able to come up with a general solution to the quintic equation until, in 1821, the Norwegian mathematician Niels Abel (pictured) used a branch of mathematics called group theory to prove that there could never be a 'quintic formula'.

The letters a, b, c etc. in Key point 4.1 are called the **coefficients** of the powers of x. The coefficient of the highest power of x in the function (given by a in Key point 4.1) is called the **lead coefficient** and the term containing the highest power of x is the **leading order term**.

Coefficients can take any value, with the restriction that the lead coefficient cannot equal zero (a polynomial of order n with a lead coefficient 0 is in fact a polynomial of order at most $n - 1$).

You should already be familiar with adding and subtracting two polynomials. To multiply two polynomials, you need to expand the brackets and collect like terms. Worked example 4.1 is one suggested way of setting out polynomial multiplication to ensure that you include all of the terms.

> ### ✔️ Gateway to A Level
>
> See Gateway to A Level section A for a reminder of expanding Brackets.

WORKED EXAMPLE 4.1

Expand $(x^3 + 3x^2 - 2)(x^2 - 5x + 4)$.

$(x^3 + 3x^2 - 2)(x^2 - 5x + 4)$
$= x^3(x^2 - 5x + 4) + 3x^2(x^2 - 5x + 4) - 2(x^2 - 5x + 4)$
$= x^5 - 5x^4 + 4x^3$
$\qquad\qquad + 3x^4 - 15x^3 + 12x^2$
$\qquad\qquad\qquad\qquad - 2x^2 + 10x - 8$
$= x^5 - 2x^4 - 11x^3 + 10x^2 + 10x - 8$

Multiply each term inside the first brackets, in turn, by the whole of the expression in the second brackets.

Then collect like terms.

EXERCISE 4A

1 Decide whether each of the following expressions are polynomials. For those that are polynomials give the degree and the lead coefficient.

a $3x^3 - 3x^2 + 2x$
b $1 - 3x - x^5$
c $5x^2 - x^{-3}$

d $9x^4 - \dfrac{5}{x}$
e $4e^x + 3e^{2x}$
f $x^4 + 5x^2 - 3\sqrt{x}$

g $4x^5 - 3x^3 + 2x^7 - 4$
h 1

2 Expand and simplify the brackets for the following expressions.

a i $(3x - 2)(2x^2 + 4x - 7)$
ii $(3x + 1)(x^2 + 5x + 6)$

b i $(2x + 1)(x^3 - 8x^2 + 6x - 1)$
ii $(2x + 5)(x^3 - 6x^2 + 3)$

c i $(b^2 + 3b - 1)(b^2 - 2b + 4)$
ii $(r^2 - 3r + 7)(r^2 - 8r + 2)$

d i $(5 - x^2)(x^4 - 2x^3 + 1)$
ii $(x - x^3)(x^3 - x - 1)$

3 In what circumstances might you want to expand brackets? In what circumstances is the factorised form better?

4 a Is it always true that the sum of a polynomial of degree n and a polynomial of degree $n - 1$ has degree n?

b Is it always true that the sum of a polynomial of degree n and a polynomial of degree n has degree n?

Section 2: Polynomial division

From Worked example 4.1 you know that:

$$x^5 - 2x^4 - 11x^3 + 10x^2 + 10x - 8 = (x^2 - 5x + 4)(x^3 + 3x^2 - 2)$$

which can also be written as:

$$\frac{x^5 - 2x^4 - 11x^3 + 10x^2 + 10x - 8}{x^2 - 5x + 4} = x^3 + 3x^2 - 2$$

However, if you had not just done the multiplication it is unlikely that you would have been able to spot this.

One way to divide two expressions is called polynomial long division:

1 Divide the leading order term in the numerator by the leading order term in the denominator. This is the leading order term of the answer.

 Tip

The resultant polynomial, when one polynomial is divided by another, is called the 'quotient'. In this example, $x^3 + 3x^2 - 2$ is the quotient.

2   Multiply this term by the whole denominator. Subtract the resulting expression from the numerator.
3   Repeat this process until all terms have been accounted for.

There are several ways to set this process out, but a common method is given in Worked example 4.2.

⏮ **Rewind**

Another common method is to compare coefficients – this is very similar to the process shown in Chapter 1, Worked example 1.1.

WORKED EXAMPLE 4.2

Given that $(x - 4)$ is a factor of $x^3 - x^2 - 11x - 4$, find the other factor.

Divide the polynomial by $(x - 4)$ · · · · · The leading term in the divisor is x.

$$(x-4)\overline{\smash{\big)}\,x^3 - x^2 - 11x - 4}$$
$$\underline{x^2 + \ 3x + 1}$$

This is the final answer – it gets written down in stages:
To get x^2 we divide the leading term by x.

$\underline{x^3 - 4x^2}$ · · · · · · · · · This is x^2 multiplied by the divisor.

$3x^2 - 11x - 4$ · · · · · · · · These are the remaining terms. To get $+3x$ we divide $3x^2$ by x.

$\underline{3x^2 - 12x}$ · · · · · · · · This is $+3x$ multiplied by the divisor.

$x - 4$ · · · · · · · These are the remaining terms. To get $+1$ we divide x by x.

$\underline{x - 4}$ · · · · · · · This is $+1$ multiplied by the divisor.

0 · · · · · · · There is nothing left over.

Hence the other factor is $x^2 + 3x + 1$, and so:

$$x^3 - x^2 - 11x - 4 = (x - 4)(x^2 + 3x + 1)$$

EXERCISE 4B

1 You are given one factor of each polynoimal. Use polynomial division to find the other factor.

  a **i** $(x + 4)$ is one factor of $x^3 - 4x^2 - 35x - 12$

  ii $(x + 3)$ is one factor of $x^3 + x^2 - 3x + 9$

  b **i** $(x + 1)$ is one factor of $x^3 + x^2 - 2x - 2$

  ii $(x + 4)$ is one factor of $x^3 + 4x^2 + 3x + 12$

  c **i** $(2x + 5)$ is one factor of $2x^3 + x^2 - 6x + 10$

  ii $(3x - 2)$ is one factor of $3x^3 - 17x^2 + 16x - 4$

  d **i** $(x - 7)$ is one factor of $x^4 - 12x^3 + 38x^2 - 23x + 14$

  ii $(x - 8)$ is one factor of $2x^4 - 16x^3 + 3x^2 - 19x - 40$

2 Use polynomial division to simplify the following expressions.

  a **i** $\dfrac{x^3 - 3x^2 - 13x - 30}{x^2 + 3x + 5}$ **ii** $\dfrac{x^3 + 5x^2 - 5x + 63}{x^2 - 2x + 9}$

  b **i** $\dfrac{x^4 + 7x^3 + 13x^2 + 2x - 2}{x^2 + 3x - 1}$ **ii** $\dfrac{x^4 + 3x^3 - 32x^2 - 17x + 3}{x^2 - 4x - 3}$

Section 3: The factor theorem

Algebraic division allows you to factorise a polynomial if you know one factor; but finding the first factor can be difficult. To do this you use something called the **factor theorem**.

 Key point 4.2

The factor theorem states that:

$(x - a)$ is a factor of $f(x)$ if and only if $f(a) = 0$.

 Focus on ...

This is proved in Focus on ... Proof 1.

Notice that the factor theorem says two things:

- If $(x - a)$ is a factor of $f(x)$ then $f(a) = 0$.

and

- If $f(a) = 0$ then $(x - a)$ is a factor of $f(x)$.

WORKED EXAMPLE 4.3

Show that $(x + 3)$ is a factor of $f(x) = 2x^3 + x^2 - 9x + 18$.

$f(-3) = 2 \times (-3)^3 + (-3)^2 - 9 \times (-3) + 18$

$\quad = -54 + 9 + 27 + 18 = 0$

By the factor theorem if $f(-3) = 0$ then $(x + 3)$ is a factor.

Therefore $(x + 3)$ is a factor of $f(x)$.

A slightly more advanced version of the factor theorem is given in Key point 4.3.

 Key point 4.3

$(ax - b)$ is a factor of $f(x)$ if and only if $f\left(\dfrac{b}{a}\right) = 0$.

WORKED EXAMPLE 4.4

Show that $(2x - 3)$ is a factor of $f(x) = 6x^3 - 9x^2 + 8x - 12$.

$f\left(\dfrac{3}{2}\right) = 6 \times \left(\dfrac{3}{2}\right)^3 - 9\left(\dfrac{3}{2}\right)^2 + 8 \times \dfrac{3}{2} - 12$

$\quad = \dfrac{81}{4} - \dfrac{81}{4} + 12 - 12 = 0$

By the factor theorem, if $f\left(\dfrac{3}{2}\right) = 0$ then $(2x - 3)$ is a factor.

Therefore $(2x - 3)$ is a factor of $f(x)$.

WORK IT OUT 4.1

Find the value of a such that $(3x + 5)$ is a factor of $f(x) = 6x^3 + 19x^2 + ax - 10$.

Only one of these solutions is correct. Identify the errors in the incorrect solutions.

Solution 1	Solution 2	Solution 3
$f(-5) = 0$: $-750 + 475 - 5a - 10 = 0$ $5a = 285$ $a = 57$	$f\left(\dfrac{5}{3}\right) = 0$: $\dfrac{250}{9} + \dfrac{475}{9} + \dfrac{5}{3}a - 10 = 0$ $\dfrac{5a}{3} = \dfrac{617}{9}$ $a = \dfrac{617}{15}$	$f\left(-\dfrac{5}{3}\right) = 0$: $-\dfrac{250}{9} + \dfrac{475}{9} - \dfrac{5}{3}a - 10 = 0$ $\dfrac{5a}{3} = 15$ $a = 9$

Once one factor has been identified, polynomial division can be used to find the remaining factors, and then find the roots of the polynomial as in Worked example 4.5.

WORKED EXAMPLE 4.5

Solve the equation $f(x) = x^3 + x^2 - 13x + 14 = 0$.

$f(0) = 14$

$f(1) = 3$

$f(-1) = 27$

$f(2) = 0$

> Factorising would help you solve this equation. The factor theorem might help you find a factor.

Therefore $(x - 2)$ is a factor of $f(x)$.

$$
\begin{array}{r}
x^2 + 3x - 7 \\
(x-2) \,\overline{)\, x^3 + x^2 - 13x + 14} \\
\underline{x^3 - 2x^2} \\
3x^2 - 13x + 14 \\
\underline{3x^2 - 6x} \\
-7x + 14 \\
\underline{-7x + 14} \\
0
\end{array}
$$

> Polynomial division will give you the second factor.

So:

$x^3 + x^2 - 13x + 14 = (x - 2)(x^2 + 3x - 7)$

$(x - 2)(x^2 + 3x - 7) = 0$

$\Rightarrow x = 2$ or $x^2 + 3x - 7 = 0$

> If the product equals zero then one of the factors is zero.

Tip

If the expression is going to factorise nicely then you only need to try numbers that are factors of the constant term.

Tip

When questions mention factors it is often tempting to go straight to polynomial division. Always try the factor theorem first.

Continues on next page ...

$$\Rightarrow x = 2 \text{ or } x = \frac{-3 \pm \sqrt{9+28}}{2}$$

The second equation is quadratic.

So the solutions are:

$$x = 2 \text{ or } x = \frac{-3+\sqrt{37}}{2} \text{ or } x = \frac{-3-\sqrt{37}}{2}$$

A very common type of question asks to find unknown coefficients in an expression if factors are given.

WORKED EXAMPLE 4.6

$f(x) = x^3 + 4x^2 + ax + b$ has factors of $(x - 1)$ and $(x + 1)$. Find the constants a and b.

$f(1) = 0$ (1)	Apply the factor theorem with the factor $(x - 1)$. If $(x - 1)$ is a factor then $f(1) = 0$.
$1 + 4 + a + b = 0$	
$a + b = -5$	
$f(-1) = 0$ (2)	Apply the factor theorem with the factor $(x + 1)$.
$-1 + 4 - a + b = 0$	
$-a + b = -3$	
$2b = -8$ (1) + (2)	Solve the simultaneous equations in a and b.
$b = -4$	
$a = -1$	

Elevate

For a further example of this type and more practice questions, see Support sheet 4.

EXERCISE 4C

1   Decide whether each of the following expressions is a factor of $2x^3 - 3x^2 - 3x + 2$.

  a i $x - 1$ **b i** $x - 2$ **c i** $x - \frac{1}{2}$ **d i** $2x - 1$ **e i** $3x - 1$

  ii $x + 1$ **ii** $x + 2$ **ii** $x + \frac{1}{2}$ **ii** $2x + 1$ **ii** $3x + 2$

2   Fully factorise the following expressions.

  a i $x^3 + 2x^2 - x - 2$ **ii** $x^3 + x^2 - 4x - 4$

  b i $x^3 - 7x^2 + 16x - 12$ **ii** $x^3 + 6x^2 + 12x + 8$

  c i $x^3 - 3x^2 + 12x - 10$ **ii** $x^3 - 2x^2 + 2x - 15$

  d i $6x^3 - 11x^2 + 6x - 1$ **ii** $12x^3 + 13x^2 - 37x - 30$

3   Solve the following equations.

  a i $x^3 + 12 = 2x^2 + 11x$ **ii** $x^3 - x^2 - 17x = 15$

  b i $x^3 - 5x^2 + 7x - 2 = 0$ **ii** $x^3 - 6x^2 + 7x - 2 = 0$

4 Find the roots of the following equations.

  a i $x^3 - 6x^2 + 11x = 6$ **ii** $x^3 - 2x^2 + 6 = 5x$

  b i $x^3 + x^2 - x - 1 = 0$ **ii** $x^3 - 3x^2 - 10x + 24 = 0$

5 **a** Show that $(x - 2)$ is a factor of $p(x) = x^3 - 3x^2 - 10x + 24$.

  b Hence express $p(x)$ as the product of three linear factors and solve $p(x) = 0$.

6 **a** Show that $(x - 3)$ is a factor of $p(x) = x^3 - x^2 - 2x - 12$.

  b Hence show that $p(x) = 0$ only has one real root.

7 $x^3 + 7x^2 + cx + d$ has factors $(x + 1)$ and $(x + 2)$. Find the values of c and d.

8 $f(x) = x^3 - ax^2 - bx + 168$ has factors $(x - 7)$ and $(x - 3)$.

  a Find a and b.

  b Find the remaining factor of $f(x)$.

9 The polynomial $x^2 + kx - 8k$ has a factor $(x - k)$. Find the possible values of k.

10 The polynomial $x^2 - (k + 1)x - 3$ has a factor $(x - k + 1)$. Find k.

11 The polynomial $x^2 - 5x + 6$ is a factor of $2x^3 - 15x^2 + ax + b$. Find the values of a and b.

> 💡 **Hint**
>
> Note that question 5 is identical to the last part of question 4, but this is how it is often phrased in formal assessment.

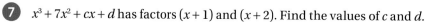

Section 4: Sketching polynomial functions

You need to know the shapes to expect for polynomial functions. The graphs of polynomials of degree zero and one are straight lines. All other polynomial graphs are smooth curves. Just as with quadratic graphs, the shape depends on the sign of the lead coefficient.

n	$y = x^n$	Positive polynomial	Negative polynomial	x-intercepts	Turning points
2	(graph of $y = x^2$)	(U-shaped curve)	(inverted-U curve)	0, 1 or 2	1
3	(graph of $y = x^3$)	(increasing cubic curve)	(decreasing cubic curve)	1, 2 or 3	0 or 2

Continued

n	$y = x^n$	Positive polynomial	Negative polynomial	x-intercepts	Turning points
4	$y = x^4$			0, 1, 2, 3 or 4	1 or 3

When a polynomial is given in factorised form, you can easily find the x-intercepts.

One fact to be aware of is how repeated roots affect the shape of the graph.

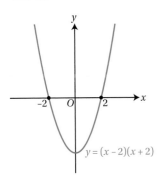

If a polynomial has a factor $(x - a)$ then the curve passes straight through the x-axis at a.

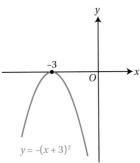

If a polynomial has a double factor $(x - a)^2$ then the curve touches the x-axis at a.

▶▶| **Fast forward**

You do not need to find the coordinates of turning points unless explicitly asked. You will learn how to do this in Chapter 14.

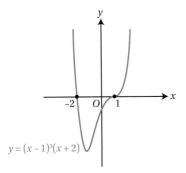

If a polynomial has a triple factor $(x - a)^3$ then the curve passes through the x-axis at a, flattening as it does so.

Once you know the x- and y-intercepts you can sketch the graph of a polynomial function. A **sketch** does not need to be to scale, but should show the correct shape and the axis intercepts. If you were asked to **draw** a graph or **plot** some points, you would do so accurately, on graph paper.

Key point 4.4

To sketch the graph of a polynomial function:

1 Decide on the basic shape by considering the order (degree) and the lead coefficient.
2 Set $x = 0$ to find the y-intercept.
3 Write in factorised form if possible.
4 Find x-intercepts.
5 Decide on how the curve meets the x-axis at each intercept.
6 Connect all this information with a smooth curve.

 Explore

For higher degree polynomials, there are more options for the shape. Use technology to investigate how many x-intercepts a polynomial of degree n can have.

WORKED EXAMPLE 4.7

Sketch the graph of $y = (2 - x)(x - 3)^2$.

This is a negative cubic.	Classify the basic shape. If you were to expand the brackets, the leading order term would be $-x^3$.
When $x = 0$, $y = 2 \times (-3)^2 = 18$	Find the y-intercept.
When $y = 0$, $x = 2$ or $x = 3$	Find the x-intercepts.
At $x = 2$ curve passes through the x-axis. At $x = 3$ curve just touches the x-axis.	Decide whether the curve crosses or touches the x-axis. This depends whether a factor is linear or squared.
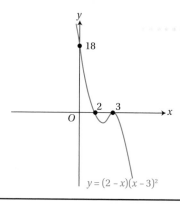	Sketch the curve.

$y = (2 - x)(x - 3)^2$

You can sometimes deduce a possible equation of a curve from its graph. If you know that a curve represents a polynomial function, the x-intercepts tell you its factors. However, there could also be a constant factor multiplying the whole equation: for example, $y = 3(x - 1)(x - 2)$ has the same x-intercepts as $y = (x - 1)(x - 2)$. You need to know the coordinates of another point on the graph (for example, the y-intercept) in order to find this constant factor.

Key point 4.5

To find the equation of a polynomial from its graph:

1 Use the shape of the graph and position of the x-intercepts to write down the factors of the polynomial.
2 Use any other point to find the constant factor.

WORKED EXAMPLE 4.8

The diagram shows the graph of a quartic polynomial. Find its equation.

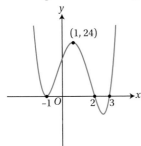

Single root at $x = 2$ and $x = 3$

Double root at $x = -1$

$y = k(x + 1)^2 (x - 2)(x - 3)$

$24 = k \times (2)^2 \times (-1) \times (-2) = 8k$

$\Rightarrow k = 3$

So the equation is $y = 3(x + 1)^2 (x - 2)(x - 3)$

Describe x-intercepts. They tell you about the factors.

Write in factorised form. Don't forget the constant factor outside the brackets.

Use the fact that when $x = 1$, $y = 24$.

EXERCISE 4D

1 Sketch the following graphs, labelling all axis intercepts.

  a i $y = 2(x - 2)(x - 3)(x - 4)$ ii $y = 7(x - 5)(x + 1)(x - 3)$

  b i $y = 4(5 - x)(x - 3)(x - 3)$ ii $y = 2(x - 1)(2 - x)(x - 3)$

  c i $y = -x(x - 4)^2$ ii $y = (x - 2)^2(x + 2)$

  d i $y = x(x^2 + 4)$ ii $y = (x + 1)(x^2 - 3x + 7)$

  e i $y = (1 - x)^2(1 + x)$ ii $y = (2 - x)(3 - x)^2$

> **Tip**
>
> Remember that a sketch does not need to be to scale. In this exercise, you don't need to find the coordinates of turning points.

2 Sketch the following graphs, labelling all axis intercepts.

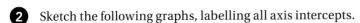

  a i $y = x(x - 1)(x - 2)(2x - 3)$ ii $y = (x + 2)(x + 3)(x - 2)(x - 3)$

  b i $y = -4(x - 3)(x - 2)(x + 1)(x + 3)$ ii $y = -5x(x + 2)(x - 3)(x - 4)$

  c i $y = (x - 3)^2(x - 2)(x - 4)$ ii $y = -x^2(x - 1)(x + 2)$

d i $y = 2(x+1)^3(x-3)$ **ii** $y = -x^3(x-4)$

e i $y = (x^2 + 3x + 12)(x+1)(3x-1)$ **ii** $y = (x+2)^2(x^2+4)$

3 Find the lowest order polynomial equation for each of the
following graphs.

a i

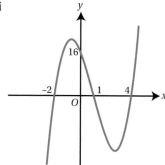

ii

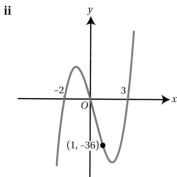

b i

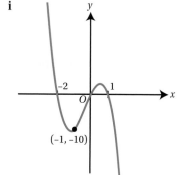

ii

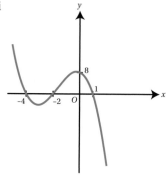

c i

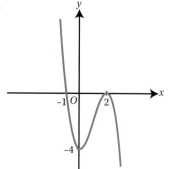

ii

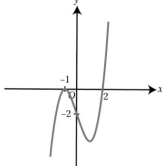

d **i**

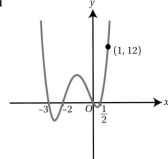

ii

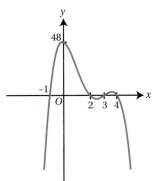

e **i**

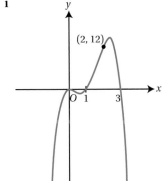

ii

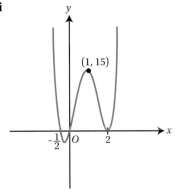

f **i**

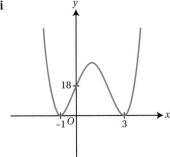

ii

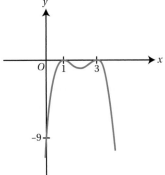

4 **a** Show that $(x - 2)$ is a factor of $f(x) = 2x^3 - 5x^2 + x + 2$.

 b Factorise $f(x)$.

 c Sketch the graph $y = f(x)$.

5 Sketch the graph of $y = 2(x + 2)^2(3 - x)$, labelling clearly any axis intercepts.

6 These two graphs both have equations of the form $y = px^3 + qx^2 + rx + s$.
Find the values of p, q, r and s for each graph.

a

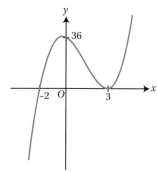

b

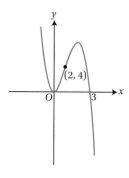

7 **a** Factorise fully $x^4 - q^4$ where q is a positive constant.

   b Hence or otherwise sketch the graph $y = x^4 - q^4$, labelling any points where the graph meets an axis.

8 **a** Sketch the graph of $y = (x - p)^2(x - q)$ where $0 < p < q$.

   b How many solutions does the equation $(x - p)^2(x - q) = k$ have when $k > 0$?

Checklist of learning and understanding

- A polynomial is an expression that is a sum of terms, each of the form ax^k.
- You can multiply two polynomials by expanding the brackets and collecting like terms.
- You can divide two polynomials by using polynomial division.
- The **factor theorem** tells you when a linear expression is a factor of a polynomial:
  - $(ax + b)$ is a factor of a polynomial $f(x)$ **if and only if** $f\left(-\dfrac{b}{a}\right) = 0$.
- You can sketch the graph of a polynomial function by using its factorised form. The factors tell you the x-intercepts. Repeated factors tell you whether the graph crosses or touches the x-axis.

Mixed practice 4

1 The diagram shows the graph with equation $y = ax^4 + bx^3 + cx^2 + dx + e$. Find the values of a, b, c, d and e.

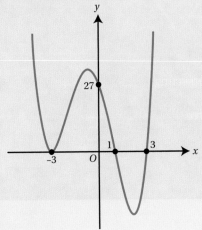

2 Show that
$$\frac{x^3 + 2x^2 - 3x - 6}{x + 2} = x^2 + bx + c$$
where b and c are integers to be found.

3 **a** Show that $(x - 2)$ is a factor of $f(x) = x^3 - 4x^2 + x + 6$.

b Factorise $f(x)$.

c Sketch the graph of $y = f(x)$.

4 Two cubic polynomials are defined by $f(x) = x^3 + (a - 3)x + 2b$, $g(x) = 3x^3 + x^2 + 5ax + 4b$, where a and b are constants.

i Given that $f(x)$ and $g(x)$ have a common factor of $(x - 2)$, show that $a = -4$ and find the value of b.

ii Using these values of a and b, factorise $f(x)$ fully. Hence show that $f(x)$ and $g(x)$ have two common factors.

© OCR, AS GCE Mathematics, Paper 4722, June 2012

5 **a** Given that $(2x - 1)$ and $(x + 2)$ are factors of $2x^3 + ax^2 + 4x + b$, find the values of a and b.

b Hence sketch the graph of $y = 2x^3 + ax^2 + 4x + b$.

6 Sketch the graph of $y = (x - a)^2(x - b)(x - c)$ where $b < 0 < a < c$.

7 The cubic polynomial $f(x)$ is defined by $f(x) = x^3 + x^2 - 11x + 10$.

i Use the factor theorem to find a factor of $f(x)$.

ii Hence solve the equation $f(x) = 0$, giving each root in an exact form.

© OCR, AS GCE Mathematics, Paper 4722, June 2011

8 The polynomial $x^2 - 4x + 3$ is a factor of the polynomial $x^3 + ax^2 + 27x + b$. Find the values of a and b.

 Elevate

For a mixture of more challenging questions, see Extension sheet 4.

5 Using graphs

In this chapter you will learn how to:

- use the link between solving simultaneous equations and intersecting graphs
- determine a number of intersections between a line and a curve
- use transformations of graphs
- use graphs and applications of direct and inverse proportion
- illustrate two-variable inequalities on a graph.

Before you start…

Chapter 3	You should know how to solve quadratic equations.	1	Solve $x^2 + x - 1 = 0$.
Chapter 3	You should know how to use the quadratic discriminant to determine the number of real solutions of a quadratic equation.	2	How many real solutions are there to the equation $x^2 + 4x + 4 = 0$?
GCSE	You should know how to solve simple linear simultaneous equations by elimination.	3	Solve these simultaneous equations. $x + 2y = 5$ $3x + 4y = 11$
Chapter 2	You should know how to solve equations involving indices.	4	Solve $2^x = 8$.
GCSE	You should know how to solve linear inequalities.	5	Solve $3x + 1 > 13$.
GCSE	You should be able to find equations for direct and inverse proportion.	6	V is inversely proportional to the square of r. When $r = 2$, $V = 12$. Find an expression for V in terms of r.

Why use graphs?

Graphs are an alternative way of expressing a relationship between two variables. Understanding the connection between graphs and equations (or inequalities), and being able to switch between the two representations, gives you a much wider variety of tools to solve mathematical problems.

Section 1: Intersections of graphs

You already know how to solve linear simultaneous equations, and how to use simultaneus equations to find the point of intersection of two straight lines. You can apply similar ideas to find intersections between curves whose equations involve quadratic functions. Whenever you are finding an intersection between two graphs, you are solving simultaneous equations. This means that the values you find for x and y must satisfy both equations.

Gateway to A Level

For revision of linear simultaneous equations, see Gateway to A Level section J.

The intersection of two graphs can always be found using technology (for example, graphing software or a graphical calculator). However, this usually only gives approximate solutions. If you need exact solutions you have to use an algebraic method. In many cases the best method is **substitution**, where you replace every occurrence of one variable in one equation by its expression from the other equation.

WORKED EXAMPLE 5.1

Find the coordinates of the points of intersection of the line $y = 2x - 1$ and the parabola $y = x^2 - 3x + 5$.

$x^2 - 3x + 5 = 2x - 1$	At the intersection points, the y-coordinates for the two curves are equal, so you can replace y in the first equation with the expression for y from the second equation.
$x^2 - 5x + 6 = 0$	This is a quadratic equation. Try to factorise.
$(x - 2)(x - 3) = 0$	
$x = 2 \text{ or } 3$	
$y = 2x - 1$	You also need to find the y-coordinates, by substituting back into one of the equations for y (both should give the same answer). Pick the first equation, as it is easier.
$x = 2: y = 2 \times 2 - 1 = 3$	
$x = 3: y = 2 \times 3 - 1 = 5$	

The coordinates are $(2, 3)$ and $(3, 5)$.

WORK IT OUT 5.1

Solve $x + y = 3$ and $y^2 + 2x^2 = 9$.

Which is the correct solution? Can you identify the errors made in the incorrect solutions?

Solution 1	Solution 2	Solution 3
Squaring $x + y = 3$ gives $x^2 + y^2 = 9$. Subtracting this from the second equation gives $x^2 = 0$ so $x = 0$. Substituting into the first equation, $y = 3$. Checking this in the second equation gives: $$3^2 + 2 \times 0^2 = 9$$	If $x + y = 3$ then $y = 3 - x$ Substituting into the second equation: $y^2 + 2x^2 = 9$ $(3 - x)^2 + 2x^2 = 9$ $9 - 6x + x^2 + 2x^2 = 9$ $3x^2 - 6x = 0$ Dividing by $3x$: $x - 2 = 0$ $x = 2$ Substituting into $y = 3 - x$: $x = 2, y = 1$	Rearranging the first equation gives $y = 3 - x$. Substituting into the second equation: $y^2 + 2x^2 = 9$ $(3 - x)^2 + 2x^2 = 9$ $9 - 6x + x^2 + 2x^2 = 9$ $3x^2 - 6x = 0$ $3x(x - 2) = 0$ $x = 0 \text{ or } 2$ Substituting into the first equation: $x = 0, y = 3$ $x = 2, y = 1$

EXERCISE 5A

1. Find the coordinates of intersection of the given curve and the given straight line.

   a i $y = x^2 + 2x - 3$ and $y = x - 1$

   a ii $y = x^2 - 4x + 3$ and $y = 2x - 6$

   b i $y = -x^2 + 3x + 9$ and $2x - y = 3$

   b ii $y = x^2 - 2x + 8$ and $x - y = 6$

2. Solve the following simultaneous equations:

   a i $x - 2y = 1$, $3xy - y^2 = 8$

   a ii $x + 2y = 3$, $y^2 + 2xy + 9 = 0$

   b i $xy = 3$, $x + y = 4$

   b ii $x + y + 8 = 0$, $xy = 15$

   c i $x + y = 5$, $y = x^2 - 2x + 3$

   c ii $x - y = 4$, $y = x^2 + x - 5$

3. Find the coordinates of the points of intersection of $y = \dfrac{1}{x}$ and $y = 2x$.

4. Solve simultaneously:

   $3^x + 2^x = 13 \qquad 3^x - 2^x = 5$

5. Solve simultaneously:

   $y = 2^x \qquad 4^x + y = 72$

6. The sum of two numbers is 8 and their product is 9.75.

   a Show that this information can be written as a quadratic equation.

   b What are the two numbers?

7. Solve the equations $xy + x = 0$, $x^2 + y^2 = 4$.

8. The equations $y = (x - 2)(x - 3)^2$ and $y = k$ have one solution for all $k < m$. Find the largest value of m.

Section 2: The discriminant revisited

Sometimes you only want to know how many intersection points there are, rather than to find their actual coordinates. The discriminant can be used to determine the number of intersections.

WORKED EXAMPLE 5.2

Find the set of values of k for which the line with equation $x + y = k$ intersects the curve with equation $x^2 - 4x + y^2 + 6y = 12$ at two distinct points.

Line equation: $y = k - x$

> Try finding the intersections in terms of k and see if that gives you any ideas.

Substitute into the equation:

$x^2 - 4x + (k - x)^2 + 6(k - x) = 12$

$\Rightarrow x^2 - 4x + k^2 - 2kx + x^2 + 6k - 6x = 12$

> At the intersection points, the y-coordinates for the two curves are equal, so you can replace y in the second equation by the expression for y from the first equation.

$\Rightarrow 2x^2 - (10 + 2k)x + k^2 + 6k = 12$

$\Rightarrow 2x^2 - (10 + 2k)x + (k^2 + 6k - 12) = 0$

> This is a quadratic equation, so write it with one side equal to zero.

Continues on next page ...

Two solutions $\therefore \Delta > 0$

$\Delta = (10+2k)^2 - 8(k^2 + 6k - 12) > 0$

$\Rightarrow 100 + 40k + 4k^2 - 8k^2 - 48k + 96 > 0$

$\Rightarrow -4k^2 - 8k + 196 > 0$

$\Rightarrow k^2 + 2k - 49 < 0$

> You know that the discriminant tells you the number of solutions of a quadratic equation.

> Divide both sides by -4. Remember that this reverses the inequality.

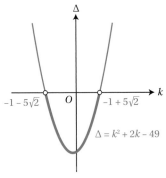

Roots: $k^2 + 2k - 49 = 0$

$k = \dfrac{-2 \pm \sqrt{4 + 4 \times 49}}{2}$

$= \dfrac{-2 \pm 2\sqrt{1 + 49}}{2}$

$= -1 \pm \sqrt{50} = -1 \pm 5\sqrt{2}$

$\therefore -1 - 5\sqrt{2} < k < -1 + 5\sqrt{2}$

> This is a quadratic inequality. To solve it, find where LHS $= 0$ and sketch the graph.

> The graph shows that the required interval is between the roots.

Tip

Questions which talk about the number of intersections are often solved using the discriminant.

▶▶ Fast forward

The equation $x^2 - 4x + y^2 + 6y = 12$ in Worked example 5.2 actually represents a circle. You will study circles in Chapter 6.

EXERCISE 5B

1. Show that the line with equation $x - y = 6$ is a tangent to the curve with equation $x^2 - 6x + y^2 - 2y + 2 = 0$.

2. Find the exact values of m for which the line $y = mx + 3$ is a tangent to the curve with equation $y = 3x^2 - x + 5$.

3. Let C be the curve with equation $4x^2 + 9y^2 = 36$. Find the exact values of k for which the line $2x + 3y = k$ is a tangent to C.

Tip

A tangent touches the curve but does not cross at that point. With quadratic equations this means that there are repeated roots so the discriminant is zero. After studying Chapter 13 you will find another way of finding the tangent to a curve. However, this type of question is still best done using the discriminant.

4 Find the values of a for which the curve $y = x^2$ never touches the curve $y = a - (x - a)^2$.

5 Show algebraically that the line $y = kx + 5$ intersects the parabola $y = x^2 + 2$ twice for all values of k.

Section 3: Transforming graphs

From previous study you may know how changing the function changes the graph as summarised in Key point 5.1.

Key point 5.1

Transformation of $y = \mathrm{f}(x)$	Transformation of graph
$y = \mathrm{f}(x) + c$	Translation c units up.
$y = \mathrm{f}(x + d)$	Translation d units to the *left*.
$y = p\mathrm{f}(x)$	Vertical stretch, scale factor p
$y = \mathrm{f}(qx)$	Horizontal stretch factor $\dfrac{1}{q}$
$y = -\mathrm{f}(x)$	Reflection in the x-axis
$y = \mathrm{f}(-x)$	Reflection in the y-axis

Tip

When c is negative the translation is down, and when d is negative it is to the right. When p or q are negative, the stretch is combined with a reflection.

Vertical transformations behave as expected, but the horizontal ones can be counter-intuitive; for example, $\mathrm{f}(x + 3)$ translates the graph to the left.

The following proof shows why that is the case. However, you can use all the results from Key Point 5.1 without proof.

PROOF 2

Prove that the graph of $\mathrm{f}(x + d)$ is a translation of the graph of $y = \mathrm{f}(x)$, by d units to the left.

Let (x_1, y_1) be a point on the graph of $y = \mathrm{f}(x)$ and (x_2, y_2) a point on the graph of $y = \mathrm{f}(x + d)$.

Define variables. You have to be very careful and **not** assume that x's are all the same or y's are all the same.

When $x_1 = x_2 + d$ then:

$y_1 = \mathrm{f}(x_1) = \mathrm{f}(x_2 + d) = y_2$

This says that if two points are d units apart horizontally, then they are at the same height.

Continues on next page ...

Hence (x_2, y_2) is d units to the left of (x_1, y_1), and so the graph of $y = f(x)$ is translated d units to the left to get the graph of $y = f(x + d)$.

Interpret your calculation geometrically and write a conclusion.

WORKED EXAMPLE 5.3

The graph of $y = x^2 + 2x$ is translated 5 units to the left. Find the equation of the resulting graph in the form $y = ax^2 + bx + c$.

If $f(x) = x^2 + 2x$, then the new graph is $y = f(x + 5)$,

Relate the transformation to function notation.

$y = (x + 5)^2 + 2(x + 5)$
$\quad = x^2 + 12x + 35$

Replace all x by $(x + 5)$ in the equation for the function.

 Tip

A translation 5 units to the left could also be described in vector notation as $\begin{pmatrix} -5 \\ 0 \end{pmatrix}$.

WORKED EXAMPLE 5.4

Describe a transformation which transforms the graph of $y = x^2 + 3x$ to the graph of $y = 4x^2 + 6x$.

Let $f(x) = x^2 + 3x$

Then $4x^2 + 6x = (2x)^2 + 3(2x) = f(2x)$

Try to relate the two equations by writing the second function in a similar way to the first.

It is a horizontal stretch with scale factor $\dfrac{1}{2}$.

Relate the function notation to the transformation.

WORKED EXAMPLE 5.5

The graph of $y = f(x)$ has a single maximum point with coordinates $(4, -3)$. Find the coordinates of the maximum point on the graph of $y = f(-x)$.

The transformation taking $y = f(x)$ to $y = f(-x)$ is a reflection in the y-axis.

Relate the function notation to the transformation.

The maximum point is $(-4, -3)$.

Reflection in the y-axis leaves y-coordinates unchanged and changes x to $-x$.

EXERCISE 5C

1 The graph of $y = f(x)$ is shown. Sketch the graph of the following functions, including the position of the minimum and maximum points.

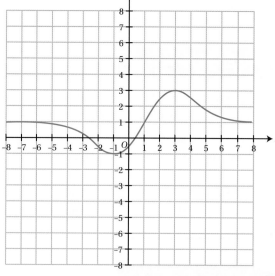

a **i** $y = f(x) + 3$ **ii** $y = f(x) + 5$

b **i** $y = f(x) - 7$ **ii** $y = f(x) - 0.5$

c **i** $y = f(x + 2)$ **ii** $y = f(x + 4)$

d **i** $y = f(x - 1.5)$ **ii** $y = f(x - 2)$

e **i** $y = 3f(x)$ **ii** $y = 5f(x)$

f **i** $y = \dfrac{f(x)}{4}$ **ii** $y = \dfrac{f(x)}{2}$

g **i** $y = f(2x)$ **ii** $y = f(6x)$

h **i** $y = f\left(\dfrac{2x}{3}\right)$ **ii** $y = f\left(\dfrac{5x}{6}\right)$

i **i** $y = -f(x)$ **ii** $y = f(-x)$

2 Find the equation of each of these graphs after the given transformation is applied:

a **i** $y = 3x^2$ after a translation of 3 units vertically up

     ii $y = 9x^3$ after a translation of 7 units vertically down

b **i** $y = 7x^3 - 3x + 6$ after a translation of 2 units down

     ii $y = 8x^2 - 7x + 1$ after a translation of 5 units up

c **i** $y = 4x^2$ after a translation of 5 units to the right

     ii $y = 7x^2$ after a translation of 3 units to the left

d **i** $y = 3x^3 - 5x^2 + 4$ after a translation of 4 units to the left

     ii $y = x^3 + 6x + 2$ after a translation of 3 units to the right

3 Find the required translations:

a **i** transforming the graph $y = x^2 + 3x + 7$ to the graph $y = x^2 + 3x + 2$

     ii transforming the graph $y = x^3 - 5x$ to the graph $y = x^3 - 5x - 4$

b **i** transforming the graph $y = x^2 + 2x + 7$ to the graph $y = (x + 1)^2 + 2(x + 1) + 7$

     ii transforming the graph $y = x^2 + 5x - 2$ to the graph $y = (x + 5)^2 + 5(x + 5) - 2$

c **i** transforming the graph $y = \sqrt{2x}$ to the graph $y = \sqrt{2x + 6}$

     ii transforming the graph $y = \sqrt{2x + 1}$ to the graph $y = \sqrt{2x - 3}$

Elevate

To explore how transformations are related to the symmetries of a graph, see Extension sheet 5.

Elevate

For more examples like this, see Support sheet 5.

4 Find the equation of the graph after the given transformation is applied.

   a **i** $y = 3x^2$ after a vertical stretch factor 7 relative to the x-axis.

      ii $y = 9x^3$ after a vertical stretch factor 2 relative to the x-axis.

   b **i** $y = 7x^3 - 3x + 6$ after a vertical stretch factor $\frac{1}{3}$ relative to the x-axis.

      ii $y = 8x^2 - 7x + 1$ after a vertical stretch factor $\frac{4}{5}$ relative to the x-axis.

   c **i** $y = 4x^2$ after a horizontal stretch factor 2 relative to the y-axis.

      ii $y = 7x^2$ after a horizontal stretch factor 5 relative to the y-axis.

   d **i** $y = 3x^3 - 5x^2 + 4$ after a horizontal stretch factor $\frac{1}{2}$ relative to the y-axis.

      ii $y = x^3 + 6x + 2$ after a horizontal stretch factor $\frac{2}{3}$ relative to the y-axis.

5 Describe the following stretches:

   a **i** transforming the graph $y = x^2 + 3x + 7$ to the graph $y = 4x^2 + 12x + 28$

      ii transforming the graph $y = x^3 - 5x$ to the graph $y = 6x^3 - 30x$

   b **i** transforming the graph $y = x^2 + 2x + 7$ to the graph $y = (3x)^2 + 2(3x) + 7$

      ii transforming the graph $y = x^2 + 5x - 2$ to the graph $y = (4x)^2 + 5(4x) - 2$

   c **i** transforming the graph $y = \sqrt{4x}$ to the graph $y = \sqrt{12x}$

      ii transforming the graph $y = \sqrt{2x+1}$ to the graph $y = \sqrt{x+1}$

6 Find the equation of the graph after the given transformation is applied.

   a **i** $y = 3x^2$ after reflection in the x-axis.

      ii $y = 9x^3$ after reflection in the x-axis.

   b **i** $y = 7x^3 - 3x + 6$ after reflection in the x-axis.

      ii $y = 8x^2 - 7x + 1$ after reflection in the x-axis.

   c **i** $y = 4x^2$ after reflection in the y-axis.

      ii $y = 7x^3$ after reflection in the y-axis.

   d **i** $y = 3x^3 - 5x^2 + 4$ after reflection in the y-axis.

      ii $y = x^3 + 6x + 2$ after reflection in the y-axis.

7 Describe the following transformations:

   a **i** transforming the graph $y = x^2 + 3x + 7$ to the graph $y = -x^2 - 3x - 7$

      ii transforming the graph $y = x^3 - 5x$ to the graph $y = 5x - x^3$

   b **i**   transforming the graph $y = x^2 + 2x + 7$ to the graph $y = x^2 - 2x + 7$

      ii   transforming the graph $y = x^2 - 5x - 2$ to the graph $y = x^2 + 5x - 2$

   c **i**   transforming the graph $y = \sqrt{4x}$ to the graph $y = \sqrt{-4x}$

      ii   transforming the graph $y = \sqrt{2x - 1}$ to the graph $y = \sqrt{-1 - 2x}$

Section 4: Graphs of $\dfrac{a}{x}$ and $\dfrac{a}{x^2}$

You need to be able to sketch the graphs of $y = \dfrac{1}{x}$ and $y = \dfrac{1}{x^2}$.

Key point 5.2

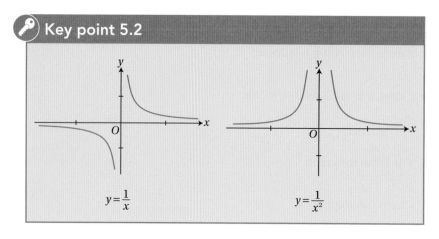

$$y = \frac{1}{x}$$
$$y = \frac{1}{x^2}$$

The graphs of $\dfrac{a}{x}$ and $\dfrac{a}{x^2}$ are very similar to the graphs in Key point 5.2.

They are vertically stretched by a factor of a.

Both graphs have two **asymptotes**. An asymptote is a line to which the curve gets closer and closer but never meets. These curves have asymptotes at $x = 0$ and $y = 0$.

EXERCISE 5D

1 **a** Write down the transformation that changes the graph of $y = \dfrac{a}{x}$ into the graph of $y = \dfrac{a}{x - d}$.

    b Hence write down the equations of the asymptotes of the graph $y = \dfrac{a}{x - d}$.

2 Show that the curve $y = \dfrac{a}{x^2}$ is a horizontal stretch of the curve $y = \dfrac{1}{x^2}$ and find the stretch factor.

3 **a** Show that the curves $y = \dfrac{a}{x}$ and $y = \dfrac{b}{x^2}$ always intersect at exactly one point, P, and find the coordinates of that point.

    b The origin and P are opposite vertices of a rectangle with sides parallel to the coordinate axes. Show that the area of this rectangle is independent of b.

4 Find a condition on m in terms of a and c so that the line $y = mx + c$ is a tangent to the curve $y = \dfrac{a}{x}$.

5 The function f(x) is a cubic polynomial. Show graphically that the curve $y = \dfrac{1}{x}$ can intersect this curve in 0, 1, 2, 3 or 4 places.

Section 5: Direct and inverse proportion

Direct proportion means that the ratio of two quantities is constant.

For example, if y is proportional to x^2 you can write $\dfrac{y}{x^2} = k$ or $y = kx^2$.

Inverse proportion means that the product of two quantities is constant.

For example, if y is inversely proportional to x^2 you write $yx^2 = k$ or $y = \dfrac{k}{x^2}$.

You can use your knowledge of graphs to sketch the graphs of two quantities if you are given information about their proportionality.

Linear functions are closely related to direct proportion: if $y = mx + c$ then $(y - c)$ is directly proportional to x.

Straight-line graphs can be used to represent or model a variety of real-life situations. In some situations, the linear model is only approximate. When making predictions, you should consider its accuracy and limitations.

 Gateway to A Level

For a reminder of calculations involving direct and inverse proportion, see Gateway to A Level section K.

 Fast forward

A common example where a straight line is used to make predictions is the line of best fit used in statistics. You will learn more about lines of best fit in Chapter 16, Section 4.

WORKED EXAMPLE 5.6

It takes me 12 minutes to drive from my house to the motorway. On the motorway, I drive at an average speed of 65 miles per hour.

a Approximately how long does it take me to drive to Leeds, which is 154 miles away?
b Write down an equation modelling the time, t hours, it takes me to drive to a city d miles away.
c Explain why this model only gives approximate times.

a Time in hours:

$0.2 + \dfrac{154}{65} = 2.57 \text{ hours}$ · · · · · · · · · · · ·

(about 2 h 34 minutes)

> Use time on motorway $= \dfrac{\text{distance}}{\text{speed}}$.
>
> 12 minutes = 0.2 hours.

b $t = 0.2 + \dfrac{d}{65}$

c The speed on the motorway is not constant.   · · · · · · · · · · · · · · · · ·

It doesn't take into account the time from getting off the motorway in Leeds.

The 154 miles distance is probably not exact; it doesn't specify where in Leeds you are going or exactly where it is measured from.   · · · · · · ·

> You are modelling the speed as constant, although in reality this is not the case.
>
> The speeds and distances quoted are probably only correct to the nearest integer.
>
> All these considerations mean that the model does not give an exact answer, but it is probably good enough to be practical.

EXERCISE 5E

1   **a**   If y is proportional to x^2 and $y = 12$ when $x = 2$, find the value of y when $x = 4$.

     b   Sketch the graph of y against x.

2   **a**   If y is proportional to $x - 4$ and $y = 1$ when $x = 6$, find y when $x = 8$.

     b   Sketch the graph of y against x.

3   **a**   If y is inversely proportional to x^2 and $y = 20$ when $x = 1$, find y when $x = 4$.

     b   Sketch the graph of y against x.

4   **a**   If y is inversely proportional to $x + 1$ and $y = 9$ when $x = 3$, find y when $x = 5$.

     b   Sketch the graph of y against x.

5   Economists use supply and demand curves to model the number of items produced and sold at a particular price. Let £ p be the price of one item. Demand (D) is the number of items that can be sold at this price. Supply (S) is the number of items that the producer will make. The graph shows supply and demand in the simplest model, where both vary linearly with price.

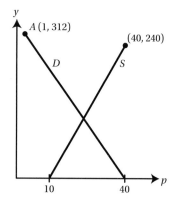

     a   Show that the equation of line D is $y_D = 320 - 8p$ and find the equation of line S.

     b   What does the value 320 in the equation of D represent? Suggest why it may not be reasonable to extend the straight line for D beyond point A.

     c   What is the maximum price that can be charged before there is no more demand?

   The market is said to be in equilibrium when supply equals demand.

     d   Find the equilibrium price of one item.

6   A provider offers two different mobile phone contracts:

     A   The set-up cost of £65, plus calls at 3 p per minute.

     B   No set-up costs, calls cost 5 p per minute.

     a   Write down an equation for the total cost, £C, of making m minutes of calls for each contract.

     b   Hence find after how many minutes of calls contract A becomes better value.

7 y is inversely proportional to x^2 and z is inversely proportional to y. Sketch a graph of z against x.

8   The strength of the Earth's gravitational field is inversely proportional to the square of the distance from the centre of the Earth. If a satellite is put into orbit, the distance to the centre of the Earth is increased by 10%. Find the percentage decrease in the gravitational field strength.

Section 6: Sketching inequalities in two variables

You can represent inequalities in one variable on a number line.
For example, the inequality $1 < x < 4$ can be represented by:

If there is also another variable, you can represent the inequality on a graph:

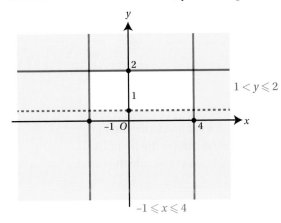

$1 < y \leqslant 2$

$-1 \leqslant x \leqslant 4$

In this graph you can see the convention that the part that satisfies the inequality is left unshaded. This is so that when you have several inequalities on one graph, the region which satisfies all the inequalities is clear.

If the inequality involves both variables you can still represent the solution by shading. For example, $y > x + 1$ is shown on the following graph. The required region has been left unshaded.

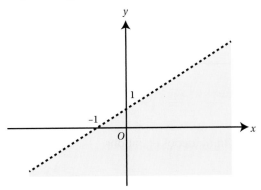

Notice that since the line $y = x + 1$ is not included it is drawn as a dashed line.

🔑 Key point 5.3

The general process for illustrating inequalities is:

- draw the associated equation on the graph, using a dashed line if the curve is not included
- test a convenient point on one side of the curve
- shade the side that does not satisfy the inequality.

WORKED EXAMPLE 5.7

a Represent the inequalities $y \geqslant x$ and $y \leqslant 1 - x^2$ on a graph.

b Find the largest value of x that satisfies these inequalities.

a

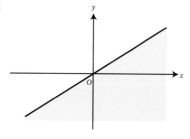

First sketch $y = x$. It is a solid line since the line is included in the inequality. You can try the point $(1, 0)$ and it does not satisfy the inequality, so you shade that side of the line.

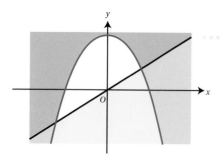

Then sketch $y = 1 - x^2$. This is a solid line since the line is included in the inequality. You can try the point $(0, 0)$ and it does satisfy the inequality, so you shade the other side of the curve.

b The largest x value corresponds to the point labelled P.

You need to find the point in the unshaded region with the largest x value.

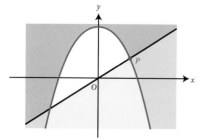

P occurs where:

To find this point you use simultaneous equations.

$x = 1 - x^2$

So $x = \dfrac{-1 \pm \sqrt{5}}{2}$

You can solve this using the quadratic formula.

So the largest value of x is $\dfrac{-1 + \sqrt{5}}{2}$

The larger solution is the one with a plus.

EXERCISE 5F

1 Illustrate the following inequalities on a graph.

a **i** $y > 1 + 2x$ **ii** $y < 2 + x$

b **i** $y + x \geqslant 1$ **ii** $y + 2x \geqslant 4$

c **i** $y > x^2$ **ii** $y > -x^2$

d **i** $y > x^2 + 3x + 2$ **ii** $y > x^2 - 7x + 6$

e **i** $y \leqslant x^2 + 2x + 1$ **ii** $y \leqslant x^2 - 7x + 10$

2 Illustrate the region $x > 0$, $y > 0$, $x + y < 4$ on a graph.

3 Illustrate the region $y \geqslant x^2$, $y < 4$ on a graph.

4 Illustrate the region $y > x^2 - 4x$ and $y < 2x - x^2$ on a graph.

5 Describe using inequalities the unshaded region in this graph.

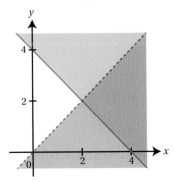

6 This region is bounded by a parabola and a straight line. Describe using inequalities the unshaded region in this graph.

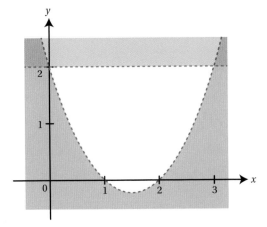

7 Find the largest integer value of x which satisfies $y < 120x - 2x^2$ and $y > 11x$.

8 Sketch $y > xy$.

Explore

Graphs of inequalities are needed to solve problems about maximising profits or minimising production time. Find out about a technique called **linear programming**.

Checklist of learning and understanding

- You can use substitution to solve simultaneous equations, which allows you to find the intersection point of two curves.
- The number of intersections of a quadratic curve and a straight line can be determined using the quadratic discriminant.
- Transforming a function results in a transformation of the graph of the function.

Transformation of $y = f(x)$	Transformation of graph
$y = f(x) + c$	Translation c up.
$y = f(x + d)$	Translation d to the **left**.
$y = pf(x)$	Vertical stretch, scale factor p relative to the x-axis
$y = f(qx)$	Horizontal stretch factor $\dfrac{1}{q}$ relative to the y-axis
$y = -f(x)$	Reflection in the x-axis
$y = f(-x)$	Reflection in the y-axis

- You should be able to sketch the graphs of $y = \dfrac{a}{x}$ and $y = \dfrac{a}{x^2}$.
- You should be able to interpret descriptions of the proportionality of two variables and to sketch the associated graph. You should also be able to use a linear model in a variety of contexts and understand that models sometimes only give approximate predictions.
- You can represent inequalities in two variables graphically by shading.

Mixed practice 5

1 Find the intersection of the graphs $x^2 + y^2 = 25$ and $x + y = 7$.

2 **a** Illustrate the region represented by the inequalities $x + y < 3$, $y \geqslant 0$, $y < 2x$.

  b Find the upper bound for the values of y that satisfy these inequalities.

3 Find the transformation that transforms the graph of $y = (x - 1)^2$ to the graph of $y = (x + 2)^2$.

4 If z is proportional to x^2 sketch the graph of z against x.

5 Two taxi companies have the following pricing structures:

  Company A charges £1.60 per kilometre.

  Company B charges £1.20 per kilometre plus £1.50 call-out charge.

  Find the length of the journey for which the two companies charge the same amount.

6 The graph of $y = f(x)$ is shown.

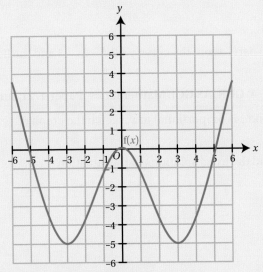

  a Sketch the graph of $y = f(x - 1) + 2$.

  b State the coordinates of the maximum point of the new graph.

7 The diagram shows a part of the graph of $y = f(x)$.

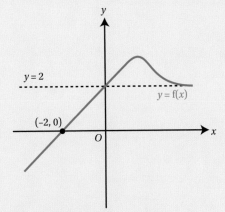

  Sketch the graph of $y = f(3x)$.

8 **i** The curve $y = x^2$ is translated 2 units in the positive x direction. Find the equation of the curve after it has been translated.

ii The curve $y = x^3 - 4$ is reflected in the x-axis. Find the equation of the curve after it has been reflected.

© **OCR, AS GCE Mathematics, Paper 4721, June 2008**

9 A doctor thinks that mass of a baby can be modelled as a linear function of age. A particular baby had a mass of 4.1 kg aged 2 weeks, and 4.8 kg aged 5 weeks.

a If M is the mass of the baby aged n weeks, show that the straight line model results in the equation $M = 0.233n + 3.63$, where the coefficients have been rounded to three significant figures.

b Give an interpretation of the values 0.233 and 3.63 in the equation in part **a**.

c The normal mass of a healthy one-year-old baby is approximately between 10 and 12 kg. Is the linear model appropriate for babies as old as one year?

10 **i** Solve the simultaneous equations
$$y = 2x^2 - 3x - 5, \qquad 10x + 2y + 11 = 0.$$

ii What can you deduce from the answer to part **i** about the curve $y = 2x^2 - 3x - 5$ and the line $10x + 2y + 11 = 0$?

© **OCR, AS GCE Mathematics, Paper 4721, January 2013**

11 Given that x is inversely proportional to y and z is proportional to x^2 sketch the graph of z against y.

12 **a** By using an appropriate substitution find the exact solutions to the equation
$$x^4 + 36 = 13x^2$$

b Hence solve the inequality $x^4 + 36 \leqslant 13x^2$.

6 Coordinate geometry

In this chapter you will learn how to:

- find the distance between two points and the midpoint of two points
- find the equation of a straight line in the form $y - y_1 = m(x - x_1)$ and $ax + by + c = 0$
- determine whether two straight lines are parallel or perpendicular
- find the equation of a circle with a given centre and radius
- solve problems involving intersections of lines and circles.

Before you start...

GCSE	You should know how to find the equation of a straight line in the form $y = mx + c$.	1	Find the equation of a straight line a with gradient 3 and y-intercept $(0, -1)$ b with gradient -2 and passing through the point with coordinates $(2, 5)$ c passing through the points with coordinates $(1, 3)$ and $(3, 9)$.
GCSE	You should know how to use the fact that parallel lines have the same gradient.	2	A straight lines passes through the points $(-1, -4)$ and $(4, p)$ and is parallel to the line with equation $y = 3x + 4$. Find the value of p.
GCSE	You should know how to solve two linear simultaneous equations.	3	Solve the simultaneous equations: $3x - 2y = 7$ $x + 3y = 12$
Chapter 3	You should know how to complete the square for an algebraic expression.	4	Write $x^2 - 4x - 3$ in the form $(x - p)^2 + q$.
Chapter 5	You should know how to solve linear and quadratic simultaneous equations, and interpret the solution as the intersection points between a line and a curve.	5	a Solve the simultaneous equations: $\quad y = x^2$ $\quad x + y = 6$ b Show that the line $y = 2x + 1$ is a tangent to the parabola $y = -x^2$.

Continues on next page ...

GCSE	You should know how to use properties of special quadrilaterals.					

6 Which of the following properties does each of these quadrilaterals have?

	Parallelogram	Rectangle	Rhombus	Square
opposite sides parallel	☐	☐	☐	☐
opposite sides equal	☐	☐	☐	☐
all four sides equal	☐	☐	☐	☐
sides perpendicular	☐	☐	☐	☐
diagonals equal	☐	☐	☐	☐
diagonals perpendicular	☐	☐	☐	☐
diagonals bisect each other	☐	☐	☐	☐

GCSE

- You should know how to use the properties of tangents and chords of circles:

- the angle in a semi-circle is a right angle

- a tangent to the circle is perpendicular to the radius at the point of contact

- the radius perpendicular to the chord bisects the chord

7 Find the angles and lengths marked with letters, giving reasons for your answers:

a

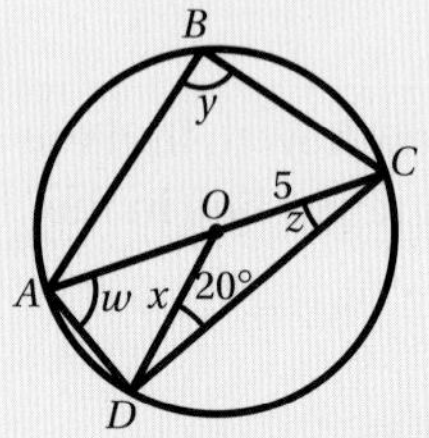

b

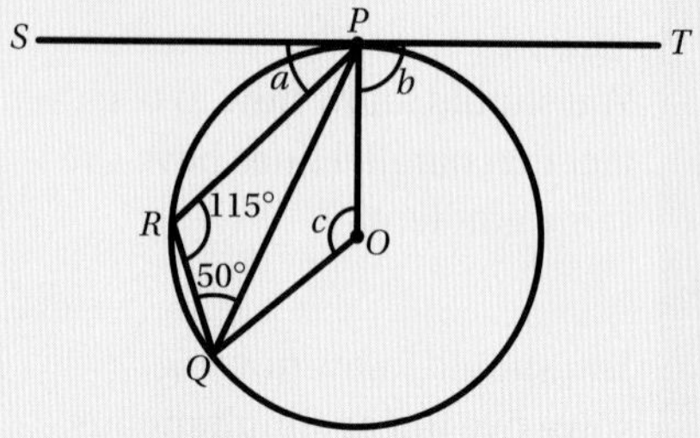

c

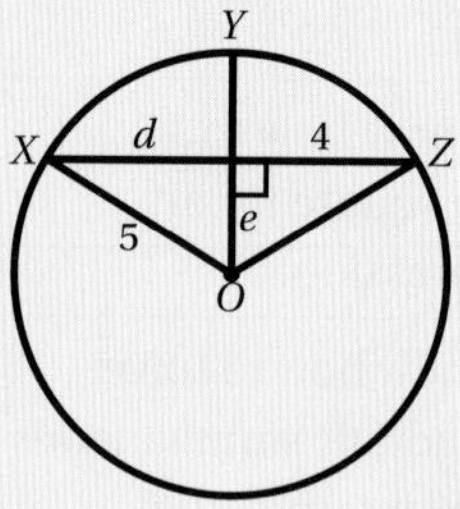

Using equations to represent geometrical shapes

Straight lines and circles are fundamental objects in geometry, and can be used to model many real-life objects. You already know several properties of lines and circles, as well as other geometrical figures made out of them, such as triangles and cones.

In this chapter you will look at using coordinates to represent lines and circles. You will use equations to represent those shapes and to find their intersections.

ⓘ Did you know?

Using equations to represent geometrical shapes is a relatively recent idea in mathematics – it was developed in the 17th century by the French philosopher and mathematician René Descartes. The Cartesian coordinate system is named after him.

Section 1: Midpoint and distance between two points

You may already have met the idea that if we have two points with coordinates (x_1, y_1) and (x_2, y_2) we can find the distance between these two points using Pythagoras' theorem.

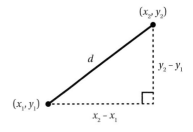

 Key point 6.1

The distance between the points (x_1, y_1) and (x_2, y_2) is $\sqrt{(x_2 - x_1)^2 + (y_2 - y_1)^2}$.

If the two points are called A and B we use the notation AB to mean the distance between the two points.

We can also find the midpoint of A and B. This is the point on halfway along the line connecting A and B. It can be found by thinking of it as the average of the coordinates of the two points.

 Key point 6.2

The midpoint of (x_1, y_1) and (x_2, y_2) is $\left(\dfrac{x_1 + x_2}{2}, \dfrac{y_1 + y_2}{2}\right)$.

 Fast forward

You will see how to prove this using vectors in Chapter 17.

WORKED EXAMPLE 6.1

The points A and B have coordinates $(-2, 4)$ and $(5, 2)$. Find:

a the exact distance AB

b the midpoint, M, of A and B.

a The distance is

$$AB = \sqrt{(x_2 - x_1)^2 + (y_2 - y_1)^2}$$

$$= \sqrt{(5 - (-2))^2 + (2 - 4)^2}$$

$$= \sqrt{7^2 + (-2)^2}$$

$$= \sqrt{53}$$

Use Key point 6.1 with $x_2 = 5, x_1 = -2$ $y_2 = 2, y_1 = 4$.

b The midpoint is

$$M = \left(\frac{x_1 + x_2}{2}, \frac{y_1 + y_2}{2}\right)$$

$$= \left(\frac{-2 + 5}{2}, \frac{4 + 2}{2}\right)$$

$$= (1.5, 3)$$

Use Key point 6.2.

Questions can also involve unknown points.

WORKED EXAMPLE 6.2

Find all points of the form (a, a) that are a distance of 5 away from the point $(0, 1)$.

The distance between the points is given by

$$5 = \sqrt{(0-a)^2 + (1-a)^2}$$

Use distance $= \sqrt{(x_2-x_1)^2 + (y_2-y_1)^2}$ and set this equal to 5.

$$= \sqrt{a^2 + 1 - 2a + a^2}$$
$$= \sqrt{2a^2 - 2a + 1}$$

Simplify the expression under the square root.

So

$$25 = 2a^2 - 2a + 1$$

Square both sides to get rid of the square root.

$$0 = 2a^2 - 2a - 24$$
$$0 = a^2 - a - 12$$
$$0 = (a-4)(a+3)$$
$$a = 4 \text{ or } -3$$

Solve the quadratic equation.

So the points are $(4, 4)$ or $(-3, -3)$.

EXERCISE 6A

1 Find the exact distance between the points.

   a **i** $(0, 0)$ and $(5, 12)$ **ii** $(3, 4)$ and $(0, 0)$

   b **i** $(1, 4)$ and $(2, 6)$ **ii** $(2, 2)$ and $(3, 5)$

   c **i** $(-1, 4)$ and $(3, 2)$ **ii** $(-1, 3)$ and $(-3, 1)$

   d **i** $(-2, -3)$ and $(-3, 0)$ **ii** $(-1, -5)$ and $(-2, -1)$

2 Find the midpoint for each of the pairs of points in question 1.

3 Find in terms of a the exact distance between the points $(a, 2a)$ and $(-2a, 8a)$ where $a > 0$.

4 The midpoint of points P and Q is $(1, 1)$. If point P has coordinates (a, b) find the coordinates of Q.

5 **a** The point A has coordinates $(0, 1)$, the point B has coordinates $(4, 4)$ and the point C has coordinates $(7, 8)$. Show that the distance AB equals the distance BC.

   b Explain why this does not mean that B is the midpoint of AC.

 Gateway to A Level

For more practice on basic questions involving distances between points and midpoints, see Gateway to A Level section L.

6 The point $(a, 2a)$ is 3 units away from the point $(3, 1)$. Find the possible values of a.

7 The set of points (x, y) are defined by the property that the distance to the point $(0, 1)$ equals y.

Find the equation connecting x and y.

8 Point A has coordinates (x_1, y_1), point B has coordinates (x_2, y_2) and point M has coordinates $\left(\dfrac{x_1 + x_2}{2}, \dfrac{y_1 + y_2}{2} \right)$.

Prove that $AM = \dfrac{1}{2} AB$.

9 The points A and B have coordinates $(-2, 4)$ and $(4a, 2a)$. M is the midpoint of A and B.

a Find and simplify in terms of a:

    i the distance AB

    ii the midpoint of A and B.

b If O is the origin show that the ratio $AB : OM$ is independent of a.

10 A spider starts at one corner of a cuboidal room with dimensions 5 m by 5 m by 5 m. It can crawl freely across the surface of the wall.

What is the shortest distance it needs to travel to get to the opposite end of the room?

Section 2: Equation of a straight line

You already know that a non-vertical straight line has an equation of the form $y = mx + c$.

In this equation, m is the **gradient** of the line and c is the **y-intercept**. If you know these two pieces of information you can simply write down the equation.

However, this is often not the information you are given. It is more common to know two points the line passes through, or the gradient and one point.

 Gateway to A Level

For a reminder and more practice of $y = mx + c$, see Gateway to A Level revision section M.

Equation of the line with a given gradient and one point

This diagram shows a straight line passing through the point with coordinates (x_1, y_1). The gradient of the line is m.

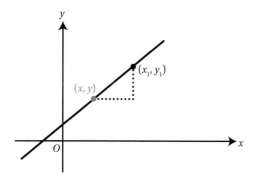

✔ **Gateway to A Level**

For revision of finding the gradient from two points on the line, see Gateway to A Level section L.

Let (x, y) be any other point on the line. The equation of the line is a rule connecting x and y. You can use the dotted triangle to write an equation for the gradient:

$$m = \frac{y - y_1}{x - x_1}$$

Rearranging this equation gives the form of the equation of the line in Key point 6.3.

 Key point 6.3

The line with gradient m through point (x_1, y_1) has equation $y - y_1 = m(x - x_1)$.

If you need to, you can rearrange the equation in Key point 6.3 into the form $y = mx + c$.

WORKED EXAMPLE 6.3

Find the equation of the line with gradient $\frac{2}{3}$ which passes through the point $(-3, 1)$. Give your answer in the form $y = mx + c$.

$y - y_1 = m(x - x_1)$

$y - 1 = \frac{2}{3}(x - (-3))$

Use the equation from Key point 6.3.

$\Leftrightarrow y - 1 = \frac{2}{3}x + 2$

Expand the brackets and rearrange.

$\Leftrightarrow y = \frac{2}{3}x + 3$

Equation of a line through two points

If you know the coordinates of two points the line passes through, you can use their coordinates to find the gradient. You can then use the method used in Worked example 6.3 to find the equation of the line.

WORKED EXAMPLE 6.4

Find the y-intercept of the line containing points $(2, -3)$ and $(-1, 4)$.

Gradient:

$$m = \frac{4-(-3)}{-1-2} = -\frac{7}{3}$$

To find the equation, you need the gradient and one point.

Equation of the line:

$$y - y_1 = m(x - x_1)$$

$$y - (-3) = -\frac{7}{3}(x - 2)$$

$$\Leftrightarrow y + 3 = -\frac{7}{3}(x - 2)$$

Now use the equation from Key point 6.3. You can use **either** of the two points.

When $x = 0$:

$$y + 3 = -\frac{7}{3}(0 - 2)$$

The y-intercept is when $x = 0$.

$$y = \frac{14}{3} - 3 = \frac{5}{3}$$

The y-intercept is $\left(0, \frac{5}{3}\right)$.

You should check that using the point $(-1, 4)$ gives the same equation.

The form $ax + by + c = 0$

Sometimes it is convenient to write the equation of a line in a form other than $y = mx + c$.

For example, when solving simultaneous equations you may want to write the equations in the form such as $3x + 2y = 7$.

You should also remember that a vertical line has an equation such as $x = 3$ that cannot be written in the form $y = mx + c$.

If you start with the equation of a line in the form $y - y_1 = m(x - x_1)$ it is easy to rearrange it into the form $ax + by + c = 0$.

This form makes it straightforward to find the x- and y-intercepts. If you want to find the gradient of a line given in this form you need to rewrite it as $y = mx + c$.

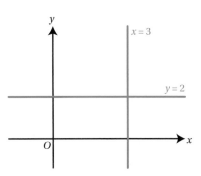

WORKED EXAMPLE 6.5

Line l passes through the point $(-2, 2)$ and has the same gradient as the line with equation $3x + 5y = 7$.

a Find the equation of l in the form $ax + by + c = 0$ where a, b and c are integers.

b The line l crosses the coordinate axes at points A and B. Find the exact distance AB.

a *Gradient:*

$3x + 5y = 7$ .... You first need to find the gradient of l. This requires rewriting $3x + 5y = 7$ in the form $y = mx + c$.

$\Leftrightarrow 5y = 7 - 3x$

$\Leftrightarrow y = \dfrac{7}{5} - \dfrac{3}{5}x$

So $m = -\dfrac{3}{5}$ .... The gradient is the coefficient of x.

Equation of l:

$y - 2 = -\dfrac{3}{5}(x - (-2))$ .... Now use $y - y_1 = m(x - x_1)$.

$\Leftrightarrow 5y - 10 = -3(x + 2)$ .... You need all the coefficients to be integers, so multiply through by 5.

$\Leftrightarrow 5y - 10 = -3x - 6$

$\Leftrightarrow 3x + 5y - 4 = 0$

b x-intercept is when $y = 0$: .... You need to find the coordinates of A and B.

$3x + 0 - 4 = 0$

$\Rightarrow x = \dfrac{4}{3}$

y-intercept is when $x = 0$:

$0 + 5y - 4 = 0$

$\Rightarrow y = \dfrac{4}{5}$

Distance between $A\left(\dfrac{4}{3}, 0\right)$ *and* $B\left(0, \dfrac{4}{5}\right)$:

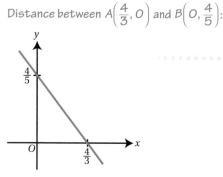

The distance between points (x_1, y_1) and (x_2, y_2) is $\sqrt{(x_1 - x_2)^2 + (y_1 - y_2)^2}$ In this case, you can also use the graph to help.

$AB = \sqrt{\left(\dfrac{4}{3}\right)^2 + \left(\dfrac{4}{5}\right)^2} = \sqrt{\dfrac{16}{9} + \dfrac{16}{25}}$

$= \sqrt{\dfrac{544}{225}}$

$= \dfrac{4\sqrt{34}}{15}$

EXERCISE 6B

1 Write down the equation of each line in the form $y - y_1 = m(x - x_1)$.

   a **i** gradient 3, through the point $(4, -1)$

      ii gradient 5, through the point $(-3, 2)$

   b **i** gradient $-\frac{1}{2}$, through the point $(-3, 1)$

      ii gradient $\frac{4}{3}$, through the point $(1, 3)$

   c **i** through points $(3, 7)$ and $(5, 15)$

      ii through points $(4, 1)$ and $(7, 10)$

   d **i** through points $(3, -1)$ and $(-4, 5)$

      ii through points $(-1, -7)$ and $(3, 2)$

2 Find the equation of each line in the form $ax + by + c = 0$ where a, b and c are integers.

   a **i** gradient -2, through the point $(-1, 3)$

      ii gradient -5, through the point $(3, -2)$

   b **i** gradient $\frac{1}{3}$, through the point $(-1, -7)$

      ii gradient $-\frac{3}{2}$, through the point $(2, -5)$

   c **i** through points $(-1, 2)$ and $(2, 7)$

      ii through point $(3, 5)$ and $(5, -4)$

   d **i** through points $(2, 1)$ and $(-3, 7)$

      ii through points $(-3, 2)$ and $(1, -5)$

3 Find the gradient, the x- and y-intercepts of the lines with the following equations:

   a **i** $y = 3x + 1$ **ii** $y = -2x + 3$

   b **i** $3x - 2y + 5 = 0$ **ii** $4x + 5y - 1 = 0$

   c **i** $3y - 3x + 5 = 0$ **ii** $y - 4x - 6 = 0$

   d **i** $4x - 3y = 7$ **ii** $5x + 2y = 3$

   e **i** $y - 3 = 2(x - 2)$ **ii** $y + 1 = 3(x - 5)$

4 Find the intersections of the following pairs of lines:

   a **i** $y = \frac{1}{2}x - 3$ and $y = x + 1$

      ii $y = \frac{2}{3}x + 2$ and $y = 2x - 2$

   b **i** $2x + 3y = 1$ and $x - 3y + 1 = 7$

      ii $3x - y = 3$ and $2x + 5y = 1$

   c **i** $5x + 2y + 3 = 1$ and $3x + 4y - 1 = 0$

      ii $4x - 2y - 1 = 0$ and $3x - 5y + 5 = 0$

> **Tip**
>
> In part d, do the lines intersect for all values of a and b?

5 **a** Find the equation of the line passing through the points with coordinates $(-4, 3)$ and $(5, -1)$. Give your answer in the form $ax + by + c = 0$ where a, b and c are integers.

   b A second line has the same gradient as the line in part **a** and passes through the point $(-4, 2)$. Find the equation of this line.

   c Find the value of k such that the point $(3k, k)$ lies on the line in part **b**.

6 A straight line has gradient $-\dfrac{2}{3}$ and passes through the point with coordinates $(2, 5)$. It cuts the coordinate axes at points P and Q. Find the area of the triangle OPQ where O is the origin.

7 Line l_1 passes through the points $(-3, -1)$ and $(10, 12)$. Line l_2 passes through the point $(-16, 12)$ and has gradient $-\dfrac{3}{2}$.

   a Find the equations of l_1 and l_2 in the form $ax + by = c$.

   b Find the coordinates of the point of intersection, P, of l_1 and l_2.

   l_1 intersects the x-axis at Q and l_2 intersects the x-axis at R.

   c Find the area of triangle PQR.

8 A line passes through the points $A(2 - 2k, k)$ and $B(k-1, 2k + 1)$, where k is a constant. The gradient of the line is $\dfrac{2}{3}$.

   a Find the value of k.

   b Find the equation of the line.

9 The line with equation $4y - 7x + 14 = 0$ crosses the coordinate axes at points A and B. M is the midpoint of AB. Find the distance of M from the origin, giving your answer in the form $\dfrac{\sqrt{p}}{q}$ where p and q are integers.

10 A line passes through the point $\left(\dfrac{p}{3}, \dfrac{2}{p}\right)$ and has gradient $-\dfrac{6}{p^2}$.

   It crosses the coordinate axes at points A and B. Show that the area of the triangle OAB is independent of p.

Section 3: Parallel and perpendicular lines

It is useful to be able to tell whether two lines are parallel or perpendicular, without having to draw them accurately. You already know how to decide whether two lines are parallel:

 Key point 6.4

Two lines are parallel if they have the same gradient.

> **Tip**
>
> The easiest way to identify the gradient is to write the equation of the line in the form $y = mx + c$.

WORKED EXAMPLE 6.6

Find the equation of the line that is parallel to $3x + 5y - 2 = 0$ and passes through the point $(-1, 3)$. Give your answer in the form $ax + by = c$ where a, b and c are integers.

$3x + 5y - 2 = 0$

$\Leftrightarrow 5y = -3x + 2$ Rearrange the equation in order to identify the gradient.

$\Leftrightarrow y = -\dfrac{3}{5}x + \dfrac{2}{5}$

Continues on next page ...

$$\therefore m = -\frac{3}{5}$$

Parallel lines have the same gradient.

Line passes through $(-1, 3)$:

$$y - 3 = -\frac{3}{5}(x + 1)$$

Use $y - y_1 = m(x - x_1)$.

$$\Leftrightarrow 5y - 15 = -3x - 3$$

Rearrange into the required form.

$$\Leftrightarrow 3x + 5y = 12$$

The diagram shows how the gradients of a pair of perpendicular lines are related.

For a line with gradient m you can draw a right-angled triangle with horizontal side 1 and vertical side m. When the line is rotated through $90°$ the horizontal and vertical distances are swapped, so that the horizontal side is m and vertical -1.

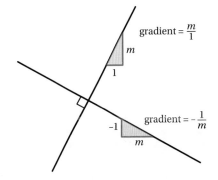

gradient $= \frac{m}{1}$

gradient $= -\frac{1}{m}$

Key point 6.5

- If a line has gradient m, the gradient of any perpendicular line is $m_1 = \frac{-1}{m}$.
- Two lines with gradients m_1 and m_2 are perpendicular if $m_1 m_2 = -1$.

Tip

Remember that a horizontal line has gradient zero and the gradient of a vertical line is undefined; so this calculation does not apply to those lines.

For example, lines with gradients $-\frac{2}{3}$ and $\frac{3}{2}$ are perpendicular because $-\frac{2}{3} \times \frac{3}{2} = -1$ and lines with gradients -2 and $\frac{1}{2}$ are perpendicular because $-2 \times \frac{1}{2} = -1$.

WORKED EXAMPLE 6.7

Points A, B and C have coordinates $A(3, -2)$, $B(p, 2)$ and $C(-1, 5)$. Find the possible values of p so that ABC is a right angle.

$$m_{AB} = \frac{4}{p-3}, \, m_{BC} = \frac{3}{-1-p}$$

$$m_{AB} m_{BC} = -1$$

The gradients of AB and BC should multiply to -1.

$$\Rightarrow \frac{4}{p-3} \times \frac{3}{-1-p} = -1$$

$$\Rightarrow 12 = -1(-p - p^2 + 3 + 3p)$$

$$\Rightarrow p^2 - 2p - 15 = 0$$

$$\Rightarrow (p-5)(p+3) = 0$$

Solve the quadratic equation.

$$\Rightarrow p = -3 \text{ or } 5$$

WORK IT OUT 6.1

Find the gradient of a line that is perpendicular to the line with equation $3x + 5y = 12$.

Which is the correct solution? Can you identify the errors made in the incorrect solutions?

Solution 1	Solution 2	Solution 3
$m = \frac{5}{3}$, so $m_1 = -\frac{3}{5}$	$m = -\frac{3}{5}$ so $m_1 = \frac{5}{3}$	$m = -\frac{3}{5}$ so $m_1 = \frac{3}{5}$

One important example of perpendicular lines is the **perpendicular bisector** of a line segment joining two points.

 **Fast forward**

You will meet another important example, the equation of a tangent to a circle, in Section 4.

WORKED EXAMPLE 6.8

Find the equation of the perpendicular bisector of the line segment joining points $(-3, 4)$ and $(5, 1)$. Give your answer in the form $ax + by = c$.

Gradient of the line segment:

$$m = \frac{1-4}{5-(-3)} = -\frac{3}{8}$$

You need the gradient of the segment to find the perpendicular gradient.

Perpendicular gradient:

$$m_1 = \frac{-1}{\left(\frac{3}{8}\right)} = \frac{8}{3}$$

Midpoint of the segment joining $(-3, 4)$ to $(5, 1)$:

The perpendicular bisector passes through the midpoint of the line segment.

$$x = \frac{-3+5}{2} = 1$$

$$y = \frac{4+1}{2} = \frac{5}{2}$$

Equation of the line:

$$y - \frac{5}{2} = \frac{8}{3}(x-1)$$

$$\Leftrightarrow 6y - 15 = 16x - 16$$

$$\Leftrightarrow 16x - 6y = 1$$

EXERCISE 6C

1 Find the gradient of a line perpendicular to the given line.

a i $3y = 5x - 2$ **ii** $6y = x - 7$

b i $4x = 2y - 3$ **ii** $5x + 3 = 2y$

c i $y = 4 - 2x$ **ii** $y = 1 - 3x$

d i $3x - 7y + 1 = 0$ **ii** $x - 5y + 3 = 0$

2 Determine whether each pair of lines is parallel, perpendicular or neither.

a i $y = 3 - 4x$ and $y = \frac{1}{4}x - 5$ **ii** $y = 3 - x$ and $y = 5 - x$

b i $3x - y + 7 = 0$ and $y - 3x + 5 = 0$ **ii** $5x - 2y + 3 = 0$ and $2y - 5x + 3 = 0$

c i $7x + 2y - 3 = 0$ and $2x - 7y + 4 = 0$ **ii** $2x + 4y - 4 = 0$ and $4x + 2y + 1 = 0$

d i $5x + 3y - 1 = 0$ and $3y - 5x + 2 = 0$ **ii** $2y - 7x = 3$ and $7x + 2y = 7$

3 a Show that the point $P(1, 4)$ lies on the line l_1 with equation $5x - 2y + 3 = 0$.

b Line l_2 passes through P and is perpendicular to l_1. Find the equation of l_2 in the form $ax + by + c = 0$ where a, b and c are integers.

4 Points A and B have coordinates $A(-2, 3)$ and $B(1, 5)$. O is the origin. Show that the triangle ABO is right-angled, and find its area.

5 a Find the coordinates of the midpoint of the line segment connecting points $A(5, 2)$ and $B(-1, 7)$.

b Hence find the equation of the perpendicular bisector of AB, giving your answer in the form $y = mx + c$.

6 a Find the equation of the line that is parallel to the line with equation $2x + 3y = 6$ and passes through the point $(-4, 1)$.

b The two lines cross the x-axis at points P and Q. Find the distance PQ.

7 Point P has coordinates $(0, 7)$ and point R has coordinates $(12, 4)$. Point Q lies on the x-axis and PQR is a right angle. Find the possible coordinates of Q, giving your answers in surd form.

8 Points P and Q have coordinates $(-4, 3)$ and $(5, 1)$. Find the equation of the perpendicular bisector of PQ in the form $ax + by + c = 0$ where a, b and c are integers.

9 Point M has coordinates $(3, 5)$. Points A and B lie on the coordinate axes and have coordinates $(0, p)$ and $(q, 0)$, so that $A\hat{M}B$ is a right angle.

a Show that $5p + 3q = 34$.

b Given that $p = 4$, find the value of q and the exact area of the quadrilateral $AOBM$ (where O is the origin).

10   Line l has equation $x - 2y + 3 = 0$ and point P has coordinates $(-1, 6)$.

     a   Find the equation of the line through P that is perpendicular to l.

     b   Hence find the shortest distance from P to l.

11   Four points have coordinates $A(k, 2)$, $B(k + 1, k + 2)$, $C(k - 3, k + 4)$ and $D(k - 4, 4)$.

     a   Show that $ABCD$ is a parallelogram for all values of k.

     b   Find the value of k for which $ABCD$ is a rectangle.

 Gateway to A Level

For a reminder of the properties of the parallelogram and rhombus, see Gateway to A Level section N.

Section 4: Equation of a circle

In this section you will see how to find an equation of a circle with a given centre and radius. As an example, consider the circle with centre at the point $C(7, 5)$ and radius $r = 4$ as shown in the diagram.

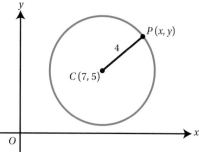

 Explore

Find out as much as you can about a curve called an ellipse. What is it? In what ways is it similar to a circle and how is it different?

An equation of a circle is a rule satisfied by the coordinates of all the points on the circle. Let P be a point on the circle with coordinates (x, y). The distance CP equals the radius of the circle. Using the formula for the distance (or Pythagoras' theorem):

$$(x - 7)^2 + (y - 5)^2 = 4^2$$

This equation is satisfied by the coordinates of any point of the circle. This result is generalised in Key point 6.6.

You can use the equation to check whether a point lies on, inside or outside a given circle.

Key point 6.6

The circle with centre (a, b) and radius r has equation $(x - a)^2 + (y - b)^2 = r^2$.

WORKED EXAMPLE 6.9

A circle has radius 5 and the coordinates of its centre are $(-3, 6)$.

   a   Write down the equation of the circle.

   b   Determine whether the following points lie on, inside or outside the circle:

     i $M(2, 6)$ **ii** $N(3, 1)$

Continues on next page …

a $(x-(-3))^2+(y-6)^2=5^2$

Take care with negative numbers.

$\Leftrightarrow (x+3)^2+(y-6)^2=25$

b i Point M:

$(2+3)^2+(6-6)^2=5^2+0^2=25$

Substitute the coordinates into the equation of the circle.

Point M lies on the circle.

ii Point N:

$(3+3)^2+(1-6)^2=6^2+(-5)^2=61$

$61>25$, so the point is further than 5 units from the centre of the circle.

Point N lies outside the circle.

If you are given an equation of a circle, you can identify the centre and radius. You may need to complete the square first.

 Rewind

Completing the square was covered in Chapter 3, Section 3.

WORKED EXAMPLE 6.10

Find the radius and the coordinates of the centre of the circle with equation $x^2-3x+y^2+4y=12$.

$\left(x-\dfrac{3}{2}\right)^2-\left(\dfrac{3}{2}\right)^2+(y+2)^2-2^2=12$

Complete the square for both x and y.

$\Leftrightarrow \left(x-\dfrac{3}{2}\right)^2+(y+2)^2=12+\dfrac{9}{4}+4$

Rearrange into the form $(x-a)^2+(y-b)^2=r^2$.

$\Leftrightarrow \left(x-\dfrac{3}{2}\right)^2+(y+2)^2=\dfrac{73}{4}$

The centre is $\left(\dfrac{3}{2},-2\right)$ and the radius is $\dfrac{\sqrt{73}}{2}$.

Remember that the number on the right is r^2.

If you are given three points you can draw a circle passing through them (unless the three points lie in a straight line). Finding the centre and radius of the circle involves a long calculation. However there is one special case where you can use a circle theorem to simplify the calculation.

 Fast forward

See question 8 in Exercise 6D for how to find a circle determined by three points.

✔ **Gateway to A Level**

For a reminder and more practice of circle theorems, see Gateway to A Level section O.

WORKED EXAMPLE 6.11

Points $A(3, 9)$, $B(4, 2)$ and $C(11, 3)$ lie on a circle.

a Show that AC is a diameter of the circle.

b Hence find the equation of the circle.

a $m_{AB} = \dfrac{2-9}{4-3} = -7$

$m_{BC} = \dfrac{3-2}{11-4} = \dfrac{1}{7}$

> If AC is a diameter then ABC is a right angle. You can check this by finding the gradients of AB and BC.

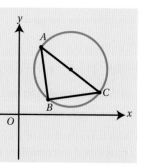

$m_{AB}m_{BC} = -1$ so AB is perpendicular to BC.

> Perpendicular lines have $m_1 m_2 = -1$.

Since $ABC = 90°$, AC is a diameter of the circle.

b Find the centre:

$M = \left(\dfrac{3+11}{2}, \dfrac{9+3}{2} \right) = (7, 6)$

> You need to find the centre and the radius. Since AC is a diameter, the centre is the midpoint of AC.

Find the radius:

$AC^2 = (11-3)^2 + (3-9)^2 = 100$

> The radius is half the distance AC.

$AC = 10$

$\therefore r = 5$

$(x-7)^2 + (y-6)^2 = 25$

> Now use the equation of a circle.

EXERCISE 6D

1 Find the equation of the circle with the given centre and radius.

   a **i** centre $(3, 7)$, radius 4   **ii** centre $(5, 1)$, radius 6

   b **i** centre $(3, -1)$, radius $\sqrt{7}$ **ii** centre $(-4, 2)$, radius $\sqrt{5}$

2 Write down the centre and radius of the following circles:

   a **i** $(x-2)^2 + (y+3)^2 = \dfrac{9}{4}$ **ii** $(x+1)^2 + (y+5)^2 = \dfrac{4}{25}$

   b **i** $(x-3)^2 + \left(y-\dfrac{1}{2}\right)^2 = 6$ **ii** $\left(x+\dfrac{3}{4}\right)^2 + \left(y-\dfrac{1}{5}\right)^2 = 3$

3 Find the centre and radius of the following circles:

   a **i** $x^2 + 4x + y^2 - 6y + 4 = 0$ **ii** $x^2 - 8x + y^2 + 2y + 8 = 0$

   b **i** $x^2 - 2x + y^2 + 6y + 1 = 0$ **ii** $x^2 - 10x + y^2 + 4y - 1 = 0$

   c **i** $x^2 + 5x + y^2 - y + 2 = 0$ **ii** $x^2 - 3x + y^2 + 7y - 3 = 0$

   d **i** $x^2 + y^2 - 5y = 12$ **ii** $x^2 + y^2 + 3x = 10$

4 Determine whether each point lies on, inside or outside the given circle.

   a i point $(1, 7)$, circle centre $(-2, 3)$, radius 5   **ii** point $(2, -1)$, circle centre $(-3, 3)$, radius $\sqrt{41}$

   b i point $(-1, 1)$, circle centre $(3, 6)$, radius 5   **ii** point $(2, 1)$, circle centre $(5, -1)$, radius 7

5 **a** Write down the equation of the circle with centre $(-6, 3)$ and radius $\sqrt{117}$.

   b Find the coordinates of the points where the circle cuts the y-axis.

6 **a** Find the centre and the radius of the circle with equation $x^2 - 5x + y^2 + y = 3$.

   b Determine whether the point $A(-1, 3)$ lies inside or outside the circle.

7 A circle with centre $(3, -5)$ and radius 7 crosses the x-axis at points P and Q. Find the exact distance PQ.

8 Points A, B and C have coordinates $A(-7, 3)$, $B(3, 9)$ and $C(12, -6)$.

   a Show that ABC is a right angle.

   b Find the distance AC.

   c Hence find the equation of the circle passing through the points A, B and C.

9 The circle with equation $(x - p)^2 + (y + 3)^2 = 26$ where p is a positive constant passes through the origin.

   a Find the value of p.

   b Determine whether the point $(3, 2)$ lies inside or outside the circle.

10 A diameter of a circle has endpoints $P(a, b)$ and $Q(c, d)$. Let $Z(x, y)$ be any other point on the circle.

   a Write down the size of the angle PZQ.

   b Hence prove that the equation of the circle can be written as $(x - a)(x - c) + (y - b)(y - d) = 0$.

Section 5: Solving problems with lines and circles

In this section you will solve a variety of problems involving lines and circles. You start by looking at intersections, which involves solving simultaneous equations.

> **⏮ Rewind**
>
> Before starting this section, you may want to review the circle theorems listed at the start of this chapter.

For the intersection of a line and a circle, there are three possibilities, shown in these diagrams:

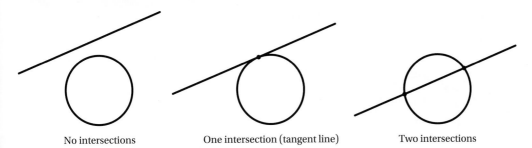

    No intersections   One intersection (tangent line)   Two intersections

Because the equation of the circle is quadratic, you can use the discriminant to determine whether there are two, one or no intersections.

> **⏮ Rewind**
>
> See Chapter 5, Sections 1 and 2, for a reminder of quadratic simultaneous equations.

WORKED EXAMPLE 6.12

A circle has centre (3, 2). Find the radius of the circle so that the circle is tangent to the line with equation $x + 5y = 20$.

Equation of the circle: $(x-3)^2 + (y-2)^2 = r^2$

Equation of the line: $x + 5y = 20 \Rightarrow x = 20 - 5y$

> Start by writing both equations and trying to find the intersection.

Intersection: $(17 - 5y)^2 + (y-2)^2 = r^2$

> Substitute x from the equation of the line into the equation of the circle.

$\Leftrightarrow (289 - 170y + 25y^2) + (y^2 - 4y + 4) = r^2$

$26y^2 - 174y + (293 - r^2) = 0$

> Write in standard quadratic form in order to find the discriminant.

Tangent means one solution so the discriminant is zero:

$174^2 - 4(26)(293 - r^2) = 0$

$\Rightarrow 104r^2 - 196 = 0$

$\Rightarrow r^2 = \dfrac{49}{26}$

$\Rightarrow r = 1.37$

> The radius of the circle is a positive number.

To find the equation of the tangent to a circle at a given point you can use one of the circle theorems: that the tangent is perpendicular to the radius at the point of contact. You can therefore find the gradient of the tangent by using $m_1 m_2 = -1$ for perpendicular lines.

Focus on ...

Focus on ... Problem solving 1 explores alternative methods of solving the problem from the previous worked example.

Key point 6.7

- The tangent to the circle is perpendicular to the radius at the point of contact.
- The normal is the line containing the point of contact and the centre of the circle.

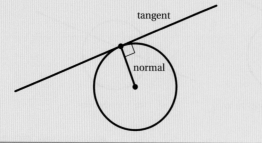

Fast forward

The line that is perpendicular to the tangent at the point of contact is called a **normal** to the curve. In the case of the circle, the normal is the same line as the radius of the circle.

You will learn about tangents and normals to other curves in Chapter 13.

WORKED EXAMPLE 6.13

Find the equation of the tangent and normal to the circle $(x-3)^2 + (y+5)^2 = 5$ at the point $(2, -7)$.

Coordinates of the centre: $(3, -5)$

Gradient of the radius:

$$m_1 = \frac{-7-(-5)}{2-3} = \frac{-2}{-1} = 2$$

You can tell that $(2, -7)$ does indeed lie on the circle because $(-1)^2 + (-2)^2 = 5$. The tangent is perpendicular to the radius, which is the line connecting $(2, -7)$ to the centre.

Gradient of the tangent:

$$m_1 m_2 = -1 \Rightarrow m_2 = -\frac{1}{2}$$

Tangent passes through $(2, -7)$:

$$y-(-7) = -\frac{1}{2}(x-2)$$

Now use the equation of a straight line.

$$\Rightarrow y = -\frac{1}{2}x - 6$$

Normal: $y-(-7) = 2(x-2)$

$$\Rightarrow y = 2x - 11$$

The normal is the line connecting $(2, -7)$ to the centre. You already know that its gradient is 2.

Intersection of two circles

There are five possibilities for the relative position of two distinct circles. A clever way to distinguish between them involves comparing the distance between their centres to the radii of the circles.

 Elevate

For another example of finding a tangent to a circle, see Support sheet 6.

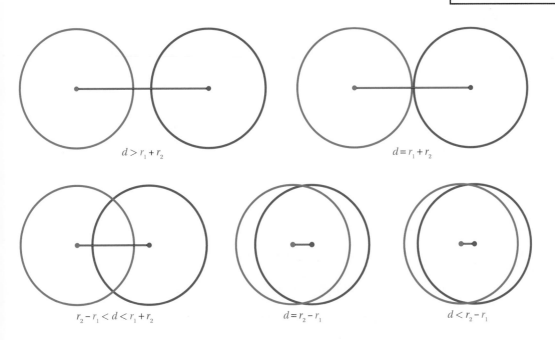

$d > r_1 + r_2$

$d = r_1 + r_2$

$r_2 - r_1 < d < r_1 + r_2$

$d = r_2 - r_1$

$d < r_2 - r_1$

WORKED EXAMPLE 6.14

Two circles have equations $x^2 - 6x + y^2 - 20y + 45 = 0$ and $(x - 15)^2 + (y - 5)^2 = r^2$.

a In the case $r = 7$ show that the two circles intersect at two different points.

b Given that the two circles are externally tangent to each other, find the value of r.

a $x^2 - 6x + y^2 - 20y + 45 = 0$

$\Leftrightarrow (x - 3)^2 + (y - 10)^2 - 9 - 100 + 45 = 0$

$\Leftrightarrow (x - 3)^2 + (y - 10)^2 = 64$

> You need to compare the distance between the centres to the radii of the circles. So first you need to identify the centre and radius of both circles.

The first circle has centre (3, 10) and radius 8.

The second circle has centre (15, 5) and radius 7.

The distance between the centres is

$d = \sqrt{(3 - 15)^2 + (10 - 5)^2} = 13$

> The distance between the centres is less than the sum of the radii but more than their difference.

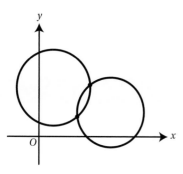

So the two circles intersect.

b

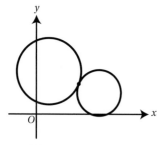

> 'Externally tangent' means that they touch on the outside. The distance between the centres is equal to the sum of the radii.

$8 + r = 13$

$\Rightarrow r = 5$

Finding points of intersection of two circles can be difficult, as it involves solving two simultaneous quadratic equations. However, there are some special cases where it is possible to use the substitution method as you did when intersecting a circle with a line.

WORKED EXAMPLE 6.15

Find the coordinates of the points of intersection of the circles $(x-2)^2 + y^2 = 36$ and $(x-2)^2 + (y-10)^2 = 64$.

From the first equation:

$(x-2)^2 = 36 - y^2$

> You need to solve the two simultaneous equations. The term $(x-2)^2$ is common to both equations so you can substitute it from one equation into the other.

Substitute into the second:

$36 - y^2 + (y-10)^2 = 64$

$\Rightarrow 36 - y^2 + y^2 - 20y + 100 = 64$

$\Rightarrow 20y = 72$

$\Rightarrow y = 3.6$

$(x-2)^2 + 3.6^2 = 36$

> Now substitute back to find the x–coordinates.

$\Rightarrow (x-2)^2 = 23.04$

$\Rightarrow x - 2 = \pm 4.8$

$\therefore x = 6.8 \text{ or } -2.8$

The coordinates are (6.8, 3.6) and

(−2.8, 3.6).

EXERCISE 6E

1 Find the equations of the following:

    a **i** tangent to the circle $x^2 - 2x + y^2 = 15$ at the point $(1, 4)$

       ii tangent to the circle $x^2 + y^2 + 6y = 25$ at the point $(-3, 2)$

    b **i** normal to the circle $x^2 + 4x + y^2 - 6y = 0$ at the point $(1, 1)$

       ii normal to the circle $x^2 - 4x + y^2 = 9$ at the point $(5, 2)$

    c **i** tangent to the circle with centre $(1, 2)$ and radius $\sqrt{5}$ at the point $(3, 3)$

       ii tangent to the circle with centre $(-3, 1)$ and radius $\sqrt{32}$ at the point $(1, 5)$

2 Determine whether the line and the circle intersect. Where they do, find the coordinates of the point(s) of intersection.

    a **i** $x^2 + 3x + y^2 = 24$ and $y = 2x + 1$ **ii** $x^2 - 5x + y^2 + y = 17$ and $y = 2x - 1$

    b **i** $x^2 - 12x + y^2 - 10y + 41 = 0$ and $2x - y + 3 = 0$ **ii** $x^2 + y^2 = 32$ and $x + y = 8$

    c **i** $x^2 + y^2 - 10y + 9 = 0$ and $x - y = 7$ **ii** $x^2 - 8x + y^2 - 6y = 25$ and $x + y = 20$

3 Determine whether the two circles intersect, are disjointed or tangent to each other, or whether one circle is completely inside the other one.

    a   **i** $(x-3)^2+(y-5)^2=16$ and $(x+1)^2+(y-2)^2=25$

        ii $(x+2)^2+(y-1)^2=64$ and $(x-1)^2+(y+2)^2=64$

    b   **i** $(x-4)^2+(y+1)^2=20$ and $(x+3)^2+(y-5)^2=17$

        ii $x^2+(y-2)^2=10$ and $(x-3)^2+(y+3)^2=12$

    c   **i** $x^2+y^2=30$ and $(x+1)^2+(y-1)^2=6$

        ii $(x+3)^2+(y-2)^2=9$ and $(x+7)^2+(y+1)^2=4$

4 Line l_1 has equation $5x-2y=7$ and line l_2 is perpendicular to l_1 and passes through the point $(-3, 1)$. Find the coordinates of the point of intersection of the two lines.

5 **a** Show that the point $P(-3, 2)$ lies on the circle with equation $(x-1)^2+(y+2)^2=32$.

    b Write down the coordinates of the centre of the circle.

    c Find the equation of the tangent to the circle at P.

6 Line l_1 has equation $2x+y-10=0$ and line l_2 is perpendicular to l_1 and crosses the x-axis at the point $A(-2, 0)$.

    a Find the equation of l_2.

    b Find the coordinates of M, the point of intersection of l_1 and l_2.

    c Line l_1 crosses the x-axis at B. Find the exact area of the triangle AMB.

7 The circumcircle of a triangle is the circle containing all three vertices.

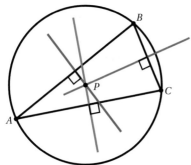

    Its centre is the point of intersection of the perpendicular bisectors of the sides.

    A triangle has vertices $A(1, 3)$, $B(5, 7)$ and $C(2, 9)$.

    a Find the equations of the perpendicular bisectors of AB and AC.

    b Find the coordinates of their intersection, P. This is the centre of the circumcircle.

    c Find the equation of the perpendicular bisector of BC and verify that it also passes through P.

    d Find the exact value of the radius of the circumcircle of triangle ABC.

8 A circle with centre $C(2, 5)$ passes through the origin.

    a Find the equation of the circle.

    b Show that the point $A(0, 10)$ lies on the circle.

B is another point of the circle such that the chord AB is perpendicular to the radius OC (extended).

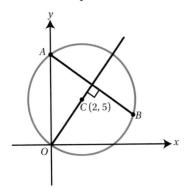

    c Find the length of AB correct to three significant figures.

9 Circle C_1 has centre $(-2, 5)$ and radius 7. Circle C_2 has centre $(12, 5)$.

    a Given that the two circles are tangent to each other, find the two possible values for the radius of C_2.

    b Given instead that the radius of C_2 is 16, find the coordinates of the intersection points of C_1 and C_2.

10 A circle with centre at the origin passes through the point $(2, 6)$. The tangent to the circle at $(2, 6)$ cuts the coordinate axes at points P and Q. Find the area of the triangle OPQ.

11 Find the values of k for which the line $y = kx$ is tangent to the circle with centre $(3, 6)$ and radius 2.

12 The line $3x - y = 3$ is tangent to the circle with centre $(5, -1)$ and radius r. Find the value of r.

13 The circle with centre at the origin and radius 5 cuts the negative y-axis at point B. Point $A(4, 3)$ lies on the circle. Let M be the midpoint of the chord AB. The line through O and M cuts the circle at the point P, as shown in the diagram.

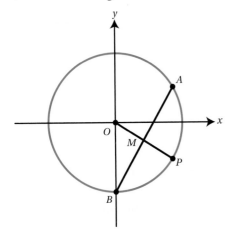

    a Find the coordinates of M.

    b Show that the quadrilateral $OAPB$ is not a rhombus.

14 A circle has equation $x^2 + y^2 - 10x - 10y + 25 = 0$.

   a Show that the circle is tangent to both coordinate axes.

   b Show that the point $M(8, 9)$ lies on the circle.

The diagram shows the circle and the tangent at M.

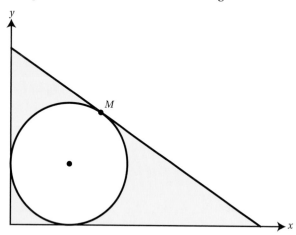

   c Find the exact value of the shaded area.

15 Find a condition on a and b so that the curve $x^2 + y^2 = 1$ touches the curve $(x - a)^2 + (y - b)^2 = r^2$ at exactly one point.

Checklist of learning and understanding

- Given two points $A(x_1, y_1)$ and $B(x_2, y_2)$:
  - the distance $AB = \sqrt{(x_2 - x_1)^2 + (y_2 - y_1)^2}$
  - the midpoint of AB is $\left(\dfrac{x_1 + x_2}{2}, \dfrac{y_1 + y_2}{2} \right)$.
- The equation of the straight line through the points (x_1, y_1) and (x_2, y_2) is $y - y_1 = m(x - x_1)$:
  - the gradient is given by $m = \dfrac{y_2 - y_1}{x_2 - x_1}$
  - the equation of a line is often written in the form $y = mx + c$ or $ax + by + c = 0$.
- Parallel lines have the same gradient.
- The gradients of perpendicular lines satisfy $m_1 m_2 = -1$.
- A circle with centre (a, b) and radius r has equation $(x - a)^2 + (y - b)^2 = r^2$.
  - You may need to complete the square in order to find the centre and radius.
- You can find the intersection of two lines, a line and a circle, or (sometimes) two circles by solving simultaneous equations.
  - You can tell whether two circles intersect, are disjoint or tangent to each other by comparing the sum and the difference of the radii of the circles to the distance between their centres.
- A tangent to a circle is perpendicular to the radius at the point of contact. The normal is in the direction of the radius.
- A radius that is perpendicular to a chord bisects that chord.
- An angle in a semi-circle is a right angle. It follows that, if A, B and C are three points on a circle and ABC is a right angle, then AC is a diameter of the circle.

Mixed practice 6

1 Find the radius of the circle $x^2 - 8x + y^2 + 6y = 144$.

2 Line l_1 has equation $3x - 2y + 7 = 0$.

    a Point $A(2k, 2k + 1)$ lies on l_1. Find the value of k.

    b Point B has coordinates $(-2, p)$. Find the value of p so that AB is perpendicular to l_1.

    c Line l_2 is parallel to l_1 and passes through B. Find the equation of l_2 in the form $ax + by + c = 0$ where a, b and c are integers.

    d l_2 crosses the x-axis at the point C. Find the coordinates of C.

3 Circle C has equation $x^2 - 2x + y^2 - 10y - 19 = 0$.

    a Find the coordinates of the centre, P, of the circle.

    b Show that point $A(7, 2)$ lies on the circle.

Point M has coordinates $(1, -1)$. Line l is perpendicular to PA and passes through M. It cuts PA at the point S.

    c Find the coordinates of S.

4 A circle has equation $x^2 + y^2 + 6x - 4y - 4 = 0$.

    i Find the centre and radius of the circle.

    ii Find the coordinates of the points where the circle meets the line with equation $y = 3x + 4$.

        © OCR, AS GCE Mathematics, Paper 4721, January 2010

5 $y = -3x + 5$ is tangent to the circle C at the point $(4, -7)$. The centre of C is at the point $(k - 4, k + 3)$. Find the value of k.

6 Consider the points $A(4, 3)$, $B(3, -2)$ and $C(9, 2)$.

    a Show that BAC is a right angle.

    b Hence find the equation of the circle through A, B and C.

    c Find the equation of the tangent to the circle at B. Give your answer in the form $ax + by + c = 0$ where a, b and c are integers.

7 A circle has centre $(3, 0)$ and radius 5. The line $y = 2x + k$ intersects the circle in two points. Find the set of possible values of k, giving your answers in surd form.

8 A circle has centre $C(7, 12)$ and passes through the point $D(4, 10)$. The tangent to the circle at D cuts the coordinate axes at points A and B. Find the area of these triangles:

    a AOB **b** ABC

9 The points $A(-3, 7)$ and $B(5, -1)$ are endpoints of the diameter of a circle. Find the equation of the circle in the form $x^2 + ax + y^2 + by + c = 0$.

10 Find the exact values of k for which the line $y = kx + 3$ is tangent to the circle with centre $(6, 3)$ and radius 2.

11 **i** Find the equation of the circle with radius 10 and centre $(2, 1)$, giving your answer in the form $x^2 + y^2 + ax + by + c = 0$.

   ii The circle passes through the point $(5, k)$ where $k > 0$. Find the value of k in the form $p + \sqrt{q}$.

   iii Determine, showing all working, whether the point $(-3, 9)$ lies inside or outside the circle.

   iv Find an equation of the tangent to the circle at the point $(8, 9)$.

© OCR, AS GCE Mathematics, Paper 4721, June 2008

12 Find the shortest distance from the point $(-3, 2)$ to the line with equation $3x + 2y = 19$.
Give your answer in exact form.

13 Show that each of the circles $x^2 - 6x + y^2 + 10y + 18 = 0$ and $x^2 - 14x + y^2 - 6y + 49 = 0$ lies entirely outside the other one.

14 A circle has centre $(5, 7)$. It crosses the x-axis at points $A(2, 0)$ and $B(p, 0)$, where $p > 2$.

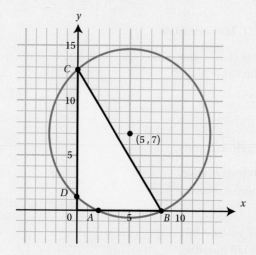

a Find the value of p and write down the equation of the circle.

b The circle crosses the y-axis at points C and D. Find the area of the quadrilateral $ABCD$.

 Elevate

For a selection of more challenging problems, see Extension sheet 6.

7 Logarithms

In this chapter you will learn how to:

- undo exponential functions using an operation called a logarithm
- use laws of logarithms
- use logarithms to find exact solutions of some exponential equations
- use a special number called e.

Before you start...

GCSE	You should know how to work with expressions involving exponents.	1	Answer 'true' or 'false': a $2 \times 3^2 = 36$ b when $x = 25$, $4x^{\frac{1}{2}} = 10$ c $(2 \times 3)^7 = 2^7 \times 3^7$ d $\dfrac{1}{2x^3} = 2^{-3} x^{-3}$
GCSE	You should know how to evaluate fractional and negative powers.	2	Evaluate the following without a calculator: a $27^{\frac{4}{3}}$ b $9^{-\frac{3}{2}}$
Chapter 2	You should know how to use laws of indices.	3	Write the following in the form x^p: a $x^2 \times \sqrt{x}$ b $\dfrac{x\sqrt{x}}{x^2}$
GCSE	You should know how to solve equations involving fractions.	4	Solve this equation. $\dfrac{x+1}{2x-3} = 2$
Chapter 3	You should know how to solve quadratic equations.	5	Solve these equations. a $(x-1)(x+3) = 5$ b $2x^2 - \dfrac{1}{x^2} = 1$

Discovering logarithms

If you were asked to solve $x^2 = 3$ for $x \geqslant 0$ then you could either find a decimal approximation (for example by using a calculator or trial and improvement) or take the square root:

$$x = \sqrt{3}$$

This statement just says that 'x is the positive value that, when squared, gives 3'.

Similarly, to solve $10^x = 50$ you could use trial and improvement to seek a decimal value:

$$10^1 = 10$$
$$10^2 = 100$$

So x is between 1 and 2.

$$10^{1.5} \approx 31.6$$
$$10^{1.6} \approx 39.8$$
$$10^{1.7} \approx 50.1$$

So the answer is approximately 1.7.

Just as you can take the square root to answer the question: 'What is the number, which when squared, gives 3?', there is also a function to answer the question: 'What is the number, which when put as the exponent of 10, gives 50?' This power is called a base-10 logarithm.

In this chapter you will learn about laws of logarithms and how to use them to solve some problems involving exponential functions.

Section 1: Introducing logarithms

In the example in the introduction, the solution to the equation $10^x = 50$ can be written as $x = \log_{10} 50$. More generally, the equation $y = 10^x$ can be re-expressed as $x = \log_{10} y$. In fact, the base does not need to be 10, but could be any positive value other than 1.

 Key point 7.1

Converting between index and logarithmic forms:

$$a = b^c \Leftrightarrow c = \log_b a$$

 Tip

Remember that the symbol $\Leftrightarrow$ means that the statements are equivalent and you can switch between them.

WORKED EXAMPLE 7.1

Evaluate without a calculator:

a $\log_2 8$ b $\log_{10} 0.01$ c $\log_{25} 5$

a $\log_2 8 = 3$ Ask the question: '2 raised to what power equals 8'?

b $\log_{10} 0.01 = -2$ Because $10^{-2} = \dfrac{1}{10^2} = \dfrac{1}{100} = 0.01$.

c $\log_{25} 5 = \dfrac{1}{2}$ Because $25^{\frac{1}{2}} = \sqrt{25} = 5$.

Whenever you raise a positive number to an exponent, whether it is a positive or negative exponent, the answer is always positive. So there is **no** answer to a question such as 'to what power do you raise 10 to get -3?'

Key point 7.2

The logarithm of a negative number or zero is **not** a real number.

 Fast forward

It is possible to take logarithms of negative numbers if you use complex numbers. This is a new type of number you will meet if you study Further Mathematics in Pure Core Student Book 1, Chapter 3.

Two common bases have abbreviations for their logarithms. Since a decimal system of counting is commonly used, base 10 is the default base for a logarithm, so that $\log_{10} x$ is usually written simply as $\log x$.

There is also a special number, called e, which is important when studying rates of change. e $(\approx 2.718\,28)$ is an irrational number. The logarithm in base e is called the natural logarithm, denoted by $\ln x$. Although it looks different, $\ln x$ follows all the same rules as other logarithms.

 Fast forward

You will look at the number e in more detail in Chapter 8.

 Key point 7.3

- $\log_{10} x$ is written as $\log x$.
- $\log_e x$ is written as $\ln x$.

Since taking a logarithm **reverses** the process of raising to a power, the facts listed in Key point 7.4 follow:

 Tip

Your calculator has special buttons for log and ln. Some calculators can also evaluate logs in other bases.

 Key point 7.4

- $\log_a(a^x) = x$
- $a^{\log_a x} = x$

These are referred to as the **cancellation principles**. This sort of 'cancellation', similar to squaring a square root, is frequently useful when simplifying logarithm expressions, but you can only apply it when the base of the logarithm and the base of the exponential match and are immediately adjacent in the expression.

 Did you know?

Logarithms were introduced by the Scottish mathematician John Napier (1550–1617). He originally studied logarithms in base $\frac{1}{e}$.

WORKED EXAMPLE 7.2

Simplify:

a $\ln(e^5)$ **b** $10^{2 + \log 3}$

a $\ln(e^5) = 5$ Apply the first cancellation principle (with base e) from Key point 7.4.

b $10^{2 + \log 3} = 10^2 \times 10^{\log 3}$ Use the laws of indices.

     $= 100 \times 3$ Apply the second cancellation principle (with base 10)
     $= 300$ from Key point 7.4.

You can also use the fact that logarithms reverse raising to a power to solve equations and rearrange formulae.

WORKED EXAMPLE 7.3

Make x the subject of each equation.

a $\log_2 x = y + 3$ **b** $\log_x (y + 1) = 2$

a $\log_2 x = y + 3$

     $x = 2^{y+3}$ Use $\log_b a = c \Leftrightarrow b^c = a$ (Key point 7.1).

b $\log_x (y + 1) = 2$

     $x^2 = y + 1$ Use $\log_b a = c \Leftrightarrow b^c = a$ (Key point 7.1).

     $x = \sqrt{y+1}$ The base of a logarithm has to be positive, so you do not need to use $\pm$.

WORKED EXAMPLE 7.4

Find the exact solution to the equation $3 \ln (2 + x) = 6$.

$\ln (2 + x) = 2$ Divide both sides by 3 to get the logarithm by itself.

$e^{\ln(2+x)} = e^2$
$2 + x = e^2$ Turn each side into a power with e as the base; then e and ln will cancel.

$x = e^2 - 2$ Now just solve for x. You are asked for an exact answer so this is the form to leave it in. You should not try to write it as a decimal.

Remember that $\log x$ represents a single value, so it can be treated like any algebraic expression, In particular, $\log x \times \log x = (\log x)^2$.

 Tip

$(\log x)^2$ is **not** the same as $\log (x^2)$.

WORKED EXAMPLE 7.5

Expand and simplify: **a** $(\log x + 1)(\log x - 3)$ **b** $\dfrac{(\ln x)^2 - 4}{\ln x + 2}$

a $(\log x + 1)(\log x - 3) = (\log x)^2 + \log x - 3 \log x - 3$ Expand the brackets as normal.

     $= (\log x)^2 - 2 \log x - 3$ Group like terms.

b $\dfrac{(\ln x)^2 - 4}{\ln x + 2} = \dfrac{(\ln x - 2)(\ln x + 2)}{\ln x + 2}$ Factorise the numerator (difference of two squares).

     $= \ln x - 2$ Cancel common factors in the numerator and denominator.

EXERCISE 7A

1 Evaluate the following without using a calculator:

a **i** $\log_3 27$ **ii** $\log_4 16$

b **i** $\log_5 5$ **ii** $\log_3 3$

c **i** $\log_{12} 1$ **ii** $\log_{15} 1$

d **i** $\log_3 \dfrac{1}{3}$ **ii** $\log_4 \dfrac{1}{64}$

e **i** $\log_4 2$ **ii** $\log_{27} 3$

f **i** $\log_8 \sqrt{8}$ **ii** $\log_2 \sqrt{2}$

g **i** $\log_8 4$ **ii** $\log_{81} 27$

h **i** $\log_{25} 125$ **ii** $\log_{16} 32$

i **i** $\log_4 2\sqrt{2}$ **ii** $\log_9 81\sqrt{3}$

j **i** $\log_{25} 0.2$ **ii** $\log_4 0.5$

2 Use a calculator to evaluate each of the following, giving your answer correct to 3 s.f.

a **i** $\log 50$ **ii** $\log\left(\dfrac{1}{4}\right)$

b **i** $\ln 0.1$ **ii** $\ln 10$

c **i** $\log_3 8.5$ **ii** $\log_5 0.6$

d **i** $\log_{0.2} 3$ **ii** $\log_{0.8} 0.6$

3 Find an equivalent form for each of the following expressions:

a **i** $7\log x - 2\log x$ **ii** $2\log x + 3\log x$

b **i** $(\log x - 1)(\log y + 3)$ **ii** $(\log x + 2)^2$

c **i** $\dfrac{\log a + \log b}{\log a \log b}$ **ii** $\dfrac{(\log a)^2 - 1}{\log a - 1}$

4 Make x the subject of the following:

a **i** $\log_3 x = y$ **ii** $\log_4 x = 2y$

b **i** $\log_a x = 1 + y$ **ii** $\log_a x = y^2$

c **i** $\log_x 3y = 3$ **ii** $\log_x y = 2$

d **i** $y = 2 + \ln x$ **ii** $\ln y = \ln x - 2$

5 Find the value of x in each of the following:

a **i** $\log_2 x = 5$ **ii** $\log_2 x = 4$

b **i** $\log_5 25 = 5x$ **ii** $\log_{49} 7 = 2x$

c **i** $\log_x 36 = 2$ **ii** $\log_x 10 = \dfrac{1}{2}$

In questions 6 to 11, you must show detailed reasoning. This means that you need to use algebraic rearrangement rather than, for example, the equation solver on your calculator.

> **Tip**
>
> Although you can evaluate logarithms on a calculator, this exercise will help you develop your understanding of this new concept.

> **Tip**
>
> There are often different ways of expressing the answer but usually only one 'sensible' one.

6 Solve the equation $\log_{10}(9x+1)=3$.

7 Solve the equation $\log_8\sqrt{1-x}=\frac{1}{3}$.

8 Find the exact solution to the equation $\ln(3x-1)=2$.

9 Solve the equation $3(1+\log x)=6+\log x$.

10 Find all values of x that satisfy $(\log_3 x)^2=4$.

11 Solve the simultaneous equations:

$$\log_3 x+\log_5 y=6 \qquad \log_3 x-\log_5 y=2$$

12 Evaluate $\sqrt[6]{(\pi^4+\pi^5)}$.

What do you notice about this result?

Section 2: Laws of logarithms

There is a series of laws that hold when performing arithmetic with exponents. There are corresponding laws that apply to logarithms. To investigate this it is useful to look at some examples:

1   $\log_2 4=2$ $\log_2 8=3$ $\log_2 32=5$

2   $\log_{10}1000=3$ $\log_{10}10=1$ $\log_{10}10\,000=4$

3   $\log_3 27=3$ $\log_3\left(\frac{1}{9}\right)=-2$ $\log_3(3)=1$

In each case it seems that when you add two logs with the same base you get the log of the product. You can put this into an algebraic rule.

$$\log_a(xy)=\log_a x+\log_a y$$

This can be derived from the laws of indices.

PROOF 3

Prove that $\log_a(xy)=\log_a x+\log_a y$.

Let $P=\log_a x$ and $Q=\log_a y$

> Often in proofs it is useful to define certain parts that you are interested in, and then manipulate them using known laws.

So $x=a^P$ and $y=a^Q$

> You don't have many algebraic properties of logarithms to work with. You need to use the defining feature of logarithms (Key point 7.1) to turn it into something you are more familiar with: index form.

So $xy=a^P\times a^Q=a^{(P+Q)}$

> You can now try to apply the laws of indices to xy.

Taking logs of both sides:
$\log_a(xy)=\log_a a^{P+Q}$

> You want $\log_a(xy)$ so you need to take logs of both sides.

$=P+Q$

> Using the cancellation principle (Key point 7.4).

$=\log_a x+\log_a y$

> Substitute back in to write the answer in terms of x and y.

Other laws can be derived in a similar way.

🔍 **Explore**

The initial purpose of logarithms was as a calculation aid. Because they turn multiplication into addition and division into subtraction, they were used to multiply and divide large numbers. Find out how this was done using 'log tables'.

🔑 **Key point 7.5**

$$\log_a\left(\frac{x}{y}\right) = \log_a x - \log_a y$$

$$\log_a x^k = k \log_a x$$

It is useful to remember these special values:

🔑 **Key point 7.6**

For any base $a > 0$, $\log_a a = 1$.

The logarithm of 1 is always 0, irrespective of the base.

$$\log_a 1 = 0$$

💡 **Tip**

A useful particular case of the third law is when $k = -1$:

$$\log_a \frac{1}{x} = -\log_a x$$

These laws can be used to manipulate expressions involving logarithms.

💡 **Tip**

Note that, since $\ln x$ is just a logarithm in base e, $\ln e = 1$ and $\ln 1 = 0$.

WORKED EXAMPLE 7.6

If $x = \log_{10} a$ and $y = \log_{10} b$, express $\log_{10} \dfrac{100a^2}{b}$ in terms of x and y.

$\log_{10} \dfrac{100a^2}{b} = \log_{10} 100a^2 - \log_{10} b$ · · · · · · Use laws of logs to isolate $\log_{10} a$ and $\log_{10} b$. First, using the law relating to the log of a fraction...

$\quad = \log_{10} 100 + \log_{10} a^2 - \log_{10} b$ · · then the log of a product...

$\quad = \log_{10} 100 + 2\log_{10} a - \log_{10} b$ · · then the log of an exponent.

$\quad = 2 + 2 \log_{10} a - \log_{10} b$ · · · · · · $\log_{10} 100 = 2$.

$\quad = 2 + 2x - y$

WORK IT OUT 7.1

If $e^{2y} = x + 2$ write y in terms of x.

Which is the correct solution? Can you identify the errors made in the incorrect solutions?

Solution 1	Solution 2	Solution 3
$2y = \ln(x+2)$ $\quad = \ln x + \ln 2$ So $y = \dfrac{\ln x + \ln 2}{2}$	$2y = \ln(x+2)$ $y = \dfrac{1}{2}\ln(x+2)$ $y = \ln\sqrt{x+2}$	$2y = \ln(x+2) = \ln x \times \ln 2$ So $y = \dfrac{1}{2}\ln x \times \dfrac{1}{2}\ln 2$

The laws of logarithms can also be used to solve equations. The usual tactic is to combine all the logarithms into one.

 Tip

It is important to know what you **cannot** do with logarithms and not make up your own rules!

WORKED EXAMPLE 7.7

Solve the equation $\log_2 x + \log_2(x+4) = 5$.

$\log_2 x + \log_2(x+4) = 5$

$\log_2(x(x+4)) = 5$

Rewrite one side as a single logarithm.

$2^{\log_2(x(x+4))} = 2^5$

Undo the logarithm by raising 2 to the power of both sides.

$x^2 + 4x = 32$

Use the cancellation principle.

$x^2 + 4x - 32 = 0$

$(x+8)(x-4) = 0$

Solve the quadratic equation.

$x = -8$ or $x = 4$

When $x = -8$:

LHS: $\log_2(-8) + \log_2(-4)$ is not real so this solution does not work.

Check your solution in the original equation.

When $x = 4$:

LHS: $\log_2 4 + \log_2 8 = 2 + 3 = 5 = $ RHS

So $x = 4$ is the only solution.

State the final solution.

Tip

Checking your solutions is about more than looking for an arithmetic error. It is possible to introduce false solutions through algebraic manipulation.

EXERCISE 7B

In this exercise, you must show detailed reasoning.

1 Given $b > 0$, simplify each of the following:

a **i** $\log_b b^4$ **ii** $\log_b \sqrt{b}$

b **i** $\log_{\sqrt{b}} b^3$ **ii** $\log_b b^2 - \log_b \sqrt{b}$

2 If $x = \log a$, $y = \log b$ and $z = \log c$, express the following in terms of x, y and z:

a **i** $\log b^7$ **ii** $\log a^2 b$

b **i** $\log\left(\dfrac{ab^2}{c}\right)$ **ii** $\log\left(\dfrac{a^2}{bc^3}\right)$

c **i** $\log\left(\dfrac{100}{bc^5}\right)$ **ii** $\log(5b) + \log(2c^2)$

d **i** $\log a^3 - 2\log ab^2$ **ii** $\log(4b) + 2\log(5ac)$

3 Solve the following for x:

a **i** $\log_3\left(\dfrac{2+x}{2-x}\right) = 1$ **ii** $\log_2(7x+4) = 5$

b **i** $\log_3 x - \log_3(x-6) = 1$ **ii** $\log_8 x - 2\log_8\left(\dfrac{1}{x}\right) = 1$

c **i** $\log_3(x-7) + \log_3(x+1) = 2$ **ii** $2\log(x-2) - \log(x) = 0$

4 Find the value of x for which $3\log_b x = \log_b 64$.

5 Solve the equation $\ln x = 2\ln 9 - \ln 3$.

6 Solve the equation $\log(3x+6) = \log(3) + 1$.

7 If $x = \log a$, $y = \log b$ and $z = \log c$ express the following in terms of x, y and z:

a $\log(a^2 b)$ **b** $\log\left(\dfrac{100a}{\sqrt{c}}\right)$

8 If $a = \ln 2$ and $b = \ln 5$ find in terms of a and b:

a $\ln 50$ **b** $\ln 0.16$

9 Find the exact solution of the equation $2\ln x + \ln 9 = 3$ giving your answer in the form Ae^B where A and B are rational numbers.

10 Solve the equation $\log(x+5) - 1 = \log(x-1)$.

11 Solve the equation $\log_2(x+2) = 3 - \log_2 x$.

12 Solve the equation $\log(x^2 + 1) = 1 + 2\log(x)$.

Elevate

For a further example and more practice of this type of question, see Support sheet 7.

Section 3: Solving exponential equations

One of the main purposes of logarithms is to make it possible to solve equations with the unknown in the exponent. By taking logarithms the unknown becomes a factor, which is easier to deal with.

 Key point 7.7

To solve an equation with the unknown in the power, take logarithms (to any base) of both sides.

WORKED EXAMPLE 7.8

Find the exact solution of the equation $3^{x-2} = 5$.

$3^{x-2} = 5$	Take logarithms of both sides. You can use any base. Here base 10 is used.
$\log(3^{x-2}) = \log 5$	
$(x-2)\log 3 = \log 5$	Use the rule $\log a^p = p \log a$.
$x \log 3 - 2 \log 3 = \log 5$	Multiply out the brackets to isolate the term with x.
$x \log 3 = \log 5 + 2 \log 3$	Collect terms without x and divide by the coefficient of x.
$x = \dfrac{\log 5 + 2\log 3}{\log 3}$	

There is often more than one correct way to write an answer in terms of logarithms. See if you can work out which one of the answers in Work it out 7.2 is an alternative way of solving the equation in Worked example 7.8.

WORK IT OUT 7.2

Check each of these solutions to the equation $3^{x-2} = 5$.

Which is the correct solution? Can you identify the errors made in the incorrect solutions?

Solution 1	Solution 2	Solution 3
$x - 2 = \log_3 5$ $x = \log_3 5 + 2$	$\ln(3^{x-2}) = \ln 5$ $(x-2)\ln 3 = \ln 5$ $x - 2 = \ln\left(\dfrac{5}{3}\right)$ $x = \ln\left(\dfrac{5}{3}\right) + 2$	$(x-2)\log 3 = \log 5$ $x \log 3 = 2 \log 3 + \log 5 = \log 45$ So, $x = \dfrac{\log 45}{\log 3} = \log 42$

The strategy of taking logs of both sides works particularly well when the unknown appears in the power on both sides of the equation. Again, you can choose any base (**unless** a particular base is specified in the question).

WORKED EXAMPLE 7.9

Solve the equation $2^{x+3} = 5^{x-1}$ giving your answer in the form $\dfrac{\ln p}{\ln q}$.

$(x+3)\ln 2 = (x-1)\ln 5$	Take logs of both sides. The question says to use ln.
$x\ln 2 + 3\ln 2 = x\ln 5 - \ln 5$	Expand the brackets.
$3\ln 2 + \ln 5 = x\ln 5 - x\ln 2$	Group terms with x on one side and terms without x on the other.
$3\ln 2 + \ln 5 = x(\ln 5 - \ln 2)$	You can factorise the expression on the right so that x occurs only once in the equation.
$\ln(2^3 \times 5) = x\ln\left(\dfrac{5}{2}\right)$	Use rules of logarithms to combine into a single log on each side.
$x = \dfrac{\ln 40}{\ln 2.5}$	You can now divide by the coefficient of x to get the answer in the required form.

WORK IT OUT 7.3

Solve the equation $3 \times 2^x = 7^{x-2}$.

Which is the correct solution? Can you identify the errors made in the incorrect solutions?

Solution 1	Solution 2	Solution 3
$\log 3 \times \log(2^x) = \log(7^{x-2})$	$\ln 3 + x\ln 2 = (x-2)\ln 7$	$6^x = 7^{x-2}$
$\log 3 \times x\log 2 = (x-2)\log 7$	$\ln 3 + 2\ln 7 = x\ln 7 - x\ln 2$	$x = (x-2)\log_6(7)$
$x\log 3 \times x\log 2 = x\log 7 - 2\log 7$	$x = \dfrac{\ln 147}{\ln 3.5}$	$x = x\log_6 7 - \log_6 49$
$x\log 6 - x\log 7 = -2\log 7$		$\log_6 49 = x(\log_6 7 - 1)$
$x\log\left(\dfrac{7}{6}\right) = 2\log 7$		$x = \dfrac{\log_6 49}{\log_6 7 - 1}$
$x = \dfrac{\log(49)}{\log\left(\dfrac{7}{6}\right)}$		

EXERCISE 7C

In this exercise, you must show detailed reasoning.

1 Solve for x, giving your answers correct to 3 s.f.

   a **i** $3 \times 4^x = 90$ **ii** $1000 \times 1.02^x = 10\,000$

   b **i** $6 \times 7^{x+1} = 1.2$ **ii** $5 \times 2^{2x-5} = 94$

   c **i** $3^{2x} = 4^{x-1}$ **ii** $5^x = 6^{x-1}$

   d **i** $3 \times 2^{3x} = 7 \times 3^{3x-2}$ **ii** $4 \times 8^{x-1} = 3 \times 5^{2x+1}$

2 Solve the following equations, giving your answers in terms of natural logarithms.

   a **i** $2 \times 3^x = 5$ **ii** $5 \times 7^x = 3$

   b **i** $4e^x = 1$ **ii** $3e^x = 1$

   c **i** $2^{2x} = 5$ **ii** $10^{2x} = 7$

   d **i** $2^{3x+1} = 10$ **ii** $5^{2x-3} = 4$

   e **i** $2^{x+1} = 5^x$ **ii** $5^{x-2} = 3^x$

   f **i** $2^{3x} = 3e^x$ **ii** $e^{2x} = 5 \times 2^x$

   g **i** $5 \times 3^x = 8^{x+2}$ **ii** $3^{2x+1} = 7 \times 2^{x-2}$

   h **i** $3 \times 2^{3x} = 7 \times 3^{3x-2}$ **ii** $4 \times 8^{x-1} = 3 \times 5^{2x+1}$

3 Solve the equation $5^{4x+3} = 28$, giving your answer correct to 3 s.f.

4 Find the exact solution of the equation $4 \times 3^{x-5} = 1$.

5 Find, in terms of the natural logarithm, the exact solution of the equation $e^{3-2x} = 10$.

6 Find the exact solution of the equation $10^x = 5 \times 2^{3x}$, giving your answer in the form $x = \dfrac{\log p}{q + \log r}$, where p, q and r are integers.

7 Solve the equation $2^{3x-1} = 5^{2-x}$ giving your answer in the form $x = \dfrac{\log_6 49}{\log_6 7 - 1}$ where a and b are integers.

8 If $3^x \times 4^{2x+1} = 6^{x+2}$, show that $x = \dfrac{\ln 9}{\ln 8}$.

Section 4: Disguised quadratics

It is usually impossible to simplify expressions such as $3^x + 5^x$ which contain powers with different bases. This means that you cannot (algebraically) solve the equation $3^x + 5^x = 17$. However, there is a special type of equation that looks very similar to this but which can be solved exactly, by writing it as a quadratic equation.

 Rewind

You already met these 'disguised quadratics' in Chapter 3, Section 6.

▶▶❙ Fast forward

You will meet disguised quadratics again in Chapter 10, Section 7 on trigonometry.

WORKED EXAMPLE 7.10

Find the exact solution of the equation $4^x + 2^x = 12$.

$4^x + 2^x = 12$ .... | $4^x = (2^2)^x = (2^x)^2$

$(2^x)^2 + 2^x = 12$

Let $y = 2^x$. .... | Make a substitution to turn the equation into a

Then $y^2 + y = 12$ | quadratic.

$y^2 + y - 12 = 0$ .... | Solve the quadratic.

$(y + 4)(y - 3) = 0$

$y = -4$ or 3

$2^x = -4$ is impossible. .... | No real power of a positive number can be negative.

When $2^x = 3$: .... | The other solution for y **does** give a valid solution

$x \log 2 = \log 3$ | for x.

$x = \dfrac{\log 3}{\log 2}$

EXERCISE 7D

1 Find the exact solution(s) of each equation.

a **i** $4^x - 5 \times 2^x + 6 = 0$ **ii** $9^x - 6 \times 3^x + 8 = 0$

b **i** $9^x - 8 \times 3^x = 9$ **ii** $25^x - 5^x = 6$

c **i** $e^{2x} + 16e^x = 80$ **ii** $e^{2x} - 9e^x + 20 = 0$

d **i** $25^x - 15 \times 5^x + 50 = 0$ **ii** $4^x - 7 \times 2^x + 12 = 0$

e **i** $\log_4 x = (\log_4 x^2)^2$ **ii** $(\log_3 x)^2 - 3\log_3 x + 2 = 0$

2 **a** By letting $y = 3^x$, show that $3^{2x} - 3^{x+2} + 20 = 0$ can be written in the form $y^2 - 9y + 20 = 0$.
     b Hence solve $3^{2x} - 3^{x+2} + 20 = 0$, giving your answer correct to 3 s.f.

3 Find exact solutions of the equation $4^x - 10 \times 2^x + 16 = 0$.

4 Solve the equation $2e^{2x} - 9e^x + 4 = 0$ giving your answers in the form $k \ln 2$.

5 Solve the equation $5^{2x+1} - 14 \times 5^x - 3 = 0$.

6 Solve, in exact form, the equation $e^x = 8 - 15e^{-x}$.

Checklist of learning and understanding

- Logarithms answer the question: 'To what power do I need to raise b to get a?'
  - You can convert between logarithmic and index forms: $c = \log_b a \Leftrightarrow b^c = a$.
- You can only take a logarithm of a positive number.
- Cancellation rules can be used to simplify some expressions:
  - $\log_a a^x = x = a^{\log_a x}$
- Logarithms in base 10 are written as $\log x$.
- Logarithms in base e (natural logarithms) are written as $\ln x$.
- Logarithms obey the following laws:
  - $\log_a (xy) = \log_a x + \log_a y$
  - $\log_a \left(\dfrac{x}{y}\right) = \log_a x - \log_a y$
  - $\log_a \left(\dfrac{1}{x}\right) = -\log_a x$
  - $\log_a x^k = k \log_a x$
  - $\log_a 1 = 0$ and $\log_a a = 1$ for any base $a > 0$.
- Many exponential equations can be solved by taking a logarithm of both sides and using log rules.
- Some equations can be turned into quadratic equations by using a substitution of the form $y = a^x$.

Mixed practice 7

In this exercise, you must show detailed reasoning.

1 Solve $\log_5\left(\sqrt{x^2+49}\right)=2$.

2 If $8^x=16$, then x equals:

  a $\log_{16}8$ **b** $\sqrt[8]{16}$ **c** $\dfrac{16}{8}$ **d** $\dfrac{4}{3}$

3 Given that $a=\log x$, $b=\log y$ and $c=\log z$ (with all logs being to the base 10), express the following in terms of a, b, c and integers:

  a $\log\dfrac{x^2\sqrt{y}}{z}$ **b** $\log\sqrt{0.1x}$ **c** $\log_{100}\left(\dfrac{y}{z}\right)$

4 Solve the equation $3e^{2x+1}=17$, giving your answer to 3 s.f.

5 Solve the equation $4\log_a x=\log_a 81$.

6 Given that $\log_x 4=9$, find the value of x correct to 3 s.f.

7 If $\log_a y+\log_a 7=4$, express y in terms of a.

8 The curve $y=3^{2x-1}$ intersects the line $y=4$ at the point P. Find the exact value of the x-coordinate of P.

9 Solve the simultaneous equations:

  $\ln x+\ln y^2=8$

  $\ln x^2+\ln y=6$

10 Given that $4\log_b x-\log_b 9=2$, express b in terms of x.

11 Given that $\log_5 y=8$, find the value of $\log_5(125y)$.

12 If $y=\ln x-\ln(x+2)+\ln(4-x^2)$, express x in terms of y.

13 Solve, correct to 3 s.f., $3^{2x}-3^{x+1}-10=0$.

14 Solve the equation $\log(x^2+1)=1+2\log x$.

15 Use logarithms to solve the equation $3^{2x+1}=5^{200}$, giving the value of x correct to 3 significant figures.

© OCR, AS GCE Mathematics, Paper 4722, June 2007

16 **a** Given that $\log_a x=p$ and $\log_a y=q$, express the following in terms of p and q.

  i $\log_a(xy)$ **ii** $\log_a\left(\dfrac{a^2x^3}{y}\right)$

  b **i** Express $\log_{10}(x^2-10)-\log_{10}x$ as a single logarithm.

  ii Hence solve the equation $\log_{10}(x^2-10)-\log_{10}x=2\log_{10}3$.

© OCR, AS GCE Mathematics, Paper 4722, January 2009

17 Find the exact value of x satisfying the equation $2^{3x-2}\times 3^{2x-3}=$ 36^{x-1} giving your answer in simplified form $\dfrac{\ln p}{\ln q}$ where $p,q\in\mathbb{Z}$.

18 Solve the equation $5\times 4^{x-1}=\dfrac{1}{3^{2x}}$ giving your answer in the form $x=\dfrac{\ln p}{\ln q}$ where p and q are rational numbers.

19 Find the exact solutions to $e^x+e^{-x}=4$.

20 Find the values of x for which $(\log_3 x)^2=\log_3 x^3-2$.

> **⬇ Elevate**
>
> For a selection of more challenging questions, see Extension sheet 7.

8 Exponential models

In this chapter you will learn:

- about graphs of exponential functions
- why exponential functions are often used in modelling
- how to use logarithms to transform curved graphs into straight lines.

Before you start…

Chapter 7	You should be able to use the number e and natural logarithms.	1	Simplify each expression. a $\ln(5e^2)$ b $e^{1 + \ln(5)}$
Chapter 7	You should be able to use the laws of logarithms.	2	If $y = 100x^3$ write $\log y$ in the form $n + k \log x$.
Chapter 5	You should be able to transform graphs.	3	Describe the effect of changing $y = f(x)$ into $y = f(2x)$.
Chapter 6	You should be able to work with equations of straight lines.	4	What is the gradient of $3y + 2x = 5$?
		5	Find, in the form $y = mx + c$, the equation of this line:

Why use exponential models?

In many situations in the real world the rate of growth of a quantity is approximately proportional to the amount that is there. For example, the more people there are in a country, the more babies will be born. It turns out that the only functions that have this property are exponential functions of the form $y = Ca^x$.

Section 1: Graphs of exponential functions

This is the graph of $y = 2^x$:

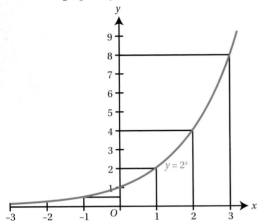

For very large positive values of x, the y value approaches infinity, and for very large negative values of x the y value approaches (but never reaches) 0. In this case, you would say that the x-axis is an **asymptote** to the graph.

If you look at the graphs of exponential functions with different bases you can start to make some generalisations.

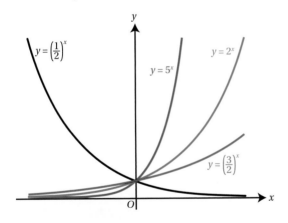

⏮ Rewind

You may notice that the black line is a reflection of the blue line. This is because $\left(\frac{1}{2}\right)^x = (2^{-1})^x = 2^{-x}$. You know from Chapter 5, Section 3 that replacing x by $-x$ results in the graph being reflected in the y-axis.

🔑 Key point 8.1

For all the graphs $y = a^x$:

- the y-intercept is always $(0, 1)$ because $a^0 = 1$
- the graph of the function lies entirely above the x-axis
- the x-axis is an asymptote.

If $a > 1$, then as x increases so does y. This is called **exponential growth**.

If $0 < a < 1$, then as x increases, y decreases. This is called **exponential decay**.

Gradient of an exponential graph

For an exponential growth graph the gradient also increases with x. In fact, the gradient is exactly proportional to the y value at every point on the graph.

You can find the gradient of a curved graph by drawing a tangent and calculating its gradient. The diagram shows some tangents to the graph of $y = 2^x$.

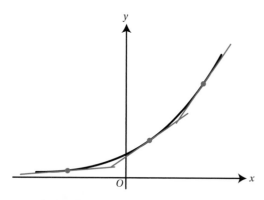

x	−1	0	1	2
y	0.5	1.0	2.0	4.0
Gradient	0.35	0.7	1.4	2.8

The table shows the y values and the gradient for each of the points. You can check that gradient $\approx 0.69y$.

You can do a similar calculation for the graph of $y = 3.5^x$ and find that the gradient $\approx 1.25y$.

These examples suggest that the constant of proportionality depends on the base of the exponential. There is one special value of the base where this constant is 1 so that the gradient at any point is exactly equal to the y value. This value is the number e that you met in Chapter 7.

 Key point 8.2

The gradient of e^x equals e^x.

 Tip

Remember that $e \approx 2.7$ Since $e > 1$, e^x is a type of exponential growth, while $e^{-x} = \left(\frac{1}{e}\right)^x$ represents exponential decay.

You can extend this result to exponential functions of the form e^{kx} for any constant k.

 Key point 8.3

The gradient of e^{kx} equals ke^{kx}.

PROOF 4

Prove that the gradient of e^{kx} is ke^{kx}.

Consider the graph of $y = e^x$ and $y = e^{kx}$.

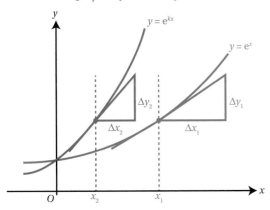

> You can compare the two graphs using the fact that they are related by a horizontal stretch.

A triangle is drawn from the tangent on the blue graph. The gradient is $\dfrac{\Delta y_1}{\Delta x_1} = e^{x_1}$.

The red graph is a horizontal stretch, factor $\dfrac{1}{k}$, of everything on the blue graph, including the triangle.

This means that $\Delta y_2 = \Delta y_1$ but $\Delta x_2 = \dfrac{\Delta x_1}{k}$.

So the gradient of the red line at this point is $\dfrac{\Delta y_2}{\Delta x_2} = k\dfrac{\Delta y_1}{\Delta x_1} = ke^{x_1}$.

> You already know that $\dfrac{\Delta y_1}{\Delta x_1} = e^{x_1}$.

But we also have $x_2 = \dfrac{x_1}{k}$ so $x_1 = kx_2$.

> You now need to write the gradient in terms of the x-coordinate of the point on the red graph.

So the gradient of the red line when $x = x_2$ is ke^{kx_2}.

In general the gradient of e^{kx} is ke^{kx}.

WORKED EXAMPLE 8.1

a   Find the gradient of $e^{1.2x}$ when $x = 2.6$.
b   Find the value of x when the gradient of $e^{1.2x}$ equals 15.
c   Find the gradient of the graph of $y = e^{1.2x}$ at the point where $y = 6.5$.

a   gradient $= 1.2e^{1.2x}$

> The gradient equals 1.2 times the value of the function.

   When $x = 2.6$:

   the gradient $= 1.2e^{1.2 \times 2.6}$

   $\qquad\qquad = 27.2$ (3 s.f.)

b $1.2e^{1.2x} = 15$

> You found the expression for the gradient in part **a**.

   $e^{1.2x} = 12.5$

> This is an exponential equation. Isolate the exponential term and then use logarithms.

   $1.2x = \ln(12.5)$

   $x = 2.1$ (2 s.f.)

c   gradient $= 1.2y$

> The gradient is proportional to the y-value. You have found that the gradient $= 1.2e^{1.2x}$ and $y = e^{1.2x}$ so the gradient $= 1.2y$.

   $\qquad = 1.2 \times 6.5$

   $\qquad = 7.8$

Changing the base of an exponential

The gradient of other exponential functions is more difficult to find. Luckily, any exponential function can be converted into an exponential with base e.

WORKED EXAMPLE 8.2

Given that 3^x can be written in the form e^{kx}, find the value of k.

   $3^x = e^{kx}$

   $\Rightarrow \ln(3^x) = \ln(e^{kx})$

> This is an exponential equation, so take a logarithm of each side. Since you want to find k, choose base e.

   $\Rightarrow x\ln 3 = kx$

> We can compare coefficients of x.

   So $k = \ln 3$

🔑 Key point 8.4

Any exponential function a^x can be written in the form e^{kx}.

- If $a > 1$, k is positive and e^{kx} represents exponential **growth**.
- If $a < 1$, k is negative and e^{kx} represents exponential **decay**.

WORKED EXAMPLE 8.3

a Write $\left(\dfrac{3}{4}\right)^x$ in the form e^{kx} giving the value of k to three significant figures.

b Hence find the gradient of $\left(\dfrac{3}{4}\right)^x$ when $x = 2.5$.

a
$$\left(\frac{3}{4}\right)^x = e^{kx}$$

$$\Rightarrow \ln\left(\frac{3}{4}\right)^x = kx \qquad\cdots\cdots\cdots\cdots\cdots\quad \text{Take ln of both sides to solve the equation for } k.$$

$$\Rightarrow x \ln\left(\frac{3}{4}\right) = kx \qquad\cdots\cdots\cdots\cdots\quad \text{We can compare the coefficients of } x.$$

$$\Rightarrow k = \ln\left(\frac{3}{4}\right) \approx -0.288$$

b The gradient of $e^{-0.288x}$ is $-0.288e^{-0.288x}$ $\quad$ The gradient of e^{kx} is ke^{kx}.

When $x = 2.5$:

gradient $= -0.288e^{-0.288 \times 2.5}$

$\qquad = -0.14$ (2 s.f.)

EXERCISE 8A

1 Match each exponential graph with its equation.

a **i** $y = 1.5^x$

    ii $y = e^x$

    iii $y = 0.7^x$

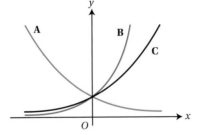

b **i** $y = e^{1.5x}$

    ii $y = e^{2.3x}$

    iii $y = e^{-2x}$

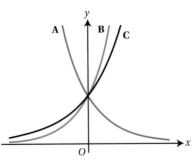

c **i** $y = e^{-0.5x}$

    ii $y = e^{-1.7x}$

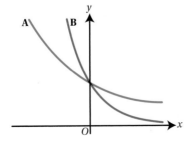

2 Find an expression for the gradient of each function.

    a i $e^{3.2x}$ **ii** $e^{0.6x}$

    b i $e^{-1.3x}$ **ii** e^{-x}

3 Find the gradient of each graph at the given value of x.

    a $y = e^{3.5x}$ when $x = 0.8$ **b** $y = e^{2.9x}$ when $x = -1.2$

    c $y = e^{-1.2x}$ when $x = 3.6$ **d** $y = e^{-0.5x}$ when $x = -0.9$

4 Find the gradient of each graph at the given value of y.

    a i $y = e^{1.5x}$ when $y = 17$ **ii** $y = e^{4x}$ when $y = 0.6$

    b i $y = e^{-0.6x}$ when $y = 3.5$ **ii** $y = e^{-x}$ when $y = 0.5$

5 Find the gradient of the graph of $y = e^{1.5x}$ when:

    a $x = -2.1$ **b** $y = 12$.

6 For the graph of $e^{-2.3x}$:

    a find the gradient when $y = 0.5$

    b find the value of x where the gradient is -2.5.

7 The graph of $y = e^{kx}$ has gradient 26 at the point where $y = 8$.

    a Find the value of k.

    b Find the gradient of the graph when $x = -1$.

8 The gradient of the graph of $y = e^{ax}$ at the point where $y = 4.6$ equals -1.2. Find the value of x at the point where the gradient is -5.

9 **a** Find the value of k so that $8^x = e^{kx}$.

    b Hence find the gradient of the graph of $y = 8^x$ at the point where $x = -0.5$.

10 **a** Find the value of p such that $0.3^x = e^{px}$.

    b Hence find the gradient of the curve $y = 0.3^x$ at the point where $y = 0.065$.

Section 2: Graphs of logarithms

You need to know the graph of the natural logarithm function.

🔑 Key point 8.5

The graph of $y = \ln(x)$:

- passes through the point $(0, 1)$
- has the y-axis as a vertical asymptote.

You can combine these facts with your knowledge of other graphs and graph transformations to solve a variety of problems.

EXERCISE 8B

1 **a** On the same diagram sketch the graphs of $y = \ln(x)$ and $y = \dfrac{2}{x}$.

 b Hence state the number of solutions of the equation $x\ln(x) = 2$.

2 Sketch the graphs of $y = \ln(x)$ and $y = \ln(x - 2)$ on the same diagram. Label all intercepts with the coordinate axes.

3 Let k be a positive constant. Use a graphical method to prove that the equation $kx + \ln(x) = 0$ has exactly one solution.

4 The graph of $y = \ln(x)$ can be transformed into the graph of $y = \ln(3x)$ either by a translation or by a stretch. Find the translation vector and the scale factor of the stretch.

5 **a** Sketch the graphs of $y = 2\ln(x)$ and $y = \ln(x + 3)$ on the same graph.

 b Find the exact solution of the equation $2\ln(x) = \ln(x + 3)$.

6 Given that $\log_{10}(x) = k\ln(x)$:

 a by raising 10 to the power of both sides, show that $k = \dfrac{1}{\ln 10}$

 b describe fully the transformation that transforms the graph of $y = \ln(x)$ to the graph of $y = \log_{10}(x)$.

Section 3: Exponential functions and mathematical modelling

You know that the gradient of an exponential function $y = e^{kx}$ is proportional to the y value. This means that if a quantity grows (or decays) exponentially, then its **rate of change** (the rate at which one variable changes in relation to another variable) is proportional to the quantity itself.

There are many situations where the rate of change of a quantity is proportional to its size. Here are some examples:

- A population increases at a rate proportional to its size.
- The rate of a chemical reaction is proportional to the amount of the reactant.
- The rate of radioactive decay is proportional to the amount of the substance remaining.
- The value of an investment that is subject to compound interest increases exponentially.

Exponential population growth is an example of a **mathematical model** where you try to capture the important part of a real-world situation using equations. Mathematical models are rarely perfect, so you should always be aware that they might not always work in predicting the real world. For example, there may be other factors that affect the rate of population growth (such as environmental conditions) that are not included in the exponential model.

In Section 1 of this chapter, you only considered exponential functions of the form $y = a^x$ or $y = e^{kx}$.

> **Explore**
>
> The exponential function is the only function where the gradient is proportional to the y-value. Can you find a proof? It relies on the fact that exponential is the only function for which $f(x + y) = f(x)f(y)$.

> **Focus on ...**
>
> You can use technology to investigate how different factors affect population growth. See Focus on ... Modelling 1.

All of these functions have the value 1 when $x = 0$. If you want an exponential model in which the initial value is different from 1 (such as in Worked example 8.4), you need to modify the equation by including another constant.

In many exponential models the quantity varies with time, so in this section you will use t to denote the independent variable.

WORKED EXAMPLE 8.4

The number of bacteria in a culture medium is modelled by the equation $N = 1000 \times 2^{4t}$ where t is the number of hours elapsed since 8 a.m.

a What was the size of the population at 8 a.m?
b At what time will the population first reach one million?
c What does this model predict about the size of the population in the long term? Explain why this is not a realistic prediction.

a $N = 1000 \times 2^0 = 1000$ This is when $t = 0$.

b $1000 \times 2^{4t} = 1000\,000$ You are solving the equation $N = 1000\,000$.

$2^{4t} = 1000$ Isolate the term containing t.

$\log(2^{4t}) = \log 1000$ Take logarithms of both sides.

$4t \log 2 = 3$ Use the rule $\log_a x^p = p \log_a x$.

$t = \dfrac{3}{4 \log 2} = 2.49$ Divide both sides by $4 \log 2$.

The population will first reach 1 million at 10:29 on the same day. $0.49 \times 60 = 29$ so this is 2 hours 29 minutes after 8 a.m.

c The model predicts that the population will increase faster and faster.

This is not realistic, as the growth will eventually be limited (for example, by lack of food or space).

     The exponential function grows with an increasing gradient. This is not realistic in the long term – there are lots of different reasons why the growth might slow down, so there are many possible answers here.

🔑 **Key point 8.6**

For a function of the form $y = Ae^{kt}$:

- the initial value (when $t = 0$) is A
- the rate of growth is $ky = kAe^{kt}$.

WORKED EXAMPLE 8.5

The mass (m grams) of one of the substances in a chemical reaction is modelled by the equation $m = Ae^{-1.2t}$ where t seconds is the time since the start of the reaction. The initial mass of the substance was 72 g.

a State the value of A.
b Find the rate at which the mass is decreasing 5 seconds after the start of the reaction.

a $A = 72$ .... A is the value of m when $t = 0$.

b When $t = 5$: .... The rate of change is $-1.2m$, so you need to find m first.

$m = 72e^{-1.2 \times 5} = 0.178$

The rate of change is

$-1.2m = -1.2 \times 0.178$

$= -0.214$

The mass is decreasing at the rate of .... The negative rate means that the amount is **decreasing**.
0.214 grams per second.

WORK IT OUT 8.1

A population grows according to the exponential model $N = 250e^{0.02t}$ where t is measured in months. Find the rate at which the population is increasing after 7 months.

Which of the following solutions is correct? Identify the mistakes in the other two.

Solution 1	Solution 2	Solution 3
The rate of change of e^{kx} is ke^{kx} so the rate of growth is:	The rate of change of e^{kx} is ke^{kx} so the rate of growth is:	Initial population is 250.
$0.02e^{0.02t} = 0.02e^{0.14}$	$250 \times 0.02e^{0.02t} = 5e^{0.14}$	Population after 7 months is $250e^{0.02 \times 7} = 288$
$= 0.023$	$= 5.75$	So the rate of growth is $\frac{288-250}{7} = 5.43$

Sometimes you need to use experimental data to find the parameters in the model.

WORKED EXAMPLE 8.6

A simple model of a population of bacteria states that the number of bacteria (N thousand) grows exponentially, so that $N = Ae^{kt}$ where t is time in minutes since the start of the experiment.

Initially, there were 2000 bacteria in the dish and after 5 minutes this number has grown to 7000.

a Find the values of constants A and k.
b According to this model, how many bacteria will there be in the dish after another 5 minutes?
c Give two reasons why this model will not provide a good prediction for the number of bacteria in the dish 12 hours later.

Continues on next page ...

137

a When $t = 0$:

$$2 = Ae^0 \Rightarrow A = 2$$

When $t = 5$:

$$7 = 2e^{5k}$$

$$e^{5k} = 3.5$$

$$k = \frac{1}{5}\ln 3.5 \,(= 0.251)$$

b $N = 2e^{10k}$

$$= 24.5$$

The model predicts that there will be 24 500 bacteria.

c The model predicts that the bacteria population will continue growing indefinitely, but in reality it will eventually slow down as food and space become limiting factors.

The information given in the model is only approximate so in 12 hours errors in this information may make the prediction far off the correct value.

> Use the equation for $t = 0$ and $t = 5$.
> Remember that N is in thousands.

> Use logarithms to solve the equation for k.

> In another 5 minutes, $t = 10$.

> Notice that, instead of using the value of k found in part **a**, you could use the fact that $e^{10k} = (e^{5k})^2 = 3.5^2$.

> You are not expected to have any technical biological knowledge, but you may need to apply general experience of the real world to interpreting and criticising models.

> There are many other possible criticisms of this model, so anything relevant would be acceptable.

🔘 Focus on...

In focus on … Modelling 1 you can explore some modifications to the population growth model.

WORKED EXAMPLE 8.7

A population of flies grows exponentially, so that its size can be modelled by the equation $N = Ae^{kt}$, where N is the number of flies after t weeks. At the time $t = 0$, the population size is 2400 and it is increasing at the rate of 80 flies per week. Find the values of A and k.

When $t = 0$, $N = A$,

so $A = 2400$

The rate of increase is kN, so:

$$2400k = 80$$

$$k = \frac{1}{30}$$

> A is the initial value.

> This is an exponential equation, so the rate of increase of N is kN.

EXERCISE 8C

1 An amount of £C is invested in an account giving $p\%$ annual interest.

  a Find an expression for the value of the investment after 1 year in each case.

   i The interest is compounded annually.

   ii $\dfrac{p}{2}\%$ interest is compounded twice a year.

   iii $\dfrac{p}{4}\%$ interest is compounded four times a year.

  b If $\dfrac{p}{n}\%$ is compounded n times a year, explain why the value of the investment after one year is $V = C\left(1 + \dfrac{p}{100n}\right)^{n}$.

  c Investigate the behaviour of the sequence $\left(1 + \dfrac{1}{n}\right)^{n}$ as n increases.

  d For the case of a (not very realistic!) 100% interest rate, find an expression for the value of the investment after x years when the interest is compounded continuously.

2 In a yeast culture cell numbers are given by $N = 100e^{1.03t}$ where t is measured in hours after the cells are introduced to culture.

  a What is the initial number of cells?

  b How many cells will be present after 6 hours?

  c How long will it take for the population to reach one thousand?

  d At what rate will the population be growing at that point?

3 An algal population grows by 10% every day on the surface of a pond, and the area it covers can be modelled by the equation $y = k \times 1.1^{t}$ where t is measured in days. At 9 a.m. on Tuesday it covered $10\ \text{m}^2$. What area will it cover by 9 a.m. on Friday?

4 A technology company is interested in predicting the number of mobile phones in the world. The number of mobile phones in billions (N) in t years is predicted to follow the model $N = 2e^{0.1t} + 1$

  a According to the model, how many mobile phones are currently in the world?

  b How many mobile phones does the model predict will exist in 10 years' time? Give your answer to 3 significant figures.

5 The mass of a piece of plutonium (M grams) after t seconds is given by $M = ke^{-0.01t}$.

  a Sketch the graph of M against t.

  b How long will it take to reach 25% of its original mass?

Explore

The procedure described in question 1 leads to one way to define the number e. What other definitions of e can you find?

Did you know?

π and e have many similar properties. Both are **irrational**, meaning that they cannot be written as a ratio of two whole numbers and both are **transcendental**, meaning that they cannot be written as the solution to a polynomial equation with integer coefficients. The proof of these facts is intricate but beautiful.

6 A population size is increasing according to an exponential model $N = N_0 e^{at}$ where t is time measured in days. Initially the population size is 450 and is increasing at a rate of 90 per hour.

    a Find the values of N_0 and a.

    b At what rate is the population increasing when its size is 750?

    c How long will the population size take to reach 2000?

7 A radioactive substance decays so that the rate of decay (measured in atoms per day) is numerically equal to 40% of the number of atoms remaining at that time. Initially there were 500 atoms. Write an equation to model the number of atoms N at time t days.

8 The value of a new car is £6800. One year later the value has decreased to £5440.

    a Assuming the value continues to decrease by the same percentage every year, write the model for the price of the car in the form $V = Pe^{kt}$.

    b What does this model predict the value of the car will be in 10 years' time?

9 The population of Great Britain is currently 70 million and is predicted to grow by 2% each year due to births and deaths.

    a Write down a model for the population of Great Britain, P, at a time n years from now.

    b Give two reasons why this model might not be valid when predicting the population of Great Britain in 2100.

10 A bowl of soup is served at a temperature 35 °C above room temperature. Every 5 minutes, the temperature difference between the soup and the room air decreases by 30%. Assume that the room air temperature remains constant at 20°C. Then the temperature difference between the room and the soup, T°C, can be modelled by $T = ka^t$, where t is the time (minutes) since the soup was served.

    a At what temperature will the soup be 7 minutes after serving?

    b If the soup was put into a thermos flask instead of a bowl, determine how this would affect the value of:

        i k **ii** a.

11 The speed (V metres per second) of a parachutist t seconds after jumping from an aeroplane is modelled by the expression $V = 40 (1 - 3^{-0.1t})$.

    a Find the initial speed.

    b What speed does the model predict that he will eventually reach?

12 The model $I = 100e^{-2x}$ is used to estimate the intensity of light (I) at a distance x metres away from a bulb.

a By what factor has the light intensity dropped between 0 m and 1 m away from the bulb?

b Prove that every 1 m further from the bulb produces the same factor reduction in light intensity.

Section 4: Fitting models to data

In Worked example 8.6 you found the values of parameters A and k in the model $N = Ae^{kt}$ by using the information about the number of bacteria when $t = 0$ and $t = 5$. In many real-life situations, models are not exact, or there may be inaccuracies in the measurements. This means that if you used the number of bacteria when, say, $t = 10$ you would get slightly different values for N and k.

To get a more reliable result it may be a good idea to use data from more than two measurements. Suppose you measure the number of bacteria every 5 minutes for half an hour. If you plot your results you might get a graph like the one here. It is very difficult to draw an exponential curve that best fits the points. There is a clever trick that turns this curve into a straight line.

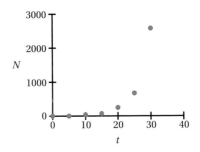

The equation for the population size is $N = Ae^{kt}$.
You can take a logarithm of both sides:

$$\ln N = \ln(Ae^{kt})$$
$$= \ln A + \ln e^{kt}$$
$$= \ln A + kt$$

If you write $y = \ln N$ (and remember that $\ln A$ and k are constants), you may notice that this is the equation of a straight line:

$$y = kt + \ln A$$

So, if you plot the data points with t on the x-axis and $\ln N$ on the y-axis, they should roughly follow a straight line with gradient k and y-intercept $\ln A$.

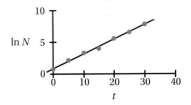

But you know how to draw a line of best fit and find its gradient and y-intercept.

In the example, you can find from the graph that the y-intercept is 0.8 and the gradient is $\dfrac{8-0.8}{30} = 0.24$. So:

$$k = 0.24 \text{ and } \ln A = 0.8$$
$$\Rightarrow A = e^{0.8} = 2.2$$

Therefore, the experimental data suggest that the model for the bacterial population growth is $N = 2.2e^{0.24t}$.

You can perform a similar calculation when the base of the exponential is unknown. In that case you can take logarithms in any base (it is common to use base 10 or base e).

◀◀ **Rewind**

See Chapter 6, Section 3 for a reminder of equations of straight lines.

▶▶ **Fast forward**

Ⓐ You will learn more about lines of best fit in Chapter 16, Section 4.

Key point 8.7

If $y = kb^x$ then $\log y = \log k + x \log b$.

- The graph of $\log y$ against x is a straight line with gradient $\log b$ and y-intercept $\log k$.

 Did you know?

This type of graph, where you take a logarithm of one variable but not the other, is called a semi-log graph.

WORKED EXAMPLE 8.8

The mass of a piece of radioactive material decays exponentially, according to the model $M = Cb^t$, where M is the mass in grams, t is the time in seconds and C and b are constants. A physicist measures the mass several times and plots the points on a graph with t on the x-axis and $\log M$ on the y-axis. The line of best fit has equation $\log M = 1.3 - 1.8t$.

Estimate the values of C and b.

If $M = Cb^t$ then:

$\log M = \log C + \log(b^t)$ .... | Take logs of both sides to transform to an equation of a straight line.

$\quad = \log C + t \log b$ .... | Use rules of logs.

So

$\log C + t \log b = 1.3 - 1.8t$ .... | $\log C$ and $\log b$ are numbers that should match the coefficients in the straight line equation.

$\Rightarrow \log C = 1.3$ and $\log b = -1.8$

$\quad C = 10^{1.3} \approx 20$

$\quad b = 10^{-1.8} \approx 0.016$ .... | Remember that the logs are in base 10.

A variation on the method used in Worked example 8.7 can also be used for models of the form $y = ax^n$ where x is in the base of the exponential and the power is unknown. In this case, you need to take a logarithm of both variables in order to get a straight line graph. This is called a log–log graph.

 Did you know?

Many natural and man-made phenomena follow so-called power laws of the form $y = ax^n$. Examples include the distribution of common words, the sizes of cities and corporations, and Kepler's law for planetary orbits.

 Key point 8.8

If $y = ax^n$ then $\log y = \log a + n \log x$.

The graph of $\log y$ against $\log x$ is a straight line with gradient n and y-intercept $\log a$.

WORKED EXAMPLE 8.9

A scientist thinks that variables x and y are related by an equation of the form $y = ax^n$.

She collects the data and plots a scatter graph with $\log x$ on the horizontal axis and $\log y$ on the vertical axis. The points follow a straight line with gradient 2.6 and y-intercept -0.9. Find the values of a and n, and hence write an equation for y in terms of x.

If $y = ax^n$ then

$\log y = \log a + \log(x^n)$

$\qquad = \log a + n \log x$

gradient: $n = 2.6$

intercept: $\log a = -0.9 \Rightarrow a = 10^{-0.9} \approx 0.13$

So: $y \approx 0.13x^{2.6}$

> Take logs of both sides to identify the gradient and the intercept.

> This is a straight line with gradient n and y-intercept $\log a$.

▶▶| Fast forward

If you study the Statistics option of Further Mathematics you will learn how to use your calculator to find the equation of the line of best fit on a scatter graph. You will then be able to apply these techniques to real experimental data.

EXERCISE 8D

1 In each of the following examples variables x and y are related by $y = Ab^x$ You are given the equation of a straight line of $\ln(y)$ as a function of x. Find the values of the constants A and b.

a $\ln y = 1.2x + 0.7$ **b** $\ln y = 3.1 - 0.6x$ **c** $\ln y = 2.3x - 4$

2 In each of the following examples variables x and y are related by $y = Cx^n$. You are given the equation of a straight line of $\ln(y)$ as a function of $\ln(x)$. Find the values of the constants C and n.

a $\ln y = 0.7 \ln x + 1.2$ **b** $\ln y = 2.1 \ln x - 4.7$ **c** $\ln y = 2 - 0.9 \ln x$

3 A zoologist is studying the growth of a population of fish in a lake. He thinks that the size of the population can be modelled by the equation $N = Ae^{kt}$ where N is the number of fish and t is the number of months since the fish were first introduced into the lake.

a The zoologist collected some data and wants to plot them on the graph in order to check whether his proposed model is suitable. Assuming his model is correct, state which of the following graphs will produce approximately a straight line.

   A N against $\log t$ **B** $\log N$ against t **C** $\log N$ against $\log t$

You may now assume that the proposed model is correct.

b Initially, 150 fish are introduced into the lake. Write down the value of A.

c After 10 months there are 780 fish in the lake. Find the value of k.

d Comment on the suitability of this model for predicting the number of fish in the long term.

⤓ Elevate

For more practice of questions like this, see Support sheet 8.

4 It is known that a population of bacteria can be modelled by the equation $N = 1500e^{bt}$, where N is the number of bacteria at time t hours.

   a Explain the significance of the number 1500 in the equation.

   b When $t = 0$, the population is growing at the rate of 500 bacteria per hour. Find the value of b.

   c According to this model, how long will it take for the number of bacteria to reach 1 million?

5 A scientist is modelling exponential decay of the amount of substance in a chemical reaction. She proposes a model of the form $M = Kc^t$ where M is the mass of the substance in grams, t is the time in seconds since the start of the reaction, and K and c are constants. The mass of the substance is recorded for the first six seconds of the reaction. The graph of $\ln(M)$ against t is shown.

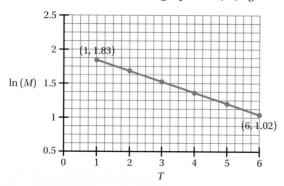

   a The points are found to lie on a straight line. Find its equation, giving parameters to 2 significant figures.

   b Hence find the values of K and c.

   c How long, to the nearest second, will it take for the mass of the substance to fall below 1 gram?

6 A model for the size of the population of a city predicts that the population will grow according to the equation $P = Ct^n$ where P thousand is the number of people and t is the number of years since the measurements began. The graph shows $y = \ln(P)$ plotted against $x = \ln(t)$.

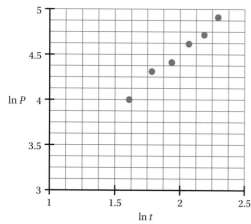

   a Draw a line of best fit on the graph and find its equation in the form $y = mx + c$.

b Hence estimate the values of C and n.

c According to this model, after how many years will the population first exceed 200 000?

 Elevate

For more applications of logarithms see Extension sheet 8.

7 A scientist is investigating the population of mice in a field. She collected some data over a period of time, and recorded it on a graph. Let N denote the number of mice at time t weeks. The graph of $y = \ln N$ against t has equation $y = 5.8 + 0.16t$.

a Find the equation for the size of the population at time t weeks.

b Find the rate at which the population is growing after 8 weeks.

8 a A common model used in population growth is called the logistic function. It predicts that the population N is related to the time t by the formula

$$N = \frac{1}{1 + Je^{-bt}}$$

Find an expression, in terms of N, which can be plotted against t to form a straight line if a population follows this model. Write down an expressions for the gradient and the intercept of the line in terms of b and J.

b By comparing the long-term predictions of the logistic function and normal exponential growth explain why the logistic function is a better model for population growth than normal exponential growth.

Checklist of learning and understanding

- For all the graphs $y = a^x$:
    - The y-intercept is always $(0, 1)$, because $a^0 = 1$.
    - The graph of the function lies entirely above the x-axis.
    - The x-axis is an asymptote.
- If $a > 1$, then as x increases so does y. This is called exponential growth.
- If $0 < a < 1$, then as x increases, y decreases. This is called exponential decay.
- Exponential functions are often used to model situations where the rate of growth is proportional to the amount present.
    - The gradient of e^{kx} equals ke^{kx}.
    - In a model of the form $y = Ae^{kt}$ the initial value is A and the rate of change equals ky.
- The graph of $y = \ln(x)$:
    - passes through $(1, 0)$
    - has the y-axis as an asymptote.
- Logarithms can be used to turn some curved graphs into straight lines. This is used to estimate parameters in models.

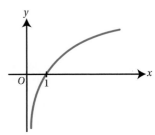

- If $y = kb^x$ then $\log y = \log k + x \log b$

The graph of $\log y$ against x is a straight line with gradient $\log b$ and y-intercept $\log k$.

- If $y = ax^n$ then $\log y = \log a + n \log x$

The graph of $\log y$ against $\log x$ is a straight line with gradient n and y-intercept $\log a$.

Mixed practice 8

1　**a**　Sketch the graph of $y = e^{0.8x}$.

　　b　Find the gradient of your graph at the point where $x = 3$.

　　c　Use your graph to determine the number of solutions of
　　　　the equation $e^{0.8x} = \dfrac{1}{x}$.

2　The amount of substance in a chemical reaction is
　　decreasing according to the equation $m = 32e^{-0.14t}$ where m
　　grams is the mass of the substance t seconds after the start of
　　the reaction.

　　a　State the amount of the substance at the start of the reaction.

　　b　At what rate is the amount of substance decreasing 3
　　　　seconds after the start of the reaction?

　　c　How long will it take for the amount of substance to halve?

3　Use graphs to determine the number of solutions of the
　　equation $\ln x = \dfrac{3}{x^2}$.

4　The volume of a blob of algae (V) in cm^3 in a jar is modelled
　　by $V = 0.4 \times 2^{0.1t}$ where t is the time in weeks after the
　　observation begins.

　　a　What is the initial volume of the algae?

　　b　How long does it take for the volume of algae to double?

　　c　Give two reasons why the model would not be valid for
　　　　predicting the volume in 10 years' time.

5　A rumour spreads exponentially through a school. When
　　school begins (at 9 a.m.) 18 people know it.
　　By 10 a.m. 42 people know it.

　　Let N be the number of people who know the rumour after t
　　minutes.

　　a　Find constants A and k so that $N = Ae^{kt}$.

　　b　How many people know the rumour at 10:30?

　　c　There are 1200 people in the school. According to the
　　　　exponential model at what time will everyone know the
　　　　rumour?

6　A patient is being treated for a condition by having insulin
　　injected. The level of insulin (I) in the blood t minutes
　　after the injection is given by $I = 10e^{-0.05t} + 2$, measured in
　　microunits per millilitre (μU/ml).

　　a　What is the level of insulin immediately after the
　　　　injection?

　　b　There is a danger of coma if insulin levels fall below 1.8
　　　　μU/ml. According to the model, will this level be reached?
　　　　Justify your answer.

7 It is thought that the global population of tigers is falling exponentially. Estimates suggest that in 1970 there were 37 000 tigers but by 1980 the number had dropped to 22 000.

a A model of the form $T = ka^n$ is suggested, connecting the number of tigers (T) with the number of years (n) after 1970.

    i Show that $22\,000 = ka^{10}$.

    ii Write another similar equation and solve them to find k and a.

b What does the model predict the tiger population will be in 2020?

c When the population reaches 1000, the tiger population will be described as 'near extinction'. In which year will this happen?

8 A zoologist believes that the population of fish in a small lake is growing exponentially. He collects data about the number of fish every 10 days for 50 days. The data are given in this table:

Time (days)	0	10	20	30	40	50
Number of fish	35	42	46	51	62	71

The zoologist proposes a model of the form $N = Ae^{kt}$ where N is the number of fish and t is time in days. In order to estimate the values of the constant A and k he plots a graph with t on the horizontal axis and $\ln N$ on the vertical axis.

a Explain why, assuming the zoologist's model is correct, this graph will be approximately a straight line.

b Complete the table of values for the graph:

t	0	10	20	30	40	50
$\ln N$	3.56	3.74	3.83	3.93		4.26

c Find the equation of the line of best fit for this table. (Do not draw the graph.) Hence estimate the values of A and k.

d Use this model to predict the number of fish in the lake when $t = 260$.

e The zoologist finds that the number of fish in the lake after 260 days is actually 720. Suggest one reason why the observed data does not fit the prediction.

9 Quantities m and t are related by an equation of the form $m = at^p$ where a and p are constants. The graph of $\log m$ against $\log t$ is a straight line that passes through the points $(2, 5)$ and $(4, 0)$. Find the values of a and p.

 Tip

You can use technology to find the equation of the line of best fit.

10 A substance is decaying in such a way that its mass, m kg, at a time t years from now is given by the formula $m = 240e^{-0.04t}$.

    i Find the time taken for the substance to halve its mass.

    ii Find the value of t for which the mass is decreasing at a rate of 2.1 kg per year.

© OCR, AS GCE Mathematics, Paper 4723, June 2007

11 The mass, M grams, of a certain substance is increasing exponentially so that, at time t hours, the mass is given by $M = 40e^{kt}$, where k is a constant. The following table shows certain values of t and M.

t	0	21	63
M		80	

    i In either order,

        a find the values missing from the table,

        b determine the value of k.

    ii Find the rate at which the mass is increasing when $t = 21$.

© OCR, AS GCE Mathematics, Paper 4723, January 2009

12 Radioactive decay can be modelled using an equation of the form $m = m_0 e^{-kt}$ where m is the mass of the radioactive substance at time t, m_0 is the initial mass and k is a positive constant. The half-life of a radioactive substance is the length of time it takes for half of the substance to decay. A particular radioactive substance has a half-life of 260 years. Find the value of k.

13 The speed, $V \text{ m s}^{-1}$, of a parachutist, t seconds after jumping from the aeroplane, is modelled by the equation $V = 42(1 - e^{-0.2t})$.

    a What is the initial speed of the parachutist?

    b What is the maximum speed that the parachutist could reach?

    c When the parachutist reaches 22 m s^{-1} he opens the parachute. For how long is he falling before he opens his parachute?

14 When a cup of tea is first made its temperature is 98 °C. After two minutes the temperature has reached 94 °C. The room temperature is 22 °C and the difference between the temperature of the tea and the room temperature decreases exponentially.

    a Let T be the temperature of the tea and t be the time, in minutes, since the tea was made. Find the constants C and t so that $T - 22 = Ce^{-kt}$.

    b Find the time it takes for the tea to cool to 78 °C.

9 Binomial expansion

In this chapter you will learn:

- how to expand an expression of the form $(a + b)^n$ for any positive integer n
- how to find individual terms in the expansion of $(a + b)^n$ for any positive integer n
- how to use partial expansions of $(a + bx)^n$ to find an approximate value for a number raised to a positive integer power
- about the notations $n!$ and ^nC_r.

Before you start...

GCSE	You should know how to evaluate expressions involving powers, including using the correct order of operations.	1 Evaluate 2×3^2.
GCSE	You should know how to use the rules of indices.	2 a Evaluate $(2x^3)^4$. b Simplify $x^4 \times x^7$. c Simplify $\dfrac{x^{12}}{x^3}$.
GCSE	You should know how to multiply out two brackets.	3 Expand $(2x + 3)^2$.
Chapter 3	You should know how to solve quadratic equations using the formula or factorising.	4 Solve $x^2 + 5x + 4 = 0$.

What is binomial expansion?

A **binomial expression** is one which contains two terms. For example, $a + b$.

Finding a power of such a binomial expression can be performed by expanding brackets. For example, $(a + b)^7$ can be found by calculating, at length:

$$(a+b)(a+b)(a+b)(a+b)(a+b)(a+b)(a+b)$$

This is time consuming and mistakes can easily be made, but fortunately there is a much quicker approach, called the **binomial expansion**.

Section 1: The binomial theorem

To see how you might rapidly expand an expression of the form $(a + b)^n$ for an integer power n first look at some expansions of $(a + b)^n$ done using the slow method of multiplying out brackets repeatedly. The table shows the results for $n = 0, 1, 2, 3$ and 4. In the right-hand column the coefficients and powers in the expansions are coloured to emphasise the pattern.

$(a+b)^0$	$= 1$	$= 1a^0b^0$
$(a+b)^1$	$= a+b$	$= 1a^1b^0 + 1a^0b^1$
$(a+b)^2$	$= a^2 + 2ab + b^2$	$= 1a^2b^0 + 2a^1b^1 + 1a^0b^2$
$(a+b)^3$	$= a^3 + 3a^2b + 3ab^2 + b^3$	$= 1a^3b^0 + 3a^2b^1 + 3a^1b^2 + 1a^0b^3$
$(a+b)^4$	$= a^4 + 4a^3b + 6a^2b^2 + 4ab^3 + b^4$	$= 1a^4b^0 + 4a^3b^1 + 6a^2b^2 + 4a^1b^3 + 1a^0b^4$

There are several patterns:

- The powers of a and b in each term (coloured blue) always add up to n.
- Each power of a from 0 up to n is present in one of the terms, with the corresponding complementary power of b.
- The pattern of coefficients (coloured in red) in each line is symmetrical.

 Key point 9.1

The **binomial theorem** states that for any positive integer n,

$$(a+b)^n = {}^nC_0 a^n b^0 + {}^nC_1 a^{n-1} b^1 + {}^nC_2 a^{n-2} b^2 + \dots + {}^nC_n a^0 b^n$$

This will appear in your formula book.

For example, the calculation for the expansion of $(a+b)^4$ is:

$$(a+b)^4 = {}^4C_0 a^4 b^0 + {}^4C_1 a^3 b^1 + {}^4C_2 a^2 b^2 + {}^4C_3 a^1 b^3 + {}^4C_4 a^0 b^4$$

The numbers ${}^nC_r$ are called **binomial coefficients** because they are the constants in the expansions of expressions of the form $(a+b)^n$.

 Key point 9.2

Binomial coefficients can be found using the ${}^nC_r$ button on your calculator or from Pascal's triangle.

${}^nC_r$ can also be written as $\dbinom{n}{r}$ or ${}_nC_r$.

 Tip

You can use either ${}^nC_r$ or $\dbinom{n}{r}$, but you need to recognise both.

Pascal's triangle is constructed by adding two adjacent numbers to produce the number below them in the next row, as shown in the diagram.

To find the binomial coefficient ${}^4C_2$ in Pascal's triangle, look at the row starting 1, 4 ... The coefficients in this row are:

$${}^4C_0 \quad {}^4C_1 \quad {}^4C_2 \quad {}^4C_3 \quad {}^4C_4$$

So ${}^4C_2$ is the third number in this row, which is 6.

In Key point 9.1, a and b can be replaced by any number, letter or expression.

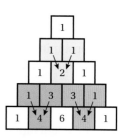

Tip

The binomial coefficient ^nC_r is the $(r+1)$th number in the row starting $1, n \ldots$ in Pascal's triangle.

WORKED EXAMPLE 9.1

Expand and simplify $(2+x)^4$.

$(2+x)^4 = {^4C_0}(2)^4(x)^0 + {^4C_1}(2)^3(x)^1 + {^4C_2}(2)^2(x)^2$
$\qquad\qquad + {^4C_3}(2)^1(x)^3 + {^4C_4}(2)^0(x)^4$ .... Use the formula from Key point 9.1.

$\qquad = 1(16)(1) + 4(8)(x) + 6(4)(x^2)$ .... Find the binomial coefficients (the red
$\qquad\quad + 4(2)(x^3) + 1(1)(x^4)$ numbers) either from your calculator or by
looking at Pascal's triangle: you want the
row starting $1, 4 \ldots$

$\qquad = 16 + 32x + 24x^2 + 8x^3 + x^4$

Remember that anything raised to the power
of 0 is 1.

You need to be careful when there is a minus sign or a number in front of x.

WORKED EXAMPLE 9.2

a Expand and simplify $(3x-5)^3$.

b Hence find the expansion of $(3x^3-5)^3$.

a $(3x-5)^3 = (3x+(-5))^3$

$\qquad = {^3C_0}(3x)^3(-5)^0 + {^3C_1}(3x)^2(-5)^1 + {^3C_2}(3x)^1$ .... Use the formula from Key point 9.1.
$\qquad\quad (-5)^2 + {^3C_3}(3x)^0(-5)^3$

$\qquad = 1(27x^3)(1) + 3(9x^2)(-5) + 3(3x)(25) + 1(1)$ .... Find the binomial coefficients from your
$\qquad\quad (-125)$ calculator or from Pascal's triangle.

$\qquad = 27x^3 - 135x^2 + 225x - 125$

Be careful with powers:

$(3x)^3 = 27x^3$

$(-5)^2 = 25$, but $(-5)^3 = -125$

b $(3x^3-5)^3 = 27(x^3)^3 - 135(x^3)^2 + 225(x^3) - 125$ ..... Replace x by x^3 in the expansion in part **a**.

$\qquad\qquad = 27x^9 - 135x^6 + 225x^3 - 125$ .... Use laws of indices to simplify.

Sometimes you want to find a particular term, rather than the whole expansion.

WORKED EXAMPLE 9.3

Find the coefficient of $x^5 y^3$ in the expansion of $(x + 2y)^8$.

The required term is $^8C_3 \, (x)^5 \, (2y)^3$.	Write down the required term in the form $^nC_r(a)^{n-r}\,(b)^r$. $a = x, \, b = 2y, \, r = 3, \, n = 8$
$^8C_3 = 56$ $(x)^5 = x^5$ $(2y)^3 = 8y^3$	Calculate the binomial coefficient and apply the powers to the bracketed terms.
The term is $56 \, (x^5)(8y^3) = 448x^5 y^3$ The coefficient is 448.	Combine the elements to calculate the coefficient.

💡 **Tip**

A question might ask you to give the term or just the coefficient. Make sure that you answer the question posed.

WORK IT OUT 9.1

Expand $(1 + 2x)^4$.

Which is the correct solution? Can you identify the errors made in the incorrect solutions?

Solution 1	Solution 2	Solution 3
$= 1^4 + {}^4C_1(2x) + {}^4C_2(2x)^2$ $+ {}^4C_3(2x)^3 + {}^4C_4(2x)^4$ $= 1 + 8x + 24x^2 + 32x^3 + 16x^4$	$= 1 + 4 \times 2x + 6 \times 2x^2 + 4 \times 2x^3 + 2x^4$ $= 1 + 8x + 12x^2 + 8x^3 + 2x^4$	$= 1^4 (2x)^0 + 1^3 (2x)^1 + 1^2 (2x)^2$ $+ 1^1 (2x)^3 + 1^0 (2x)^4$ $= 1 + 2x + 4x^2 + 8x^3 + 16x^4$

EXERCISE 9A

1 Use your calculator to find these binomial coefficients:

a **i** $^7C_3$ **ii** $^9C_2$

b **i** $^9C_0$ **ii** $^6C_0$

c **i** $\binom{8}{7}$ **ii** $\binom{10}{8}$

2 Expand and simplify the following:

a i $(2-x)^5$ **ii** $(3+x)^6$

b i $(2-3x)^4$ **ii** $(2x-7)^3$

c i $(3x+y)^5$ (first 3 terms only)   **ii** $(2c-d)^4$ (first 3 terms only)

d i $(2x^2-3x)^3$ **ii** $(2x^{-1}+5y)^3$

e i $\left(2x+\dfrac{1}{x}\right)^3$ **ii** $\left(x-\dfrac{3}{x}\right)^4$

3 **a** Find the coefficient of xy^3 in the expansion of $(x+y)^4$.

b Find the coefficient of x^3y^4 in the expansion of $(x+y)^7$.

c Find the coefficient of ab^6 in the expansion of $(a+b)^7$.

d Find the coefficient of a^5b^3 in the expansion of $(a+b)^8$.

4 **a** Find the coefficient of y^3 in:

i $(2-3y)^4$ **ii** $(5+y)^4$

b Find the term in y^4 in:

i $(x-2y)^7$ **ii** $(y-2x)^7$

c Find the coefficient of b^3 in:

i $\left(2-\dfrac{1}{2}b\right)^5$ **ii** $(17+3b)^5$

5 Find the expansion of $(3+x)^3$.

6 Determine which term in the expansion of $(1-2y)^5$ has the given coefficient:

a 80   **b** −80

7 Find the coefficient of x^3 in the expansion of $(1-5x)^9$.

8 Find the term in x^2 in the expansion of $(3-2x)^7$.

9 Find the first four terms in the expansion of $(y+3y^2)^6$ in ascending powers of y.

10 **a** Find the expansion of $(1+2x)^4$.

b Expand $\left(\dfrac{x+2}{x}\right)^4$.

11 Find the coefficient of x^2 in the expansion of $\left(x+\dfrac{1}{x}\right)^8$.

12 The expansion of $(x+ay)^n$ contains the term $60x^4y^2$.

a Write down the value of n.   **b** Find the value of a.

13 Complete and simplify the expansion of $\left(2z^2+\dfrac{3}{z}\right)^4$ that begins $16z^8+96z^5$.

14 The expansion of $\left(3x^2y+\dfrac{5x}{y}\right)^n$ begins with $27x^6y^3+135x^5y$.

a Write down the value of n.

b Complete and simplify the expansion.

15 Find the constant term in the expansion of $(x-2x^{-2})^9$.

16 Find the term in x^5 in $\left(x^2-\dfrac{3}{x}\right)^7$.

17 Find the term that is independent of x in the expansion of $\left(2x-\dfrac{5}{x^2}\right)^{12}$.

Section 2: Calculating the binomial coefficients

Although in many problems you can use your calculator or Pascal's triangle to find binomial coefficients, sometimes you may need to use a formula. This formula contains the **factorial** function $n!$

 Key point 9.3

$n! = n \times (n-1) \times \ldots \times 2 \times 1$ for $n \in \mathbb{N}$

$0!$ is defined to be 1.

Using this function, it is possible to find a formula for the binomial coefficients.

 Key point 9.4

$$^nC_r = \frac{n!}{r!(n-r)!}$$

This will appear in your formula book.

 Fast forward

Binomial coefficients are also used to evaluate binomial probabilities, as you will learn in Chapter 17, Section 3.

You will see how to prove this formula if you study the Statistics option of Further Mathematics.

WORKED EXAMPLE 9.4

Show that $^6C_4 = 15$.

$$^6C_4 = \frac{6!}{4! \times (6-4)!} = \frac{6!}{4! \times 2!}$$

Use the formula with $n = 6$ and $r = 4$.

$$= \frac{6 \times 5 \times 4 \times 3 \times 2 \times 1}{(4 \times 3 \times 2 \times 1) \times (2 \times 1)}$$

Use the definition of $n!$ to write out each term in full.

Then cancel factors from the numerator and denominator.

$$= \frac{6 \times 5}{2} = 15$$

Finally, evaluate what is left.

This method of cancelling factors that appear in the numerator and denominator can be used to provide an alternative (often more useful) version of the formula for ^nC_r:

$$^nC_r = \frac{n!}{r!(n-r)!}$$

$$= \frac{(n) \times (n-1) \times \ldots \times (n-r+1) \times (n-r) \ldots \times 3 \times 2 \times 1}{r! \times ((n-r) \times \ldots \times 3 \times 2 \times 1)}$$

$$= \frac{n \times (n-1) \times \ldots \times (n-r+1)}{r!}$$

 Tip

You can remember the last formula by noting that there are r numbers in both the numerator and the denominator. For example,

$$^7C_3 = \frac{7 \times 6 \times 5}{3 \times 2 \times 1}.$$

Key point 9.5 gives the expressions for $r = 0$, 1 and 2.

Key point 9.5

$$^nC_0 = 1$$

$$^nC_1 = n$$

$$^nC_2 = \frac{n(n-1)}{2}$$

These expressions are useful when part of an expansion has been given and you need to find the power.

WORKED EXAMPLE 9.5

The first three terms of the expansion of $(1 + 2x)^n$ is given by $1 + ax + 112x^2$.

Find the values of n and a.

$$(1+2x)^n = \binom{n}{0}(1)^n + \binom{n}{1}(1)^{n-1}(2x) + \binom{n}{2}(1)^{n-2}(2x)^2 + \ldots$$

Write out the expansion of the left-hand side in terms of n.

$$= 1 + n(2x) + \frac{n(n-1)}{2}4x^2 + \ldots$$

$$= 1 + 2nx + 2n(n-1)x^2 + \ldots$$

Now use the expressions from Key point 9.5 for $\binom{n}{0}$, $\binom{n}{1}$ and $\binom{n}{2}$.

Comparing coefficients of x^2:

$$2n(n-1) = 112$$

$$2n^2 - 2n - 112 = 0$$

$$n^2 - n - 56 = 0$$

$$(n-8)(n+7) = 0$$

$$n = 8, -7$$

You are given that the coefficient of x^2 is 112 (whereas you don't know the coefficient of x), so equating coefficients of x^2 allows you to solve for n.

$n = 8$ as n must be positive.

Comparing coefficients of x:

$$2n = a$$

$$a = 16$$

Now that you know n you can equate coefficients of x to find a.

EXERCISE 9B

1   Use the formula to evaluate these binomial coefficients:

   a   i $^7C_2$ ii $^5C_2$

   b   i $^{10}C_3$ ii $^{12}C_3$

   c   i $\binom{8}{1}$ ii $\binom{15}{1}$

   d   i $\binom{15}{0}$ ii $\binom{9}{0}$

e i $^{12}C_{12}$ **ii** $^{8}C_{8}$

f i $\binom{7}{6}$ **ii** $\binom{12}{11}$

2 Find the value of n in each equation.

a i $^{n}C_{1} = 10$ **ii** $^{n}C_{1} = 13$

b i $\binom{n}{2} = 45$ **ii** $\binom{n}{2} = 66$

3 If $(2 + x)^n = 32 + ax + \dots$

  a find the value of n **b** find the value of a.

4 If $(1 + 2x)^n = 1 + 20x + ax^2 + \dots$

  a find the value of n **b** find the value of a.

5 If $\left(1 + \dfrac{x}{2}\right)^n = 1 + ax + \dfrac{33}{2}x^2 + \dots$

  a find the value of n **b** find the value of a.

6 Given that $^{n}C_{k} = {}^{n}C_{k+1}$ write n in terms of k.

7 This question explores why binomial coefficients appear in Pascal's triangle.

Consider the expansions of $(a + b)^2$ and $(a + b)^3$:

$$(a + b)^2 = 1a^2 + 2ab + 1b^2$$

$$(a + b)^3 = (a + b)(1a^2 + 2ab + 1b^2)$$

$$= 1a^3 + 2a^2b + 1ab^2$$
$$+ 1a^2b + 2ab^2 + 1b^3$$

In the expansion of $(a + b)^3$, the coefficient of a^2b (which is 3) is found by adding $2a^2b$ and $1a^2b$. This exactly corresponds to the way that you get from one row of Pascal's triangle to the next row:

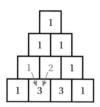

a Multiply out $(a + b)(a + b)^3$ in a similar way to show which two coefficients add up to give the coefficient of a^2b^2 in the expansion of $(a + b)^4$.

b Try some other examples to see how multiplying out successive powers of $(a + b)$ leads to Pascal's triangle.

 Elevate

For more questions on identities involving binomial coefficients, see Extension sheet 9.

Explore

Find out about many interesting patterns that appear in Pascal's triangle. Which of them can you explain by using the binomial expansion?

Section 3: Applications of the binomial theorem

There are two common applications of the binomial theorem:

- Simplifying a more complex expansion (usually multiplying a binomial expansion by another bracket).
- Making approximations to numbers raised to a positive integer power.

WORKED EXAMPLE 9.6

Use the binomial theorem to expand and simplify $(5-3x)(2-x)^4$.

$(2-x)^4 = 1(2)^4 + 4(2)^3(-x) + 6(2)^2(-x)^2 + 4(2)^1(-x)^3 + 1(-x)^4$ ⟶ First expand $(2-x)^4$

$\qquad = 16 - 32x + 24x^2 - 8x^3 + x^4$

So $(5-3x)(2-x)^4 = (5-3x)(16 - 32x + 24x^2 - 8x^3 + x^4)$ ⟶ Then multiply by $(5-3x)$ in the normal way.

$\qquad = 5[16 - 32x + 24x^2 - 8x^3 + x^4]$

$\qquad\quad -3x[16 - 32x + 24x^2 - 8x^3 + x^4]$

$\qquad = 80 - 208x + 216x^2 - 112x^3 + 29x^4 - 3x^5$

Sometimes you are only interested in one of the terms, rather than the whole expansion.

WORKED EXAMPLE 9.7

a Find the first three terms in the expansion of $(1+2x)^6$.

b Hence find the coefficient of x^2 in the expansion of $(1-x+2x^2)(1+2x)^6$.

a $(1+2x)^6 = 1(1)^6 + 6(1)^5(2x)^1 + 15(1)^4(2x)^2 + ...$ ⟶ You can stop after the first three terms.

$\qquad\quad = 1 + 12x + 60x^2 + ...$ ⟶ Be careful with the final term: $(2x)^2 = 4x^2$.

b $(1-x+2x^2)(1+12x+60x^2...)$ ⟶ You only need the first three terms of the binomial expansion, as after that all terms have powers of x^3 or higher.

The x^2 term is: ⟶ There are three ways to get the x^2 term: $1 \times 60x^2, -x \times 12x$ and $2x^2 \times 1$.

$60x^2 - 12x^2 + 2x^2 = 50x^2$

So the coefficient of x^2 is 50.

When x is very small, as the powers of x become larger their values become smaller. So the first few terms of a binomial expansion may be used to approximate the entire expansion.

🔑 Key point 9.6

If the value of x is close to zero, large powers of x will be extremely small.

WORKED EXAMPLE 9.8

a Find the first three terms in ascending powers of x of the expansion of $(2-x)^5$.

b Use your answer to **a** to find an approximate value of 1.99^5.

a The first 3 terms of $(2-x)^5$ are

$1(2)^5 + 5(2)^4(-x)^1 + 10(2)^3(-x)^2 = 32 - 80x + 80x^2$

> You know the coefficients for $n=5$.

b $2-x=1.99$

$x=0.01$

> You need to choose a value of x so that $(2-x)^5 = 1.99^5$, i.e. so that $2-x=1.99$.

$1.99^5 \approx 32 - 80(0.01) + 80(0.01^2)$

$= 32 - 0.8 + 0.008 = 31.208$

> Now just evaluate the first three terms of the series at $x=0.01$ to give an approximation for 1.99^5.

EXERCISE 9C

1 a Expand and simplify $(1+2x)^5$.

   b Expand and simplify $(3-x)(1+2x)^5$.

2 a Find the first four terms, in ascending powers of x, in the expansion of $(2-5x)^7$.

   b Hence find the coefficient of x^3 in the expansion of $(1+2x)(2-5x)^7$.

3 a Find the first three terms in the expansion of $(3-5x)^4$.

   b Using a suitable value of x, use your answer to find a 5 significant figure approximation for 2.995^4.

4 a Find the first three terms in the expansion of $(8+2x)^5$.

   b Use your answer, with a suitable value of x, to find an approximate value of 8.02^5.

5 a Find the first three terms in the expansion of $(2+3x)^7$.

   b Hence find an approximation to:

   i 2.3^7 ii 2.03^7.

   c Which of your answers in part **b** provides a more accurate approximation? Justify your answer.

6 a Find the first three terms in the expansion of $(4-x)^7$.

   b Hence find the coefficient of x^2 in the expansion of $(2+2x-x^2)(4-x)^7$.

7 a Expand $\left(e+\dfrac{2}{e}\right)^5$.   b Simplify $\left(e+\dfrac{2}{e}\right)^5 + \left(e-\dfrac{2}{e}\right)^5$.

> **Elevate**
>
> For a further example of this type and more practice questions, see Support sheet 9.

8 **a** Write the expression $(1+x)^n (1-x)^n$ in the form $(f(x))^n$.

    b Find the first three non-zero terms of the expansion of $(1-x)^{10}$ $(1+x)^{10}$ in ascending powers of x.

9 Find the coefficient of x^5 in the expansion of $(1+3x)(1+x)^7$.

Checklist of learning and understanding

- The expansion of $(a+b)^n$ can be found directly using the formula:

$$(a+b)^n = {}^nC_0 a^n b^0 + {}^nC_1 a^{n-1} b^1 + {}^nC_2 a^{n-2} b^2 + \ldots + {}^nC_n a^0 b^n$$

- The binomial coefficients, written ${}^nC_r$ or $\binom{n}{r}$, are given by the formula:

$${}^nC_r = \frac{n!}{r!(n-r)!}$$

where $n! = n \times (n-1) \times \ldots \times 3 \times 2 \times 1$ and $0! = 1$.

- Approximations for numbers raised to a positive integer power can be made using the first few terms of a binomial expansion $(a+bx)^n$. This is valid when bx is small, so that terms with higher powers are negligibly small.

Mixed practice 9

1 $^nC_2 = \dfrac{n!}{2!6!}$. What is the value of n?

2 Find the coefficient of x^5 in the expansion of $(2-x)^{12}$.

3 Fully expand and simplify $(2x^{-1} + 5y)^3$.

4 Find the coefficient of $x^2 y^6$ in $(3x + 2y^2)^5$.

5 $a = 2 - \sqrt{2}$. Using binomial expansion or otherwise, express a^5 in the form $m + n\sqrt{2}$.

6 Find the constant term in the expansion of $(x^3 - 2x^{-1})^4$.

7 Fully expand and simplify $\left(x^2 - \dfrac{2}{x}\right)^4$.

8 The constant term in the expansion of $\left(x^2 + \dfrac{a}{x^4}\right)^9$ is $-\dfrac{28}{9}$. What is the value of a?

9 Find the coefficient of d^{11} in the expansion of $(2 + 5d)(1 + d)^{14}$.

10 Find the coefficient of x^6 in the expansion of $(1 - x^2)(1 + x)^5$.

11 **i** Find the binomial expansion of $(2x + 5)^4$, simplifying the terms.

    ii Hence show that $(2x + 5)^4 - (2x - 5)^4$ can be written as $320x^3 + kx$, where the value of the constant k is to be stated.

    iii Verify that $x = 2$ is a root of the equation $(2x + 5)^4 - (2x - 5)^4 = 3680x - 800$, and find the other possible values of x.

© OCR, AS GCE Mathematics, Paper 4722, January 2008

12 The expansion of $(2x + ay)^n$ contains the term $20x^3 y^2$.

    a Write down the value of n.

    b Find the value of a where a is positive.

    c Find the first four terms in ascending powers of y.

    d Hence or otherwise, find 20.05^n correct to the nearest hundred. You do not need to justify the accuracy of your approximation.

13 Find the coefficient of x^2 in the expansion of $\left(2x + \dfrac{1}{\sqrt{x}}\right)^5$.

14 $(1 + ax)^n = 1 + 10x + 40x^2 + \dots$

Find the values of a and n.

15 **a** Sketch the graph of $y = (x + 2)^3$.

    b Find the binomial expansion of $(x + 2)^3$.

    c Find the exact value of 2.01^3.

    d Solve the equation $x^3 + 6x^2 + 12x + 16 = 0$.

16 In the binomial expansion of $(k + ax)^4$ the coefficient of x^2 is 24.

    i Given that a and k are both positive, show that $ak = 2$.

    ii Given also that the coefficient of x in the expansion is 128, find the values of a and k.

    iii Hence find the coefficient of x^3 in the expansion.

© OCR, AS GCE Mathematics, Paper 4722, January 2009

From general to specific

In Chapter 4, Key point 4.2 states the factor theorem. One part of this theorem says:

> **Given that f(x) is a polynomial, and that f(a) = 0, then ($x - a$) is a factor of f(x).**

This is actually a specific case of a more general result, called the remainder theorem:

> **Let f(x) be a polynomial and suppose you can write f(x) $\equiv$ ($x - a$)q(x) + r for some polynomial $q(x)$. Then r = f(a).**

> ▶▶) **Fast forward**
>
> **A** The remainder theorem can be interpreted as saying that, when f(x) is divided by ($x - a$), the remainder is f(a). You will study the remainder theorem in more detail in Student Book 2.

PROOF 5

Proof of the remainder theorem:

$f(x) \equiv (x - a)q(x) + r$ ⋯⋯ Start with the given expression.

$\Rightarrow f(a) = (a - a)q(a) + r$ ⋯ You can substitute any value of x in the above identity. $x = a$ is useful because it makes one term equal to zero.

$f(a) = r$

Questions

1 Where in the proof did you use the fact that q(x) is a polynomial? Does f(x) have to be a polynomial?

2 Adapt the given proof to find the remainder when f(x) is divided by ($bx - a$).

3 Use the remainder theorem to prove the factor theorem.

4 The full statement of the factor theorem is:

($x - a$) is a factor of a polynomial f(x) **if and only if** f(a) = 0.

This statement comprises of two implications:

- f(a) = 0 $\Rightarrow$ ($x - a$) is a factor of f(x)
- ($x - a$) is a factor of f(x) $\Rightarrow$ f(a) = 0

  a Prove the second implication: If ($x - a$) is a factor of f(x), then f(a) = 0.

  b Did you need to use the remainder theorem in your proof?

Alternative approaches

When faced with an unfamiliar problem, you might be happy if you could just get the solution, by whatever method. However, once you have solved the problem, it is worth thinking about whether there is an alternative strategy. This helps confirm that your solution is correct but, more importantly, it gives you an opportunity to reflect on which approach is best for what type of question.

In Worked example 6.12 in Chapter 6, Section 5, you solved the following problem:

> **A circle has centre (3, 2). Find the radius of the circle so that the circle is tangent to the line with equation $x + 5y = 20$.**

Strategy 1

This is the method used in Worked example 6.12:

- Write the equations of the circle with unknown radius:

$$(x - 3)^2 + (y - 2)^2 = r^2$$

- The equation for the intersection of this circle with the line rearranges to:

$$26y^2 - 174 + (293 - r^2) = 0$$

- If the circle is tangent to the line this has only one solution, so the discriminant is zero:

$$174^2 - 4(26)(293 - r^2) = 0$$

- This gives the solution $r = 1.37$.

Strategy 2

This uses the fact that the tangent is perpendicular to the radius at the point of contact. You don't know the coordinates of the point where the line touches the circle, but you know it lies on the line $x + 5y = 20$.

This means that for every point on the line, $x = 20 - 5y$, so you can write the unknown coordinates as $(20 - 5y, y)$.

The line connecting this unknown point to the centre (3, 2) needs to be perpendicular to $x + 5y = 20$.

- Write down the gradient of the line $x + 5y = 20$.
- Write down the gradient of a perpendicular line.
- Hence write an equation for the gradient of the line connecting (3, 2) to $(20 - 5y, y)$.

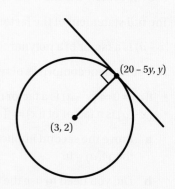

You should find that the coordinates of the point of contact are $\left(\frac{85}{26}, \frac{87}{26}\right)$.

Now you can find the radius, which is the distance of this point from the centre.

Strategy 3

This is based on the same fact as strategy 2, but you find the coordinates of the point of contact by intersecting the line $x + 5y = 20$ with the line perpendicular to it and passing through the centre $(3, 2)$. See if you can carry out this strategy for yourself.

Strategy 4

This also uses the fact that the radius is perpendicular to the tangent, but you will find the length of the radius directly, without finding the coordinates of the point of contact first. Instead, you will create a right-angled triangle and find its area in two different ways.

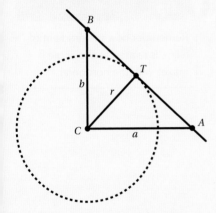

Draw lines parallel to the coordinate axes to form a right-angled triangle ACB. You can calculate the area of this triangle in two different ways:

$$\text{Area} = \frac{1}{2}ab = \frac{1}{2}r(AB)$$

Points A and B are on the line $x + 5y = 20$ so you can find their coordinates:

- A has the same y-coordinate as C ($y = 2$). Show that $a = 7$.
- B has the same x-coordinate as C ($x = 3$). Show that $b = \frac{7}{5}$.
- Show that the length of AB is $\sqrt{\dfrac{1274}{25}}$.

So the area equation gives:

$$\frac{1}{2}(7)\left(\frac{7}{5}\right) = \frac{1}{2}r\sqrt{\frac{1274}{25}}$$

$$\Rightarrow r = 1.37$$

> ⏮ **Rewind**
>
> This is the same method used to find the shortest distance from a point to a line in question 10 in Exercise 6C.

Questions

1 This is from question 7 from Exercise 6D:

A circle with centre $(3, -5)$ and radius 7 crosses the x-axis at points P and Q. Find the exact distance PQ.

    a Solve the problem by writing the equation of the circle and finding the coordinates of points P and Q.

    b Draw a diagram and label some lengths. Hence use a geometrical method to solve the problem.

2 How many different ways can you find to solve this problem?

Find the shortest distance from the origin to the line with equation $5x + 12y = 60$

3 This is question 10 from Mixed practice 6:

Find the exact values of k for which the line $y = kx + 3$ is tangent to the circle with centre $(6, 3)$ and radius 2.

    a Solve the problem by finding a quadratic equation for intersections and using the discriminant.

    b Draw a diagram and find a different way to solve the problem.

    c Would the second method work if the equation of the tangent was $y = kx + 2$ instead of $y = kx + 3$?

4 Circle C_1 has centre at the origin and radius 1. Circle C_2 has centre $(4, 3)$ and radius r. Find the value of r so that the two circles touch.

 Tip

Remember how the gradient of a line is related to the angle it makes with the horizontal.

Using data to modify the model

In Chapter 8 you learnt that you can use an exponential function to model population growth. This basic model is based on the following assumption:

The population growth is proportional to the size of the population.

 Fast forward

In Chapter 13, you will learn that this statement can be written as an equation: $\dfrac{dN}{dt} = kN$.

Questions

The simple population model leads to the equation $N = Ae^{kt}$ where N is the size of the population at time t and $k > 0$ is a constant.

 a Plot the graph of N against t for various values of A and k.

b What do the constants A and k represent, in the context of this model?

c Suppose you observe the size of the population at two specific times. For example, $N = 35$ when $t = 5$ and $N = 152$ when $t = 11$. Use technology to find approximate values of A and k.

d Can you use algebra to find the values of A and k?

e At a later time, you acquire a third observation: $N = 340$ when $t = 18$. What does this tell you about your model?

In a modified model, the population is assumed to have a maximum capacity (for example, limited by the amount of food or space available). The rate of growth is proportional both to the size of the population and to the remaining space.

This is called a **logistic** model, and leads to the equation:

$$N = \frac{ACe^{kt}}{C - A + Ae^{kt}}$$

 a Which of the parameters (A, C or k) represents the initial population size?

b Investigate this equation for various values of the parameters. Which parameter represents the maximum capacity?

c Use technology to find approximate values of the parameters which fit with the three observed data values: $(5, 35)$, $(11, 152)$ and $(18, 340)$.

Now consider the population model $N = Ae^{-kt}$ where k is a positive constant.

3 **a** What is the effect of the negative sign in the equation? How can you interpret this in the context of this problem?

  b What does this model predict will happen to the population in the long term?

To counteract population decline, individuals can be added to the population. (For example, this could model controlled immigration in a country where the death rate is larger than the birth rate.)

In a simple immigration model, new individuals are added at a constant rate D.

This model leads to the following equation:

$$N = \frac{D}{k} - \frac{1}{k}(D - kA)e^{-kt}$$

 4 **a** Which parameter represents the initial population?

  b According to this model, what happens to the population in the long term?

  c Explain what happens, and why, in the case when $D = kA$.

 5 A population of a small country was 7 430 000. Ten years later, the population has fallen to 7 026 000.

  a For a simple exponential model, $N = Ae^{-kt}$, find the value of the constants A and k.

  b By what factor does the population decrease each year? Given that the annual birth rate is 4.7 babies per 1000 people, estimate the annual death rate.

  c To counteract the population decline, the government proposes a controlled immigration programme (like the one you used in question 4). They want to aim for a stable long-term population of about 7 200 000.

    i What annual immigration target should they set?

    ii What assumptions about the immigrant population need to be made for the model prediction (a long-term population of 7 200 000) to be valid?

 Tip

You should find that the behaviour depends on whether $D > kA$ or $D < kA$.

 Explore

Find out about other modifications to the population growth models, for example those incorporating seasonal variation.

CROSS-TOPIC REVIEW EXERCISE 1

1 **Any calculations in your written solution to this question must show detailed reasoning.**

 a Find the exact value of $3\log 5 - \log 20 + \log 16$.

 b Given that $x = \ln 2$, $y = \ln 3$ and $z = \ln 5$, express $\ln\left(\dfrac{45}{4}\right)$ in terms of x, y and z.

 c If $\ln K = 2 - \ln c$, find and simplify an expression for K in terms of c.

2 **a i** Write $x^2 - 6x + 5$ in the form $(x - h)^2 - k$.

 ii Describe a single transformation that transforms the graph of $y = x^2$ into the graph of $y = x^2 - 6x + 5$.

 iii Sketch the graph of $y = x^2 - 6x + 5$.
   Mark the coordinates of the axes intercepts and the minimum point.

 b i Add the graph of $y = x - 1$ to your sketch.

 ii Solve the equation $x^2 - 6x + 5 = x - 1$.

 iii Using shading identify the region that satisfies $y \geqslant x^2 - 6x + 5$ **and** $y \leqslant x - 1$ (leave the area that satisfies the inequality unshaded).

3 **a** Show that $(x - 3)$ is a factor of $p(x) = 2x^3 - 5x^2 - 6x + 9$.

 b Factorise $p(x)$ completely.

 c Hence sketch the graph of $y = p(x)$.

 d Sketch the graph of $y = 2(x + 2)^3 - 5(x + 2)^2 - 6(x + 2) + 9$.

4 The circle with centre $(12, 9)$ and radius $\sqrt{145}$ intersects the x-axis at points A and B and the y-axis at points C and D. Find the area of the quadrilateral $ABDC$.

5 **Any calculations in your written solution to this question must show detailed reasoning.**

 Find the exact solutions of the equation $3e^{2x} - 7e^x + 2 = 0$.

6 The diagram shows the graph with equation $y = C + Ae^{-kt}$.
 The graph passes through the point $P(2, 3)$.

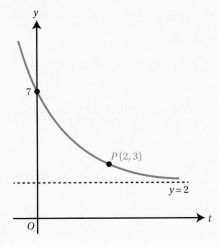

 a Write down the value of C and the value of A.

 b Find the exact value of k.

7 **a** Expand and simplify $(1 + x)^4 + (1 - x)^4$.

   b Hence show that $\left(\sqrt{2}+1\right)^4 + \left(\sqrt{2}-1\right)^4$ is an integer and find its value.

8 Number x satisfies the equation $x^2 = 3x - 1$.

   a Show that $x + \dfrac{1}{x} = 3$.

   b **i** Expand $\left(x + \dfrac{1}{x}\right)^2$ and $\left(x + \dfrac{1}{x}\right)^3$.

   ii Hence find the values of $x^2 + \dfrac{1}{x^2}$ and $x^3 + \dfrac{1}{x^3}$.

9 The graph of $y = \ln x$ can be transformed into the graph of $y = \ln kx$ using either a horizontal stretch or a vertical translation.

   a State the stretch factor of the horizontal stretch.

   b Find the vertical translation vector.

10 Given that $\binom{n}{2} = k$ express n in terms of k.

11 It is claimed that the number of plants of a certain species in a particular locality is doubling every 9 years. The number of plants now is 42. The number of plants is treated as a continuous variable and is denoted by N. The number of years from now is denoted by t.

   i Two equivalent expressions giving N in terms of t are $N = A \times 2^{kt}$ and $N = Ae^{mt}$
   Determine the value of each of the constants A, k and m.

   ii Find the value of t for which $N = 100$, giving your answer to 3 s.f.

   iii Find the rate at which the number of plants will be increasing at a time 35 years from now.

© **OCR, AS GCE Mathematics, Paper 4723, June 2008**

12 Show that the graph of $y = x^2 - (m + 3)x + (m + 1)$ crosses the x-axis for all values of m.

13 **a** Given that $y = e^x + e^{-x}$, express x in terms of y.

   b **i** Given that x is a real number, find the set of possible values of y.

   ii For a fixed y from this set, show that the sum of all the possible values of x is zero.

14 **a** Sketch the graph of $y = 6b^x$ where b is a constant and $b > 1$. Label the coordinates of any points of intersection with the axes.

   b The point P on the curve $y = 6b^x$ has its y-coordinate equal to $54b^2$. Show that the x-coordinate of P can be written as $2(1 + \log_b 3)$.

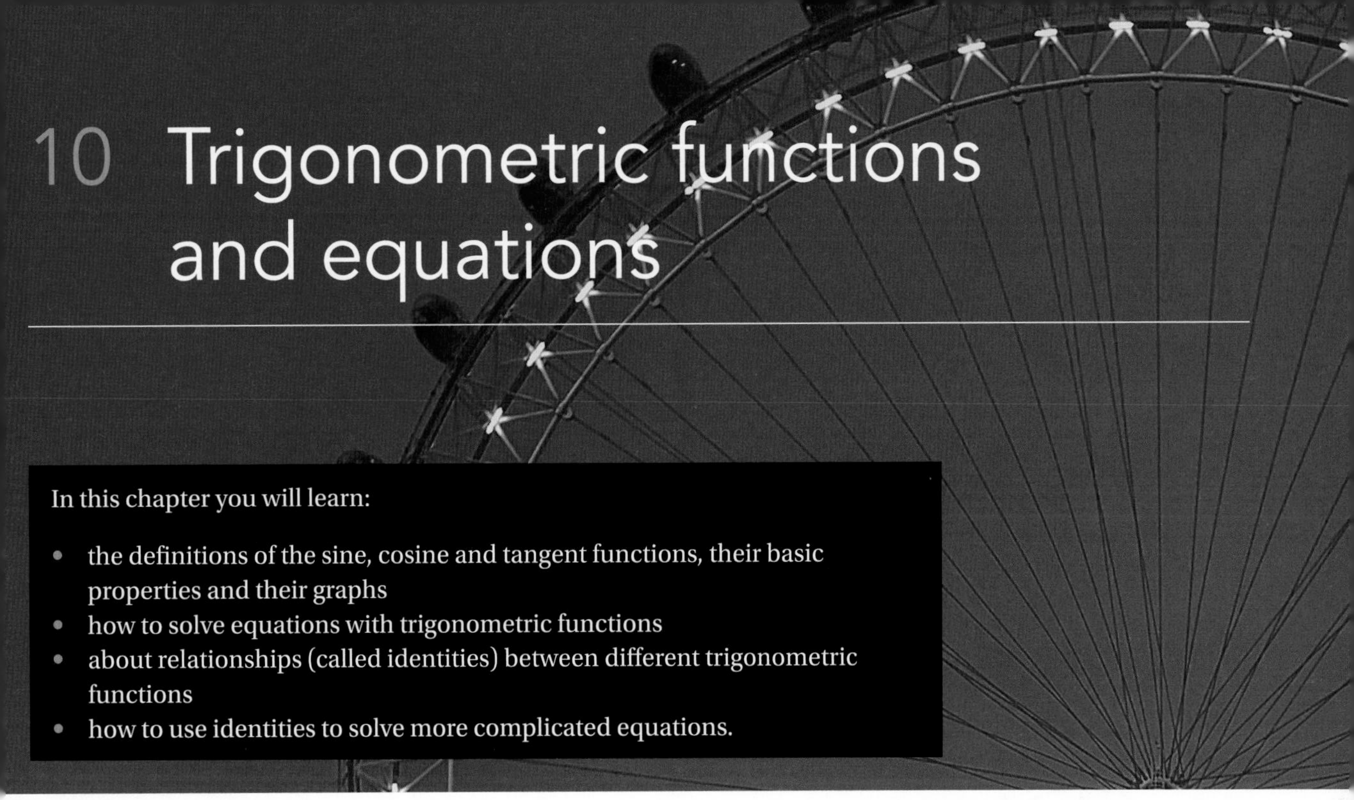

10 Trigonometric functions and equations

In this chapter you will learn:

- the definitions of the sine, cosine and tangent functions, their basic properties and their graphs
- how to solve equations with trigonometric functions
- about relationships (called identities) between different trigonometric functions
- how to use identities to solve more complicated equations.

Before you start...

GCSE	You should know how to use trigonometry in right-angled triangles to find unknown lengths.	1 Find the value of x in the diagram. 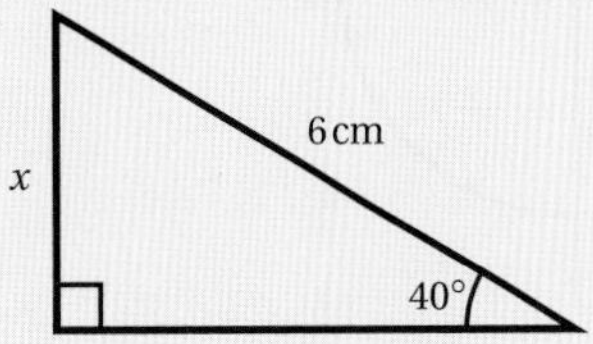
GCSE	You should know how to use trigonometry in right-angled triangles to find unknown angles.	2 Find the value of θ in the diagram. 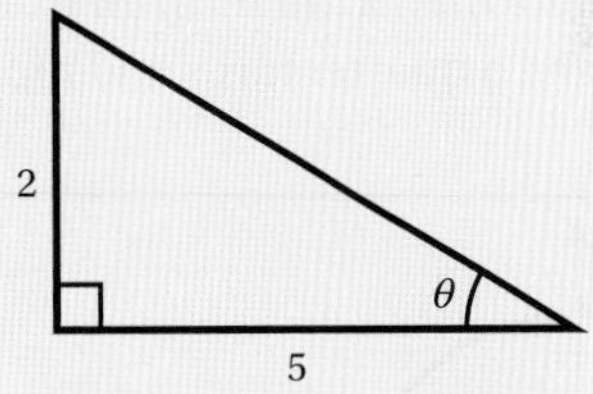
GCSE	You should know how to use Pythagoras' theorem in a right-angled triangle.	3 The two shorter sides of a right-angled triangle are 5 and 12. Find the length of the hypotenuse.
Chapter 3	You should know how to solve quadratic equations by using the formula or factorising.	4 Solve $x^2 - 2x + 1 = 0$.
Chapter 3	You should know how to solve equations that are quadratic in a function of the unknown.	5 Solve the equation $(\ln x)^2 - 2\ln x = 3$.

What are trigonometric functions?

There are many real-life situations in which something repeats at regular Intervals. For example, the height of a fairground ride, the tides of the sea or the vibration of a guitar string. All of these can be modelled using the trigonometric functions sine, cosine and tangent.

You first met sine, cosine and tangent when working with angles in a triangle. In this chapter, you will find out how they can be used in a variety of other contexts.

Section 1: Definitions and graphs of the sine and cosine functions

You've already used trigonometric functions in right-angled triangles but in these triangles no angle can exceed 90°. If we want to use trigonometric functions for other purposes it will be useful to have a more general definition.

To do this, consider a circle of radius 1 centred at the origin (the 'unit circle'). As a point *P* moves anti-clockwise around the circumference, an angle is formed between *OP* and the horizontal, for example angle *AOP* in the diagram is 60°.

Gateway to A Level

For a reminder of using trigonometry in right-angled triangles see Gateway to A Level section P.

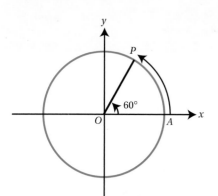

Any angle can be defined in this way. If the angle is greater than 360° the point *P* rotates more than a full turn, for example in the diagram point *P* has rotated one and a quarter turns and represents 450°.

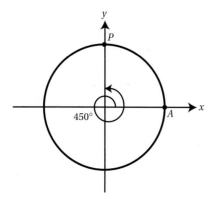

If the angle is negative then point *P* rotates clockwise.

For an angle θ, the sine and cosine functions are then defined in terms of the distance of the point *P* to the axes.

Key point 10.1

- sin θ is the distance of the point P above the horizontal axis (its y-coordinate).
- cos θ is the distance of the point P to the right of the vertical axis (its x-coordinate).

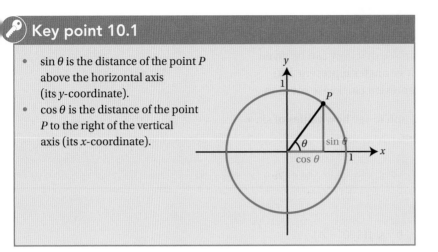

With this definition we can draw the graphs of $y = \sin x$ and $y = \cos x$ for any value of x.

The graph of $y = \sin x$

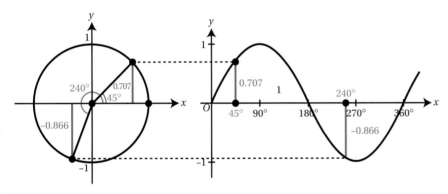

Key point 10.2

This is the graph of $y = \sin x$.

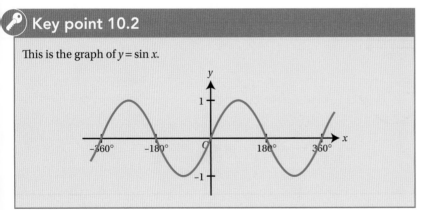

The graph repeats after 360°. The sine function is **periodic** with **period** 360°, which means that $\sin(x + 360°) = \sin(x)$ for all x.

You can also see that the minimum possible value of $\sin x$ is −1 and the maximum value is 1. The sine function has **amplitude** 1. Amplitude is the maximum 'height' of a periodic function, i.e. half of the distance from the minimum value of y to the maximum value of y.

Tip

For a periodic function with period p:

$f(x + p) = f(x)$ for all x.

You might think that considering negative angles or angles beyond 360° would not have any practical use. However, if you think about angles as measuring the amount of rotation you can see that they can be given a concrete meaning. By convention, positive angles represent anti-clockwise rotation and negative angles represent clockwise rotation.

You can use the symmetries of the sine graph to see how values of $\sin x$ for various angles are related to each other.

WORKED EXAMPLE 10.1

Given that $\sin a = 0.6$ find the value of:

a $\sin(180° - a)$ **b** $\sin(180° + a)$.

a

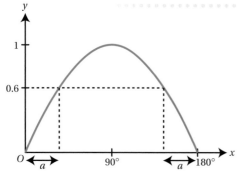

The graph has a vertical line of symmetry at $x = 90°$, so $\sin(180° - a)$ is the same as $\sin a$.

$\sin(180° - a) = 0.6$

b

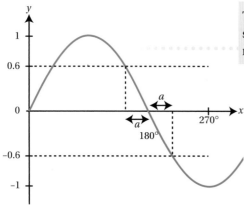

The part of the graph below the x-axis is the same shape as the part above. So $\sin(180° + a)$ is the negative of $\sin a$.

$\sin(180° + a) = -0.6$

There are several other similar relationships that you can find from the graph. They will be useful when solving trigonometric equations.

🔑 Key point 10.3

- $\sin x \equiv \sin(180° - x)$
- $\sin x \equiv \sin(x + 360°)$
- $\sin(180° + x) \equiv \sin(-x) \equiv -\sin x$

The graph of $y = \cos x$

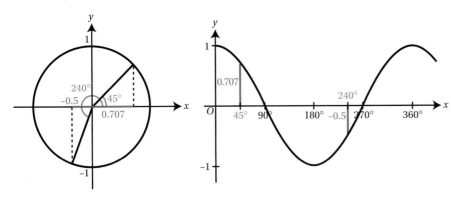

🔑 **Key point 10.4**

The graph of $y = \cos x$

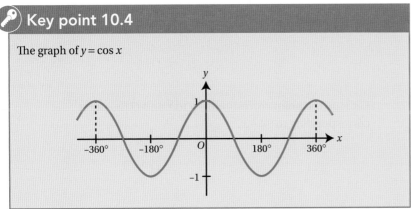

You can see that the cosine function is also periodic with period 360° and has amplitude 1.

You can use the symmetry of the graph to find relationships between values of $\cos x$ for different angles.

WORKED EXAMPLE 10.2

If $\cos 20° = c$, find two values of x between 0° and 360° for which $\cos x = -c$.

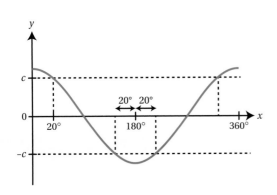

$x_1 = 180° - 20° = 160°$ ········· The two values are 20° away from 180° on either side.

$x_2 = 180° + 20° = 200°$

Key point 10.5

- $\cos x \equiv \cos(-x)$
- $\cos x \equiv \cos(x + 360°)$
- $\cos(180° - x) \equiv \cos(180° + x) \equiv -\cos x$

The unit circle definition can be used to establish a connection between the sine and cosine functions.

WORKED EXAMPLE 10.3

Given that $\sin x = 0.4$, find the value of

a $\cos(90° - x)$ **b** $\cos(x + 90°)$

a

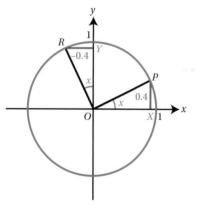

Let P be the point corresponding to x and Q the point corresponding to $90 - x$.

$\cos(90° - x) = 0.4$

$\cos(90° - x) = QY$

b

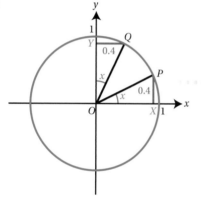

R is the point corresponding to $90 + x$.

$\cos(90° + x) = -0.4$

$\cos(90 + x) = RY$, but this is in the negative direction on the x-axis.

 Key point 10.6

- $\sin x \equiv \cos(90° - x)$
- $\cos x \equiv \sin(90° - x)$

Tip

These relationships can also be seen by noting that the graph of $y = \cos x$ is obtained from the graph of $y = \sin x$ by translating it 90° to the left and vice versa.

WORKED EXAMPLE 10.4

Find the two values of x in the interval $0° \leqslant x \leqslant 360°$ for which $\sin x = \cos 20°$.

$\cos(90° - x) = \cos 20°$ .... Use $\sin x = \cos(90° - x)$ so that both sides are in terms of the same trigonometric function.

Also, $\cos(90° - x) = \cos(-20°)$ .... Since $\cos x = \cos(-x)$, $\cos 20° = \cos(-20°)$.

$\therefore 90° - x = 20°$ or $-20°$ .... Remove the cos function from both sides.

$x = 70°$ or $110°$

EXERCISE 10A

1 Use your calculator to evaluate the following, giving your answers to 3 s.f.

a i $\sin 42°$ **ii** $\cos 168°$

b i $\sin(-50°)$ **ii** $\cos(-227°)$

2 Use graphs to find the value of:

a i $\sin 90°$ **ii** $\sin 360°$

b i $\cos 0°$ **ii** $\cos(-180°)$

c i $\sin(-90°)$ **ii** $\cos 450°$

3 Given that $\cos 40° = 0.766$ (3 s.f.) find the value of:

a $\cos 400°$ **b** $\cos 320°$

c $\cos(-220)°$ **d** $\cos 140°$

4 Given that $\sin 130° = 0.766$ (3 s.f.) find the value of:

a $\sin 490°$ **b** $\sin 50°$

c $\sin(-130)°$ **d** $\sin 230°$

5 **a** Sketch the graph of $y = \sin x$ for:

  i $0° \leqslant x \leqslant 180°$ **ii** $90° \leqslant x \leqslant 360°$

  b Sketch the graph of $y = \cos x$ for:

  i $-180° \leqslant x \leqslant 180°$ **ii** $0° \leqslant x \leqslant 270°$

6 Simplify $\sin(x + 360°) + \sin(x + 540°)$.

7 Prove that $\cos(180° + x) + \cos(180° - x) = k\cos x$ where k is a constant to be found.

8 If $\cos x = a$, show that $\sin(x - 90°) = ka$ where k is a constant to be found.

9 Simplify $\sin x + \sin(x + 90°) + \sin(x + 180°) + \sin(x + 270°) + \sin(x + 360°)$.

10 Find all values of x that satisfy $\cos x = \sin(\ln 3)$ for $-360° < x < 360°$, giving your answers in exact form.

> **⬇ Elevate**
>
> For more challenging questions on periodic functions, see Extension sheet 10.

Section 2: Definition and graph of the tangent function

You can now define another trigonometric function, the **tangent** function. This is defined as the ratio between the sine and the cosine functions.

 Key point 10.7

$$\tan x \equiv \frac{\sin x}{\cos x}$$

This is consistent with your previous knowledge of the tangent function.

If $\sin x = \frac{o}{h}$ and $\cos x = \frac{a}{h}$ then $\frac{\sin x}{\cos x} = \frac{o/h}{a/h} = \frac{o}{a}$, which is how you previously defined $\tan x$.

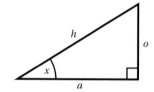

You may notice that there is a problem with this definition. When $\cos x$ is zero, you cannot divide by it. Thus the tangent function is undefined for values of x where $\cos x = 0$ (which is when $x = 90°$, $270°$ and so on).

You can also see that $\tan x = 0$ whenever $\sin x = 0$, which is when $x = 0°$, $180°$, $360°$, etc.

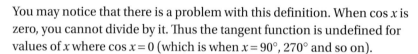 **Key point 10.8**

This is the graph of $y = \tan x$.

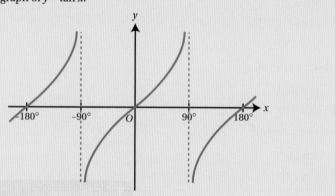

The tangent function is periodic with period $180°$:

$$\tan x = \tan (x + 180°) = \tan (x + 360°) = \ldots$$

It is undefined for $x = 90°$, $270°$, etc. The lines $x = 90°$, $270°$, etc. are vertical asymptotes.

 Rewind

Asymptotes were discussed in Chapter 5, Section 4.

EXERCISE 10B

1 Sketch the graph of $y = \tan x$ for:

    a $0° \leqslant x \leqslant 360°$ **b** $-90° \leqslant x \leqslant 270°$

2 Use your calculator to evaluate the following, giving your answers to 3 s.f.

    a **i** $\tan 32°$ **ii** $\tan 168°$

    b **i** $\tan (-540°)$ **ii** $\tan (-128°)$

3 Given that $\tan 20° = 0.364$ (3 s.f.) use the tangent graph to find the following:

    a $\tan 380°$ **b** $\tan(-160°)$

    c $\tan 160°$ **d** $\tan(-200°)$

4 Use the properties of sine and cosine to express the following in terms of $\tan x$:

    a $\tan(90° - x)$ **b** $\tan(x + 90°)$

    c $\tan(-270° - x)$ **d** $\tan(540° - x)$

5 Simplify $\tan(x + 360°) - \tan(180° - x)$.

6 Find the two exact values of x in the interval $-180 \leqslant x \leqslant 180$ for which $\tan x° = \tan e°$.

7 Let $\tan x = t$.

    Express $\dfrac{\tan(360° - x)}{\tan(270° - x)}$ in terms of t.

Section 3: Exact values of trigonometric functions

Although values of trigonometric functions are generally difficult to find without a calculator, there are a few special numbers for which exact values are easily found. The method relies on properties of special right-angled triangles.

WORKED EXAMPLE 10.5

Find the exact values of $\sin 30°$, $\cos 30°$ and $\tan 30°$.

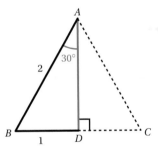

If a right-angled triangle has a 30° angle, then the third angle is 60°, so this is half of an equilateral triangle.

You can choose any length for the side of the equilateral triangle. Let $AB = 2$; then $BD = 1$.

$AD^2 = 2^2 - 1^2$

    $= 3$

To find AD use Pythagoras' theorem.

$\therefore AD = \sqrt{3}$

$\sin 30° = \dfrac{o}{h} = \dfrac{1}{2}$

You can now use the definitions of sin, cos and tan.

$\cos 30° = \dfrac{a}{h} = \dfrac{\sqrt{3}}{2}$

$\tan 30° = \dfrac{o}{a} = \dfrac{1}{\sqrt{3}}$

You can also find exact values for certain angles greater than 90° by considering symmetries of the trigonometric graphs.

WORKED EXAMPLE 10.6

Show that $\cos 135° = -\dfrac{\sqrt{2}}{2}$.

From the cos graph:

$\cos 135° = -\cos 45°$ .... You cannot have $135°$ in a right-angled triangle, so look at the cos graph.

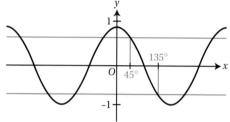

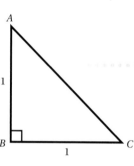

Now use a right-angled triangle with one angle $45°$. This triangle is isosceles.

Let $AB = 1$

Then $BC = AB = 1$

$AC = \sqrt{1^2 + 1^2}$ .... Use Pythagoras' theorem to find the hypotenuse.

$\quad = \sqrt{2}$

So: $\cos 45° = \dfrac{1}{\sqrt{2}} = \dfrac{\sqrt{2}}{2}$ .... You can now find $\cos 45°$, rationalising the denominator.

And so $\cos 135° = -\dfrac{\sqrt{2}}{2}$ .... And hence $\cos 135°$.

The results for other special values are summarised in Key point 10.9.

🔑 Key point 10.9

	0°	30°	45°	60°	90°	120°	135°	150°	180°
sin	0	$\dfrac{1}{2}$	$\dfrac{\sqrt{2}}{2}$	$\dfrac{\sqrt{3}}{2}$	1	$\dfrac{\sqrt{3}}{2}$	$\dfrac{\sqrt{2}}{2}$	$\dfrac{1}{2}$	0
cos	1	$\dfrac{\sqrt{3}}{2}$	$\dfrac{\sqrt{2}}{2}$	$\dfrac{1}{2}$	0	$-\dfrac{1}{2}$	$-\dfrac{\sqrt{2}}{2}$	$-\dfrac{\sqrt{3}}{2}$	−1
tan	0	$\dfrac{1}{\sqrt{3}}$	1	$\sqrt{3}$	not defined	$-\sqrt{3}$	−1	$-\dfrac{1}{\sqrt{3}}$	0

💡 **Tip**

Notice the pattern in the values of sin and cos:

$0, \dfrac{1}{2}, \dfrac{\sqrt{2}}{2}, \dfrac{\sqrt{3}}{2}, 1\left(=\dfrac{\sqrt{4}}{2}\right)$.

You should understand how these exact values are derived, as illustrated in the previous examples, and need to be able to use them in calculations, but you can check the values on your calculator.

EXERCISE 10C

Do not use your calculator in this exercise.

1 Find the exact value of:

a $\cos 45°$ b $\sin 135°$

c $\cos 225°$ d $\tan 225°$

e $\sin 210°$ f $\cos 210°$

g $\tan 210°$ h $\tan 330°$

2 Evaluate the following, simplifying as far as possible.

a $1 - \sin^2 30°$ b $1 + \tan^2 30°$

c $\sin 45° + \sin 60°$ d $\cos 60° - \cos 30°$

> **Tip**
>
> The notation $\sin^2 x$ means $(\sin x)^2$. This is not the same as $\sin(x^2)$.

3 Show that:

a $\sin 60° \cos 30° + \cos 60° \sin 30° = \sin 90°$ b $\sin^2 45° + \cos^2 45° = 1$

c $\cos^2 30° - \sin^2 30° = \cos 60°$ d $\left(1 + \tan 60°\right)^2 = 4 + 2\sqrt{3}$

4   a Show that $\sin 60° + \tan 30° = \dfrac{5\sqrt{3}}{6}$.

     b Given that $1 - 2\sin^2 60° = \cos A$, find one possible value of A.

5   a Find the exact value of $\cos 150° - \cos 120°$.

     b Paul thinks that $\cos A - \cos B = \cos(A - B)$.

     Use a counter example to disprove this statement.

6 Show that $\dfrac{\sin 30° + \sin 45°}{\cos 30° + \cos 45°} = \sqrt{6} + \sqrt{3} - \sqrt{a} + b$ where a and b are constants to be found.

Section 4: Trigonometric identities

You have already seen one example of an identity in this chapter: $\dfrac{\sin x}{\cos x} = \tan x$. There are many other identities involving trigonometric functions. The most important of these is:

> **Tip**
>
> Many books write $\dfrac{\sin x}{\cos x} \equiv \tan x$ to emphasise that the expression is an identity (true for **all** values of x) rather than an equation (only true for some values of x which need to be found). However, mathematicians often use the equals sign in identities, unless there could be confusion.

🔑 Key point 10.10

$\sin^2 x + \cos^2 x = 1$ for all x.

Because of the way it is derived, $\sin^2 x + \cos^2 x = 1$ is sometimes called the Pythagorean identity.

PROOF 6

This result follows from considering the definitions of $\sin x$ and $\cos x$ on the unit circle.

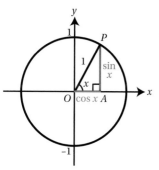

If the point P represents the angle x, then $AP = \sin x$ and $OA = \cos x$.

The triangle OAP is right angled, with hypotenuse 1, so by Pythagoras' theorem $\sin^2 x + \cos^2 x = 1$.

On the previous diagram both $\sin x$ and $\cos x$ are positive. However, since they are being squared, the proof also applies when they have negative values.

You have already seen examples where you used the values of $\sin x$ and $\cos x$ to find the value of $\tan x$. Using the Pythagorean identity, you only need to know the value of one of the functions to find the possible values of the other two.

WORKED EXAMPLE 10.7

Given that $\sin x = \dfrac{1}{3}$ find the possible values of:

a $\cos x$ **b** $\tan x$.

a $\sin^2 x + \cos^2 x = 1$

Use the identity $\sin^2 x + \cos^2 x = 1$ to relate cos to sin.

$$\left(\frac{1}{3}\right)^2 + \cos^2 x = 1$$

$$\cos^2 x = 1 - \frac{1}{9}$$

$$\cos^2 x = \frac{8}{9}$$

$$\therefore \cos x = \pm\sqrt{\frac{8}{9}}$$

Remember $\pm$ when taking the square root.

$$= \pm\frac{2\sqrt{2}}{3}$$

b $\tan x = \dfrac{\sin x}{\cos x}$

Use the identity $\tan x = \dfrac{\sin x}{\cos x}$ to relate tan to sin and cos.

$$= \frac{\frac{1}{3}}{\pm\frac{2\sqrt{2}}{3}}$$

Substitute in the values of sin and cos.

$$= \pm\frac{\sqrt{2}}{4}$$

Notice that for a given value of sin x, there are two possible values of cos x (positive and negative).

You can specify one of the two possible values by restricting x to a particular quadrant.

WORKED EXAMPLE 10.8

If $\tan x = -2$ and $90° < x < 180°$ find the value of $\cos x$.

$\tan x = -2$	To introduce cos you need to use $\tan x = \dfrac{\sin x}{\cos x}$.
$\dfrac{\sin x}{\cos x} = -2$	
$\sin x = -2\cos x$	
$\sin^2 x = 4\cos^2 x$	To remove sin so that you only have cos, use $\sin^2 x + \cos^2 x = 1$.
$1 - \cos^2 x = 4\cos^2 x$	
$5\cos^2 x = 1$	
$\cos^2 x = \dfrac{1}{5}$	
$\cos x = \pm\dfrac{1}{\sqrt{5}}$	
$90° < x < 180° \Rightarrow \cos x < 0$	Since x is between $90°$ and $180°$, cos x is negative. (You can see this from the graph.)
$\therefore \cos x = -\dfrac{1}{\sqrt{5}} = -\dfrac{\sqrt{5}}{5}$	

You can use known identities to derive new ones. For example, multiplying both sides of the Pythagorean identity by 3 gives:

$$3\sin^2 x + 3\cos^2 x = 3$$

You can also rearrange an identity, just as you would with an equation. For example, you can rearrange the Pythagorean identity to get:

$$\cos^2 x = 1 - \sin^2 x$$

You can also substitute one identity into another. For example, you can write $\tan x = \dfrac{\sin x}{\cos x}$ as $\cos x = \dfrac{\sin x}{\tan x}$ and substitute it into the identity to get:

$$\frac{\sin^2 x}{\tan^2 x} = 1 - \sin^2 x$$

Finally, it is important to realise that in each of these identities the variable x can be replaced by any other variable or expression, as long as each occurrence of x is replaced by the same thing. This means that, for example:

$$\sin^2(2x + 1) + \cos^2(2x + 1) = 1 \text{ and } \frac{\sin 2x}{\cos 2x} = \tan 2x.$$

You can combine these ideas with algebraic manipulations, such as simplifying algebraic fractions or the difference of two squares, to prove even more identities.

Rewind

Proving new trigonometric identities is an example of proof by deduction, which you met in Chapter 1, Section 4, where you start from given assumptions and use known facts to reach a conclusion.

WORKED EXAMPLE 10.9

Prove the identity $\sin^4 x - \cos^4 x = 2\sin^2 x - 1$.

$\text{LHS} = \sin^4 x - \cos^4 x$	You need to prove that the two sides are equal. One way to do this is to start with the left-hand side (LHS) and transform it until you make it look like the right-hand side (RHS).
$= (\sin^2 x - \cos^2 x)(\cos^2 x + \sin^2 x)$	In this case, you can start by using the difference of two squares.
$= (\sin^2 x - \cos^2 x)(1)$	The expression in the second bracket always equals 1.
$= \sin^2 x - (1 - \sin^2 x)$	The expression you want to get on the RHS contains $\sin x$ only, so use $\sin^2 x + \cos^2 x = 1$ to replace $\cos^2 x$ by $1 - \sin^2 x$.
$= 2\sin^2 x - 1$	The final expression equals the required RHS, so you have completed the proof.
$= \text{RHS}$	

$\therefore$ proved

Trigonometric identities often involve fractions. When simplifying expressions with fractions, you should always look for common denominators.

WORKED EXAMPLE 10.10

Prove the identity $\sin x \cos x = \dfrac{\tan x}{1 + \tan^2 x}$.

$\text{RHS} = \dfrac{\tan x}{1 + \tan^2 x}$ $= \dfrac{\frac{\sin x}{\cos x}}{1 + \frac{\sin^2 x}{\cos^2 x}}$	The RHS looks more complicated, so start there and try to simplify. Since the required answer on the LHS involves sin and cos, you should start by writing $\tan x$ as $\dfrac{\sin x}{\cos x}$.
$= \dfrac{\frac{\sin x}{\cos x} \times \cos^2 x}{\cos^2 x + \frac{\sin^2 x}{\cos^2 x} \times \cos^2 x}$	To simplify this 'double fraction', multiply top and bottom by the common denominator, which is $\cos^2 x$.
$= \dfrac{\sin x \cos x}{\cos^2 x + \sin^2 x}$	
$= \sin x \cos x$	The expression in the denominator always equals 1.
$= \text{LHS}$	

$\therefore$ proved

EXERCISE 10D

Do not use your calculator in this exercise, and give all your answers in surd form.

1 **a** Find the exact values of $\cos x$ and $\tan x$ given that:

    i $\sin x = \frac{1}{3}$ and $0° < x < 90°$ **ii** $\sin x = \frac{4}{5}$ and $0° < x < 90°$

  b Find the exact values of $\sin \theta$ and $\tan \theta$ given that:

    i $\cos \theta = -\frac{1}{3}$ and $180° < \theta < 270°$ **ii** $\sin \theta = -\frac{3}{4}$ and $180° < \theta < 270°$

  c Find the exact value of $\cos x$ if:

    i $\sin x = \frac{1}{5}$ and $90° < x < 180°$ **ii** $\sin x = -\frac{1}{2}$ and $270° < x < 360°$

  d Find the exact value of $\tan x$ if:

    i $\cos x = \frac{3}{5}$ and $0° < x < 180°$ **ii** $\cos x = -1$ and $90° < x < 270°$

  e **i** Find the possible values of $\cos x$ if $\tan x = \frac{2}{3}$.

    ii Find the possible values of $\sin x$ if $\tan x = -\frac{1}{2}$.

2 Find the exact value of:

  a $3\sin^2 x + 3\cos^2 x$ **b** $\sin^2 5x + \cos^2 5x$

  c $-2\cos^2 2x - 2\sin^2 2x$ **d** $\dfrac{3}{2\sin^2 4x} - \dfrac{3}{2\tan^2 4x}$

3 **a** Express $3\sin^2 x + 4\cos^2 x$ in terms of $\sin x$ only.

  b Express $\cos^2 x - \sin^2 x$ in terms of $\cos x$ only.

4 Prove the following identities:

  a **i** $(\sin x + \cos x)^2 + (\sin x - \cos x)^2 = 2$

    ii $(2\sin x - \cos x)^2 + (\sin x + 2\cos x)^2 = 5$

  b **i** $\sin \theta \tan \theta + \cos \theta = \dfrac{1}{\cos \theta}$

    ii $\dfrac{\cos^2 \theta}{\sin \theta} = \dfrac{1}{\sin \theta} - \sin \theta$

5 $\cos \theta = \frac{2}{3}$ and $270° < \theta < 360°$. Find the exact value of:

  a $\sin \theta$ **b** $\tan \theta$

6 If $\tan \theta = 3$ find, in exact form, the possible values of $\sin \theta$.

7 If $s = \sin x$ and $90° < x < 180°$, express $\cos x$ in terms of s.

8 Express the following in terms of $\cos x$ only:

  a $3 - 2\tan^2 x$ **b** $\dfrac{1}{1 + \tan^2 x}$

9 Simplify fully the expression $\left(\dfrac{1}{\sin x} - \dfrac{1}{\tan x}\right)\left(\dfrac{1}{\sin x} + \dfrac{1}{\tan x}\right)$.

10 Show that for all x, $2\tan^2 2x - \dfrac{2}{\cos^2 2x} = k$ stating the value of the constant k.

11 If $t = \tan x$ express the following in terms of t:

    a $\cos^2 x$ **b** $\sin^2 x$

    c $\cos^2 x - \sin^2 x$ **d** $\dfrac{2}{\sin^2 x} + 1$

 12 Prove the following identities:

    a $\dfrac{\sin\theta}{\cos\theta} + \dfrac{\cos\theta}{\sin\theta} = \dfrac{1}{\sin\theta\cos\theta}$ **b** $\dfrac{1}{\cos\theta} + \tan\theta = \dfrac{\cos\theta}{1 - \sin\theta}$

13 Prove the identity $\dfrac{1}{\cos\theta} - \cos\theta = \sin\theta\tan\theta$.

Section 5: Introducing trigonometric equations

In order to solve equations it will be important that you can undo trigonometric functions. If you were told that the sine of a value is 0.6 the original value is not easy to find. To do this you need to undo the sine function using the inverse function of sine, written as arcsin x or $\sin^{-1} x$.

The inverse cosine function is called arccos x or $\cos^{-1} x$. The inverse tangent function is called arctan x or $\tan^{-1} x$.

Suppose you want to find the x values which satisfy $\sin x = 0.6$. By applying inverse sine to both sides of the equation you get

$\sin x = 0.6$

$\quad x = \sin^{-1} 0.6$

$\qquad = 36.9°$ (to 3 s.f.)

The inverse sine function only gives you one solution. However, looking at the graph of $y = \sin x$ you can see that there are many values that satisfy this equation.

 Rewind

You already know how to use $\sin^{-1}$, $\cos^{-1}$ and $\tan^{-1}$ to find angles in a triangle.

 Tip

Calculators usually do not have a button labelled arcsin; use the $\boxed{\sin^{-1}}$ button (usually found as $\boxed{\text{SHIFT}} + \boxed{\sin}$) instead.

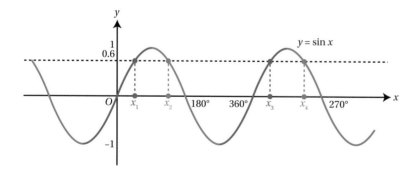

The solutions come in pairs – one solution in the green section of the graph and one in the blue section (for example, x_1 and x_2). The inverse sine function will always give you a solution in the green section that passes through the origin. To get from the first pair (x_1 and x_2) to the second pair (x_3 and x_4) you add 360°.

 Tip

The curve between 0° and 180° has line symmetry about the line $x = 90°$. If $x_1 = 36.9°$, what will x_2 be?

Key point 10.11

To find the possible values of x satisfying $\sin x = a$:

- use your calculator to find $x_1 = \sin^{-1} a$
- the second solution is given by $x_2 = 180° - x_1$
- other solutions are found by adding or subtracting $360°$ to any solution already found.

Tip

Always use the ANS button or the stored value rather than the rounded answer when doing subsequent calculations.

WORKED EXAMPLE 10.11

Find all possible values of $\theta \in [0°, 360°]$ for which $\sin \theta = -0.3$.
Give your answers to 1 decimal place.

$\sin^{-1}(-0.3) = -17.5°$

> Start by taking the inverse sine (which gives a solution that is not in the required interval).

$180° - (-17.5°) = 197.5°$

> Another solution is given by $180° - \theta$ (which is in the required interval).

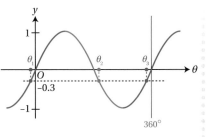

> Sketch the graph to see how many solutions there are in the required interval.

There are two solutions.

$-17.5° + 360° = 342.5°$

> The first solution $(-17.5°)$ is not in the required interval. However, you can see from the graph that adding $360°$ produces another solution that is.

$\theta = 197.5°, 342.5°$

> State the complete list of solutions.

You can apply a similar analysis to the equation $\cos x = k$.

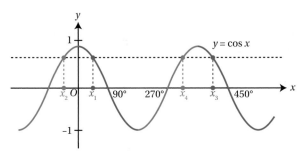

The solutions again come in pairs – one solution in the green section of the graph and one in the blue section (for example, x_1 and x_2). The inverse cosine function will always give you a solution in the green section closest to the origin.

 Key point 10.12

To find the possible values of x satisfying $\cos x = a$:

- use your calculator to find $x_1 = \cos^{-1} a$
- the second solution is given by $x_2 = -x_1$
- other solutions are found by adding or subtracting $360°$ to any solution already found.

 Tip

If you are looking for positive solutions, then the second solution can be found directly as $x_2 = 360° - x_1$.

It can be difficult to foresee how many times to add or subtract $360°$ to make sure that you have found all the solutions in a given interval. Drawing a graph can help here. You can then see how many solutions you are looking for and where they are.

WORKED EXAMPLE 10.12

Find the values of $-180° < x < 360°$ for which $\cos x = \dfrac{\sqrt{2}}{2}$.

$x_1 = \cos^{-1}\left(\dfrac{\sqrt{2}}{2}\right) = 45°$ .... Start by taking the inverse cosine.

$x_2 = -45°$ .... The second solution is given by $-x_1$.

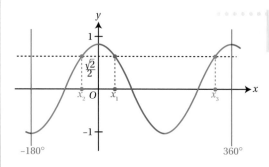 .... Sketch the graph to see how many solutions there are in the required interval.

There are 3 solutions.

$x_3 = -45° + 360° = 315°$ .... Add $360°$ to x_2 to find the other solution. Notice that adding $360°$ to x_1 would take you outside the interval.

$\therefore x = -45°, 45°, 315°$ .... State the complete list of solutions.

The procedure for solving equations of the type $\tan x = a$ is slightly different, because the tangent function has period $180°$ rather than $360°$.

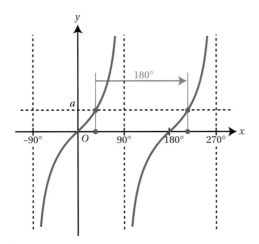

🔑 **Key point 10.13**

To find the possible values of x satisfying $\tan x = a$:

- use your calculator to find $x_1 = \tan^{-1} a$
- other solutions are found by adding or subtracting multiples of $180°$.

WORKED EXAMPLE 10.13

Solve the equation $\tan x = 2.5$ for $-180° < x < 540°$. Give your answers to 3 s.f.

$x_1 = \tan^{-1} 2.5 = 68.2°$

> Start by taking the inverse tangent.

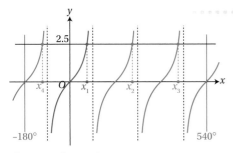

> Sketch the graph to see how many solutions there are in the required interval.

There are four solutions.

$x_2 = x_1 + 180° = 248°$

$x_3 = x_2 + 180° = 428°$

> The other solutions are found by adding or subtracting $180°$.

$x_4 = x_1 - 180° = -112°$

$\therefore x = -112°, 68.2°, 248°, 428°$

> List the complete set of solutions.

EXERCISE 10E

In this exercise, you must show detailed reasoning. This means that you can't, for example, use graphs or the equation solver function on your calculator. You need to use algebraic rearrangement and inverse trigonometric functions.

1 Evaluate the following, giving your answer in degrees correct to one decimal place.

a i $\sin^{-1} 0.7$ **ii** $\sin^{-1} 0.3$

b i $\cos^{-1}(-0.62)$ **ii** $\cos^{-1}(-0.75)$

c i $\tan^{-1} 6.4$ **ii** $\tan^{-1}(-7.1)$

2 Find the values of x between $0°$ and $360°$ for which:

a i $\sin x = \dfrac{1}{2}$ **ii** $\sin x = \dfrac{\sqrt{2}}{2}$

b i $\cos x = \dfrac{1}{2}$ **ii** $\cos x = \dfrac{\sqrt{3}}{2}$

c i $\tan x = 1$ **ii** $\tan x = \sqrt{3}$

d i $\sin x = -\dfrac{\sqrt{3}}{2}$ **ii** $\sin x = -\dfrac{1}{2}$

e i $\cos x = -\dfrac{1}{\sqrt{2}}$ **ii** $\cos x = -1$

f i $\tan x = -\dfrac{1}{\sqrt{3}}$ **ii** $\tan x = -1$

> ⏮ **Rewind**
>
> Question 2 involves exact values of trigonometric functions, which are summarised in Key Point 10.9.

3 Solve these equations in the given interval. Give your answers to one decimal place.

a i $\sin x = 0.45$ for $x \in [0°, 360°]$ **ii** $\sin x = 0.7$ for $x \in [0°, 360°]$

b i $\cos x = -0.75$ for $-180° \leqslant x \leqslant 180°$ **ii** $\cos x = -0.2$ for $-180° \leqslant x \leqslant 180°$

c i $\tan \theta = \dfrac{1}{3}$ for $0° \leqslant \theta \leqslant 720°$ **ii** $\tan \theta = \dfrac{4}{3}$ for $0° \leqslant \theta \leqslant 720°$

d i $\sin t = -\dfrac{2}{3}$ for $t \in [-180°, 360°]$ **ii** $\sin t = -\dfrac{1}{4}$ for $t \in [-180°, 360°]$

4 Solve the following equations.

a i $2\sin \theta + 1 = 1.2$ for $0° < \theta < 360°$ **ii** $4\sin x + 3 = 2$ for $-90° < x < 270°$

b i $3\cos x - 1 = \dfrac{1}{3}$ for $0° < x < 360°$ **ii** $5\cos x + 2 = 4.7$ for $0° < x < 360°$

c i $3\tan t - 1 = 4$ for $-180° < t < 180°$ **ii** $5\tan t - 3 = 8$ for $0° < t < 360°$

5 Find the values of x between $-180°$ and $180°$ for which $2\sin x + 1 = 0$.

6 Solve the equation $3\tan x + 5 = 0$ for $0° \leqslant x \leqslant 360°$.

7 Solve $2\cos x = \sqrt{3}$ for $x \in [-360°, 360°]$.

8 Find all values of θ in the interval $0° \leqslant \theta \leqslant 360°$ for which $\sin \theta° (3\cos \theta° - 2) = 0$.

9 Solve $(\tan x + 1)(5\sin x - 2) = 0$ for $0° \leqslant x \leqslant 360°$.

10 Show by a counter example that $\tan^{-1} x \neq \dfrac{\sin^{-1} x}{\cos^{-1} x}$.

11 Show by a counter example that $\sin^{-1}(\sin x)$ is **not** always x.

Section 6: Transformations of trigonometric graphs

If you solve the equation $\sin x = 0.6$ for $0° \leqslant x \leqslant 360°$, you can see from the graph that there are two solutions:

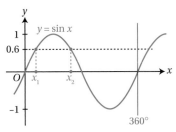

If you solve the equation $\sin 2x = 0.6$ for $0° \leqslant x \leqslant 360°$ you can see from the graph that there are four solutions:

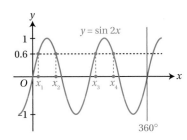

> **Rewind**
>
> Remember that replacing x by $2x$ results in the graph being 'squashed' in the horizontal direction.

You need to extend your methods to deal with equations like this. A substitution is a useful way of doing this.

WORKED EXAMPLE 10.14

Solve $3 \sin(2x) + 1 = 0$ for $x \in [0°, 360°]$. Give your answers to one decimal place.

$A = 2x$ .... Make a substitution: replace $2x$ by a single letter A.

If $x \in [0°, 360°]$ then $A \in [0°, 720°]$. .... Rewrite the interval in terms of A.

$3\sin(A) + 1 = 0$ .... Rearrange into the form $\sin(A) = k$.

$\sin(A) = -\dfrac{1}{3}$

$\sin A = -\dfrac{1}{3}$

$\sin^{-1}\left(-\dfrac{1}{3}\right) \approx -19.47°$ (outside interval) ..... Find the solutions to 2 d.p., then round at the end.

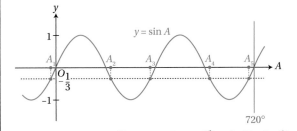

Continues on next page ...

There are four solutions. Solve the equation for A.

$A_2 = 180° - (-19.47°) = 199.47°$

$A_3 = -19.47° + 360° = 340.53°$

$A_4 = 199.47° + 360° = 559.47°$

$A_5 = 340.53° + 360° = 700.53°$

$x = \dfrac{A}{2}$  Transform the solutions back into x.

$\quad = 99.7°, 170.3°, 279.7°, 350.3°$ to 1 d.p.

A summary of this procedure is given in the four-step process.

🔑 Key point 10.14

1 Make a substitution (such as $A = 2x$).
2 Change the interval for x into the interval for A.
3 Solve the equation in the usual way.
4 Transform the solutions back into the original variable.

💡 Tip

Make sure you do not round your answers until the end.

WORK IT OUT 10.1

Solve $\tan 3x = 1$ for $-180° < x < 180°$.

Which is the correct solution? Can you identify the errors made in the incorrect solutions?

Solution 1	Solution 2	Solution 3
Let $A = 3x$	Let $A = 3x$	Let $A = 3x$
$A_1 = \tan^{-1}(1) = 45°$ $A_2 = 45 - 180 = -135°$ $x = \dfrac{A}{3}$ $\quad = 15°, -45°$	$-180° < x < 180°$ $\Rightarrow -540° < A < 540°$ $A_1 = \tan^{-1}(1) = 45°$ $\therefore x_1 = 15°$ $x_2 = 15 + 180 = 195$ $x_3 = 195 + 180 = 375$ $x_4 = 15 - 180 = -165$ $x_5 = -165 - 180 = -345$ $x_6 = -345 - 180 = -525$ $x = -525°, -345°, -165°, 15°,$ $\quad\quad 195°, 375°$	$-180° < x < 180°$ $\Rightarrow -540° < A < 540°$ $A_1 = \tan^{-1}(1) = 45°$ $A_2 = 45 + 180 = 225$ $A_3 = 225 + 180 = 405$ $A_4 = 45 - 180 = -135$ $A_5 = -135 - 180 = -315$ $A_6 = -315 - 180 = -495$ $x = \dfrac{A}{3}$ $\quad = -165°, -105°, -45°, 15°,$ $\quad\quad 75°, 135°$

Worked example 10.15 shows this method in a more complicated situation.

WORKED EXAMPLE 10.15

Solve the equation $3\cos(2x + 10°) = 2$ for $-180° \leqslant x \leqslant 180°$. Give your answers to 3 s.f.

$A = 2x + 10$ .... Make a substitution.

If $-180° \leqslant x \leqslant 180°$ then .... Rewrite the interval.

$-360° \leqslant 2x \leqslant 360°$

$-350° \leqslant 2x + 10° \leqslant 370°$

So $-350° \leqslant A \leqslant 370°$

$3\cos(A) = 2$ .... Write the equation in the form $\cos(A) = k$.

$\cos(A) = \dfrac{2}{3}$

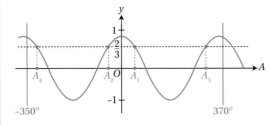

There are four solutions:

$A_1 = \cos^{-1}\left(\dfrac{2}{3}\right) = 48.19°$ .... Solve the equation for A.

$A_2 = -48.19°$

$A = 48.19° + 360° = 408.19°$ – not in range

$A_3 = -48.19° + 360° = 311.81°$

$A_4 = 48.19° - 360° = -311.81°$

$x = \dfrac{A - 10}{2}$ .... Transform the solutions back into x.

$\quad = -161°, -29.1°, 19.1°, 151°$ (3 s.f.)

Worked example 10.16 revisits the tangent function and exact values.

WORKED EXAMPLE 10.16

Solve the equation $3\tan\left(\dfrac{1}{2}\theta - 30°\right) = \sqrt{3}$ for $0° \leqslant \theta \leqslant 720°$.

$A = \dfrac{1}{2}\theta - 30°$ .... Make a substitution.

Continues on next page ...

If $0° \leqslant \theta \leqslant 720°$ then

$0° \leqslant \dfrac{1}{2}\theta \leqslant 360°$

So $-30° \leqslant \dfrac{1}{2}\theta - 30° \leqslant 330°$

$3\tan\left(\dfrac{1}{2}\theta - 30°\right) = \sqrt{3}$

$\tan\left(\dfrac{1}{2}\theta - 30°\right) = \dfrac{\sqrt{3}}{3}$

Rewrite the interval.

Rearrange the equation into the form $\tan(A) = k$.

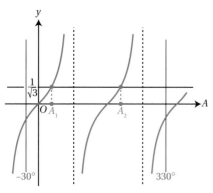

There are two solutions:

$A_1 = \tan^{-1}\left(\dfrac{\sqrt{3}}{3}\right) = 30°$

$A_2 = 30° + 180° = 210°$

Solve the equation for A.

$\theta = 2(A + 30°)$

$= 120°, 480°$

Transform the solutions back into θ.

EXERCISE 10F

In this exercise, you must show detailed reasoning. This means that you can't, for example, use graphs or the equation solver function. You need to use algebraic rearrangement and inverse trigonometric functions.

1 Solve the following equations in the interval $0° \leqslant x \leqslant 360°$ giving your answers to 3 s.f.

    a **i** $\sin 2x = 0.7$ **ii** $\sin 3x = -0.2$

    b **i** $\cos 3x = -0.4$ **ii** $\cos 4x = 1$

    c **i** $\tan 4x = 1.5$ **ii** $\tan 2x = -2$

2 Solve the following equations in the interval $-180° \leqslant \theta \leqslant 180°$ giving your answers to 3 s.f.

    a **i** $\sin(\theta + 40°) = 0.25$ **ii** $\sin(\theta - 25°) = -0.75$

    b **i** $\cos(\theta - 50°) = -0.9$ **ii** $\sin(\theta + 10°) = 0.3$

    c **i** $\tan(\theta - 45°) = 2$ **ii** $\tan(\theta + 60°) = -3$

3 Find the exact solutions of the equation $\tan 3x = \sqrt{3}$ for $0° < x < 180°$.

4 Solve $2\cos(2x)+1=0$ for $x\in[-180°, 180°]$.

5 Find the values of θ in the interval $-360° < \theta < 360°$ for which $3\sin\left(\frac{\theta}{2}\right)=-2$.

6 Solve $2\tan\left(\frac{\theta}{3}\right)=5$ for $0° < \theta < 540°$.

7 Find the values of x in the interval $-360° < x < 360°$ for which $2\sin(2x+30°)+\sqrt{3}=0$.

8 Solve $2\cos(3x-50°)-\sqrt{2}=0$ for $-90° < x < 90°$.

9 Solve the equation $\dfrac{\cos 2x+0.5}{1-\cos 2x}=2$ for $x\in(-180°, 180°)$.

10 Find the values of x in the interval $-\sqrt{180°} < x < \sqrt{180°}$ for which $\sin(x^2)=\frac{1}{2}$.

Section 7: More complex trigonometric equations

You have already seen how to solve equations that are in the form 'trigonometric function of unknown = constant'. However, sometimes you need to get the equation into this form first. There are three tactics that are often used:

- Look for disguised quadratics.
- Take everything over to one side and factorise.
- Use trigonometric identities.

> **Tip**
>
> Remember that $\cos^2\theta$ means $(\cos\theta)^2$.

WORKED EXAMPLE 10.17

Solve the equation $\cos^2\theta=\frac{4}{9}$ for $\theta\in[0°, 360°]$. Give your answers correct to one decimal place.

$\cos^2\theta=\frac{4}{9}$ ⟶ First find possible values of $\cos\theta$.

$\cos\theta=\pm\frac{2}{3}$ ⟶ Remember $\pm$ when taking the square root.

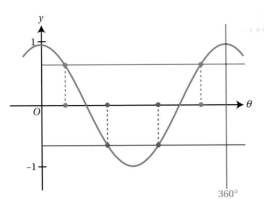

Sketch the graph to see how many solutions there are in the required interval.

There are two solutions to each.

When $\cos\theta=\frac{2}{3}$:

$\cos^{-1}\left(\frac{2}{3}\right)=48.2°$

Solve each equation separately.

$\theta_1=48.2°$

$\theta_2=360°-48.2°=311.8°$

Continues on next page ...

When $\cos\theta = -\frac{2}{3}$:

$$\cos^{-1}\left(-\frac{2}{3}\right) = 131.8°$$

$\theta_1 = 131.8°$

$\theta_2 = 360° - 131.8° = 228.2°$

$\theta = 48.2°, 131.8°, 228.2°, 311.8°$ .... List all the solutions.

WORKED EXAMPLE 10.18

Solve the equation $3\sin^2 x - 5\sin x + 1 = 0$ for $0° < x < 360°$.

$$\sin x = \frac{5 \pm \sqrt{5^2 - 4 \times 3 \times 1}}{2 \times 3}$$ .... This is a disguised quadratic equation in $\sin x$. If you cannot factorise it, use the quadratic formula.

$$= 1.434 \text{ or } 0.2324$$

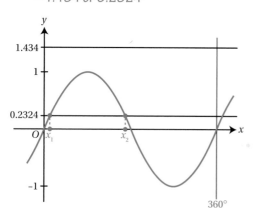

.... Sketch the graph to see how many solutions there are.

There are two solutions.

$\sin x = 1.434 > 1$ is impossible. .... $\sin x$ is always between -1 and 1, so only one of the values is possible.

$\sin x = 0.2324$ .... You can now solve the equation as usual.

$\sin^{-1}(0.2324) = 13.4°$

$x_1 = 13.4°$

$x_2 = 180 - 13.4 = 167°$

$\therefore x = 13.4°, 167°$

◄◄ Rewind

You may want to revisit Chapter 3, Section 5 on disguised quadratics.

WORKED EXAMPLE 10.19

Solve the equation $3 \sin x \cos x = 2 \sin x$ for $-180° \leqslant x \leqslant 180°$.

$3 \sin x \cos x = 2 \sin x$

$3 \sin x \cos x - 2 \sin x = 0$

$\sin x\,(3 \cos x - 2) = 0$

This equation contains both sin and cos. However, both sides have a factor of $\sin x$, so you can make one side of the equation equal to zero and factorise.

$\sin x = 0$ or $\cos x = \dfrac{2}{3}$

You then have two separate equations, each containing only one trig function.

When $\sin x = 0$:

$\sin^{-1} 0 = 0$

Solve each equation separately.

Remember to sketch the graph for each equation to see how many solutions there are.

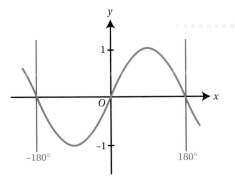

$x_1 = 0°$

$x_2 = 180° - 0° = 180°$

$x_3 = 180° - 360° = -180°$

When $\cos x = \dfrac{2}{3}$:

$\cos^{-1}\left(\dfrac{2}{3}\right) = 48.2°$

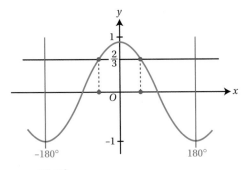

$x_1 = 48.2°$

$x_2 = -48.2°$

$\therefore x = -180°, -48.2°, 0°, 48.2°, 180°$

List all the solutions.

EXERCISE 10G

1 Solve the following equations in the interval $0° \leqslant x \leqslant 360°$ giving your answers to 3 s.f.

   a **i** $3 \sin^2 \theta = 2$ **ii** $3 \tan^2 \theta = 5$

   b **i** $\tan^2 x - \tan x - 6 = 0$ **ii** $3 \cos^2 x + \cos x - 2 = 0$

   c **i** $4 \cos^2 x - 11 \cos x + 6 = 0$ **ii** $5 \sin^2 x + 6 \sin x - 8 = 0$

   d **i** $3 \sin^2 x + \sin x = 0$ **ii** $4 \tan^2 x + 5 \tan x = 0$

2 Solve the following equations in the interval $-180° \leqslant \theta \leqslant 180°$ giving your answers to 3 s.f.

   a **i** $2 \sin \theta - 5 \sin \theta \cos \theta = 0$ **ii** $4 \cos \theta + 5 \sin \theta \cos \theta = 0$

   b **i** $4 \sin \theta \cos \theta = \cos \theta$ **ii** $3 \sin \theta = 5 \sin \theta \cos \theta$

3 Find the values of $x \in (-360°, 360°)$ for which $2 \sin x \cos x = \cos x$.

4 **a** Given that $2 \sin^2 x - 3 \sin x = 2$, find the exact value of $\sin x$.

   b Hence solve the equation $2 \sin^2 x - 3 \sin x = 2$ for $0° < x < 360°$.

5 Solve the equation $\tan^2 x = \tan x + 12$ for $-180° \leqslant x \leqslant 180°$. Give your answers to 1 decimal place.

6 Find the values of θ in the interval $0° < \theta < 360°$ for which $2 \sin 2\theta = \sqrt{3} \sin 2\theta \cos 2\theta$.

7 Solve the equation $3 \cos^2 3x + 7 \cos 3x + 2 = 0$ for $x \in [0°, 180°]$.

Using identities to solve equations

When there is more than one trigonometric function in an equation, it is often useful to use an identity to eliminate one of the functions.

WORKED EXAMPLE 10.20

Find all values of θ in the interval $[-180°, 180°]$ that satisfy the equation $2 \sin^2 \theta + 3 \cos \theta = 1$.

$2 \sin^2 \theta + 3 \cos \theta = 1$

$2(1 - \cos^2 \theta) + 3 \cos \theta = 1$

The equation contains both sin and cos. Because you have $\sin^2$ you can use $\sin^2 x + \cos^2 x = 1$ to replace $\sin^2 \theta$ by $1 - \cos^2 \theta$.

$2 - 2 \cos^2 \theta + 3 \cos \theta = 1$

$2 \cos^2 \theta - 3 \cos \theta - 1 = 0$

This is a disguised quadratic equation in $\cos \theta$, so write it in the standard form.

$\cos \theta = 1.78 \text{ or } -0.281$

Solve it using your calculator or the quadratic formula.

$\cos \theta = 1.78$ is impossible.

cos is always between −1 and 1.

Continues on next page ...

$\cos \theta = -0.281$: .... Solve the equation as normal.

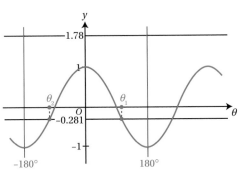

There are two solutions:

$\theta_1 = \cos^{-1}(-0.281) = 106°$

$\theta_2 = -106°$

$\therefore \theta = -106°, 106°$

WORKED EXAMPLE 10.21

Solve the equation $\sin \theta + \sqrt{3} \cos \theta = 0$ for $-360° < \theta < 360°$.

$\sin \theta + \sqrt{3} \cos \theta = 0$ .... The equation involves both sin and cos. It is
inefficient to use $\sin^2 x + \cos^2 x = 1$ to eliminate one
$\sin \theta = -\sqrt{3} \cos \theta$ of them as neither is squared.

$\dfrac{\sin \theta}{\cos \theta} = -\sqrt{3}$

$\tan \theta = -\sqrt{3}$ .... Instead rearrange and use $\dfrac{\sin \theta}{\cos \theta} = \tan\theta$.

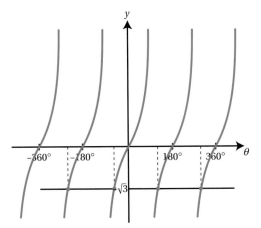

$\theta_1 = \tan^{-1}(-\sqrt{3}) = -60°$

$\theta_2 = -60° + 180° = 120°$ .... Solve this equation as normal.

$\theta_3 = 120° + 180° = 300°$

$\theta_4 = -60° - 180° = -240°$

$\therefore \theta = -240°, -60°, 120°, 300°$

WORKED EXAMPLE 10.22

Solve the equation $4 \sin 2x = \tan 2x$ in the interval $0° \leqslant x \leqslant 180°$.

$4 \sin 2x = \tan 2x$

> The only identity you can use here is the one for tan.

$4 \sin 2x = \dfrac{\sin 2x}{\cos 2x}$

$4 \sin 2x \cos 2x = \sin 2x$

> Multiply both sides by $\cos 2x$.

$4 \sin 2x \cos 2x - \sin 2x = 0$

$\sin 2x (4 \cos 2x - 1) = 0$

> Although you have both sin and cos, both sides contain $\sin 2x$, so you can make one side of the equation equal to zero and factorise.

$\sin 2x = 0$ or $\cos A = \dfrac{1}{4}$

Let $A = 2x$

> We now have two equations, each of which only has one trig function.

$0° \leqslant x \leqslant 180°$
$\Rightarrow 0° \leqslant A \leqslant 360°$

> Now solve each equation separately.

When $\sin A = 0$:

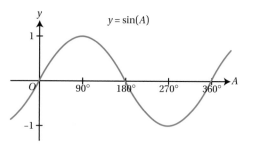

$A = 0°, 180°, 360°$

$x = 0°, 90°, 180°$

When $\cos A = \dfrac{1}{4}$:

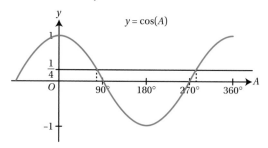

$\cos^{-1}\left(\dfrac{1}{4}\right) = 75.5$

$A = 75.5°$ or $360 - 75.5° = 284°$

$x = 37.8°, 142°$

$\therefore x = 0°, 37.8°, 90°, 142°, 180°$

> List all the solutions.

WORK IT OUT 10.2

Solve the equation $\tan x = 2\sin x$ for $x \in [0, 360°]$.

Which is the correct solution? Can you identify the errors made in the incorrect solutions?

Solution 1	Solution 2	Solution 3
$\dfrac{\sin x}{\cos x} = 2\sin x$	$\dfrac{\sin x}{\cos x} = 2\sin x$	$\dfrac{\sin x}{\cos x} = 2\sin x$
$\sin x = 2\sin x \cos x$	$\sin x = 2\sin x \cos x$	$\sin x = 2\sin x \cos x$
$\sin x = 0$ or $1 = 2\cos x$	$\sin x(1 - 2\cos x) = 0$	$1 = 2\cos x$
$x = 0$ or $\cos^{-1}\left(\dfrac{1}{2}\right) = 60°$	$\sin x = 0$ or $\cos x = \dfrac{1}{2}$	$\cos x = \dfrac{1}{2}$
	$x = 0, 180°, 360°, 60°, 300°$	$x = 60°, 300°$

EXERCISE 10H

1. By using the identity $\tan x = \dfrac{\sin x}{\cos x}$ solve the following equations for $0° \leqslant x \leqslant 180°$.

   a i $3\sin x = 2\cos x$ ii $3\sin x = 5\cos x$

   b i $7\cos x - 3\sin x = 0$ ii $\sin x - 5\cos x = 0$

2. Use the identity $\sin^2 x + \cos^2 x = 1$ to solve the following equations for x in the interval $[0°, 360°]$.

   a i $7\sin^2 x + 3\cos^2 x = 5$ ii $\sin^2 x + 4\cos^2 x = 2$

   b i $3\sin^2 x - \cos^2 x = 1$ ii $\cos^2 x - \sin^2 x = 1$

3. Find the values of x in the interval $0° < x < 360°$ for which $\sin 2x + \cos 2x = 0$.

4. Solve $\dfrac{\cos\theta}{\sin\theta} - 2 = 0$ for $\theta \in [-180°, 180°]$.

5. Solve $\sin x + \dfrac{\sin^2 x}{\cos x} = 0$ for $0° \leqslant x \leqslant 360°$.

6. Solve the equation $\sin x \tan x = \sin^2 x$ for $-180° \leqslant x \leqslant 180°$.

7. Solve the equation $5\sin^2 \theta = 4\cos^2 \theta$ for $-180° \leqslant \theta \leqslant 180°$. Give your answers to the nearest $0.1°$.

8. Solve the equation $2\cos^2 t - \sin t - 1 = 0$ for $0° \leqslant t \leqslant 360°$.

9. Find the values of x in the interval $-180° \leqslant x \leqslant 180°$ that satisfy $4\cos^2 x - 5\sin x - 5 = 0$.

10. a Given that $\cos^2 t + 5\cos t = 2\sin^2 t$, find the exact value of $\cos t$.

    b Hence solve the equation $\cos^2 t + 5\cos t = 2\sin^2 t$ for $t \in [0°, 360°]$.

11. a Given that $6\sin^2 x + \cos x = 4$, find the exact values of $\cos x$.

    b Hence solve the equation $6\sin^2 x + \cos x = 4$ for $0° \leqslant x \leqslant 360°$ giving your answers to 3 s.f.

12. a Show that the equation $2\sin^2 x - 3\sin x \cos x + \cos^2 x = 0$ can be written in the form $2\tan^2 x - 3\tan x + 1 = 0$.

    b Hence solve the equation $2\sin^2 x - 3\sin x \cos x + \cos^2 x = 0$ giving all solutions in the interval $-180° < x < 180°$.

 Elevate

For a further example of this type and more practice questions, see Support sheet 10.

Checklist of learning and understanding

- The sine and cosine functions can be defined using the unit circle:

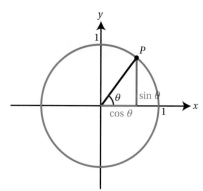

- The sine and cosine functions are periodic with period 360°.

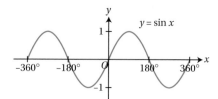 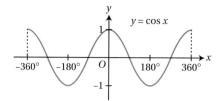

- These relationships can be seen from the unit circle or the graph:

    - $\sin x \equiv \cos(90° - x)$

    - $\cos x \equiv \sin(90° - x)$

- The tangent function is defined by the identity: $\tan x \equiv \dfrac{\sin x}{\cos x}$.
  It is periodic with period 180°.

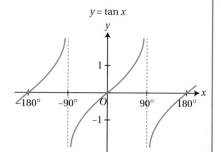

- To solve trigonometric equations, you should use the
  following procedure:

    - first rearrange into the form $\sin x = k$, $\cos x = k$ or $\tan x = k$

    - always draw a graph to see how many solutions there are

    - find one solution (for tan) or the first two solutions (for sin and cos)

        - $\sin x = k$: $x_1 = \sin^{-1} k$, $x_2 = 180° - x_1$

        - $\cos x = k$: $x_1 = \cos^{-1} k$, $x_2 = -x_1$

        - $\tan x = k$: $x_1 = \tan^{-1} k$, $x_2 = x_1 + 180°$

    - other solutions are found by adding or subtracting multiples of 180° (for tan) or 360° (for sin and cos).

- If the angle in the function in the trigonometric equation has been transformed:

    - make a substitution (such as $A = 2x$)

    - change the interval for x into the interval for A

    - solve the equation in the usual way

    - transform the solutions back into the original variable.

- The identities $\sin^2 x + \cos^2 x \equiv 1$ and $\tan x \equiv \dfrac{\sin x}{\cos x}$ can be used to solve some trigonometric equations.
  This often leads to disguised quadratic equations.

Mixed practice 10

1 If $\cos(x + 180°) = a$ what is the value of $\cos x$?

2 Solve the equation $\tan x = -0.62$ for $x \in (-90°, 270°)$ giving your answers to the nearest $0.1°$.

3 Solve the equation $\sqrt{2} \sin \theta + 1 = 0$ for $-360° < \theta < 360°$.

4 Find the values of x in the interval $0° < x < 720°$ for which $2\cos\left(\frac{1}{2}x + 45°\right) = \sqrt{3}$.

5 Solve, to 3 s.f., the equation $7\sin^2 \theta = 9\cos^2 \theta$ for $-180° \leqslant \theta \leqslant 180°$.

6 **i** Show that the equation $2\sin^2 x = 5\cos x - 1$ can be expressed in the form $2\cos^2 x + 5\cos x - 3 = 0$.

   ii Hence solve the equation $2\sin^2 x = 5\cos x - 1$, giving all values of x between $0°$ and $360°$.

© OCR, AS GCE Mathematics, Paper 4722, January 2010

7 **a** Show that the equation $\cos \theta - 2\sin^2 \theta + 2 = 0$ can be expressed in the form $2\cos^2 \theta + \cos \theta = 0$.

   b Hence find all values of $\theta \in [0°, 360°]$ for which $\cos \theta - 2\sin^2 \theta + 2 = 0$.

8 How many solutions are there to the equation $\sin^2 2x = \frac{1}{4}$ in the interval $-180° < x < 180°$?

9 The diagram shows the graph of the function $f(x) = a \sin(bx)$.
Find the values of a and b.

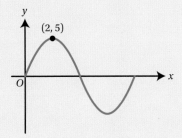

10 Find the values of x that satisfy the equation $6\cos^2 x = \cos x + 2$, within the interval $0 \leqslant x \leqslant 360°$.

Write your solutions to 3 significant figures.

11 Prove the identity $\dfrac{2}{\cos^2 x} - \tan^2 x = 2 + \tan^2 x$.

12 **i** Show that the equation $2\sin x = \dfrac{4\cos x - 1}{\tan x}$ can be expressed in the form $6\cos^2 x - \cos x - 2 = 0$.

   ii Hence solve the equation $2\sin x = \dfrac{4\cos x - 1}{\tan x}$, giving all values of x between $0°$ and $360°$.

© OCR, AS GCE Mathematics, Paper 4722, January 2013

13 Prove the identity $\dfrac{1}{1 + \cos x} + \dfrac{1}{1 - \cos x} = \dfrac{2}{\sin^2 x}$.

14 **i** Show that $\dfrac{\sin^2 x - \cos^2 x}{1 - \sin^2 x} \equiv \tan^2 x - 1$.

   ii Hence solve the equation $\dfrac{\sin^2 x - \cos^2 x}{1 - \sin^2 x} = 5 - \tan x$, for $0° \leqslant x \leqslant 360°$.

© OCR, AS GCE Mathematics, Paper 4722, June 2010

15 Show that $\tan x + \dfrac{1}{\tan x} = \dfrac{\tan x}{\sin^2 x}$.

16 Find all values of x in the interval $-90° < x < 90°$ that satisfy $6\cos^2 2x = \sin 2x + 4$.

17 **a** Find the values of k for which the equation $4x^2 - kx + 1 = 0$ has a repeated root.

 b Show that the equation $4\sin^2\theta = 5 - k\cos\theta$ can be written as $4\cos^2\theta - k\cos\theta + 1 = 0$.

 c Let $f_k(\theta) = 4\cos^2\theta - k\cos\theta + 1$.

  i State the number of values of $\cos\theta$ that satisfy the equation $f_4(\theta) = 0$.

  ii Find all the values of $\theta \in [-360°, 360°]$ that satisfy the equation $f_4(\theta) = 0$.

  iii Find the value of k for which $x = 1$ is a solution of the equation $4x^2 - kx + 1 = 0$.

  iv For this value of k, find the number of solutions of the equation $f_k(\theta) = 0$ for interval $\theta \in [-360°, 360°]$.

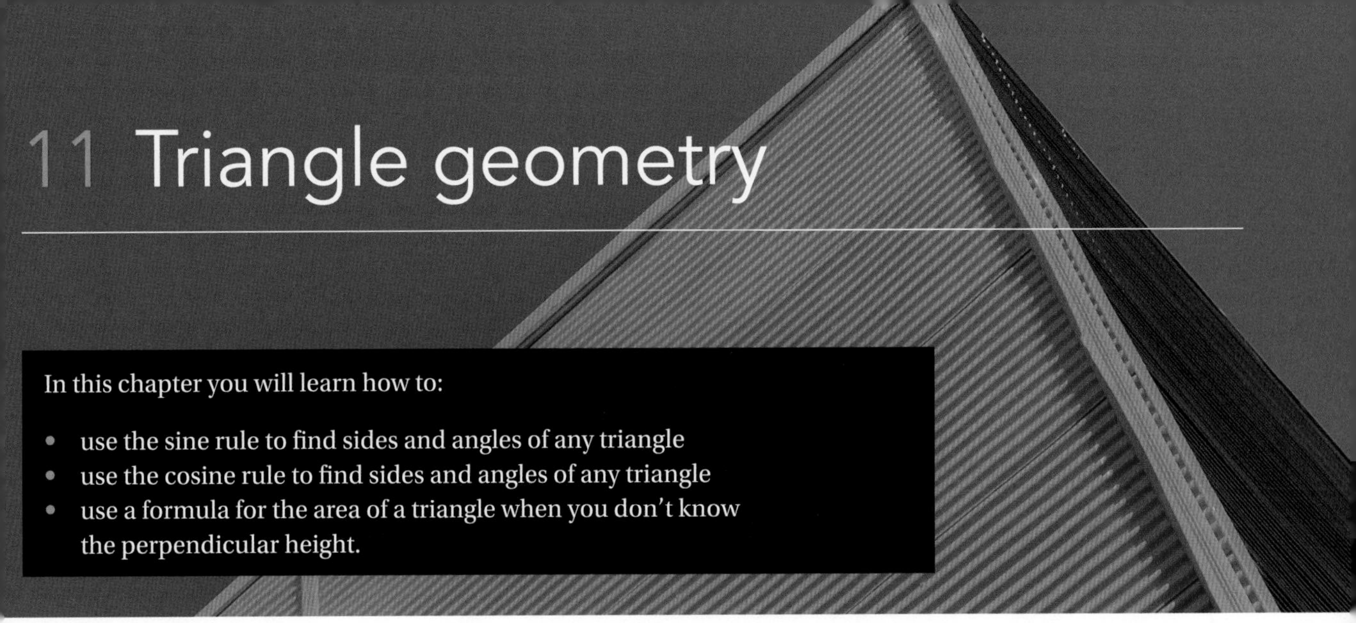

11 Triangle geometry

In this chapter you will learn how to:

- use the sine rule to find sides and angles of any triangle
- use the cosine rule to find sides and angles of any triangle
- use a formula for the area of a triangle when you don't know the perpendicular height.

Before you start…

GCSE	You should know how to use trigonometry in right-angled triangles.	1 Find the angle marked x in the diagram. 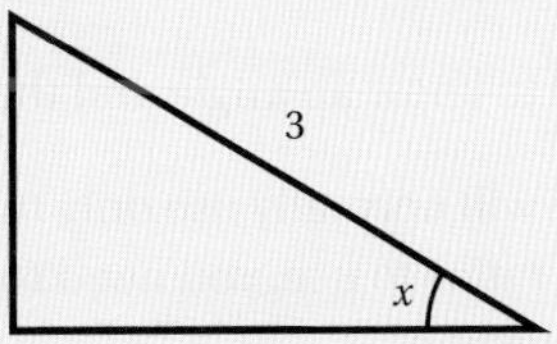 *(diagram of right-angled triangle with sides 2 and 3, angle x)*
GCSE	You should know how to use three-figure bearings.	2 Point A is a on a bearing of 290° from B. Find the bearing of B from A.
Chapter 3	You should know how to solve quadratic equations using the formula or factorising.	3 Solve $x^2 + 5x + 4 = 0$.
Chapter 10	You should know how to solve trigonometric equations.	4 Solve the equation $\sin x = 0.15$ for $0° < x < 180°$.

Trigonometry and triangles

The first steps in developing trigonometry were made by Babylonian astronomers as early as the 2nd millennium BCE. It is thought that Egyptians used some trigonometric calculations when building the pyramids. It was further developed by Greek, Islamic and Indian mathematicians to solve problems in land measurement, building and astronomy.

In this chapter you will use what you already know about trigonometric functions, as well as develop some new results to enable you to calculate lengths and angles in triangles.

✓ Gateway to A Level

For a reminder of using trigonometry in right-angled triangles see Gateway to A Level section P.

Section 1: The sine rule

You can use trigonometry to calculate sides and angles in triangles without a right angle.

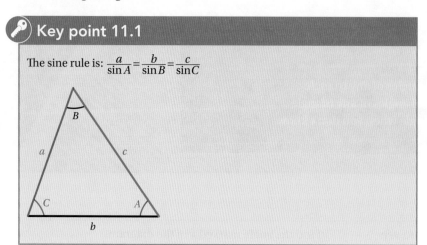

> ### 🔑 Key point 11.1
>
> The sine rule is: $\dfrac{a}{\sin A} = \dfrac{b}{\sin B} = \dfrac{c}{\sin C}$

📷 Focus on …

Focus on … Proof 2 shows you how to prove the sine rule for any triangle.

To use the sine rule you need to know an angle and the opposite side.

When using the sine rule you will normally use only two of the three ratios. To decide which ratios to use, you need to look at what information is given in the question.

WORKED EXAMPLE 11.1

Find the length of side AC.

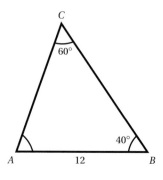

$$\frac{12}{\sin 60^\circ} = \frac{AC}{\sin 40^\circ}$$

You are given length AB and the angles opposite sides AB and AC, so use the sine rule with those two sides.

$$AC = \frac{12 \sin 40^\circ}{\sin 60^\circ}$$

$$= 8.91 \text{ to 3 s.f.}$$

💡 Tip

Give your answer to three significant figures, unless the question requests otherwise.

You can also use the sine rule to find angles:

WORKED EXAMPLE 11.2

Find the size of the angle marked θ. Give your answer to one decimal place.

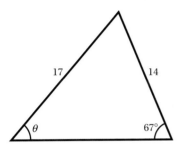

$$\frac{17}{\sin 67°} = \frac{14}{\sin \theta}$$

You have an angle opposite one of the sides, and want the angle opposite the other known side, so use the sine rule.

$$\sin \theta = \frac{14 \sin 67°}{17} = 0.758 \ldots$$

$$\therefore \theta = \sin^{-1} 0.758 \ldots = 49.3° \text{ (1 d.p.)}$$

Although you can write down this intermediate answer to 3s.f., you should use the unrounded value in subsequent calculations.

Notice that you can also find the third angle even though you do not know the length of the side opposite. Having found θ using the sine rule, you could deduce that the final angle must equal $180° - 67° - \theta = 63.7°$.

The ambiguous case

You should remember from your work on trigonometric equations that there is more than one value of θ with $\sin \theta = 0.758$. Does this mean that Worked example 11.2 has more than one possible answer? Another solution of the equation $\sin \theta = 0.758$ is $180° - 49.3° = 130.7°$.

However, as one of the other angles is $67°$, this is impossible, because all three angles of the triangle must add up to $180°$, and $130.7 + 67 = 197.7 > 180$.

All other possible values of θ are outside the interval $(0°, 180°)$, so cannot be angles of a triangle. In this example, there is only one possible value of angle θ.

Worked example 11.3 shows that this is not always the case.

 Rewind

See Chapter 10, Section 5 for more on solving trigonometric equations.

WORKED EXAMPLE 11.3

Find the size of the angle marked θ, giving your answer to the nearest degree.

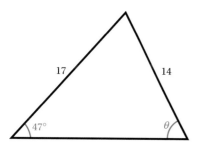

$\dfrac{17}{\sin\theta} = \dfrac{14}{\sin47°}$ .... Use the sine rule with the two given sides.

$\therefore \sin\theta = \dfrac{17\sin47°}{14} = 0.888\ldots$

$\sin^{-1} 0.888\ldots = 62.6°$ ...... Find the two possible values of θ.
(nearest degree)

$\therefore \theta = 62.6°$ or $180° - 62.6°$
$\qquad = 117.4°$

$62.6 + 47 = 109.6 < 180$ .... Check whether both solutions are possible: do the two angles add up to less than $180°$?

$117.4 + 47 = 164.4 < 180$

$\therefore \theta = 63°$ or $117°$ ...... Both solutions are possible.

> ### Tip
>
> The question will often alert you to look for two possible answers. For example by specifying that θ is obtuse. However, if it doesn't, you should check whether the second solution is possible by finding the sum of the known angles.

This diagram shows the two possible triangles. In both triangles, length 14 is opposite angle 47°, with another side having length 17. As illustrated, if the two triangles are placed adjacent to each other, together they form an isosceles triangle with base angle 47° and matched sides of length 17.

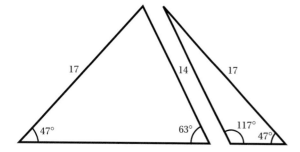

🗝 Key point 11.2

When using the sine rule to find an angle, there may be two possible solutions.

WORK IT OUT 11.1

In triangle ABC, $AB = 10$ cm, $AC = 12$ cm and angle $ABC = 70°$. Find the size of angle ACB.

Which is the correct solution? Can you identify the errors made in the incorrect solutions?

Solution 1	Solution 2	Solution 3
$\dfrac{\sin 70°}{12} = \dfrac{\sin x}{10}$ $\sin x = \dfrac{10 \sin 70°}{12} = 0.783$ $x = \sin^{-1}(0.783) = 51.5°$	$\dfrac{\sin x}{12} = \dfrac{\sin 70°}{10}$ $\sin x = 1.13$ There are no solutions.	$\dfrac{\sin 70°}{12} = \dfrac{\sin x}{10}$ $\sin x = \dfrac{10 \sin 70°}{12} = 0.783$ $\sin^{-1}(0.783) = 51.5°$ So $x = 51.5°$ or $128°$

EXERCISE 11A

Unless stated otherwise, give your answers to three significant figures.

1 Find the lengths of the sides marked with letters.

a i

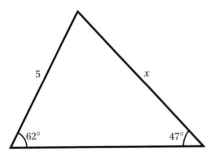

ii

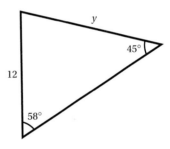

b i

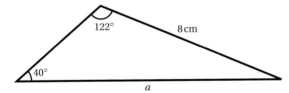

ii

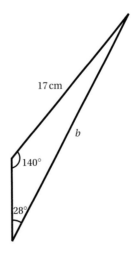

2 Find the angles marked with letters, checking whether there is more than one solution.

a i

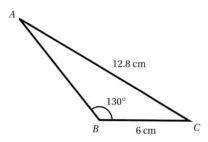

6.2 cm

4.8 cm

x

80°

ii

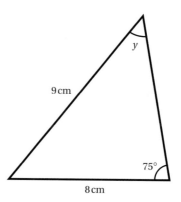

9 cm

y

75°

8 cm

b i

8 cm

12 cm

z

40°

ii

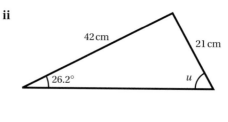

42 cm

21 cm

26.2°

u

c i

6.2 cm

75°

a

5.2 cm

ii

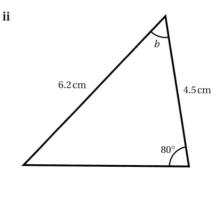

6.2 cm

4.5 cm

b

80°

3 Find all the unknown sides and angles of triangle ABC.

A

12.8 cm

130°

B

6 cm

C

4 In triangle ABC, $AB = 6$ cm, $BC = 8$ cm, $ACB = 35°$. Show that there are two possible triangles with these measurements and find the remaining side and angles for each.

5 In the triangle shown in the diagram, $AB = 6$, $AC = 8$, $AD = 5$ and angle $ADB = 75°$. Find the length of the side BC.

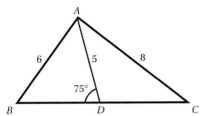

6 A balloon is tethered to a peg in the ground by a 20 m string, which makes an angle of 72° to the horizontal. An observer on the same side of the peg as the balloon notes that the angle of elevation from him to the balloon is 41° and his angle of depression to the peg is 10°. Find the horizontal distance of the observer from the peg.

7 Show that it is impossible to draw a triangle ABC with $AB = 12$ cm, $AC = 8$ cm and angle $ABC = 47°$.

Section 2: The cosine rule

If you have two sides and the angle between them or all three side lengths, you **cannot** use the sine rule. For example, can you find the length of the side AB in the triangle shown in the diagram?

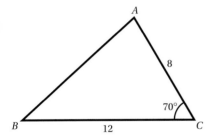

The sine rule for this triangle says: $\dfrac{AB}{\sin 70°} = \dfrac{8}{\sin B} = \dfrac{12}{\sin C}$

But you do not know either of the angles B or C, so it is impossible to find AB from this equation. We need a different strategy.

🔑 Key point 11.3

The cosine rule: $c^2 = a^2 + b^2 - 2ab \cos C$

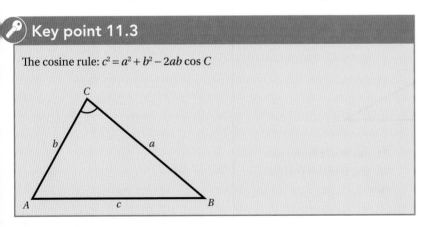

💡 Tip

See Focus on ... Proof 2 for the proof of the cosine rule.

📷 Focus on ...

See Focus on ... Proof 2 for the proof.

There is nothing special about the letters a, b and c in the formula in Key point 11.3. You can use any variables you like. The important thing is that the angle in '$\cos C$' is opposite the side on the left-hand side of the equation.

WORKED EXAMPLE 11.4

Find the length of the side PQ.

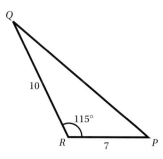

$PQ^2 = 7^2 + 10^2 - 2 \times 7 \times 10 \times \cos 115°$ . . . .

> When you are given two sides and the angle between them, use the cosine rule.

$PQ^2 = 208.16\ldots$

$PQ = \sqrt{208.16\ldots} = 14.4 \ (3\,\text{s.f.})$

You can also use the cosine rule to find an angle if you know all three sides of a triangle. To help with this, there is a rearrangement of the cosine rule.

 Key point 11.4

$$\cos C = \frac{a^2 + b^2 - c^2}{2ab}$$

WORKED EXAMPLE 11.5

Find the size of the angle ACB correct to the nearest degree.

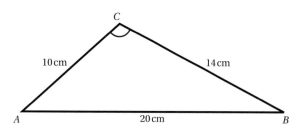

$\cos C = \dfrac{196 + 100 - 400}{2 \times 14 \times 10}$ . . . .

> As you don't know any angles, use the cosine rule.

$\qquad = -\dfrac{104}{280}$

$\qquad = -0.371\ldots$

$C = \arccos(-0.371\ldots) = 112°$
(nearest degree)

 Tip

Remember that $\arccos(x)$ is another way of writing $\cos^{-1} x$.

When using the cosine rule there is no second solution for the angle. This is because the equation $\cos x = c$ has only one solution between $0°$ and $180°$.

It is possible to use the cosine rule even when the given angle is not opposite the required side. You may need to solve a quadratic equation.

WORKED EXAMPLE 11.6

Find the possible lengths of the side marked a.

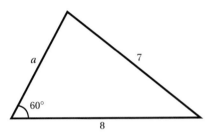

$7^2 = a^2 + 8^2 - 2a \times 8 \cos 60°$ .... As all three sides are involved in the question, you can use the cosine rule. The known angle is opposite the side marked 7.

$49 = a^2 + 64 - 8a$ .... $\cos 60° = \dfrac{1}{2}$

$a^2 - 8a + 15 = 0$ .... Solve the quadratic equation.

$(a - 3)(a - 5) = 0$

$a = 3$ or 5

It is also possible to answer Worked example 11.6 using the sine rule twice, first to find the angle opposite the side marked 8, and then to find side a. Try to see if you can get the same answers.

Worked example 11.7 illustrates how to select which of the two rules to use. For both the sine and cosine rules, you need to know three measurements in a triangle to find a fourth one.

Elevate

For a further example of choosing between the sine and cosine rules, and for more practice questions, see Support sheet 11.

WORKED EXAMPLE 11.7

In the triangle shown in the diagram, $AB = 6.5$ cm, $AD = 7$ cm, $CD = 5.8$ cm, angle $ABC = 52°$ and $AC = x$. Find the value of x correct to one decimal place.

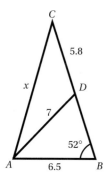

Sine rule in triangle ABD; let angle $ADB = \theta$:

$$\frac{6.5}{\sin \theta} = \frac{7}{\sin 52°}$$

The only triangle in which you know three measurements is ABD. You know two side lengths and an angle opposite one of these, so use the sine rule to find angle ADB.

$$\sin \theta = \frac{6.5 \sin 52°}{7} = 0.7317\ldots$$
$$\theta = \sin^{-1} 0.7317\ldots = 47.0° \text{ (1 d.p.)}$$

$$180° - 47.0° = 133°, 133° + 52° > 180°$$

$\therefore$ there is only one solution: $\theta = 47.0°$

Are there two possible solutions?

$$ADC = 180° - 47.0° = 133°$$

In triangle ADC, you know two sides and want to find the third. If you knew angle ADC, you could use the cosine rule. But you can find this angle easily.

Cosine rule in triangle ADC:

Now use the cosine rule.

$$x^2 = 7^2 + 5.8^2 - 2 \times 7 \times 5.8 \cos 133°$$

$$x^2 = 138$$
$$x = \sqrt{138} = 11.7 \, cm \text{ (3 s.f.)}$$

EXERCISE 11B

 Find the lengths of the sides marked with letters.

a i

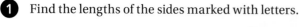
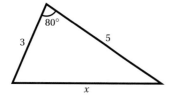

ii

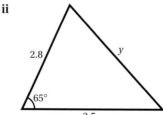

b i

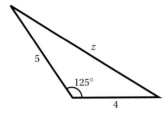

ii

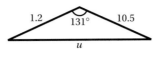

2 Find the angles marked with letters.

a i

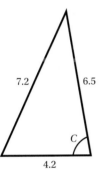

ii

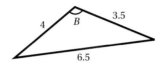

b i

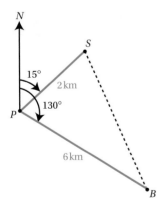

ii

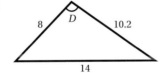

3 **a** Triangle PQR has sides $PQ = 8$ cm, $QR = 12$ cm, $RP = 7$ cm. Find the size of the largest angle.

b Triangle ABC has sides $AB = 4.5$ cm, $BC = 6.2$ cm, $CA = 3.7$ cm. Find the size of the smallest angle.

> 💡 **Tip**
>
> The largest angle in a triangle is opposite the longest side.

4 Ship S is 2 km from the port on a bearing of 15° and boat B is 6 km from the port on a bearing of 130°, as illustrated in the diagram.

Find the distance between the ship and the boat.

> ✓ **Gateway to A level**
>
> For a reminder of bearings, see Gateway to A Level section N.

5 A cyclist rides from H for 15 km on a bearing of 55° until she reaches A. She then changes direction and rides for 25 km on a bearing of 160 from A to B. Find her distance from H when she is at B.

6 Find the value of x in this diagram.

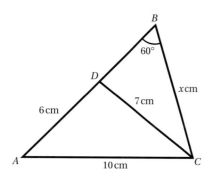

7 In triangle ABC, $AB = (x-3)$ cm, $BC = (x+3)$ cm, $AC = 8$ cm and $\angle BAC = 60°$. Find the value of x.

8 The longest side of a triangle has length $(3x - 10)$ cm. The other two sides have lengths $(x-2)$ cm and $(x+2)$ cm. The largest angle is $120°$. Find the value of x.

9 In triangle KLM, $KL = 4$, $LM = 7$ and angle $LKM = 45°$. Find the exact length of KM.

Section 3: Area of a triangle

One way to calculate the area of a triangle is $\frac{1}{2}$ base $\times$ height. There is another formula using two sides and the angle between them.

> ### 🔑 Key point 11.5
>
> The area of the triangle is given by: Area $= \frac{1}{2}ab\sin C$
>
>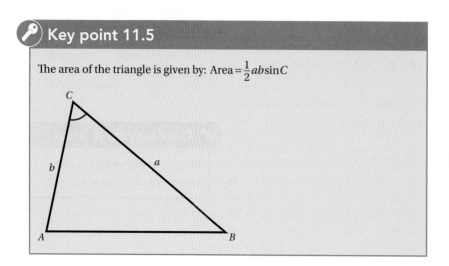

> ### 🔍 Explore
>
> There is also a formula for the area of a triangle if you know all three of its sides. Find out about Heron's formula.

WORKED EXAMPLE 11.8

The area of the triangle shown in the diagram is 52 cm². Find the two possible values of angle *ABC*, correct to one decimal place.

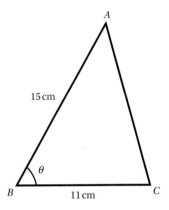

$$\frac{1}{2}(11 \times 15)\sin \theta = 52$$ .... Use formula for the area of a triangle.

$$\sin \theta = \frac{2 \times 52}{11 \times 15} = 0.630\ldots$$ .... Remember that with sin there are two possible answers.

$$\theta = \sin^{-1} 0.630 \ldots = 39.1° \ (1 \ d.p.)$$

$$\theta = 39.1° \ or \ 180° - 39.1° = 140.9° \ (1 \ d.p.)$$

Worked example 11.9 combines the sine rule with the area of the triangle, working with exact values.

WORKED EXAMPLE 11.9

For triangle *PQR* shown in the diagram:

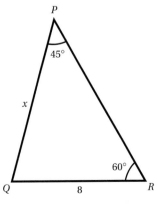

a calculate the exact value of *x*

b find the area of the triangle.

Continues on next page ...

$$\frac{8}{\sin 45°} = \frac{x}{\sin 60°}$$ ········· Since you know two angles and a side, use the sine rule.

$$\frac{8}{\frac{\sqrt{2}}{2}} = \frac{x}{\frac{\sqrt{3}}{2}}$$ ········· You need the exact value of x, so use $\sin 45° = \frac{\sqrt{2}}{2}$ and $\sin 60° = \frac{\sqrt{3}}{2}$.

$$\frac{16}{\sqrt{2}} = \frac{2x}{\sqrt{3}}$$

$$x = \frac{16\sqrt{3}}{2\sqrt{2}}$$

$$x = 4\sqrt{6}$$

$PQR = 180 - 60 - 45 = 75°$ ········· To use the formula for the area of the triangle, you need angle PQR.

$$Area = \frac{1}{2}(8 \times 4\sqrt{6})\sin 75°$$

$$= 37.9 \, (3 \text{ s.f.})$$

EXERCISE 11C

1 Calculate the areas of these triangles.

a i

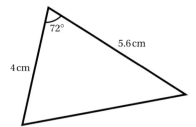

ii

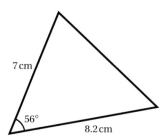

b i

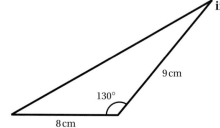

ii

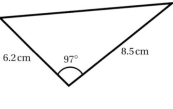

2 Each triangle has the area shown. Find two possible values of each marked angle.

a

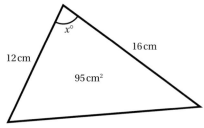

b

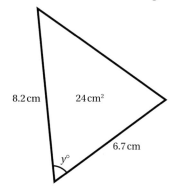

3️⃣ In triangle LMN, $LM = 12$ cm, $MN = 7$ cm, and $LMN = 135°$. Find the length of the side LN and the area of the triangle.

4️⃣ An equilateral triangle has area $25\sqrt{3}$ cm². Find the length of each side.

5️⃣ In triangle ABC, $AB = x + 3$, $BC = x$ and angle $ABC = 150°$.

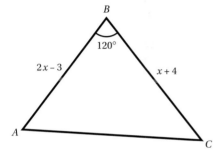

The area of the triangle is 10. Find the value of x.

6️⃣ In triangle ABC, $AB = 2x - 3$, $BC = x + 4$ and angle $ABC = 120°$.

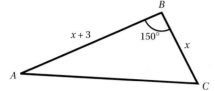

The area of the triangle is $39\sqrt{3}$. Find the value of x.

7️⃣ In triangle PQR, $PQ = 8$ cm, $RQ = 7$ cm, and $RPQ = 60°$. Find the exact difference in areas between the two possible triangles.

📎 Checklist of learning and understanding

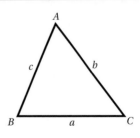

- To find a side when two angles and a side are given, or an angle when two sides and a non-included angle are given, use the **sine rule**:
  - $\dfrac{a}{\sin A} = \dfrac{b}{\sin B} = \dfrac{c}{\sin C}$
- When using the sine rule to find an angle, there may be two possible answers: A and $180 - A$.
- To find a side when two sides and the angle between them are given, or an angle when all three sides are given, use the cosine rule:
  - $c^2 = a^2 + b^2 - 2ab \cos C$
  - $\cos C = \dfrac{a^2 + b^2 - c^2}{2ab}$
- To find the area of a triangle when two sides and the included angle are known, use the formula:
  - Area $= \dfrac{1}{2} ab \sin C$

Mixed practice 11

1 In triangle ABC, $AB = 6.2$ cm, $CA = 8.7$ cm and angle $ACB = 37.5°$. Find the two possible values of ABC.

2 A vertical tree of height 12 m stands on horizontal ground. The bottom of the tree is at the point B. Observer A, standing on the ground, sees the top of the tree at an angle of elevation of $56°$.

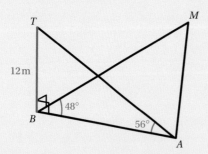

a Find the distance of A from the bottom of the tree.

Another observer, M, stands the same distance away from the tree, and $ABM = 48°$

b Find the distance AM.

3 The diagram shows triangle ABC, with $AB = 9$ cm, $AC = 17$ cm and angle $BAC = 40°$.

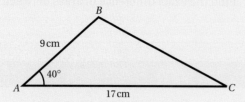

i Find the length of BC.

ii Find the area of triangle ABC.

iii D is a point on AC such that angle $BDA = 63°$. Find the length of BD.

© OCR, AS GCE Mathematics, Paper 4722, June 2011

4 The lengths of the three sides of a triangle are 6.4 cm, 7.0 cm and 11.3 cm.

i Find the largest angle in the triangle.

ii Find the area of the triangle.

© OCR, AS GCE Mathematics, Paper 4722, June 2009

5 In triangle ABC, $AB = 2\sqrt{3}$, $AC = 10$ and angle $BAC = 150°$. Find the exact length of BC.

6 In the obtuse angled triangle KLM, $LM = 6.1$ cm, $KM = 4.2$ cm and angle $KLM = 42°$.

Find the area of the triangle.

7 In triangle ABC, angle $AB = 10$ cm, $BC = 8$ cm and $CA = 7$ cm.

  a Find the exact value of $\cos(\angle ABC)$

  b Find the exact value of $\sin(\angle ABC)$.

  c Find the exact value of the area of the triangle.

8 In triangle ABC, $AB = 5$, $AC = x$ and the angle at A is θ. M is the midpoint of the side AC.

  a Use the cosine rule to find an expression for MB^2 in terms of x and θ.

  b Given that $BC = MB$, show that $\cos\theta = \dfrac{3x}{20}$.

  c If $x = 5$, find the value of the angle θ such that $MB = BC$.

9 Two radar stations, A and B, are 20 km apart. B is due east of A. Station B detects a ship on a bearing of $310°$. The same ship is 15 km from station A.

  a Find the two possible bearings of the ship from station A.

  b Hence find the distance between the two possible positions of the ship.

10 A regular pentagon has area 200 cm². Find the length of each side.

11 In triangle ABC, $AB = 10$, $BC = 5$, $CA = x$ and angle $CAB = \theta$.

  a Show that $x^2 - 20x\cos\theta + 75 = 0$.

  b Find the range of values of $\cos\theta$ for which the equation in part **a** has real roots.

  c Hence find the set of values of θ for which it is possible to construct triangle ABC with the given measurements.

 Elevate

See Extension sheet 11 for challenge questions involving triangle geometry.

12 Vectors

In this chapter you will learn how to:

- represent vectors using the base vectors **i** and **j**
- find the magnitude and direction of a vector
- perform algebraic operations on vectors given in different forms
- recognise when two vectors are parallel
- find unit vectors
- work with positions and displacements of points in the plane
- use vectors to solve problems about geometrical figures.

Before you start...

GCSE	You should know how to represent vectors on a grid and write them as column vectors.	1	Write this as a column vector:
GCSE	You should know how to use Pythagoras' theorem and trigonometry in right-angled triangles.	2	Find the length of the side BC and the size of the angle ABC.
Chapter 3	You should know how to solve quadratic equations, and recognise when a quadratic equation has no solutions.	3	State the number of solutions of the equation $6x^2 + 9x + 1 = 0$.

Where can we use vectors?

A **vector** is a quantity that has both **magnitude** (size) and **direction**. You may be familiar with examples such as velocity and force. By contrast, **scalar** quantities (quantities such as mass, that have magnitude but no direction) can be fully described by a single number. In pure mathematics, vectors can be to represent displacement from one point to another, and thus to describe geometrical figures. They also have many applications in spatial modelling problems, for example describing flight paths or positions of characters in a computer game.

In this chapter you will learn about different ways to represent vectors and use them to solve geometrical problems.

Section 1: Describing vectors

You already know that there are two ways to describe a vector. You can draw an arrow, or write it as a column vector.

- The arrow shows the magnitude and the direction of the vector explicitly.
- The numbers in a column vector are called the **components** of the vector. For example, the column vector $\begin{pmatrix} 5 \\ -3 \end{pmatrix}$ has horizontal component 5 and vertical component −3.

Another way of writing a vector in **component form** is using the **i** and **j** notation. Vectors of length one unit in the horizontal and vertical directions are denoted by **i** and **j** respectively. These vectors are called **base vectors**. You can then express any vector in terms of **i** and **j**, as shown in the diagram. 2**i** and 3**j** are called **component vectors** of 2**i** + 3**j**.

To emphasise that something is a vector, rather than a scalar (number), we use bold type (for example, **a** = 3**i** + 2**j**). When writing by hand, you should **underline** the letters representing vectors.

Fast forward

In Chapters 21 and 22 you will use vectors to work with forces.

Gateway to A level

For a reminder of column vector notation see Gateway to A Level section Q.

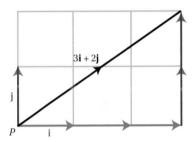

WORKED EXAMPLE 12.1

a Write vectors **a**, **b** and **c** using **i**, **j** notation.

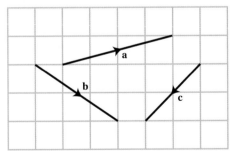

b Write the following as column vectors: $\mathbf{p} = 4\mathbf{i} - 4\mathbf{j}$ $\mathbf{q} = 2\mathbf{j}$ $\mathbf{r} = \mathbf{j} - 4\mathbf{i}$

a $\underline{a} = 4\underline{i} + \underline{j}$

    $\underline{b} = 3\underline{i} - 2\underline{j}$

    $\underline{c} = -2\underline{i} - 2\underline{j}$

> The coefficient of **i** represents the number of horizontal units and the coefficient of **j** the number of vertical units. Positive directions are to the right and up.

Continues on next page ...

b $\underline{p} = \begin{pmatrix} 4 \\ -4 \end{pmatrix}$ ··········   This means 4 units in the horizontal direction and −4 in the vertical direction.

     $\underline{q} = \begin{pmatrix} 0 \\ 2 \end{pmatrix}$ ··········   There are zero units in the **i**-direction, so the horizontal component is 0.

     $\underline{r} = \begin{pmatrix} -4 \\ 1 \end{pmatrix}$ ··········   Be careful: **i** and **j** are given in the opposite order to normal!

Magnitude and direction

If you are given a vector in component form (written to show its components, either as a column vector or using **i**, **j** base vectors) you can find its magnitude and direction.

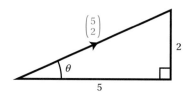

> ### 💡 Tip
>
> When finding the direction of a column vector it is important to draw a diagram to be sure that the correct angle is being calculated.

The magnitude of the vector is its length, which and you can find by using Pythagoras' theorem. The direction is described by giving an angle.

 ### Key point 12.1

The **magnitude (modulus)** of a vector is its length.

If $\mathbf{a} = \begin{pmatrix} p \\ q \end{pmatrix}$ then $|\mathbf{a}| = \sqrt{p^2 + q^2}$.

The **direction** of a vector is the angle it makes with the positive horizontal direction. It can be found from the right-angled triangle formed by the vector and its components.

> ### 💡 Tip
>
> By convention, the *x*-axis is called the horizontal axis and the *y*-axis the vertical axis, even if they are both in the horizontal plane.

The magnitude of a vector can never be negative. The only vector with zero magnitude is $\begin{pmatrix} 0 \\ 0 \end{pmatrix}$ called the **zero vector**.

WORKED EXAMPLE 12.2

   a   Find the magnitude of the vector $\mathbf{a} = 5\mathbf{i} + 3\mathbf{j}$ and the angle it makes with the direction of **i**.

   b   Find the direction of the vector $\mathbf{b} = \begin{pmatrix} -4 \\ 7 \end{pmatrix}$.

a

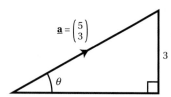

Draw a diagram and mark the required angle. The direction of **i** is to the right.

Continues on next page ...

$|a| = \sqrt{25 + 9}$

$= \sqrt{34}$ .... Use Pythagoras' theorem to find the length (magnitude).

$\tan \theta = \dfrac{3}{5}$ (3 s.f.)

$\theta = 31.0°$

The direction is at $31°$.

b .... The required angle is marked in green.

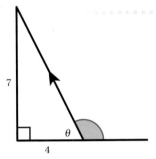

$\tan \theta = \dfrac{7}{4}$

$\theta = 60.3°$ .... Use a right-angled triangle to find θ first.

The direction is at $180 - \theta = 120°$.

WORK IT OUT 12.1

Find the direction of the vector $-5\mathbf{i} + 2\mathbf{j}$.

Which is the correct solution? Can you identify the errors made in the incorrect solutions?

Solution 1	Solution 2	Solution 3
$\tan^{-1}\left(\dfrac{2}{-5}\right) = -21.8°$ So the angle is $21.8°$.	$\tan^{-1}\left(\dfrac{2}{5}\right) = 21.8°$ $180 - 21.8 = 158$ So the angle is $158°$.	$\tan^{-1}\left(\dfrac{5}{2}\right) = 68.2°$ $180 - 68.2 = 112$ So the angle is $112°$.

You can also use trigonometry to find the components of a vector if you know its magnitude and direction.

▶▶│ Fast forward

(A) This method will be particularly useful when you learn about resolving forces in the mechanics section in Student Book 2.

WORKED EXAMPLE 12.3

Vector **v** has magnitude 7 and has direction 62°. Write **v** as a column vector.

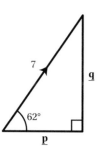

Draw a diagram showing the given information and the components (labelled **p** and **q**).

$\underline{v} = \begin{pmatrix} \underline{p} \\ \underline{q} \end{pmatrix}$

$\underline{p} = 7 \cos 62° = 3.29$

You have a right-angled triangle with a known hypotenuse and one angle, so use trigonometry.

$\underline{q} = 7 \sin 62° = 6.18$

$\therefore \underline{v} = \begin{pmatrix} 3.29 \\ 6.18 \end{pmatrix}$

Unit vectors

Vectors of length one are often very useful, so are given a special name.

🔑 **Key point 12.2**

A **unit vector** is a vector whose magnitude is one.

💡 **Tip**

You have already met two special examples of unit vectors: the base vectors **i** and **j**.

WORKED EXAMPLE 12.4

a Which of the following is a unit vector?

$$\mathbf{a} = \begin{pmatrix} -1 \\ 2 \end{pmatrix} \qquad \mathbf{b} = \begin{pmatrix} \frac{1}{\sqrt{3}} \\ \sqrt{\frac{2}{3}} \end{pmatrix}$$

b Find two possible values of t such that $\mathbf{c} = (12t)\mathbf{i} - (9t)\mathbf{j}$ is a unit vector.

a $|\underline{a}| = \sqrt{1+4}$

$= \sqrt{5} \neq 1$

Use Pythagoras' theorem to find the magnitudes.

 $|\underline{b}| = \sqrt{\dfrac{1}{3} + \dfrac{2}{3}}$

$= 1$

$\underline{b}$ is a unit vector.

A unit vector has magnitude one.

Continues on next page ...

b $|\underline{c}| = \sqrt{144t^2 + 81t^2}$ .... Find the magnitude of **c** in terms of t ...

$= \sqrt{225t^2}$

$|\underline{c}| = 1$

.... and make it equal to 1.

$\Rightarrow \sqrt{225t^2} = 1$

$\Rightarrow 225t^2 = 1$ .... Square both sides of the equation.

$\Rightarrow t^2 = \dfrac{1}{225}$

$\Rightarrow t = \pm\dfrac{1}{15}$

EXERCISE 12A

1. Write the following vectors using **i**, **j** notation:

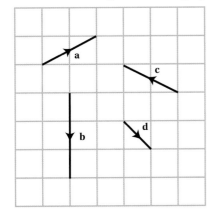

2. Represent the following vectors on a grid:

   a **i** $\begin{pmatrix} 3 \\ -5 \end{pmatrix}$ **ii** $\begin{pmatrix} -2 \\ -4 \end{pmatrix}$

   b **i** $-4\mathbf{i} + 3\mathbf{j}$ **ii** $2\mathbf{i} - \mathbf{j}$

   c **i** $6\mathbf{j}$ **ii** $-2\mathbf{i}$

3. For each vector from question 2 find:

   A the magnitude

   B the direction (anticlockwise angles are positive)

   C the angle it makes with the direction of **j**.

4. Decide which of the following are unit vectors:

   a $\dfrac{1}{2}\mathbf{i} + \dfrac{1}{3}\mathbf{j}$ **b** $-\mathbf{j}$

   c $(\cos\theta)\mathbf{i} + (\sin\theta)\mathbf{j}$ **d** $(3\cos\theta)\mathbf{i} + (3\sin\theta)\mathbf{j}$

5. Find the values of c such that $(2c)\mathbf{i} + (5c)\mathbf{j}$ is a unit vector.

6 $\begin{pmatrix} 3k \\ -2k \end{pmatrix}$ is a unit vector. Find the possible values of k.

7 Find the values of t such that the vector $\begin{pmatrix} 4t+10 \\ -2t \end{pmatrix}$ has magnitude $2\sqrt{10}$.

8 Vector **v** has magnitude 12 and is 27° clockwise from the **j**-direction. Find:

   a   the direction of **v**

   b   the components of **v**.

9 Vector **b** has magnitude $2\sqrt{3}$ and direction 150°. Write **b** as a column vector, giving your answers in surd form.

Section 2: Operations with vectors

In order to use vectors to solve problems you need to be able to perform some algebraic operations with them: adding, subtracting and multiplying by a scalar.

Adding vectors

If two vectors are represented by arrows then you can perform vector addition by joining the starting point of the second vector to the end point of the first. If the vectors are given in component form, you just add the corresponding components. The sum of two vectors is also called the **resultant vector**.

What if the two vectors are not in this position? Remember that vectors represent a length in a given direction, but don't tell you anything about **where** this length actually is. So vectors can be 'moved around' as long as the magnitude and direction remain unchanged.

▶▶) **Fast forward**

If you study Further Mathematics, in Pure Core Student Book 1 you will learn two different ways of multiplying one vector by another.

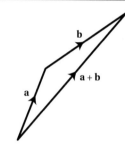

💡) **Tip**

Two vectors do not have to start and finish at the same points to be equal. They just need to have the same length and point in the same direction.

WORKED EXAMPLE 12.5

   a   Add vectors **a** and **b** as arrows on the grid.

   b   Write **a** and **b** as column vectors and hence find **a** + **b** as a column vector.

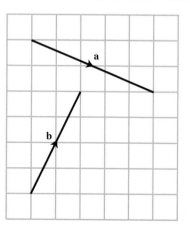

Continues on next page ...

a

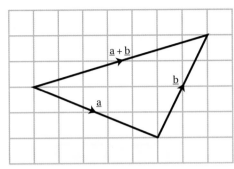

$a + b$

b

a

b $\underline{a} = \begin{pmatrix} 5 \\ -2 \end{pmatrix}$, $\underline{b} = \begin{pmatrix} 2 \\ 4 \end{pmatrix}$

$\underline{a} + \underline{b} = \begin{pmatrix} 5+2 \\ -2+4 \end{pmatrix}$ · · · · · · · · · · · · · · · · · · Add the components.

$= \begin{pmatrix} 7 \\ 2 \end{pmatrix}$

Another way of visualising vector addition is as a diagonal of the parallelogram formed by the two vectors. In this case the vectors are moved so that they have a common starting point.

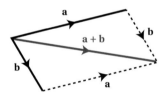

Subtracting vectors

Making a vector negative reverses the direction of the vector. Subtracting a vector is the same as adding its negative. So to subtract two vectors you need to reverse the direction of the second vector and then add it to the first. In component form you subtract corresponding components.

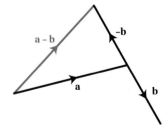

$$\begin{pmatrix} 4 \\ 1 \end{pmatrix} - \begin{pmatrix} 1 \\ -2 \end{pmatrix} = \begin{pmatrix} 4 \\ 1 \end{pmatrix} + \begin{pmatrix} -1 \\ 2 \end{pmatrix}$$

$$= \begin{pmatrix} 3 \\ 3 \end{pmatrix}$$

The difference of two vectors can also be represented by the diagonal of the parallelogram formed by the two vectors: the arrow points from the end of **b** towards the end of **a**.

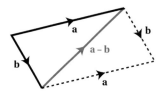

Scalar multiplication (multiplying a vector by a number) changes the magnitude (length) of the vector, leaving the direction the same. If the scalar is negative the vector will point in the opposite direction (but still along the same line). In component form, each component is multiplied by the scalar.

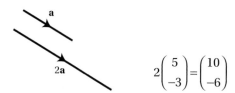

$$2\begin{pmatrix} 5 \\ -3 \end{pmatrix} = \begin{pmatrix} 10 \\ -6 \end{pmatrix}$$

> **Tip**
>
> In this paragraph the word 'direction' seems ambiguous: in the first instance it refers to the line along which the arrow lies, and in the second to the way the arrow is pointing. You need to be clear which meaning is being used.

WORKED EXAMPLE 12.6

Given the vectors $\mathbf{a} = \begin{pmatrix} 4 \\ -3 \end{pmatrix}$, $\mathbf{b} = \begin{pmatrix} -1 \\ 1 \end{pmatrix}$ and $\mathbf{c} = \begin{pmatrix} 11 \\ -9 \end{pmatrix}$, find scalars k and m such that $k\mathbf{a} - m\mathbf{b} = \mathbf{c}$.

$k\underline{a} - m\underline{b} = \begin{pmatrix} 4k \\ -3k \end{pmatrix} - \begin{pmatrix} -m \\ m \end{pmatrix}$ ⟶ Write $k\mathbf{a} - m\mathbf{b}$ in component form ...

$\quad = \begin{pmatrix} 4k+m \\ -3k-m \end{pmatrix}$

$k\underline{a} - m\underline{b} = c$

$\begin{pmatrix} 4k+m \\ -3k-m \end{pmatrix} = \begin{pmatrix} 11 \\ -9 \end{pmatrix}$ ⟶ ... and compare it to **c**.

$\begin{cases} 4k+m = 11 \\ -3k-m = -9 \end{cases}$ ⟶ Both components have to be equal.

$\Rightarrow k = 2, m = 3$ ⟶ Solve simultaneous equations.

Equal and parallel vectors

Two vectors are equal if they have the same magnitude and same direction. All their components are equal. They may have different start and end points.

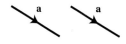

Parallel vectors are scalar multiples of each other.

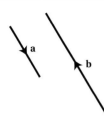

$\begin{pmatrix} 3 \\ -2 \end{pmatrix}$ is parallel to $\begin{pmatrix} -9 \\ 6 \end{pmatrix}$ since $\begin{pmatrix} -9 \\ 6 \end{pmatrix} = -3\begin{pmatrix} 3 \\ -2 \end{pmatrix}$

 Key point 12.3

If vectors **a** and **b** are parallel then you can write $\mathbf{b} = t\mathbf{a}$ for some scalar t.

 Tip

Remember that multiplying by a negative scalar will change the way the arrow is pointing.

WORKED EXAMPLE 12.7

Given vectors $\mathbf{a} = \begin{pmatrix} 1 \\ 2 \end{pmatrix}$ and $\mathbf{c} = \begin{pmatrix} -2 \\ 5 \end{pmatrix}$, find the value of scalar p such that $\mathbf{a} + p\mathbf{c}$ is parallel to the vector $\begin{pmatrix} 10 \\ 23 \end{pmatrix}$.

$\underline{a} + p\underline{c} = \begin{pmatrix} 1 \\ 2 \end{pmatrix} + \begin{pmatrix} -2p \\ 5p \end{pmatrix}$ .... You can write $\mathbf{a} + p\mathbf{c}$ as a single column vector.

$= \begin{pmatrix} 1-2p \\ 2+5p \end{pmatrix}$

Parallel to $\begin{pmatrix} 10 \\ 23 \end{pmatrix}$: .... If two vectors are parallel, then they are scalar multiples of each other.

$\begin{pmatrix} 1-2p \\ 2+5p \end{pmatrix} = t\begin{pmatrix} 10 \\ 23 \end{pmatrix}$ for some scalar t.

$\Rightarrow \begin{cases} 1-2p = 10t \\ 2+5p = 23t \end{cases}$ .... If two vectors are equal then all their components are equal.

$\Rightarrow \begin{cases} 10t + 2p = 1 \\ 23t - 5p = 2 \end{cases}$ .... Solve simultaneous equations: you only need to find p, so eliminate t.

$\Rightarrow \begin{cases} 230t + 46p = 23 \\ 230t - 50p = 20 \end{cases}$

$\Rightarrow 96p = 3$

$\Rightarrow p = \dfrac{1}{32}$

You can use scalar multiplication to find a vector with a given magnitude in the same direction as a given vector. In particular, you can find a unit vector in a given direction.

WORKED EXAMPLE 12.8

Find two unit vectors parallel to $\begin{pmatrix} 3 \\ 4 \end{pmatrix}$.

Let $\underline{a} = t\begin{pmatrix} 3 \\ 4 \end{pmatrix} = \begin{pmatrix} 3t \\ 4t \end{pmatrix}$ .... If a vector is parallel to $\begin{pmatrix} 3 \\ 4 \end{pmatrix}$ you can write it as $t\begin{pmatrix} 3 \\ 4 \end{pmatrix}$.

Then

$|\underline{a}| = 1$ ....

$\sqrt{(3t)^2 + (4t)^2} = 1$

$9t^2 + 16t^2 = 1^2$

$25t^2 = 1$

A unit vector has magnitude 1.

You can find the magnitude of a vector using Pythagoras' theorem.

$t = \pm\sqrt{\dfrac{1}{25}}$ .... Don't forget $\pm$ when taking a square root.

$= \pm\dfrac{1}{5}$

$\therefore \underline{a} = \pm\dfrac{1}{5}\begin{pmatrix} 3 \\ 4 \end{pmatrix}$

$= \begin{pmatrix} 0.6 \\ 0.8 \end{pmatrix}$ or $\begin{pmatrix} -0.6 \\ -0.8 \end{pmatrix}$

The two possible vectors are shown in this diagram.

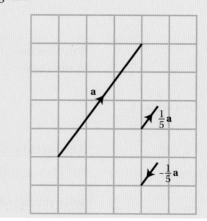

EXERCISE 12B

1 Represent vectors **a**, **b** and **c** by arrows on the grid.

   a $\mathbf{a} = \mathbf{u} + \mathbf{v}$, $\mathbf{b} = -2\mathbf{u}$, $\mathbf{c} = \mathbf{v} - \mathbf{u}$

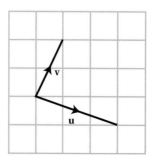

b $\mathbf{a} = 3\mathbf{v}, \mathbf{b} = \mathbf{u} - \mathbf{v}, \mathbf{c} = \mathbf{u} + \mathbf{v}$

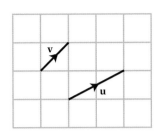

2 Let $\mathbf{a} = \begin{pmatrix} 7 \\ 1 \end{pmatrix}$, $\mathbf{b} = \begin{pmatrix} 5 \\ -2 \end{pmatrix}$ and $\mathbf{c} = \begin{pmatrix} 1 \\ 1 \end{pmatrix}$. Find the following vectors:

a   i $3\mathbf{a}$ ii $4\mathbf{b}$

b   i $\mathbf{a} - \mathbf{b}$ ii $\mathbf{b} + \mathbf{c}$

c   i $2\mathbf{b} + \mathbf{c}$ ii $\mathbf{a} - 2\mathbf{b}$

d   i $\mathbf{a} + \mathbf{b} - 2\mathbf{c}$ ii $3\mathbf{a} - \mathbf{b} + \mathbf{c}$

3 Let $\mathbf{a} = \mathbf{i} + 2\mathbf{j}$, $\mathbf{b} = \mathbf{i}$ and $\mathbf{c} = 2\mathbf{i} - \mathbf{j}$. Find the following vectors:

a   i $-6\mathbf{b}$ ii $4\mathbf{a}$

b   i $\mathbf{c} - \mathbf{a}$ ii $\mathbf{a} - \mathbf{b}$

c   i $\mathbf{a} - \mathbf{b} + 2\mathbf{c}$ ii $4\mathbf{c} - 3\mathbf{b}$

4 Given that $\mathbf{a} = 4\mathbf{i} - 2\mathbf{j}$, find the vector $\mathbf{b}$ such that:

a $\mathbf{a} + \mathbf{b}$ is the zero vector   c $\mathbf{a} - \mathbf{b} = \mathbf{j}$

b $2\mathbf{a} + 3\mathbf{b}$ is the zero vector   d $\mathbf{a} + 2\mathbf{b} = 3\mathbf{i}$

> **Tip**
>
> A zero vector is a vector with magnitude equal to zero.

5 Decide which of the following vectors are parallel:

a   i $\begin{pmatrix} -4 \\ 1 \end{pmatrix}$ and $\begin{pmatrix} -8 \\ 2 \end{pmatrix}$ ii $\begin{pmatrix} 3 \\ -1 \end{pmatrix}$ and $\begin{pmatrix} -6 \\ 2 \end{pmatrix}$

b   i $\begin{pmatrix} 2 \\ 5 \end{pmatrix}$ and $\begin{pmatrix} 4 \\ 9 \end{pmatrix}$ ii $\begin{pmatrix} 3 \\ -1 \end{pmatrix}$ and $\begin{pmatrix} -6 \\ -2 \end{pmatrix}$

c   i $3\mathbf{i} - 4\mathbf{j}$ and $1.5\mathbf{i} - 2\mathbf{j}$ ii $9\mathbf{i} - 2\mathbf{j}$ and $4.5\mathbf{i} + 2\mathbf{j}$

6 Given that $\mathbf{a} = \begin{pmatrix} -1 \\ 1 \end{pmatrix}$ and $\mathbf{b} = \begin{pmatrix} 5 \\ 3 \end{pmatrix}$ find vector $\mathbf{x}$ such that $3\mathbf{a} + 4\mathbf{x} = \mathbf{b}$.

7 Given that $\mathbf{a} = 3\mathbf{i} - 2\mathbf{j}$, $\mathbf{b} = \mathbf{i} - \mathbf{j}$ and $\mathbf{c} = \mathbf{i}$, find the value of the scalar t such that $\mathbf{a} + t\mathbf{b} = \mathbf{c}$.

8 Given that $\mathbf{a} = \begin{pmatrix} 2 \\ 0 \end{pmatrix}$ and $\mathbf{b} = \begin{pmatrix} 3 \\ 1 \end{pmatrix}$, find the value of the scalar p such that $\mathbf{a} + p\mathbf{b}$ is parallel to the vector $\begin{pmatrix} 3 \\ 2 \end{pmatrix}$.

9 Given that $\mathbf{x} = 2\mathbf{i} + 3\mathbf{j}$ and $\mathbf{y} = 4\mathbf{i} + \mathbf{j}$, find the value of the scalar λ such that $\lambda\mathbf{x} + \mathbf{y}$ is parallel to vector $\mathbf{j}$.

10 Given that $\mathbf{a} = \mathbf{i} - \mathbf{j}$, $\mathbf{b} = 2q\mathbf{i} + \mathbf{j}$ and that $p\mathbf{a} + \mathbf{b}$ is parallel to vector $\mathbf{i} + \mathbf{j}$, express q in terms of p.

11 Find the value of k such that the vector $\begin{pmatrix} 3k+1 \\ k-3 \end{pmatrix}$ is parallel to $\begin{pmatrix} -4 \\ 1 \end{pmatrix}$.

12 Find two vectors of magnitude 20 in the same direction as $\begin{pmatrix} 6 \\ -8 \end{pmatrix}$.

13 Find two vectors of magnitude 3 in the same direction as $\begin{pmatrix} 4 \\ 2 \end{pmatrix}$.

14 Find two unit vectors in the same direction as $\begin{pmatrix} -2 \\ 1 \end{pmatrix}$.

15 **a** Show that vectors $v = \begin{pmatrix} t-1 \\ 2t+1 \end{pmatrix}$ and $u = \begin{pmatrix} t^2-1 \\ 2t^2+3t+1 \end{pmatrix}$ are parallel for all values of t.

   b Find the value of t for which the two vectors are equal.

Elevate

For another example and more practice of questions like this, see Support sheet 12.

Section 3: Position and displacement vectors

Vectors are used to represent displacements between points. You can think of a vector as describing how to get from one point to another.

For example, to get from A to B in this diagram you need to move 5 units to the right and 3 units up. This can be represented by the **displacement** vector $\overrightarrow{AB} = \begin{pmatrix} 5 \\ 3 \end{pmatrix}$.

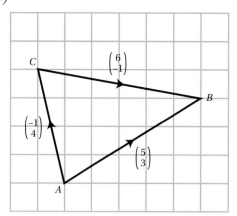

If you now have a third point, C, there are two different ways of getting from A to B: either directly or via C. Both of those journeys represent the same total displacement, so you can write $\overrightarrow{AB} = \overrightarrow{AC} + \overrightarrow{CB}$ or, using components, $\begin{pmatrix} 5 \\ 3 \end{pmatrix} = \begin{pmatrix} -1 \\ 4 \end{pmatrix} + \begin{pmatrix} 6 \\ -1 \end{pmatrix}$.

- If one displacement is followed by another, the total displacement is represented by the sum of the two displacement vectors.
- Multiplying a displacement vector by a scalar represents a displacement in the same direction but different distance.
- Making a displacement negative represents travelling the same distance in the opposite direction.

WORKED EXAMPLE 12.9

The diagram shows points M, N, P, Q such that $\overrightarrow{MN} = 3\mathbf{i} - 2\mathbf{j}$, $\overrightarrow{NP} = \mathbf{i} + \mathbf{j}$ and $\overrightarrow{MQ} = -2\mathbf{j}$.

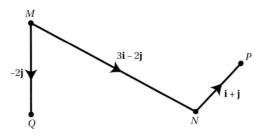

a Write the following vectors in component form:

   i $\overrightarrow{MP}$ **ii** $\overrightarrow{PQ}$

b Add a point R to the diagram such that $\overrightarrow{PR} = -2\overrightarrow{PM}$.

a i $\overrightarrow{MP} = \overrightarrow{MN} + \overrightarrow{NP}$ You can get from M to P via N.

    $= (3\underline{i} - 2\underline{j}) + (\underline{i} + \underline{j})$

    $= 4\underline{i} - \underline{j}$

ii $\overrightarrow{PM} = -\overrightarrow{MP}$ You can get from P to Q via M. You have already found $\overrightarrow{MP}$.

    $= -4\underline{i} + \underline{j}$

   $\overrightarrow{PQ} = \overrightarrow{PM} + \overrightarrow{MQ}$ Getting from P to R is in the opposite direction as getting from P to M.

    $= (-4\underline{i} + \underline{j}) + (-2\underline{j})$

    $= -4\underline{i} - \underline{j}$

b

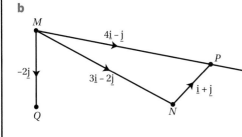

Displacement vectors tell you how to get from one point to another, but nothing about where the points actually are. To describe the position of a point you need a fixed **origin**, defined as $(0, 0)$ and labelled O. Then the the vector $\overrightarrow{OP}$, connecting the origin to a point P is called the **position vector** of P.

It is common to denote the position vector by the same letter as the point: for example, $\overrightarrow{OA} = \mathbf{a}$.

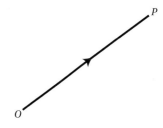

If you know position vectors of two points A and B you can find the displacement $\overrightarrow{AB}$ as shown in the diagram.

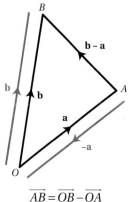

$$\overrightarrow{AB} = \overrightarrow{OB} - \overrightarrow{OA}$$

 Key point 12.4

If points A and B have position vectors $\mathbf{a}$ and $\mathbf{b}$ then $\overrightarrow{AB} = \mathbf{b} - \mathbf{a}$.

Tip

Remember that $\overrightarrow{AB}$ means the vector from A to B.

Tip

You can think of this as being the 'journey' $-\mathbf{a}$ followed by $\mathbf{b}$.

WORKED EXAMPLE 12.10

Points P and Q have position vectors $\overrightarrow{OP} = \begin{pmatrix} 3 \\ -5 \end{pmatrix}$ and $\overrightarrow{OQ} = \begin{pmatrix} -2 \\ 1 \end{pmatrix}$.

Find the displacement vector $\overrightarrow{PQ}$.

$\overrightarrow{PQ} = \overrightarrow{OQ} - \overrightarrow{OP}$ .... Use the result from Key point 12.4.

$= \begin{pmatrix} -2 \\ 1 \end{pmatrix} - \begin{pmatrix} 3 \\ -5 \end{pmatrix}$

$= \begin{pmatrix} -5 \\ 6 \end{pmatrix}$

Position vectors are closely related to coordinates. If the base vectors $\mathbf{i}$ and $\mathbf{j}$ have directions along the coordinate axes, then the components of the position vector are simply the coordinates of the point.

WORKED EXAMPLE 12.11

Points A and B have coordinates $(3, -1)$ and $(5, 0)$, respectively.

a Write as column vectors:

   i   the position vectors of A and B ii the displacement vector $\overrightarrow{AB}$

b Find the position vector of the point C such that $\overrightarrow{CA} = -4\mathbf{i} + 2\mathbf{j}$.

a i $\underline{a} = \begin{pmatrix} 3 \\ -1 \end{pmatrix}$ $\underline{b} = \begin{pmatrix} 5 \\ 0 \end{pmatrix}$

> The components of the position vectors are the coordinates of the point.

  ii $\overrightarrow{AB} = \underline{b} - \underline{a}$

> Use $\overrightarrow{AB} = \mathbf{b} - \mathbf{a}$.

$$= \begin{pmatrix} 5 \\ 0 \end{pmatrix} - \begin{pmatrix} 3 \\ -1 \end{pmatrix}$$

$$= \begin{pmatrix} 2 \\ 1 \end{pmatrix}$$

b $-4\underline{i} + 2\underline{j} = (3\underline{i} - \underline{j}) - \underline{c}$

> Use $\overrightarrow{CA} = \mathbf{a} - \mathbf{c}$.

$\underline{c} = (3\underline{i} - \underline{j}) - (-4\underline{i} + 2\underline{j})$

> Rearrange to find the position vector of C.

$= 7\underline{i} - 3\underline{j}$

Distance between two points

🔑 Key point 12.5

If points A and B have position vectors $\mathbf{a}$ and $\mathbf{b}$, then the distance between them, AB, is equal to the magnitude of the vector $\overrightarrow{AB}$:

$$AB = \left|\overrightarrow{AB}\right| = |\mathbf{b} - \mathbf{a}|$$

WORKED EXAMPLE 12.12

a Find the distance between points A and B with position vectors $\mathbf{a} = \begin{pmatrix} -3 \\ 2 \end{pmatrix}$ and $\mathbf{b} = \begin{pmatrix} -4 \\ 0 \end{pmatrix}$.

b Point C has position vector $\mathbf{c} = \begin{pmatrix} 2 \\ p \end{pmatrix}$. Find the exact values of p such that $AC = 3AB$.

a $\underline{b} - \underline{a} = \begin{pmatrix} -4 \\ 0 \end{pmatrix} - \begin{pmatrix} -3 \\ 2 \end{pmatrix}$

> First find the vector $\overrightarrow{AB} = \mathbf{b} - \mathbf{a}$

$$= \begin{pmatrix} -1 \\ -2 \end{pmatrix}$$

Continues on next page …

$$\therefore AB = \sqrt{1^2 + 2^2}$$

$$= \sqrt{5}$$

Then find the magnitude using Pythagoras' theorem.

b $\underline{c} - \underline{a} = \begin{pmatrix} 2 \\ p \end{pmatrix} - \begin{pmatrix} -3 \\ 2 \end{pmatrix}$

First find an expression for the vector $\overrightarrow{AC} = \mathbf{c} - \mathbf{a}$ in terms of p.

$$= \begin{pmatrix} 5 \\ p-2 \end{pmatrix}$$

$$AC = \sqrt{5^2 + (p-2)^2}$$

Then find the magnitude using Key point 12.1.

$$AC = 3AB$$

$$\sqrt{25 + (p-2)^2} = 3\sqrt{5}$$

Form an equation.

$$25 + (p-2)^2 = 45$$

Square both sides to get rid of the root.

$$(p-2)^2 = 20$$

$$p - 2 = \pm\sqrt{20}$$

$$p = 2 \pm 2\sqrt{5}$$

You don't need to expand the brackets. Square root, remembering $\pm$.

WORK IT OUT 12.2

Points P and Q have coordinates $P(-1, 3)$ and $Q(7, -2)$. Find the vector $\overrightarrow{QP}$.

Which is the correct solution? Can you identify the errors made in the incorrect solutions?

Solution 1	Solution 2	Solution 3
$\overrightarrow{QP} = \mathbf{p} - \mathbf{q}$	$\overrightarrow{QP} = \mathbf{p} + \mathbf{q}$	$\overrightarrow{QP} = \mathbf{q} - \mathbf{p}$
$= \begin{pmatrix} -1 \\ 3 \end{pmatrix} - \begin{pmatrix} 7 \\ -2 \end{pmatrix}$	$= \begin{pmatrix} -1 \\ 3 \end{pmatrix} + \begin{pmatrix} 7 \\ -2 \end{pmatrix}$	$= \begin{pmatrix} 7 \\ -2 \end{pmatrix} - \begin{pmatrix} -1 \\ 3 \end{pmatrix}$
$= \begin{pmatrix} -8 \\ 5 \end{pmatrix}$	$= \begin{pmatrix} 6 \\ 1 \end{pmatrix}$	$= \begin{pmatrix} 8 \\ -5 \end{pmatrix}$

EXERCISE 12C

1 **a** Write down the following displacement vectors in component form:

    i from A to C **ii** from C to B

    iii from B to C **iv** from D to A

  b Copy the grid and mark on points P, Q and R so that:

    i $\overrightarrow{AP} = \begin{pmatrix} 3 \\ -2 \end{pmatrix}$ **ii** $\overrightarrow{QC} = \begin{pmatrix} -1 \\ 3 \end{pmatrix}$ **iii** $\overrightarrow{RD} = \begin{pmatrix} 0 \\ 4 \end{pmatrix}$

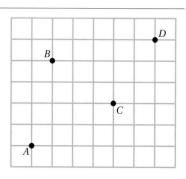

2 Four points have coordinates $A(-1, 3)$, $B(3, -3)$, $C(0, -5)$ and $D(-3, -2)$. Write the following vectors in component form:

  a i the position vector of A **ii** the position vector of B

  b i the displacement from B to D **ii** the displacement from C to B

  c i $\overrightarrow{AB}$ **ii** $\overrightarrow{DA}$

3 Points A, B, C and D are as in question 2. Find the coordinates of the points satisfying the following conditions:

  a i point P such that $\overrightarrow{AP} = \begin{pmatrix} 3 \\ -2 \end{pmatrix}$ **ii** point Q such that $\overrightarrow{CQ} = \begin{pmatrix} -4 \\ 1 \end{pmatrix}$

  b i point R such that $\overrightarrow{RB} = \begin{pmatrix} 2 \\ -1 \end{pmatrix}$ **ii** point S such that $\overrightarrow{SD} = \begin{pmatrix} -5 \\ -2 \end{pmatrix}$

  c i point X such that $\overrightarrow{AX} = 3\overrightarrow{AB}$ **ii** point Y such that $\overrightarrow{BY} = 2\overrightarrow{BD}$

  d i point Z such that $\overrightarrow{CZ} = -2\overrightarrow{AB}$ **ii** point W such that $\overrightarrow{DW} = -4\overrightarrow{CA}$

4 Points A, B, C and D have position vectors $\mathbf{a} = 3\mathbf{i} - 7\mathbf{j}$, $\mathbf{b} = -3\mathbf{i} + 6\mathbf{j}$, $\mathbf{c} = \mathbf{i} - 5\mathbf{j}$, $\mathbf{d} = -4\mathbf{j}$.
Find the following distances:

  a i AB **ii** CD

  b i DA **ii** BC

5 The diagram shows four points P, Q, R and S such that $\overrightarrow{PQ} = 4\mathbf{i} - 3\mathbf{j}$, $\overrightarrow{QR} = \mathbf{i} + 2\mathbf{j}$ and $\overrightarrow{RS} = 2\mathbf{i} + 5\mathbf{j}$.

Express the following vectors in component form:

  a $\overrightarrow{PR}$ **b** $\overrightarrow{SP}$

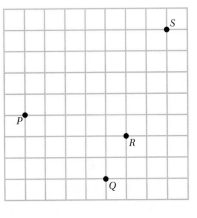

6 Points A, B, C and D have coordinates $A(3, -2)$, $B(-4, 1)$, $C(1, -5)$, and $D(0, 7)$.

  a Write $\overrightarrow{AC}$ and $\overrightarrow{DB}$ as column vectors.

  b Find the coordinates of the point E such that $\overrightarrow{AE} = \begin{pmatrix} -3 \\ 5 \end{pmatrix}$.

7 Points A, B and C have coordinates $A(1, 3)$, $B(5, -1)$, and $C(2, -8)$.

Point D is such that $\overrightarrow{AD} = \overrightarrow{BC} + (2x)\overrightarrow{AB} + (3y)\overrightarrow{AC} = \overrightarrow{AB} + (2x)\overrightarrow{AC} + (3y)\overrightarrow{BC}$.

Find the coordinates of D.

8 $\overrightarrow{AB} = \begin{pmatrix} 6 \\ -3 \end{pmatrix}$ and $\overrightarrow{AC} = \dfrac{4}{3}\overrightarrow{AB}$.

  a Write down $\overrightarrow{AC}$.

Point P is such that $AP = 2BP$.

  b If $\overrightarrow{AP} = \begin{pmatrix} r \\ q \end{pmatrix}$, write down vectors $\overrightarrow{BP}$ and $\overrightarrow{CP}$ in terms of r and q.

  c Show that CP is independent of the values of r and q and evaluate it.

Section 4: Using vectors to solve geometrical problems

In this section you will learn how to describe and prove various properties of geometrical figures.

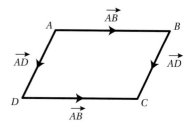

Special shapes

Consider four points A, B, C and D such that $\overrightarrow{AB} = \overrightarrow{DC}$.
This means that the opposite sides AB and DC are parallel and have equal length, so the shape is a parallelogram. It follows that the other two sides are also equal and parallel, so $\overrightarrow{BC} = \overrightarrow{AD}$.

One special type of parallelogram is a rhombus, which has all four sides of equal length. This means that vectors $\overrightarrow{AB}$ and $\overrightarrow{BC}$ have equal magnitudes. Note that they are not equal vectors because they don't have the same direction.

> ✔ **Gateway to A level**
>
> For a reminder of the properties of special quadrilaterals see Gateway to A Level section N.

> ⏩ **Fast forward**
>
> Other special types of parallelogram are a rectangle and a square; they have right angles. If you study Further Mathematics in Pure Core Student Book 1 you will learn how to find the angle between two vectors.

> 🔑 **Key point 12.6**
>
> If $\overrightarrow{AB} = \overrightarrow{DC}$ then $ABCD$ is a parallelogram.
> If in addition $\left|\overrightarrow{AB}\right| = \left|\overrightarrow{BC}\right|$ then $ABCD$ is a rhombus.

WORKED EXAMPLE 12.13

Four points have coordinates $A(2, -1)$, $B(k, k+1)$, $C(2k-3, 2k+2)$ and $D(k-1, k)$.

a Show that $ABCD$ is a parallelogram for all values of k.
b Find the value of k for which $ABCD$ is a rhombus.

a $\overrightarrow{AB} = \begin{pmatrix} k \\ k+1 \end{pmatrix} - \begin{pmatrix} 2 \\ -1 \end{pmatrix}$ .... For a parallelogram you need to show that $\overrightarrow{AB} = \overrightarrow{DC}$.

$= \begin{pmatrix} k-2 \\ k+2 \end{pmatrix}$

$\overrightarrow{DC} = \begin{pmatrix} 2k-3 \\ 2k+2 \end{pmatrix} - \begin{pmatrix} k-1 \\ k \end{pmatrix}$

$= \begin{pmatrix} k-2 \\ k+2 \end{pmatrix}$

$\overrightarrow{AB} = \overrightarrow{DC}$ so $ABCD$ is a parallelogram.

Continues on next page ...

b $\left|\overrightarrow{AB}\right| = \sqrt{(k-2)^2 + (k+2)^2}$ · · · · · · · · · · · For a rhombus $\left|\overrightarrow{AB}\right| = \left|\overrightarrow{BC}\right|$ so find expressions for these two distances...

$\overrightarrow{BC} = \begin{pmatrix} 2k-3 \\ 2k+2 \end{pmatrix} - \begin{pmatrix} k \\ k+1 \end{pmatrix}$

$= \begin{pmatrix} k-3 \\ k+1 \end{pmatrix}$

$\left|\overrightarrow{BC}\right| = \sqrt{(k-3)^2 + (k+1)^2}$

$\left|\overrightarrow{AB}\right| = \left|\overrightarrow{BC}\right|$ · ... and then make them equal.

$\Rightarrow (k-2)^2 + (k+2)^2 = (k-3)^2 + (k+1)^2$ · · · Square both sides to get rid of the roots.

$2k^2 + 8 = 2k^2 - 4k + 10$

$4k = 2$

$k = \dfrac{1}{2}$

Straight lines

If points A, B and C lie in a straight line then vectors $\overrightarrow{AB}$ and $\overrightarrow{BC}$ are parallel, so $\overrightarrow{BC} = t\,\overrightarrow{AB}$ for some scalar t. This scalar gives the ratio of the lengths BC and AB.

Points that lie on a straight line are said to be **collinear**.

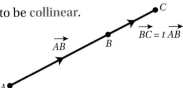

WORKED EXAMPLE 12.14

Three points have coordinates $A(-3, 2)$, $B(6, 5)$ and $C(12, 7)$.

a Show that A, B and C lie on a straight line.
b Find the ratio $AB : BC$.

a $\overrightarrow{AB} = \begin{pmatrix} 6 \\ 5 \end{pmatrix} - \begin{pmatrix} -3 \\ 2 \end{pmatrix}$ · · · · · · · · · · You need to show that $\overrightarrow{AB}$ and $\overrightarrow{BC}$ are parallel. First find these two vectors.

$= \begin{pmatrix} 9 \\ 3 \end{pmatrix}$

$\overrightarrow{BC} = \begin{pmatrix} 12 \\ 7 \end{pmatrix} - \begin{pmatrix} 6 \\ 5 \end{pmatrix}$

$= \begin{pmatrix} 6 \\ 2 \end{pmatrix}$

Continues on next page ...

If points A, B and C
lie on a straight line: $\overrightarrow{BC} = t\overrightarrow{AB}$

> You need to get the same value of t for both
> components.

$$\begin{cases} 6 = 9t \Rightarrow t = \dfrac{2}{3} \\ 2 = 3t \Rightarrow t = \dfrac{2}{3} \end{cases}$$

$$\therefore \overrightarrow{BC} = \frac{2}{3}\overrightarrow{AB}$$

Since AB and BC are parallel and
contain a common point B, A, B
and C lie on a straight line.

> Conclude that A, B and C lie on a straight line.

b $BC = \dfrac{2}{3}AB$

> Since $\overrightarrow{BC} = \frac{2}{3}\overrightarrow{AB}$, the length $BC = \frac{2}{3}AB$.

$$\therefore AB : BC = 3 : 2$$

Midpoints

Consider points A and B with position vectors $\mathbf{a}$ and $\mathbf{b}$ and let M be the
midpoint of AB. Then you can express the position vector of M in terms
of $\mathbf{a}$ and $\mathbf{b}$.

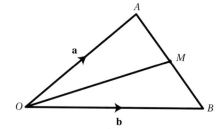

 Key point 12.7

The midpoint of the line segment connecting points with position vectors $\mathbf{a}$
and $\mathbf{b}$ has position vector $\frac{1}{2}(\mathbf{a}+\mathbf{b})$.

PROOF 7

$$\overrightarrow{OM} = \overrightarrow{OA} + \frac{1}{2}\overrightarrow{AB}$$

> You can get from O to M by going from O to A and then
> half-way from A to B.

$$= \mathbf{a} + \frac{1}{2}(\mathbf{b} - \mathbf{a})$$

> You know that $\overrightarrow{OA} = \mathbf{a}$ and $\overrightarrow{AB} = \mathbf{b} - \mathbf{a}$.

$$= \frac{1}{2}\mathbf{a} + \frac{1}{2}\mathbf{b}$$

$$= \frac{1}{2}(\mathbf{a} + \mathbf{b})$$

In Worked example 12.15 we use vectors to prove that the diagonals of
a parallelogram bisect each other. In Mixed practice 12 question 13 you
can prove this result in general.

WORKED EXAMPLE 12.15

Points A, B and C have position vectors $\mathbf{a} = \begin{pmatrix} 3 \\ -5 \end{pmatrix}$, $\mathbf{b} = \begin{pmatrix} 4 \\ 2 \end{pmatrix}$ and $\mathbf{c} = \begin{pmatrix} -3 \\ -1 \end{pmatrix}$

a Find the position vector of the point D such that $ABCD$ is a parallelogram.

M is the midpoint of the diagonal AC.

b Find the position vector of M.

c Show that M is also the midpoint of BD.

a $\overrightarrow{AB} = \overrightarrow{DC}$

For a parallelogram, $\overrightarrow{AB} = \overrightarrow{DC}$.

$\begin{pmatrix} 4 \\ 2 \end{pmatrix} - \begin{pmatrix} 3 \\ -5 \end{pmatrix} = \begin{pmatrix} -3 \\ -1 \end{pmatrix} - \underline{d}$

Use $\overrightarrow{AB} = \mathbf{b} - \mathbf{a}$ and $\overrightarrow{DC} = \mathbf{c} - \mathbf{d}$.

$\begin{pmatrix} 1 \\ 7 \end{pmatrix} = \begin{pmatrix} -3 \\ -1 \end{pmatrix} - \underline{d}$

$\underline{d} = \begin{pmatrix} -3 \\ -1 \end{pmatrix} - \begin{pmatrix} 1 \\ 7 \end{pmatrix}$

Rearrange to find **d**.

$= \begin{pmatrix} -4 \\ -8 \end{pmatrix}$

b $\underline{m} = \frac{1}{2}(\underline{a} + \underline{c})$

Using the result for the midpoint from Key point 12.7.

$= \frac{1}{2}\left(\begin{pmatrix} 3 \\ -5 \end{pmatrix} + \begin{pmatrix} -3 \\ -1 \end{pmatrix} \right)$

$= \frac{1}{2}\begin{pmatrix} 0 \\ -6 \end{pmatrix}$

$= \begin{pmatrix} 0 \\ -3 \end{pmatrix}$

c $\overrightarrow{BM} = \begin{pmatrix} 0 \\ -3 \end{pmatrix} - \begin{pmatrix} 4 \\ 2 \end{pmatrix}$

If M is half-way between B and D then $\overrightarrow{BM} = \overrightarrow{MD}$.
You could also have used the condition that if M is the midpoint of BD then $\mathbf{m} = \frac{1}{2}(\mathbf{b} + \mathbf{d})$.

$= \begin{pmatrix} -4 \\ -5 \end{pmatrix}$

$\overrightarrow{MD} = \begin{pmatrix} -4 \\ -8 \end{pmatrix} - \begin{pmatrix} 0 \\ -3 \end{pmatrix}$

$= \begin{pmatrix} -4 \\ -5 \end{pmatrix}$

$\overrightarrow{BM} = \overrightarrow{MD}$ so M is the midpoint of BD.

Vectors are very useful for proving that two lines are parallel, even if they don't have the same length. Worked example 12.16 combines midpoints with parallel lines.

 Tip

Remember that two vectors are parallel if one is a scalar multiple of the other.

WORKED EXAMPLE 12.16

The vertices of triangle ABC have position vectors $\mathbf{a}$, $\mathbf{b}$ and $\mathbf{c}$. M and N are the midpoints of sides AB and AC.

a Express the position vectors of M and N in terms of $\mathbf{a}$, $\mathbf{b}$ and $\mathbf{c}$.

b Prove that MN is parallel to and half the length of BC.

a M is the midpoint of AB so $\underline{m} = \frac{1}{2}(\underline{a}+\underline{b})$

> Find the position vectors of midpoints using the result from Key point 12.7.

N is the midpoint of AC so $\underline{n} = \frac{1}{2}(\underline{a}+\underline{c})$

b $\overrightarrow{BC} = \underline{c} - \underline{b}$

$\overrightarrow{MN} = \underline{n} - \underline{m}$

> You want to compare vectors $\overrightarrow{MN}$ and $\overrightarrow{BC}$.

$\quad = \frac{1}{2}(\underline{a}+\underline{c}) - \frac{1}{2}(\underline{a}+\underline{b})$

> Use the result from part **a** on $\overrightarrow{MN}$.

$\quad = \frac{1}{2}\underline{c} - \frac{1}{2}\underline{b}$

$\overrightarrow{MN} = \frac{1}{2}\overrightarrow{BC}$

> Since $\overrightarrow{MN} = \frac{1}{2}\overrightarrow{BC}$ the two vectors are parallel.

So MN is parallel to BC and half its length.

EXERCISE 12D

1 The diagram shows a parallelogram $ABCD$ with $\overrightarrow{AB} = \mathbf{a}$ and $\overrightarrow{AD} = \mathbf{b}$. M is the midpoint of BC and N is the midpoint of CD. Express the following vectors in terms of $\mathbf{a}$ and $\mathbf{b}$:

a i $\overrightarrow{BC}$ **ii** $\overrightarrow{AC}$

b i $\overrightarrow{CD}$ **ii** $\overrightarrow{ND}$

c i $\overrightarrow{AM}$ **ii** $\overrightarrow{MN}$

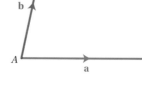

2 In the parallelogram $ABCD$, $\overrightarrow{AB} = \mathbf{a}$ and $\overrightarrow{AD} = \mathbf{b}$. M is the midpoint of BC, Q is the point on the extended line AB such that $BQ = \frac{1}{2}AB$ and P is the point on the extended line BC such that $BC : CP = 3 : 1$, as shown on the diagram. Express the following vectors in terms of $\mathbf{a}$ and $\mathbf{b}$:

a i $\overrightarrow{AP}$ **ii** $\overrightarrow{AM}$

b i $\overrightarrow{QD}$ **ii** $\overrightarrow{MQ}$

c i $\overrightarrow{DQ}$ **ii** $\overrightarrow{PQ}$

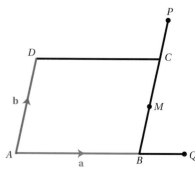

3 For the coordinate sets given, determine whether the three points A, B and C are collinear. If they are, find the ratio $AB : BC$.

a i $A(3, 8), B(-1, 2), C(51, 80)$ **ii** $A(4, -1), B(6, 3), C(11, 13)$

b i $A(2, 1), B(-11, 14), C(4, 3)$ **ii** $A(3, 5), B(1, 7), C(-6, 3)$

c i $A(4, 2a), B(1, 3a + 2), C(10, 4)$ **ii** $A(4, 2a), B(1, 2a + 1), C(7, 2a - 1)$

d i $A(a^2 + 2a, 3), B(a^2 + a - 1, 1), C(3a^2 + 2a - 2, 4a - 1)$

  ii $A(a^2 - 2a, 5), B(a^2 + a + 2, 5), C(a^2 + 2a, -4)$

4 The points A and B have position vectors $\mathbf{a} = 7\mathbf{i} + 18\mathbf{j}$ and $\mathbf{b} = -3\mathbf{i} + 6\mathbf{j}$.
Find the position vector of the midpoint of AB.

5 $\overrightarrow{AB} = \begin{pmatrix} 3 \\ -7 \end{pmatrix}$ and $\overrightarrow{CA} = \begin{pmatrix} -9 \\ 21 \end{pmatrix}$.

Show that A, B and C are collinear and find the ratio $AB : BC$.

6 Points A, B and C have position vectors $\mathbf{a} = \begin{pmatrix} 3 \\ -5 \end{pmatrix}$, $\mathbf{b} = \begin{pmatrix} -1 \\ 4 \end{pmatrix}$ and $\mathbf{c} = \begin{pmatrix} 4 \\ 5 \end{pmatrix}$.

a Find the position vector of the point D such that $ABCD$ is a parallelogram.

b Determine whether $ABCD$ is a rhombus.

7 Points A, B, C and D have position vectors.

$\mathbf{a} = \begin{pmatrix} 3 \\ -1 \end{pmatrix}$, $\mathbf{b} = \begin{pmatrix} 5 \\ 0 \end{pmatrix}$, $\mathbf{c} = \begin{pmatrix} 7 \\ 8 \end{pmatrix}$ and $\mathbf{d} = \begin{pmatrix} 4 \\ 3 \end{pmatrix}$.

Point E is the midpoint of BC.

a Find the position vector of E.

b Show that $ABED$ is a parallelogram.

8 The vertices of a quadrilateral $PQRS$ have coordinates $P(-2, 1)$, $Q(5, -3)$, $R(6, 0)$ and $S(-1, 5)$.
The midpoints of the sides PQ, QR, RS and SP are A, B, C and D.

Prove that $ABCD$ is a parallelogram.

9 Points A and B have position vectors $\mathbf{a} = \begin{pmatrix} 2 \\ 1 \end{pmatrix}$ and $\mathbf{b} = \begin{pmatrix} -1 \\ 3 \end{pmatrix}$. Point C lies on the line segment AB so that
$AC : BC = 2 : 3$. Find the position vector of C.

10 Points A, B, C and D have position vectors $\mathbf{a}$, $\mathbf{b}$, $\mathbf{c}$ and $\mathbf{d}$.

M is the midpoint of AB and N is the midpoint of BC.

P is the midpoint of CD and Q is the midpoint of AD.

By finding the vectors $\overrightarrow{MN}$ and $\overrightarrow{QP}$, prove that $MNPQ$ forms a parallelogram.

11 Points A and B have coordinates $A(10, 1)$ and $B(2, 7)$. Point C lies on the line segment AB such that
$AC : BC = x : 1 - x$, where $0 < x < 1$.

a Find the coordinates of C, in terms of x.

b Point D has coordinates $D(3, 2)$ and $CD = \sqrt{26}$. Find x.

12 $\;$ $ABCD$ is a parallelogram with $\overrightarrow{AB} = \mathbf{p}$ and $\overrightarrow{BC} = \mathbf{q}$. Let M be the midpoint of the diagonal AC.

$\quad$ **a** $\;$ Express $\overrightarrow{AM}$ in terms of $\mathbf{p}$ and $\mathbf{q}$.

$\quad$ **b** $\;$ Show that M is also a midpoint of the diagonal BD.

13 $\;$ Four points have coordinates $A(2, -1)$, $B(k, k+1)$, $C(2k-3, 3k+2)$ and $D(k-1, 2k)$.

$\quad$ **a** $\;$ Show that $ABCD$ is a parallelogram for all values of k.

$\quad$ **b** $\;$ Show that there is no value of k for which $ABCD$ is a rhombus.

Checklist of learning and understanding

- A vector is a quantity that has both magnitude and direction.
- The magnitude (modulus) of vector $\mathbf{a}$ is written $|\mathbf{a}|$. The direction is the angle it makes with the positive x-axis.
- There are several ways to represent a vector:
  - by drawing a directed arrow: in this case the magnitude of the vector is represented by the length of the arrow
  - by stating its components, either as a column vector or by using base vectors $\mathbf{i}$ and $\mathbf{j}$

  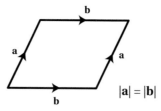
  $$\begin{pmatrix} a_1 \\ a_2 \end{pmatrix} = a_1\mathbf{i} + a_2\mathbf{j}$$

  - by stating its magnitude and direction.
- You can perform three operations with vectors: adding, subtracting and multiplying by a scalar.
- If vectors $\mathbf{a}$ and $\mathbf{b}$ are parallel then $\mathbf{b} = t\mathbf{a}$ for some scalar t.
- A unit vector is a vector with magnitude 1.
- Vectors can represent positions of points or displacements between two points.
- The position vector of a point is a vector from the origin to that point.
  - If points A and B have position vectors $\mathbf{a}$ and $\mathbf{b}$ then the displacement from A to B is $\overrightarrow{AB} = \mathbf{b} - \mathbf{a}$.
  - The distance between two points is the magnitude of the displacement between them: $AB = \left| \overrightarrow{AB} \right| = |\mathbf{b} - \mathbf{a}|$.
- Vectors can be used to solve problems and prove properties of geometrical shapes. Some of the most useful properties are:
  - If a shape is a parallelogram then the vectors corresponding to the opposite sides are equal.
  - If the shape is a rhombus then the vectors corresponding to all four sides have equal magnitudes.

$$|\mathbf{a}| = |\mathbf{b}|$$

- The midpoint of the line segment joining points with position vectors $\mathbf{a}$ and $\mathbf{b}$ has position vector $\frac{1}{2}(\mathbf{a}+\mathbf{b})$.
- You can use vectors to show that two lines are parallel.

Mixed practice 12

1 Points A and B have position vectors $\mathbf{a} = 3\mathbf{i} - \mathbf{j}$ and $\mathbf{b} = 2\mathbf{j}$. Find the exact distance between A and B.

2 **a** Given the points $P(-5, 2)$ and $Q(1, -3)$, write vector $\overrightarrow{PQ}$ in the form $a\mathbf{i} + b\mathbf{j}$.

b Point R is such that $\overrightarrow{RQ} = \mathbf{i} - 4\mathbf{j}$. Find the coordinates of R.

3 Points A and B have position vectors $\mathbf{a} = \begin{pmatrix} 12 \\ -7 \end{pmatrix}$ and $\mathbf{b} = \begin{pmatrix} -3 \\ 5 \end{pmatrix}$.

M is the midpoint of AB.

a Find the position vector of M.

b Find the exact distance BM.

4 Points A, B and C have position vectors $\mathbf{a} = 3\mathbf{i} - \mathbf{j}$, $\mathbf{b} = \mathbf{i} + 2\mathbf{j}$ and $\mathbf{c} = 4\mathbf{i} + \mathbf{j}$. Point D is such that $ABCD$ is a parallelogram. Find the position vector of D.

5 The diagram shows points P, Q and R such that $\overrightarrow{PQ} = \mathbf{a}$ and $\overrightarrow{PR} = 3\mathbf{b}$.

Points M and N are on PQ and PR such that $PM = \frac{1}{3}PQ$ and $\overrightarrow{PN} = \mathbf{b}$.

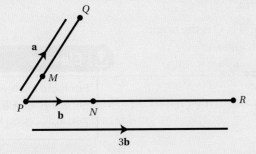

Express $\overrightarrow{MN}$ in terms of $\mathbf{a}$ and $\mathbf{b}$ and hence prove that MN is parallel to QR.

6 OAB is a triangle with $\overrightarrow{OA} = \mathbf{a}$ and $\overrightarrow{OB} = \mathbf{b}$. M is the midpoint of AB and G is a point on OM such that $OG : GM = 2 : 1$. N is the midpoint of OA. Use vectors to prove that the points B, G and N are collinear.

7 Find the magnitude of the vector $(3 \sin \theta)\underline{\mathbf{i}} + (5 \cos \theta)\underline{\mathbf{j}}$ in terms of θ.

8 Points M and N have coordinates $M(-6, 1)$ and $N(3, 5)$. Find a unit vector parallel to $\overrightarrow{MN}$.

9 Points P and Q have coordinates $(1, -8)$ and $(10, -2)$. N is a point on PQ such that $PN : NQ = 1 : 2$.

a Find the coordinates of N.

b Calculate the magnitudes of $\overrightarrow{OP}$, $\overrightarrow{ON}$ and $\overrightarrow{PN}$. Hence show that ONP is a right angle.

10 Points A, B, C and D have position vectors **a**, **b**, **c** and **d**. M, N, P and Q are midpoints of AB, BC, CD and DA.

   a Express vectors $\overrightarrow{MN}$ and $\overrightarrow{PQ}$ in terms of **a**, **b**, **c** and **d**.

   b What type of quadrilateral is $MNPQ$?

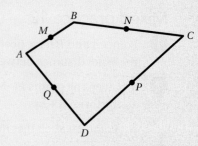

11 Points A and B have position vectors **a** and **b**. O is the origin and point P is such that $OAPB$ is a parallelogram.

   a Write down the position vector of P in terms of **a** and **b**.

   b Find the position vector of M, the midpoint of AP.

   Point Q lies on OP. Let $\overrightarrow{OQ} = t\overrightarrow{OP}$.

   c Express $\overrightarrow{BQ}$ in terms of t, **a** and **b**. Hence find the value of t for which BQM is a straight line.

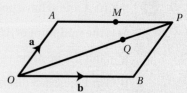

12 Points P and Q have position vectors $p = \begin{pmatrix} 5 \\ 2 \end{pmatrix}$ and $q = \begin{pmatrix} 2 \\ 3 \end{pmatrix}$.

Point H lies on PQ and $\overrightarrow{PH} = t\overrightarrow{PQ}$, with $0 < t < 1$.

Let O be the origin.

   a Express the vector $\overrightarrow{OH}$ and its length in terms of t.

   b Hence find the minimum possible distance of H from the origin, giving your answer in exact form.

13 Points A and B have position vectors **a** and **b**. O is the origin and point P is such that $OAPB$ is a parallelogram.

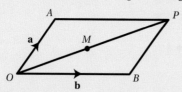

Elevate

For more challenging geometry problems, see Extension sheet 12.

M is the midpoint of OP.

   a Show that M lies on AB and determine the ratio $AM : MB$.

   b What conclusion can you make about the diagonals of a parallelogram?

13 Differentiation

In this chapter you will learn how to:

- sketch the gradient function for a given curve
- find the gradients of curves from first principles – a process called differentiation
- differentiate x^n
- use differentiation to decide whether a function is increasing or decreasing.

Before you start...

Chapter 2	You should know how to work with indices.	1	Write the following in the form $nx^a + mx^b$. a $\sqrt[3]{x^2} - \dfrac{5}{2x}$ b $\dfrac{2+x}{\sqrt{x}}$
Chapter 3	You should know how to solve linear and quadratic inequalities.	2	Solve these inequalities: a $3x - 4 \geqslant 5x + 2$ b $x^2 - 4x - 12 \geqslant 0$
Chapter 6	You should know how to find the gradient of a straight line.	3	Find the gradient of the line that passes through the point $(-1, 4)$ and $(7, -2)$.
Chapter 9	You should know how to work with the binomial expansion.	4	Expand $(2+x)^3$.

What is differentiation?

In real life, things change: planets move, babies grow, prices rise and fall. Calculus is the study of change, and one of its most important tools is differentiation – finding the rate at which the y-coordinate of a curve is changing when the x-coordinate changes. For a straight-line graph, this rate of change was given by the gradient of the line. In this chapter you will apply the same idea to curves, where the gradient is different at different points.

Section 1: Sketching derivatives

You first need to establish exactly what is meant by the gradient of a curve. You know what this means for a straight line, so we can use this idea to make a more general definition.

Key point 13.1

The gradient of a curve at a point P is the gradient of the tangent to the curve at that point.

◀◀ Rewind

You have already met tangents in Chapters 5 and 6.

A tangent to a curve at a point is a straight line which touches the curve without crossing it at that point.

Note that when we say that the tangent at P does not cross the curve, we mean this in a 'local' sense: the tangent does not cross the curve close to the point P but it can intersect a different part of the curve (as shown in the diagram).

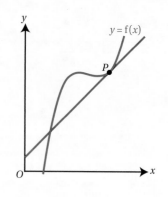

▶▶ Fast forward

> **A** It is in fact possible for a tangent at a point to cross the curve at that point; this happens at a point of inflection. You will learn about this in Student Book 2, Chapter 12.

The **derivative** (or **gradient function**) of a function f(x) is another function that gives the gradient of the graph of $y = $ f(x) at any point. It is often useful to be able to sketch the derivative of a given function.

WORKED EXAMPLE 13.1

Sketch the derivative of this function:

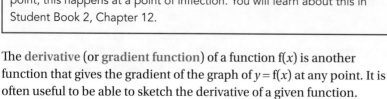

Imagine a point moving along the curve from left to right. Track the tangent of the curve at the moving point and form the graph of its gradient.

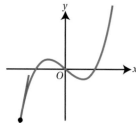
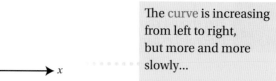

The curve is increasing from left to right, but more and more slowly...

... so the gradient is positive and falling.

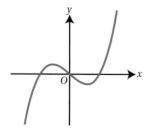

The tangent is horizontal...

... so the gradient is zero.

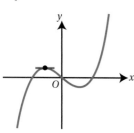
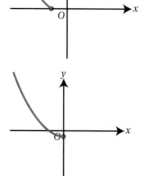
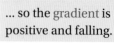

The curve is now decreasing...

... so the gradient is negative.

Continues on next page ...

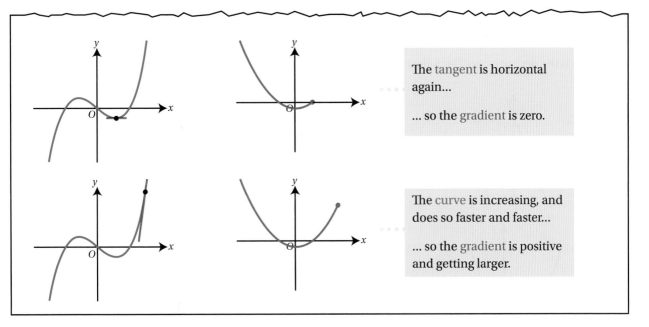

The tangent is horizontal again...

... so the gradient is zero.

The curve is increasing, and does so faster and faster...

... so the gradient is positive and getting larger.

The relationship between the graph of a function and its derivative can be summarised as follows:

🔑 Key point 13.2

- When the graph is **increasing** the gradient is positive.
- When the graph is **decreasing** the gradient is negative.
- When the tangent is horizontal the gradient is zero. A point on the graph where this happens is called a **stationary point**.

▶▶ Fast forward

You will examine stationary points in detail in Chapter 14.

WORKED EXAMPLE 13.2

The diagram shows the graph of the gradient function f'(x).

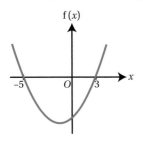

a   Is the function f(x) increasing or decreasing at the point $x = 2$?

b   The graph of $y = f(x)$ has two stationary points. Write down their x-coordinates.

a    The function f(x) is decreasing.

   The gradient is negative at $x = 2$.

b $x = -5$ and $x = 3$.

   Stationary points occur where the gradient is zero, which is where the graph of $y = f'(x)$ crosses the x-axis.

EXERCISE 13A

1 Sketch the derivatives of the following functions, showing any intercepts with the x-axis.

a i

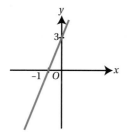

ii

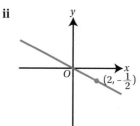

b i

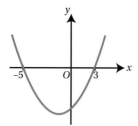

ii

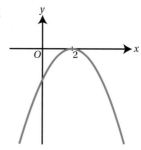

c i

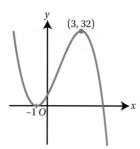

ii

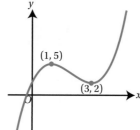

d i

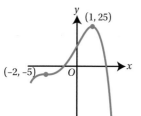

ii

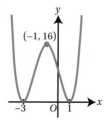

e i

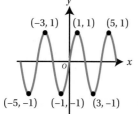

ii

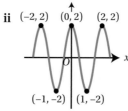

f i

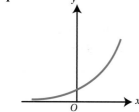

ii

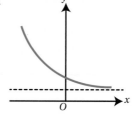

2 Each of the following represents a graph of a function's derivative. Sketch a possible graph for the original function, indicating any stationary points.

a
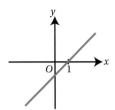

b
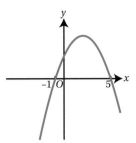

c
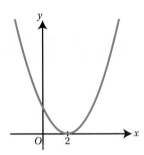

d
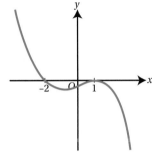

3 Decide whether each of the following statements is true or false. For the statements that are false, give a counter example.

a At a point where the derivative is positive the original function is positive.

b If the original function is negative then the derivative is also negative.

c The derivative crossing the axis corresponds to a stationary point on the graph.

d When the derivative is zero the graph is at a local maximum or minimum point.

e If the derivative function is always positive then part of the original function is above the x-axis.

f At the lowest value of the original function the derivative is zero.

Section 2: Differentiation from first principles

The line segment between two points on a curve is called a **chord**.

The diagram shows the chord PQ. You can see that the closer the point Q is to P, the closer the gradient of the chord is to the gradient of the tangent at P.

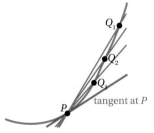

> ◀◀ **Rewind**
>
> Remember that in Section 1, the gradient of a curve at a given point was defined as the gradient of the tangent to the curve at that point.

You can use this idea to find the gradient of a function at a given point, P.

For example, to find the gradient to $y = x^2$ at the point P where $x = 3$, consider a chord from P to the point Q with a slightly larger x-coordinate, $x = 3 + h$.

The gradient of the chord, m, is:

$$m = \frac{y_2 - y_1}{x_2 - x_1}$$

$$= \frac{(3+h)^2 - 9}{(3+h) - 3}$$

$$= \frac{9 + 6h + h^2 - 9}{h}$$

$$= \frac{6h + h^2}{h}$$

$$= 6 + h$$

Tip

The letter h just denotes a small distance.

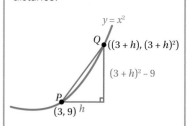

If the point Q now approaches P, then h tends to 0 and so m tends to 6

Therefore, you can say that when $x = 3$, the gradient of $y = x^2$ is 6.

To denote this idea of the distance h approaching zero, use $\lim\limits_{h \to 0}$ which reads as 'the limit as h tends to 0'.

The process of finding $\lim\limits_{h \to 0}$ of the gradient of the chord is called **differentiation from first principles**.

This method can be used to find the gradient at a general point on any function $f(x)$:

Did you know?

The credit for developing calculus in the 17th century is usually given to Gottfried Leibniz and Isaac Newton. However, there is evidence that the idea of considering small changes in the value of a function had been used many centuries earlier.

Key point 13.3

$$f'(x) = \lim_{h \to 0} \frac{f(x+h) - f(x)}{h}$$

The expression $f'(x)$ is called the **derivative** of $f(x)$. It can also be denoted as f', y' or $\dfrac{dy}{dx}$ where $y = f(x)$. So, in this example, we can write $f'(3) = 6$, or $\dfrac{dy}{dx} = 6$ when $x = 3$.

The process of finding the derivative is called **differentiation**.

You can use this definition to find the derivative of simple polynomial functions.

Tip

'Differentiation from first principles' means finding the derivative using this definition, rather than any of the rules you will meet in the later sections.

WORKED EXAMPLE 13.3

Prove, using differentiation from first principles, that for $f(x) = x^2 + x$, $f'(x) = 2x + 1$.

$$f'(x) = \lim_{h \to 0} \frac{f(x+h) - f(x)}{h}$$

$$= \lim_{h \to 0} \frac{(x+h)^2 + (x+h) - (x^2 + x)}{h}$$

Use the formula with $f(x) = x^2 + x$, so that $f(x+h) = (x+h)^2 + (x+h)$.

Continues on next page ...

$$= \lim_{h \to 0} \frac{x^2 + 2xh + h^2 + x + h - x^2 - x}{h}$$

Expand $(x+h)^2$ and simplify the expression.

$$= \lim_{h \to 0} \frac{2xh + h^2 + h}{h}$$

$$= \lim_{h \to 0} (2x + h + 1)$$

Then divide top and bottom by h.

$$= 2x + 1$$

Finally, let $h \to 0$.

EXERCISE 13B

1 Prove from first principles that the derivative of the function $f(x) = 8$ is zero.

2 Let $f(x) = -4x$.

Use differentiation from first principles to find $f'(x)$.

3 Let $y = 3x^2$.

Find $\dfrac{dy}{dx}$ from first principles.

4 Using differentiation from first principles, prove that the derivative of $x^2 + 1$ is $2x$.

5 Differentiate $f(x) = x^2 - 6x$ from first principles.

6 Let $y = x^2 - 3x + 4$.

Using differentiation from first principles, find y'.

7 **a** Expand $(x + h)^3$.

b Hence find from first principles the derivative of $y = x^3$.

8 $f(x) = 3x^3 + 2$.

Find $f'(x)$ from first principles.

9 **a** Expand $(x + h)^4$.

b Hence prove from first principles that if $f(x) = x^4$, then $f'(x) = 4x^3$.

10 A curve has equation $y = 4x^3$. Points A and B lie on the curve and have x-coordinates a and $a + h$, respectively.

a Find and simplify an expression, in terms of a and h, for the gradient of the chord AB.

b Find, in terms of a, the limit of this gradient when h tends to zero.

c What does your answer to part **b** represent?

11 If k is a constant, prove that the derivative of $kf(x)$ is $kf'(x)$.

12 If $y = f(x) + g(x)$, prove that $y' = f'(x) + g'(x)$.

Elevate

For more challenging questions on differentiation from first principles, see Extension sheet 13.

Section 3: Rules of differentiation

In the previous exercise (questions 7 and 9) you found that the derivative of x^3 is $3x^2$, and that the derivative of x^4 is $4x^3$. This suggests a general rule for differentiating functions of the form $y = x^n$.

> **Key point 13.4**
>
> If $y = x^n$ then: $\qquad\qquad \dfrac{dy}{dx} = nx^{n-1}$

> **Fast forward**
>
> **A** In Student Book 2 you will use a method called 'implicit differentiation' to extend this proof to all rational powers.

The result in Key point 13.2 is proved here for positive integers using differentiation from first principles, but the result is true (and you will need to use it) for **all** rational powers – positive and negative.

PROOF 8

$\dfrac{dy}{dx} = \lim\limits_{h \to 0} \dfrac{(x+h)^n - x^n}{h}$

Use the formula with $f(x) = x^n$.

$= \lim\limits_{h \to 0} \dfrac{x^n + \binom{n}{1}x^{n-1}h + \binom{n}{2}x^{n-2}h^2 + \ldots + h^n - x^n}{h}$

Expand $(x+h)^n$ using the binomial expansion.

$= \lim\limits_{h \to 0} \dfrac{\binom{n}{1}x^{n-1}h + \binom{n}{2}x^{n-2}h^2 + \ldots + h^n}{h}$

Simplify...

$= \lim\limits_{h \to 0} \left[\binom{n}{1}x^{n-1} + \binom{n}{2}x^{n-2}h + \ldots + h^{n-1} \right]$

and then divide top and bottom by h.

$= \binom{n}{1}x^{n-1}$

Let $h \to 0$.

$= nx^{n-1}$

$\binom{n}{1} = n$

WORKED EXAMPLE 13.4

Let $y = x^6$. Find $\dfrac{dy}{dx}$.

$\dfrac{dy}{dx} = 6x^{6-1}$

$\qquad = 6x^5$

Use $\dfrac{dy}{dx} = nx^{n-1}$.

WORKED EXAMPLE 13.5

For $y = x^{-5}$, find $\dfrac{dy}{dx}$.

$\dfrac{dy}{dx} = -5x^{-5-1}$ ⋯⋯⋯⋯⋯⋯⋯⋯⋯⋯⋯⋯⋯⋯ Use $\dfrac{dy}{dx} = nx^{n-1}$.

$= -5x^{-6}$

WORKED EXAMPLE 13.6

Differentiate $f(x) = x^{\frac{1}{4}}$.

$f'(x) = \dfrac{1}{4}x^{\frac{1}{4}-1}$ ⋯⋯⋯⋯⋯⋯⋯⋯⋯⋯⋯⋯⋯ Use $f'(x) = nx^{n-1}$.

$= \dfrac{1}{4}x^{-\frac{3}{4}}$

WORKED EXAMPLE 13.7

Find the derivative of $f(x) = x$.

$f(x) = 1x^{1-1}$ ⋯⋯⋯⋯⋯⋯⋯⋯⋯⋯⋯⋯⋯ Use $f'(x) = nx^{n-1}$.

$= x^0$

$= 1$ ⋯⋯⋯⋯⋯⋯⋯⋯⋯⋯⋯⋯⋯ Remember that $x^0 = 1$.

The results in Exercise 13B also suggest the properties of differentiation (they were in fact proved in questions 11 and 12).

Key point 13.5

- If $y = kf(x)$, where k is a constant, then $y' = kf'(x)$.
- If $y = f(x) + g(x)$, then $y' = f'(x) + g'(x)$.

Tip

Key point 13.5 just says that you can differentiate a function and then multiply by a constant, and that you can differentiate terms of a sum separately.

Explore

Some functions don't have derivatives at all points. For example, try finding the derivative of $y = \sqrt{x}$ at $x = 0$. Can you explain why this is the case by looking at the graph?

WORKED EXAMPLE 13.8

Find the derivative of $f(x) = 5x^3$.

$f'(x) = 5 \times 3x^2$ .... Differentiate x^3 and then multiply by 5.

$\qquad = 15x^2$

WORKED EXAMPLE 13.9

Find $\dfrac{dy}{dx}$ for $y = 8$.

$y = 8x^0$ .... Using the fact that $x^0 = 1$ you can write $y = 8$ as $y = 8x^0$.

$\dfrac{dy}{dx} = 8 \times 0x^{0-1}$ .... Now you can apply $\dfrac{dy}{dx} = nx^{n-1}$.

$\qquad = 0$ .... As 0 is now a factor, the whole expression is zero.

From Worked example 13.9 you can see that the derivative of the function $f(x) = c$ for any constant c will always be zero. This corresponds to the fact that the gradient of the horizontal line $y = c$ is zero everywhere.

 Tip

You do not need to write out $c = cx^0$ every time you differentiate $y = c$. You just need to know that the derivative will always be zero.

WORKED EXAMPLE 13.10

A curve has equation $y = x^4 - 4x^{\frac{1}{2}} + 5x - 3$. Find $\dfrac{dy}{dx}$.

$\dfrac{dy}{dx} = 4x^3 - 4 \times \dfrac{1}{2}x^{-\frac{1}{2}} + 5$ .... Differentiate each term separately. Remember that the derivative of a constant is zero, so the -3 vanishes.

$\qquad = 4x^3 - 2x^{-\frac{1}{2}} + 5$

EXERCISE 13C

1 Differentiate the following:

a **i** $y = x^4$ **ii** $y = x^6$

b **i** $y = 3x^7$ **ii** $y = -4x^5$

c **i** $y = -x$ **ii** $y = 3x$

d **i** $y = 10$ **ii** $y = -3$

e **i** $y = \dfrac{1}{3}x^6$ **ii** $y = -\dfrac{3}{4}x^2$

f **i** $y = 4x^3 - 5x^2 + 2x - 8$ **ii** $y = 2x^4 + 3x^3 - x$

g **i** $y = 7x - \dfrac{x^3}{2}$ **ii** $y = 2 - 5x^4 + \dfrac{x^5}{5}$

2 Find $f'(x)$ for the following functions:

a **i** $f(x) = x^{\frac{3}{2}}$ **ii** $f(x) = x^{\frac{2}{3}}$

b **i** $f(x) = 8x^{\frac{1}{2}}$ **ii** $f(x) = 6x^{\frac{4}{3}}$

c **i** $f(x) = \dfrac{4}{9}x^{\frac{3}{4}}$ **ii** $f(x) = \dfrac{3}{5}x^{\frac{5}{6}}$

d **i** $f(x) = 3x^4 - 15x^{\frac{2}{5}} - 2$ **ii** $f(x) = x^3 - \dfrac{3}{5}x^{\frac{5}{3}} + \dfrac{4}{3}x^{\frac{1}{2}}$

e **i** $f(x) = x^{-1}$ **ii** $f(x) = x^{-3}$

f **i** $f(x) = x^{-\frac{1}{2}}$ **ii** $f(x) = x^{-\frac{2}{3}}$

g **i** $f(x) = -6x^{-\frac{4}{3}}$ **ii** $f(x) = -8x^{-\frac{3}{4}}$

h **i** $f(x) = 5x - \dfrac{8x^{-\frac{5}{2}}}{15}$ **ii** $f(x) = -\dfrac{7x^{-\frac{3}{7}}}{3} + \dfrac{4x^{-6}}{3}$

3 Find $\dfrac{dy}{dx}$ for the following:

a **i** $y = 4x^{2.7}$ **ii** $y = 3x^{3.5}$

b **i** $y = 5x^{0.6}$ **ii** $y = -3x^{0.4}$

c **i** $y = -2x^{-0.7}$ **ii** $y = 4x^{-1.5}$

4 A curve has equation $y = x^2 - 3x^{\frac{1}{2}} + 5$. Find $\dfrac{dy}{dx}$.

5 Given $f(x) = 4x^3 - 3x^2 + 2x^{-\frac{3}{2}}$, find $f'(x)$.

6 Find the derivative of the function $f(x) = 12x^{-\frac{1}{3}} + \dfrac{5x^{\frac{2}{5}}}{6}$.

Section 4: Simplifying into terms of the form ax^n

Notice that there is no rule in Key point 13.5 for differentiating products of functions, $y = f(x)g(x)$, or quotients of functions, $y = \dfrac{f(x)}{g(x)}$.

Before these can be differentiated, they need to be converted into terms of the form ax^n. This is often done by using the laws of indices.

▶▶ **Fast forward**

Ⓐ Some expressions cannot be simplified using laws of indices. In Student Book 2 you will learn different rules for differentiating products and quotients.

WORKED EXAMPLE 13.11

$y = (x + 2)(x - 5)$. Find $\dfrac{dy}{dx}$.

$y = (x + 2)(x - 5)$

$= x^2 - 3x - 10$ | Expand the brackets.

$\dfrac{dy}{dx} = 2x - 3$ | Then differentiate.

◀◀ **Rewind**

If you need to review the laws of indices, see Chapter 2.

WORKED EXAMPLE 13.12

A curve has equation $y = \dfrac{1}{x^3}$. Find y'.

$y = \dfrac{1}{x^3}$

$= x^{-3}$ | First rewrite the function in the form x^n using the laws of indices.

$y' = -3x^{-4}$ | Then differentiate.

WORKED EXAMPLE 13.13

Find the derivative of $f(x) = x^2 \sqrt{x}$.

$f(x) = x^2 \sqrt{x}$

$= x^2 x^{\frac{1}{2}}$ | First rewrite the function in the form x^n using the laws of indices.

$= x^{2 + \frac{1}{2}}$

$= x^{\frac{5}{2}}$

$f'(x) = \dfrac{5}{2} x^{\frac{5}{2} - 1}$ | Then differentiate.

$= \dfrac{5}{2} x^{\frac{3}{2}}$

WORKED EXAMPLE 13.14

Differentiate $y = \dfrac{2x-6}{\sqrt{x}}$.

$y = \dfrac{2x-6}{\sqrt{x}}$ .... You need to write this as a sum of terms of the form x^n.

$ = \dfrac{2x-6}{x^{\frac{1}{2}}}$

$ = 2x^{1-\frac{1}{2}} - 6x^{-\frac{1}{2}}$

$ = 2x^{\frac{1}{2}} - 6x^{-\frac{1}{2}}$

$y' = 2 \times \dfrac{1}{2}x^{\frac{1}{2}-1} - 6\left(-\dfrac{1}{2}\right)x^{-\frac{1}{2}-1}$ .... Now differentiate each term separately.

$ = x^{-\frac{1}{2}} + 3x^{-\frac{3}{2}}$

WORK IT OUT 13.1

Three students' attempts to differentiate $f(x) = \dfrac{x^2 - 3x}{x^3}$ are shown.

Which is the correct solution? Can you identify the errors made in the incorrect solutions?

Solution 1	Solution 2	Solution 3
$f(x) = \dfrac{x^2 - 3x}{x^3}$	$f(x) = \dfrac{x^2 - 3x}{x^3}$	$f(x) = \dfrac{x^2 - 3x}{x^3}$
$f'(x) = \dfrac{2x - 3}{3x^2}$	$= x^{-1} - 3x^{-2}$	$= x^{-3}\left(x^2 - 3x\right)$
	$f'(x) = -x^{-2} + 6x^{-3}$	$f'(x) = -3x^{-4}\left(2x - 3\right)$

EXERCISE 13D

1 Find $\dfrac{dy}{dx}$ for the following:

   a **i** $y = \sqrt[3]{x}$ **ii** $y = \sqrt[5]{x}$

   b **i** $y = 8\sqrt[4]{x}$ **ii** $y = \dfrac{\sqrt{x}}{3}$

   c **i** $y = -\dfrac{1}{x}$ **ii** $y = \dfrac{1}{x^4}$

   d **i** $y = \dfrac{3}{x^2}$ **ii** $y = -\dfrac{2}{5x^{10}}$

e **i** $y = \dfrac{1}{\sqrt{x}}$ **ii** $y = \dfrac{1}{\sqrt[3]{x}}$

f **i** $y = -\dfrac{10}{\sqrt[5]{x}}$ **ii** $y = \dfrac{8}{3\sqrt[4]{x}}$

2 Find $f'(x)$ for the following:

a **i** $f(x) = (2x - 3)(x + 4)$ **ii** $f(x) = 3x(x - 5)$

b **i** $f(x) = \sqrt{x}(4x + 3)$ **ii** $f(x) = \sqrt[3]{x}(x - 1)$

c **i** $f(x) = \left(\sqrt{x} + 2x\right)^2$ **ii** $f(x) = \left(\sqrt[4]{x} - 4\right)^2$

d **i** $f(x) = \left(x + \dfrac{1}{x}\right)^2$ **ii** $f(x) = \left(x + \dfrac{2}{x}\right)\left(x - \dfrac{2}{x}\right)$

3 Differentiate the following:

a **i** $f(x) = \dfrac{3x - 2}{x}$ **ii** $f(x) = \dfrac{1 + 4x^2}{2x}$

b **i** $f(x) = \dfrac{\sqrt{x} - 3}{x^2}$ **ii** $f(x) = \dfrac{x^2 + 4}{\sqrt{x}}$

4 Differentiate $y = x^2(3x - 4)$.

5 A curve has equation $y = 2\sqrt{x}\left(x^3 + 4\right)$. Find y'.

6 $y = \sqrt[5]{x^4}$. Find $\dfrac{dy}{dx}$.

7 Find the derivative of the function $f(x) = \dfrac{8}{3\sqrt[4]{x^3}}$.

8 A curve has equation $y = \dfrac{3x^5 - 2x}{x^2}$.

a Express $y = \dfrac{3x^5 - 2x}{x^2}$ in the form $y = ax^p + bx^q$.

b Hence find $\dfrac{dy}{dx}$.

9 $f(x) = \dfrac{(x + 1)(x + 9)}{x}$

Show that $f'(x) = \dfrac{(x - 3)(x + 3)}{x^2}$.

10 $f(x) = \dfrac{9x^2 + 3}{2\sqrt[3]{x}}$. Find $f'(x)$.

11 Find the derivative of the curve $y = \dfrac{\left(2\sqrt{x} - 3\right)^2}{\sqrt{x^3}}$.

Section 5: Interpreting derivatives and second derivatives

The derivative $\dfrac{dy}{dx}$ has two related interpretations:

- It is the gradient of the graph of y against x.
- It measures how fast y changes when x is changed – this is called the **rate of change** of y with respect to x.

To calculate the gradient (or the rate of change) at any particular point, you simply substitute the value of x into the equation for the derivative.

 Tip

Your calculator may be able to find the gradient at a given point, but it cannot give you the expression for the derivative.

WORKED EXAMPLE 13.15

Find the gradient of the graph $y = 4x^3$ at the point where $x = 2$.

$\dfrac{dy}{dx} = 12x^2$	The gradient is given by the derivative, so find $\dfrac{dy}{dx}$.
When $x = 2$, $\dfrac{dy}{dx} = 12 \times 2^2 = 48$	Substitute the given value for x.
So the gradient is 48.	

If you know the gradient of a graph at a particular point, you can find the value of x at that point. This involves solving an equation.

WORKED EXAMPLE 13.16

Find the values of x for which the graph of $y = x^3 - 7x + 1$ has gradient 5.

$\dfrac{dy}{dx} = 3x^2 - 7$	The gradient is given by the derivative.
$\dfrac{dy}{dx} = 5$ $3x^2 - 7 = 5$	You know that $\dfrac{dy}{dx} = 5$ so you can form an equation.
$3x^2 = 12$	
$x^2 = 4$	
$x = 2$ or -2	

Increasing and decreasing functions

The sign of the gradient at a point tells you whether the function is increasing or decreasing at that point.

🔍 Key point 13.6

- If $\dfrac{dy}{dx}$ is positive the function is increasing – as x gets larger, so does y.
- If $\dfrac{dy}{dx}$ is negative the function is decreasing – as x gets larger, y gets smaller.

⏩ **Fast forward**

In Chapter 14 you will find out what happens when $\dfrac{dy}{dx} = 0$.

A function can increase on some intervals and decrease on others.

WORKED EXAMPLE 13.17

Find the range of values of x for which the function $f(x) = 2x^3 - 6x$ is decreasing.

$f'(x) = 6x^2 - 6$ .... First find the derivative.

$f'(x) < 0$

$6x^2 - 6 < 0$ .... A decreasing function has negative gradient.

$6(x^2 - 1) < 0$ .... This is a quadratic inequality. To solve it, first sketch the graph.

$6(x - 1)(x + 1) < 0$

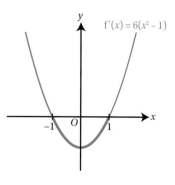

$\therefore -1 < x < 1$ .... The graph is below the x-axis between the two intercepts.

Some functions increase (or decrease) for all values of x.

⏪ **Rewind**

See Chapter 3 for a reminder of quadratic inequalities.

WORKED EXAMPLE 13.18

Show that the function $f(x) = 3x^3 + 5x$ is increasing for all x.

$f'(x) = 9x^2 + 5$ .... The derivative tells us whether a function is increasing or decreasing.

Since $x^2 \geqslant 0$, $f'(x) > 0$ for all x. .... Squares can never be negative.

Hence $f(x)$ is always increasing. .... Positive derivative means that the function is increasing.

WORK IT OUT 13.2

Is the function $f(x) = 5x - 3x^2$ increasing or decreasing at $x = -2$?

Which is the correct solution? Can you identify the errors made in the incorrect solutions?

Solution 1	Solution 2	Solution 3
$f(-2) = 5(-2) - 3(-2^2)$	$f'(x) = 5 - 6x$	$f'(x) = 5 - 6x$
$= -10 + 12$	$f'(-2) = 5 + 12 = 17 > 0$	When $x = -2$:
$= 2 > 0$	So it is increasing.	$5 - 12 = -7 < 0$
So it is increasing.		So it is decreasing.

There is nothing special about the variables y and x, and any letters could be used. To emphasise which variables you are using, you call $\dfrac{dy}{dx}$ the derivative of y with respect to x.

WORKED EXAMPLE 13.19

Given that $a = \sqrt{S}$, find the positive rate of change of a with respect to S when $S = 9$.

$a = S^{\frac{1}{2}}$ — The rate of change is given by the derivative.

$\dfrac{da}{dS} = \dfrac{1}{2}S^{-\frac{1}{2}}$

$= \dfrac{1}{2\sqrt{S}}$

When $S = 9$:

$\dfrac{da}{dS} = \dfrac{1}{2\sqrt{9}} = \dfrac{1}{6}$ — Substitute the given value for S.

Higher derivatives

Since the derivative $\dfrac{dy}{dx}$ is itself a function of x, you can differentiate it with respect to x. The result is called the **second derivative**.

The second derivative is the derivative of $\dfrac{dy}{dx}$ and is given the symbol $\dfrac{d^2y}{dx^2}$ or $f''(x)$. It measures the rate of change of the gradient.

You can differentiate again to find the third derivative $\left(\dfrac{d^3y}{dx^3}\text{ or }f'''(x)\right)$, fourth derivative $\left(\dfrac{d^4y}{dx^4}\text{ or }f^{(4)}(x)\right)$, and so on.

WORKED EXAMPLE 13.20

Let $f(x) = 5x^3 - 4x$.

a Find $f''(x)$.

b Find the rate of change of the gradient of the graph of $y = f(x)$ at the point where $x = -1$.

c Show that, when $x = 0.1$, the graph of $y = f(x)$ is decreasing, but its gradient is increasing. Hence sketch the graph of $y = f(x)$ near $x = 0.1$.

a $f'(x) = 15x^2 - 4$

  $f''(x) = 30x$

> Differentiate $f(x)$ and then differentiate the result.

b $f''(-1) = -30$

> The rate of change of the gradient means the second derivative.

c $f'(0.1) = 15 \times 0.1^2 - 4$

  $= -3.85 < 0$

> A decreasing function has a negative gradient.

So the function is decreasing.

$f''(0.1) = 30 \times 0.1 = 3 > 0$

So the gradient is increasing.

> The rate of change of gradient is $f''(0.1)$. If this is positive, the gradient is increasing.

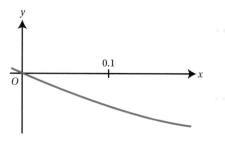

> $f(x)$ is decreasing, which means that the graph is going down (looking from left to right).

> The gradient is increasing, but it is negative. This means that it is getting less negative, and so the graph is becoming less steep.

EXERCISE 13E

1 Write the following rates of change as derivatives.

a The rate of change of z as t changes.

b The rate of change of Q with respect to P.

c How fast R changes when m is changed.

d How quickly the volume of a balloon (V) changes over time (t).

e The rate of increase of the cost of apples (y) as the mass of the apple (x) increases.

f The rate of change of the rate of change of z as y changes.

g The second derivative of H with respect to m.

2 a i If $f = 5x^{\frac{1}{3}}$ what is the derivative of f with respect to x?

    ii If $p = 3q^5$ what is the derivative of p with respect to q?

b **i** Differentiate $d = 3t + 7t^{-1}$ with respect to t.

    ii Differentiate $r = c + \frac{1}{c}$ with respect to c.

c **i** Find the second derivative of $y = 9x^2 + x^3$ with respect to x.

    ii Find the second derivative of $z = \frac{3}{t}$ with respect to t.

3 **a** **i** If $y = 5x^2$ find $\frac{dy}{dx}$ when $x = 3$.

    ii If $y = x^3 + \frac{1}{x}$ find $\frac{dy}{dx}$ when $x = 1.5$.

  b **i** If $A = 7b + 3$ find $\frac{dA}{db}$ when $b = -1$.

    ii If $\Phi = \theta^2 + \theta^{-3}$ find $\frac{d\Phi}{d\theta}$ when $\theta = 0.1$.

  c **i** Find the gradient of the graph of $A = x^3$ when $x = 2$.

    ii Find the gradient of the tangent to the graph of $z = 2a + a^2$ when $a = -6$.

> **Tip**
>
> Φ is the Greek letter phi. This is the capital form of the letter.

  d **i** How quickly does $f = 4T^2$ change as T changes when $T = 3$?

    ii How quickly does $g = y^4$ change as y changes when $y = 2$?

  e **i** What is the rate of increase of W with respect to p when p is -3 if $W = -p^2$?

    ii What is the rate of change of L with respect to c when $c = 6$ if $L = 7\sqrt{c} - 8$?

4 **a** **i** If $y = ax^2 + (1 - a)x$ where a is a constant, find $\frac{dy}{dx}$.

    ii If $y = x^3 + b^2$ where b is a constant, find $\frac{dy}{dx}$.

  b **i** If $Q = \sqrt{ab} + \sqrt{b}$ where b is a constant, find $\frac{dQ}{da}$.

    ii If $D = 3(av)^2$ where a is a constant, find $\frac{dD}{dv}$.

5 **a** **i** If $y = x^3 - 5x$ find $\frac{d^2y}{dx^2}$ when $x = 9$.

    ii If $y = 8 + 2x^4$ find $\frac{d^2y}{dx^2}$ when $x = 4$.

  b **i** If $S = 3A^2 + \frac{1}{A}$ find $\frac{d^2S}{dA^2}$ when $A = 1$.

    ii If $J = v - \sqrt{v}$ find $\frac{d^2J}{dv^2}$ when $v = 9$.

  c **i** Find the second derivative of B with respect to n if $B = 8n$ and $n = 2$.

    ii Find the second derivative of g with respect to r if $g = r^7$ and $r = 1$.

6 **a** **i** If $y = 3x^3$ find x at the point where $\frac{dy}{dx} = 36$.

    ii If $y = x^4 + 2x$ find x at the point where $\frac{dy}{dx} = 6$.

b i If $y = 2x + \dfrac{8}{x}$ find y at the point where $\dfrac{dy}{dx} = -30$.

ii If $y = \sqrt{x} + 3$ find y at the point where $\dfrac{dy}{dx} = \dfrac{1}{6}$.

c i If $y = 3x^3$ find x at the point where $\dfrac{d^2y}{dx^2} = -54$.

ii If $y = \dfrac{2}{x}$ find x at the point where $\dfrac{d^2y}{dx^2} = \dfrac{1}{2}$.

7 a i Find the interval in which $x^2 - x$ is an increasing function.

ii Find the interval in which $x^2 + 2x - 5$ is a decreasing function.

b i Find the range of values of x for which $x^3 - 3x$ is an increasing function.

ii Find the range of values of x for which $x^3 + 2x^2 - 5$ is a decreasing function.

c i Find the interval in which the gradient of $y = x^3 - 3x$ is decreasing.

ii Find the interval in which the gradient of $y = 2x^3 - x^2$ is increasing.

8 a Find the rate of change of $y = \dfrac{3}{\sqrt{x}}$ at the point where $x = 9$.

b Is the gradient increasing or decreasing at this point?

9 Find the rate of change of the gradient of $f(x) = \sqrt{x} + \dfrac{1}{x}$ when $x = 4$.

10 Find the range of values of x for which the function $y = 3x^3 - 4x + 1$ is decreasing.

11 Find the values of x for which the graph of $\dfrac{1}{3}x^3 - x^2 - 12x + 1$ has gradient 3.

12 Find the x-coordinates of the points on the curve $y = x^4 - 12x^2 + 3x - 1$ where $\dfrac{d^2y}{dx^2} = 0$.

13 Show that $y = x^3 + kx + c$ is always increasing if $k > 0$.

14 Find all points of the graph of $y = x^2 - 2x + 1$ where the gradient equals the y-coordinate.

15 Find the range of x-values for which $f(x) = x^3 - 6x^2 + 5$ is an increasing function.

16 The function $f(x) = 12x - 2x^2 - \dfrac{1}{3}x^3$ is increasing for $a < x < b$. Find the constants a and b.

17 Find the interval in which the gradient of the graph of $y = 7x - x^2 - x^3$ is decreasing.

18 In what interval is the gradient of the graph $y = \dfrac{1}{4}x^4 + x^3 - \dfrac{1}{2}x^2 - 3x + 6$ decreasing?

19 Find the range of values of x for which the function $f(x) = x^3 - 6x^2 + 9x + 2$ is decreasing but its gradient is increasing.

20 Find an alternative expression for $\dfrac{d^n}{dx^n}(x^n)$.

Elevate

For more practice of increasing and decreasing functions see Support sheet 13.

Checklist of learning and understanding

- The gradient (or the derivative) of a function at the point P is the gradient of the tangent to the function's graph at that point.
- To find the derivative of a function you differentiate.
    - Differentiation from first principles:
    $$f'(x)=\lim_{h\to 0}\frac{f(x+h)-f(x)}{h}$$
    - If $f(x) = ax^n$, then $f'(x) = anx^{n-1}$.

    - The derivative of a sum is the sum of the derivatives of each term.
- The derivative at a point tells you the rate of change of the y-coordinate at that point.
- You can use the derivative to tell whether a function is increasing or decreasing:
    - If $\frac{dy}{dx}>0$ the function is increasing.

    - If $\frac{dy}{dx}<0$ the function is decreasing.
- The second derivative, $\frac{d^2y}{dx^2}$, gives you the rate of change of gradient.

Mixed practice 13

1 Find the gradient function of $f(x) = \dfrac{3x-2}{\sqrt{x}}$.

2 A curve has equation $y = (4x^2 - 1)(3 - x)$. Find $\dfrac{dy}{dx}$.

3 $f(x) = \dfrac{x^2 - 4}{2x}$. Find $f''(2)$.

4 Given that $f(x) = 3\sqrt{x} - \dfrac{2}{\sqrt{x}}$ find:

   a $f'(x)$

   b the gradient of the graph of $y = f(x)$ at the point where $x = 4$.

5 $f(x) = x^2 + bx + c$. If $f(1) = 2$ and $f'(2) = 12$ find the values of b and c.

6 **a** Find the gradient of the curve $y = 3\sqrt{x} - 2$ at the point where it crosses the x-axis.

   b Is the curve increasing or decreasing at this point? Give a reason for your answer.

7 Find the range of values of x for which the function $y = 3x^2 - 4x$ is increasing.

8 Find the rate of change of the gradient of $y = x^2 - 2\sqrt{x}$ at the point where $x = 9$.

9 Given that $y = \dfrac{5}{x^2} - \dfrac{1}{4x} + x$, find:

   i $\dfrac{dy}{dx}$,   **ii** $\dfrac{d^2y}{dx^2}$.

© OCR, AS GCE Mathematics, Paper 4721, January 2011

10 $y = x^2 + ax - 7$ is increasing for $x > 5$. Find a.

11 What is the rate of change of the gradient of $y = x^3 + 4x^2 - 2x + 1$ at $x = \tfrac{1}{2}$?

12 This graph shows the gradient function, $f'(x)$, of a function $f(x)$. Which of the following is definitely true at the point A?

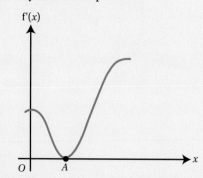

  A $f(x)$ has a minimum   **B** $f(x)$ has a maximum   **C** $f(x) = 0$ **D** $f''(x) = 0$

13 The diagram shows part of the curve $y = x^2 + 5$. The point A has coordinates $(1, 6)$. The point B has coordinates $(a, a^2 + 5)$, where a is a constant greater than 1. The point C is on the curve between A and B.

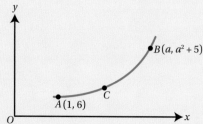

i   Find by differentiation the value of the gradient of the curve at the point A.

ii The line segment joining the points A and B has gradient 2.3. Find the value of a.

iii State a possible value for the gradient of the line segment joining the points A and C.

© OCR, AS GCE Mathematics, Paper 4721, January 2010

14 Use differentiation from first principles to find $\dfrac{dy}{dx}$ for $y = x^3 - 5x$.

15 The diagram shows the graph of $y = f'(x)$.

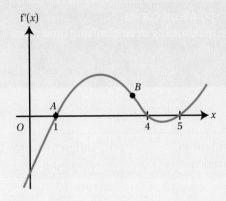

a   State the value of the gradient of the graph of $y = f(x)$ at the point marked A.

b   Is the function $f(x)$ increasing or decreasing at the point marked B?

c   Sketch the graph of $y = f(x)$.

16 Find the coordinates of the point on the curve $y = \sqrt{x} + 3x$ where the gradient is 5.

17 Find the gradient of the graph of $y = \dfrac{1}{2\sqrt{x}}$ at the point where the y-coordinate is 3.

18 $f(x) = ax^3 + bx^{-2}$ where a and b are constants. $f'(1) = 18$ and $f''(1) = 18$.
Find a and b.

19 $f(x) = \sqrt{x^3} + 15\sqrt{x}$
Find the values of x for which the gradient of $f(x)$ is 9.

20 Find the range of values of x for which the gradient of the graph $y = x^4 - 2x^2 + 3$ is decreasing.

14 Applications of differentiation

In this chapter you will learn how to:

- find the equations of tangents and normals to curves at given points
- find maximum and minimum points on curves
- solve problems which involve maximising or minimising quantities.

Before you start…

Chapter 13	You should know how to differentiate functions involving x^n.	1	Differentiate the following: a $\dfrac{3x^4 - 2}{5x^2}$ b $\dfrac{3}{2\sqrt{x}}$
Chapter 13	You should know how to evaluate second derivatives.	2	Given that $y = \dfrac{3}{2x^2}$ evaluate $\dfrac{d^2y}{dx^2}$ when $x = -2$.
Chapter 6	You should know how to find the equation of a straight line.	3	Find the equation of the line through the point $(-2, 1)$ with gradient 3.
Chapter 6	You should know how to find the equation of a perpendicular to a line.	4	Find the equation of the perpendicular to the line with gradient $\dfrac{3}{4}$ that passes through the point $(2, -3)$.

Where can you use differentiation?

You can apply the techniques from the Chapter 13 to solve a variety of problems. You will first look at graphs of functions, learning how to find equations of tangents and normals. These have applications in mechanics when studying collisions, as well in pure mathematics when defining 'curvature' of a graph. You will then turn to finding coordinates of maximum and minimum points and solving practical problems where you need to minimise or maximise quantities, such as production costs.

Section 1: Tangents and normals

The **normal** to a curve at a given point is a straight line that crosses the curve at that point and is perpendicular to the tangent.

You know from the previous chapter that the gradient of the tangent at a point is the value of the curve's gradient at that point; this can be found by substituting the value of x into the equation for the derivative $\dfrac{dy}{dx}$.

The gradient of the normal can then be found by using the fact that if two lines with gradients m_1 and m_2 are perpendicular, then $m_1 m_2 = -1$.

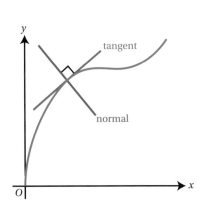

Once you have the gradient you can use it, together with the coordinates of the point, to find the equations of the tangent and normal.

 Rewind

See Chapter 6, Section 1 for a reminder of how to find the equation of the line with a given point and gradient.

WORKED EXAMPLE 14.1

A curve has equation $y = x^3 - 5x^2 - x^{\frac{3}{2}} + 22$.

Find the equations of:

a   the tangent   b   the normal

to the curve at the point $(4, -2)$.

In each case give your answer in the form $ax + by + c = 0$ where a, b, c are integers.

a $y' = 3x^2 - 10x - \dfrac{3}{2}x^{\frac{1}{2}}$ First find y'.

   At $x = 4$,   Then evaluate the derivative at $x = 4$.
   This will give the gradient of the tangent at $x = 4$.

   $y' = 3(4)^2 - 10(4) - \dfrac{3}{2}(4)^{\frac{1}{2}}$

   $= 48 - 40 - 3$

   $= 5$

   Equation of the tangent: Use $y - y_1 = m(x - x_1)$ to find the equation of the straight line with gradient 5, passing through $(4, -2)$.

   $y - (-2) = 5(x - 4)$

   $y + 2 = 5x - 20$

   $5x - y - 22 = 0$

b   Gradient of the normal: Find the gradient of the normal, using $m_1 m_2 = -1$.

   $m_n = \dfrac{-1}{5}$

   Equation of the normal: Use the equation of the line again. The coordinates of the point are the same, but now use the gradient of the normal.

   $y - (-2) = \dfrac{-1}{5}(x - 4)$

   $5y + 10 = -x + 4$

   $x + 5y + 6 = 0$

The procedure for finding the equations of tangents and normals is summarised in Key point 14.1.

Key point 14.1

For the point on the curve $y = f(x)$ with $x = a$:

- the gradient of the tangent is $f'(a)$
- the gradient of the normal is $-\dfrac{1}{f'(a)}$
- the coordinates of the point are $x_1 = a$, $y_1 = f(a)$.

To find the equation of the tangent or the normal, use $y - y_1 = m(x - x_1)$ with the appropriate gradient.

Harder questions may give you some information about the tangent and require you to find other information.

WORKED EXAMPLE 14.2

The tangent at point P on the curve $y = x^2 + 1$ passes through the origin. Find the possible coordinates of P.

Let P have coordinates (p, q) .... You want to find the equation of the tangent at P, but you don't know the coordinates.

Then $q = p^2 + 1$ .... As P lies on the curve, (p, q) must satisfy $y = x^2 + 1$.

$\dfrac{dy}{dx} = 2x$ .... The gradient of the tangent is given by $\dfrac{dy}{dx}$ when $x = p$.

When $x = p$:

$\dfrac{dy}{dx} = 2p$

$\therefore m = 2p$

Equation of the tangent: .... Write the equation of the tangent, remembering it passes through (p, q).

$y - q = 2p(x - p)$

$y - (p^2 + 1) = 2p(x - p)$

Passes through $(0, 0)$: .... The tangent passes through the origin, so set $x = 0$, $y = 0$.

$0 - (p^2 + 1) = 2p(0 - p)$

$-p^2 - 1 = -2p^2$

$p^2 = 1$

$p = 1 \text{ or} -1$

When $p = 1$, $q = 2$ .... Now use $q = p^2 + 1$ to find the corresponding values of q.

When $p = -1$, $q = 2$

So the coordinates of P are $(1, 2)$ or $(-1, 2)$.

 Tip

Notice that letters other than x and y are used for the unknown coordinates at the point P, as x and y will appear in the equation of the tangent, $y - y_1 = m(x - x_1)$.

WORK IT OUT 14.1

Find the equation of the normal to the curve $y = \dfrac{3}{x}$ at the point where $x = 2$.

Which is the correct solution? Can you identify the errors made in the incorrect solutions?

Solution 1	Solution 2	Solution 3
$\dfrac{dy}{dx} = -\dfrac{3}{x^2}$	$\dfrac{dy}{dx} = -\dfrac{3}{x^2}$	$\dfrac{dy}{dx} = -\dfrac{3}{x^2}$
$x = 2, m = -\dfrac{3}{2^2} = -\dfrac{3}{4}, y = \dfrac{3}{2}$	$x = 2, m = \dfrac{2^2}{3} = \dfrac{4}{3}, y = \dfrac{3}{2}$	so normal $m = \dfrac{x^2}{3}$
equation:	equation:	$x = 2, y = \dfrac{3}{2}$
$y - \dfrac{3}{2} = -\dfrac{3}{4}(x - 2)$	$y - \dfrac{3}{2} = \dfrac{4}{3}(x - 2)$	equation:
$3x + 4y = 12$	$8x - 6y = 7$	$y - \dfrac{3}{2} = \dfrac{x^2}{3}(x - 2)$
		$y = \dfrac{x^3}{3} - \dfrac{2}{3}x^2 + \dfrac{3}{2}$

WORKED EXAMPLE 14.3

The point P on the curve $y = \dfrac{a}{x}$ has x-coordinate 3. The normal to the curve at P is parallel to the line $x - 3y + 6 = 0$. Find the constant a.

Normal at P is parallel to:

$x - 3y + 6 = 0$

$$y = \frac{1}{3}x + 2$$

Rearrange the equation into the form $y = mx + c$ to find the gradient of the normal.

So, gradient of curve at P is

$m = -\dfrac{1}{\frac{1}{3}}$

$ = -3$

Find the gradient of the tangent at P using $m_1 m_2 = -1$.

$y = ax^{-1}$

$y' = -ax^{-2}$

The gradient of the curve is given by y'.

When $x = 3$,

$y' = -a(3)^{-2}$

$ = -\dfrac{a}{9}$

Evaluate at $x = 3$.

Therefore,

$-\dfrac{a}{9} = -3$

$a = 27$

The gradient of the tangent and the gradient of the curve at P are the same, so set them equal and solve for a.

EXERCISE 14A

1 Find the equation of the tangent and normal at the following points. In each case, give your answer in the form $ax + by + c = 0$.

   a **i** $y = 2x^2 - 4x$ at $(1, -2)$ **ii** $y = x^2 - 6x + 9$ at $(1, 24)$

   b **i** $y = \dfrac{3}{x}$ at $(-3, -1)$ **ii** $y = -\dfrac{6}{x^2}$ at $\left(2, -\dfrac{3}{2}\right)$

   c **i** $y = x + \dfrac{12}{\sqrt{x}}$ at $(4, 10)$ **ii** $y = 4\sqrt[3]{x} - \dfrac{x}{2}$ at $(8, 4)$

2 Find the equation of the tangent to the curve $y = \dfrac{x^2 + 4}{\sqrt{x}}$ at the point where $x = 4$.

3 Find the equation of the normal to the curve $y = 2x - \dfrac{3}{\sqrt{x}}$ at the point where $x = 4$.

4 The normal to the curve with equation $y = 2x^3 - 4x$ at the point $x = 2$ crosses the x-axis at P. Find the coordinates of P.

5 The tangent to the graph of $y = \dfrac{3}{x^2}$ at $x = 3$ crosses the coordinate axes at the points A and B. Find the area of the triangle AOB, where O is the origin.

6 Find the equations of the tangents to the curve $y = 2x^3 - 9x^2 + 12x + 1$ which are parallel to the x-axis.

7 Find the x-coordinates of the points on the curve $y = x^3 - 2x^2$ where the tangent is parallel to the normal at the point $(1, -1)$.

8 The normal to the curve $y = ax^3 + bx^2$ at the point $(1, 2)$ is parallel to the line $x - 2y + 14 = 0$. Find a and b

9 The tangent to the curve $y = p\sqrt{x} + qx$ at the point $\left(1, -\dfrac{7}{6}\right)$ is parallel to the line $2x + 3y - 12 = 0$. Find p and q.

10 Given that $f(x) = \dfrac{2}{x}$, find the coordinates of the point where the tangent to $y = f(x)$ at $x = 1$ intersects the normal to $y = f(x)$ at $x = -2$.

11 Find the coordinates of the point where the tangent to the curve $y = x^3 - 3x^2$ at $x = 2$ meets the curve again.

12 Find the coordinates of the point on the curve $y = (x - 1)^2$ where the normal passes through the point $(0, 0)$.

13 $y = -\dfrac{1}{2}x + c$ is the equation of a normal to the curve $y = x^2 + 5x + 4$. Find the constant c.

14 A tangent is drawn on the graph $y = \dfrac{k}{x}$ at the point where $x = a$ $(a > 0)$. The tangent intersects the y-axis at P and the x axis at Q. If O is the origin, show that the area of the triangle OPQ is independent of a.

15 Show that the tangent to the curve $y = x^3 - x$ at the point with x-coordinate a meets the curve again at a point with x-coordinate $-2a$.

 Tip

You could use a graphical calculator to help with question 12.

Elevate

For more questions with tangents and normals, see Extension sheet 14.

Section 2: Stationary points

In real life, you might be interested in maximising profits or minimising the drag on a car. You can use calculus to mathematically describe such problems.

The quantity you wish to maximise or minimise often depends on another variable. For example, the profit might depend on the selling price of the item. You can represent this relationship on a graph.

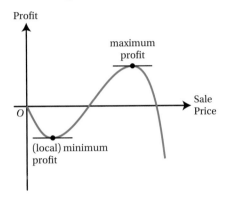

The gradients at both the local maximum and the local minimum point on this graph are zero.

Key point 14.2

To find local maximum and local minimum points, solve the equation $\dfrac{dy}{dx} = 0$.

You use the terms local maximum and local minimum because it is possible that the largest or smallest value of the whole function occurs at the endpoint of the graph, or that there are several points that have gradient zero. The points that you have found are just the largest or smallest values of y in their local area.

For this function, $y = f(x)$, defined for $x_A \leqslant x \leqslant x_F$:

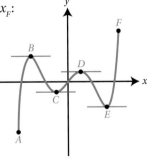

- B and D are local maximum points
- C and E are local minimum points
- A is the point where y is smallest
- F is the point where y is largest.

Points such as B, C, D and E, which have a gradient of zero, are called **stationary points**.

WORKED EXAMPLE 14.4

Find the coordinates of the stationary points of $y = 2x^3 - 15x^2 + 24x + 8$.

$\dfrac{dy}{dx} = 6x^2 - 30x + 24$ .... First differentiate.

For stationary points $\dfrac{dy}{dx} = 0$: .... Then solve the equation $\dfrac{dy}{dx} = 0$.

$6x^2 - 30x + 24 = 0$

$x^2 - 5x + 4 = 0$

$(x - 4)(x - 1) = 0$

$x = 1$ or $x = 4$

When $x = 1$: .... Remember to find the y-coordinate for each point.

$y = 2(1)^3 - 15(1)^2 + 24(1) + 8$

$= 19$

When $x = 4$:

$y = 2(4)^3 - 15(4)^2 + 24(4) + 8$

$= -8$

Therefore, stationary points are: ...... State the coordinates.

$(1, 19)$ and $(4, -8)$

The calculation in Worked example 14.4 does not tell you whether the stationary points you found are maximum or minimum points. To decide this, we need to look at how the gradient changes on either side of the stationary point.

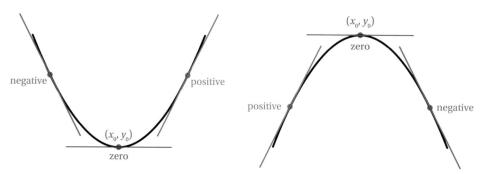

It can be seen from these diagrams that for a minimum point the gradient goes from negative to positive. This means that the gradient is increasing, so the rate of change of the gradient, $\dfrac{d^2y}{dx^2}$, is positive. For a maximum point, the gradient goes from positive to negative, so $\dfrac{d^2y}{dx^2}$ is negative. This test does not tell us what happens to the gradient if $\dfrac{d^2y}{dx^2}$ is zero.

 **Key point 14.3**

Given a stationary point (x_0, y_0) of a function $y = f(x)$:

- if $\dfrac{d^2y}{dx^2} < 0$ at x_0 then (x_0, y_0) is a local **maximum**

- if $\dfrac{d^2y}{dx^2} > 0$ at x_0 then (x_0, y_0) is a local **minimum**

- if $\dfrac{d^2y}{dx^2} = 0$ at x_0 then no conclusion can be drawn.

 Tip

It is common to simply say 'maximum' instead of 'local maximum' when the intended meaning is clear.

If a question asks you to 'classify' or 'determine the nature of' the stationary points on a curve, you need to decide whether each point is a local maximum or a local minimum.

WORKED EXAMPLE 14.5

Find and classify the stationary points of the curve $y = 2x^3 - 15x^2 + 24x + 8$ from Worked example 14.4.

Stationary points:
(1,19) and (4,−8)

You have already found the stationary points.

$\dfrac{d^2y}{dx^2} = 12x - 30$

Find the second derivative.

At $x = 1$:
$\dfrac{d^2y}{dx^2} = 12(1) - 30$

Evaluate the second derivative at the stationary point with $x = 1$.

$= -18 < 0$

$\dfrac{d^2y}{dx^2} < 0$ so the point is a local maximum.

∴ (1,19) is a maximum

At $x = 4$:

$\dfrac{d^2y}{dx^2} = 12(4) - 30$

Evaluate the second derivative at the stationary point with $x = 4$.

$= 18 > 0$

$\dfrac{d^2y}{dx^2} < 0$ so the point is a local minimum.

∴ (4,−8) is a minimum

Tip

Remember to solve $\dfrac{dy}{dx} = 0$ first, then substitute the x-value into $\dfrac{d^2y}{dx^2}$ to test whether the points are maximum or minimum. Do not try to solve the equation $\dfrac{d^2y}{dx^2} = 0$.

Fast forward

A You will see in Student Book 2 that there is another type of stationary point other than a maximum or minimum.

One use of stationary points is to find the largest and smallest values of a function for a given set of x-values.

 **Fast forward**

A You will see in Student Book 2 that this is related to the *range* of a function.

 Tip

Remember that the largest/smallest value of a function in a given interval could occur at the endpoint(s) of the interval instead of at the local maximum/minimum.

WORKED EXAMPLE 14.6

Find the largest and smallest values of $f(x) = 2x^3 - 6x + 3$ for $-2 \leqslant x \leqslant 3$.

Endpoints:

Evaluate the function at the endpoints; it may have a greater value at an endpoint than it does at any local maximum and/or be less than any local minimum.

$f(-2) = 2(-2)^3 - 6(-2) + 3$

$\quad = -1$

$f(3) = 2(3)^3 - 6(3) + 3$

$\quad = 39$

Stationary points:

Stationary points give local minimum and maximum values. Solve $f'(x) = 0$ to find any.

$f'(x) = 0$

$6x^2 - 6 = 0$

$6(x - 1)(x + 1) = 0$

$x = 1 \text{ or } -1$

$f(1) = 2(1)^3 - 6(1) + 3$

Find the value of the function at the stationary points. Second derivative analysis is not needed; the maximum and minimum values of the function must be either at endpoints or at stationary points.

$\quad = -1$

$f(-1) = 2(-1)^3 - 6(-1) + 3$

$\quad = 7$

So, the largest value of $f(x)$ is 39.

$f(-2)$ is the same as at the local minimum, but $f(3)$ is larger than at the local maximum.

The smallest value of $f(x)$ is -1

$-1 \leqslant f(x) \leqslant 39$

EXERCISE 14B

1 Find and classify the stationary points on the following curves.

a **i** $y = x^3 - 5x^2$ **ii** $y = 1 + 24x^2 - x^3$

b **i** $y = x^4 - 8x^2$ **ii** $y = x^4 - 2x^2 + 3$

c **i** $y = 2x - \dfrac{1}{x}$ **ii** $y = 3x^2 + \dfrac{9}{x}$

d **i** $y = 2\sqrt{x} - 3x$ **ii** $y = \dfrac{1}{\sqrt{x}} + 3x$

> ⬇ **Elevate**
>
> See Support sheet 14 for more practice.

2 Find and classify the stationary points on the curve $y = x^3 + 3x^2 - 24x + 12$.

3 Prove that the curve $y = x^3 - 3x^2 + 4x - 1$ has no stationary points.

4 $f(x) = \dfrac{9x^2 + 1}{x}$

a Find the x-coordinates of the stationary points on the curve $y = f(x)$.

b Determine whether each is a maximum or minimum point.

5 Find the coordinates of the stationary point on the curve $y = x - \sqrt{x}$ and determine its nature.

6 **a** Find the coordinates of the stationary points on the curve with equation $y = x^2 \left(6\sqrt[3]{x} - 7 \right)$.

b Establish whether each is a maximum or minimum point.

7 The curve $y = x^3 + 10x^2 + kx - 2$ has a stationary point at $x = -8$.

a Find the x-coordinate of the other stationary point.

b Determine the nature of both stationary points.

8 The curve $y = ax^2 + bx - 2$ has a minimum point at $x = -2$ and passes through the point $(1, 13)$. Find a and b.

9 $f(x) = 4 - 9x + 6x^2 - x^3, \ -2 \leqslant x \leqslant 4$

Find the largest and smallest values of $f(x)$.

10 $f(x) = -\dfrac{1}{4}x^4 - x^3 + 2x^2 - 10$

Show that $f(x) \leqslant 22$ for all x.

11 **a** Find the stationary points of the curve $y = 3x^4 - 16x^3 + 18x^2 + 6$.

b Find the set of values of c for which the equation $3x^4 - 16x^3 + 18x^2 + 6 = c$ has four real roots.

12 Find and classify in terms of k the stationary points on the curve $y = kx^3 + 6x^2$.

Section 3: Optimisation

You can now apply results from the previous section to solve practical problems which involve maximising or minimising quantities.

WORKED EXAMPLE 14.7

The distance travelled, in metres, by a paper aeroplane of mass w grams where $w > 1$ is

$$s = \left(1 - \frac{1}{\sqrt{w}}\right)\left(\frac{5}{w}\right)$$

a Find the mass the aeroplane needs to be to travel its maximum distance.

b Find this maximum distance.

a $s = \left(1 - \frac{1}{\sqrt{w}}\right)\left(\frac{5}{w}\right)$ .... | Expand the brackets and write terms in the form ax^n using laws of indices.

$= \dfrac{5}{w} - \dfrac{5}{w\sqrt{w}}$

$= 5w^{-1} - 5w^{-\frac{3}{2}}$

$\dfrac{ds}{dw} = -5w^{-2} + \dfrac{15}{2}w^{-\frac{5}{2}}$ .... | Then find the maximum by solving $\dfrac{ds}{dw} = 0$.

Stationary points:

$\dfrac{ds}{dw} = 0$

$-5w^{-2} + \dfrac{15}{2}w^{-\frac{5}{2}} = 0$

$\dfrac{15}{2}w^{-\frac{5}{2}} = 5w^{-2}$

$3w^{-\frac{5}{2}} = 2w^{-2}$ .... | Multiply through by 2 and divide by 5.

$\dfrac{3}{w^{\frac{5}{2}}} = \dfrac{2}{w^2}$ .... | Rewrite without the negative indices.

$3 = \dfrac{2w^{\frac{5}{2}}}{w^2}$ .... | Multiply through by $w^{\frac{5}{2}}$.

$3 = 2w^{\frac{1}{2}}$ .... | Simplify.

$\sqrt{w} = \dfrac{3}{2}$ .... | Solve for w.

$w = \dfrac{9}{4}g$

Nature of stationary point: .... | You know that there is a stationary point at this value of w but you need to check that this is a maximum.

$\dfrac{d^2s}{dw^2} = 10w^{-3} - \dfrac{75}{4}w^{-\frac{7}{2}}$

When $w = \dfrac{9}{4}$:

$\dfrac{d^2s}{dw^2} = -0.22 < 0$

$\therefore$ maximum

Continues on next page ...

b Maximum value of s:

$$s = \left(1 - \frac{1}{\sqrt{\frac{9}{4}}}\right)\left(\frac{\frac{5}{9}}{\frac{9}{4}}\right)$$

$$= \left(1 - \frac{2}{3}\right)\left(\frac{20}{9}\right)$$

$$= \frac{20}{27}m$$

Find the maximum value of the distance by evaluating the original expression for s at $w = \frac{9}{4}$.

In some examples, a function appears to depend on two different variables. However, these two variables will always be related by a **constraint**, a condition that allows one of the variables to be eliminated. You can then follow the normal procedure for finding maxima or minima.

The two common types of constraints are:

- A shape has a fixed perimeter, area or volume – this gives an equation relating different variables (height, length, radius...).
- A point lies on a given curve – this gives a relationship between x and y.

📷 **Focus on ...**

Focus on ... Problem solving 2 looks at choosing the right variables in this sort of optimisation problem.

WORKED EXAMPLE 14.8

A wire of length 12 cm is bent to form a rectangle.

a Show that the area, A, is given by $A = 6x - x^2$ where x is the width of the rectangle.
b Find the maximum possible area.

a Let the length of the rectangle be y.

Then $A = xy$

Introduce a variable, y, for the length in order to write an expression for the area (which is to be maximised).

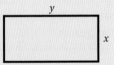

$P = 2x + 2y$

Since perimeter $P = 12$,

$12 = 2x + 2y$

$6 = x + y$

$y = 6 - x$

Use the information about the perimeter to form a second equation (the constraint).

Make y the subject.

So

$A = xy$

$= x(6 - x)$

$= 6x - x^2$

Substitute into the expression for A in order to eliminate y and express A as a function of x only.

Continues on next page ...

b Stationary points:

$$\frac{dA}{dx} = 6 - 2x = 0$$

$$x = 3$$

Find the value of x at which the maximum of A occurs by solving $\frac{dA}{dx} = 0$.

Nature of stationary point:

$$\frac{d^2A}{dx^2} = -2 < 0$$

$\therefore$ maximum

Check that the stationary point is a maximum.

Maximum value of A is

$$A = x(6 - x)$$

$$= 3(6 - 3)$$

$$= 9 \, cm^2$$

Find the maximum value of A by substituting $x = 3$ into $A = x(6 - x)$.

 Explore

Worked example 14.8 is an example of the isoperimetric problem – to find the shape with the fixed perimeter and maximum area. Find out more about it – it has some very interesting applications.

Tip

Don't forget to substitute the value of x that maximises/minimises the quantity back into the original expression to find the maximum/minimum value of that quantity.

WORKED EXAMPLE 14.9

An open-top cylindrical can has base radius r and height h.

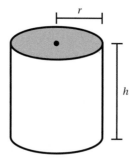

The external surface area $A = 243\pi$ cm^2.

a Show that the volume, V, is given by $V = \frac{\pi}{2}(243r - r^3)$.

b Hence find the maximum capacity of the can.

Continues on next page ...

a $V = \pi r^2 h$

Write down an expression for the quantity to be maximised.

$A = \pi r^2 + 2\pi r h$

The surface area is made up of the area of the base (πr^2) and the curved surface area of the cylinder ($2\pi r h$).

Since $A = 243\pi$,

Use the information about the surface area to form a second equation (the constraint).

$243\pi = \pi r^2 + 2\pi r h$

$243 = r^2 + 2rh$

$h = \dfrac{243 - r^2}{2r}$

Make h the subject.

So

$V = \pi r^2 \left(\dfrac{243 - r^2}{2r} \right)$

Substitute into the expression for V in order to eliminate h and express V as a function of r only.

$= \dfrac{\pi r^2}{2r}(243 - r^2)$

$= \dfrac{\pi r}{2}(243 - r^2)$

$= \dfrac{\pi}{2}(243r - r^3)$

b Stationary points:

Find the value of r at which the maximum of V occurs by solving $\dfrac{dV}{dr} = 0$.

$\dfrac{dV}{dr} = 0$

$\dfrac{\pi}{2}(243 - 3r^2) = 0$

$243 - 3r^2 = 0$

$r^2 = 81$

$r = 9 \quad (r > 0)$

Nature of stationary point:

Check that the stationary point is a maximum.

$\dfrac{d^2V}{dr^2} = \dfrac{\pi}{2}(-6r)$

$= -3\pi r$

$= -3\pi(9)$

$= -27\pi < 0$

$\therefore$ maximum

Maximum value of V is

Don't forget to find the maximum value of V by substituting $r = 9$ into $V = \dfrac{\pi}{2}(243r - r^3)$.

$V = \dfrac{\pi}{2}(243r - r^3)$

$= \dfrac{\pi}{2}(243(9) - (9)^3)$

$= 729\pi \, \text{cm}^3$

✔ **Gateway to A level**

If you need a reminder about volume and area, see Gateway to A Level section R.

✔ **Gateway to A level**

For a reminder of changing the subject of the formula, and substituting one formula into another, see Gateway to A Level section S.

WORKED EXAMPLE 14.10

Let A be a point on the curve $y = x^2$ with x-coordinate a.

Let L be the distance from A to the point $P\left(2, \frac{1}{2}\right)$.

a   Write down an expression for L^2 in terms of a.
b   Find the minimum possible value of L^2.
c   Hence write down the coordinate of the point on the curve $y = x^2$ that is closest to the point $P\left(2, \frac{1}{2}\right)$.

Rewind

You will need the formula for the distance between two points from Chapter 6.

a   *The coordinates of A are (a, a^2)*

For any point of the curve, the y-coordinate equals x^2.

The distance between A and P is

$$L^2 = (a-2)^2 + \left(a^2 - \frac{1}{2}\right)^2$$

Use $L^2 = (x_2 - x_1)^2 + (y_2 - y_1)^2$.

b $L^2 = a^2 - 4a + 4 + a^4 - a^2 + \dfrac{1}{4}$

$$= a^4 - 4a + \frac{17}{4}$$

Before differentiating to find stationary points, you need to expand the brackets.

$$\frac{d(L^2)}{da} = 4a^3 - 4$$

Stationary points:

$$\frac{d(L^2)}{da} = 0$$

$$4a^3 - 4 = 0$$

$$4(a^3 - 1) = 0$$

$$a = 1$$

Nature of stationary point:

$$\frac{d^2(L^2)}{da^2} = 12a^2$$

$$= 12(1)$$

$$= 12 > 0$$

$\therefore$ *minimum*

Check that the stationary point is a minimum.

The minimum value of L^2 is:

$$L^2 = 1^4 - 4 + \frac{17}{4}$$

$$= \frac{5}{4}$$

The question was to find the minimum value of L^2.

c   *From part b, the minimum value of L is when $a = 1$, so the point is*

$$A(a, a^2) = (1, 1)$$

The minimum of L occurs at the same value of a as the minimum of L^2.

Note that the minimum distance from P to the curve is $\dfrac{\sqrt{5}}{2}$.

EXERCISE 14C

1 **a** **i** Find the maximum value of xy given that $x + 2y = 4$.

ii Find the maximum possible value of xy given that $3x + y = 7$.

b **i** Find the minimum possible value of $a + b$ given that $ab = 3$ and $a, b > 0$.

ii Find the minimum possible value of $2a + b$ given that $ab = 4$ and $a, b > 0$.

c **i** Find the maximum possible value of $4r^2h$ if $2r^2 + rh = 3$ and $r, h > 0$.

ii Find the maximum possible value of rh^2 if $4r^2 + 3h^2 = 12$ and $r, h > 0$.

2 A rectangle has width x metres and length $30 - x$ metres.

a Find the maximum area of the rectangle.

b Show that as x changes the perimeter stays constant and find the value of this perimeter.

3 The sector of a circle with radius r has perimeter 40 cm.

The sector has area A.

a Show that $A = 20r - r^2$.

b **i** Find the value of r for which A is a maximum.

ii Show that this does give a maximum.

4 A square sheet of card of side 12 cm has four squares of side x cm cut from the corners. The sides are then folded to make a small open box.

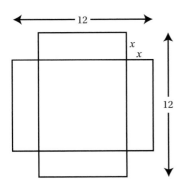 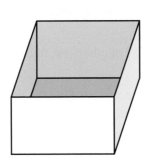

a Show that the volume, V, is given by $V = x(12 - 2x)^2$.

b Find the value of x for which the volume is the maximum possible, and prove that it is a maximum.

5 Prove that the minimum possible value of the sum of a positive real number and its reciprocal is 2.

6 A solid cylinder has radius r and height h.

The total surface area of the cylinder is 450 cm².

   a Find an expression for the volume of the cylinder in terms of r only.

   b Hence find the maximum possible volume, justifying that the value found is a maximum.

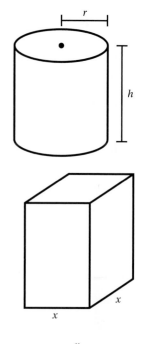

7 A closed carton is in the shape of a cuboid. The base is a square of side x.

The total surface area is 486 cm².

   a Find an expression for the volume of the carton in terms of x only.

   b Hence find the maximum possible volume, justifying that the value found is a maximum.

8 A certain type of chocolate is sold in boxes that are in the shape of a triangular prism. The cross-section is an equilateral triangle of side x cm. The length is y cm.

The volume of the box needs to be 128 cm³.

The manufacturer wishes to minimise the surface area.

   a Show that $A = \sqrt{3}\left(\dfrac{512}{x} + \dfrac{x^2}{2}\right)$.

   b Find the minimum value of A.

   c Prove that the value found is a minimum.

9 A cone of radius r and height h has volume 81π.

   a Show that the curved surface area of the cone is given by
$$S = \pi\sqrt{r^4 + \dfrac{243^2}{r^2}}.$$

It is required to make the cone so that the curved surface area is the minimum possible.

   b By considering stationary points of S^2, or otherwise, find the radius and the height of the cone.

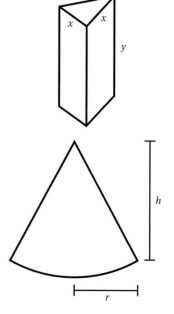

10 The sum of two numbers x and y is 6, and $x, y \geqslant 0$. Find the two numbers if the sum of their squares is the:

   a minimum possible   **b** maximum possible.

11 The time in minutes taken to melt 100 g of butter (t) depends upon the percentage of the butter that is made of saturated fats (p), as shown in the following function:

$$t = \frac{p^2}{10\,000} + \frac{p}{100} + 2$$

Find the maximum and minimum times to melt 100 g of butter.

12 A 20 cm piece of wire is bent to form an isosceles triangle with base b.

   a Show that the area of the triangle is given by $A = \frac{1}{2}\sqrt{100b^2 - 10b^3}$.

   b Show that the area of the triangle is the largest possible when the triangle is equilateral.

13 The sum of the squares of two positive numbers is a. Prove that their product is the maximum possible when the two numbers are equal.

14 Find the coordinates of the point on the curve $y = x^2$, $x \geqslant 0$, closest to the point $(0, 4)$.

15 A cylinder of radius 6 cm and height 6 cm fits perfectly inside a cone, leaving a constant ring of width x around the base of the cylinder.

   a Show that the height, h, of the cone is $h = \frac{36}{x} + 6$.

   b Find the volume of the cone in terms of x.

   c Hence find the minimum value of the volume, justifying that the value you have found is a minimum.

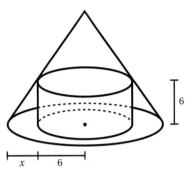

Checklist of learning and understanding

- The **tangent** to a curve at a point (x_0, y_0) has gradient equal to $\frac{\mathrm{d}y}{\mathrm{d}x}$ evaluated at that point.
- The **normal** to the curve at a point (x_0, y_0) is perpendicular to the tangent at that point.
- **Stationary points** of a function are points where the gradient is zero, i.e. $\frac{\mathrm{d}y}{\mathrm{d}x} = 0$.
- The second derivative can be used to determine the nature of a stationary point. At a stationary point (x_0, y_0):

  - if $\frac{\mathrm{d}^2 y}{\mathrm{d}x^2} < 0$ at x_0 then (x_0, y_0) is a maximum

  - if $\frac{\mathrm{d}^2 y}{\mathrm{d}x^2} > 0$ at x_0 then (x_0, y_0) is a minimum

  - if $\frac{\mathrm{d}^2 y}{\mathrm{d}x^2} = 0$ at x_0 then no conclusion can be drawn.

Mixed practice 14

1 $y = f(x)$ has a stationary point, P, at $x = 2$. What is the equation of the tangent at P?

Choose from the following options:

A $y = f'(2)$ **B** $x = 2$ **C** $y = f(2)$ **D** $x = -\dfrac{1}{2}$

2 Find the equation of the tangent to the curve $y = x^2 - \dfrac{3}{x}$ at the point where $x = 2$.
Give your answer in the form $ax + by = c$ where a, b and c are integers.

3 Find the equation of the normal to the curve $y = (x - 2)^3$ when $x = 2$.

4 Find the x-coordinates of the stationary points on the graph of $y = \dfrac{x^3}{6} - x^2 + x$
and determine their nature.

5 A curve C has equation $y = \dfrac{1}{4}x^4 - 2x^3 + 4x^2 - 1$.

  a Find the coordinates of the stationary points on C.

  b Determine the nature of each stationary point.

6 A rectangle is drawn inside the region bounded by the curve $y = 4 - x^2$ and the x-axis, so that two of the vertices lie on the axis and the other two on the curve.

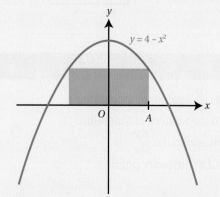

Find the coordinates of vertex A so that the area of the rectangle is the maximum possible.

7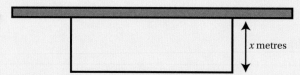

The diagram shows a rectangular enclosure, with a wall forming one side. A rope, of length 20 metres, is used to form the remaining three sides. The width of the enclosure is x metres.

  i Show that the enclosed area, A m^2, is given by $A = 20x - 2x^2$.

  ii Use differentiation to find the maximum value of A.

© OCR, AS GCE Mathematics, Paper 4721, June 2007

8 $y = \dfrac{1}{3}x^3 - ax^2 + 3ax + 1$ where $a \neq 0$ has one stationary point. What is the value of a?

9 The curve $y = ax^3 + bx^2 + 8x - 1$ has stationary points at $x = \dfrac{1}{3}$ and $x = 4$. Find a and b.

10 $f(x) = x^2 - 4x\sqrt{x} + 4x - 3$

Show that the curve $y = f(x)$ has two stationary points and determine whether each is a maximum or minimum.

11 A function is defined by $f(x) = x^3 - 9x$ for $-2 \leqslant x \leqslant 5$.

   a Find the coordinates of the stationary points on the curve $y = f(x)$.

   b Find the minimum and maximum values of $f(x)$.

12 The tangent to the graph of $y = \dfrac{1}{x^2}$ at the point where $x = 3$ crosses the coordinate axes at points M and N. Find the exact area of the triangle MON.

13 A car tank is being filled with petrol such that the volume in the tank in litres (V) over time in minutes (t) is given by $V = 300(t^2 - t^3) + 4$ for $0 < t < 0.5$.

   a How much petrol was initially in the tank?

   b After 30 seconds the tank was full. What is the capacity of the tank?

   c At what time is petrol flowing in at the greatest rate?

14 A gardener is planting a lawn in the shape of a sector of a circle joined to a rectangle. The sector has radius r and angle $\dfrac{2\pi}{3}$ radians.

He needs the area, A, of the lawn to be 200 m^2.

A fence is to be built around the perimeter of the lawn.

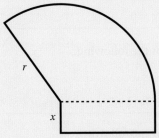

   a Show that the length of the fence, P, is given by $P = 2r + \dfrac{400}{r}$.

   b Hence find the minimum length of fence required, justifying that this value is a minimum.

15 **i** Find the coordinates of the stationary point on the curve $y = 3x^2 - \dfrac{6}{x} - 2$.

   ii Determine whether the stationary point is a maximum point or a minimum point.

© OCR, AS GCE Mathematics, Paper 4721, June 2011

16 The line $y = 24(x - 1)$ is tangent to the curve $y = ax^3 + bx^2 + 4$ at $x = 2$.

   a Use the fact that the tangent meets the curve to show that $2a + b = 5$.

   b Use the fact that the tangent has the same gradient as the curve to find another relationship between a and b.

   c Hence find the values of a and b.

   d The line meets the curve again. Find the coordinates of the other point of intersection.

17 On the curve $y = x^3$ a tangent is drawn from the point (a, a^3) and a normal is drawn from the point $(-a, -a^3)$. The tangent and the normal meet on the y-axis. Find the value of a.

18 The curve $y = ax^2 + \dfrac{24}{x}$ has a stationary point at $y = 18$. Find a.

15 Integration

In this chapter you will learn how to:

- reverse the process of differentiation (this process is called integration)
- find the equation of a curve given its derivative and a point on the curve
- find the area between a curve and the x-axis.

Before you start…

Chapter 3	You should know how to solve quadratic and cubic equations by factorising.	1 Solve the following equations: a $3x^2 - 4x = 0$ b $x^3 - 4x^2 = 0$ c $x^3 - 5x = 0$
Chapter 13	You should know how to differentiate expressions of the form ax^n.	2 Find $\dfrac{dy}{dx}$ for the following: a $y = 3x^2 - x$ b $y = x^{\frac{1}{2}} - 3x^{-\frac{2}{3}} + 2$
Chapter 13	You should know how to convert expressions to the form ax^n in order to differentiate.	3 Find $\dfrac{dy}{dx}$ for the following: a $y = \dfrac{3}{2x^2}$ b $y = 3x\sqrt{x}$

What is integration?

As in many areas of mathematics, as soon as you learn a new process you must then learn how to undo it. Reversing differentiation answers the question: If you know the equation for the gradient of a curve, can you find the equation of the curve itself?

This question is important because, in many applications, the rate of change is easier to measure or model than the quantity itself. For example, acceleration, which is the rate of change of velocity, can be calculated if you know the forces acting on an object. You can then 'undifferentiate' the equation for acceleration to find the equation for velocity.

It turns out that undoing the process of differentiation opens up the possibility of answering another, seemingly unconnected problem: how to find the area under a curve. As you will learn in the mechanics chapters, this enables you to find distance travelled from a velocity–time graph.

▶▶ **Fast forward**

See Chapters 19 and 20 for more about motion.

Section 1: Rules for integration

If you know the function describing a curve's gradient, you can find the equation of the curve by 'undoing' the differentiation. This process of reversing differentiation is known as **integration**.

For example, if $\dfrac{dy}{dx} = 2x$ you know that the original function, y, must have contained x^2. However, it could have been $y = x^2 + 2$ or $y = x^2 - \dfrac{2}{3}$ or in fact $y = x^2 + c$, for any constant c.

All of these functions have $\dfrac{dy}{dx} = 2x$, as the derivative of any constant is zero. Without further information, it is impossible to know what the constant was in the original function, so you say:

If $\dfrac{dy}{dx} = 2x$, then $y = x^2 + c$

or, equivalently, using the integration symbol:

$$\int 2x\, dx = x^2 + c$$

Here, the dx simply states that the integration is taking place with respect to the variable x in exactly the same way that in $\dfrac{dy}{dx}$ it states that the differentiation is taking place with respect to x. You could equally well write, for example:

$$\int 2t\, dt = t^2 + c$$

This relationship between differentiation and integration is so important that it is given a special name.

▶▶ **Fast forward**

You will see how to find the constant of integration in Section 4.

🔑 Key point 15.1

The fundamental theorem of calculus:

$\int f(x)\, dx = F(x) + c$ means that $f(x) = \dfrac{d}{dx} F(x)$

This just means that integration is the reverse of differentiation.

💡 **Tip**

A This theorem implies that the processes of integration and differentiation are inverses of each other.

Reversing the formula you know for differentiation gives the rule for integration.

🔑 Key point 15.2

$\int x^n\, dx = \dfrac{1}{n+1} x^{n+1} + c$ for any $n \neq -1$

💡 **Tip**

It may be helpful to think of this in words: 'add one to the power and divide by the new power'.

🔍 Explore

The statement in Key point 15.1 is one way to define integration. It can also be defined using areas, as you will find out in the next chapter. The full statement of the fundamental theorem of calculus says that the two definitions are equivalent; find out how to prove this.

💡 **Tip**

Note the condition $n \neq -1$, which ensures that you are not dividing by zero.

WORKED EXAMPLE 15.1

If $\dfrac{dy}{dx} = x^3$ find y.

$y = \displaystyle\int x^3 \, dx$ .... Integrate to get y.

$= \dfrac{1}{3+1} x^{3+1} + c$ .... Use $\displaystyle\int x^n \, dx = \dfrac{1}{n+1} x^{n+1} + c$.

$y = \dfrac{1}{4} x^4 + c$

💡 **Tip**

Don't forget the $+ c$. It is a part of the answer and you **must** write it every time.

WORKED EXAMPLE 15.2

Find $\displaystyle\int x^{-4} \, dx$.

$\displaystyle\int x^{-4} \, dx = \dfrac{1}{-4+1} x^{-4+1} + c$ ... Use $\displaystyle\int x^n \, dx = \dfrac{1}{n+1} x^{n+1} + c$.

$= -\dfrac{1}{3} x^{-3} + c$

WORKED EXAMPLE 15.3

If $f'(x) = x^{\frac{1}{2}}$ find $f(x)$.

$f(x) = \displaystyle\int x^{\frac{1}{2}} \, dx$ .... Integrate $f'(x)$ to get $f(x)$.

$= \dfrac{1}{\frac{1}{2}+1} x^{\frac{1}{2}+1} + c$ .... Use $\displaystyle\int x^n \, dx = \dfrac{1}{n+1} x^{n+1} + c$.

$= \dfrac{1}{\frac{3}{2}} x^{\frac{3}{2}} + c$ .... Simplify.

$= \dfrac{2}{3} x^{\frac{3}{2}} + c$

Some important properties of integration follow directly from the properties on differentiation given in Key point 13.4.

🔑 **Key point 15.3**

- $\displaystyle\int k\,f(x) \, dx = k \int f(x) \, dx$ where k is a constant.

- $\displaystyle\int f(x) + g(x) \, dx = \int f(x) \, dx + \int g(x) \, dx$.

💡 **Tip**

Key point 15.3 just says that you can integrate a function and then multiply by a constant, and that you can integrate terms of a sum separately.

WORKED EXAMPLE 15.4

Find $\int 3x^5 \, dx$.

$\int 3x^5 \, dx = 3 \times \dfrac{1}{6} x^6 + c$ .... Integrate x^5 and then multiply by 3.

$\qquad = \dfrac{1}{2} x^6 + c$

WORKED EXAMPLE 15.5

Find $\int 7 \, dx$.

$\int 7 \, dx = \int 7x^0 \, dx$ .... Using the fact that $x^0 = 1$ you can write 7 as $7x^0$.

$\qquad = 7 \times \dfrac{1}{1} x^1 + c$ .... Now integrate x^0.

$\qquad = 7x + c$

From Worked example 15.5 you can see that $\int k \, dx = kx + c$ for any constant k.

> 💡 **Tip**
>
> You do not need to write out $k = kx^0$ every time you integrate $y = k$. You just need to know that the integral will always be $kx + c$.

WORKED EXAMPLE 15.6

A curve has equation $\dfrac{dy}{dx} = 4x^{-\frac{1}{2}} - 3x + 8$. Find an equation for y in terms of x.

$y = \int 4x^{-\frac{1}{2}} - 3x + 8 \, dx$ .... Integrate to find y.

$\quad = 4 \times \dfrac{1}{\frac{1}{2}} x^{\frac{1}{2}} - 3 \times \dfrac{1}{2} x^2 + 8x + c$ .... Integrate each term separately. Remember that the integral of a constant, k, is just kx.

$\quad = 8x^{\frac{1}{2}} - \dfrac{3}{2} x^2 + 8x + c$

EXERCISE 15A

1 Find y for the following:

a i $\dfrac{dy}{dx} = x^5$ ii $\dfrac{dy}{dx} = x^6$ b i $\dfrac{dy}{dx} = 3x^2$ ii $\dfrac{dy}{dx} = -5x^4$

c i $\dfrac{dy}{dx} = 2x^3$ ii $\dfrac{dy}{dx} = -3x^7$ d i $\dfrac{dy}{dx} = x$ ii $\dfrac{dy}{dx} = -4x$

e i $\dfrac{dy}{dx} = 0$ ii $\dfrac{dy}{dx} = 1$ f i $\dfrac{dy}{dx} = -\dfrac{1}{6}$ ii $\dfrac{dy}{dx} = \dfrac{1}{3} x^8$

g i $\dfrac{dy}{dx} = \dfrac{14x^6}{5}$ ii $\dfrac{dy}{dx} = \dfrac{10x}{7}$ h i $\dfrac{dy}{dx} = 3x^5 - x + 4$ ii $\dfrac{dy}{dx} = 2x^4 + 4x^3 - 8x - 1$

i i $\dfrac{dy}{dx} = \dfrac{x^2}{2} + 2x - \dfrac{3}{4}$ ii $\dfrac{dy}{dx} = x^2 - \dfrac{3x^5}{8}$

2 Find the following integrals:

a **i** $\int x^{\frac{2}{3}}\,dx$ **ii** $\int x^{\frac{1}{3}}\,dx$ **b** **i** $\int 5x^{\frac{2}{3}}\,dx$ **ii** $\int 14x^{\frac{3}{4}}\,dx$

c **i** $\int \frac{5}{4}x^{\frac{1}{4}}\,dx$ **ii** $\int -\frac{3}{2}x^{\frac{1}{2}}\,dx$ **d** **i** $\int -\frac{7x^{\frac{4}{3}}}{6}\,dx$ **ii** $\int \frac{14x^{\frac{2}{5}}}{15}\,dx$

e **i** $\int 5x - 7x^{\frac{5}{2}}\,dx$ **ii** $\int 6 + \frac{x}{3} - 12x^{\frac{1}{2}}\,dx$ **f** **i** $\int x^{-2}\,dx$ **ii** $\int x^{-3}\,dx$

g **i** $\int x^{-\frac{1}{3}}\,dx$ **ii** $\int x^{-\frac{1}{4}}\,dx$ **h** **i** $\int -4x^{-\frac{2}{3}}\,dx$ **ii** $\int -5x^{-\frac{3}{2}}\,dx$

i **i** $\int x^{-\frac{1}{2}} - \frac{6x^{-4}}{5}\,dx$ **ii** $\int 3x^{-5} + 7x^{-\frac{1}{6}}\,dx$

3 Find the following integrals:

a **i** $\int 3\,dt$ **ii** $\int 7\,dz$ **b** **i** $\int q^5\,dq$ **ii** $\int r^{10}\,dr$

c **i** $\int 12g^{\frac{3}{5}}\,dg$ **ii** $\int 6y^{\frac{7}{2}}\,dy$ **d** **i** $\int 5a^{-\frac{3}{4}}\,da$ **ii** $\int 7p^{-\frac{4}{3}}\,dp$

4 If $f'(x) = \frac{x^3}{2} - 6x^{-\frac{5}{3}} + 2$, find $f(x)$.

5 Find $\int x^{\frac{3}{2}} - x^{-\frac{3}{2}}\,dx$.

6 Find $\int \frac{x^5 - 3x^{-3} + x}{2}\,dx$.

Section 2: Simplifying into terms of the form ax^n

Just as for differentiation, before you can integrate products or quotients of functions they need to be converted into terms of the form ax^n, often by using the laws of indices.

 Fast forward

A In Student Book 2 you will learn methods for integrating some products and quotients.

WORKED EXAMPLE 15.7

Find $\int (2x - 1)(x + 3)\,dx$.

$\int (2x-1)(x+3)\,dx = \int 2x^2 + 5x - 3\,dx$ Expand the brackets.

$= \frac{2}{3}x^3 + \frac{5}{2}x^2 - 3x + c$ Then integrate.

💡 **Tip**

You can't integrate products and quotients of functions separately; that is:

$$\int f(x)g(x)\,dx \neq \int f(x)\,dx \times \int g(x)\,dx$$

$$\int \frac{f(x)}{g(x)}\,dx \neq \frac{\int f(x)\,dx}{\int g(x)\,dx}$$

WORK IT OUT 15.1

Three students are trying to find the following integral:

$$\int 2x\left(x^2 - 2\right)dx$$

Which is the correct solution? Can you identify the errors made in the incorrect solutions?

Solution 1	Solution 2	Solution 3
$\int 2x\left(x^2-2\right)dx$	$\int 2x\left(x^2-2\right)dx$	$\int 2x\left(x^2-2\right)dx$
$=\int 2x^3 - 4x\,dx$	$=\dfrac{2x^2}{2}\left(\dfrac{x^3}{3}-2x\right)+c$	$=2x\int x^2 - 2\,dx$
$=\dfrac{2x^4}{4}-\dfrac{4x^2}{2}+c$	$=x^2\left(\dfrac{x^3}{3}-2x\right)+c$	$=2x\left(\dfrac{x^3}{3}-2x\right)+c$
$=\dfrac{x^4}{2}-2x^2+c$		

WORKED EXAMPLE 15.8

Find $\displaystyle\int \frac{1}{x^2}\,dx$.

$\displaystyle\int \frac{1}{x^2}\,dx = \int x^{-2}\,dx$ ······· First rewrite the function in the form x^n using the laws of indices.

$\qquad\qquad = -x^{-1} + c$ ········· Then integrate.

WORKED EXAMPLE 15.9

Find $\displaystyle\int 5x^2\sqrt[3]{x}\,dx$.

$\displaystyle\int 5x^2\sqrt[3]{x}\,dx = \int 5x^2\,x^{\frac{1}{3}}\,dx$ ···· First rewrite the function in the form ax^n using the laws of indices.

$\qquad\qquad = \int 5x^{\frac{7}{3}}\,dx$

$\qquad\qquad = 5\times\dfrac{3}{10}x^{\frac{10}{3}}+c$ ···· Then integrate: dividing by $\dfrac{10}{3}$ is the same as multiplying by $\dfrac{3}{10}$.

$\qquad\qquad = \dfrac{3}{2}x^{\frac{10}{3}}+c$

WORKED EXAMPLE 15.10

Find $\int \dfrac{(x-3)^2}{\sqrt{x}}\,dx$.

$\int \dfrac{(x-3)^2}{\sqrt{x}}\,dx = \int \dfrac{x^2-6x+9}{\sqrt{x}}\,dx$ .... Expand the brackets first.

$= \int \dfrac{x^2-6x+9}{x^{\frac{1}{2}}}\,dx$ .... Then replace $\sqrt{x}$ with $x^{\frac{1}{2}}$.

$= \int x^{2-\frac{1}{2}}-6x^{1-\frac{1}{2}}+9x^{-\frac{1}{2}}\,dx$ .... Simplify using the laws of indices.

$= \int x^{\frac{3}{2}}-6x^{\frac{1}{2}}+9x^{-\frac{1}{2}}\,dx$

$= \dfrac{2}{5}x^{\frac{5}{2}}-6\times\dfrac{2}{3}x^{\frac{3}{2}}+9\times2x^{\frac{1}{2}}+c$ .... Then integrate: dividing by $\frac{3}{2}$ is the same as multiplying by $\frac{2}{3}$; dividing by $\frac{1}{2}$ is the same as multiplying by 2.

$= \dfrac{2}{5}x^{\frac{5}{2}}-4x^{\frac{3}{2}}+18x^{\frac{1}{2}}+c$

EXERCISE 15B

1 Find the following integrals:

a **i** $\int \sqrt{x}\,dx$ **ii** $\int \sqrt[4]{x}\,dx$ **b** **i** $\int 6\sqrt[5]{x}\,dx$ **ii** $\int \dfrac{\sqrt[3]{x}}{6}\,dx$

c **i** $\int \dfrac{1}{x^3}\,dx$ **ii** $\int -\dfrac{1}{x^7}\,dx$ **d** **i** $\int -\dfrac{8}{x^5}\,dx$ **ii** $\int \dfrac{10}{3x^6}\,dx$

e **i** $\int \dfrac{1}{\sqrt{x}}\,dx$ **ii** $\int \dfrac{1}{\sqrt[3]{x}}\,dx$ **f** **i** $\int -\dfrac{15}{\sqrt[6]{x}}\,dx$ **ii** $\int \dfrac{9}{8\sqrt[4]{x}}\,dx$

2 Find the following integrals:

a **i** $\int (2x+3)(x+1)\,dx$ **ii** $\int 3x^2(x-2)\,dx$

b **i** $\int \sqrt{x}(5x+4)\,dx$ **ii** $\int \sqrt[3]{x}(2x^2+3)\,dx$

c **i** $\int (\sqrt[4]{x}+3x)^2\,dx$ **ii** $\int (\sqrt{x}-x^2)^2\,dx$

d **i** $\int (x-\dfrac{1}{x})^2\,dx$ **ii** $\int (2x+\dfrac{1}{x^2})(2x-\dfrac{1}{x^2})\,dx$

3 Find the following integrals:

a **i** $\int \dfrac{7x-2}{x^3}\,dx$ **ii** $\int \dfrac{2+5x}{4x^3}\,dx$ **b** **i** $\int \dfrac{\sqrt{x}-3}{x^2}\,dx$ **ii** $\int \dfrac{x^2-6x}{\sqrt{x}}\,dx$

4 Find $\int 10x\sqrt{x}\,dx$.

5 Find $\int x^2(\sqrt[3]{x}-12)\,dx$.

6 Find $\int 9\sqrt[4]{x^5}\,dx$.

7 Find $\int \dfrac{1}{3\sqrt[3]{x^2}}\,dx$.

8 Find $\int\left(\dfrac{1}{\sqrt{x}}-1\right)dx$.

9 Find $\int\dfrac{1}{3x^3}+\dfrac{1}{4x^4}\,dx$.

10 $f(x)=\dfrac{6+x}{\sqrt[3]{x}}$.

    a Express $f(x)$ in the form ax^n+bx^m.   **b** Hence find $\int\dfrac{6+x}{\sqrt[3]{x}}\,dx$.

11 $y=\dfrac{(x+2)(x-2)}{2\sqrt{x}}$

    a Show that $y=ax^{\frac{3}{2}}+bx^{-\frac{1}{2}}$ where a and b are constants to be found.

    b Hence find $\int y\,dx$.

12 Show that $\int 12\sqrt{x}-\dfrac{4}{\sqrt{x}}\,dx=8\sqrt{x}(x-1)+c$.

13 Find $\int\dfrac{(x+4)^2}{8x\sqrt{x}}\,dx$.

Section 3: Finding the equation of a curve

Consider again $\dfrac{dy}{dx}=2x$ which you encountered at the start of this chapter.
You know that the original function has equation $y=x^2+c$ for some constant value c.

If you are also told that the curve passes through the point $(1,-1)$, you can specify which of the family of curves your function must be, and find c.

Worked example 15.11 illustrates the general procedure for finding the equation of a curve given its gradient function.

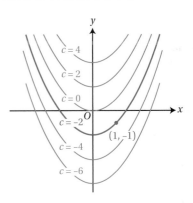

WORKED EXAMPLE 15.11

The gradient of a curve is given by $\dfrac{dy}{dx}=3x^2-8x+5$ and the curve passes through the point $(1,-4)$. Find the equation of the curve.

$y=\displaystyle\int 3x^2-8x+5\,dx$ To find y from $\dfrac{dy}{dx}$ you need to integrate. Don't forget $+c$.

$\quad=x^3-4x^2+5x+c$

When $x=1$, $y=-4$:

$-4=(1)^3-4(1)^2+5(1)+c$ Substitute in $x=1$, $y=-4$ in order to find c.

$-4=1-4+5+c$

$\quad c=-6$

$\therefore\ y=x^3-4x^2+5x-6$ State the final equation.

Key point 15.4

To find the equation for y given the gradient $\dfrac{dy}{dx}$ and one point (p, q) on the curve:

- integrate $\dfrac{dy}{dx}$ to get an equation for y in terms of x, remembering $+c$
- find the value of c by substituting $x = p$ and $y = q$ into the equation
- rewrite the equation for y, using the value of c that has been found.

 Fast forward

Equations with second derivatives occur frequently in the work on velocity and acceleration – see Chapter 19.

Sometimes you know the second derivative; in that case, you need to integrate twice to find the equation of the original curve. Be careful: you will need to add a different constant each time you integrate.

WORKED EXAMPLE 15.12

A curve has second derivative $\dfrac{d^2 y}{dx^2} = 3 - 6x$.

It passes through the point $(1, 2)$ and its gradient at this point is -3. Find the equation of the curve.

$\dfrac{dy}{dx} = \displaystyle\int 3 - 6x \, dx$ · · · · · · · · · Integrating the second derivative once gives the first derivative.

$\quad = 3x - 3x^2 + c$

When $x = 1$, $\dfrac{dy}{dx} = -3$: · · · · · · You can find c by using the given value of the gradient at $x = 1$.

$\quad -3 = 3 - 3 + c$

$\quad c = -3$

$\therefore \dfrac{dy}{dx} = 3x - 3x^2 - 3$ · · · · · · State the full equation for the derivative.

$y = \displaystyle\int 3x - 3x^2 - 3 \, dx$ · · · · · · Now integrate again to find y. There will be another constant.

$\quad = \dfrac{3x^2}{2} - x^3 - 3x + d$

When $x = 1$, $y = 2$: · · · · · · Now use the given x and y values to find d.

$\quad 2 = \dfrac{3}{2} - 1 - 3 + d$

$\quad d = \dfrac{9}{2}$

$\therefore y = \dfrac{3x^2}{2} - x^3 - 3x + \dfrac{9}{2}$ · · · · · · Finally state the equation for y.

WORK IT OUT 15.2

Three students attempt to solve the following problem:

A curve has $\dfrac{d^2 y}{dx^2} = 3x^2$ When $x = 2$, $y = 3$ and $\dfrac{dy}{dx} = -1$ Find the equation of the curve.

Which is the correct solution? Can you identify the errors made in the incorrect solutions?

Continues on next page ...

Solution 1	Solution 2	Solution 3
$\dfrac{dy}{dx} = \int 3x^2\,dx$	$\dfrac{dy}{dx} = \int 3x^2\,dx$	$\dfrac{dy}{dx} = \int 3x^2\,dx$
$\quad = x^3 + c$	$\quad = x^3 + c$	$\quad = x^3 + c$
$y = \int x^3 + c\,dx$	$y = \int x^3 + c\,dx$	When $x = 2$:
$\quad = \dfrac{x^4}{4} + cx + c$	$\quad = \dfrac{x^4}{4} + cx$	$\dfrac{dy}{dx} = -1$:
When $x = 2, y = 3$:	When $x = 2, y = 3$:	$-1 = 2^3 + c$
$3 = 4 + 2c + c$	$3 = 4 + 2c$	$c = -9$
$3 = 4 + 3c$	$c = -\dfrac{1}{2}$	$y = \int x^3 - 9\,dx$
$c = -\dfrac{1}{3}$		$\quad = \dfrac{x^4}{4} - 9x + d$
	$\therefore y = \dfrac{x^4}{4} - \dfrac{1}{2}x$	When $x = 2, y = 3$:
$\therefore y = \dfrac{x^4}{4} - \dfrac{1}{3}x - \dfrac{1}{3}$		$3 = 4 - 18 + d$
		$d = 17$
		$\therefore y = \dfrac{x^4}{4} - 9x + 17$

EXERCISE 15C

1 Find the equation of the curve if:

a i $\dfrac{dy}{dx} = x$ and the curve passes through $(-2, 7)$ **ii** $\dfrac{dy}{dx} = 6x^2$ and the curve passes through $(0, 5)$

b i $\dfrac{dy}{dx} = \dfrac{1}{x^2}$ and the curve passes through $(1, -1)$ **ii** $\dfrac{dy}{dx} = \dfrac{1}{x^2}$ and the curve passes through $(1, 3)$

c i $\dfrac{dy}{dx} = 3x - 5$ and the curve passes through $(2, 6)$ **ii** $\dfrac{dy}{dx} = 3 - 2x^3$ and the curve passes through $(1, 5)$

d i $\dfrac{dy}{dx} = 3\sqrt{x}$ and the curve passes through $(9, -2)$ **ii** $\dfrac{dy}{dx} = \dfrac{1}{\sqrt{x}}$ and the curve passes through $(4, 8)$

2 Find the equation of the curve if:

a i $\dfrac{d^2y}{dx^2} = 6x$ and the curve has gradient 2 at the point $(1, 5)$

ii $\dfrac{d^2y}{dx^2} = \dfrac{6}{x^3}$ and the curve has gradient -1 at the point $(1, 3)$

b i $f''(x) = 1 - 2x$, $f'(2) = 1$ and $f(2) = -1$

ii $f''(x) = 3x^2 - x$, $f'(1) = 3$ and $f(1) = 10$

3 A curve has gradient $\dfrac{dy}{dx} = x - \dfrac{1}{x^2}$ and passes through the point $(1, 3)$. Find the equation of the curve.

4 $f'(x) = \dfrac{2x - 1}{\sqrt{x}}$ and $f(4) = 2$. Find $f(x)$.

5 $f'(x) = \sqrt{x}\,(5x - 4)$ and $f(1) = \dfrac{19}{3}$. Find $f(4)$.

6 The gradient of a curve at any point is directly proportional to the x-coordinate of that point. The curve passes through point A with coordinates $(3, 2)$. The gradient of the curve at A is 12. Find the equation of the curve.

7 The gradient of a curve is $\dfrac{dy}{dx} = x^2 - 4$.

    a Find the x-coordinate of the maximum point, justifying that it is a maximum.

    b Given that the curve passes through the point $(0, 2)$ show that the y-coordinate of the maximum point is $7\frac{1}{3}$.

8 A curve has second derivative $\dfrac{d^2y}{dx^2} = 2 - x^2$.

    At the point $(1, 3)$ the gradient of the curve is 5. Find the equation of the curve in the form $y = f(x)$.

9 $f''(x) = 12x - \dfrac{5}{\sqrt[3]{x}}$, $f'(1) = -\dfrac{9}{2}$ and $f(0) = 2$.

    Find $f(8)$.

10 The gradient of the normal to a curve at any point is equal to the square of the x-coordinate at that point. If the curve passes through the point $(2, 3)$ find the equation of the curve in the form $y = f(x)$.

Section 4: Definite integration

Until now you have been carrying out a process known as **indefinite integration**: indefinite in the sense that you have an unknown constant each time, for example:

$$\int x^2 \, dx = \frac{1}{3}x^3 + c$$

There is also a process called **definite integration**, which gives a numerical answer. Evaluate the indefinite integral at two points and take the difference of the two results:

$$\int_2^3 x^2 \, dx = \left[\frac{1}{3}x^3 + c \right]_2^3$$

$$= \left(\frac{1}{3} \times 3^3 + c \right) - \left(\frac{1}{3} \times 2^3 + c \right)$$

$$= 6\frac{1}{3}$$

The numbers 2 and 3 are known as the **limits of integration**; 2 is the lower limit and 3 is the upper limit.

Notice the square bracket notation, which means that the integration has taken place but the limits have not yet been applied.

> **Tip**
>
> The constant of integration cancels in the subtraction, so there is no need to include it in the calculation at all.

> **Tip**
>
> You may be able to evaluate definite integrals on your calculator. Even when you are asked to find the exact value of an integral, you can use your calculator to check the answer.

WORKED EXAMPLE 15.13

Evaluate $\displaystyle\int_2^4 x^3 - 2x \, dx$.

$$\int_2^4 x^3 - 2x \, dx = \left[\frac{1}{4}x^4 - x^2 \right]_2^4$$

    Integrate, using square brackets to indicate that the integration has taken place but the limits are still to be applied.

$$= \left(\frac{1}{4} \times 4^4 - 4^2 \right) - \left(\frac{1}{4} \times 2^4 - 2^2 \right)$$

    Evaluate at the upper and lower limits and subtract.

$$= (64 - 16) - (4 - 4)$$

$$= 48$$

WORKED EXAMPLE 15.14

Find the exact value of $\int_8^9 \frac{3}{\sqrt{x}} \, dx$.

$$\int_8^9 \frac{3}{\sqrt{x}} \, dx = \int_8^9 3x^{-\frac{1}{2}} \, dx$$

First rewrite in the form ax^n.

$$= \left[3 \times 2x^{\frac{1}{2}} \right]_8^9$$

Then integrate: dividing by $\frac{1}{2}$ is the same as multiplying by 2.

$$= \left[6x^{\frac{1}{2}} \right]_8^9$$

$$= \left(6 \times 9^{\frac{1}{2}} \right) - \left(6 \times 8^{\frac{1}{2}} \right)$$

Evaluate at the upper and lower limits and subtract.

$$= 6\sqrt{9} - 6\sqrt{8}$$

Write the fractional power as a root in order to evaluate.

$$= 18 - 12\sqrt{2}$$

Remember that $\sqrt{8} = \sqrt{4 \times 2} = 2\sqrt{2}$.

EXERCISE 15D

1 Evaluate the following definite integrals, giving exact answers.

a i $\int_2^6 x^3 \, dx$ ii $\int_4^5 x^4 \, dx$ b i $\int_{-2}^2 3x^5 \, dx$ ii $\int_{-3}^3 2x^2 \, dx$

c i $\int_{-3}^{-1} 6x^2 - 3 \, dx$ ii $\int_{-4}^{-2} 3x^2 - 4 \, dx$ d i $\int_1^4 x^2 + x \, dx$ ii $\int_{-2}^1 3x^2 - 5x \, dx$

e i $\int_4^9 2\sqrt{x} \, dx$ ii $\int_8^{27} 6\sqrt[3]{x} \, dx$ f i $\int_1^{16} \frac{6}{\sqrt{x}} \, dx$ ii $\int_{-3}^{-1} \frac{3}{x^2} \, dx$

g i $\int_{-4}^{-2} 1 + \frac{2}{x^2} \, dx$ ii $\int_{-3}^{-1} 2x - \frac{1}{x^2} \, dx$

2 Evaluate this following integral, giving your answer in the form $a + b\sqrt{2}$: $\int_2^8 3\sqrt{x} - 2x \, dx$

3 Show that $\int_1^3 9\sqrt{x} - \frac{4}{\sqrt{x}} \, dx = a + b\sqrt{3}$, where a and b are integers to be found.

4 Find the following in terms of k: $\int_1^k 2 - \frac{1}{x^2} \, dx$

5 Find the following in terms of a: $\int_{-a}^2 x^2(4x - 3) \, dx$

6 Find the value of a such that $\int_1^a \sqrt{t} \, dt = 42$.

7 $\int_{-2}^p 1 - \frac{10}{3x^2} \, dx = -\frac{2}{3}$

Find all possible values of p.

8 Given that $\int_3^9 f(x) \, dx = 7$ evaluate $\int_3^9 2f(x) + 1 \, dx$.

9 Given that $\int_{-1}^4 f(x) \, dx = 10$ evaluate $\int_{-1}^4 \frac{f(x)}{2} + x - 1 \, dx$.

10 **a** **i** Evaluate $\displaystyle\int_3^5 2x\,dx$. **ii** Evaluate $\displaystyle\int_5^3 2x\,dx$.

    b **i** Find an expression for $\displaystyle\int_b^a 2x\,dx$.

       ii Find an expression for $\displaystyle\int_a^b 2x\,dx$.

    c Suggest a general relationship between $\displaystyle\int_b^a f(x)\,dx$ and $\displaystyle\int_a^b f(x)\,dx$.

11 **a** Find the definite integral $\displaystyle\int_1^a x^2\,dx$ in terms of a.

    b Let $f(a)=\displaystyle\int_1^a x^2\,dx$. Find $f'(a)$.

    c Find $f'(a)$ for each of the following:

       i $f(a)=\displaystyle\int_2^a x^2\,dx$ **ii** $f(a)=\displaystyle\int_{-1}^a x^2\,dx$

       What do you notice?

    d Find $f'(a)$ for each of the following, and comment on your results:

       i $f(a)=\displaystyle\int_0^a 4x^3-2x\,dx$ **ii** $f(a)=\displaystyle\int_1^a \frac{3}{x^2}\,dx$ **iii** $f(a)=\displaystyle\int_{-2}^a 1-3x^2\,dx$

Section 5: Geometrical significance of definite integration

Now you have a method that gives a numerical value for an integral, the natural question to ask is: What does this number mean? The (somewhat surprising) answer is that the definite integral represents the area under a curve. More precisely, $\displaystyle\int_a^b f(x)\,dx$ is the area enclosed between the graph of $y=f(x)$, the x-axis and the lines $x=a$ and $x=b$.

i) Did you know?

The ancient Greeks had methods for finding gradients of curves and areas under graphs. However, it took over 2000 years to develop the theory which formally proves that the two are related; that areas can be found by reversing differentiation. This was finally accomplished in the 17th century by Isaac Newton and Gottfried Leibniz.

Key point 15.5

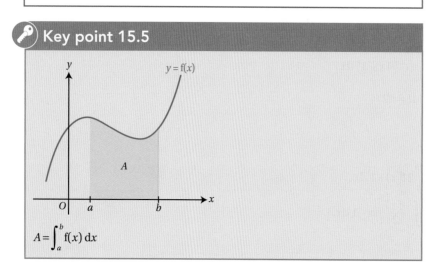

$A=\displaystyle\int_a^b f(x)\,dx$

WORKED EXAMPLE 15.15

Find the exact area enclosed between the graph of $y = 5x - x^2$, the x-axis and the lines $x = 1$ and $x = 3$.

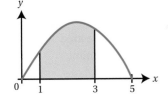

Sketch the graph and shade the required area.

$\text{Area} = \displaystyle\int_1^3 5x - x^2 \, \mathrm{d}x$

Write down the required definite integral. The limits are given by the x-coordinates at the end of the shaded region.

$= \left[\dfrac{5}{2}x^2 - \dfrac{1}{3}x^3 \right]_1^3$

Integrate and write in square brackets, then evaluate the expression at the limits and subtract.

$= \left(\dfrac{5}{2} \times 9 - \dfrac{1}{3} \times 27 \right) - \left(\dfrac{5}{2} - \dfrac{1}{3} \right)$

$= \dfrac{34}{3}$

When the curve is entirely below the x-axis the integral will give you a negative value. The area should be taken to be the positive value.

▶▶) Fast forward

Ⓐ In Student Book 2 you will learn that this can be written using the modulus function:

$$A = \int_a^b |f(x)| \, \mathrm{d}x$$

WORKED EXAMPLE 15.16

Find the area A shaded in the diagram.

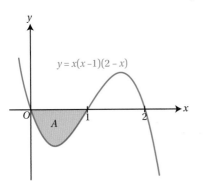

$y = x(x-1)(2-x)$

Continues on next page …

$$\int_0^1 x(x-1)(2-x)\,dx = \int_0^1 -x^3 + 3x^2 - 2x\,dx$$

Expand the brackets.

$$= \left[-\frac{1}{4}x^4 + x^3 - x^2 \right]_0^1$$

Then integrate and evaluate at the limits.

$$= \left(-\frac{1}{4} + 1 - 1 \right) - (0)$$

$$= -\frac{1}{4}$$

The integral gives a negative value because the area is under the x-axis. The area is a positive number.

$$\therefore A = \frac{1}{4}$$

The relationship between integrals and areas is a bit more complicated when some parts of the curve are above the axis and other parts are below it. Those parts above the axis contribute positively to the area, but parts below the axis contribute negatively. To calculate the total area you must separate out the sections above the axis and those below the axis.

🔍 Explore

Another difficulty with finding areas arises when the graph has a vertical asymptote. For example, try working out $\int_{-2}^2 \frac{1}{x^2}\,dx$. This is called an 'improper integral'. It turns out that sometimes regions that appear to be infinite still have a finite area.

WORKED EXAMPLE 15.17

a Find $\int_1^4 x^2 - 4x + 3\,dx$.

b Sketch the graph of $y = x^2 - 4x + 3$. Hence find the area enclosed between the x-axis, the curve $y = x^2 - 4x + 3$ and the lines $x = 1$ and $x = 4$.

a $\int_1^4 x^2 - 4x + 3\,dx = \left[\frac{1}{3}x^3 - 2x^2 + 3x \right]_1^4$

$= \left(\frac{1}{3}(4)^3 - 2(4)^2 + 3(4) \right) - \left(\frac{1}{3}(1)^3 - 2(1)^2 + 3(1) \right)$

Integrate and evaluate at the upper and lower limits.

$= \left(\frac{4}{3} \right) - \left(\frac{4}{3} \right)$

$= 0$

Continues on next page ...

b

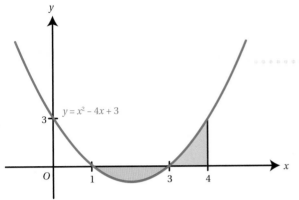

You can see that the required area is made up of two parts, so evaluate each of them separately.

$$\int_1^3 x^2 - 4x + 3 \ dx = \left[\frac{1}{3}x^3 - 2x^2 + 3x \right]_1^3$$

$$= (0) - \left(\frac{4}{3} \right)$$

$$= -\frac{4}{3}$$

The integral for the part of the curve below the axis is negative, but the area must be positive.

$\therefore$ Area below the axis is $\dfrac{4}{3}$

$$\int_3^4 x^2 - 4x + 3 \ dx = \left[\frac{1}{3}x^3 - 2x^2 + 3x \right]_3^4$$

$$= \left(\frac{4}{3} \right) - (0)$$

$$= \frac{4}{3}$$

The area of the part above the axis is found as normal.

$\therefore$ Area above the axis is $\dfrac{4}{3}$

Total area $= \dfrac{4}{3} + \dfrac{4}{3} = \dfrac{8}{3}$

Now add the two areas together.

The fact that the integral in worked example 15.17 was zero can be interpreted as meaning that the area above the axis is exactly cancelled by the area below the axis.

 Tip

Always sketch the graph first (if it is not given) when asked to find an area.

WORK IT OUT 15.3

Find the total area enclosed by the graph of $y = x^3 - 5x^2 + 6x$ and the x-axis.

Which is the correct solution? Can you identify the errors made in the incorrect solutions?

Solution 1	Solution 2	Solution 3
The x-intercepts are 0, 2, 3. $$\int_0^3 x^3 - 5x^2 + 6x \; \mathrm{d}x$$ $$= \left[\frac{1}{4}x^4 - \frac{5}{3}x^3 + 3x^2\right]_0^3 = \frac{9}{4}$$	The x-intercepts are 0, 2, 3. $$\int_0^2 x^3 - 5x^2 + 6x \; \mathrm{d}x$$ $$+ \int_2^3 x^3 - 5x^2 + 6x \; \mathrm{d}x$$ $$= \left(\frac{8}{3} - 0\right) + \left(\frac{9}{4} - \frac{8}{3}\right) = 2.25$$	The x-intercepts are 0, 2, 3. $$\int_0^2 x^3 - 5x^2 + 6x \; \mathrm{d}x = \frac{8}{3} - 0 = \frac{8}{3}$$ $$\int_2^3 x^3 - 5x^2 + 6x \; \mathrm{d}x = \frac{9}{4} - \frac{8}{3}$$ $$= -\frac{5}{12}$$ $$\text{Area} = \frac{8}{3} + \frac{5}{12} = \frac{37}{12}$$

EXERCISE 15E

1 Find the shaded areas.

a i

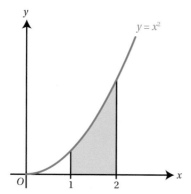

ii

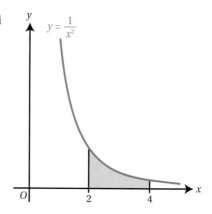

b i

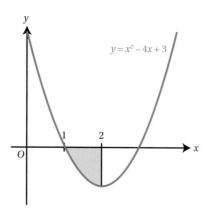

ii

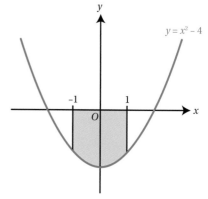

c **i**

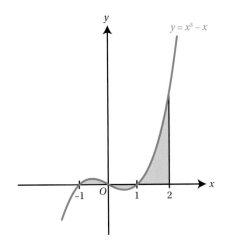

ii

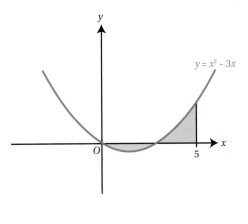

2 Find the following areas. You may want to sketch the graph first.

a **i** Between the curve $y = x^2 + 2$, the x-axis and the lines $x = 2$ and $x = 5$.

ii Between the curve $y = 2x^2 + 1$, the x-axis and the lines $x = 1$ and $x = 2$.

b **i** Enclosed between the graph of $y = 4 - x^2$ and the x-axis.

ii Enclosed between the graph of $y = x^2 - 1$ and the x-axis.

c **i** Enclosed between the curve $y = x^2 - 9x$ and the x-axis.

ii Enclosed between the curve $y = x^3 - 3x^2 + 2x$ and the x-axis.

Elevate

For a reminder and more practice of questions like this on finding areas, see Support sheet 15.

3 A part of the graph of $y = x^2 - 4x + 3$ is shown here. The curve crosses the x-axis at $x = 1$. The shaded region is enclosed by the curve, the x-axis and the lines $x = 0$ and $x = 2$.

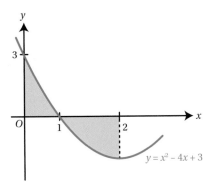

Find the area of the shaded region.

4 The diagram shows the graph of $y = \sqrt{x}$. The shaded area is 18.

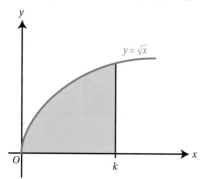

Find the value of k.

5 **a** Find $\displaystyle\int_0^3 x^2 - 1 \, dx$.

b The graph of $y = x^2 - 1$ is shown in the diagram. The shaded region is bounded by the curve, the x-axis and the lines $x = 0$ and $x = 3$.

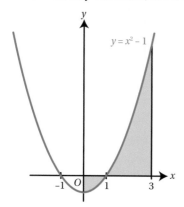

Find the area of the shaded region.

6 **a** Factorise $x^2 - 7x + 10$.

b Find the area enclosed by the curve $y = 7x - x^2 - 10$ and the x-axis.

7 **a** Write down the coordinates of the points where the graph of $y = x^2 - kx$ crosses the x-axis.

b The area shaded in the diagram is bounded by the curve $y = x^2 - kx$, the x-axis and the lines $x = 0$ and $x = 3$. The area below the x-axis equals the area above the x-axis. Find the value of k.

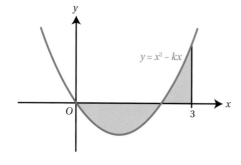

8 **a** Evaluate $\displaystyle\int_0^3 x^2 + 2 \, dx$.

   b The diagram shows a part of the curve with equation $y = x^2 + 2$.
   The shaded region is bounded by the curve, the y-axis and the
   line $y = 11$.

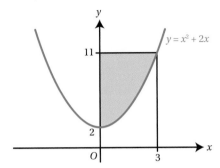

   Find the area of the shaded region.

9 Find the area enclosed between the curve $y = 1 - 8x^3$, the y-axis
and the line $y = -63$.

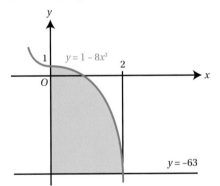

10 The diagram shows the graphs of $y = 36 - x^2$ and $y = 18x - x^2$.
The shaded region is bounded by the two curves and the x-axis.

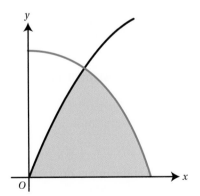

Find the area of the shaded region.

11 The curve in the diagram has equation $y = \sqrt{x}$.

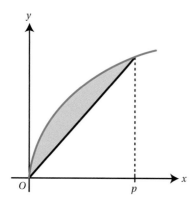

Find the shaded area in terms of p.

12 The diagram shows a part of the parabola $y = a^2 - x^2$. Point P has x-coordinate $\frac{a}{2}$.

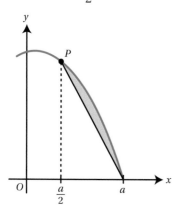

Find the shaded area in terms of a.

📎 Checklist of learning and understanding

- Integration is the reverse process of differentiation.
- If you know $\frac{dy}{dx}$, the indefinite integral gives an expression for y with an unknown constant of integration. You can find this constant if you know the coordinates of a point on the curve.
- For all rational $n \neq -1$:

$$\int x^n \, dx = \frac{1}{n+1} x^{n+1} + c$$

- The definite integral $\int_a^b f(x) \, dx$ is found by evaluating the integrated expression at the upper limit b and then subtracting the integrated expression evaluated at the lower limit a.
- The **area** between the curve, the x-axis and lines $x = a$ and $x = b$ is given by $A = \int_a^b f(x) \, dx$ provided that the part of the curve between $x = a$ and $x = b$ lies entirely above the x-axis.
- If the curve goes **below** the x-axis, then the integral of the part below the axis will be **negative**. To find the total area you need to find areas of the parts below and above the axis separately.

Mixed practice 15

1 A curve has gradient $\dfrac{dy}{dx} = 3x - \sqrt{x}$ and passes through the point $(4, -1)$. Find the equation of the curve.

2 Find the indefinite integral $\displaystyle\int \dfrac{1 + x\sqrt{x}}{x^2}\, dx$.

3 Given that $f'(x) = (1 - x)(\sqrt{x} + 2)$, and that $f(1) = 3$, find an expression for $f(x)$.

4 **a** Find the exact value of $\displaystyle\int_2^{2\sqrt{3}} 3 - \dfrac{12}{x^2}\, dx$.

Give your answer in the form $a + b\sqrt{3}$, where a and b are integers.

b The curve in the diagram has equation $y = 3 - \dfrac{12}{x^2}$. The curve crosses the x-axis at $x = 2$. The shaded region is bounded by the curve, the y-axis and the lines $y = 0$ and $y = 2$.

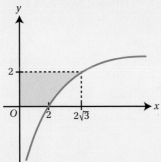

Find the area of the shaded region.

5 **i** Find $\displaystyle\int (x^2 - 2x + 5)\, dx$.

ii Hence find the equation of the curve for which $\dfrac{dy}{dx} = x^2 - 2x + 5$ and which passes through the point $(3, 11)$.

© OCR, AS GCE Mathematics, Paper 4722, June 2012

6 Given that $f(x) = \displaystyle\int 4x + 5\, dx$, find $f'(x)$.

7 **a** Find $\displaystyle\int (x^2 + 4)(x - 6)\, dx$.

b The diagram shows the curve $y = 6x^{\frac{2}{3}}$ and part of the curve $y = \dfrac{8}{x^2} - 2$, which intersect at the point $(1, 6)$.

Use integration to find the area of the shaded region enclosed by the two curves and the x-axis.

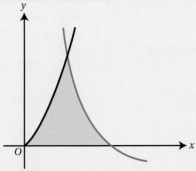

© OCR, AS GCE Mathematics, Paper 4722, January 2012

8 $f'(x) = \dfrac{4x^2 - 3\sqrt{x}}{x}$ and $f(1) = 2$.

Find $f(4)$.

9 $\displaystyle\int_1^a 2x - 3\,dx = 6,\ a > 0$

What is the value of a?

10 **a** Find the positive value of a for which $\displaystyle\int_0^a x^3 - x\,dx = 0$.

b For this value of a, find the total area enclosed between the x-axis and the curve $y = x^3 - x$ for $0 \leqslant x \leqslant a$.

11 Find the area enclosed between the graph of $y = k^2 - x^2$ and the x-axis, giving your answer in terms of k.

12 Let $f(x) = 2x^3 - 3x^2 - 3x + 2$.

a **i** Show that $(x - 2)$ is a factor of $f(x)$ and hence factorise $f(x)$ completely.

ii Sketch the graph of $y = f(x)$, labelling clearly the points where the curve crosses the coordinate axes.

b Find the exact area enclosed by the x-axis and the graph of $y = f(x)$.

13 The diagram shows the graph of $y = x^n$ for $n > 1$.

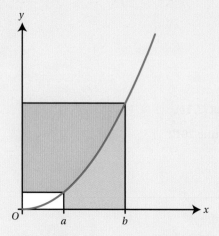

a **i** Write down an expression for the area of the white rectangle.

ii B is the area of the blue shaded region. Find an expression for B in terms of a, b and n.

b The pink area is three times as large as the blue area. Find the value of n.

 Tip

You don't need an expression for the pink area to do this question.

14 The diagram shows a parabola with equation $y = a^2 - x^2$.
The parabola crosses the x-axis at points A and B, and the
y-axis at point C.

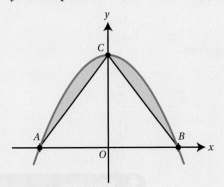

a i Write down the coordinates of A, B and C.

   ii Find, in terms of a, the area of the shaded region.

b Point P lies on the parabola. The x-coordinate of P is p.

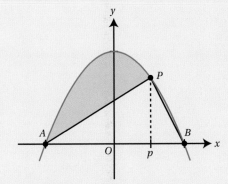

The value of p varies between the x-coordinates of A and B.

Find the minimum value of the shaded area.

15 A part of the curve with equation $y = 4 - x^2$ is shown in the
diagram. Point P has coordinates $(p, 4 - p^2)$ and point Q has
coordinates $(2, 0)$.

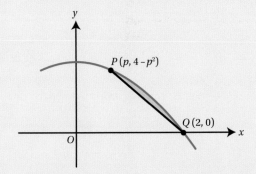

The shaded region is bounded by the curve and the chord
PQ. Show that the area of the shaded region is $\frac{1}{6}(2 - p)^3$.

16 The function f(x) has a stationary point at (3, 19) and
f''(x) = $6x+6$.

   a Determine the nature of the stationary point at (3, 19).

   b Find an expression for f(x).

17 The diagram shows the graph of $y = 6\sqrt{x}$ and the tangent to
the graph at the point (9, 18). The tangent crosses the y-axis
at the point B.

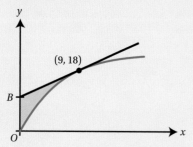

Find the area of the shaded region.

 Elevate

For more challenging question
on integration and areas see
Extension sheet 15.

Breaking the problem down

The aim of this section is to show you how you can prove new results by breaking them down into previously known ones. You will use as examples the sine and cosine rules.

We start with a specific example. Consider a triangle with $AB = 7$, $\angle BAC = 55°$ and $\angle ACB = 80°$. What is the length BC?

 Tip

When writing a proof, we need to know which results we can assume. Here we will assume that you can use trigonometry in right-angled triangles.

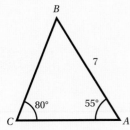 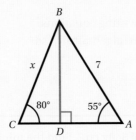

There are no right angles in the diagram, but we can create some by drawing the line BD perpendicular to AC.

We now have two right-angled triangles, which share the side BD.

- Write an expression for BD using triangle ABD.
- Write an expression for BD using triangle BCD.
- Comparing the two expressions for BD, we get:

$$x \sin 80° = 7 \sin 55° \qquad (*)$$

and rearranging gives:

$$x = \frac{7 \sin 55°}{\sin 80°} = 5.82$$

Questions

1 Use the given example to write a general proof of the sine rule: $\dfrac{a}{\sin A} = \dfrac{b}{\sin B} = \dfrac{c}{\sin C}$.

2 How is the diagram different if the angle C is obtuse? Does the proof still work?

3 Use this diagram, and your knowledge of right-angled triangles and Pythagoras' theorem, to prove the cosine rule: $c^2 = a^2 + b^2 - 2ab \cos C$.

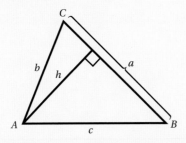

Choosing variables

Solving a problem often starts with writing some equations to represent the situation. While in exam questions you are often told things like 'express the volume in terms of r', in real applications you need to decide for yourself which variables are relevant to the question. Sometimes there is more than one possible choice, and some choices need simpler equations than others.

This section focuses on selecting variables and writing equations. Some of the resulting equations cannot be solved algebraically, so you will solve the equations using technology.

WORKED EXAMPLE

A closed cylindrical can has a fixed volume of 540π cm³. Find the minimum possible surface area of the can.

Let r be the radius and h the height of the cylinder.

> Define variables: the surface area depends on the radius and the height of the can.

Surface area: $S = 2\pi r^2 + \pi rh$

> Write an expression for the surface area.

Volume: $V = \pi r^2 h = 540\pi$

> The surface area depends on two variables. You can eliminate one of them by using the expression for the volume.

$\Rightarrow h = \dfrac{540}{r^2}$

> You now have a choice: you can express h in terms of r, or r in terms of h.

$\Rightarrow S = 2\pi r^2 + \pi r\left(\dfrac{540}{r^2}\right)$

> The latter would involve square roots, so choose the former.

$S = 2\pi r^2 + \dfrac{540\pi}{r}$

> You can use graphing software to sketch the graph of S against r and find the minimum value.

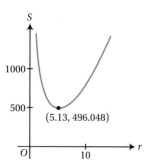

(5.13, 496.048)

The graph shows that the minimum value of the surface area is 496 cm².

Questions

1 Two people attempt to push-start a car on a horizontal road. One person pushes with a force of 100 N; the other with a force of 80 N. The car starts to accelerate constantly at $0.15\,\text{m s}^{-2}$. Assuming these are the only horizontal forces acting, find the mass of the car.

2 A sledge of mass m kg is pushed horizontally through the snow by a force of 40 N. There is resistance to its motion of magnitude 10 N as shown in the diagram.

If the sledge is accelerating at $1.5\,\text{m s}^{-2}$, find its mass.

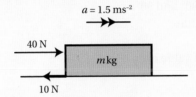

3 Two forces F_1 and F_2 act on a particle as shown.

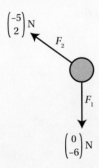

A third force, F_3, is added so that the resultant force on the particle is 2 N to the right.

Find:

a the magnitude of F_3

b the direction F_3 makes with the direction of motion.

The sunrise equation

The 'sunrise equation' can be used to calculate the approximate time the sun rises and sets at a specified location on Earth on a specified day.

$$H = \left| \frac{1}{15} \arccos \left[-\tan(L) \tan \left(23.44 \sin \left(\frac{360(D + 284)}{365} \right)^\circ \right) \right] \right|$$

In this equation:

- H is the number of hours before local noon when sunrise occurs. 'Local noon' is when the sun is directly overhead at that particular location. (You may need to add an hour for summer time.)
- L is the latitude. It is measured in degrees, between $-90°$ and $90°$; points in the northern hemisphere have positive latitude.
- D is the day of the year, with $D = 1$ being 1 January.
- The modulus sign, $|\ |$, means that you take the positive value even if the value of arccos is negative.
- Sunset occurs H hours after local noon.

As well as calculating the times of sunrise and sunset, the equation can be used to generate a 'Day and night world map', which shows the parts of the world that are in daylight at a particular point in time.

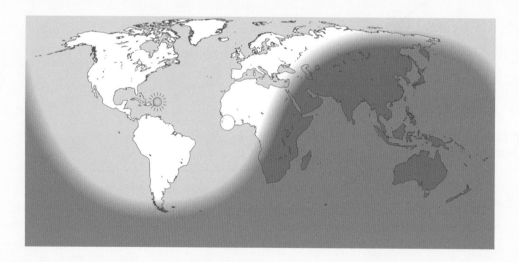

Questions

1. London is at the latitude of around 53° north. Work out the time that the formula predicts sunrise will occur on:

   a 16 February

   b 5 July.

2. Predict the time of sunset, relative to local noon, in Rio de Janeiro (about 22° south) on 12 August. What would you need to consider to find the actual time of sunset?

3. Sydney, Australia, is at about 33° south. Find the approximate length of the day (the time between sunrise and sunset) in Sydney on:

   a 8 March

   b 26 August.

4. State the largest possible value of $23.44 \sin x$. Hence find the length of the longest day in Cairo, located at 30° north.

5. Use the sunrise equation to show that, on the days of the vernal and autumnal equinoxes (20 March and 22 September) there are exactly 12 hours of daylight, regardless of the location on Earth.

6. Show that, when $L > 66.5$, there are values of D for which it is not possible to find H. What does this mean?

7. Plot the graph of H against D when:

   a $L = 55$ (for example, Edinburgh)

   b $L = 70$ (for example, Hammerfest, Norway).

8. Plot the graph of H against L for:

   a 6 September

   b 6 January.

9. What value of D should you use for 29 February in a leap year? Does the exact choice make much of a difference?

10. The constant 365 in the formula represents the number of the days in a year. A year actually has 365.25 days. Would using this value make significant difference to any of the answers you found?

11. Try to interpret the other constants in the equation.

12. What other modelling assumptions do you think have been made in forming this equation?

CROSS-TOPIC REVIEW EXERCISE 2

1 For the function $f(x) = ax^3 + bx^2 + 4x - 3$, given that $f'(2) = 0$ and $f''(2) = 10$, find $a, b \in \mathbb{R}$.

2 Find the exact period of the function $f(x) = \sin 4x + \sin 6x$.

3 In this diagram, $\overrightarrow{AB} = \overrightarrow{DC} = \mathbf{a}$ and $\overrightarrow{BC} = \overrightarrow{AD} = \mathbf{b}$. Q is the midpoint of AD and points M, N, P and Q are such that $AM : MB = 2 : 1$, $DN : NC = 2 : 7$, $BP : PC = 3 : 1$.

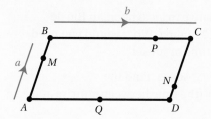

a Express $\overrightarrow{MP}$ and $\overrightarrow{QN}$ in terms of $\mathbf{a}$ and $\mathbf{b}$.

b Hence show that MP and QN are parallel.

4 Do not use a calculator in this question. Find the exact solutions of the equation $\sin 2\theta = \sqrt{3}\cos 2\theta$ for $0 \leqslant \theta \leqslant 180°$.

5 A polynomial is defined by $f(x) = x^3 - 5x^2 - x + 5$.

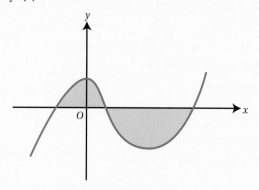

a Show that $(x + 1)$ is a factor of $f(x)$, and factorise $f(x)$ completely.

b The graph of $y = f(x)$ is shown in the diagram. Find the exact value of the shaded area.

6 Consider the function: $f(x) = \dfrac{(x-2)(x-6)}{\sqrt{x}}$.

a Show that this can be written in the form $f(x) = x^a - 8x^b + 12x^c$ giving the values of the real numbers a, b and c.

b Find the equation of the normal to $f(x)$ at the point $x = 4$.

c The normal intersects the x-axis at the point P and the y-axis at the point Q.

    i State the coordinates of P and Q.

    ii Give the exact area of the triangle POQ.

7 **a** Show that $\dfrac{1}{\cos x} - \cos x = \sin x \tan x$.

b Given that $\sin x - \cos x = \dfrac{1}{\sin x} - \dfrac{1}{\cos x}$

    i Show that $\tan x = 1$.

    ii Hence find the value of $x \in [180°, 360°]$.

8 The diagram shows the graph of $y = 9 - x^2$ and the tangent to the graph at $x = 1$. Find the shaded area.

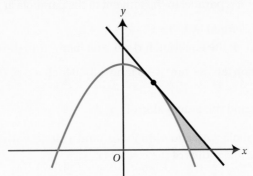

9 The triangle in the diagram has sides $AB = x + 1$, $BC = x + 3$, and $CA = 2x + 1$ and angle $B = 120°$.

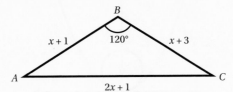

Find the value of x.

10 **a** Expand and simplify $(x + h)^4 - x^4$.

b Hence prove from first principles that the derivative of x^4 is $4x^3$.

11 A curve has gradient $f'(x) = 2x - 6$ and passes through the point $(2, 0)$.

a Find the equation of the curve.

b Find the equation of the normal to the curve at the point $(2, 0)$.

c Find the coordinates of the points where the normal intersects the curve again.

12 The diagram shows curves with equations $y = (x - 3)^2$ and $y = a(x - p)^2 + q$. The point $(4, 5)$ is the minimum point of this second curve.

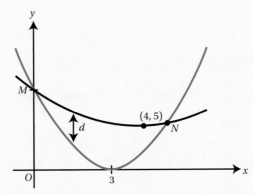

a Find the values of a, p and q.

b Find the coordinates of the intersection points, M and N, of the two curves.

c The vertical distance between the two curves is denoted by d, as shown in the diagram. Write an expression for d in terms of x. Hence find the maximum vertical distance between the two curves, on the part of the curves between points M and N.

13 The point $A(3, 4)$ lies on the circle with equation $x^2 + y^2 = 25$. The point B lies on the parabola $y = 10 - x^2$. The tangent to the circle at A is parallel to the tangent to the parabola at B. Find the coordinates of B.

14 **a** The polynomial $f(x)$ is defined by $f(x) = x^3 - x^2 - 3x + 3$.
Show that $x = 1$ is a root of the equation $f(x) = 0$, and hence find the other two roots.

b Hence solve the equation $\tan^3 x - \tan^2 x - 3\tan x + 3 = 0$ for $0 \leqslant x \leqslant 180°$.

15 Given that $A = \arcsin\left(\frac{1}{3}\right)$, find the exact value of $\cos A$.

16 The diagram shows a parabola with equation $y = ax^2$ and a circle, with the centre on the y-axis, that passes through the origin. The radius of the circle is r.

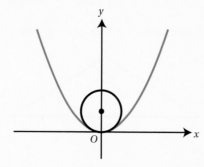

a Show that the y-coordinates of any intersections of the circle and the parabola satisfy the equation $y^2 - 2yr + \frac{y}{a} = 0$.

b Hence find, in terms of a, the largest value of r for which the circle and the parabola have only one common point.

17 **a** Simplify $(a^2 + b^2)^2 - 2a^2b^2$.

Hence show that $\cos^4 \theta + \sin^4 \theta = 1 - 2\sin^2 \theta \cos^2 \theta$.

b Show that $(\cos \theta - \sin \theta)^4 = (1 - 2\sin \theta \cos \theta)^2$.

18 **a** Sketch the graph of $y = \tan\left(\frac{1}{2}x\right)$ for $-360° \leqslant x \leqslant 360°$.

On the same axes, sketch the graph of $y = 3\cos\left(\frac{1}{2}x\right)$ for $-360° \leqslant x \leqslant 360°$, indicating the point of intersection with the y-axis.

b Show that the equation $\tan\left(\frac{1}{2}x\right) = 3\cos\left(\frac{1}{2}x\right)$ can be expressed in the form
$3\sin^2\left(\frac{1}{2}x\right) + \sin\left(\frac{1}{2}x\right) - 3 = 0.$

Hence solve the equation $\tan\left(\frac{1}{2}x\right) = 3\cos\left(\frac{1}{2}x\right)$ for $-360° \leqslant x \leqslant 360°$.

16 Working with data

In this chapter you will learn how to:

- interpret statistical diagrams including stem-and-leaf diagrams, histograms, scatter diagrams, cumulative frequency curves and box-and-whisker plots
- calculate standard deviation for data
- work with grouped data
- understand correlation and use a regression line
- clean data to remove outliers.

Before you start…

GCSE	You should know how to interpret basic statistical diagrams such as pie charts and bar charts.	1	Find the percentage decrease in the stock price after a financial crash in the following bar chart.
GCSE	You should know how to calculate the mean, median and mode of a set of data.	2	Find the mean, median and mode of: 1, 1, 4, 5, 9, 10
GCSE	You should know how to calculate the range and interquartile range of a set of data.	3	Find the range and interquartile range of: 12, 15, 18, 18, 19, 16, 14, 20, 12

Why collect data?

Statistics is an incredibly important part of mathematics in the real world. It provides the tools to collect, organise and analyse large amounts of data. For example, the government uses statistical analysis to plan public services such as building schools and hospitals.

At first, it might seem as if statistics is just about representing data through either diagrams or calculations. However, as you progress through statistics you will see that it is about making inferences about a larger group on the basis of a **sample**. Medical trials and pre-election polls are both examples of using samples to make a prediction about a whole population.

Although many statistical methods were developed more than 200 years ago, technological advances in the last few decades have enabled the analysis of much larger quantities of data, making statistics one of the most common applications of mathematics.

Section 1: A reminder of statistical diagrams

Histograms

Large amounts of data are often sorted into groups (called classes). With **continuous data**, these classes need to cover all possible data values in the range; this means that there are no gaps between classes. For example, if you have a sample of heights between 120 cm and 200 cm, you might split them into classes as follows:

Group	$120 \leqslant h < 160$	$160 \leqslant h < 180$	$180 \leqslant h < 200$
Frequency	60	40	50

You could draw this bar chart for this data.

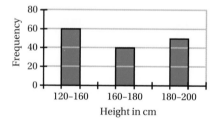

However, this bar chart is misleading. The first class has the greatest frequency, but that might be due to the fact that it covers a wider range of height than the other classes. You can overcome this problem by using a **histogram**, which looks a lot like a bar chart but the horizontal scale is continuous and the frequency is equal to area rather than height. This means that the vertical scale is **frequency density**. The equation for frequency density is given in Key point 16.1.

Key point 16.1

$$\text{Frequency density} = \frac{\text{frequency}}{\text{class width}}$$

Tip

Notice the use of inequality signs to define the classes. In practice, continuous data is usually rounded. It is therefore important to know where to put someone whose height is recorded as 180 cm.

Gateway to A Level

For a reminder of and practice with basic statistical diagrams, see Gateway to A Level section T.

Elevate

You can use bar charts, pie charts, dot plots, histograms and cumulative frequency diagrams to explore real data in the Large Data Set section on the Cambridge Elevate digital platform.

Tip

The class width is the difference between the largest and smallest possible value in the class.

If you plot the previous data on a histogram, it shows much more clearly the shape of the distribution.

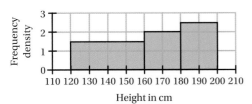

Tip

If all the class widths are equal, the histogram will have the same shape as the bar chart. However, it is still preferable to use frequency density on the vertical axis.

WORKED EXAMPLE 16.1

Use this histogram to estimate the probability of living between 5 km and 6 km away from school.

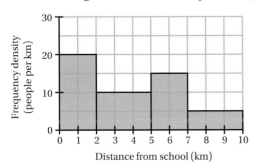

Class	0 to 2	2 to 5	5 to 7	7 to 10
width	2	3	2	3
Frequency density	20	10	15	5
Frequency	40	30	30	15

Convert the frequency densities to frequencies using the equation:
frequency = frequency density × class width

So the total frequency is $40 + 30 + 30 + 15 = 115$
The area from 5 to 6 is $1 × 15 = 15$ people, so the
probability is $\dfrac{15}{115} ≈ 0.13$

Did you know?

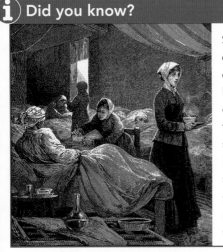

Some of the first users of statistical diagrams (in the 18th and 19th centuries) include Florence Nightingale and the political economist William Playfair. The term 'histogram' was coined by the statistician Karl Pearson. Florence Nightingale (1820–1910) used statistical evidence to convince the government to improve healthcare provision for military personnel during the Crimean War.

Cumulative frequency graphs

A **cumulative frequency diagram** is a curve showing the data values on the horizontal axis and cumulative frequency on the vertical axis. You have already met cumulative frequency diagrams in your previous studies. Although these are diagrams, their main purpose is not to provide a visual representation of the data – histograms are much better at that. They are mainly used to estimate the **median** and **quartiles** of grouped data.

Cumulative frequency is the total number of data items less than or equal to a particular value.

WORKED EXAMPLE 16.2

This table shows the masses of a sample of eggs. Find the cumulative frequency for the upper bound of each class.

Mass of eggs, x, in g	Frequency
$100 < x \leqslant 120$	26
$120 < x \leqslant 140$	52
$140 < x \leqslant 160$	84
$160 < x \leqslant 180$	60
$180 < x \leqslant 200$	12

Mass of eggs, x, in g	Cumulative frequency
$x \leqslant 120$	26
$x \leqslant 140$	78
$x \leqslant 160$	162
$x \leqslant 180$	222
$x \leqslant 200$	234

The cumulative frequency is found by adding on the number in each class to the cumulative frequency of the previous class and is recorded against the upper bound for the class.
For example, 26 eggs had mass up to 120 g, $26 + 52 = 78$ had mass up to 140 g, etc.

Once you have the cumulative frequency you can draw a cumulative frequency diagram. This has the data values along the horizontal axis and the cumulative frequency up the vertical axis. In Worked example 16.2, you can see that 26 eggs weighed 120 g or less, 78 eggs weighed 140g or less, and so on. Therefore you should plot the cumulative frequency against the upper bound of each class.

Also, notice that you have an additional point you can plot. You know from the data table that there are no eggs that weigh less than 100 g. You can then produce this cumulative frequency diagram.

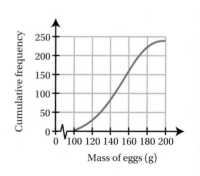

Once you have the cumulative frequency graph you can use it to estimate the median and the quartiles. The median is the value corresponding to the middle data item. On the graph, this corresponds to drawing a horizontal line at half the total frequency until it meets the curve, then a vertical line down to find the median value.

To find the quartiles you follow a similar process but with horizontal lines at one quarter and three quarters of the total frequency.

WORKED EXAMPLE 16.3

Estimate the median and interquartile range of the eggs data in Worked example 16.2.

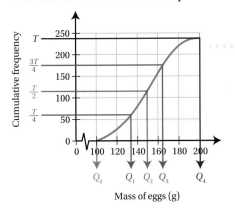

The total frequency (T) is 234, so draw lines across from the vertical axis at $0.5 \times 234 = 117$ for the median, and at $0.75 \times 234 = 175.5$ and $0.25 \times 234 = 58.5$ for the upper and lower quartiles. Where these horizontal lines meet the cumulative frequency curve, draw down to the horizontal axis to find the values of the median and quartiles.

Median (Q_2) $\approx 150\,g$

Upper quartile (Q_3) $\approx 165\,g$

Lower quartile (Q_1) $\approx 135\,g$

IQR $= Q_3 - Q_1 \approx 30\,g$

Read off the values on the horizontal axis shown by the constructed lines. The accuracy of the quartiles will depend on the scale of the graph and the smoothness of the line drawn. Here, the values are given to the nearest 5.

The median and quartiles are specific examples of **percentiles**, which tell you what data value is a given percentage of the way through the data when it is put in order. The median is therefore the 50th percentile and the lower quartile is the 25th percentile.

WORKED EXAMPLE 16.4

a Find the 90th percentile of the mass of eggs in Worked example 16.2.
b 10% of eggs are classed as extra large. At what mass is an egg classed as extra large?

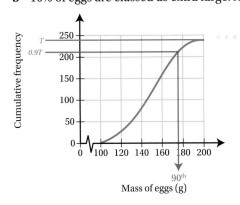

The total frequency is 234, so draw a line across from the vertical axis at $0.9 \times 234 \approx 211$.

a From the diagram the 90th percentile is approximately 175 g.

Read off the values on the horizontal axis shown by the constructed line.

b Eggs with mass greater than 175 g are classified as extra large.

Box-and-whisker plots

A useful way of visually representing the information found from a cumulative frequency diagram is a **box-and-whisker plot**. The 'box' extends from the lower quartile to the upper quartile, with the vertical line marking the median. The 'whiskers' connect the ends of the box to the maximum and minimum data values.

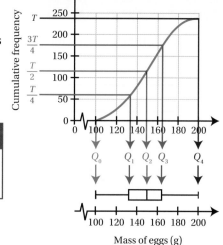

> **▶▶I) Fast forward**
>
> In Section 5 you will see that if the data contains outliers you can mark them as crosses on the box-and-whisker plot.

Box-and-whisker plots are useful when comparing two sets of data.

WORKED EXAMPLE 16.5

These box-and-whisker plots show the incomes of a large sample of people in the UK and the USA. Make two comments comparing the distributions of incomes.

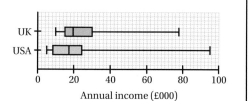

The median income in the UK is slightly higher than in the USA, so people get paid a little more on average.

You should make one comment on average...

Both the range and the interquartile range of the USA income is higher, so they have a larger spread of incomes.

and one comment on spread.

Stem-and-leaf diagrams

The diagrams you have met so far are all used for grouped data. They are very good for showing the distribution of the data, but the detail of the individual results is lost. A **stem-and-leaf diagram** is a way of recording all the data values by sorting it in rows according to the first digit(s), thus organising them into groups to show the overall distribution. This is only practical for moderately large sets of data.

Stem-and-leaf diagrams can be used to compare two distributions, or to find the median and quartiles.

WORKED EXAMPLE 16.6

This back-to-back stem-and-leaf diagram shows the heights (in cm) of a group of 20 boys and a group of 25 girls.

boys		girls
8	12	6 6 7 9 9
9 8 4	13	0 1 1 3 4 7 7 8 8
9 9 7 6 4 4 1 0 0	14	1 2 2 2 5 8 9
3 3 2 1 1 1 0	15	0 0 1 4

key: 12|6 means 126 (cm)

a   How tall is the tallest girl?
b   Find the median height of the boys.
c   Compare the distributions of heights of the two groups.

a   The tallest girl in the list has height recorded as 15|4, which means 154 cm.

The 'key' beside the diagram tells you what the numbers mean.

b   The 10th value is 146 and the 11th 147, so the median height of the boys is 146.5 cm.

There are 20 boys, so the median is the average of the 10th and 11th numbers.

Count along to find them, remembering that the boys' heights on each line go from right to left!

c   Boys are taller on average.

You can comment on three things: the average...

The spread of the heights is similar for both groups.

the spread ...

The girls' distribution is more symmetrical.

and the shape of the distribution.

EXERCISE 16A

1   For each of the following data sets:

a   draw a histogram

b   draw a cumulative frequency diagram

c   estimate from your cumulative frequency diagram the median and interquartile range

d   draw a box-and-whisker plot.

A x is the time, in minutes, taken to travel to work.

x	Frequency
$0 < x \leqslant 15$	19
$15 < x \leqslant 30$	15
$30 < x \leqslant 45$	7
$45 < x \leqslant 60$	5
$60 < x \leqslant 90$	4

B x is the age, in years, of residents in a village.

x	Frequency
$0 < x \leqslant 15$	17
$15 < x \leqslant 30$	23
$30 < x \leqslant 45$	42
$45 < x \leqslant 60$	21
$60 < x \leqslant 90$	5

💡 **Tip**

Technology should normally be used to draw statistical diagrams so that you can focus on interpreting them. However, you may find that question 1 is helpful in developing your understanding.

2 For each of these histograms find the probability that the value of *x* is between 1 and 2.

a i

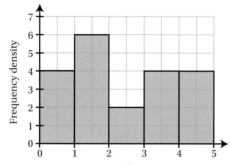

ii

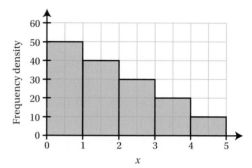

b i

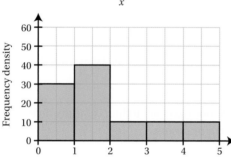

ii

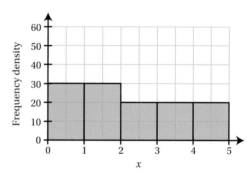

c i

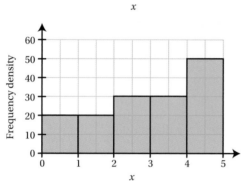

ii

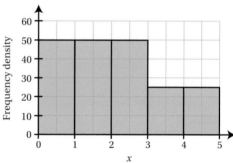

3 From the box-and-whisker plot shown, state the median and interquartile range.

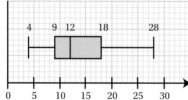

4 80 students were asked to solve a simple word puzzle and their times, in seconds, were recorded. The results are shown on the cumulative frequency graph.

a Estimate the median.

The middle 50% of students took between *c* and *d* seconds to solve the puzzle.

b Estimate the values of *c* and *d*.

c Hence estimate the interquartile range.

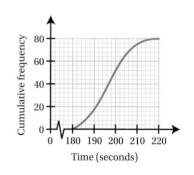

5 This cumulative frequency curve indicates the amount of time 200 students spend travelling to school.

a Estimate the percentage of students who spend between 30 and 50 minutes travelling to school.

b If 80% of the students spend more than x travelling to school, estimate the value of x.

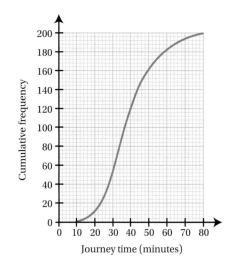

Journey time (minutes)

6 These box-and-whisker plots show the results of students in a History test and an English test.

a Compare the results in the two tests.

b What is the probability that a randomly chosen student scores more than 50% in the History test?

c State one further piece of information you would need to know to decide if the History test was easier than the English test.

d State one important feature of the data that is not conveyed by the box-and-whisker plot.

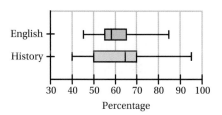

Percentage

7 These box-and-whisker plots show waiting times for two telephone banking services.

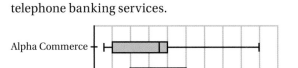

Waiting time in minutes

a What is the interquartile range of the waiting time for Beta Bank?

b If I need my calls to be answered within 5 minutes, which bank should I choose? What is the probability of getting the call answered within 5 minutes?

c If I need my calls to be answered within 15 minutes, which bank should I choose? What is the probability of getting the call answered within 15 minutes?

8 The histogram shows the wages of employees in a company.

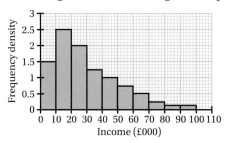

Income (£000)

a Use the histogram to estimate the probability of a randomly chosen employee earning between £20 000 and £25 000.

b The diagram shows four box-and-whisker plots labelled A, B, C and D. Explain which one corresponds to the data in the histogram.

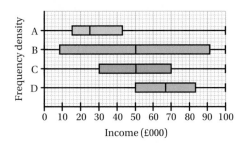

9 The stem-and-leaf diagram shows the times, in seconds, that two groups of 20 students took to complete a task.

Group 1		Group 2
8 8 6	1	6 6 7 9 9 9
9 8 5 4 4 3 2	2	0 1 1 3 4 7 8 8
9 9 7 6 4 4 1 0 0 0	3	1 2 2 4 8 9

key: 1|4 means 14s

a Find the median and interquartile range of the times for Group 2.

b Calculate the mean time for Group 2.

c Without doing any further calculations, write two comments comparing the times for the two groups.

10 Match each histogram with the cumulative frequency diagram coming from the same data.

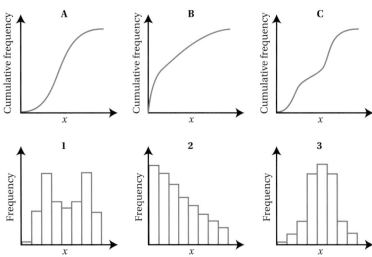

11 A histogram is drawn for the following data.

x	$0 < x \leqslant 2$	$2 < x \leqslant 5$
Frequency	a	ab

The height of the bar over the $0 < x \leqslant 2$ group is h. Find, in terms of b and h only, the height of the bar over the $2 < x \leqslant 5$ group.

Section 2: Standard deviation

The **range** is the difference between the largest and smallest values in a data set and the **interquartile range** is the difference between the lower and upper quartiles of a data set. These are both measures of spread. However, **neither** takes into account **all** of the data. There is another measure called the **standard deviation**, usually given the symbol σ (the Greek letter lower case sigma). This does take into account all of the data. It is a measure of the mean difference of each data point from the mean.

Consider the data 2, 5, 8. The mean, which is usually given the symbol $\bar{x}$, is 5.

You can look at the difference of each data point from the mean.

x	$x - \bar{x}$
2	–3
5	0
8	3

The mean of the differences is zero because the negative values cancel out the positive values. This will always be the case so it is no good as a measure of spread. However, if you square the difference you eliminate the negative values.

x	$(x - \bar{x})^2$
2	9
5	0
8	9

The average is given by adding up all the values of $(x - \bar{x})^2$ and dividing by n, the number of data items. In mathematics the symbol Σ (the Greek letter capital sigma), is used to mean 'add up all the terms'. In this case, the sum of the numbers in the right column is 18 so their average is $18 \div 3 = 6$.

You then need to undo the squaring to get a measure that has the same units as x. This means that the standard deviation for this set of data is $\sqrt{6}$.

Key point 16.2

Standard deviation: $\sigma = \sqrt{\dfrac{\Sigma(x - \bar{x})^2}{n}}$

Standard deviation can be thought of as the 'root mean square deviation from the mean'. Look at the formula in Key point 16.2 to see how this is an accurate definition. There is an alternative formula for the standard deviation which is sometimes easier to calculate.

Key point 16.3

$$\sigma = \sqrt{\dfrac{\Sigma x^2}{n} - \bar{x}^2}$$

This can be written as $\sigma^2 = \overline{x^2} - \bar{x}^2$

✔ Gateway to A Level

For a reminder of measures of average and spread, see Gateway to A Level section U.

Elevate

You will practise using spreadsheets to calculate measures of average and spread in the Large Data Set section on the Cambridge Elevate digital platform.

🔍 Explore

Try finding out about other possible measures of spread. If, instead of squaring, you simply ignore any negative signs you will get another measure of the spread called the absolute deviation. However, this is not used very widely because it does not have some of the beautiful properties of the standard deviation, which you will meet if you study Further Mathematics.

📷 Focus on …

Focus on … Proof 3 shows you the proof that the formulae in Key points 16.2 and 16.3 are equivalent.

💡 Tip

Notice that the mean of x^2 is different from the mean squared.

The **variance**, σ^2, is the square of the standard deviation. It has some very useful mathematical properties.

You now know how to calculate different measures of spread, including: range, interquartile range and standard deviation. Worked example 16.7 illustrates all three of these. There are several alternative ways to find quartiles from a list of data values; some give slightly different answers. We illustrate one possible method here, but you can use whichever way you are already familiar with.

▶▶ **Fast forward**

You will learn more about variance in the Statistics option in Further Mathematics.

✔ **Gateway to A Level**

For more practice of finding quartiles see Gateway to A Level section U.

WORKED EXAMPLE 16.7

In this question you must show detailed reasoning.

Find the range, interquartile range and standard deviation of the following numbers:

1, 12, 9, 9, 15, 7, 5

range $= 15 - 1 = 14$

Interquartile range:

1, 5, 7, 9, 9, 12, 15 ....

LQ $= 5$, UQ $= 12$, so IQR $= 7$

| Order the data then split into two halves. Because there is an odd number, you discard the middle number. Then find the midpoint of each half. |

Standard deviation:

	x	x^2
	1	1
	5	25
	7	49
	9	81
	9	81
	12	144
	15	225
Sums:	58	606

Square each data value.

Find the sum of x and of x^2.

$$\sigma = \sqrt{\frac{606}{7} - \left(\frac{58}{7}\right)^2}$$

$$= \sqrt{17.918}$$

$$\approx 4.23 \text{ (3 s.f.)}$$

In many naturally occurring measurements, about two thirds of the data will be less than one standard deviation away from the mean. This can serve as a useful quick check (even though you should not draw any firm conclusions from a small data set): in worked example 16.7, two data items (1 and 15) out of seven are more than 4.23 away from the mean (8.29). In a large data set, nearly all the data will be within two standard deviations of the mean, and anything more than three standard deviations away is very unusual.

Although you need to understand how to use the formula, in practice you can use your calculator to find the mean and standard deviation. Be careful: different calculators use different symbols for standard deviation (for example, σ or s_n). Make sure you know which option to

▶▶ **Fast forward**

Most calculators also have an option to calculate s_{n-1} which is used to estimate the population standard deviation from a sample. You will only use this if you study the Statistics option in Further Mathematics.

choose! Whatever symbol your calculator uses, in your solution you should use σ for standard deviation.

You will often be given data in the form of summary statistics, where you are told the sum of all the data values and the sum of their squares. You can then use the formula from Key point 16.3 to find the standard deviation.

WORKED EXAMPLE 16.8

Deepti records the length of time, t minutes, it takes her to cycle to school on 18 separate days. Her results are summarised as follows: $\sum t = 295.2$, $\sum t^2 = 5222.6$. Find the mean and standard deviation of the times.

$\bar{t} = \dfrac{295.2}{18} = 16.4$ minutes

> The mean is the sum of all the values divided by the number of values.

$\sigma^2 = \dfrac{\sum t^2}{18} - (\bar{t})^2$

$= \dfrac{5222.6}{18} - 16.4^2$

> Use the formula from Key point 16.3. Find the variance first and then square root the answer. Note that you have already calculated the mean.

$= 21.18$

$\sigma = \sqrt{21.18} = 4.6$ minutes

> The units of standard deviation are the same as the units of the original data.

Comparing sets of data

You already know how to use the median and inter-quartile range to compare two sets of data. The advantage of using mean and standard deviation is that they take into account all of the data, whereas the IQR only tells you about the spread of the middle half. On the other hand, if a data set contains outliers, mean and standard deviation may not be a good representation of the whole data set.

> ⏭️ **Fast forward**
>
> In Section 5 you will learn how to use standard deviation to identify outliers.

WORKED EXAMPLE 16.9

A school football team consists of eleven players with a mean age 16.3 years and standard deviation 0.6 years. The school orchestra has 20 members with a mean age 15.8 years and standard deviation 1.4 years.

a Compare the ages of the football team players and the orchestra members.

The orchestra conductor is a teacher who is 62 years old.

b Find the mean age of all the orchestra members, including the conductor.

c A student says that the orchestra members are on average older than the football team members. Comment on this statement.

a The football team are older on average, but have a smaller spread of ages.

> You should make one comment comparing an average and one comment comparing spread of ages.

b new mean $= \dfrac{20 \times 15.8 + 62}{21}$

$= 18$ years

> Find the sum of the students' ages, then add the conductor's age and divide by the total number of people.

c This is not a useful comparison, because the mean for the orchestra is affected by one extreme value.

> The mean is not a good measure of average age of the orchestra because one person is much older than the rest.

WORK IT OUT 16.1

Find the standard deviation of the following data: 2, 4, 5, 9.

Which is the correct solution? Can you identify the errors made in the incorrect solutions?

Solution 1	Solution 2	Solution 3
$\bar{x} = \dfrac{2+4+5+9}{4} = 5$ $\Sigma(x-\bar{x})^2 = (-3)^2 + (-1)^2 + 0^2 + 4^2 = 26$ $\sigma = \sqrt{\dfrac{26}{4}} \approx 2.55$	$\Sigma x = 20$ so $\Sigma x^2 = 400$ $\overline{x^2} = \dfrac{400}{4} = 100$ $\bar{x} = \dfrac{20}{4} = 5$ So standard deviation is $100 - 5^2 = 75$	From calculator, standard deviation is 2.94.

EXERCISE 16B

1 For each set of data, calculate the standard deviation and interquartile range.

   a   **i**   19.0, 23.4, 36.2, 18.7, 15.7   **ii**   0.4, −1.3, 7.9, 8.4, −9.4

   b   **i**   28, 31, 54, 28, 17, 30   **ii**   60, 18, 42, 113, 95, 23

   c   **i**   1, 2, 1, 3, 5   **ii**   3, −2, 4, −2, 5, 2

2 Sets of data are summarised by the information given. For each set of information find the standard deviation.

   a   **i** $\Sigma(x-\bar{x})^2 = 42.9,\ n = 10$ **ii** $\Sigma(x-\bar{x})^2 = 8.9,\ n = 10$

   b   **i** $\Sigma x = 49,\ \Sigma x^2 = 339,\ n = 8$ **ii** $\Sigma x = 329,\ \Sigma x^2 = 22\,135,\ n = 8$

   c   **i** $\bar{x} = 66.6,\ \overline{x^2} = 4512.6$ **ii** $\bar{x} = 24.8,\ \overline{x^2} = 1072.4$

3 The ordered set of data 5, 5, 7, 8, 9, x, 13 has interquartile range equal to 7.

   a Find the value of x.

   b Find the standard deviation of the data set.

4 10 data items have a sum of 468 and the sum of the squares of the data is 27 172.

   a Find the mean of the data.

   b Find the variance of the data.

5 The speed, x, in mph, of 10 serves by Tim, a professional tennis player, is summarised as follows:

$\Sigma x = 1245,\ \Sigma x^2 = 156\,403$

   a Find the mean speed of the serves.

   b Find the standard deviation in the speed of the serves.

   c Andy is another professional tennis player. The variance in the speed of Andy's serves is 89.6 mph^2. Which player appears to be more consistent in their serving speed?

6 The scores in a Physics test were: 81, 36, 73, 78, 74, 75.

   a Find the standard deviation of these scores.

Elevate

For more practice finding standard deviation from summary statistics see Support sheet 16.

b The standard deviation of the results of the same set of students in a Chemistry test was 5.91. Give two reasons why it would not be appropriate to use a comparison of these two standard deviations to determine whether students were more consistent in Physics or Chemistry.

Tip

In question 6, you can use a calculator to find the standard deviation.

7 Consider the five numbers, 2, 5, 9, x and y. The mean of the numbers is 5 and the variance is 6. Find the value of xy.

8 The mean IQ of a class of 9 students is 121 and the variance is 226. Another student joins the class and the variance changes to 239.4. What are the possible values of the IQ of the new student?

9 **a** Explain why for any piece of data $x - \bar{x}$ is less than the range.

b By considering the formula $\sigma = \sqrt{\dfrac{\Sigma(x - \bar{x})^2}{n}}$ prove that the standard deviation is always strictly less than the range.

Elevate

You can use Extension sheet 16 to explore different ways of comparing sets of data.

Section 3: Calculations from frequency tables

It is very common to summarise large amounts of data in a frequency table. This is a list of all the values that the data takes, along with how often they occur. You could convert this into a list of all the data values and calculate the statistics as you did previously. However, there is a formula that you can use to find the mean more quickly.

Tip

Your calculator may be able to work with frequency tables. You can always use it to check your answer, but you may also be required to use the formula.

Key point 16.4

$\bar{x} = \dfrac{\Sigma fx}{n}$ where f is the frequency of each x value and n is the total frequency.

You can work out $\overline{x^2}$ in a similar way, giving the following formula for the variance.

Key point 16.5

$\sigma^2 = \dfrac{\Sigma fx^2}{n} - \bar{x}^2$

WORKED EXAMPLE 16.10

Find the median, mean and standard deviation of the number of passengers observed in cars passing a school.

Passengers	Frequency
0	32
1	16
2	2
3 or more	0

median = average of 25th and 26th numbers so median = 0

There are $32 + 16 + 2 = 50$ data items so the median is the average of 25th and 26th data items. Both of these equal 0.

$\Sigma fx = (32 \times 0) + (16 \times 1) + (2 \times 2)$
$= 20$ passengers

The total number of passengers is: none in the first group, 16 in the second group and 4 in the third group.

Continues on next page ...

$\bar{x} = 20 \div 50 = 0.4$

> The total frequency is $32 + 16 + 2 = 50$.
> Always sense check your answer – here, 0.4 passengers per car seems reasonable. It does not have to be rounded as means do not have to be achievable numbers.

$\Sigma fx^2 = (32 \times 0) + (16 \times 1) + (2 \times 4) = 24$

> To find the standard deviation you need to first calculate the mean of the squares.

$\sigma^2 = \dfrac{24}{50} - 0.4^2 = 0.32$

> Using Key point 16.5.

$\sigma = 0.566$ to 3 s.f.

In the calculations in Worked example 16.9, you knew the exact data values, but when you are dealing with grouped data, you no longer have this level of precision. In order to assess the mean and standard deviation, your best and simplest assumption is that all the original values in a group were located at the centre of the group, called the **mid-interval value**. To find the centre of the group you take the mean of the largest and the smallest possible values in the group.

WORKED EXAMPLE 16.11

Find the mean and standard deviation of the mass of eggs produced by a chicken farm. Explain why these answers are only estimates.

Mass of eggs, in g	Frequency
$[100,120)$	26
$[120,140)$	52
$[140,160)$	84
$[160,180)$	60
$[180,200)$	12

x	f	fx	fx^2
110	26	2860	314 600
130	52	6760	878 800
150	84	12 600	1 890 000
170	60	10 200	1 734 000
190	12	2280	433 200
Sum:	234	34 700	5 250 600

> Make a table assuming each data value lies in the centre of its group.

$\bar{x} = \dfrac{\Sigma fx}{n} = \dfrac{34\,700}{234} = 148.3g \ (4\text{s.f.})$

> Your calculator should be able to give you the values of Σfx and Σfx^2. You should write those down as evidence of your method.

$\sigma^2 = \dfrac{\Sigma fx^2}{n} - \bar{x}^2$

$= \dfrac{5250\,600}{234} - 148.3^2 = 448.4$

Continues on next page ...

Therefore $\sigma = 21.2\,g$ (3 s.f.) .... Always do a sense check – in this case 21.2 g seems like a sensible measure of spread as it is significantly smaller than the range. You can also check that about two thirds of the data (about 150 values) lie within one standard deviation of the mean (between about 130 and 170).

These answers are only estimates because we have assumed that all the data in each group is at the centre, rather than using the actual data values.

◀◀ Rewind

This bracket notation to describe intervals was introduced in Chapter 1, Section 2.

Sometimes the endpoints of the intervals shown in the table are not the actual smallest and largest possible values in that group. For example, when measuring length in centimetres it is common to round the values to the nearest integer, so 10–15 actually means [9.5, 15.5). To find the mid-interval values you must first identify the actual interval boundaries.

WORKED EXAMPLE 16.12

Estimate the mean of the following data, which relates to the age of a sample of young people in years. Give your answer accurate to 3 significant figures.

Age	Frequency
10 to 12	27
13 to 15	44
16 to 19	29

Group	x	f	fx
[10,13)	11.5	27	310.5
[13,16)	14.5	44	638
[16,20)	18	29	522
Sum:		100	1470.5

Carefully decide on the upper and lower interval boundaries. There should be no 'gaps' between the groups, because age is continuous. Age is a little bit tricky because you are 17 years old until your 18th birthday.

$$\bar{x} = \frac{\sum fx}{n} = \frac{1470.5}{100} = 14.7 \text{ years (3 s.f.)}$$

Enter midpoints and frequencies into your calculator.

EXERCISE 16C

1 Calculate the mean, standard deviation and the median for each of these data sets.

a i

x	Frequency
0	16
1	22
2	8
3	4
4	0

ii

x	Frequency
–1	10
0	8
1	5
2	1
3	1

b i

x	Frequency
10	7
12	19
14	2
16	0
18	2

ii

x	Frequency
0.1	16
0.2	15
0.3	12
0.4	9
0.5	8

2 Calculate estimates of the mean and standard deviation of each of the following sets of data. Use statistical functions on your calculator.

a i x is the time taken to complete a puzzle in seconds.

x	Frequency
[0, 15)	19
[15, 30)	15
[30, 45)	7
[45, 60)	5
[60, 90)	4

ii x is the mass of plants in grams.

x	Frequency
[50, 100)	17
[100, 200)	23
[200, 300)	42
[300, 500)	21
[500, 1000)	5

b i x is the length of fossils found in a geological dig, to the nearest centimetre.

x	Frequency
0 to 4	71
5 to 10	43
11 to 15	22
16 to 30	6

ii x is the power consumption of light bulbs, to the nearest watt.

x	Frequency
90 to 95	17
96 to 100	23
101 to 105	42
106 to 110	21
111 to 120	5

c **i** x is the age of children in a hospital ward.

x	Frequency
0 to 2	12
3 to 5	15
6 to 10	7
11 to 16	6
17 to 18	3

ii x is the value of tips paid in a restaurant, rounded down to the nearest pound.

x	Frequency
0 to 5	17
6 to 10	29
11 to 20	44
21 to 30	16
31 to 50	8

3 A group is described as '17–20'. State the upper and lower boundaries of this group if it is measuring:

a age in completed years

b number of pencils

c length of a worm to the nearest centimetre

d hourly earnings, rounded up to a whole number of pounds.

4 The bar chart shows the outcome of a survey into the number of cars owned in each household in a small town called Statham.

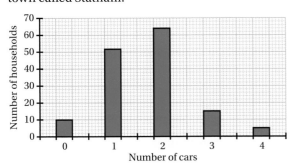

a Copy and complete this table using the graph:

Number of cars	0	1	2	3	4
Number of households	10	52			

b Hence find the mean and standard deviation of the number of cars in a household.

c The survey is also conducted in a nearby town called Mediton where the mean is found to be 2.17 cars per household with standard deviation 1.12. Make two comparisons, in context, between the two towns.

5 The mass of food eaten by 50 dogs during a week was measured to the nearest kg:

Mass (kg)	1 or 2	3 or 4	5 or 6	7 or 8
Frequency	12	20	16	2

a Estimate the mean and standard deviation of the masses.

b State two ways in which the accuracy of these estimates could be improved if the observations were to be repeated.

6 In a sample of 50 boxes of 12 eggs, the number of broken eggs per box is shown.

Number of broken eggs per box	0	1	2	3	4	5	6
Number of boxes	17	8	7	7	6	5	0

a Find the median number of broken eggs per box.

b Calculate the mean number of broken eggs per box.

c Calculate the variance of the data.

d The packaging process for the eggs is changed. In a new sample of 50 boxes the mean number of broken eggs was 1.92 and the variance was 2.84. Give one reason to support someone who argues:

  i   the new packaging process is better

  ii the new packaging process is worse

  iii there is no difference between the two packaging processes.

7 A student is investigating the ways teachers from different schools travel to work. For a large number of schools, he recorded the percentage of teachers who cycle to work. He summarised the information in a histogram.

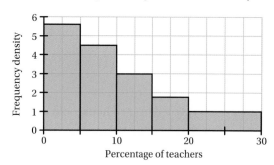

a Use the graph to calculate estimates of the mean and standard deviation of the percentage of teachers who cycle to work.

b What assumptions have you made in your calculations in part **a**?

c Explain with reference to the graph why the median will be below the mean for this set of data.

8 The standard deviation of this data is $0.8k$ where k is a positive constant.

x	Frequency
1	8
p	2

a Explain why there will be two possible values for p for each value of k.

b Find expressions for p in terms of k.

c Given that the mean is 2.2, find the value of k.

9 The mean of the data in the table is 32 and the variance is 136. Find the possible values of p and q.

x	Frequency
20	12
40	q
p	8

10 Amy and Bob are both playing a game on their computer. Amy's average score on both level one and level two is higher than Bob's. Show that it is possible for Bob to still have a higher overall average across levels one and two.

Section 4: Scatter diagrams and correlation

So far, you have only been interested in one variable at a time, such as someone's height or their IQ. But now you would like to see whether there is a relationship between two variables. By gathering two data values from an individual source, say a person's age and mass, you can investigate any potential relationship. Data that comes in pairs in this fashion is said to be **bivariate**.

When you have two sets of data, their relationship might be independent – when you know one variable it gives you no information about the other one. For example, the IQ and the house number of a randomly chosen person. Alternatively, the variables may be in a fixed relationship – when you know one variable you know exactly what the other one will be. For example the length of a side of a randomly created cube and the volume of the cube. However, usually it is somewhere in between – if you know one value you can make a better guess at the value of the other variable, but not be certain. For example, your mark in paper 1 and mark in paper 2 of a Maths exam. The **correlation** of the two variables describes where the relationship lies on this spectrum.

In this course, you shall focus on linear correlation – the extent to which two variables are related by a relationship of the form $y = mx + c$. If the gradient of the linear relationship is positive you describe the correlation as positive, and if the gradient is negative you describe the correlation as negative.

These relationships are often best illustrated using a scatter diagram:

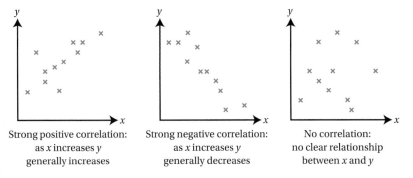

Strong positive correlation: as x increases y generally increases

Strong negative correlation: as x increases y generally decreases

No correlation: no clear relationship between x and y

Rather than simply describing the relationship in words you can find a numerical value to represent the linear correlation. The **correlation coefficient**, r, is a measure of the strength of the relationship between two variables. It can take values between –1 and 1.

You need to know how to interpret the value of r:

Value of r	Interpretation
$r \approx 1$	Strong positive linear correlation
$r \approx 0$	No linear correlation
$r \approx -1$	Strong negative linear correlation

If $r = \pm 1$ it is perfect correlation – the data lies exactly along a straight line.

Explore

There are many different measures of correlation. This one is often referred to as Pearson's product moment correlation coefficient (or PPMCC). Find out about other measures such as Spearman's Rank or Kendall's Tau.

Just because $r = 0$ does not mean that there is no relationship between the two variables – it just means that there is no **linear** relationship. This graph shows data which has a correlation coefficient of zero, but there is clearly a relationship:

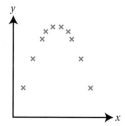

Scatter diagrams can also reveal if there are two separate groups within the data:

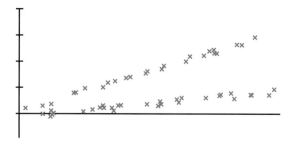

Elevate

You will find more practice of interpreting scatter graphs in the Large Data Set section on the Cambridge Elevate digital platform.

While the product moment correlation coefficient can give a measure of correlation between two variables, it is important to realise that just because r might be close to ± 1, a change in one variable does not necessarily **cause** a change in the other. Such a correlation might be simply coincidence or due to a third, hidden variable.

For example, there might be a strong correlation between ice cream sales and instances of drowning at beaches in a given location. Clearly, eating more ice cream does not cause drowning; instead, the hidden variable of temperature could cause both to rise.

Tip

You may want to remember the phrase 'correlation does not imply causation'.

WORKED EXAMPLE 16.13

Decide which of the following graphs has a correlation coefficient of –0.94. Justify your answer.

A

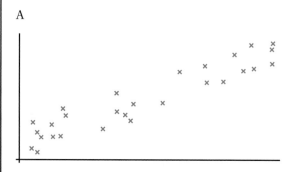

B

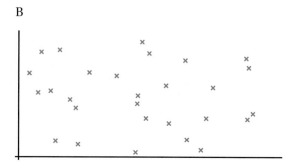

Continues on next page ...

C

D

Diagram A has a positive correlation.

Diagram B has no correlation.

Diagram C has strong negative correlation.

Diagram D has perfect negative correlation.

$r = -0.94$ indicates strong (but not perfect) negative correlation which is in diagram C.

Once you have established from the correlation coefficient that there is a linear relationship it is often useful to draw in a line of best fit, sometimes called a **regression line**.

When interpreting regression lines you should always consider whether the data actually follows a linear trend – either by looking at the correlation coefficient or the scatter diagram. You should also be aware that if you are using the regression line to predict values outside the range of the observed data – called **extrapolation** – your answer may be less valid.

 Explore

Find out about a method for calculating lines of best fit called 'least squares regression'.

Fast forward

A In Student Book 2, Chapter 19, you will see a method for deciding if a calculated correlation coefficient is evidence of a genuine linear relationship between the two variables. Until then, you will not have to deal with correlation coefficients where the interpretation is ambiguous.

EXERCISE 16D

 1 For each of the following sets of bivariate data describe the correlation you would expect to see.

a The distance someone lives from school and the time it takes them to travel to school.

b A person's height and their income.

c The age of a car and the number of miles driven.

d The distance travelled by a car going at constant speed and the time it has travelled.

e The age of a school student and the time taken to run 100 m.

f The value of a house and the number of bedrooms.

g The average age of adults in a village and the percentage of adults who cycle to work.

2 Describe the correlation shown in each of these scatter diagrams.

a

b

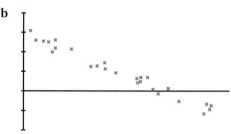

c

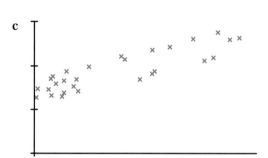

d

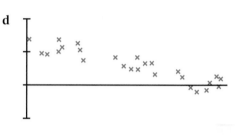

e

f

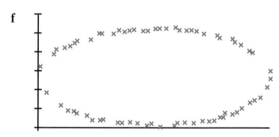

g

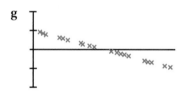

h

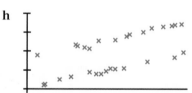

3 The correlation coefficient between the speed of a computer processor and its life expectancy is 0.984, based on a sample of 50 processors.

  a Interpret this correlation coefficient.

  b Does this result imply that processor speed affects the life expectancy? Explain your answer.

4 A road safety group has tested the braking distance of cars of 20 different ages. The correlation coefficient between a car's age and braking distance is 0.92.

  a Interpret the correlation coefficient.

  b Nicole says that this provides evidence that older cars tend to have longer stopping distances. State with a reason whether you agree with her.

5 The masses of babies (Y kg) at age X months is measured for a sample of 100 babies between 0 and 18 months.

  a The correlation coefficient is found to be 0.88. Describe what this suggests about the relationship between mass and age for babies.

  b The equation of the line of best fit is found to be $Y = 0.5X + 3.2$. Interpret in context the meaning in this equation of:

    i 0.5   **ii** 3.2

  c Explain why this line of best fit would not be an appropriate model to predict the mass of a 14-year-old boy.

6 The number of years since starting primary school (x) and 100 m times (t seconds) of 20 students was measured. The output from a spreadsheet gave the following information:

$$t = 24.8 - 0.609x \qquad r = -0.24 \qquad r^2 = 0.0576$$

  a Interpret in context the values in the output of:

    i 24.8   **ii** 0.609

  b Give two reasons why it would not be appropriate to use this model to predict the 100 m time of a 60-year-old.

7 Match the scatter diagrams with the following values of r:

  a $r = 0.98$ **b** $r = -0.34$ **c** $r = -0.93$ **d** $r = 0.58$

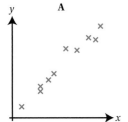 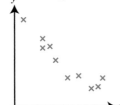 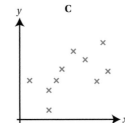 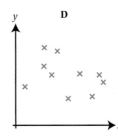

8 The heights and ages of 30 trees in a forest were measured and plotted on this scatter diagram.

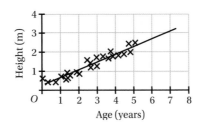

The correlation coefficient is 0.96.

  a Use the line of best fit to estimate the height of a tree that is

    i 3 years old   **ii** 7 years old.

  b Comment on the validity of your answers to part **a**.

9   This graph shows a connected scatter plot of the lowest frequency produced by a sample of 6 speakers against their power.

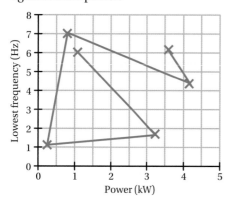

a   Use the line provided to estimate, where possible, the lowest frequency if the power is:

   i   3.5 kW   **ii**   2 kW

b   Explain why it is not appropriate to connect the data using straight lines in this way.

c   Describe a situation in which it would be appropriate to connect the points using straight lines in this way.

10   Decide which of the following statements are true for the bivariate data and which are false?

a   If $r = 0$ there is no relationship between the two variables.

b   If $Y = kX$ then $r = 1$.

c   If $r < 0$ then the gradient of the line of best fit is negative.

d   As r increases then so does the gradient of the line of best fit.

Section 5: Outliers and cleaning data

When dealing with real-world data there are sometimes errors, missing data or extreme values that can distort your results. In this section you will look at some standard ways to identify problematic data and how to deal with it.

Often the most useful thing to do is to look at your data graphically. If the underlying pattern is strong, **outliers** can become obvious. For example, on the following scatter diagram, the red point does not seem to follow the trend of the other points.

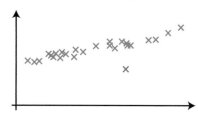

There are also some standard calculations that you can use to check for outliers.

The first is that an outlier is any number more than 1.5 interquartile ranges away from the nearest quartile.

WORKED EXAMPLE 16.14

A group of people were asked to name as many characters from *Harry Potter* as possible in one minute. The results are illustrated in this box-and-whisker plot. Determine if there are any outliers in the data set using the definition that an outlier is any data value lying more than 1.5 interquartile ranges away from the nearest quartile.

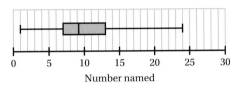

Number named

Lower quartile: 7

Upper quartile: 13

Interquartile range: 6

> Read off the quartiles from the plot to find the IQR.

Upper quartile plus 1.5 IQR

$= 13 + 1.5 \times 6 = 22$

Lower quartile minus 1.5 IQR

$= 7 - 1.5 \times 6 = -2$

> Find the largest and smallest values that are not outliers.

Smallest value is 1 which is not an outlier.

Largest value is 24 which is an outlier.

> Look at largest and smallest values.

Hence there is at least one outlier in the data set.

> The box plot does not show the exact distribution of the data values along the right-hand 'whisker', so it's impossible to tell whether there are any other outliers.

Another possible method is to classify anything more than two standard deviations from the mean as an outlier.

WORKED EXAMPLE 16.15

The wages of workers in a factory are (in thousands of pounds):

x	10	16	20	145
f	18	14	4	1

Use the definition of an outlier as anything more than two standard deviations from the mean to determine if the wage of £145 000 is an outlier.

Use your calculator:

$\bar{x} = 17$

> Use your calculator to find the mean and standard deviation.

$\sigma = 21.633...$

Two standard deviations from the mean is

$17 + 2 \times 21.633... = 60.266...$

> Use the full accuracy from your calculator rather than the quoted rounded value.

$145 > 60.266...$ so £145 000 is an outlier.

Once you have found that something is an outlier you must then decide whether or not to include it in your calculation. This often requires you to look at the data in context.

If the outlier is clearly an error (for example, the wrong units being used or an impossible value) then it should be excluded from the data.

If there are several outliers it might be a distinctly different group which should be analysed separately.

Otherwise, it might simply be that there is an unusual value in your data. This does not mean that it is an error. Unless you have a good reason to exclude it you should keep it in your analysis but report the presence of outliers.

When using large data sets, you will often find that some of the data are missing. You should consider how the missing values may affect the results of your calculations.

⬇ Elevate

You will find practice of how to deal with missing data in a real data set in the Large Data Set section on the Cambridge Elevate digital platform.

💡 Tip

You may be asked to add to diagrams in order to interpret data.

ℹ Did you know?

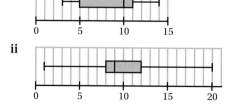

There is a famous story (probably not entirely accurate) that NASA satellites first 'discovered' a hole in the ozone layer in the 1970s but an automatic error checker decided it was an anomalous reading so it was ignored until nearly ten years later. Sometimes outliers are potentially the most interesting part of the data.

EXERCISE 16E

1 Determine, using the definition of an outlier as more than 1.5 IQR from the nearest quartile, if there are outliers in the following sets of data.

a i

ii

b i

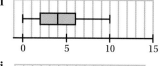

ii

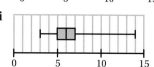

2 Determine if the following data contain outliers, defined as data more than 2 standard deviations from the mean.

a i 1, 5, 5, 7, 14   **ii** 80, 85, 90, 90, 125

b i –3, 8, 8, 10, 14, 15, 16   **ii** 0, 26, 26, 28, 29, 30, 64

3 A biologist collects mass and length information on a sample of ants from a forest. He finds the correlation coefficient is 0.22, so concludes that there is not a strong linear relationship between mass and length. A colleague suggests that he should draw a scatter diagram to illustrate the data, which is shown here.

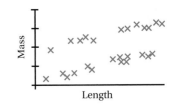

What statistical advice would you give the biologist?

4 30 people attempted to complete a level on a computer game. This box-and-whisker plot shows the number of attempts required.

a Find the interquartile range for this set of data.

b If outliers are defined as more than 1.5 IQR from the nearest quartile, then show that there must be an outlier in the data.

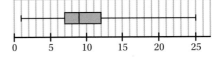

5 The following cumulative frequency graph shows the marks of 100 students in a test.

Use the definition that an outlier is more than 1.5 IQR from the nearest quartile to show that there are no outliers in this data.

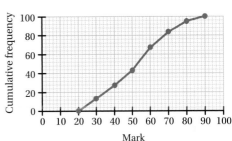

6 A survey is conducted in a large school to find out the mean height of all students in years 7 to 13. In each situation described below the data set contains some missing data. Explain whether the calculated mean is likely to be an underestimate, an overestimate or close to the actual mean.

a The basketball team were away.

b 5% of the whole school were ill.

c All of Year 7 were out on a Geography trip.

7 All 560 Year 12 students at a college did a Maths test, on which the maximum possible mark was 70. Unfortunately, one teacher forgot to record the marks for his class of 18 students. The mean mark for the remaining 542 students is 48. Find the minimum and maximum possible mean mark for all 560 students.

8 This scatter diagram shows the number of matches on a tennis court in a week (N) against the average temperature in that week (T).

The mean number of matches per week is 46.4 with standard deviation 7.80.

a Use of the tennis court is known to increase noticeably during the first week of the Wimbledon tennis tournament. What was the average temperature during that week?

b The data point corresponding to the first week of Wimbledon is removed. Without further calculation, determine:

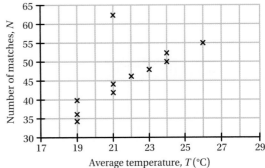

i Will the mean number of matches per week increase or decrease?

ii Will the standard deviation in the number of matches increase or decrease?

9 A runner uses a smartwatch to track the time taken (t in minutes) and distance covered (d in km) on her run each day for a seven day week.

a The times taken are summarised by $\Sigma t = 440$, $\Sigma t^2 = 28\,040$. Find the mean and standard deviation of the times taken.

b The data is tabulated and illustrated in the scatter diagram as follows:

	Time (min)	Distance (km)
Monday	62	18
Tuesday	49	15
Wednesday	75	23
Thursday	62	14
Friday	66	20
Saturday	59	17
Sunday	67	20

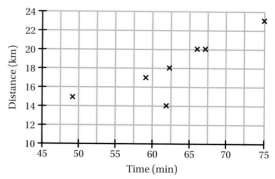

Six of the days were sunny but on one day it was raining and windy. Which day was this?

c Remove the day with bad weather and recalculate the mean and standard deviation of the times.

d The equation of the regression line for the sunny days is $d = 0.314t - 0.957$.
Use this equation to estimate the speed of the runner.

e Would it be appropriate to use this regression line to estimate the time the runner would take to complete a 40 km race? Justify your answer.

10 **a** A doctor measures the level of infection markers in 6 samples of blood. The mean of the values is 18 with a variance of $\frac{631}{3}$. The largest value is 50. Show that this is an outlier, using the definition that outliers are more than 2 standard deviations away from the mean.

b Find the mean and standard deviation if the value of 50 is removed.

11 **a** Find the maximum and minimum value of $8x^2 - 576x + 11\,826$ for $0 \leqslant x \leqslant 50$.

b A group of nine students took a test, marked out of 50. The mark for one of the students did not get recorded. For the remaining eight students, the mean mark was 36 and the standard deviation was 4.5. Find the smallest and largest possible standard deviation for all nine students.

12 In this question, define an outlier as being more than two standard deviations from the mean.

a The standard deviation of a set of data is 9 with range 50. Prove that there must be an outlier in the data.

b Consider the following data set:

x	Frequency
0	p
30	q

Show that 30 is an outlier if $p > 4q$.

c Hence show that if a data set has a standard deviation of 9 with range 30 it is possible for there to be an outlier. (Hint: try $q = 3$.)

d Show using a counter example that if a data set has standard deviation 9 and range 30 it is not certain that there is an outlier. (Hint: Consider a data set with three values: 0, 15 and 30.)

✎ Checklist of learning and understanding

- **Histograms** are a useful visual summary of data, giving an immediate impression of centre and spread.
- In a histogram, the area represents frequency. The vertical axis represents **frequency density**.
- **Cumulative frequency diagrams** are useful for finding the median and the interquartile range and also facilitate the construction of a **box-and-whisker plot**, another good visual summary of data.
- A **stem-and-leaf diagram** shows the distribution of the data while displaying all the values.
- The centre of the data can be measured using the **mean**, **median** or **mode**. The spread around the centre can be measured using the **range**, **interquartile range** or **standard deviation**.
- The square of the standard deviation is called the **variance**.
- If the data has been grouped you can estimate the mean and standard deviation by assuming that every data value is at the centre of each class.
- The **correlation coefficient** is a value between -1 and 1 which measures the strength of linear relationship between two variables.
- The **regression line** can be drawn on a scatter diagram for a set of **bivariate data**. It should only be used if there is significant linear correlation and there is not too much extrapolation.
- Graphs or calculations can be used to identify **outliers** in data, which then may need to be removed.

Mixed practice 16

1 A sample of discrete data is drawn from a population and given as 115, 108, 135, 122, 127, 140, 139, 111, 124.

Find:

a the interquartile range

b the mean

c the variance.

2 $\Sigma(x - \bar{x})^2 = 12$ and $n = 3$. Find the value of the standard deviation.

3 A student takes the bus to school every morning. She records the length of the time, in minutes, she waits for the bus on 12 randomly chosen days. The data set is summarised by $\Sigma x = 49$ and $\Sigma x^2 = 305.7$.

a Find the mean.

b Find the variance.

4 This box-and-whisker plot shows the lengths of corn snakes (x) in cm.

Use the definition that an outlier is more than 1.5 IQR from the closest quartile to find the range of values that would be outliers. Hence show that there are no outliers for this data.

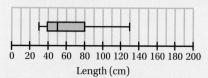

Length (cm)

5 a Use a counter example with two data items to show that $\overline{x^2} = \bar{x}^2$ is not always true.

b If $\overline{x^2} = \bar{x}^2$ find the standard deviation of the data. Hence provide an example of a set of data containing two items which has $\overline{x^2} = \bar{x}^2$.

6 40 people were asked to guess the length of a certain road. Each person gave their guess, l km, correct to the nearest kilometre. The results are summarised below.

l	10–12	13–15	16–20	21–30
Frequency	1	13	20	6

i a Use appropriate formulae to calculate estimates of the mean and standard deviation of l.

b Explain why your answers are only estimates.

ii A histogram is to be drawn to illustrate the data. Calculate the frequency density of the block for the 16–20 class.

iii Explain which class contains the median value of l.

iv Later, the person whose guess was between 10 km and 12 km changed his guess to between 13 km and 15 km. Without calculation, state whether the following will increase, decrease or remain the same:

    a the mean of l,   **b** the standard deviation of l.

    © **OCR, AS GCE Mathematics, Paper 4732, January 2010**

7   **a**   From this chart calculate an estimate of the mean and the standard deviation of the data.

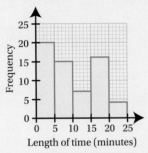

    b   The chart shows the distribution of the length of time, in minutes, Tom has to wait for a bus in the morning. Find the probability that, on a randomly selected day, he has to wait between 15 and 25 minutes.

8   Jenny must sit 4 papers for an exam. All papers have an equal weight when their marks are combined. The mean of the first 3 papers Jenny has sat is 72% with a standard deviation of 8%.

    a   If she wants to get a mean of 75% overall what is the lowest percentage she can get in her fourth paper?

    b   What is the highest possible mean she can get?

    c   If she does get the highest possible mean, what is her new standard deviation?

9   This cumulative frequency diagram gives the speed, v, of 50 cars in mph as they travel past a motorway checkpoint.

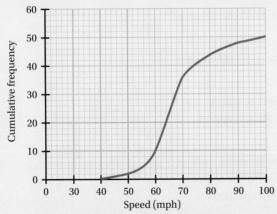

    a   From the diagram find the median speed.

    b   Any car travelling above 75 mph will be stopped by the police. How many of these cars will be stopped?

c   The middle 50% of speeds lie between a and b where $a < b$. Find the values of a and b.

d   Copy and complete the following frequency table.

v	Frequency
$40 < v \leqslant 50$	2
$50 < v \leqslant 60$	9
$60 < v \leqslant 70$	
$70 < v \leqslant 80$	
$80 < v \leqslant 90$	
$90 < v \leqslant 100$	

e   Hence estimate the mean and the standard deviation in the speeds.

f   Use the definition of an outlier as anything more than 2 standard deviations from the mean to show that some of the observed speeds are outliers. Decide, with justification, whether these speeds need to be removed for a valid analysis.

10   A geographer is studying data on the area (A) and population (P) of various cities in a country. He displays his data on a scatter diagram.

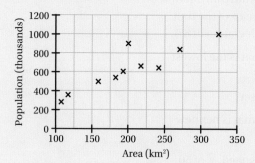

The mean population of the cities studied is 604 thousand.

a   What is the advantage of displaying the data on a scatter diagram rather than two histograms?

b   Describe the correlation of the data shown by the scatter graph.

c   One of the cities completely fills an island so that as its population has grown it has not been able to expand. What is the area of the island?

d   In the rest of the analysis, the city on the island is removed from the data. What effect does this have on the mean population of the cities studied? Explain your answer.

e   The regression line of the remaining cities has equation $P = 3.05A - 3.26$. Interpret the value 3.05 in the context of the cities.

f The capital of the country has an area of 1600 km². Why would it not be valid to use the regression line to predict the population of the capital?

11 The test marks of 14 students are displayed in a stem-and-leaf diagram, as shown below.

0	
1	2 6
2	1 3 5
3	$w\,x\,4\,8\,y\,z$
4	6 7 7

Key: 1|6 means 16 marks

i Find the lower quartile.

ii Given that the median is 32, find the values of w and x.

iii Find the possible values for the upper quartile.

iv State one advantage of a stem-and-leaf diagram over a box-and-whisker plot.

v State one advantage of a box-and-whisker plot over a stem-and-leaf diagram.

© OCR, AS GCE Mathematics, Paper 4732, June 2012

12 The four populations A, B, C and D are the same size and have the same range.

Histograms for the four populations are shown.

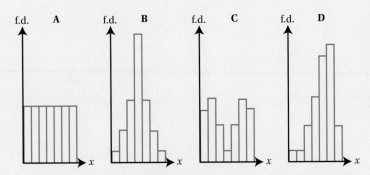

a Each of these three box-and-whisker plots corresponds to one of the four populations. Write the letter of the correct population for each of α, β and γ.

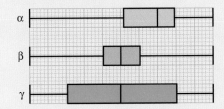

Tip

γ is a Greek letter pronounced gamma. This is the lower case form of the letter.

b Each of these three cumulative frequency diagrams corresponds to one of the four populations. Write the letter of the correct population for each of **i**, **ii** and **iii**.

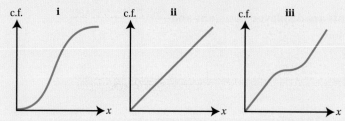

13 The mean of a set of 10 data items is 115 and the variance is 154. Another piece of data is discovered and the new mean is 114. What is the new variance?

14 If the sum of 20 pieces of data is 1542, find the smallest possible value of Σx^2.

17 Probability

In this chapter you will learn how to:

- work out combined probabilities when you are interested in more than one outcome
- work out the probability of a sequence of events occurring
- construct and use a table showing probabilities of all possible outcomes in a given situation (probability distributions)
- calculate probabilities in a situation when an experiment is repeated several times (binomial distribution).

Before you start…

GCSE	You should be able to find probabilities by listing all possible outcomes (sample space) of a single event or a combination of two events.	1	One spinner has the numbers 1 to 5 written on it, and another has the letters A to D. What is the probability of getting an A and a 3 when the two spinners are spun?
GCSE	You should know how to use tree diagrams to determine probabilities of successive events, and to calculate probabilities of combined events.	2	A bag contains 7 red and 3 yellow sweets. A sweet is taken out of the bag and eaten. This is done three times. Find the probability that 3 red sweets are picked.
Chapter 9	You should know how to calculate factorials and binomial coefficients.	3	Use your calculator to find the following: a $7!$ b $\dfrac{7!}{3!}$ c $^{7}C_{3}$ d $\dbinom{5}{5}$ e $^{10}C_{0}$

Why study probability?

Probability is the study of events that depend on chance. Knowing how likely a certain outcome is, even if you cannot predict it with certainty, is important in estimating the risk of events such as earthquakes and disease outbreaks.

You already know how to calculate probabilities of simple events, such as rolling a 6 on a dice or picking an ace from a pack of cards. In this chapter, you will review the concepts of independent and mutually exclusive events, and use them to calculate more complicated probabilities; for example, several events happening at the same time or one after the other.

 Fast forward

Probability theory also underpins the statistical tests you will meet in Chapter 18.

It is often useful to have a list of all possible outcomes in a given situation together with the probability of each outcome. This is called a **probability distribution**. A particularly important distribution, called the **binomial distribution**, can be used to model the number of successful outcomes in a series of repeated experiments. It has applications from medical trials to predicting election results from exit polls.

Section 1: Combining probabilities

You are often interested in probabilities of more than one outcome. For example, your university offer may require you to get an A or a B in Mathematics. Suppose you are told that last year 33% of all candidates achieved an A and 18% achieved a B in Mathematics. You can then work out that the probability of getting an A or a B is $0.33 + 0.18 = 0.51$, or 51%. You can write this as $P(A \text{ or } B) = 0.51$.

But what if, instead, your offer asks for an A in Mathematics **or** Economics? Last year 20% of all candidates got an A in Economics; so is the probability of getting an A in at least one of the subjects $0.33 + 0.20 = 0.53$? The answer is no, because those who got an A in Mathematics and those who got an A in Economics are not two separate groups of people – there are those who got an A in both. In fact, unless you know how many got two As, it is impossible to find the probability of getting this combination of grades.

The events 'getting an A in Mathematics' and 'getting a B in Mathematics' are **mutually exclusive**. This means that they cannot both happen at the same time; the probability of both happening together is zero. The events from the second example, 'getting an A in Mathematics' and 'getting an A in Economics', are **not** mutually exclusive because it is possible for both of them to happen at the same time.

Gateway to A Level

For a reminder of and practice with basic probability calculations, see Gateway to A Level section V.

Key point 17.1

Events A and B are mutually exclusive if it is impossible for both of them to happen at the same time:

$$P(A \text{ and } B) = 0$$

If events are mutually exclusive, their probabilities can be added:

$$P(A \text{ or } B) = P(A) + P(B)$$

WORKED EXAMPLE 17.1

A fair six-sided dice is rolled once. In each case, state whether the two events are mutually exclusive, and write down $P(A)$, $P(B)$ and $P(A \text{ or } B)$.

a A: rolling a 5; B: rolling a 6.
b A: rolling an even number; B: rolling a prime number.

Continues on next page ...

a *A* and *B* are mutually exclusive.

$$P(A) = \frac{1}{6}, P(B) = \frac{1}{6}$$ .... It is not possible to roll a 5 and a 6 at the same time.

$$P(A \text{ or } B) = \frac{2}{6}$$ .... The probabilities can be added.

b *A* and *B* are not mutually exclusive. ...... It is possible to get a number that is both even and prime (2).

$$P(A) = \frac{3}{6}, P(B) = \frac{3}{6}$$ .... There are three even numbers (2, 4, 6) and three prime number (2, 3, 5).

$$P(A \text{ or } B) = \frac{5}{6}$$ .... The probabilities cannot be added; you have to count all possible outcomes (2, 3, 4, 5, 6).

When two events are not mutually exclusive, there is a possibility that they can both happen at the same time. Can the probability of both events happening together be worked out from their individual probabilities?

Consider again the example of Mathematics and Economics grades. Let *M* be the event 'getting an A in Mathematics' and *E* the event 'getting an A in Economics'. As previously, suppose that P(*M*) = 0.33 and P(*E*) = 0.20. What is P(*M* and *E*)?

Here are two possible situations that fit in with these numbers. The numbers in cells show percentages. For example, in the first table, the percentage of candidates with an A in Mathematics is 15 + 18 = 33: 15% also got an A in Economics and the other 18% did not.

> **▶▶ Fast forward**
>
> **A** You may remember the formula P(*A* or *B*) = P(*A*) + (*B*) − P(*A* and *B*) from the GCSE course. You will meet it again if you study Venn diagrams in Student Book 2.

> **▶▶ Fast forward**
>
> **A** You may have met conditional probability at GCSE, and you will meet it again in Student Book 2 if you study the full A level course.

		Economics grade		Total
		A	not A	
Maths grade	A	15	18	33
	not A	5	62	67
Total		20	80	100

		Economics grade		Total
		A	not A	
Maths grade	A	6.6	26.4	33
	not A	13.4	53.6	67
Total		20	80	100

Both examples have P(*M*) = 0.33 and P(*E*) = 0.20. But in the first situation P(*M* and *E*) = 0.15 and in the second P(*M* and *E*) = 0.066. This suggests that P(*M* and *E*) depends on more than just the individual probabilities of *M* and *E*. In fact, it depends on how the two events influence each other – how the probability of one event changes when you know the outcome of the other. This is called **conditional probability**.

There is one important special case when the probability of two events happening together can be easily calculated: when the two events do not affect each other. You say that the events are **independent**.

> **🔍 Explore**
>
> Explore applications of independence of random events. This is an important concept in both legal and medical trials

Key point 17.2

Events A and B are independent if knowing the outcome of A does not affect the probability of B.

For independent events:

$$P(A \text{ and } B) = P(A) \times P(B)$$

If A and B are independent then A' and B' are also independent, as are A and B', and B and A'.

WORKED EXAMPLE 17.2

Two dice are rolled simultaneously. What is the probability that both dice show a prime number?

Let the two events be:

$A = $ 'The first dice shows a prime number'

$B = $ 'The second dice shows a prime number'

Then $P(A) = \dfrac{3}{6}, P(B) = \dfrac{3}{6}$ .... There are three prime numbers on a dice: 2, 3, 5.

A and B are independent, so

$P(A \text{ and } B) = P(A) \times P(B)$

$\qquad = \dfrac{3}{6} \times \dfrac{3}{6}$ .... Knowing the result for the first dice does not affect probabilities for the second dice.

$\qquad = \dfrac{1}{4}$

 Tip

You can also answer the question in Worked example 17.2 by using a sample space table showing all possible outcomes.

	1	2	3	4	5	6
1		\	\		\	
2	/	X	X	/	X	/
3	/	X	X	/	X	/
4		\	\		\	
5	/	X	X	/	X	/
6		\	\		\	

Each cell in the 6 × 6 table corresponds to a possible outcome of a roll of two dice. The outcomes where the first dice shows a prime number are marked /, and the outcomes where the second dice shows a prime number are marked \. This means that the outcomes where both numbers are prime are marked X.

You can see that 9 out of 36 possible outcomes have both dice showing prime numbers, so the required probability is $\dfrac{9}{36} = \dfrac{1}{4}$.

WORKED EXAMPLE 17.3

A biased coin has the probability $\frac{2}{3}$ of showing heads. The coin is tossed three times. Find the probability of getting either three heads or three tails.

$P(3 \text{ heads}) = P(\text{heads}) \times P(\text{heads}) \times P(\text{heads})$ ···· | The three tosses are independent, so multiply the probabilities for each one.

$$= \frac{2}{3} \times \frac{2}{3} \times \frac{2}{3}$$

$$= \frac{8}{27}$$

$P(3 \text{ tails}) = P(\text{tails}) \times P(\text{tails}) \times P(\text{tails})$

$$= \frac{1}{3} \times \frac{1}{3} \times \frac{1}{3}$$

$$= \frac{1}{27}$$

$P(3 \text{ heads or } 3 \text{ tails}) = \frac{8}{27} + \frac{1}{27} = \frac{1}{3}$ ········ | The events 'getting three heads' and 'getting three tails' are mutually exclusive, so find the probability of each and add them together.

💡 **Tip**

In examples like Worked example 17.3 you may find it helpful to think of a tree diagram (which you may have met in your previous study, and will cover in more detail in Student Book 2).

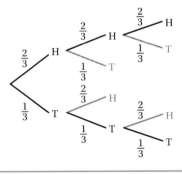

✅ **Gateway to A level**

For a reminder of tree diagrams, see Gateway to A Level section W.

One important example of mutually exclusive events is an event and its **complement**: in statistics, 'complement' means the event not happening. Since either an event or its complement must occur, the total probability is 1.

🔑 **Key point 17.3**

The complement of an event A is the event "not A" or A': $P(A) + P(A') = 1$.

The equation in Key point 17.3 is very useful because sometimes the complement is much simpler to evaluate than the event itself.

WORKED EXAMPLE 17.4

A fair dice is rolled five times. Find the probability of getting at least one six.

$$P(\text{at least one six}) = 1 - P(\text{no sixes})$$

There are several possible ways to get at least one six (you could get 1, 2, 3, 4 or 5).

But the complement of the event 'at least one six' is 'no sixes', which can happen in only one way: if each dice shows 'not a six'.

$$= 1 - \left(\frac{5}{6}\right)^5$$

The five rolls are independent, so you need to multiply five probabilities of 'not a six'.

$$= 0.598 \ (3 \text{ s.f.})$$

💡 **Tip**

The complement of an event can be represented on a Venn diagram, which you may have met in your previous studies (and will cover in more detail in Student Book 2). For example, if it is known that 40% of people have blue eyes and 25% of people have brown eyes, then the event 'a person has neither blue nor brown eyes' is the complement of the event 'a person has blue eyes or brown eyes', and is represented by the shaded region on this Venn diagram:

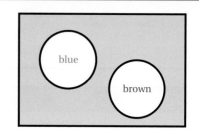

The probability of this event is:

P(a person has neither blue eyes nor brown eyes) = 1 − 0.4 − 0.25 = 0.35

EXERCISE 17A

1 Which of these events are mutually exclusive? For those events that are mutually exclusive, find P(A or B).

a On a fair six-sided dice:

   i A: rolling a multiple of 3; B: rolling a multiple of 4.

   ii A: rolling an even number; B: rolling a multiple of 5.

b One card is selected from a standard pack of 52 cards.

   i A: selecting a king; B: selecting a red card.

   ii A: selecting an ace; B: selecting a spade.

c Two fair dice are rolled and the scores are added.

   i A: the total is a multiple of 6; B: the total is less than 5.

   ii A: the total is greater than 7; B: the total is less than 9.

d A bag contains four green and six yellow balls. A ball is taken out of the bag, its colour noted, and then returned to the bag. Another ball is then selected.

   i A: both balls are green; B: both balls are yellow.

   ii A: the first ball is green; B: the second ball is green.

e   A bag contains four green and six yellow balls. Two balls are taken out without replacement.

   i   *A*: the first ball is green; *B*: the second ball is green.

   ii   *A*: both balls are green; *B*: both balls are yellow.

2   Which pairs of events from question 1 are independent? For those that are, calculate P(*A* and *B*) and P(*A*) × P(*B*).

3   Two events, *A* and *B*, have probabilities P(*A*) = *p* and P(*B*) = *q*.

   a   Write down an expression for P(*A* and *B*) in the following situations:

   i   *A* and *B* are independent   ii   *A* and *B* are mutually exclusive.

   b   If two events are independent, can they also be mutually exclusive?

4   A coin is biased so that the probability of getting tails is $\frac{3}{4}$. The coin is tossed twice. Find the probability that:

   a   the coin shows heads both times   b   the coin shows heads at least once.

5   Two fair six-sided dice are rolled. Find the probability that the product of the scores is 6.

6   Daniel has three blocks with letters C, A and T written on them. He arranges the blocks in a row randomly.

   a   Write down all possible arrangements of the three letters.

   b   Find the probability that the blocks make the word 'CAT' or 'ACT'.

7   A fair six-sided dice is rolled once. Define events as:

   A: the dice shows an even number; *B*: the dice shows a prime number.

   a   Find P(*A* and *B*).

   b   Determine whether events *A* and *B* are independent.

8   300 students in Years 9, 10 and 11 at a school were asked to say which of Biology, Chemistry and Physics is their favourite science. The results are shown in this table.

Year group	Biology	Chemistry	Physics	Total
Year 9	41	29	27	97
Year 10	35	36	34	105
Year 11	37	30	31	98
Total	113	95	92	300

   a   Find the probability that a randomly chosen student:

   i   prefers Chemistry   ii   is in Year 11 and doesn't prefer Biology.

   b   Determine whether the event 'the student is in Year 9' and the event 'the student's favourite science is Physics' are independent.

9   A fair four-sided spinner, with numbers 1 to 4 written on it, is spun three times. Find the probability of getting either three 1s or three 4s.

10   A fair coin is tossed three times. Determine the probability that it shows:

   a   three tails   b   at least one head.

11   The probability that a student is late for a lesson is 0.15, independently of any other students.

   a   Find the probability that at least one of the 12 students in a class is late.

   b   Is the assumption of independence reasonable in this case? Explain your answer.

Section 2: Probability distributions

So far you have only been asked to calculate the probability of a specific event, or a combination of events happening. But sometimes you are interested in probabilities of all possible outcomes in a given situation. For example, if you roll two dice and add up the scores you can get 11 possible outcomes: any integer between 2 and 12. The probabilities of those outcomes are not all equal; a total of 7 is more likely than a total of 12.

The list of all possible outcomes together with their probabilities is called a probability distribution. This information is best displayed in a table. In the AS course you only work with **discrete** probability distributions – ones where all possible outcomes can be listed (though the list may be infinite!).

 **Fast forward**

> **A** If you study the A level course you will also meet continuous distributions, which can take any value in a given range, in Student Book 2.

WORKED EXAMPLE 17.5

Two fair dice are rolled and their scores are added. Find the probability distribution of the total.

Possible outcomes for the total:

	1	2	3	4	5	6
1	2	3	4	5	6	7
2	3	4	5	6	7	8
3	4	5	6	7	8	9
4	5	6	7	8	9	10
5	6	7	8	9	10	11
6	7	8	9	10	11	12

The numbers in the table show the total score of the two dice.

The probability distribution of the total:

Total	2	3	4	5	6	7	8	9	10	11	12
Probability	$\frac{1}{36}$	$\frac{2}{36}$	$\frac{3}{36}$	$\frac{4}{36}$	$\frac{5}{36}$	$\frac{6}{36}$	$\frac{5}{36}$	$\frac{4}{36}$	$\frac{3}{36}$	$\frac{2}{36}$	$\frac{1}{36}$

Each combination of scores is equally likely, so each has a probability of $\frac{1}{36}$.

So, for example, $P(\text{total}=5)=\frac{4}{36}$, because the total of 5 can be obtained in 4 different ways.

The table in Worked example 17.5 is an example of a **sample space table**, which is a way of listing all possible outcomes of an event.

The probabilities in a probability distribution cannot be just any numbers.

 Key point 17.4

The total of all the probabilities of a probability distribution must always equal 1.

📷 **Focus on ...**

Probability distributions of combined events can be difficult to find theoretically. Focus on ... Modelling 3 shows you how to use computer simulation to find probability distributions.

WORKED EXAMPLE 17.6

In a game at a fair, a ball is thrown at a rectangular target. The dimensions of the target (in metres) are as shown in the diagram. The probability of hitting each region is proportional to its area. The prize for hitting a region is the number of chocolates equal to the number shown in that region. Find the probability distribution of the number of chocolates won.

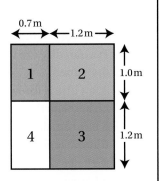

Let x = the number of chocolates won

x	1	2	3	4
$P(X=x)$	$0.7k$	$1.2k$	$1.44k$	$0.84k$

The probability is proportional to the area so write $p = k \times$ area.

$0.7k + 1.2k + 1.44k + 0.84k = 1$

$4.18k = 1$

To find k, use the fact that the probabilities add up to 1.

$k = 0.239$ (3 s.f.)

So the distribution is:

x	1	2	3	4
$P(X=x)$	0.167	0.287	0.344	0.201

Sometimes a probability distribution can be given by a formula.

Sometimes the notation used here can be confusing. X is the name of the **random variable** (a variable whose value depends on chance); x is the **value** it takes. For example, $P(X=2) = 0.287$.

WORKED EXAMPLE 17.7

A probability distribution is given by $P(X=x) = kx$ for $x = 1, 2, 3$. Find $P(X=2)$.

$P(X=2) = 2k$

Replace x by the particular value of X.

To find k:

$k + 2k + 3k = 1$

Use the fact that all probabilities add up to 1.

$\Rightarrow k = \dfrac{1}{6}$

You may find it helpful to show the probability distribution in a table:

x	1	2	3
$P(X=x)$	k	$2k$	$3k$

So $P(X=2) = 2 \times \dfrac{1}{6} = \dfrac{1}{3}$

EXERCISE 17B

1 For each of the following, draw a table to represent the probability distribution.

a A fair coin is thrown three times. T is the number of tails obtained.

b Two fair dice are thrown. D is the difference between the larger and the smaller score, or zero if they are the same.

c A fair dice is thrown once. X is calculated as half the result if the dice shows an even number, or one higher than the result if the dice shows an odd number.

d A bag contains six red and three green counters. Two counters are drawn at random from the bag without replacement. G is the number of green counters remaining in the bag.

e Karl picks a card at random from a standard pack of 52 cards. If he draws a diamond, he stops; otherwise, he replaces the card and continues to draw cards at random, with replacement, until he has either drawn a diamond or has drawn a total of 4 cards. C is the total number of cards drawn.

f Two fair four-sided spinners, each labelled 1, 2, 3 and 4, are spun. X is the product of the two values shown.

2 Find the missing value k for each probability distribution.

a i

x	3	7	9	11
$P(X=x)$	$\frac{1}{2}$	$\frac{1}{4}$	$\frac{1}{8}$	k

ii

x	1	2	3	4
$P(X=x)$	$2k$	$3k$	$2k$	k

b i

x	1	2	3	4
$P(X=x)$	k	$4k$	k	$2k$

ii

x	1	2	3	4
$P(X=x)$	$\frac{k}{2}$	k	$\frac{k}{3}$	$\frac{k}{2}$

c i $P(Y=y)=ky$ for $y=1, 2, 3, 4$

ii $P(X=x)=\dfrac{k}{x}$ for $x=1, 2, 3, 4$

3 A six-sided dice is biased with the probabilities of each outcome as shown in the table:

Score	1	2	3	4	5	6
Probability	$\frac{1}{12}$	$\frac{1}{6}$	$\frac{1}{12}$	$\frac{1}{4}$	$2k$	$3k$

a Find the value of k.

b The dice is rolled once. Find the probability that the score is more than 4.

4 The number of students absent from a Mathematics lesson on any particular day follows the probability distribution:

Number of absentees	0	1	2	3	4	5
Probability	0.15	0.21	k	0.26	0.12	0.07

a Find the value of k.

b Find the probability that at most 2 students are absent.

5 Ben and Anna both take three shots at a goal. The table shows the probability distribution of the number of goals each of them scores.

Number of goals	0	1	2	3
Probability	0.2	0.3	0.4	0.1

a Find the probability that Anna scores at least one goal.

b Find the probability that both Ben and Anna score three goals.

6 A fair four-sided spinner, with numbers 1 to 4 written on it, is spun twice and the scores are added.

   a Find the probability distribution of the total.

   b Find the probability that the total is at least 6.

7 A teacher randomly selects how many questions to set for homework after each lesson. The probability distribution of the number of questions is:

Number	2	3	4	5	6
Probability	a	0.1	0.3	0.3	b

The probability that the teacher sets fewer than four questions is 0.2.
Find the values of a and b.

8 A probability distribution of X is given by $P(X = x) = k(x + 1)$ for $x = 2, 3, 4, 5, 6$.

   a Show that $k = 0.04$.

   b Find $P(X \geqslant 4)$.

9 A four-sided dice is biased. The probability of each possible score is shown.

Score	1	2	3	4
Probability	$\frac{1}{3}$	$\frac{1}{4}$	k	$\frac{1}{5}$

   a Find the value of k.

   b Find the probability that the total score is four after two rolls.

10 Ronnie and Jimmy are playing snooker. They both try to pot two balls.

For Ronnie, the probability distribution of the number of successful pots is:

Number of pots	0	1	2
Probability	0.1	0.2	0.7

For Jimmy, the probability distribution is:

Number of pots	0	1	2
Probability	0.3	0.5	0.2

Assuming that their performance is independent, find the probability that, between them:

   a they pot exactly one ball

   b they pot at least one ball.

11 $P(X \leqslant x) = kx^2$ for $x = 1, 2, 3$.

   a Find the value of k.

   b What is the probability distribution of X?

12 $P(X = x) = \frac{1}{9}$ for integers in the range $[-k, k]$.

   a Find the value of k.

   b If $Y = X^2$ find the probability distribution of Y.

Section 3: The binomial distribution

Some probability distributions occur in lots of different contexts. Consider the following questions:

- A fair six-sided dice is rolled four times. What is the probability of getting exactly two fives?
- A fair coin is tossed ten times. What is the probability that it shows heads at least six times?
- A multiple choice test has 20 questions, each with five possible answers, only one of which is right. A student guesses the answer to each question, with an equal probability of guessing any answer correctly. What is the probability that he gets fewer than five correct answers?

All of these questions involve a similar scenario:

- An action is repeated several times (a dice roll, a coin toss, an attempt to answer a question). These repeats are called 'trials'.
- Possible outcomes can be split into two groups, usually labelled 'success' and 'failure' (five or not a five; heads or tails; right or wrong answer).
- You are interested in the probability of one of the outcomes happening a given number of times.

This type of situation is very common, so it is worth asking whether there is a general rule or formula for calculating the probability. In order to establish the formula, you must first ensure that certain conditions are satisfied.

> ### 🔑 Key point 17.5
>
> The **binomial distribution** models the number of successful outcomes from repeated trials, provided the following conditions are satisfied:
>
> - the number of trials is fixed
> - each outcome can be classified as either 'success' or 'failure'
> - the trials are independent of each other
> - the probability of success is the same in each trial.
>
> If n is the number of trials, p the probability of a success and X denotes the number of successes, you can write $X \sim B(n, p)$.

The probabilities for the binomial distribution can be found using your calculator. You need to specify the number of trials (n), the probability of success (p) in a single trial and the required number of successes.

WORKED EXAMPLE 17.8

Decide whether each of the following situations can be modelled using the binomial distribution. If not, say which of the conditions is not satisfied. If yes, find the required probability.

a A fair dice is rolled until it shows a six. Find the probability of getting two fours.
b Tom and Jerry play eight games of chess. The probability that Tom wins a game is 0.6, independently of any other game. Find the probability that Tom wins exactly four games.

Continues on next page ...

c   A student is trying to answer 20 quiz questions. The probability of getting the first question right is 0.9, but the probability halves for each subsequent question. What is the probability that he answers 10 questions correctly?

d   In a particular village, 63% of five-year-olds attend the local primary school. What is the probability that in a group of 15 friends, at least 10 attend that school?

e   The probability that it rains on any particular day is 0.3. Assuming the days are independent, find the probability that it rains on more than four days in a week.

---

a   Not binomial; the number of trials is not constant.

> The first thing to check is that the situation has a fixed number of trials.

b   Binomial, $n = 8$, $p = 0.6$

$P(X = 4) = 0.232$

> All the conditions are satisfied. Use your calculator to find the probability.

c   Not binomial; the probability of success is not constant.

> There is a fixed number of trials, but the probability changes every time.

d   Not binomial; the trials are not independent.

> If one child attends the school it is more likely that their friends do as well.

e   Binomial, $n = 7$, $p = 0.3$

$P(X > 4) = P(X = 5, 6 \text{ or } 7)$

> All the conditions are satisfied. The required probability is for 5, 6 or 7 days.

$= P(X = 5) + P(X = 6) + P(X = 7)$

$= 0.0288$

> The three outcomes are mutually exclusive, so their probabilities can be added.

In practice, it may not always be clear that all of the necessary conditions are satisfied, and you may need to make some assumptions in order to be able to use the binomial distribution. For example, if you want to use the binomial distribution to calculate the probability of guessing 8 out of 20 correct answers in a quiz, you need to assume that the different guesses are independent of each other, and that the probability of guessing correctly does not change from one question to the next.

The conditions 'fixed number of trials' and 'outcomes classified as either success or failure' are usually given as a part of the description of the situation in the question. For example, you may be told that a quiz has 20 questions and that you are interested in the number of correct answers. The other two conditions, 'independent trials' and 'constant probability of success', are additional modelling assumptions that you need to make if they are not explicitly given.

You may also need to make further assumptions about the exact values of n and p. For example, when calculating the probability of getting five heads out of 12 coin tosses, you may need to assume that the coin is fair so that $p = \frac{1}{2}$.

 Tip

You only need to assume things that are not explicitly given in the question. For example, if you are told that a coin is fair, then $p = \frac{1}{2}$ would not be an additional assumption.

WORK IT OUT 17.1

On historical evidence, Carol estimates that the probability that it rains on any particular day is 0.08. Carol wants to calculate the probability that it rains on exactly three days in a week. What further assumptions does she need to make so that the number of rainy days in a week can be modelled by the distribution B(7, 0.08)?

Which of the following answers is correct? Explain the error with the incorrect answers.

Solution 1	Solution 2	Solution 3
One day being rainy is independent of any other day being rainy.	The number of days in a week is constant.	The probability that it rains on any given day is constant.

WORKED EXAMPLE 17.9

Alessia is going to roll 10 dice and wants to find the probability of getting more than two 5s. She says that, in order to justify a binomial distribution as a model for the number of 5s, she must assume that the rolls are independent of each other, and that all the dice are fair.

a Explain which part of Alessia's statement is incorrect.
b What assumption does she need to make about the probability of getting a 5 on each dice?

Daniel says that the number of 5s can be modelled by the distribution $B\left(10, \frac{1}{6}\right)$.

c State two assumptions that Daniel needs to make.

a It is not necessary to assume that the dice are fair.

It is true that the rolls need to be independent. This is almost certainly justified in the case of rolling dice repeatedly.

The binomial distribution only requires that the probability of success is constant, but does not specify a value for it.

b That the probability of rolling a 5 is the same for each dice.

For example, if all the dice were biased so that the probability of rolling a five was $\frac{1}{2}$ for each dice, the conditions for binomial distribution would still be satisfied.

c The rolls are independent of each other. All the dice are fair.

Daniel wants to use a specific probability, so he does need to assume that all the dice are fair. (The assumption of independence is almost certainly justified in this case.)

Note that he does not need to assume that the number of rolls is constant, as the question already states that there are ten rolls.

Cumulative probabilities

In the final part of Worked example 17.8 you were asked to find the probability of more than one outcome. This is straightforward when there are only three probabilities to add up, but what if there were 20 trials and you wanted to find the probability of more than 11 successes? Would you have to add all the probabilities from $P(X = 12)$ to $P(X = 20)$?

 Tip

Make sure you can distinguish between the single probability and the cumulative probability functions on your calculator.

Fortunately, calculators usually have a function to calculate the probability of getting up to (and including) a specified number of successes – this is called a **cumulative probability**. For example, if $n = 20$ and $p = 0.3$ you can find that $P(X \leqslant 7) = 0.772$. You can also find the probability of getting more than a certain number of successes, for example:

$$P(X > 11) = 1 - P(X \leqslant 11)$$
$$= 1 - 0.995$$
$$= 0.005$$

If you want to find the probability of getting more than 5 but fewer than 10 successes, this is:

$$P(5 < X < 10) = P(X \leqslant 9) - P(X \leqslant 5)$$

You can see this by looking at the number line.

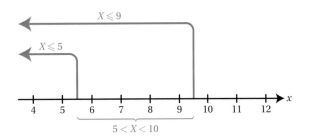

WORKED EXAMPLE 17.10

Anita shoots at a target 15 times. The probability that she hits the target on any shot is 0.6, independently of the other shots. Find the probability that she hits the target more than 5 but at most 10 times.

Let X be the number of times Anita hits the target. Then	There is a fixed number of trials and you are interested in the number of successes, so this is a binomial distribution.
$X \sim B(15, 0.6)$	
$P(5 < X \leqslant 10) = P(X \leqslant 10) - P(X \leqslant 5)$	Express the required probability in terms of cumulative probabilities
$\qquad = 0.7827 - 0.0338$	
$\qquad = 0.749 \,(3 \text{ s.f.})$	

Tip

When you are using a calculator to find probabilities, you should still use correct mathematical notation (not calculator notation) in your answer. You must show what distribution you used and which probabilities you have found from your calculator.

WORK IT OUT 17.2

Four students are trying to answer the following question:

Anna shoots at a target 15 times. The probability that she hits the target on any shot is 0.6, independently of the other shots. Find the probability that she hits the target at least 6 times.

Which is the correct solution? Can you identify the errors made in the incorrect solutions?

Solution 1	Solution 2	Solution 3	Solution 4
$P(X \geqslant 6) = 1 - P(X \leqslant 6)$	$P(X > 6) = 1 - P(X \leqslant 6)$	$P(X > 6) = 1 - P(X \leqslant 5)$	$P(X \geqslant 6) = 1 - P(X \leqslant 5)$
$= 1 - 0.095$	$= 1 - 0.095$	$= 1 - 0.034$	$= 1 - 0.034$
$= 0.905$	$= 0.905$	$= 0.966$	$= 0.966$

The formula for binomial probabilities

So far, you have used a calculator to find probabilities for the binomial distribution. But how are those probabilities calculated?

Consider the first example from the start of this section: a dice is rolled four times; what is the probability of getting exactly two fives?

There are four trials so $n = 4$. If you label a five as a 'success' then $p = \frac{1}{6}$. The probability of a 'failure' is therefore $\frac{5}{6}$. X stands for the number of fives, so you are interested in $P(X = 2)$.

One way of getting exactly two fives is if on the first two rolls you get a five and on the last two rolls you get something else. The probability of this happening is $\frac{1}{6} \times \frac{1}{6} \times \frac{5}{6} \times \frac{5}{6} = \left(\frac{1}{6}\right)^2 \left(\frac{5}{6}\right)^2$.

But this is not the only way in which two fives can occur. The two fives may be on the first and third, or second and fourth rolls. This can be illustrated on a tree diagram.

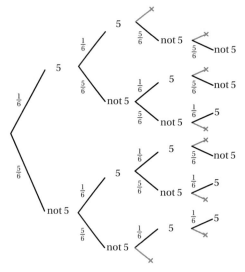

> ✔ **Gateway to A Level**
>
> For a reminder of tree diagrams for working with probabilities, see Gateway to A Level section W.

Each of the required paths has the same probability, $\left(\frac{1}{6}\right)^2 \left(\frac{5}{6}\right)^2$ because two of the outcomes are a five and two are something else. The number of paths leading to the outcome 'two fives' is 6 so $P(X = 2) = 6\left(\frac{1}{6}\right)^2 \left(\frac{5}{6}\right)^2$.

This reasoning can be generalised. Suppose that there are n trials, the probability of a success is p and you are interested in the probability of obtaining r successes. If you imagine representing this on a tree diagram, each relevant path will have probability $p^r (1-p)^{n-r}$, because r of the outcomes are successes (with probability p) and the remaining $n - r$ outcomes are failures (with probability $1 - p$). It turns out that the number of paths that give r successes is given by the binomial coefficient $\binom{n}{r}$.

This leads to the general formula for the probabilities of the binomial distribution.

Key point 17.6

If $X \sim B(n,p)$ then:

$$P(X=x)=\binom{n}{x}p^x(1-p)^{n-x} \quad \text{for } x=0,1,2\ldots n$$

 Rewind

You met binomial coefficients in Chapter 9 when studying the binomial expansion. You can find them either on your calculator, from Pascal's triangle, or using the formula in Key point 9.3.

This will appear in your formula book.

You may find it surprising that the same binomial coefficients appear in both binomial expansion and the binomial probabilities formula. To see why this is the case, consider multiplying out $(a+b)^n$. When you expand the brackets, each term contains either an 'a' or a 'b' from each bracket. For example:

$$(a+b)(a+b)(a+b) = aaa + aab + aba + abb + baa + bab + bba + bbb$$

You can represent this on a tree diagram:

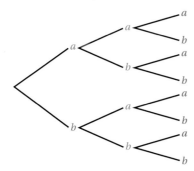

This is exactly the same tree diagram as you would use to show the possible outcomes of a binomial distribution with three trials, but you would replace a by p and b by $1-p$. Therefore, for example, the binomial probability $P(X=2)$ has the same form as the term containing $a^2 b$ in the binomial expansion.

Now consider the binomial expansion of $(p+q)^n$, where $q=1-p$:

$$(p+q)^n = p^n + \binom{n}{1}p^{n-1}q + \binom{n}{2}p^{n-2}q^2 + \cdots + q^n$$

Each term on the right is equal to one of the binomial probabilities, and the left-hand side equals 1 (since $p+q=1$). Hence this equation proves that the sum of all the probabilities in the binomial distribution equals 1 (as should be the case for any probability distribution).

When you know the values of n and p you can always use a calculator to find binomial probabilities. However, the formula from Key point 17.6 is useful when one of the parameters is unknown.

WORKED EXAMPLE 17.11

Ten students take a test. They all have a probability of p of passing, independent of the results of other students. X is the number of students passing the test.

If $P(X=6)=4P(X=4)$, find the value of p.

$P(X=6)=\binom{10}{6}p^6(1-p)^4$	Use the formula to write expressions for $P(X=6)$ and $P(X=4)$.
$\quad=210p^6(1-p)^4$	
$P(X=4)=\binom{10}{4}p^4(1-p)^6$	
$\quad=210p^4(1-p)^6$	
So $210p^6(1-p)^4=840p^4(1-p)^6$	Write the equation given in terms of these expressions.
$p^2=4(1-p)^2$	You can divide by $210\,p^4(1-p)^4$ if $p\neq0,1$.
$p=2(1-p)$	You only need to consider the positive root, since both sides must be positive.
$p=2-2p$	
$3p=2$	
$p=\dfrac{2}{3}$	

EXERCISE 17C

1 In each example, decide whether the situation can be modelled using the binomial distribution. If not, give a reason why it cannot. If it can be, identify the distribution and the required probability (you don't need to calculate the probability).

a A fair coin is tossed 20 times. What is the probability of getting exactly 15 heads?

b Elsa enjoys answering quiz questions. On average she get 78% of the answers right. What is the probability that in a particular quiz, she gets 9 out of the first 10 questions right?

c A bag contains a large number of balls, with an equal proportion of red, blue and green balls. 20 balls are chosen at random. Find the probability that 5 are red and 8 are green.

d A drawer contains 5 black socks and 10 red socks. 6 socks are drawn at random without replacement. Find the probability that at least two black socks are drawn.

e It is known that 2% of a large population carry a gene for diabetes. If 100 people are chosen at random, what is the probability of getting at least 1 person with this gene?

Elevate

For more practice finding cumulative binomial probabilities, see Support sheet 17.

2 Given that $X \sim B(8, 0.2)$, calculate:

a **i** $P(X=3)$ **ii** $P(X=4)$

b **i** $P(X \leqslant 3)$ **ii** $P(X \leqslant 2)$

c **i** $P(X>3)$ **ii** $P(X>4)$

d **i** $P(X<5)$ **ii** $P(X<3)$

e **i** $P(X \geqslant 3)$ **ii** $P(X \geqslant 1)$

f **i** $P(3<X \leqslant 6)$ **ii** $P(1 \leqslant X \leqslant 4)$

g **i** $P(1<X<5)$ **ii** $P(2<X<7)$

h **i** $P(3 \leqslant X \leqslant 7)$ **ii** $P(2 \leqslant X \leqslant 5)$

3 In each question identify the distribution, write down the required probability and find it using your calculator.

a Jake beats Marco at chess in 70% of their games. Assuming that this probability is constant and that the results of games are independent of each other, what is the probability that Jake will beat Marco in at least 16 of their next 20 games?

b On a television channel, the news is shown at the same time each day. The probability that Salia watches the news on a given day is 0.35. Calculate the probability that on 5 consecutive days she watches the news on exactly 3 days.

c Sandy is playing a computer game and needs to accomplish a difficult task at least three times in five attempts in order to pass the level. There is a 1-in-2 chance that he will accomplish the task each time he tries, unaffected by how he has done before. What is the probability that he will pass to the next level?

4 Given that $Y \sim B\left(5, \frac{1}{2}\right)$, use the formula to find the exact value of:

a **i** $P(Y=1)$ **ii** $P(Y=0)$

b **i** $P(Y \geqslant 1)$ **ii** $P(Y \leqslant 1)$

c **i** $P(Y>4)$ **ii** $P(Y \leqslant 3)$

5 15% of students at a large school travel by bus. A random sample of 20 students is taken.

a Explain why the number of students in the sample who travel by bus is only approximately a binomial distribution.

b Use the binomial distribution to estimate the probability that exactly five of the students travel by bus.

6 A Biology test consists of eight multiple choice questions. Each question has four options: only one of which is correct. At least five correct answers are required to pass the test. Chen does not know the answers to any of the questions, so answers each question at random.

a What is the probability that Chen answers exactly five questions correctly?

b What is the probability that Chen manages to pass the test?

7 0.8% of people in the country have a particular cold virus at any time. On a single day, a doctor sees 80 patients.

a What is the probability that exactly two of them have the virus?

b What is the probability that three or more of them have the virus?

c State an assumption you have made in these calculations.

8 On a fair dice, which is more likely: rolling 3 sixes in 4 throws or rolling a five or a six in 5 out of 6 throws?

ⓘ Did you know?

Question 8 is the problem which was posed to Pierre de Fermat in 1654 by a professional gambler who could not understand why he was losing. It inspired Fermat (with the assistance of Pascal) to set up probability as a rigorous mathematical discipline. Fermat was a French mathematician and lawyer.

---

9 This question is intended to help you understand the difference between 'constant probability' and 'independent trials', which are both required for the binomial distribution.

a A bag contains six red and four blue balls. A ball is taken at random and not replaced. This is repeated three times, so that in total three balls are selected.

   i Find the probability that the second ball is red.

   ii Find the probability that the third ball is red.

   iii Find the probability that the first and the second balls are both red. Hence use the formula $P(A \text{ and } B) = P(A) \times P(B)$ to show that the events 'the first ball is red' and 'the second ball is red' are not independent.

   iv Find the probability that exactly one of the three balls is red. Compare this to $P(X = 1)$ when $X \sim B(3, 0.6)$.

b Repeat parts **i–iv** if the three balls are selected with replacement.

10 In each of the following situations discuss whether the trials are independent and whether the probability of success is constant (i.e. the probability of success on the nth trial is not dependent on n).

a Pulling socks from a drawer; success is pulling a red sock out.

b Consecutive rolls of a fair dice; success is rolling a 6.

c Each member of the class flips a fair coin. If 'heads', they write down the first letter of their first name. If 'tails', they write the last letter; success is writing a vowel.

11 A fair coin is tossed ten times. What is the probability that it shows heads at least six times?

12 A multiple choice test has 20 questions, each with five possible options, only one of which is right. A student guesses the answer to each question, with an equal probability of guessing any answer correctly.

    a What is the probability that he gets fewer than five correct answers?

    b State a further assumption you made in your calculation in part **a**.

13 On a particular day, 20 babies are born at a certain hospital. Denote by G the number of girls.

    a State two assumptions you need to make so that G can be modelled by the distribution B(20, 0.5).

    b Under these assumptions, find the probability that more than 15 of the babies are girls.

14 At a certain college, it is known that on average the probability that a student is late in the morning is 0.07. Let X denote the number of students in a class of 24 who are late on a particular morning.

    a In order to model X by a binomial distribution, it is necessary to assume that the probability of being late is the same for every student. Is this a reasonable assumption?

    b State a further condition required for X to follow a binomial distribution. Would it be reasonable to assume that this condition is met in this context?

15 $X \sim B(8, p)$. If $P(X = 5) = P(X = 6)$ find the value of p.

16 X is a binomial random variable, where the number of trials is 4 and the probability of success of each trial is p. Find the possible values of p if $P(X = 2) = 0.3456$.

17 Over a one-month period, Ava and Sven play a total of n games of tennis. The probability that Ava wins any game is 0.4. The result of each game played is independent of any other game played. Let X denote the number of games won by Ava over the one-month period.

    a Show that $P(X = 2)$ can be given as $P(X = 2) = \dfrac{2n(n-1)}{9} \times 0.6^n$.

    b If the probability that Ava wins two games is 0.121 correct to three decimal places, find the value of n.

 Tip

To do question 17b you need to try some values of n or use tables on your calculator.

18 X is a random variable following B(n, 0.8). If $P(X = n) = 64P(X = 0)$, find n.

19 If $X \sim B(n, p)$ and $P(X = 4) = P(X = 5)$ find n in terms of p.

Checklist of learning and understanding

- **Mutually exclusive** events satisfy $P(A \text{ and } B) = 0$. Their probabilities can be added: $P(A \text{ or } B) = P(A) + P(B)$
- An event and its **complement** are mutually exclusive, and $P(A) + P(A') = 1$.
  The probability of the complement is sometimes easier to find.
- For **independent** events, $P(A \text{ and } B) = P(A) \times P(B)$. If A and B are independent then so are A' and B', A' and B, and A and B'.
- A **probability distribution** is a list of all possible outcomes and their probabilities.
- All probabilities in a probability distribution must add up to 1.
- **Cumulative probability** is the probability of obtaining up to and including a given outcome.
- The **binomial distribution** is a model for the number of successes when an experiment is repeated several times. If there are n trials and the probability of success is p, the distribution is denoted by $B(n, p)$.
- For the binomial distribution to be a good model, the following conditions must be satisfied:
  - The number of trials is constant.
  - Each trial has two possible outcomes.
  - The probability of success is the same for each trial.
  - The trials are independent.
- The probabilities for the binomial distribution can be found using your calculator, or the formula:

$$P(X = x) = \binom{n}{x} p^x (1-p)^{n-x} \quad \text{for } x = 0, 1, 2 \ldots n$$

Mixed practice 17

1 A factory making bottles knows that, on average, 1.5% of its bottles are defective. Find the probability that, in a randomly selected sample of 20 bottles, at least 1 bottle is defective.

2 The mark on a Physics test is an integer between 1 and 5 inclusive. The distribution of test grades is given in this table:

Mark	1	2	3	4	5
Probability	0.05	0.23	0.35	k	0.21

   a Find the value of k.

   b Find the probability that a randomly selected student scores at least a 3 in the test.

   c Write down the most likely mark in this test.

3 A spinner has four equal sections with numbers 1, 2, 5 and 7 written on them. The spinner is spun twice. Find the probability distribution of the positive difference between the scores (larger minus smaller).

4 When a boy bats at baseball, the probability that he hits the ball is 0.4. In practice he gets pitched 12 balls. Let X denote the total number of balls he hits. Assuming that his attempts are independent, find:

   a $P(X=3)$ **b** $P(X>5)$

5 A probability distribution of a variable X is shown in this table:

x	2	3	4	5	6
$P(X=x)$	p	0.2	0.3	0.3	q

   a Write down the value of $p+q$.

   b Given that $P(X \geqslant 4)=0.75$, find the values of p and q.

6 Given that $X \sim B(8, 0.65)$, find:

   a $P(X<6)$ **b** $P(X=8)$ **c** $P(5 \leqslant X<7)$

7 When Robyn shoots an arrow at a target, the probability that she hits the target is 0.6. In a competition she has eight attempts to hit the target. If she gets at least 7 hits on target she will qualify for the next round.

   a Find the probability that she hits the target exactly 4 times.

   b Find the probability that she fails to qualify for the next round.

   c What assumption did you need to make in your answers in parts **a** and **b**?

8 A test is marked on the scale from 1 to 5. The cumulative distribution of test scores is shown in the table:

Grade (s)	1	2	3	4	5
P (grades $\leqslant s$)	0.32	0.48	0.65	0.82	1

Find the percentage of candidates whose grade was:

a 2   **b** between 3 and 5 inclusive.

9 A student has the probability 0.7 of answering a question correctly, independently of any other questions.

Find the probability that, in a test containing 15 questions, the student gets more than seven but fewer than 12 correct answers.

10 A biased coin has probability p of showing heads. The coin is tossed 6 times. The probability that it shows no heads is 0.072. Find the value of p correct to two significant figures.

11 Sasha and Elijah both roll a fair six-sided dice.

a Find the probability distribution of the difference between the scores (Sasha's score – Elijah's score).

b Hence find the probability that Elijah gets a higher score than Sasha.

12 **i** A biased coin is thrown twice. The probability that it shows heads both times is 0.04. Find the probability that it shows tails both times.

ii Another coin is biased so that the probability that it shows heads on any throw is p. The probability that the coin shows heads exactly once in two throws is 0.42. Find the possible values of p.

© **OCR, AS GCE Mathematics, Paper 4732, June 2007**

13 A company producing light bulbs knows that the probability that a new light bulb is defective is 0.5%.

a Find the probability that a pack of six light bulbs contains at least one defective one.

b Hamish buys 20 packs of six light bulbs. Find the probability that more than 4 of the boxes contain at least one defective light bulb.

14 A fair coin is tossed repeatedly until it shows tails.

a Find the probability that the first five tosses all show heads.

b Hence find the probability that the first tails appear on the sixth toss.

15 The probability that a student forgets to do homework is 5% independently of other students. If at least one student forgets to do homework, the whole class has to do a test.

   a There are 12 students in a class. Find the probability that the class will have to do a test.

   b For a class with n students, write down an expression for the probability that the class will have to do a test.

   c Hence find the smallest number of students in the class such that the probability that the class will have to do a test is at least 80%.

16 Two fair dice are rolled and the difference between the two scores is recorded (larger − smaller).

   a Find the probability distribution of the recorded number.

   b This experiment is repeated ten times. Find the probability that the recorded number is zero on more than three occasions.

17 Four fair six-sided dice are rolled. Let X be the largest number rolled.

   a Explain why $P(X \leqslant k) = \left(\frac{k}{6}\right)^{4}$, for $k = 1, 2, \ldots 6$.

   b Copy and complete the following probability distribution table.

x	1	2	3	4	5	6
$P(X = x)$		$\frac{15}{1296}$	$\frac{65}{1296}$			$\frac{671}{1296}$

Elevate

For a selection of more challenging problems, see Extension sheet 17.

18 A fair six-sided dice is rolled until the fourth 6 is obtained.

   a Find the probability that there are exactly three 6s in the first seven rolls.

   b Hence find the probability that the fourth 6 is obtained on the eighth roll.

18 Statistical hypothesis testing

In this chapter you will learn how to:

- recognise the difference between a sample and a population
- use different types of sampling methods
- use the vocabulary associated with hypothesis tests
- conduct a hypothesis test using the binomial distribution to test if a proportion has changed.

Before you start...

Chapter 17	You should know how to calculate cumulative probabilities for a binomial distribution.	1	Given that $X \sim B(25, 0.6)$, find: a $P(X \leqslant 15)$ b $P(X \geqslant 17)$
Chapter 17	You should be able to deduce parameters of a binomial distribution in context.	2	It is known that, on average, 35 out of 50 people like coffee. For a random sample of 12 people, let X be the number of those who like coffee. State the distribution of X, including any parameters.

What is hypothesis testing?

The aim of statistics is to find out various things about a population. Here are some examples of questions you might ask:

- What is the mean height of all 17-year-old boys in the UK?
- What is the range of ages of all professional football players?
- What proportion of the electorate intend to vote for a particular political party in the next election?

It is often impossible to collect all the required data, so you use samples to make inferences about the whole population. A sample value can only give you an estimate of the **population parameter** (this is some numerical characteristic of the population, such as mean or range). How good this estimate is depends on the size and quality of the sample. The first part of this chapter looks at issues around sampling and using samples. Once you have used a sample to find an estimate of the population parameter it would be useful to know how accurate this estimate is likely to be. This question is in general very difficult to answer and requires some advanced probability theory. The second part of this chapter looks at a slightly simpler question, asking whether the parameter value has changed from a previously known, or assumed one. This leads to the **hypothesis test**, a procedure for determining whether a given sample provides significant evidence that a population parameter (for example, mean/spread/ proportion) has changed from a previously known or assumed value. The hypothesis test is one of the most commonly used statistical tools.

Section 1: Populations and samples

Suppose you wanted to know the average height of all adults in the UK. One way to find out would be to measure everyone's height. This is called a **census**. It involves collecting information about the entire **population** – all the individuals of interest (in this example this would be all UK adults). A large organisation may be able to carry out such a survey; indeed, the UK government undertakes a census every ten years in order to plan public services.

For a small organisation or an individual, a census is mostly not an option, because of the time and costs involved. Census data sets also take a very long time to analyse (although modern technology has made this less of a problem). This means that it is not possible for you to find out the exact average height of all UK adults. But you can try to estimate it by taking a sample – measuring heights of part of the population. The average of the sample will most likely be different from the population average. However, if the sample is selected well, it may provide a reasonable estimate.

There are situations where it is impossible to carry out a census, even if a large amount of time and money is available. One example is if it is impossible to identify, or get access to, all members of the population. For example, suppose a zoologist wanted to find out the average mass of an ant. It is impossible to find all the ants in the world, or tell which ones you have not yet measured. Another situation is when the process of collecting data destroys the object being measured. For example, a manufacturer needs to know what maximum load can be placed on a shelf. Testing the whole population would mean breaking all the shelves.

Once you have selected a sample and collected the data you can apply to it any of the techniques you learnt in Chapter 16 – you can draw statistical diagrams, calculate averages, measures of spread or correlation. You then need to decide what this tells you about the whole population.

WORKED EXAMPLE 18.1

A clothing company carries out a survey to find out the average and the range of heights of 17-year-old girls in the UK. A sample of 200 girls from a large sixth form college has a mean height of 158 cm and a range of 28 cm.

a   Is the true population mean more likely to be larger or smaller than 158 cm?

b   State one possible reason why taking a sample from a single college may not result in a good estimate for the mean height.

c   Siobhan says that 28 cm is a good estimate for the range. Priya says that the range is almost certainly larger than 28 cm. Explain who is right.

Continues on next page ...

a The sample mean is equally likely to be larger or smaller than the true population mean. · · · · This should be the case if the sample has been selected well.

b For example, the college might be · · · · located in an area populated by an ethnic group which is on average taller or shorter than the whole population. The part of the population from which the sample was taken may not be typical of the entire country.

c It is unlikely that both the shortest and the tallest 17-year-old girl in the country go to this particular college. So Priya is right, the sample range will be smaller than the population range.

Explore

It turns out that all measures of spread tend to be underestimated by a sample. However, in the case of the variance there is a change to the formula you met in Chapter 16, Section 2, which provides a better estimate. Find out about 'unbiased estimates' – you will meet them if you study the Statistics option of Further Mathematics.

A sample is often used to find an estimate of a population **parameter** (some numerical characteristic of the population, such as its mean or variance). If you want a sample to provide a good estimate of a population parameter then the sample needs to be **representative** of the population. This means that the distribution of the values in the sample is roughly the same as in the whole population. This will not be the case if the sampling procedure is **biased**. For example, if you wanted to find out about people's attitudes to music and you selected a sample from those attending a particular concert, then this sample would contain an unusually large number of fans of a particular type of music.

WORKED EXAMPLE 18.2

Comment on possible sources of bias in each of these samples:

a The basketball team as a sample of students at a college used to estimate the average height of all students.

b A sample of people from a particular political party's conference used to find out about the UK population's attitudes to taxation.

c A sample taken from those in a waiting room at a doctor's surgery for a survey to find out how many days people in the country have had off sick this year.

Continues on next page ...

a   Basketball players are on average taller than the general population.

b   Attitudes to taxation tend to be related to political affiliation, so members of a particular party will have attitudes not representative of the wider population.

c   People at a doctor's surgery are likely to have poorer health than the general population.

There are several different methods for selecting samples. This section looks at which of them are most likely to lead to representative samples. It is important to remember, however, that even a good (unbiased) sampling method can lead to an unrepresentative sample. This is because the process of sampling is inherently random so there is always a possibility that, for example, only extreme values are selected. The aim of a good sampling method is to minimise the probability of this happening.

Simple random sample

This is the type of sample most people have in mind when they talk about random samples.

Key point 18.1

Simple random sampling is a procedure where every possible sample (of a given size) has an equal chance of being selected.

Many common sampling techniques do not produce a simple random sample. For example, it is common to include equal numbers of each gender when selecting a sample for a social science study. This is not a simple random sample because a sample consisting of all females has probability zero of being selected. Another example would be selecting names from a list by choosing the starting point randomly and then taking every tenth name. There are perfectly good reasons for selecting samples in this way in certain situations, you just need to be aware that they are not simple random samples.

Common methods for generating a simple random sample include lottery machines and random number generators. When using these methods, it is a common practice to sample without replacement; this means that you do not include the same individual more than once. If the population is large, it is possible to do this for any reasonably sized sample.

WORKED EXAMPLE 18.3

A student wants to take a sample of students from his college. He has a list of all students, numbered 1 to 478. He uses a random number generator on his calculator, which can generate three-digit random numbers between 001 and 999, inclusive. The first ten numbers he obtains are:

237, 155, 623, 078, 523, 078, 003, 381, 554, 263

Suggest which could be the first four students in his sample.

237, 155,	Skip 623, as there is no student with this number.
78,	078 stands for student number 78.
3	Skip 523 because there is no student with this number, and skip 78 because it has already been included.

Opportunity sampling

Ensuring a simple random sample is remarkably difficult. A large part of the difficulty stems from the fact that it may not be possible to get the list of all the members of the population to which you can then apply the sampling procedure, or to obtain measurements from all the individuals you wish to sample. **Opportunity sampling** avoids these difficulties by sampling only from those individuals who are available and willing to take part.

 Key point 18.2

Opportunity sampling involves choosing respondents based upon their availability and convenience.

This clearly does not produce a simple random sample, but it may be the only possible option and it may still produce a good estimate of the population parameters you are interested in. However, in some situations it can introduce bias if the group consists of very similar members. It might, therefore, not be generalisable. For example, if you ask your friends which subject they like most there is no guarantee that the majority of your school shares that opinion; it would therefore not be wise to draw conclusions about the whole school based on this sample.

WORKED EXAMPLE 18.4

Del wishes to take a sample of residents from her neighbourhood. She decides to ask some people waiting at the bus stop.

a   What sort of sample is this?
b   Is the sample likely to be representative if her question is about
   i   attitudes to the environment   ii   their favourite football team?

a   Opportunity sample

b i   The sample may not be representative
       because people who use public transport are
       arguably more likely to have 'green' attitudes.

   ii   The sample could be representative, · · · · · · | You may be able to think of possible sources of
        as there is no obvious link between | bias here; for example, linked to age.
        use of public transport and football.

Systematic sampling

A simple random sample might just happen to include only people from London, or only people with the first name John. If these outcomes would be problematic, an alternative is **systematic sampling**. This requires a list of all participants ordered in some way.

🔑 **Key point 18.3**

Systematic sampling means taking participants at regular intervals from a list of the population, with the starting point chosen at random.

WORKED EXAMPLE 18.5

A sample is formed by taking a telephone book and calling the person at the top of each page.

a   State the name given to this type of sampling.
b   Explain why this is not simple random sampling.

The calls are made at between 10 a.m. and 2 p.m. on a Wednesday to enquire about the number of children in the household.

c   Suggest a reason why the mean value calculated will be biased.

a   Systematic sample

b   Not all samples are equally likely – e.g. the sample
    with all the people at the bottom of each page
    has zero probability of being selected.

c   People without children may be working · · · · · · | There are many possible reasons biasing the
    at this time, so they may not answer. | mean in either direction. Any valid, well-
    This would mean the calculated mean is higher | reasoned argument would be acceptable.
    than it should be.

Stratified sampling

A simple random sample might not be representative of the overall population. There may be more pensioners, or men, or people with Mathematics A level in your sample than the background population. One way to overcome this is to use a stratified sample. First you need to decide in advance which factors you think might be important. You separate the population by these factors and within each group you take a simple random sample. The size of each sample is in proportion to the size of the group.

 Key point 18.4

> Stratified sampling is splitting the population into groups based on factors relevant to the research, then random sampling from each group in proportion to the size of that group.

WORKED EXAMPLE 18.6

A school is made up of 250 girls and 150 boys. A sample of size 80 is to be chosen, stratified between boys and girls. How many girls must be included in the sample?

The proportion of the school which is girls is $\dfrac{250}{250+150} = \dfrac{5}{8}$

The total school population is $250 + 150 = 400$.

$\dfrac{5}{8}$ of 80 is 50.

Calculate this fraction of the sample of 80.

Quota sampling

Stratified sampling is excellent in principle, but it is often not practical. You need to have access to every member of the population to make a random sample. A common alternative is to use opportunity sampling instead of simple random sampling within each group.

 Key point 18.5

> Quota sampling is splitting the population into groups based on factors relevant to the research, then opportunity sampling from each group until a required number of participants are found.

WORKED EXAMPLE 18.7

A market researcher is required to sample 100 men and 100 women in a supermarket to find out how much they are spending on that day.

a State the name given to this type of sampling.
b Explain why this method is used rather than stratified sampling.
c State one disadvantage of this method.

a Quota sampling

b The researcher would have to know in advance who was going to be shopping on that day to create a random sample, and this is not feasible.

c The people who stop to talk to the researcher might not be representative.

> There are several other disadvantages too!

Cluster sampling

One of the main concerns in real-world sampling is cost. Creating a list of all members of a population and travelling or contacting the sample may be very difficult and expensive. One method that tries to make the process more efficient is **cluster sampling**. Like stratified sampling, this involves splitting the population into groups, called clusters. Unlike stratified sampling, these clusters do not have to be based on factors relevant to the research – they may be based just on convenience.

Key point 18.6

Cluster sampling is splitting the population into clusters based on convenience, then randomly choosing some clusters to study further.

In stratified sampling, all groups are sampled in proportion to their size, but in cluster sampling only some of the clusters are chosen (at random) to be studied. This makes it less accurate than stratified sampling, as choosing an unrepresentative cluster can have a large effect on the outcome.

WORKED EXAMPLE 18.8

Jacob wants to estimate the percentage of people in the UK who travel to work by train. He selects five local authorities at random and uses their information to work out the mean.

a State the name given to this type of sampling.
b Describe the difference between this sampling and a stratified sample across local authorities.

a Cluster sample

b Only some local authorities are chosen in this sample. If it were a stratified sample, values would be chosen from all local authorities and combined in proportion to the size of the local authority.

Comparing sampling methods

Method	Advantage	Disadvantage
Random methods		
Simple random	Produces an unbiased sample.	Hard to do in practice. Needs a list of the entire population and everybody to respond. Time consuming and expensive.
Systematic	Avoids unwanted clustering of data. Practically easier than using random number generators.	Needs a list of the entire population. Less random than simple random as no longer independent.
Stratified	Produces a sample representative over the factors identified.	Needs a list of the entire population with additional information about each member. Time consuming and expensive. Determining which factors to consider is not always obvious.
Cluster	Cheaper and easier than other random methods.	Less accurate than other random methods – clusters may not be representative.
Non-random methods		
Opportunity sample	Cheap and convenient.	May introduce bias and not be generalisable.
Quota sample	Ensures the sample is representative over the factors identified.	May introduce bias and not be generalisable.

Elevate

You will learn how to carry out different sampling methods, and explore how different samples can lead to different conclusions about the population, in the Large Data Set section on the Cambridge Elevate digital platform.

Focus on ...

Obtaining a good sample can be very difficult in practice. Focus on ... Problem solving 3 looks at some famous examples of experimental design in statistics.

Did you know?

The issue of how big a sample to use is of vital importance to statisticians. A sample of size 200 is not twice as good as a sample of size 100. This is not just a rule of thumb – you can prove it using some advanced ideas in statistics that you will meet if you study the Statistics option of Further Mathematics.

EXERCISE 18A

1 Comment on possible sources of bias in the following samples:

a Determining the attitude towards university tuition fees in the UK by asking sixth form students.

b Finding out about British people's perception of the cost of food by asking people in supermarkets to estimate the cost of a pint of milk.

c Measuring the average height of people in the UK using a sample taken from a school.

d Predicting the outcome of the 1948 US presidential election by a telephone survey of US citizens.

2 Name the type of sampling described in each of these situations:

a A zoologist is investigating different flies in a forest. She knows there are roughly equal numbers of male and female flies so she puts up fly paper that attracts female flies and fly paper that attracts male flies. She waits until each paper has 20 flies on it and then takes the paper down.

b A doctor believes that drug resistance may depend on the age of the patient. She knows that 20% of patients in the hospital are less than 18 years old and 30% are over 65. She makes a simple random sample to choose four aged under 18, ten people aged between 18 and 65 and six over 65.

c There are about 4000 professional footballers in England playing for 92 clubs. To estimate the fitness of professional footballers 10 clubs are chosen at random and fitness tests are conducted on a random sample of players at those clubs.

d The names of all students in a school are put into a hat and a sample is formed from the first 10 names taken out.

e To find the average population of countries a list of all countries is written in alphabetical order and the 3rd, 13th, 23rd … counties are chosen and investigated.

f To determine the outcome of the next election you ask everybody in your class how they will vote.

3 In order to find out the mean and standard deviation of masses of a particular breed of cat, Dougal measures a random sample of 20 cats. The results are summarised as follows:

$$\sum w = 51, \ \sum w^2 = 138.32$$

a Find the mean mass and show that the standard deviation of this sample is 0.64 to 2 decimal places.

b Is the standard deviation of the whole population likely to be larger or smaller than 0.64?

c Dougal hopes to obtain a more accurate estimate for the mean by taking a sample of size 100. The mean of this sample is 2.63. Is this necessarily a better estimate of the population mean than the one found in part **a**? Explain your answer.

4 An ecologist wants to study the proportion of adult fish in the North Sea. She believes that 40% of fish in the North Sea are cod, 40% are haddock and 20% are of other varieties. She catches fish until she has 20 cod, 20 haddock and 10 of other varieties.

a Explain why a random sampling method is not feasible in this situation.

b State the name of sampling method used.

c Why might this method be better than an opportunity sample of the first 20 fish caught?

5 Larissa wants to find out how many students at her college travel by train. She decides to conduct a survey on a simple random sample of 70 students. Describe how she could obtain such a sample.

6 Dineth is investigating attitudes to healthy eating for his Biology project. He decides to interview ten students while waiting in a queue at a burger bar.

   a State the name for this type of sampling.

   b Identify one possible source of bias in Dineth's sample.

7 Lenka needs to take a simple random sample of five students at her college to take part in her psychology experiment. She obtains the list of all 847 students and uses a random number function on her calculator to generate random numbers. Her calculator produces three-digit random numbers from 001 to 999. It produces the following numbers:

     016, 762, 938, 537, 016, 722, 886, 152, 721

   Suggest which five students Lenka should select for her sample.

8 A psychologist is studying the reading age of people in a city. He wants to create a stratified sample. He thinks that gender and age are important. According to census data, 40% of the city is female and the median age is 42 for both genders.

   a Copy and complete this table to show the number of people in each category required in a sample of 80 people.

	Female	Male
Under 42		
42 or over		

   b State one advantage of stratified sampling over quota sampling.

   c Explain why quota sampling might be preferable in this situation.

9 A shop has 40 staff in each of 10 branches in different parts of the country. The owner wants to find out about staff wellbeing. She wants to interview a sample of 20 staff. The following suggestions are made as to how to choose the sample.

   A Pick four branches at random and then interview five randomly chosen people at each branch.

   B Use a random number generator to pick 20 staff from all staff.

   C Get the manager of each branch to select two staff members to send for interview.

   D Use a 20-sided dice to randomly select two members from each branch to send for interview.

   a Name the method of sampling for each suggested method.

   b Which method is likely to give the most accurate answer?

   c Why might method **A** be used instead of method **B**?

10 A polling firm wants to investigate the voting intentions of a London borough. They have access to details of all registered voters in the borough so make a numbered list and use a random number generator to select 100 participants. They send a questionnaire to each person selected and study the responses. Explain why this will not necessarily produce a simple random sample.

 Elevate

Poor sampling methods can lead to misleading results. See Extension sheet 18 for some examples.

11 A school is attended by 500 girls and 500 boys. A simple random sample is obtained by selecting names from a box (without replacement) to get a sample of 10 students.

a Find the probability that the students are all boys.

b If names are put back in the box it is possible that the same student gets picked more than once.

    i Find the probability of someone being picked more than once.

    ii Find the probability of any one student being picked using this method.

c What is the percentage difference between the probability of all 10 students being boys in the situations described in **a** and **b**?

d Instead of simple random sampling an opportunity sample is taken by choosing the first 10 students a teacher sees on the playground. Without further calculation explain whether this will increase or decrease the probability of all 10 students being boys.

Tip

Why might this sampling method not be completely random?

 Focus on …

This problem is looked at in more detail in Focus on … Problem solving 3.

Section 2: Introduction to hypothesis testing

This section looks at using a sample to make inferences about the population. Consider the following questions:

- A particular drug is known to cure a disease in 78% of cases. A new drug is trialled on 100 patients and 68 of them were cured. Does this mean that the new drug is less effective than the old one?
- A sociologist believes that more boys than girls are born during war time. In a sample of 200 babies born in countries at war, 126 were boys. Do these data support the sociologist's theory?
- In the last general election, Party Z won 36% of the vote. An opinion poll surveys 100 people and finds that 45 support Party Z. Does this imply that their share of the vote will change in the next election?

In all these questions you are trying to find out whether the proportion of the population with a certain characteristic is different from a previously known or assumed value, by calculating the corresponding proportion from a sample. You would not expect the sample proportion to be exactly the same as the population proportion. If you took a different sample you may well get a different proportion. This means that a sample, however large, cannot provide a definitive answer to the question; it can only suggest what the answer is likely to be.

One common procedure for answering this type of question is called a 'hypothesis test'. It requires the question to be phrased in a specific way.

Fast forward

A In the AS course you only look at hypothesis tests for the population proportion using the binomial distribution. In Student Book 2 you will also meet a hypothesis test for the population mean.

Key point 18.7

A **hypothesis test** is a procedure for answering a question of the following type:

- Does a sample provide significant evidence that a population parameter (mean/spread/proportion) has changed from a previously known or assumed value?

Look at the first example given in this section. The old drug cured 78% of patients. In a trial of a new drug, 68 out 100 patients in a sample were cured; this number is called the **test statistic**. The question is:

- Does this sample provide sufficient evidence that the new population proportion is smaller than 78%?

The key phrase here is **sufficient evidence**. The sample proportion of $\frac{68}{100} = 68\%$ seems significantly smaller than 78%, but it could happen even if the population proportion is still the same. So how likely would this be?

To calculate this probability you need to assume that the population proportion hasn't changed. This is our 'default position', or **null hypothesis**, which is tested against an **alternative hypothesis**, which represents the idea you have that there has been a change.

Key point 18.8

The null hypothesis, denoted H_0, specifies the previous or assumed population proportion.

The alternative hypothesis, denoted H_1, specifies how you think the proportion may have changed.

So in the example, the null hypothesis is:

H_0: The proportion of cured patients is 78%.

and the alternative hypothesis is:

H_1: The proportion of cured patients is less than 78%.

The question now becomes:

- Does the sample provide sufficient evidence against the null hypothesis and in favour of the alternative hypothesis?

If the population proportion of cured patients is still 78%, then the probability of any particular patient being cured is 0.78. You have a sample of 100 patients, so the number of cured patients can be modelled by the binomial distribution B(100, 0.78). The number of 'successes' in the sample is 68. You are looking for evidence that the population proportion is smaller than 0.78; if this were the case, the number of cured patients would be smaller than expected under the null hypothesis. Therefore, you want to find the probability of 68 or fewer patients being cured:

If $X \sim B(100, 0.78)$ then $P(X \leqslant 68) = 0.0134$.

So if the new drug is as good as the old drug, there is a probability of around 1.3% that only 68 or fewer out of a sample of 100 patients get cured.

Is this sufficiently 'unlikely' to conclude that the population proportion for the new drug must be smaller than 78%? This is a matter of judgement, and may be different in different contexts. You need to decide on what probability is 'sufficiently small'. This is called the **significance level** of the test.

The significance level of a hypothesis test specifies the probability that is sufficiently small to be accepted as evidence against the null hypothesis.

If you assume that H_0 is correct, then the probability of the observed, or more extreme, sample value is called the *p*-value.

Tip

You will normally state the hypotheses in terms of the parameter value. For example:

H_0: $p = 0.78$, H_1: $p < 0.78$,

where p is the proportion of cured patients.

Tip

It is very important that you find $P(X \leqslant 68)$ and not $P(X = 68)$. You can remember this as 'the probability of the observed value, or more extreme'.

Key point 18.9

If the p-value is smaller than the significance level, you have sufficient evidence against H_0 and you can reject it in favour of H_1. Otherwise, the sample does not provide sufficient evidence against H_0 and you should not reject it.

Common significance levels used in practice are between 1% and 10%. If you conduct your test at the 1% significance level, then the p-value 0.0134 is greater than the significance level, so you don't have sufficient evidence that the population proportion has decreased. However, if you use a 5% significance level then you do have sufficient evidence that the new drug cures less than 78% of the patients.

Key point 18.10

A hypothesis test for a population proportion includes the following steps:

1 State the null and alternative hypotheses, defining any parameters.
2 Decide on the significance level.
3 State the distribution of the test statistic, assuming the null hypothesis is true.
4 Using this distribution calculate the probability of observing the test statistic, or more extreme. This is the p-value.
5 Compare the p-value to the significance level. If the p-value is smaller than the significance level, there is sufficient evidence to reject the null hypothesis.
6 Interpret the conclusion in context, remembering to make it clear that the conclusion is not a statement of certainty, but of significance.

Notice that there are two possible conclusions you can reach from a hypothesis test:

- the sample provides sufficient evidence to reject H_0 in favour of H_1

or

- the sample does not provide sufficient evidence to reject H_0.

In the latter case, you cannot say that H_0 is correct, just that you have not found sufficient evidence to reject it.

Once you have reached a conclusion, it is important to interpret it in the context of the question. So in the previous example you need to write something like 'There is sufficient evidence that the new drug is less effective', rather than just 'There is sufficient evidence that the proportion is less than 78%'.

 Tip

You should always use the word 'evidence' in your conclusion, to make it clear that it is not certain.

WORK IT OUT 18.1

Which of these conclusions to hypothesis tests are incorrectly written, and why?

1 Reject H_0. The proportion of red flowers has decreased.
2 There is sufficient evidence to reject H_0, and thus sufficient evidence that the proportion has increased.
3 There is insufficient evidence to reject H_0. The proportion of girls in the club is probably still 45%.
4 Accept H_0, as there is insufficient evidence that the percentage of A grades has increased.
5 There is evidence to accept H_0; the dice isn't biased.

WORKED EXAMPLE 18.9

A sociologist believes that more boys than girls are born during war time. In a sample of 200 babies born in countries at war, 116 were boys.

Do these data support the sociologist's theory at the 5% significance level?

Let p be the proportion of boys in the population.	You want to find out whether there is evidence that the proportion of boys is more than $\frac{1}{2}$.
$H_0: p = 0.5$ $H_1: p > 0.5$	So the null hypothesis is that the proportion is $\frac{1}{2}$ and the alternative hypothesis is that it is greater.
Let X be the number of boys in a sample of 200 babies. If H_0 is correct then $X \sim B(200, 0.5)$. Test statistic: $X = 116$	The test statistic is the number of boys in the sample. Since you are looking for evidence that the population proportion is greater than 0.5, you need to find the probability of observing this number, or more, if H_0 is correct.
$P(X \geqslant 116) = 1 - P(X \leqslant 115)$ $= 0.0141$	Use your calculator to find the cumulative probability.
$0.0141 < 0.05$	Compare the probability to the significance level. Large probability means that the event is 'not unlikely'.
so there is sufficient evidence to reject H_0.	The conclusion is not definite – you must use the phrase 'sufficient/insufficient evidence'.
At the 5% significance level, there is evidence to support the sociologist's theory.	The conclusion needs to be interpreted in the context of the question.

In Worked example 18.9, the alternative hypothesis was that the population proportion has increased. This is called a **one-tail test**. Sometimes you might have a reason to believe that the population proportion has changed, but you can't predict in which direction. In this case you have to do a **two-tail test**. The only difference is that you need to compare the p-value to half the significance level, because both very small and very large values of the test statistic would provide evidence against H_0.

For example, the diagram shows the binomial distribution $B(100, p)$ under $H_0: p = 0.36$. The blue and the green regions both correspond to probabilities of 5%. So observing the sample in either the blue or the green section would lead you to reject the null hypothesis at the 10% significance level.

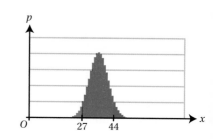

Key point 18.11

- In a one-tail test the alternative hypothesis is of the form $p < \alpha$ or $p > \alpha$. You need to compare the p-value to the significance level.
- In a two-tail test the alternative hypothesis is of the form $p \neq \alpha$. You need to compare the p-value to half the significance level.

In the third question at the start of this section, we wanted to know whether the proportion of voters supporting a particular political party has **changed**. Without any further information you cannot anticipate whether the proportion has increased or decreased, so you have to do a two-tail test.

WORKED EXAMPLE 18.10

In the last general election, Party Z won 36% of the vote. An opinion poll surveys 100 people and finds that 45 support Party Z.

Does this provide sufficient evidence at the 10% significance level that the proportion of voters who support Party Z has changed?

Let p be the proportion of voters supporting Party Z.

H_0: $p = 0.36$

H_1: $p \neq 0.36$

Start by stating the hypotheses. This is a two-tail test because you are looking for evidence of change, rather than just increase or decrease. Remember to define the meaning of the parameter p.

Let X be the number of supporters of Party Z in a sample of 100 people.

If H_0 is true, $X \sim B(100, 0.36)$.

If H_0 is correct, the number of supporters in a sample will follow a binomial distribution with the probability given in H_0.

Test statistic: $P(X = 45)$

$P(X \geqslant 45) = 1 - P(X \leqslant 44)$

$= 0.0397$

Since 45 out of 100 is more than 36%, you need to calculate the probability in the 'right tail'.

$0.0397 < 0.05$ so there is sufficient evidence to reject H_0.

The significance level is 10%, so for a two-tail test you compare the p-value to half the significance level, which is 5%, or 0.05.

There is evidence, at the 10% significance level, that the proportion of voters who support Party Z has changed.

Remember to interpret the conclusion in the context of the question, making it clear that it is not certain.

Tip

Be sure to think carefully about whether you have a one-tail or two-tail test. Remember to halve the significance level in each tail with a two-tail test.

WORK IT OUT 18.2

A dice is rolled 5 times and 3 sixes are observed. Test at the 5% significance level if the dice is biased.

Which is the correct solution? Can you identify the errors made in the incorrect solutions?

Solution 1	Solution 2	Solution 3
$H_0: p = \dfrac{1}{6}$	$H_0: p = \dfrac{1}{6}$	$H_0: p = \dfrac{1}{6}$
$H_1: p \neq \dfrac{1}{6}$	$H_1: p > \dfrac{1}{6}$	$H_1: p \neq \dfrac{1}{6}$
$X \sim B\left(5, \dfrac{1}{6}\right)$	$X \sim B\left(5, \dfrac{1}{6}\right)$	$X \sim B\left(5, \dfrac{1}{6}\right)$
$P(X = 3) = 0.032 < 0.05$ So reject H_0.	$P(X \geqslant 3) = 0.032 < 0.05$ So reject H_0.	$P(X \geqslant 3) = 0.035 > 0.025$ So there is not sufficient evidence to reject H_0.

EXERCISE 18B

1 Write down the null and alternative hypotheses for the following tests, defining the meaning of any parameters.

a **i** Daniel wants to test whether the proportion of children in his school who like football is higher than 60%.

   ii Elsa wants to find out whether the proportion of households with a pet is higher than 1 in 3.

b **i** The proportion of faulty components produced by a machine was 6% and the manager wants to check whether this has decreased following a service.

   ii Joseph thinks that fewer than half of all children eat 5 or more pieces of fruit a day and wants to confirm this by using a hypothesis test.

c **i** Sofia has a coin which she thinks is biased, and wants to use a hypothesis test to check this.

   ii Max knows that, last year, 26% of entries in AS level Psychology were graded 'A' and wants to check whether this proportion has changed.

2 In each question you are given null and alternative hypotheses (where p stands for the population proportion), the significance level and the observed data. Decide whether or not there is sufficient evidence to reject the null hypothesis.

a **i** $H_0: p = 0.3$, $H_1: p > 0.3$, significance level 5%, observed 15 successes out of 40 trials

   ii $H_0: p = 0.6$, $H_1: p > 0.6$, significance level 10%, observed 23 successes out of 45 trials

b i $H_0: p = 0.5$, $H_1: p < 0.5$, significance level 10%, observed 18 successes out of 40 trials

ii $H_0: p = 0.45$, $H_1: p < 0.45$, significance level 3%, observed 23 successes out of 60 trials

c i $H_0: p = 0.4$, $H_1: p \neq 0.4$, significance level 8%, observed 35 successes out of 100 trials

ii $H_0: p = 0.8$, $H_1: p \neq 0.8$, significance level 5%, observed 17 successes out of 20 trials

3 It is known that in the UK, 63% of households own at least one car. David, who lives in a big city, believes that in his neighbourhood car ownership is lower than this. He uses a hypothesis test, based on the binomial distribution, to confirm this.

a State suitable null and alternative hypotheses for his test.

David surveys a random sample of 50 households in his neighbourhood and finds that 29 of them own at least one car.

b Use this data to test David's hypothesis at the 10% significance level. State your conclusion clearly.

4 The 2011 census found that 68% of 16- to 19-year-olds in a particular town attended a sixth form college. In 2015 a sample of 60 teenagers in this age range was surveyed and it was found that 46 of them attended a sixth form college.

Is there evidence, at the 5% significance level, that the proportion of 16- to 19-year-olds attending a sixth form college has increased?

5 Rahul has a six-sided dice that he believes is biased so that the probability of rolling a 3 is smaller than $\frac{1}{6}$. He rolls the dice 30 times and gets four 3s.

Does this provide sufficient evidence to support Rahul's belief?

6 In a certain local authority, the proportion of workers who drive to work is known to be 33%. In a sample of 28 teachers from a particular college, 12 drive to work. Is there evidence, at the 5% significance level, that the teachers at this college are more likely to drive to work than the average for the local authority?

7 An established treatment for a particular disease is known to be effective in 82% of the cases. A doctor devises a new treatment that she believes is even more effective. She uses the treatment on a random sample of 50 patients and finds that the new treatment is effective in 43 cases.

Does this data support the doctor's belief at the 2% significance level?

8 A teacher knows that in his old school, a third of all sixth-formers had a younger sibling at the school. He moves to a new school and wants to find out whether this proportion is different. He asks a sample of 60 sixth-formers, and finds that 27 of them have a younger sibling at the school.

 Elevate

For further examples and practice of hypothesis testing see Support sheet 18.

Conduct a hypothesis test at the 5% significance level to decide whether there is evidence that the proportion of sixth-formers with a younger sibling at the new school is different from the old school.

9 Angela is playing a board game with her friends, but thinks the dice is biased and that a 6 is rolled too infrequently. In the subsequent 40 rolls of the dice she got only three 6s.

Test Angela's belief at the 10% significance level.

10 A large athletics club had the same running coach for several years. Records show that 28% of his athletes could run 100 metres in under 12 seconds. The club brings in a new coach and over the following year, 26 out of a sample of 75 athletes recorded 100-metre times under 12 seconds.

Do these data support the hypothesis that the proportion of athletes who can run 100 metres in under 12 seconds has changed? Use the 5% significance level for your test.

11 The proportion of students in Year 13 in favour of a new uniform is known to be 70%. Rhianna wants to find out whether the proportion in Year 12 is the same. She proposes to test the null hypothesis $H_0: p = 0.7$ against two different alternative hypotheses, $H_1: p < 0.7$ and $H_2: p \neq 0.7$, using the 10% significance level.

Rhianna asks a sample of 25 Year 12 students. The data give her sufficient evidence to reject H_0 in favour of H_1, but not in favour of H_2.

How many students in Rhianna's sample were in favour of the new uniform?

12 A student tests the hypothesis $H_0: p = 0.4$ against $H_1: p > 0.4$, where p is the proportion of brown cats of a particular breed.

In a sample of 80 cats of this breed 40 were brown, and this leads him to reject the null hypothesis.

What can you say about the significance level he used for his test?

13 A doctor wants to find out whether the proportion of people suffering from a certain genetic condition has decreased from its previous value, q. She decides to conduct a hypothesis test at the 5% significance level, using a sample of 120 patients. However, after doing some calculations, she realises that, even if none of her sample had the condition, this would not provide sufficient evidence that the proportion has decreased from q.

Find the maximum possible value of q.

Section 3: Critical region for a hypothesis test

Suppose you toss a coin 200 times and get 86 heads. Does this provide evidence that the coin is biased and that the probability of heads is less than $\frac{1}{2}$?

You can now do a hypothesis test to address this question. If you conduct a hypothesis test using a 1% significance level, you will find that there is insufficient evidence that the coin is biased.

The next logical question to ask is: How many heads would provide sufficient evidence that the coin is biased?

WORKED EXAMPLE 18.11

In order to find out whether a coin is biased against heads, Roberto decides to test the hypotheses

$$H_0: p = \frac{1}{2} \text{ against } H_1: p < \frac{1}{2}$$

where p is the probability of the coin showing heads. He tosses the coin 200 times and uses the 1% level of significance.

What is the greatest number of heads he can observe and still have sufficient evidence that the coin is biased?

Let X be the number of heads out of 200 coin tosses.	State the distribution of the test statistic if the null hypothesis is true.
If H_0 is true, $X \sim B\left(200, \frac{1}{2}\right)$	
Significance level is 1%, so look for a number k such that $P(X \leqslant k) < 0.01$	
$P(X \leqslant 85) = 0.020 > 1\%$	You know from the previous example in the text that 86 heads does not provide sufficient evidence, so try values smaller than 86.
$P(X \leqslant 84) = 0.014 > 1\%$	
$P(X \leqslant 83) = 0.0097 < 1\%$	

In order to have sufficient evidence against H_0 at the 1% significance level, Roberto would need to observe 83 or fewer heads out of 200 coin tosses.

The range of values of the test statistic found in Worked example 18.11 ($X \leqslant 83$) is called the **critical region** for the test.

Key point 18.12

The **critical region** (or **rejection region**) for a test is the set of values of the test statistic that provide sufficient evidence to reject the null hypothesis.

The value at the edge of the critical region is called the **critical value**.

The **acceptance region** is the set of values of the test statistic that do not provide sufficient evidence to reject the null hypothesis.

Tip

The name 'acceptance region' is misleading: you should never say that you accept the null hypothesis, only that you don't have suffcient evidence to reject it.

So in Worked example 18.11 the critical value is 83, the critical region is $X \leqslant 83$ and the acceptance region is $X \geqslant 84$.

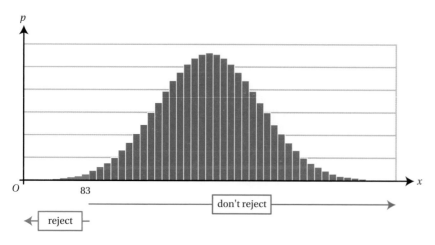

Note that the form of the critical region depends on the form of the alternative hypothesis. If you were looking for evidence that the population proportion has increased, the critical region would be of the form $X \geqslant k$.

WORKED EXAMPLE 18.12

The proportion of students getting an A in AS Mathematics is currently 33%. A publisher produces a new textbook that they hope will lead to improved performance. They trial their textbook with a sample of 120 students and want to test their hypothesis at the 5% significance level.

Find the critical region for this test.

Let p be the proportion of A grades.	You should always start by stating the hypotheses. Remember to define the meaning of p.
$H_0: p = 0.33$	
$H_1: p > 0.33$	The null hypothesis states the current, known proportion.
Let X be the number of A grades in the sample of 120 students.	Next state the distribution you are going to use.
If H_0 is true then $X \sim B(120, 0.33)$	
$P(X \geqslant 47) = 1 - P(X \leqslant 46)$ $= 0.091 > 5\%$ $P(X \geqslant 48) = 1 - P(X \leqslant 47)$ $= 0.064 > 5\%$	If H_0 were true you would expect around $120 \times 0.33 \approx 40$ A grades, so you only need to check values of X larger than 40. Use your calculator to find the probabilities.
$P(X \geqslant 49) = 1 - P(X \leqslant 48)$ $= 0.044 < 5\%$ The critical region is $X \geqslant 49$.	Look for the first probability smaller than the significance level.

Tip

Some calculators can do 'inverse binomial distribution' which tells you where to look for the critical value. You still need to show the probability calculations, as illustrated in Worked example 18.12.

Once you have found the critical region you can easily tell whether a value of the test statistic provides sufficient evidence against the null hypothesis.

> ### 🔑 Key point 18.13
>
> If the value of the test statistic is inside the critical region you have sufficient evidence to reject H_0.

> ### 💡 Tip
>
> The critical value is included in the critical (rejection) region.

So if, for example, 52 out of the 120 students got A grades, the publisher would have sufficient evidence to claim that their textbook leads to improved performance.

As with any conclusion from a statistical investigation, there is no proof that the improvement was actually caused by the textbook – there could be other factors. Perhaps more importantly, since you are only using a sample, there is no guarantee that the proportion of A grades for the whole population has increased. It is possible that the selected sample was unrepresentative, and that most other samples would result in a smaller proportion of A grades.

The meaning of the significance level

To judge how reliable your test is, it is useful to estimate the probability of drawing an incorrect conclusion. It is possible that your sample leads you to reject a correct null hypothesis. In Worked example 18.12, even if the proportion of A grades is still 33%, a sample could suggest that the proportion has increased. That would happen if the test statistic (the number of A grades in the sample) is in the critical region, in this case $X \geqslant 49$. But you have already found the probability of this happening: $P(X \geqslant 49) = 0.044$; so there is a 4.4% chance that you reject the null hypothesis even though it is correct.

> ### ⏩ Fast forward
>
> In Student Book 2 you will test hypotheses involving continuous distributions; in that case the probability of rejecting a correct null hypothesis will be exactly equal to the significance level.

> ### 🔑 Key point 18.14
>
> The probability of rejecting a correct null hypothesis is the same as the probability of the test statistic being in the critical region. It is always smaller than (or equal to) the significance level of the test.

WORKED EXAMPLE 18.13

A machine produces smartphone parts. Previous experience suggests that, on average, 7 in every 200 parts are faulty. After the machine was accidentally moved, a technician suspects that the proportion of faulty parts may have increased. She decides to test this hypothesis using a random sample of 85 parts.

a State suitable null and alternative hypotheses.

The technician decides that the critical region for the test should be $X \geqslant 5$. After checking her sample, she finds that 4 parts are faulty.

b State what conclusion she should draw and justify your answer.

c What is the probability of incorrectly rejecting the null hypothesis?

Continues on next page …

a $H_0: p = 0.035$

$H_1: p > 0.035$

(where p is the proportion of faulty parts)

> The null hypothesis is that the proportion hasn't changed, so the probability of a part being faulty is $\frac{7}{200} = 0.035$.

b The test statistic $X = 4$ is not in the critical region, so there is not sufficient evidence to reject H_0.

> Check whether the test statistic is in the critical region.

There is not sufficient evidence that the proportion of faulty parts has increased.

> Interpret the conclusion in the context of the question.

c If $X \sim B(85, 0.035)$ then the probability of rejecting H_0 is

$P(X \geqslant 5) = 1 - P(X \leqslant 4)$

$= 0.177$

> 'Incorrectly rejecting the null hypothesis' means that H_0 is correct (so $p = 0.035$) but the test statistic happens to be in the critical region (so $X \geqslant 5$).

Explore

It is also possible to reach a different type of incorrect conclusion: your sample may not provide sufficient evidence against H_0 even if it is incorrect. This is especially likely to happen if the proportion has changed by just a little bit. Find out about Type I and Type II errors.

EXERCISE 18C

1 Find the critical regions for the following hypothesis tests. You are given the null and alternative hypotheses, the significance level (SL) and the sample size (n).

a **i** $H_0: p = 0.6$, $H_1: p < 0.6$, SL $= 5\%$, $n = 50$

ii $H_0: p = 0.2$, $H_1: p < 0.2$, SL $= 10\%$, $n = 40$

b **i** $H_0: p = 0.5$, $H_1: p < 0.5$, SL $= 7\%$, $n = 120$

ii $H_0: p = 0.8$, $H_1: p < 0.8$, SL $= 1\%$, $n = 75$

c **i** $H_0: p = 0.6$, $H_1: p > 0.6$, SL $= 5\%$, $n = 50$

ii $H_0: p = 0.2$, $H_1: p > 0.2$, SL $= 10\%$, $n = 40$

d **i** $H_0: p = 0.5$, $H_1: p > 0.5$, SL $= 7\%$, $n = 120$

ii $H_0: p = 0.8$, $H_1: p > 0.8$, SL $= 1\%$, $n = 75$

2 For each of the tests in question 1, find the probability of incorrectly rejecting the null hypothesis.

3 Ayesha is trying to find out whether it is true that students studying A level Mathematics are more likely to be boys than girls. She sets up the following hypotheses:

$H_0: p = 0.5$, $H_1: p < 0.5$, where p is the proportion of girls studying A level Mathematics.

She uses a sample of 30 A level students from her college, and decides to test her hypotheses at the 10% significance level.

Find the critical region for her test.

4 A company is testing a new drug. They want to find out whether the drug cures a certain disease in more than 85% of cases.

   a State suitable null and alternative hypotheses, defining any parameters.

The company decide to conduct their test at the 5% significance level, using a sample of 180 patients.

   b Let X be the number of patients who are cured after using the drug. Find the critical region for the test.

5 A manufacturer knows that, in the past, 12% of the population have purchased their products. After a new advertising campaign, they believe that this proportion has increased. The marketing manager wants to test this belief using a random sample of 200 people.

   a Write down suitable null and alternative hypotheses.

The marketing manager decides that the rejection region for the test should be $X \geqslant 32$, where X is the number of people in the sample who have purchased their products.

   b After collecting the data, it is found that 30 people have purchased the manufacturer's products. What should the marketing manager conclude?

   c Find the probability of incorrectly rejecting the null hypothesis.

6 Sean has an eight-sided dice and wants to check whether it is biased by looking at the probability, p, of rolling a 4. He sets up the following hypotheses:

$$H_0 : p = \frac{1}{8} \quad H_1 : p \neq \frac{1}{8}$$

To test them he decides to roll the dice 80 times and reject the null hypothesis if the number of 4s is greater than 15 or fewer than five.

   a Let X be the number of 4s observed out of the 80 rolls. State the name given to the region $5 \leqslant X \leqslant 15$.

   b What is the probability that Sean incorrectly rejects the null hypothesis?

7 A hypothesis test is proposed to decide whether the proportion of children in a certain country who walk to school is greater than 30%.

   a State suitable hypotheses, defining any parameters.

The test is to be carried out at the 5% significance level using a random sample of 170 children.

   b Find the critical region for the test.

After the data was collected, it was found that 64 of the 170 children walked to school.

   c State the conclusion of the test.

8 A driving school has records showing that, over a long period, 72% of its students passed their test on the first attempt. Under a new management, some of the procedures have changed and they want to find out whether the pass rate has changed.

   a Defining any parameters, state suitable hypotheses.

The hypotheses are tested using a random sample of 50 students. It is decided that the null hypothesis should be accepted if between 31 and 41 (inclusive) of the students pass the test on the first attempt.

   b State the critical region for the test.

   c Find the probability of incorrectly rejecting the null hypothesis. What can be said about the significance level of the test?

🖉 Checklist of learning and understanding

- A **population** is the set of all individuals or items of interest in a statistical investigation. A **population parameter** is some numerical characteristic of the population (such as the mean or the range).
- A **sample** is a subset of the population. A **statistic** is some numerical characteristic of the sample that is used to estimate the population parameter of interest.
- A good sampling procedure avoids **bias**, so the sample is more likely to be **representative** of the population. However, even an unbiased sampling procedure may accidentally produce an unrepresentative sample.
- Some common sampling procedures include:
  - **Simple random sampling**: Each possible sample of a given size has equal probability of being selected. This can be achieved by using a random number generator.
  - **Opportunity sampling**: A sample is made up of individuals who are available and willing to take part.
  - **Systematic sampling**: Taking participants at regular intervals from a list of the population.
  - **Stratified sampling**: The proportion of members of the sample with certain characteristics is fixed to be the same as in the whole population; the individuals for each group are then selected randomly.
  - **Quota sampling**: Groups are determined as for stratified sampling, but the individuals for each group are then selected by opportunity sampling.
  - **Cluster sampling**: A number of subsets of the population (clusters) are selected, and then a simple random sample is taken from each cluster.
- A **hypothesis test** determines whether there is evidence that the value of a population parameter has changed from a previously known, or assumed one. The conclusion from a hypothesis test is never certain; two possible types of conclusion are:
  - There is insufficient evidence that the value of the population parameter has changed.
  - There is sufficient evidence that the value of the population parameter has changed.
- To carry out a hypothesis test, with a given **significance level**, for the proportion of the binomial distribution, you must follow these steps:
  1 State the null and alternative hypotheses, defining the meaning of any parameters.
  2 State the binomial distribution which the test statistic would follow if the null hypothesis was correct.
  3 Calculate the probability of observing the given value of the test statistic, or more extreme (the **p-value**).
  4 Compare this probability to the significance level. Reject the null hypothesis if the p-value is smaller than the significance level.

     In a **two-tail test**, compare the probability to half the significance level.
  5 State the conclusion of the test, interpreting it in context and making it clear that there is some uncertainty (using the word '**evidence**').
- The **critical region** (or **rejection region**) for a hypothesis test is the set of values of the test statistic that lead us to reject the null hypothesis. The remaining values form the **acceptance region**.
  - For a two-tail test, the critical region is made up of two parts.
- The probability of incorrectly rejecting the null hypothesis is equal to the probability of the critical region. This is always less than or equal to the significance level of the test.

Mixed practice 18

1 A market researcher is asked to conduct a survey outside a library. He is asked to sample 100 male library users, 100 female library users, 50 males who have not been into the library and 50 females who have not been into the library.

What type of sampling method is this?

2 The organisers of the school concert want to find out how many of the students are planning to attend the concert. The school has 48 different tutor groups, and they decide to select a sample of students in the following way:

- They choose five tutor groups randomly.
- From each tutor group, they select a random sample of ten students.

a What name is given to this type of sampling procedure?

b Explain why this procedure might not give a representative sample in this case.

The organisers later decide that they should take a simple random sample of 50 students instead.

c Describe how they might obtain such a sample.

3 Gavin has a six-sided dice that he thinks is biased and shows more 5s than it should. He wants to conduct a hypothesis test to test his belief.

a State suitable null and alternative hypotheses.

Gavin rolls the dice 75 times and obtains 18 5s.

b Conduct the test at the 5% significance level, stating your conclusion clearly.

4 Lisa, who takes the bus to school, is late for school on average once in every eight days. She has recently moved closer to the school and now walks. In the last 30 days she was late only twice.

Is there evidence, at the 10% significance level, that the probability of Lisa being late for school has decreased? State your hypotheses and your conclusion clearly.

5 A village has a population of 600 people. A sample of 12 people is obtained as follows. A list of all 600 people is obtained and a three-digit number, between 001 and 600 inclusive, is allocated to each name in alphabetical order. Twelve three-digit random numbers, between 001 and 600 inclusive, are obtained and the people whose names correspond to those numbers are chosen.

a Find the probability that the first number chosen is 500 or less.

b When the selection has been made, it is found that all of the numbers chosen are 500 or less. One of the people in the village says: 'The sampling method must have been biased'. Comment on this statement.

6 The head teacher of a school asks for volunteers from among the pupils to take part in a survey on political interests.

i Explain why a sample consisting of all the volunteers is unlikely to give a true picture of the political interests of all pupils in the school.

ii Describe a better method of obtaining the sample.

© OCR, AS GCE Mathematics, Paper 4733, June 2008

7 A doctor knows that 20% of people suffer from side effects when treated with a certain drug. He wants to see if the proportion of people suffering from side effects is lower with a new drug. He looks at a random sample of 30 people treated with the new drug.

What is the largest number of people who could suffer from side effects and still conclude at 5% significance that the new drug has a lower proportion of side effects?

8 In the UK, the proportion of families who own their home (as opposed to renting) is 64%. Sabina wants to find out whether this proportion is different in Germany. She surveys a random sample of 180 families in Germany and finds that 98 of them own their homes.

Conduct a hypothesis test at the 5% significance level to test whether the proportion of families in Germany who own their home is different from that in the UK.

9 **a** Define a simple random sample.

Aneka is investigating attitudes to sport among students at her school. She decides to carry out a survey using a sample of 70 students. There are the same number of boys and girls at the school, so Aneka randomly chooses 35 boys and 35 girls.

b **i** State the name for this type of sample.

ii Explain why in this case, this type of sample is better than a simple random sample.

One of Aneka's questions is about participation in school sports teams. She wants to find out whether more than 40% of students play for a school team. She sets up the following hypotheses: H_0: $p = 0.4$, H_1: $p > 0.4$, where p is the proportion of students who play for a school sports team.

c Find the critical region for the hypothesis test at the 10% significance level, using a sample of 70 students.

d What is the probability of incorrectly rejecting the null hypothesis?

e In Aneka's sample, 32 students play for a school team. State the conclusion of the test.

10 In a rearrangement code, the letters of a message are rearranged so that the frequency with which any particular letter appears is the same as in the original message. In ordinary German the letter e appears 19% of the time. A certain encoded message of 20 letters contains one letter e.

i Using an exact binomial distribution, test at the 10% significance level whether there is evidence that the proportion of the letter e in the language from which this message is a sample is less than in German, i.e., less than 19%.

ii Give a reason why a binomial distribution might not be an appropriate model in this context.

© **OCR, AS GCE Mathematics, Paper 4733, June 2007**

11 A test is constructed to see if a coin is biased. It is tossed 10 times and if there are 10 heads, 9 heads, 1 head or 0 heads it is declared to be biased.

For each of the following, explain whether or not it could be the significance level for this test:

a 1%   **b** 2%   **c** 10%   **d** 20%

FOCUS ON ... PROOF 3

Using mathematical notation

In Chapter 16, Section 2, you saw that there are two different formulae for standard deviation:

$$\sqrt{\sum \frac{(x-\bar{x})^2}{n}} \quad \text{and} \quad \sqrt{\frac{\sum x^2}{n} - \bar{x}^2}$$

In these formulae, x represents the individual data items, n is the number of items, $\bar{x}$ is the mean.

 Rewind

Remember from Chapter 16, Section 2, that the symbol σ (lower case sigma) is used for standard deviation.

▶▶ **Fast forward**

You will learn more about the Σ symbol (upper case sigma) if you study the Statistics option of Further Mathematics; for now, you just need to know that it means 'add up'.

Here is a proof that the two formulae are equivalent. It works with the expression under the square root (this is called the variance).

Prove: $\dfrac{\sum (x-\bar{x})^2}{n} = \dfrac{\sum x^2}{n} - \bar{x}^2$

PROOF 9

$\text{LHS} = \dfrac{\sum (x-\bar{x})^2}{n}$

$= \dfrac{\sum (x^2 - 2x\bar{x} + \bar{x}^2)}{n}$

Start by expanding the brackets on the left and see if you can simplify it to look like the expression on the right.

$= \dfrac{\sum x^2}{n} - \dfrac{\sum 2x\bar{x}}{n} + \dfrac{\sum \bar{x}^2}{n}$

There are three terms added up in the numerator. The first one looks like the first term in the expression you are trying to prove, so it seems sensible to split the sum into three parts.

$= \dfrac{\sum x^2}{n} - 2\bar{x}\dfrac{\sum x}{n} + \dfrac{n\bar{x}^2}{n}$

Now remember that you are adding up the terms corresponding to different values of x. There are n things to add in each sum.

The mean, $\bar{x}$, is a constant. The sum in the last term just says 'add $\bar{x}^2$ n times, so it equals $n\bar{x}^2$.

In the middle sum, $2\bar{x}$ is a constant multiplying each 'x', so it can be taken outside the sum.

$= \dfrac{\sum x^2}{n} - 2\overline{xx} + \bar{x}^2$

The first term is exactly what you want. The last term equals $\bar{x}^2$, but it has a + instead of –.

$= \dfrac{\sum x^2}{n} - 2\bar{x}^2 + \bar{x}^2$

But look at the middle term: $\dfrac{\sum x}{n}$ means 'add up all the values and divide by n'; this gives the mean, $\bar{x}$.

$= \dfrac{\sum x^2}{n} - \bar{x}^2 = \text{RHS, as required.}$

You have reached the expression on the right, so the proof is complete.

Questions

1 Was the use of Σ notation helpful, or did you find it confusing? Would it be easier to write something like $a + b + c...$ instead? Try rewriting the proof using different notation.

2 Somewhat surprisingly, the equivalence of the two standard deviation formulae can be used to prove a pure mathematical result about inequalities:

For any real numbers $x_1, x_2, ..., x_n$:

$$\sqrt{\frac{x_1^2 + x_2^2 + ... + x_n^2}{n}} \geqslant \frac{x_1 + x_2 + ... + x_n}{n}$$

Can you prove this result?

3 You know that skewness is a measure of how asymmetrical a distribution is. One measure of skewness is called the Pearson's coefficient of skewness, and has the formula:

$$\frac{1}{\sigma^3} \frac{\Sigma(x - \bar{x})^3}{n} \quad \text{where } \sigma \text{ is the standard deviation.}$$

Prove that this formula is equivalent to $\dfrac{1}{\sigma^3}\left(\dfrac{\Sigma x^3}{n} - 3\bar{x}\sigma^2 - \bar{x}^3\right)$.

Explore

The two expressions in the inequality are called the 'root mean squared' (RMS) and the 'arithmetic mean' (AM) of the set of n numbers. There are other types of mean as well; for example 'geometric mean' (GM) and 'harmonic mean' (HM). When all the numbers are positive, the four means always come in the same order: HM $\leqslant$ GM $\leqslant$ AM $\leqslant$ RMS. Can you find some proofs of this result?

Experimental design in statistics

Many questions about populations require extremely creative methods to get to an answer. This section looks at two examples.

1 Persuading people to reveal embarrassing traits

Psychologists used to find that when people were asked directly about traits they found embarrassing (such as their drug use, sexuality, criminal history or infidelity) they would not be truthful. Even anonymous surveys underpredicted the rates compared to a method called 'randomised response' designed by S. L. Warner in 1965. In this method people were sent to a private booth and asked to flip a coin. If they got a head on the coin flip they were asked to write 'Yes', otherwise they were asked to give an honest answer to the question. The researchers could then explain that they could estimate the overall proportion of the population answering yes, without knowing the result for any individual who answered yes.

2 How many adult cod are in the North Sea?

It is not practical to count all of the fish, so a method called 'mark and recapture' is used. A sample of fish is captured and marked then some time later another sample is taken. If we assume that the proportion of marked fish in the sample is the same as the proportion in the population, we can estimate the population size.

> **i) Did you know?**
>
> You might like to use the Internet to research this question – it turns out that the answer varies greatly depending upon definitions of 'adult cod', something which caused some controversy in the media.

Questions

1 A sample of 1000 people were asked if they had ever stolen goods from a shop. Randomised response was used.

  a If 612 people responded yes estimate the proportion of the whole population who have stolen goods from a shop.

  b Is this likely to be an underestimate or overestimate?

2 A sample of 10 000 adult cod is caught in the North Sea and marked using microchips. Some time later another sample of 10 000 adult cod is caught and one of the fish is found to have a microchip.

  a Use this information to estimate the number of adult cod.

  b What assumptions do you have to make in this calculation?

Using simulation to test statistical models

Once you have created a probability model you often want to use it to make predictions. This is useful to both check whether the outcomes predicted fit in with known facts and to use the model to influence decisions about future events. Even when the maths is very complicated you can use technology to produce a simulation.

For example, the length of a side of a square is chosen at random to be a number between 0 and 10 (not necessarily a whole number) with all values equally likely. This is called a uniform distribution. A spreadsheet can be used to do this using a command such as:

$$= 10*\text{RAND}()$$

If this is done over 1000 cells of the spreadsheet you can get a sample of random numbers between 0 and 10. This histogram illustrates one such sample.

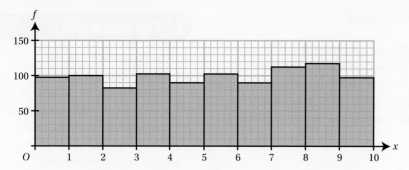

Notice that it is not a perfect uniform distribution. There are some random variations. If you repeat the experiment you will get a slightly different distribution.

Many people's intuition says that the area should also be a uniform distribution. However, you can square all of your random numbers and form a new histogram:

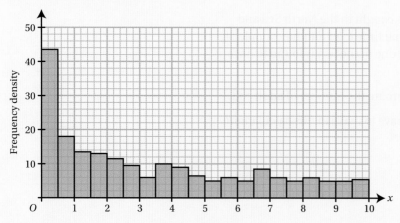

This shows the initially surprising result that the probability of small values of area is significantly higher than large values. The probability of being less than 5 is about 70.3% and the mean is about 3.4. It is possible to predict this from theory, but most modern day statistics is done using this type of simulation method – often called 'Monte Carlo simulation' because it uses random numbers.

Questions

Try to answer the following questions using Monte Carlo simulation.

1. If points are picked at random inside a square of side 1, what is the probability that they fall within a circle of diameter one centred at the centre of the square? Use the result to estimate a value of pi.

2. Every time a man moves he either takes a step left or a step right, each with probability 0.5. Find the average distance away from his starting point after 100 steps.

3. What is the distribution of an average of four values taken from the same uniform distribution? Investigate.

> ### (i) Did you know?
>
> This problem is called a 'drunken walk' and it is of huge importance in many areas, from physics (where it is used to model the movement of atoms in a gas) to finance (where it is used to model the movement of share prices).

1   What is the probability of getting an average of 3 on two rolls of a fair dice?

2   The discrete random variable X has the probability distribution:

$P(X = x) = \ln kx$ for $x = 1, 2, 3, 4$. Find the exact value of k.

3   A biased six-sided dice follows this probability distribution:

x	1	2	3	4	5	6
$P(X = x)$	0.12	0.18	p	0.27	0.22	0.08

a   Find the probability that the dice lands on either 2 or 3.

b   The dice is rolled 12 times. Find the probability that it lands on either 2 or 3 at least five times.

4   A student wants to find out how many people in her town work from home, and compare this to the national average of 11%. She thinks that this may vary according to the gender. She decides to interview people in the street until she has a sample of 20 men and 20 women.

a   i   State the name for this type of sampling.

ii   How is it different from a stratified sample?

b   In the sample of 40 people, she finds that 6 work from home. Does this provide sufficient evidence, at the 10% significance level, that the proportion of people in her town who works from home is greater than the national average?

5   i   The number of males and females in Year 12 at a school are illustrated in the pie chart. The number of males in Year 12 is 128.

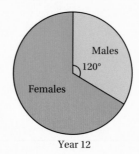

Year 12

a   Find the number of females in Year 12.

b   On a corresponding pie chart for Year 13, the angle of the sector representing males is 150°. Explain why this does not necessarily mean that the number of males in Year 13 is more than 128.

ii   All the Year 12 students took a General Studies examination. The results are illustrated in the box-and-whisker plots.

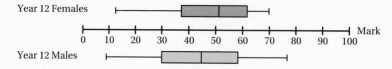

a   One student said "The Year 12 pie chart shows that there are more females than males, but the box-and-whisker plots show that there are more males than females".

Comment on this statement.

b Give two comparisons between the overall performance of the females and the males in the General Studies examination.

c Give one advantage and one disadvantage of using box-and-whisker plots rather than histograms to display the results.

iii The mean mark for 102 of the male students was 51. The mean mark for the remaining 26 male students was 59. Calculate the mean mark for all 128 male students.

© OCR, AS Mathematics, Unit 4732, June 2008

6 All students in a class recorded how long, in minutes, it took them to travel to school that morning. The results are summarised in a cumulative frequency table:

Time in minutes (t)	Cumulative frequency
$0 < t \leqslant 6$	0
$0 < t \leqslant 10$	6
$0 < t \leqslant 15$	12
$0 < t \leqslant 20$	22
$0 < t \leqslant 30$	38
$0 < t \leqslant 45$	45

a Fill in the following frequency table:

Time in minutes (t)	Frequency
$0 < t \leqslant 6$	0
$6 < t \leqslant 10$	6
$10 < t \leqslant 15$	
$15 < t \leqslant 20$	
$20 < t \leqslant 30$	
$30 < t \leqslant 45$	

b Calculate an estimate for the mean and variance of the data.

c Explain why your answer is only an estimate.

7 Three data items are collected: 3, x^2 and x. Find the minimum possible value of the mean.

8 Three data items are collected: 3, 7, x. Find the smallest possible value of the variance.

9 In 2005, a city council implemented an advertising campaign to encourage more people to use the tram system. According to their surveys, in 2003 there was an average of 4560 tram journeys per day, and this rose to 4830 in 2006.

a Give two reasons why these numbers alone do not provide evidence that a larger proportion of people are using the tram system.

b A 2003 census found that 18% of workers in the city were using the tram to get to work. A 2006 survey of 230 workers found that 52 from them used the tram. Test, at the 5% significance level, whether the proportion of workers in the city who use the tram has changed.

10 At a building site the probability, $P(A)$, that all materials arrive on time is 0.85. The probability, $P(B)$, that the building will be completed on time is 0.60. The probability that the materials arrive on time and that the building is completed on time is 0.55.

a Show that events A and B are **not** independent.

b The same company builds 25 buildings.

   i Calculate the probability that 20 of them are completed on time.

   ii What assumptions did you need to make in your calculation?

c The company made some improvements to their procedures. After this, 20 out of the next 25 buildings were completed on time. Test at the 5% significance level whether the probability of a building being completed on time has increased.

11 Bryn has a coin with a probability p of returning 'heads' when flipped.

a Show that the probability of flipping two or three 'heads' out of three coin tosses is $f(p) = 3p^2 - 2p^3$

b Sketch the graph of $y = f(p)$ for $0 \leqslant p \leqslant 1$. Indicate the coordinates of any stationary points.

c The probability of flipping two or three 'heads' out of three coin tosses is $\frac{5}{32}$.
Show that $p = \frac{1}{4}$, and explain whether there are any other solutions.

12 The mean test score of a group of eight students is 34.5 and the variance of the scores is 5.75. Another student with the score of 38 joins the group. Find the new mean and variance of the scores.

13 Aseem records his monthly expenditure over one whole year in order to help him plan his budget. He finds that his average monthly expenditure for the eight months from January to August is £620 and that his average monthly expenditure over the whole year is £586. What was his average monthly expenditure for the four months from September to December?

14 The random variable X has the probability distribution given in the table:

x	1	2	3	4
$P(X = x)$	0.26	e^{-k}	e^{-2k}	0.50

a Calculate the exact value of k.

b 70 independent observations of X are made. Find the probability that at least 30 of them are $X = 1$.

15 At a factory that makes crockery the quality control department has found that 10% of plates have minor faults. These are classed as 'seconds'. Plates are stored in batches of 12. The number of seconds in a batch is denoted by X.

   i State an appropriate distribution with which to model X. Give the value(s) of any parameter(s) and state any assumptions required for the model to be valid.

Assume now that your model is valid.

ii Find

a P($X = 3$)   b P($X \geqslant 1$)

iii A random sample of 4 batches is selected. Find the probability that the number of these batches that contain at least 1 second is fewer than 3.

© OCR, AS GCE Mathematics, Paper 4732, January 2009

16 The random variable X has the distribution B(6, p).

a Given that P($X = 4$) = 3P($X = 3$) find the value of p.

b Given instead that P($X = 4$) = 3P($X = 2$) find the value of p.

17 The probability of an event occurring is found to be $\frac{1}{7}\left(x^2 - 14x + 38\right)$ where x is known to be an integer parameter. Find all possible values of x.

18 A village has a population of 726 people. A sample of 10 people is obtained as follows. A list of all 726 people is obtained and a three-digit number, between 001 and 726 inclusive, is allocated to each name in alphabetical order. Ten three-digit random numbers, between 001 and 726 inclusive, are obtained and the people whose names correspond to those numbers are chosen.

One of the people in the village wants to estimate the probability that all 10 of the numbers chosen are 500 or less.

a Explain why this probability cannot be calculated exactly using a binomial distribution. Explain also why it is possible to get a good estimate of this probability by assuming that the selection is done with replacement.

b Hence estimate the probability that all 10 of the numbers chosen are 500 or less.

When the selection has been made, it is found that all of the numbers chosen are 500 or less. Another one of the people in the village says, 'The sampling method must have been biased.'

c Comment on this statement.

19 Introduction to kinematics

In this chapter you will learn how to:

- use the basic concepts in kinematics: displacement, distance, velocity, speed and acceleration
- use differentiation and integration to relate displacement, velocity and acceleration
- represent motion on a travel graph
- solve more complicated problems in kinematics: for example, involving two objects or several stages of motion.

Before you start...

GCSE	You should know how to find the gradient of a straight line connecting two points.	1 Consider the points $A(2, 5)$, $B(-1, 3)$ and $C(7, -2)$. Find the gradient of the straight line connecting: a A and C b B and A
Chapters 13 and 14	You should know how to differentiate polynomials.	2 a Given that $y = 3x^2 - 4x + \dfrac{5}{x}$: i find $\dfrac{dy}{dx}$ ii find the gradient of the curve when $x = -1$. b Find the coordinates of the maximum point on the graph of $y = -x^3 + 12x + 5$.
GCSE	You should know how to find areas of triangles and trapeziums.	3 Find the areas marked S and T.
Chapter 15	You should know how to use integration to find the area under a graph.	4 Find the area enclosed by the graph of $y = 6x - 3x^2$ and the x-axis. (You may find it helpful to sketch the graph first.)
Chapter 15	You should know how to find the value of a constant of integration.	5 A curve has gradient $\dfrac{dy}{dx} = 5 - 6x^2$ and passes through the point $(1, 2)$. Find the equation of the curve.

Continues on next page ...

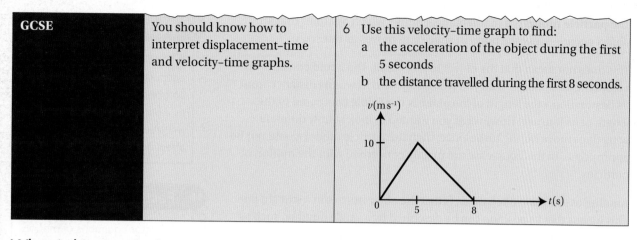

You should know how to interpret displacement–time and velocity–time graphs.

6 Use this velocity–time graph to find:
   a the acceleration of the object during the first 5 seconds
   b the distance travelled during the first 8 seconds.

What is kinematics?

Kinematics describes the motion of objects: how their position, velocity and acceleration depend on time, as well as on how they are related to each other. It is **not** concerned with what causes the motion; this comes into dynamics, which you will meet in Chapter 21. Kinematics and dynamics together form the branch of applied mathematics called mechanics.

You may have studied some mechanics before, probably within Physics. In this course, the focus is on applying mathematical techniques from previous chapters to analyse problems in mechanics. You will use vectors, trigonometry, differentiation and integration, and represent information in several different forms, mainly graphs and equations.

Section 1: Mathematical models in mechanics

The theory developed in this course is based on **mathematical models** of real-life situations. This means that some assumptions had to be made to simplify the situation, so that it can be described mathematically. It is important to consider how realistic these assumptions are, and whether improving the model would lead to substantially different results.

If you consider a car, for example, there are several different types of motion going on. The car might be travelling in a straight line, while the wheels are rotating around the axles and the wipers are moving left and right. Even if you are just interested in the position of the car, the front and the back aren't in exactly the same place. However, if all you need to know is how long it takes to drive from Newcastle to Manchester, then you can ignore all those details and consider the car as a single object, occupying a single point in space. We say that you are considering the car to be a **particle**.

The **particle model** is a mathematical model which assumes that an object occupies a single point in space and moves as one.

This does not mean that the object is very small. You could consider an aeroplane as a particle if all you were interested in was its distance from its destination – the length of the plane is negligible compared to the length of its journey. However, if you wanted to look at how different wing flaps move during turbulence, then the particle model would not be appropriate. In this course we are mainly concerned with the motion of particles.

Another assumption often made is that the object moves in a straight line. This means that its position can be described by a single number, such as its distance from its starting point. If the object is allowed to move in two or three dimensions then you need vectors to describe its position.

> ▶▶ **Fast forward**
>
> Ⓐ In Student Book 2 you will encounter situations in which an object cannot be modelled as a particle. For example, you will study **moments**, which affect how objects rotate.

> ▶▶ **Fast forward**
>
> Ⓐ Vector equations of motion are covered in Student Book 2.

WORKED EXAMPLE 19.1

The stretch of the A1(M) motorway between Junction 14 (Alconbury) and Junction 17 (Peterborough) is often cited as the longest straight stretch of UK motorway. The distance along the motorway between the two junctions is 16.8 km, while the straight line distance is 16.6 km.

A car travels along the motorway at an average speed of 110 km h^{-1}. Find the percentage difference between the times taken to travel the actual distance and the straight line distance. Hence comment whether the straight line model is appropriate for this stretch of motorway.

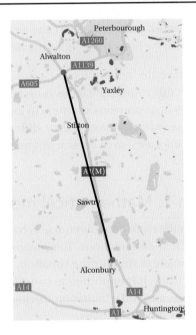

Actual time:

$$t_1 = \frac{16.8}{110} = 0.153 \text{ hours}$$

Use time $= \dfrac{\text{distance}}{\text{average speed}}$.

Straight line model:

$$t_2 = \frac{16.6}{110} = 0.151 \text{ hours}$$

Percentage difference:

$$\frac{0.153 - 0.151}{0.153} \times 100 \approx 1.3\%$$

This is a small difference, so the straight line model is appropriate.

1.3% seems an acceptable difference compared to the benefits gained from the simplicity of the straight line model.

The straight line model isn't always appropriate. For example, the M25 motorway would be better modelled as a circle.

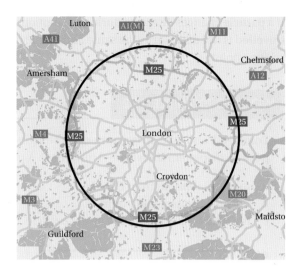

1 Discuss whether the particle model is appropriate in each of the following situations.

a You want to calculate how long it would take a car to complete the journey from Bristol to Birmingham.

b You are designing a car park.

c You want to predict the motion of a large box on a smooth floor when a force is applied at one corner.

d You want to decide how a football should be kicked so that it curves towards the goal.

2 For each of these questions, state some factors that have been ignored in the described model. Discuss how including each factor would affect the answer to the question.

a A box is modelled as a particle. The box falls from the top of a building. The only force acting on the box is gravity. How long does it take to reach the ground?

b A snooker ball is hit towards a cushion with the cue making a 30° angle with the cushion. The ball is modelled as a particle. Will it hit another ball (lying in a specified position)?

c A bus (of a given mass, modelled as a particle) travels between two cities. You are given how its speed varies with time and the fuel consumption at various speeds. How much fuel does it need?

d An aeroplane (modelled as a particle) flies between London and Tokyo. The Earth is modelled as a sphere. Assume that the aeroplane flies in a straight line, at a constant height and a constant speed. How long does it take?

Section 2: Displacement, velocity and acceleration

If the position of a particle changes with time, you can measure its **displacement** from one point to another. Displacement is a vector, because you need to specify both the **distance** and **direction** away from the starting point. If a particle can only move in one dimension, its displacement can be described by a single number. However, this number can be either positive or negative. You should always draw a diagram and make clear which direction is positive. In the rest of this chapter we will take the positive direction to be to the right unless stated otherwise.

If a particle changes direction during the motion, then the **total distance travelled** is not necessarily the same as the final distance from the starting point.

Tip

Remember that distance is a **scalar**.

WORKED EXAMPLE 19.2

Points A, B and C lie, in that order, in a straight line, with $AB = 150$ m and $BC = 260$ m. The direction of positive displacement is from A towards B. A particle travels from A to C and then from C to B. Find:

a the displacement from C to B
b the final displacement from A
c the total distance travelled by the particle.

a

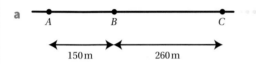

Always draw a diagram to illustrate the situation.

C to $B = -260$ m

B is to the left of C, so the displacement is negative.

b $AB = 150$ m

The particle ends up at B. This is to the right of A, so the displacement is positive.

c $AC = 150 + 260 = 410$ m
$CB = 260$ m

To find the total distance, you need to add the distance from A to C to the distance from C to B.

total distance $= AC + CB = 670$ m

If a particle travels a distance of 100 m in 20 seconds, then **on average** it travels at 5 metres per second; its **average speed** is 5 m s^{-1}. This does not mean that its speed equals 5 m s^{-1} during the whole 20-second period; you can't tell what its speed is at any particular point in time.

If you take into account the **direction** of motion as well as the speed, you get the **velocity**, which is a vector. If the particle changes direction during the motion, this means that the direction of the velocity vector is changing.

The average velocity is equal to overall displacement divided by time.

Key point 19.1

$$\text{average speed} = \frac{\text{total distance travelled}}{\text{time}}$$

$$\text{average velocity} = \frac{\text{final displacement} - \text{initial displacement}}{\text{time}}$$

The rate of change of velocity is called **acceleration**. Just like velocity, acceleration is a vector. For motion in one dimension, you represent vectors by a single number, but this number can also be positive or negative.

Tip

Speed is a scalar and velocity is a vector.

For motion in one dimension, velocity is usually denoted by the letter v and acceleration by the letter a. The units of velocity are $m\,s^{-1}$, because you divide distance (in metres) by time (in seconds). For acceleration, you divide velocity by time, so the units are $\frac{m\,s^{-1}}{s} = m\,s^{-2}$.

The basic quantities needed to describe motion of a particle are summarised in Key point 19.2.

Key point 19.2

Scalar quantities (units)	Vector quantities (units)
time $t\,(s)$	
distance $s\,(m)$	displacement $\mathbf{x}\,(m)$
speed u and $v\,(m\,s^{-1})$	velocity $\mathbf{u}$ and $\mathbf{v}\,(m\,s^{-1})$
magnitude of acceleration $a\,(m\,s^{-2})$	acceleration $\mathbf{a}\,(m\,s^{-2})$

Tip

Although displacement, velocity and acceleration are vectors, for motion in a straight line you can describe them using a single number. You will therefore denote them using italics, s (or x), v and a. This means that, for example, you use v to denote both velocity and speed – don't get confused by this! However, when you study motion in two or three dimensions you will use vector notation: $\mathbf{x}$, $\mathbf{v}$ and $\mathbf{a}$.

WORKED EXAMPLE 19.3

Three points, A, B and C, lie in a straight line, as shown in the diagram.

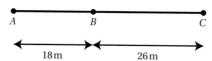

A particle starts at A, moving towards B with speed $2.5\,m\,s^{-1}$. Six seconds later, it passes B with speed $3.1\,m\,s^{-1}$. After a further 7.5 seconds it reaches C, where it stops and moves back towards B, which it passes 8.5 seconds later with speed $4.1\,m\,s^{-1}$. Find:

a   the average velocity of the particle moving from A to B
b   the average speed of the particle for the whole journey.

Continues on next page …

a $v = \dfrac{18}{6} = 3\,\text{m s}^{-1}$ ··········   average velocity $= \dfrac{\text{final displacement - initial displacement}}{\text{time}}$

b   Total distance $= AB + BC + CB$ ·····

$= 18 + 26 + 26 = 70\,\text{m}$

Total time $= 6 + 7.5 + 8.5 = 22\,\text{s}$

average speed $= \dfrac{\text{total distance}}{\text{total time}}$

$\therefore$ average speed $= \dfrac{70}{22} = 3.2\,\text{m s}^{-1}\,(2\,\text{s.f.})$ ·

The numbers in the question are given to 2 s.f., so round the final answer to the same accuracy.

In all the examples so far, you have measured distance in metres and time in seconds. These are the fundamental units of distance and time in the S.I. system. However, in real-life applications it is sometimes more convenient to use other units, such as kilometres and hours. You need to be able to convert the derived units for velocity and acceleration.

WORKED EXAMPLE 19.4

Convert:

a $2.6\,\text{ms}^{-1}$ into kilometres per hour   **b** $170\,\text{km h}^{-2}$ into m s^{-2}.

a $2.6\,\text{m s}^{-1} = \dfrac{0.0026}{\frac{1}{3600}\,\text{h}} = 9.36\,\text{km h}^{-1}$ ········

$2.6\,\text{m} = 0.0026\,\text{km}$

$1\,\text{s} = \dfrac{1}{3600}\,\text{h}$

b $170\,\text{km h}^{-2} = \dfrac{170\,000\,\text{m}}{\left(3600\,\text{s}\right)^2} = 0.0131\,\text{m s}^{-2}$ ····

$170\,\text{km} = 170\,000\,\text{m}$

$1\,\text{h} = 3600\,\text{s}$

The hours are squared.

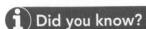

Did you know?

S.I. stands for 'Système internationale', the international system of units.
It is the most widely used metric system, in which all units can be expressed in terms of seven fundamental (base) units. It was established in the mid-20th century. The photograph shows the kilogram reference masses.

It is important to realise that you can only convert between units that measure the same type of quantity. For example, you can convert metres per second into kilometres per hour but not into kilograms per metre. Similarly, you can only add units that represent the same quantity. For example, 3 m + 42 cm = 342 cm or 3.42 m. But you cannot add 42 cm to 3 kg.

Fast forward

If you study the Mechanics option in Further Mathematics you will learn about dimensional analysis, which is a way of predicting formulae based on units.

EXERCISE 19B

Questions 1 and 2 refer to the four points, A, B, C and D, which lie in a straight line with distances between them shown in the diagram. The displacement is measured from left to right.

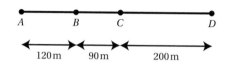

1 Find:

   a **i** the displacement from D to A **ii** the displacement from D to B

   b **i** the distance from D to B **ii** the distance from C to A

   c **i** the total displacement when a particle travels from B to C and then to A

      ii the total displacement when a particle travels from C to D and then to A

2 **a** **i** A particle travels from A to C in 23 seconds and then from C to B in 18 seconds. Find its average speed and average velocity.

      ii A particle travels from B to D in 38 seconds and then from D to A in 43 seconds. Find its average speed and average velocity.

   b **i** A particle travels from B to D in 16 seconds and then back to B in 22 seconds. Find its average speed and average velocity.

      ii A particle travels from A to C in 26 seconds and then back to A in 18 seconds. Find its average speed and average velocity.

3 Write the following quantities in the specified units, giving your answers to 3 s.f.

   a **i** $3.6\ \text{km}\,\text{h}^{-1}$ in $\text{m}\,\text{s}^{-1}$ **ii** $62\ \text{km}\,\text{h}^{-1}$ in $\text{m}\,\text{s}^{-1}$

   b **i** $5.2\ \text{m}\,\text{s}^{-1}$ in $\text{km}\,\text{h}^{-1}$ **ii** $0.26\ \text{m}\,\text{s}^{-1}$ in $\text{km}\,\text{h}^{-1}$

   c **i** $120\ \text{km}\,\text{h}^{-2}$ in $\text{m}\,\text{s}^{-2}$ **ii** $450\ \text{km}\,\text{h}^{-2}$ in $\text{m}\,\text{s}^{-2}$

   d **i** $0.82\ \text{m}\,\text{s}^{-2}$ in $\text{km}\,\text{h}^{-2}$ **ii** $2.7\ \text{m}\,\text{s}^{-2}$ in $\text{km}\,\text{h}^{-2}$

4 A particle moves with the speed of $12.3\ \text{m}\,\text{s}^{-1}$. After 5 seconds its speed is $4.3\ \text{m}\,\text{s}^{-1}$. Which of these could be its average acceleration during the 5 seconds?

   A $1.6\ \text{m}\,\text{s}^{-2}$ **B** $3.32\ \text{m}\,\text{s}^{-2}$ **C** $-1.6\ \text{m}\,\text{s}^{-2}$ **D** $-3.32\ \text{m}\,\text{s}^{-2}$

Section 3: Kinematics and calculus

In general, as a particle moves, its displacement, velocity and acceleration are constantly changing. **Equations of motion** describe how they vary with time.

$x(t)$ is normally used to denote the displacement from some reference point. The **average velocity** during the time period from $t = t_1$ to $t = t_2$ is:

$$\frac{\text{final displacement} - \text{initial displacement}}{\text{time}} = \frac{x(t_2) - x(t_1)}{t_2 - t_1}$$

If you draw a displacement–time graph, this equation says that the average velocity is the gradient of the chord between two points on the graph.

The **instantaneous velocity** at any particular point in time is given by the gradient of the tangent to the displacement graph at that point. You can think about taking the average velocity over a very small time period. This is the same process we went through when finding the gradient of a function; instantaneous velocity is the derivative of the displacement. This instantaneous velocity is itself a function of time, usually denoted by $v(t)$.

Similarly, acceleration is the rate of change of velocity with respect to time. The average acceleration is $\dfrac{\text{change of velocity}}{\text{time}}$, and the **instantaneous acceleration** is the derivative of the velocity function (and the gradient function of the velocity–time graph). Instantaneous acceleration is usually denoted by $a(t)$.

 Rewind

See Chapter 13, Section 2, if you need a reminder of how to differentiate from first principles.

🔑 **Key point 19.3**

If the displacement is given by the function $x(t)$:

- the velocity is $v(t) = \dfrac{dx}{dt}$

- the acceleration is $a(t) = \dfrac{dv}{dt} = \dfrac{d^2x}{dt^2}$

Once you have got the equations for velocity and acceleration in terms of t, you can find the values of the velocity or the acceleration at a specific point by substituting in the relevant value of t.

WORKED EXAMPLE 19.5

A toy car moves so that its displacement from a flag x metres after t seconds is given by the equation $x = 2.1 + 1.7t^2 - 0.2t^3$.

a Find the instantaneous velocity and acceleration of the car after 5 seconds.

b Find the initial displacement of the car from the flag.

c Find the average velocity during the first 5 seconds of the motion.

a $v = \dfrac{dx}{dt} = 3.4t - 0.6t^2$ | To find velocity, differentiate the displacement equation and substitute in the value of t.

When $t = 5$, $v = 2 \, \text{m s}^{-1}$

$a = \dfrac{d^2x}{dt^2} = 3.4 - 1.2t$ | To find the acceleration, differentiate again and substitute in the value of t.

When $t = 5$, $a = -2.6 \, \text{m s}^{-2}$

b   When $t = 0$, $x = 2.1 \, \text{m}$ | The initial displacement is when $t = 0$.

c   When $t = 5$, | To find average velocity, you need the final displacement from the starting point. This is the value of $x(t)$ when $t = 5$.

$x = 2.1 + 1.7 \times 5^2 - 0.2 \times 5^3 = 19.6 \, \text{m}$

The average velocity is

$v = \dfrac{19.6 - 2.1}{5} = 3.5 \, \text{m s}^{-1}$ | The average velocity is $\dfrac{\text{final displacement} - \text{initial displacement}}{\text{total time}}$

 Tip

You should not assume that the initial displacement is zero.

Sometimes you know the equation for the velocity and want to find how the displacement changes with time. This is done by integration. Since the velocity is the derivative of the displacement, it follows that the displacement is the integral of the velocity.

There are also many situations where you know the equation for acceleration in terms of time. You can integrate this equation to find velocity. You can then integrate it again to find the equation for the displacement.

 Fast forward

You will see in Chapter 21 that the acceleration is related to the force. This is why in many models you can predict the equation for acceleration.

Key point 19.4

$v(t) = \displaystyle\int a(t)\, dt$

$x(t) = \displaystyle\int v(t)\, dt$

Note that these integrals are **indefinite** integrals. This means that the result will involve a constant of integration. This can be found by using the values of v or x that are given to you (usually, but not always, when $t = 0$).

WORKED EXAMPLE 19.6

An object moves in a straight line, with the acceleration given by the equation $a = \left(3t^2 - 6t\right) \text{m s}^{-2}$ where t is measured in seconds. The initial velocity of the object is $1.6 \, \text{m s}^{-1}$.

a   Find the equation for the velocity of the particle.
b   Find the equation for the displacement from the initial position at time t.
c   Find the displacement and the velocity of the object after 2 seconds.

a $v(t) = \int 3t^2 - 6t \, dt = t^3 - 3t^2 + c$ To find the velocity, integrate the acceleration equation. Don't forget the $+c$!

    When $t = 0$, $v = 1.6$:
    $1.6 = 0 - 0 + c \Rightarrow c = 1.6$ Find the constant of integration by using the initial values of t and v.

    $\therefore v(t) = t^3 - 3t^2 + 1.6$

b $x(t) = \int t^3 - 3t^2 + 1.6 \, dt$ To find the displacement, integrate the velocity equation. There is another unknown constant to add (you should use a different letter for each new constant in a question).

    $= \dfrac{1}{4}t^4 - t^3 + 1.6t + d$

    When $t = 0$, $x = 0$:
    $0 = 0 + d \Rightarrow d = 0$ When $t = 0$ the object is at the starting point, so its displacement is zero.

    $\therefore x(t) = \dfrac{1}{4}t^4 - t^3 + 1.6t$

c   When $t = 2$:   To find the values at a specific point in time, substitute in the given value of t.

    $x(2) = -0.8 \, \text{m}$

    $v(2) = -2.4 \, \text{m s}^{-1}$

💡 **Tip**

If the displacement is measured from left to right, this means that the object is to the left of its initial position, and it is moving to the left.

If you are only interested in the change in displacement between two times (rather than finding the displacement as a function of t), you can use a definite integral.

🔑 **Key point 19.5**

The change in displacement between times t_1 and t_2 is $\displaystyle\int_{t_1}^{t_2} v(t) \, dt$.

💡 **Tip**

You will see in the next section that this is **not** always the same as distance travelled.

WORKED EXAMPLE 19.7

A particle moves in a straight line so that its velocity at time t is given by $v = 3t - t^2$.
Find the change in the displacement of the particle between $t = 2$ and $t = 5$.

$$\int_2^5 (3t - t^2)\, dt = \left[\frac{3}{2}t^2 - \frac{1}{3}t^3 \right]_2^5$$

You could find an equation for $x(t)$ and then evaluate the difference between $x(2)$ and $x(5)$. This is the same as evaluating a definite integral.

$$= -\frac{25}{6} - \frac{10}{3}$$

The particle has moved 7.5 units to the left. You should state the direction in your answer.

$$= -7.5$$

Taking the direction to the right as positive, the change in displacement is -7.5.

EXERCISE 19C

In questions 1–5, x is measured in metres, t in seconds, v in m s^{-1} and a in m s^{-2}.

1 A particle moves in a straight line. Its displacement from the point A is given by $x(t)$. Find the equations for the velocity and acceleration in terms of t if:

a **i** $x(t) = 3t^3 - 4t + 2$ **ii** $x(t) = t^4 - 3t^2 + 4t$

b **i** $x(t) = \dfrac{t^2}{5} - 4.2t$ **ii** $x(t) = -0.5t^3 + \dfrac{t^2}{3}$

2 For each part of question 1, find the values of the displacement, velocity and acceleration initially and after 3 seconds.

3 A particle moves in a straight line, with its velocity given by $v(t)$. The initial displacement from point A is $x(0)$. Find the equation for the displacement from A if:

a **i** $v(t) = 3t - 4,\ x(0) = 2$ **ii** $v(t) = 1 - 2t,\ x(0) = 1$

b **i** $v(t) = 5 - 3t^2,\ x(0) = 0$ **ii** $v(t) = t^2 - 2t,\ x(0) = 0$

4 For each part of question 3, find the displacement from A after 5 seconds.

5 A particle moves in a straight line with given acceleration $a(t)$. The initial velocity and displacement from point A are also given. Find the equations for the velocity and displacement in terms of t.

a **i** $a = 1 - 2t,\ v(0) = 3,\ x(0) = 0$ **ii** $a = 4t + 2,\ v(0) = -2,\ x(0) = 0$

b **i** $a = -5,\ v(0) = 3,\ x(0) = 5$ **ii** $a = 3,\ v(0) = -2,\ x(0) = 7$

6 A particle moves in a straight line. Its velocity, v m s^{-1}, at time t seconds is given by $v = 2.4t - 1.5t^2$.

a Find the acceleration of the particle after 2 seconds.

b Find the velocity at the point when the acceleration is zero.

c The displacement of the particle from its initial position is x m. Find an expression for x in terms of t.

7 An object moves in a straight line. t seconds after it passes point O its displacement, x m, from O is given by $x = 0.1t^3 - 1.2t^2 + 3.5t$.

a Find the speed and the magnitude of the acceleration of the object 6 seconds after passing O.

b What is the speed of the object when it first returns to O?

c Find the first time when the speed is zero, and the object's distance from O at this time.

8 A car starts from rest and moves in a straight line. Its acceleration, a m s^{-2}, is given by $a(t) = 0.12t^2 - 1.44t + 4.32$.

a Find the equations for the car's velocity and its displacement from the starting point.

b Find the velocity and the displacement at the point when the acceleration is zero.

9 A particle moves in a straight line. Its displacement from the point P is x metres and its acceleration is $a = (1 - 0.6t)$ m s^{-2}. The particle is initially 25 m from P and moving away from P with velocity 7.5 m s^{-1}.

a Find an expression for the velocity in terms of t.

b Find the particle's displacement from P after 10 seconds.

c Find the particle's displacement from P at the time when its acceleration is -2 m s^{-2}.

10 A particle moves in a straight line with acceleration $a = (2 - 6t)$ m s^{-2}, where the time is measured in seconds. When $t = 2$ its velocity is -8 m s^{-1}. Find the average velocity of the particle between $t = 5$ and $t = 8$.

Section 4: Using travel graphs

The information on how displacement and velocity change with time can be described using equations, as you did in Section 3, or represented on a graph. A visual representation gives you a good idea of the motion even without doing any detailed calculations. Moreover, in some cases the graph can be drawn even without finding the equations, and some calculations can be done straight from the graph.

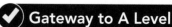

Gateway to A Level

For a reminder and more practice of travel graphs, see Gateway to A Level section X.

Displacement–time graphs

On a displacement–time graph (s–t graph), time is shown on the horizontal axis and displacement (measured from some specified reference point) on the vertical axis. Remember that the displacement can be negative – this means that the particle is on the other side of the reference point.

Tip

s is used as an alternative to x for displacement. You will usually see it on travel graphs and in constant acceleration formulae.

Key point 19.6

On a displacement–time graph:

- average velocity is the gradient of the chord between two points
- instantaneous velocity is the gradient of the tangent to the graph.

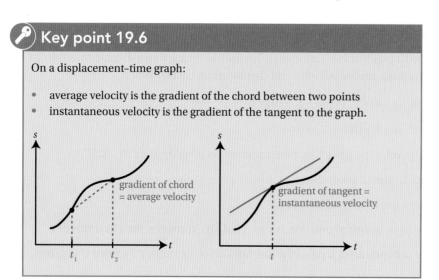

Focus on …

The concept of average velocity has some unexpected applications in pure mathematics, as explored in Focus on … Proof 4.

WORKED EXAMPLE 19.8

A small boat moves in a straight line. The graph shows its displacement, in metres, from a lighthouse.

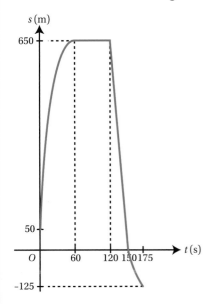

a How far from the lighthouse does the boat start?
b Describe the motion of the boat during the first 175 seconds.
c Find the velocity of the boat between 120 and 150 seconds.
d Find the average velocity for the first 175 seconds.

a The boat starts 50 m from the lighthouse.

This is the displacement when $t = 0$.

b For the first 60 seconds, the boat moves away from the lighthouse, slowing down.

The displacement is increasing.

The gradient of the graph is positive but decreasing.

For the next 60 seconds, the boat is stationary. Its velocity is zero.

The displacement is not changing.

From 120 seconds the boat moves back towards the lighthouse with constant velocity.

The displacement is decreasing.

The graph is straight, so the velocity is constant.

It passes the lighthouse at 150 seconds and continues to move away from it, slowing down.

When $t = 150$ the displacement is zero.

Negative displacement means that the boat has passed the lighthouse.

The gradient of the graph is negative and increasing (getting closer to zero) so the speed is actually decreasing.

Continues on next page ...

c $\dfrac{0-650}{30}=-21.7\,\text{m s}^{-1}\,(3\text{ s.f.})$

> Velocity is the gradient between the points (120, 650) and (150, 0).
>
> The answer should be negative.

d initial displacement $=50\,\text{m}$
   final displacement $=-125\,\text{m}$

   The average velocity is

   $\dfrac{-125-50}{175}=-1\,\text{m s}^{-1}$

> $\text{average velocity}=\dfrac{\text{final displacement}-\text{initial displacement}}{\text{time}}$

Remember that the gradient of the displacement–time graph represents the velocity. If you want to know the speed, you need to take the magnitude of the velocity. For motion in one dimension, this simply means taking the modulus of the number, so that negative numbers become positive.

WORKED EXAMPLE 19.9

The motion of a particle is represented on this displacement–time graph.

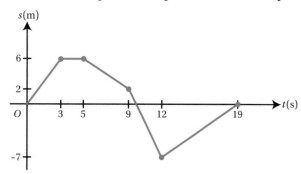

Find: **a** the maximum velocity of the particle

   b the maximum speed of the particle.

a The velocities are:

$\dfrac{6}{3}=2,$

$\dfrac{0}{2}=0,$

$\dfrac{-4}{4}=-1,$

$\dfrac{-9}{3}=-3,$

$\dfrac{7}{7}=1$

So the maximum velocity is $2\,\text{m s}^{-1}$.

> Find the velocity on each segment using
>
> $\dfrac{\text{change in displacement}}{\text{time}}$

b The maximum speed is $3\,\text{m s}^{-1}$.

> Speed is the magnitude of the velocity, for example $|-3|=3$.

Velocity–time graphs

Motion can also be shown on a velocity–time graph (v–t graph). This shows time on the horizontal axis and velocity on the vertical axis.

✓ Gateway to A level

You need to be able to find areas of triangles and trapeziums; see Gateway to A Level section R if you need a reminder.

🔑 Key point 19.7

On a velocity–time graph:

- the gradient is the acceleration
- the total area between the graph and the horizontal axis is the distance travelled.

If the graph crosses the horizontal axis, the parts of the area above and below the axes need to be added to find the total distance travelled. The difference between the area above and the area below the axis gives the displacment from the starting point (this is because the displacement equals the distance travelled to the right minus the distance travelled to the left).

WORKED EXAMPLE 19.10

The diagram shows the velocity–time graph for a particle moving in a straight line.

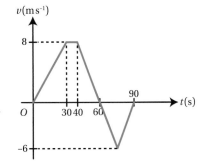

a Find the acceleration of the particle:
   i during the first 30 seconds   **ii** between $t = 40$ and $t = 60$.
b What happens when $t = 60$?
c Find the distance travelled by the particle in the first 90 seconds.
d Find the change of the displacement of the particle during the first 90 seconds.

a i $a = \dfrac{8}{30} \approx 0.267\,\mathrm{m\,s^{-2}}$ The acceleration is the gradient of the graph.

  ii $a = -\dfrac{8}{20} = -0.4\,\mathrm{m\,s^{-2}}$ Between $t = 40$ and $t = 60$ the gradient is negative.

b The particle changes direction.

                                     The velocity changes from positive to negative.

c Total distance =

    $\left(\dfrac{60 + 10}{2} \times 8\right) + \dfrac{30 \times 6}{2}$,   The distance is the total area between the x-axis and the graph, so you add the areas of the trapezium and the triangle.

    $280 + 90 = 370\,\mathrm{m}$ The change of displacement is the difference between the two areas. (The particle travels 280 m to the right and then 90 m to the left, so its displacement from the starting point is 190 m.)

d Change of displacement
    $= 280 - 90 = 190\,\mathrm{m}$

You need to be able to draw a velocity–time graph from a given description of motion. You can also write equations to find missing information.

WORKED EXAMPLE 19.11

A car moves in a straight line. When $t = 0$, it passes point P with a velocity of $12\ \text{m s}^{-1}$. It accelerates for 5 seconds with acceleration of $1.2\ \text{m s}^{-2}$ until it reaches a velocity of $V\ \text{m s}^{-1}$. It then moves with constant velocity V for T seconds and then decelerates at $0.8\ \text{m s}^{-2}$ until it comes to rest.

a Draw a velocity–time graph for the car's journey.
b Find the value of V.
c Find the time that the car spends decelerating.
d The total distance travelled by the car is $600\,\text{m}$. Find the value of T.

a

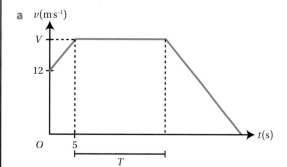

b $\dfrac{V-12}{5} = 1.2 \Rightarrow V = 18\ \text{m s}^{-1}$

> acceleration $= \dfrac{\text{change in velocity}}{\text{time}}$

c $\dfrac{0-18}{t} = -0.8 \Rightarrow t = 22.5\,\text{s}$

> The velocity changes from 18 to 0. The acceleration is negative.

d

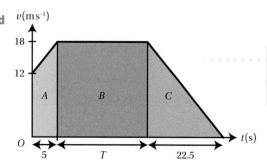

> The distance travelled is the area under the graph. You can split it into several parts; for example, as shown in the diagram.

$\dfrac{18+12}{2} \times 5 + 18T + \dfrac{22.5 \times 18}{2} = 600$

> A is a trapezium with parallel sides 12 and 18 and height 5.

$\Rightarrow 18T = 600 - 277.5 = 322.5$

> B is a rectangle with base T and height 18.

$\Rightarrow T \approx 17.9\,\text{s}$

> C is a triangle with base 22.5 and height 18.

Since the displacement and the velocity are related to each other, you should be able to draw the velocity–time graph from the displacement–time graph, and vice versa.

⏮ Rewind

This is the same as the relationship between the graph of a function and its derivative, which you met in Chapter 13, Section 1.

WORKED EXAMPLE 19.12

Match each velocity–time graph with the corresponding displacement–time graph.

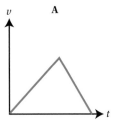
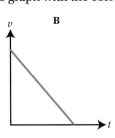
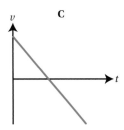
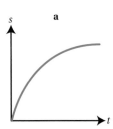
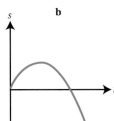
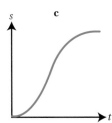

Graph **A** corresponds to graph **c**.

In graph A the velocity increases from zero and then decreases back to zero. This means that the displacement–time graph starts and ends with a zero gradient.

Graph **B** corresponds to graph **a**.

The velocity starts positive and decreases towards zero; so the gradient of the displacement graph decreases towards zero but never becomes negative.

Graph **C** corresponds to graph **b**.

The velocity starts positive but decreases to zero and then becomes negative. This means that the particle stops and turns around, so the displacement starts decreasing and eventually becomes negative (the particle goes back past the starting point).

EXERCISE 19D

1 For each velocity–time graph, find:

a the acceleration from A to B and from C to D

b the total distance travelled.

i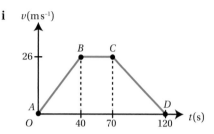

ii 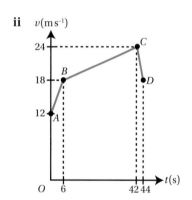   **iii**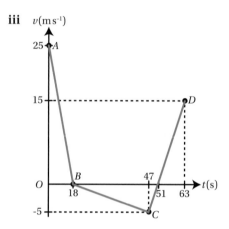

2 For each of these descriptions of motion, draw the velocity–time graph and find the total distance travelled.

a A particle accelerates uniformly from 20 m s^{-1} to 32 m s^{-1} in 15 seconds, then moves with constant speed for 25 seconds and finally decelerates uniformly and comes to rest in another 10 seconds.

b An object starts from rest and accelerates at 2.5 m s^{-2} for 12 seconds. It then moves with a constant velocity for 8 seconds and finally decelerates at 6 m s^{-2} until it comes to rest.

c A particle accelerates uniformly from 11 m s^{-1} to 26 m s^{-1} with acceleration 0.4 m s^{-2}. It then decelerates at 2 m s^{-2} until it comes to rest.

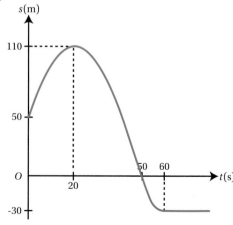

3 A particle moves in a straight line. Its displacement from point P is shown on the displacement–time graph.

a How far from P does the particle start?

b In the first 20 seconds, is the particle moving towards P or away from it?

c What happens when $t = 20$ seconds?

d What happens after 60 seconds?

e At what time does the particle pass P?

f Is the particle's speed increasing or decreasing during the first 20 seconds?

g Is the particle's speed increasing or decreasing between 50 and 60 seconds? What about its velocity?

h Find the total distance travelled by the particle in the first 60 seconds.

4 For each displacement–time graph, draw the corresponding straight line velocity–time graph:

a

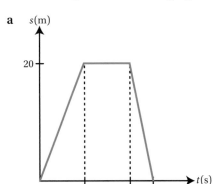

b

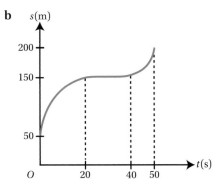

c

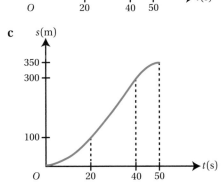

d

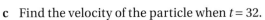

5 A car moves in a straight line. It passes the point P with a velocity of $16\,\text{m s}^{-1}$. It continues to move with constant velocity for 20 seconds and then decelerates at a constant rate of $0.8\,\text{m s}^{-2}$ until it comes to rest.

a Represent the car's journey on a velocity–time graph.

b How far from P does the car stop?

6 A particle moves in a straight line. It starts from point A when $t = 0$. Its motion during 45 seconds is represented on this velocity–time graph.

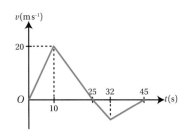

a Find the acceleration of the particle during the first 10 seconds.

b At what time does the particle change direction?

The total distance travelled by the particle is 325 m.

c Find the velocity of the particle when $t = 32$.

d How far from A is the particle at the end of the 45 seconds?

7 Sarah runs in a straight line at a constant speed of $6.2\,\text{m s}^{-1}$. When $t = 0$ she passes Helen who immediately starts running with constant acceleration of $1.3\,\text{m s}^{-2}$. Helen accelerates for 6 seconds and then continues to run at a constant speed until she catches up with Sarah.

a Draw a velocity–time graph to illustrate the motion of both girls.

b How long does it take for Helen to catch up with Sarah?

8 A particle moves in a straight line. Its velocity–time graph is shown. The total distance travelled during the 55 seconds is 275 m.

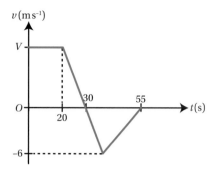

a Find the value of *V*.

b Find the deceleration of the particle when $t = 30$.

c Which of these graphs could be the displacement–time graph for the same particle?

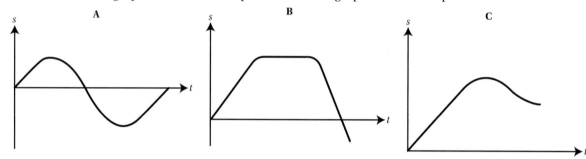

9 Peter and Sanjit are running in a race. They both start from rest.

Peter accelerates uniformly, then moves at a constant speed *V* for 5 seconds and then decelerates uniformly, coming to rest at the finish line.

Sanjit accelerates uniformly, at the same rate as Peter, to the same speed *V* and then decelerates immediately, coming to rest at the finish line. He finishes the race *x* seconds after Peter.

Find the value of *x*.

10 A particle moves in a straight line. Its velocity–time graph is shown.

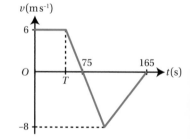

a After 165 seconds the particle returns to the starting point. Find the value of *T*.

b At what time does the particle have maximum speed?

c Draw the displacement–time graph for this particle.

Focus on …

When solving problems in Mechanics, it is important to be able to represent information in several different ways. Focus on … Problem solving 3 looks at using alternative representations.

↓ Elevate

See Extension sheet 19 for further examples of alternative representations.

Average speed and average velocity

At any point in time, speed is the magnitude of velocity. However, average speed and average velocity are not necessarily related in the same way.

If an object moves without changing direction then distance travelled can be calculated from knowing the final and initial displacements. However, finding the distance becomes more complicated if the object changes direction part-way through the motion. For example, if you move 5 m to the right and then 2 m to the left then you have travelled a distance of 7 m but your displacement has changed by +3 m.

 Rewind

Average speed and average velocity were defined in Key point 19.2.

 Tip

Here we take the positive direction to the right. Remember that distance is a scalar quantity, and displacement is a vector.

WORKED EXAMPLE 19.13

The diagram shows the displacement–time graph for a particle moving in a straight line. The displacement is measured from point A, with the positive displacement to the right.

a   Describe how the displacement and the speed of the particle are changing.

b   Find:

    i the average velocity   **ii** the average speed
                                for the whole journey.

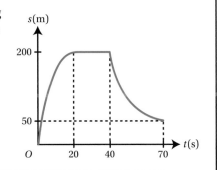

a   In the first 20 seconds the particle moves 200 m away from the starting point. Its speed is decreasing.

For the next 20 seconds the particle is stationary.

For the final 30 seconds the particle moves back towards the starting point. Its speed is decreasing. It ends up 50 m from the starting point.

In the first 20 seconds, the displacement changes from 0 to 200.
The gradient of the graph represents the speed. From 0 to 20 seconds the gradient is getting smaller.

From 40 to 70 seconds the velocity is negative and increasing, but the speed (the magnitude of the velocity) is decreasing.

b   **i**   average velocity $= \dfrac{\text{total displacement}}{\text{time}}$

$= \dfrac{50}{70} \approx 0.714\,\text{m}\,\text{s}^{-1}$ (3 s.f.)

The final displacement is 50 m from the starting point.

ii   total distance $= 200 + 150 = 350\,\text{m}$

average speed $= \dfrac{\text{total distance}}{\text{total time}}$

$= \dfrac{350}{70} = 5\,\text{m}\,\text{s}^{-1}$

The particle moves 200 m away from the starting point and then 150 m back towards it.

Remember that you can also find the change in displacement and the distance travelled from a velocity–time graph. The change in displacement is $\displaystyle\int_{t_1}^{t_2} v\,\mathrm{d}t$ while the distance is the area between the v–t graph and the axis.

 Rewind

See Key point 19.6. This difference between areas and integrals was discussed in Chapter 15, Section 5.

WORKED EXAMPLE 19.14

A particle moves with velocity $v(t) = t^3 - 7t^2 + 10t$ where t is measured in seconds and v in m s^{-1}. The diagram show the velocity-time graph of the motion. Find:

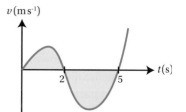

a the displacement from the starting point after 5 seconds
b the distance travelled by the particle during the first 5 seconds.
c Hence find the average velocity and the average speed of the particle.

> The velocity-time graph shows that the particle changes direction, so the distance is not the same as the change in displacement.

a $\displaystyle\int_0^5 t^3 - 7t^2 + 10t \; dt = \left[\frac{t^4}{4} - \frac{7t^3}{3} + 5t^2 \right]_0^5$

> The change in displacement is the integral between $t = 0$ and $t = 5$. This equals the final displacement from the starting point.

$\displaystyle = \left(-\frac{125}{12} \right) - (0) = -10.4 \, \text{m}$

> The negative sign means that the particle is to the left of the starting point.

b $\displaystyle\int_0^2 t^3 - 7t^2 + 10t \; dt = \left[\frac{t^4}{4} - \frac{7t^3}{3} + 5t^2 \right]_0^2$

> From $t = 0$ to $t = 2$ the particle moves to the right. The integral gives the change of displacement, which in this case is equal to the distance.

$\displaystyle = \left(\frac{16}{3} \right) - (0) = \frac{16}{3}$

$\displaystyle\int_2^5 t^3 - 7t^2 + 10t \; dt = \left[\frac{t^4}{4} - \frac{7t^3}{3} + 5t^2 \right]_2^5$

> From $t = 2$ to $t = 5$ the particle moves to the left. The change of displacement is negative. The particle has moved 15.75 m to the left.

$\displaystyle = \left(-\frac{125}{12} \right) - \left(\frac{16}{3} \right) = -15.75$

The distance is

$d = \dfrac{16}{3} + 15.75 = 21.1 \, (3 \text{ s.f.})$

> Now add the distance travelled to the right and the distance travelled to the left.

c *The average velocity is*

$\dfrac{-10.4}{5} = -2.08 \, \text{m s}^{-1}$

> To find the average velocity, use the change of displacement.

The average speed is $\dfrac{21.1}{5} \approx 4.22 \, \text{m s}^{-1}$

> To find the average speed, use the total distance.

▶| Fast forward

A If you have already studied modulus transformations (in Student Book 2, Chapter 3) you can write that the distance travelled is $\int_2^5 |t^3 - 7t^2 + 10t|\,dt$.

⬆ Elevate

For more practice finding distance from a velocity–time graph, see Support sheet 19.

EXERCISE 19E

1 For each velocity–time graph, find:

   a the average speed   **b** the average velocity.

   i

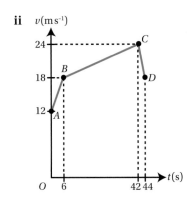

   ii   **iii**

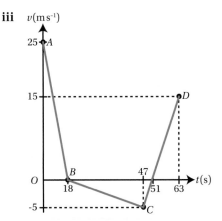

2 A particle moves in a straight line. Its motion, for the first 25 seconds, is represented on the following velocity–time graph:

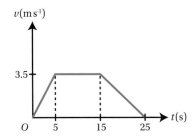

Find the average speed of the particle during the first 25 seconds.

3 The velocity of an object is given by $v(t) = 18t - 6t^2$ where time is measured in seconds and velocity in $m\,s^{-1}$.

   a Sketch the velocity–time graph for $0 \leqslant t \leqslant 3$.

   b Hence find the average speed of the particle during the first 3 seconds.

4 This displacement–time graph represents the motion of a particle moving in a straight line. The particle passes point A when $t = 0$.

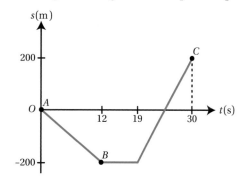

The particle is at point B when $t = 12$ and at point C when $t = 30$.

a Describe what happens between $t = 12$ and $t = 19$.

b Write down the displacement of C from A. Hence find the average velocity of the particle during the 30 seconds.

c Find the average speed of the particle during the 30 seconds.

5 The diagram shows the velocity-time graph for an object moving in a straight line. When $t = 0$ the object is at point O. The equation for the velocity is $v(t) = 3t(t-4)(t-7)$ where time is measured in seconds and velocity in metres per second.

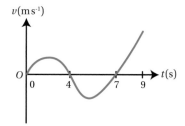

a Find the two times when the particle changes direction.

b Find the displacement of the object from O when $t = 7$.

c Find the average velocity and average speed of the object during the first 7 seconds.

6 A particle moves in a straight line, starting from rest at point P. It accelerates for 5 seconds, until it reaches a speed of 16 m s^{-1}. It maintains this speed for T seconds and then decelerates at 2 m s^{-2} until it comes to rest at point Q.

a Sketch the velocity–time graph to represent the motion of the particle.

b Given that the average speed of the particle on the journey from P to Q is 12 m s^{-1}, find the value of T.

7 A particle moves in a straight line, with its velocity given by $v = (0.05t^3 - t^2 + 4.8t) \text{ m s}^{-1}$. The particle passes point A when $t = 0$.

a Explain how you can tell that the particle is initially at rest, and find two other times when the velocity is zero.

b Find the velocity and the displacement of the particle from A when $t = 6$ s.

c Find the average speed during the first 12 seconds.

8 A particle moves in a straight line. Its velocity, v m s^{-1}, at time t seconds is given by $v(t) = (t+3)(t-2)(t-7)$. Find the average speed of the particle during the first 7 seconds.

9 The velocity of a particle is given by:

$$v(t) = \begin{cases} 5t - \dfrac{1}{2}t^2 & \text{for } 0 \leqslant t \leqslant 5 \\ 7.5 - \dfrac{1}{2}t & \text{for } 5 < t \leqslant 15 \end{cases}$$

The average speed of the particle during the first T seconds is 4 m s^{-1}. Find the value of T, where $T < 15$.

10 A particle moves in a straight line. Its displacement, x m, from point O is given by $x(t) = 24t - 3t^2$, where t is measured in seconds. The average velocity of the particle during the first T seconds is 9 m s^{-1}. Find its average speed during this time.

Tip

In question 9, the velocity suddenly jumps when $t = 5$. This can happen, for example, in a collision. The displacement still needs to be continuous.

Section 5: Solving problems in kinematics

You now have the main tools you need to solve problems in kinematics: You can use differentiation and integration to find equations for displacement, velocity and acceleration. You can also represent those quantities on travel graphs. We will now look at more complicated problems where you need to interpret the question and extract relevant information from the given context. You may also need to combine information from graphs and equations.

WORKED EXAMPLE 19.15

A boat moves in a straight line. At $t = 0$ it passes a rock and it is moving with velocity 4 m s^{-1}. Its acceleration, a m s^{-2}, is given by $a = 12 - 6t$ for $0 \leqslant t \leqslant 8$ seconds.

a Find the time when the boat changes direction.

b Find the maximum velocity of the boat.

c At what time does the boat pass the rock again?

a $v = \int 12 - 6t \, dt = 12t - 3t^2 + c$

When $t = 0$, $v = 4$ so $c = 4$

$v = 12t - 3t^2 + 4 = 0$

$\Rightarrow t = -0.309$ or 4.31

But you are only looking for positive times,

$\therefore t = 4.31$ s (3 s.f.)

The boat changes direction when the velocity changes from positive to negative. So you are looking for the time when $v = 0$.

Use the quadratic formula or the equation solver on your calculator.

Continues on next page ...

b $\dfrac{dv}{dt}=0$

When the velocity is maximum, $\dfrac{dv}{dt}=0$.

$\Rightarrow 12-6t=0$

Note that this means the same as $a=0$.

$\Rightarrow t=2\,s$

To check this is a maximum:

Check that this is a maximum by using the second derivative.

$\dfrac{d^2v}{dt^2}=-6<0$

so the stationary point is a maximum.

The maximum velocity is

Notice that $16\ ms^{-1}$ is larger than the initial velocity of $4\ ms^{-1}$. When $t=8$ the velocity is negative. So $16\ ms^{-1}$ is the maximum value in this interval.

$v(2)=24-12+4=16\ m\,s^{-1}$

c $x=\displaystyle\int 12t-3t^2+4\,dt$

If x is the displacement from the rock, you are looking for the time when $x=0$.

$\quad =6t^2-t^3+4t+d$

When $t=0, x=0$ so $d=0$

When $t=0$, the boat passes the rock, so $x=0$.

$x=6t^2-t^3+4t=0$

$\Rightarrow t\left(-t^2+6t+4\right)=0$

$\Rightarrow t=0 \text{ or } -t^2+6t+4=0$

$\Rightarrow t=0 \text{ or } -0.61 \text{ or } 6.61\,(2\,d.p.)$

The boat passes the rock again after 6.61 seconds.

You are looking for a positive value of t. (You already know that the boat passes the rock when $t=0$).

Worked example 19.15 uses some common phrases you need to understand:

- When $v=0$, the object is **instantaneously at rest** and may be changing direction.
- It reaches maximum/minimum velocity when $a=0$ (or at either end of its motion).
- It returns to the starting point when $x=x(0)$.

Tip

Be careful: $x(0)$ is the initial position, and it is not always 0.

You also need to be able to deal with two-stage problems, where the equation for velocity changes after a certain time.

WORKED EXAMPLE 19.16

A car accelerates from its parking space and moves in a straight line. Its velocity, $v\,m\,s^{-1}$, at time t seconds, satisfies:

$$v(t)=\begin{cases}14t-5t^2 & \text{for } 0\leqslant t\leqslant 2\\[2mm] 13-\dfrac{20}{t^2} & \text{for } t>2\end{cases}$$

a Find the displacement of the car from the parking space:

    i when $t=2$ **ii** when $t=5$.

Continues on next page ...

b At what time is the car 35 m from the parking space?

a **i** $x = \int_0^2 14t - 5t^2 \, dt$

From $t = 0$ to $t = 2$, the first velocity equation applies.

$$= \left[7t^2 - \frac{5}{3}t^3 \right]_0^2$$

You can find the displacement between those two times using Key point 19.5.

$$\approx 14.7 \, m$$

ii $\int_2^5 13 - \frac{20}{t^2} \, dt = \left[13t + \frac{20}{t} \right]_2^5$

From $t = 2$ to $t = 5$ you need to use the second velocity equation.

$$= 33$$

$$x = 33 + 14.7 \, m \approx 47.7 \, m$$

The change of displacement is $\int_2^5 v \, dt$, but this is measured from the point where the car was at $t = 2$, which is 14.7 m (from part **i**).

b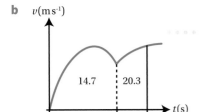

In the first 2 seconds, the car travels 14.7 m from the parking space. Therefore it gets to 35 m after more than 2 seconds, so you need to use the second equation.

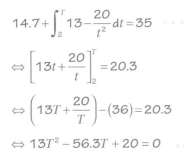

$14.7 + \int_2^T 13 - \frac{20}{t^2} \, dt = 35$

$$\Leftrightarrow \left[13t + \frac{20}{t} \right]_2^T = 20.3$$

$$\Leftrightarrow \left(13T + \frac{20}{T} \right) - (36) = 20.3$$

$$\Leftrightarrow 13T^2 - 56.3T + 20 = 0$$

$$\Leftrightarrow 0.390 \, or \, 3.94$$

$$\therefore T = 3.94 \, s \, (3 \, s.f.)$$

The total displacement of 35 m is made up of the 14.7 m travelled in the first 2 seconds, plus the displacement between $t = 2$ and $t = T$.

This can be rearranged into a quadratic equation.

You know that you are looking for a value of T above 2.

> 💡 **Tip**
>
> Note that in part b above you should first check that the car doesn't change direction; otherwise it could return to the same place more than once. You can check that the velocity is always positive for the given values of t.

> 💡 **Tip**
>
> Remember that 14.7 and 20.3 are rounded values. You should use the full values in your calculator (saved in the calculator memory from part a).

Many problems can be solved either by deriving equations or by using a travel graph. It is useful to be able to decide which method would be easier. You saw in Worked example 19.16 that multi-stage problems can be quite complicated. If the velocity–time graph is made up of straight line segments, it is easy to answer questions about displacement by using areas.

WORKED EXAMPLE 19.17

A particle moving in a straight line passes point P when $t=0$. Its velocity, $v\,\text{ms}^{-1}$, satisfies:

$$v = \begin{cases} 6.3 + 2.1t & \text{for} \quad 0 \leqslant t \leqslant 6 \\ 29.7 - 1.8t & \text{for} \qquad t > 6 \end{cases}$$

where t is measured in seconds.

a Find the particle's displacement from P when $t = 10$.
b Find the maximum displacement from P.
c Point Q has the displacement of 90 m from P.
   i Find the first time when the particle passes Q.
   ii How long does it take for the particle to return to Q?

When $t = 0$, $v = 6.3$
When $t = 6$, $v = 18.9$
When: $v = 0$: $29.7 - 1.8t = 0 \Rightarrow t = 16.5$

Since the velocity–time graph is made up of straight line segments, you don't need to use integration to find areas. So start by sketching the graph, labelling all the relevant coordinates.

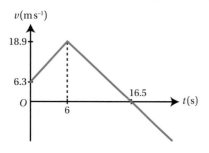

a When $t = 10$,
$$v = 29.7 - 1.8 \times 10 = 11.7\,\text{m s}^{-1}$$

The displacement is the area under the graph between $t = 0$ and $t = 10$. This is made up of two trapezia.

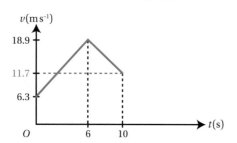

$$\frac{6}{2}(6.3 + 18.9) + \frac{4}{2}(18.9 + 11.7) = 136.8\,\text{m}\,(4\,\text{s.f.})$$

b
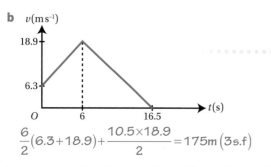

The particle moves away from P from $t = 0$ to $t = 16.5$, because that's when the velocity is positive. For $t > 16.5$ it moves back towards P. So the maximum displacement is when $t = 16.5$. The corresponding area is made up of a trapezium and a triangle.

$$\frac{6}{2}(6.3 + 18.9) + \frac{10.5 \times 18.9}{2} = 175\,\text{m}\,(3\,\text{s.f})$$

Continues on next page …

c i The displacement in the first 6 seconds:

$$\frac{6}{2}(6.3+18.9)=75.6\text{m}$$

The particle is at Q when $t=T_1$.

The displacement from $t=6$ to $t=T_1$:

$$90-75.6=14.4\text{m}$$

You can see from part **b** that the particle moves 175 m away from P and then comes back. This means that it will pass through Q twice: once in the first 16.5 seconds (when $t=T_1$) and once on the way back (when $t=T_2$).

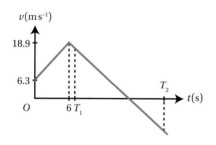

$$\int_6^{T_1} 29.7-1.8t\, dt = 14.4$$

$$\Leftrightarrow \left[29.7t-0.9t^2\right]_6^{T_1}=14.4$$

$$\Leftrightarrow \left(29.7T_1-0.9T_1^2\right)-(145.8)=14.4$$

$$\Leftrightarrow 0.9T_1^2-29.7T_1+160.2=0$$

$$\Leftrightarrow T_1=6.79 \text{ or } 26.2$$

You need to find T_1 when the area of the trapezium is 14.4. But you don't know either the base or the height. Instead, you can integrate the equation for v.

∴ The particle is at Q after 6.79 seconds.

You are looking for T_1 between 6 and 16.5.

ii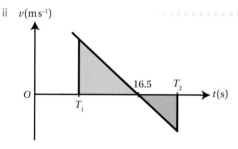

Between T_1 and T_1, the particle stops, changes direction and returns to Q. This means that the areas of the blue and the green triangles are equal, so 16.5 is the midpoint between T_1 and T_2.

$$T_2=16.5+(16.5-6.79)$$
$$=16.5+9.71$$
$$\Rightarrow T_2=26.2$$

The particle returns to Q when $t=26.2$ seconds.

> 💡 **Tip**
>
> Notice that this answer was already found from the integration in **c i**. The integral is still valid, since both values of T are in the range $t>6$.

EXERCISE 19F

1 A particle moving in a straight line passes point P when $t=0$. Its displacement from P satisfies the equation $x=3.6t-1.2t^2$ where x is measured in metres and t in seconds. Find the time when the particle changes direction.

2 Ellie runs in a straight line. At time t seconds, her displacement, x metres, from the starting point satisfies the equation $x=1.8t^2-0.2t^3$.

   a Show that that Ellie starts running from rest.

   b Find her maximum velocity.

3 A toy car's velocity, $v\,\mathrm{m\,s^{-1}}$, depends on time, $t\,\mathrm{s}$, according to the equation $v=-0.8t^2+1.44t+9.72$. Find the displacement from the starting point at the moment when the car comes to instantaneous rest, and the deceleration of the car at this point.

4 A particle moves in a straight line. Its velocity at time t seconds is $v=\left(11.2t-3t^2\right)\mathrm{m\,s^{-1}}$. The particle is at A when $t=0$. How long does it take for it to return to A?

5 The velocity of a car, $v\,\mathrm{m\,s^{-1}}$ at time t seconds, satisfies:

$$v=\begin{cases} 4t-0.5t^2 & \text{for } 0\leqslant t\leqslant 4 \\ 0.4t^2-6.4t+27.2 & \text{for } t>4 \end{cases}$$

   a Find the acceleration of the car after 5 seconds.

   b Find the car's displacement from the starting point when:

   i $t=3$ **ii** $t=10$.

6 A dog runs past a tree when $t=0$ with the speed of $3.7\,\mathrm{m\,s^{-1}}$. It accelerates for 5 seconds so that its speed satisfies $v=(u+0.4t)\,\mathrm{m\,s^{-1}}$.

   a Write down the value of u.

   For the next 5 seconds, the dog decelerates and its speed satisfies:

$$v=\left(\frac{142.5}{t^2}\right)\mathrm{m\,s^{-1}}$$

   b Find the dog's final speed.

   c Find the dog's final displacement from the tree.

   d After how long is the dog 32 m from the tree?

7 A particle moving in a straight line accelerates from rest. For the first 7 seconds its acceleration at time t seconds satisfies $a=(6.5-1.3t)\mathrm{m\,s^{-2}}$. Subsequently, the particle moves with constant acceleration. Find the equation for the velocity of the particle in terms of t when:

   a $0\leqslant t\leqslant 7$ **b** $t>7$

8 The acceleration of a particle moving in a straight line, $a\,\mathrm{m\,s^{-2}}$, satisfies $a=0.1(t-5)^2$ for $0\leqslant t\leqslant 5$ seconds. The particle is initially at rest.

   a Explain why the velocity of the particle is never negative between $t=0$ and $t=5$.

   b Find the average speed of the particle between $t=0$ and $t=5$.

   c By sketching the graph of $v(t)$, show that there is a value of t where the instantaneous speed equals the average speed.

9 A particle moves in a straight line so that its acceleration at time t seconds is given by $a = 3t^2 - 14t + 10$ (measured in $m\,s^{-2}$). The particle starts from rest when $t=0$.

   a Find the equation for the velocity of the particle in terms of t.

   b Find:

     i the maximum velocity

     ii the maximum speed of the particle in the first 5 seconds.

10 A particle is moving in a straight line, starting from point A when $t=0$. Its velocity, in $m\,s^{-1}$, is given by:

$$v = \begin{cases} 0.01\left(12t^2 - t^3\right) & \text{for} \quad 0 \leqslant t \leqslant 10 \\ 10 - 0.8t & \text{for} \quad 10 < t < 12.5 \end{cases}$$

where t is measured in seconds.

   a Find the distance travelled by the particle in the first 10 seconds.

   b After how long is the particle 17 m from A?

11 An object moves in a straight line with velocity $v = 20t^2 - t^3$. The average velocity over the first T seconds equals the instantaneous velocity after $\frac{T}{2}$ seconds. Find the value of T.

12 Cars can go over speed bumps at $5\ km\,h^{-1}$. For an average car, the maximum acceleration is $1.4\ m\,s^{-2}$ and the maximum deceleration is $3.2\ m\,s^{-2}$. How far apart should the speed bumps be placed to restrict the maximum speed to $30\ km\,h^{-1}$?

Checklist of learning and understanding

- The **displacement**, **velocity** and **acceleration** of a particle moving in a straight line are vectors: they can have a positive or a negative value.
- **Distance** (from a certain point) is the magnitude of the displacement (from that point). This is not necessarily the same as **distance travelled**.
- The **instantaneous** velocity and **instantaneous acceleration** can be **found** by differentiating the displacement equation:

$$v = \frac{dx}{dt}, \qquad a = \frac{dv}{dt}$$

- Integrating the velocity equation gives the displacement equation; integrating the acceleration equation gives the velocity equation:

$$x = \int v\,dt, \qquad v = \int a\,dt$$

- The constant of integration can be found from the initial displacement or velocity.
- The change of displacement between time t_1 and t_2 can be found using the definite integral:

$$s = \int_{t_1}^{t_2} v\,dt$$

  If the particle doesn't change direction then this integral gives the total distance travelled.
- On a velocity–time graph:
  - the acceleration is the gradient
  - the distance travelled equals the area between the graph and the t-axis.
  - The change of displacement can be found by subtracting the area below the axis from the area above the axis.
- The **average velocity** equals change of displacement divided by time. The **average speed** equals total distance divided by time.

Mixed practice 19

1 An object moves in a straight line so that its velocity, v m s^{-1}, is given by the equation $v = 3t^2 - 8t$.

   a Find the acceleration of the object after 2 seconds.

   b Find the equation for the displacement from the initial position after t seconds.

2 A particle moves in a straight line with velocity $v = (3 - t^{-2})$ m s^{-1} for $t \geqslant 1$.

   a Find the distance travelled between $t = 1$ and $t = 5$.

   b Hence find the average speed of the particle between $t = 1$ and $t = 5$.

3 The motion of a particle moving in a straight line is represented on the following velocity–time graph:

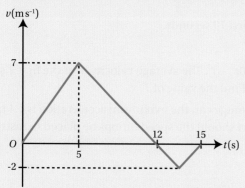

   a Find the acceleration of the particle between $t = 0$ and $t = 5$.

   b State the times when the particle is instantaneously at rest.

   c Find the average speed of the particle for the first 15 seconds.

4

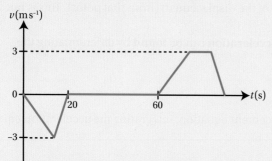

The diagram shows the (t, v) graph for a lorry delivering waste to a recycling centre. The graph consists of six straight line segments. The lorry reverses in a straight line from a stationary position on a weighbridge before coming to rest. It deposits its waste and then moves forwards in a straight line accelerating to a maximum speed of 3 m s^{-1}. It maintains this speed for 4 s and then decelerates, coming to rest at the weighbridge.

   i Calculate the distance from the weighbridge to the point where the lorry deposits the waste.

   ii Calculate the time which elapses between the lorry leaving the weighbridge and returning to it.

   iii Given that the acceleration of the lorry when it is moving forwards is 0.4 m s^{-2}, calculate its final deceleration.

© OCR, AS GCE Mathematics, Paper 4728, June 2010

5 This velocity-time graph shows the motion of a particle moving in a straight line. The total distance travelled during the 12 seconds is 360 m.

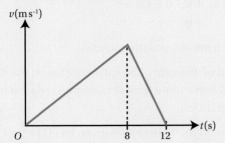

Find the acceleration of the particle during the final 4 seconds.

6 A car travels along a straight road. Its velocity, in kilometres per hour, is given by $v = 40 + 10t - 0.5t^2$ (for $0 \leqslant t \leqslant 20$), where time is measured in seconds. It passes point A when $t = 0$.

a Write an equation for the velocity in metres per second.

b Find the acceleration of the car in terms of t. Hence find the time when the car has maximum velocity.

c Find the distance of the car from A when $t = 12$.

d The car is modelled as a particle. Explain whether this is a suitable modelling assumption in the following two questions.

    i How long does the car take to overtake a stationary van of length 6.2 m?

    ii How long does the car take to pass through a tunnel of length 380 m?

7 A bus travels in a straight line. When it passes a man its speed is $8.5\,\mathrm{m\,s^{-1}}$. It decelerates uniformly until it comes to rest at the bus stop 44.2 m away.

As the bus passes the man, the man starts running at a constant velocity, $V\,\mathrm{m\,s^{-1}}$. He arrives at the bus stop at the same time as the bus.

Find the value of V.

8 A model train travels along a straight track. At time t seconds after setting out from station A, the train has velocity $v\,\mathrm{m\,s^{-1}}$ and displacement x metres from A. It is given that for $0 \leqslant t \leqslant 7$

$$x = 0.01t^4 - 0.16t^3 + 0.72t^2.$$

After leaving A the train comes to instantaneous rest at station B.

i Express v in terms of t. Verify that when $t = 2$ the velocity of the train is $1.28\,\mathrm{m\,s^{-1}}$.

ii Express the acceleration of the train in terms of t, and hence show that when the acceleration of the train is zero $t^2 - 8t + 12 = 0$.

iii Calculate the minimum value of v.

iv Sketch the (t, v) graph for the train, and state the direction of motion of the train when it leaves B.

v Calculate the distance AB.

© OCR, AS GCE Mathematics, Paper 4728, June 2008

9 A particle moves with velocity $v\,\mathrm{m\,s^{-1}}$, where:

$$v(t)=\begin{cases}0.16t^3-0.12t+10.6 & \text{for}\quad 0\leqslant t\leqslant 5\\ 40-2t & \text{for}\quad t>5\end{cases}$$

Find the two times when the particle is 200 m away from the starting point.

10 A car is travelling along a road that has a speed limit of $90\,\mathrm{km\,h^{-1}}$. The speed of cars on the road is monitored via average speed check cameras, which calculate the average speed of a car by measuring how long it takes to travel a specified distance.

The car starts from rest next to one of the cameras. Its velocity in $\mathrm{m\,s^{-1}}$ is given by $v(t)=\dfrac{1}{5}t(t-10)^2$, and it comes to rest after 10 seconds. It stays stationary for T seconds and then starts moving again with a constant acceleration of $3.5\,\mathrm{m\,s^{-2}}$. The velocity–time graph of the car's motion is shown in the diagram.

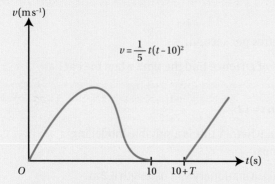

The second camera is positioned 300 m away from the first one.

a Find the time the car takes to reach the second camera after it has started from rest the second time.

b Show that the car's speed exceeded $90\,\mathrm{km\,h^{-1}}$ during both stages of motion.

c The cameras did not detect the car breaking the speed limit. Find the smallest possible value of T.

11 A particle is moving in a straight line so that its displacement from the starting point, x metres, is given by $x=0.8t^3-0.12t^4$.

Find the maximum speed of the particle during the first 6 seconds.

20 Motion with constant acceleration

In this chapter you will learn how to:

- derive equations for motion with constant acceleration
- use constant acceleration equations
- apply constant acceleration formulae to vertical motion under gravity
- solve multi-stage problems.

Before you start…

Chapter 19	You should know how to use integration to find velocity and displacement from acceleration.	1 A particle moves in a straight line. Its acceleration is given by $a = 2 - 3t^2$. a Given that its velocity at $t = 0$ is 4.2 m s^{-1} find the equation for the velocity at time t. b Given that its initial displacement from point A is 14 m, find the equation for the displacement of A at time t.
Chapter 3	You should know how to solve quadratic equations.	2 Solve the following quadratic equations: a $4.2t^2 - 11.5t + 2.6 = 0$ b $\quad 12t - 4.9t^2 = 5.2$
Chapter 3	You should know how to find the vertex of a parabola.	3 Find the coordinates of the vertex of the parabola with equation: a $y = 12.2x - 36.1x^2$ b $y = 2.1x^2 - 6.3x + 7$

Why do you need the constant acceleration formulae?

There are many situations in mechanics where the acceleration can be modelled as constant: for example, vertical motion under gravity or an object slowing down due to a constant friction force. You can use techniques from Chapter 19 to derive special equations for acceleration, velocity and displacement which apply **only** when the acceleration is constant.

Section 1: Deriving the constant acceleration formulae

If you know the acceleration of a particle, you can integrate its equation to find equations for velocity and displacement. When the acceleration is constant, you get the following formulae.

Key point 20.1

For a particle moving with constant (or uniform) acceleration a and initial velocity u:

- the velocity at time t is $v = u + at$
- the displacement from the starting point is $s = ut + \dfrac{1}{2}at^2$.

Tip

In the constant acceleration formulae, s rather than x is generally used for displacement.

WORKED EXAMPLE 20.1

Prove that if the acceleration, a, is constant and the initial velocity is u then:

a the velocity at time t is given by $v = u + at$

b the displacement from the starting point is $s = ut + \dfrac{1}{2}at^2$.

a $v = \displaystyle\int a\,dt$ Link a and v using Key point 19.5.

$ = at + c$ a is a constant so we are effectively doing $a\displaystyle\int 1\,dt$.

When $t = 0$, $v = u$:   Use the initial condition.

$u = 0 + c$

$c = u$

So $v = at + u$

i.e. $v = u + at$

b $s = \displaystyle\int v\,dt$ Link s and v using Key point 19.5.

$ = \displaystyle\int u + at\,dt$

$ = ut + \dfrac{1}{2}at^2 + d$

When $t = 0$, $s = 0$ so $d = 0$.   Since s is measured relative to the starting point.

So $s = ut + \dfrac{1}{2}at^2$

In these equations, the acceleration can be either positive or negative. Negative acceleration is called **deceleration**.

You can combine the two equations in Key point 20.1 to form another useful equation.

Key point 20.2

$s = vt - \dfrac{1}{2}at^2$

Tip

A deceleration of 3 ms⁻² is the same as an acceleration of −3 ms⁻². You would use $a = -3$ in the equation(s) in Key points 20.1 to 20.3.

This is proved in question 3 in Exercise 20A.

You can also derive these formulae by looking at a velocity–time graph. If the acceleration is constant, then the graph is a straight line with gradient a.

The method is most easily seen when considering the situation with positive acceleration and positive initial velocity.

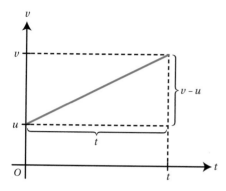 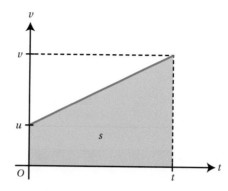

At time t, the velocity is v. Since the gradient of the graph is a,

$$a = \frac{v-u}{t}$$

$$\Leftrightarrow v = u + at$$

The area under the graph represents the distance travelled. On the graph shown, the velocity is positive so this is the same as the displacement. You can find it by using the formula for the area of a trapezium.

Key point 20.3

If the initial velocity is u and the velocity at time t is v, then $s = \frac{1}{2}(u+v)t$.

Tip

You can interpret this formula as saying that the displacement equals average velocity multiplied by time.

You can combine this equation with $v = u + at$ to derive $s = ut + \frac{1}{2}at^2$ and $s = vt - \frac{1}{2}at^2$.

Although in the derivation the velocity and acceleration were assumed to be positive, this formula for the displacement still applies when part of the v–t graph is below the t-axis. You can prove this in question 8 in Exercise 20A.

All the formulae you have derived so far are examples of equations of motion: they tell you how the velocity and the displacement vary with time.

To find an equation **not** involving time you need to eliminate t from some of the equations.

WORKED EXAMPLE 20.2

Use the equations $v = u + at$ and $s = \frac{1}{2}(u+v)t$ to derive an equation for v^2 in terms of u, a and s.

$v = u + at$

$t = \dfrac{v-u}{a}$

Make t the subject of the first equation...

Continues on next page ...

$$s = \frac{1}{2}(u+v)t$$

$$= \frac{1}{2}(u+v)\left(\frac{v-u}{a}\right)$$

and then substitute t into the second to eliminate it.

$$= \frac{v^2 - u^2}{2a}$$

Notice the difference of two squares.

$$v^2 = u^2 + 2as$$

Rearrange to make v^2 the subject.

🔍 Key point 20.4

If the initial velocity of a particle is u and it is subject to a constant acceleration a, when its displacement from the starting point is s, its velocity satisfies $v^2 = u^2 + 2as$.

Notice that this equation gives two possible values of v since you can take either the positive or the negative square root. In some situations only one of the values is relevant, but sometimes both are possible.

For example, If the particle moves away from the starting point and then back again, it will pass through a point A twice (at times labelled t_1 and t_2 on the diagram). You can see that the gradients at those two points are the same size (magnitude) but have opposite signs. This means that the particle passes A with equal speeds both times, but moving in opposite directions.

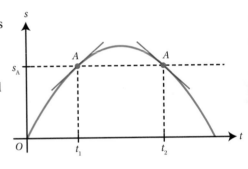

WORKED EXAMPLE 20.3

A particle moves in a straight line with uniform deceleration of 5.1 m s^{-2}. When $t = 0$ the particle is at the point A and its velocity is 14.6 m s^{-1}.

a Find the possible values of the velocity when its displacement from A is 15 m.

b Find the two times when the particle's displacement from A is 15 m.

a $v^2 = u^2 + 2as$

$\qquad = 14.6^2 + 2(-5.1)(15)$

$\qquad = 60.16$

$\therefore v = \pm 7.76 \text{ m s}^{-1}$ (3 s.f.)

You want v:

$u = 14.6$

$a = -5.1$ (remember acceleration is negative)

$s = 15$

v can be either positive or negative.

Continues on next page ...

b $s = ut + \dfrac{1}{2}at^2$

$15 = 14.6t + \dfrac{1}{2}(-5.1)t^2$

$2.55t^2 - 14.6t + 15 = 0$

$t = 1.34$ or 4.38 seconds (3 s.f.)

You can use the equation for s in terms of t with the given values of u and a. (Or you could use the values of v you have just calculated and the equation $v = u + at$.) This second equation is easier, but you would need to use value of v which is not exact.

This is a quadratic equation, so rearrange before using the formula (or your calculator). You expect to find two possible values of t.

EXERCISE 20A

In this exercise avoid early rounding of numerical answers in your working out. If you can, use the memory function on your calculator to save intermediate values, or, alternatively, work to at least 4 s.f. in your working before rounding to 3 s.f. in your final answer.

1 Use the formulae $v = u + at$ and $s = \dfrac{1}{2}(v + u)t$ to prove that $s = ut + \dfrac{1}{2}at^2$.

2 The diagram shows a velocity–time graph for a particle moving with constant acceleration a. Its speed increases from u to v in time t.

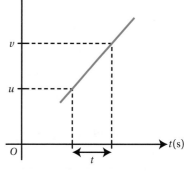

$v(\mathrm{m\,s^{-1}})$

  a Use the graph to explain why $a = \dfrac{v - u}{t}$.

  b By splitting the area under the graph into a rectangle and a triangle, show that the distance travelled during time t is given by $s = ut + \dfrac{1}{2}at^2$.

3 **a** Use the formulae $s = ut + \dfrac{1}{2}at^2$ and $v = u + at$ to derive the formula $s = vt - \dfrac{1}{2}at^2$.

  b A particle moves with constant acceleration $3.1\ \mathrm{m\,s^{-2}}$. It travels $300\ \mathrm{m}$ in the first 8 seconds. Find its speed at the end of the 8 seconds.

4 A particle starts with initial velocity u and moves with constant deceleration. After time T its velocity is v. Both u and v are positive.

  a Draw a velocity–time graph for the particle's motion during the first T seconds.

  b Hence prove that the distance travelled by the particle is $s = \dfrac{(u + v)T}{2}$.

5 **a** If the acceleration is proportional to time, so that $a = kt$, find an expression for v in terms of u, k and t.

  b Hence prove that:

  i $s = ut + \dfrac{1}{6}kt^3$ **ii** $s = \dfrac{1}{3}(2u + v)t$ **iii** $2(v - u)(2u + v)^2 = 9ks^2$.

6 Use the formulae $v = u + at$ and $s = ut + \dfrac{1}{2}at^2$ to derive the formula $v^2 = u^2 + 2as$.

7 The diagram shows velocity–time graphs for two particles. The initial speed of each particle is u.

One particle moves with constant acceleration a.

a For this particle, write down an expression for the velocity at time T.

The other particle has velocity given by $v = u + at^2$.

b Find the time when the two particles have the same velocity.

c Given that the two particles travel the same distance in time T, find the value of T.

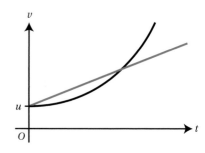

8 The diagram shows a velocity–time graph for a particle moving with constant acceleration a and initial velocity u. The velocity at time t is $-v$ and the velocity at time z is zero.

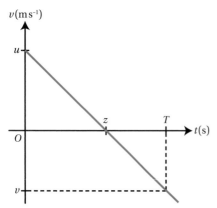

Let s denote the displacement of the particle from the starting point at time T.

Show that $s = \dfrac{1}{2}uz + \dfrac{1}{2}v(T - z)$.

Section 2: Using the constant acceleration formulae

You now have five different equations that can be used to solve problems involving motion with constant acceleration.

Selecting which one to use depends on which of the five quantities a, u, v, s and t are involved in the question.

Quantities involved	Equation
u, v, a, t	$v = u + at$
a, u, s, t	$s = ut + \dfrac{1}{2}at^2$
s, u, v, t	$s = \dfrac{1}{2}(u+v)t$
a, u, v, s	$v^2 = u^2 + 2as$
a, v, s, t	$s = vt - \dfrac{1}{2}at^2$

All five constant acceleration formulae will appear in your formula book.

If you write down what you are given in the question and what you are trying to find, you can then select the most useful equation.

WORKED EXAMPLE 20.4

A car moves with constant acceleration. When $t = 0$, it passes a junction with velocity 8.2 m s^{-1}. It passes the next junction, 320 m away, 24 seconds later. Find the car's velocity as it passes the second junction.

$s = 320$

$u = 8.2$

$t = 24$

$v = ?$

> Write down what you are given and what you are trying to find. You don't need to write units in the calculations, but remember to add them to the final answer.

$s = \dfrac{1}{2}(u + v)t$

$320 = \dfrac{1}{2}(8.2 + v)(24)$

> Looking at the table, s, u, v and t feature in the third equation: $s = \dfrac{1}{2}(u + v)t$.

$8.2 + v = \dfrac{640}{24}$

$8.2 + v = 26.7$

$v = 18.5 \text{ m s}^{-1}$

> Now solve the equation to find v.

> Remember to give correct units with your answer.

WORKED EXAMPLE 20.5

An object decelerates uniformly from 26.3 m s^{-1} to 16.2 m s^{-1}, while covering a distance of 240 m. Find its deceleration.

$s = 240$

$u = 26.3$

$v = 16.2$

$a = ?$

> Write down what you are given and what you are trying to find.

> Make sure you get u and v the right way round.

$v^2 = u^2 + 2as$

$16.2^2 = 26.3^2 + 2a(240)$

$480a = 16.2^2 - 26.3^2$

$480a = -429.25$

$a = -0.894 \text{ m s}^{-2} \text{ (3 s.f.)}$

So the deceleration is 0.894 m s^{-2}.

> s, u, v and a feature in the fourth equation: $v^2 = u^2 + 2as$

> Solve for a.

> Give your answer as a positive **deceleration**, remembering to include units.

WORKED EXAMPLE 20.6

Imogen is walking down the street when she sees a bus at the bus stop 25 m away. She starts accelerating uniformly at 0.9 m s^{-2} and reaches the bus stop 4 seconds later. Find her velocity when she arrives at the bus stop.

$s = 25$

$a = 0.9$ Write down what you are given and what you are trying to find.

$t = 4$

$v = ?$

$s = vt - \dfrac{1}{2}at^2$ Choose the equation that links s, a, t and v.

$25 = 4v - \dfrac{1}{2} \times 0.9 \times 4^2$ Put in the numbers and rearrange.

$\quad = 4v - 7.2$

$32.2 = 4v$

$v = 8.05 \text{ m s}^{-1}$

EXERCISE 20B

1. Choose an appropriate formula to answer each question.

   a. Find the values of u and s when:

      i $a = 2.4 \text{ m s}^{-2}$, $v = 18 \text{ m s}^{-1}$, $t = 6$ s   ii $a = 0.6 \text{ m s}^{-2}$, $v = -21 \text{ m s}^{-1}$, $t = 3.5$ s

   b. Find the values of t and v when:

      i $u = 13 \text{ m s}^{-1}$, $a = -1.2 \text{ m s}^{-2}$, $s = 60$ m   ii $u = 20 \text{ m s}^{-1}$, $a = -3 \text{ m s}^{-2}$, $s = 40$ m

   c. Find the values of a and t when:

      i $u = 12 \text{ m s}^{-1}$, $v = 6 \text{ m s}^{-1}$, $s = 120$ m   ii $u = -3 \text{ m s}^{-1}$, $v = 16 \text{ m s}^{-1}$, $s = 120$ m

   d. Find the values of a and s when:

      i $u = 5 \text{ m s}^{-1}$, $v = -6 \text{ m s}^{-1}$, $t = 6$ s   ii $u = 8 \text{ m s}^{-1}$, $v = -5 \text{ m s}^{-1}$, $t = 10$ s

2. A car accelerates uniformly from rest to 12.45 m s^{-1} in 6.5 seconds. Find:

   a. the acceleration

   b. the distance travelled during this time.

3. A cyclist is travelling at the speed of 4.2 m s^{-1}. She accelerates uniformly at 0.3 m s^{-2} for 7 seconds. Find:

   a. her final speed

   b. the distance she travels in the 7 seconds.

4. A particle reduces its speed from 16.3 m s^{-1} to 7.5 m s^{-1} while travelling 120 m.

   a. Find the constant acceleration of the particle.

   b. Find the distance the particle would travel in another 5 seconds.

5. A particle starts from rest and accelerates uniformly at 2.5 m s^{-2}. How long will it take to travel 250 m?

6   A particle reduces its speed from 20 m s⁻¹ to 8.2 m s⁻¹ while travelling 100 m. Assuming it continues to move with the same constant acceleration, how long will it take to travel another 20 m?

7   A particle moves with constant deceleration of 3.6 m s⁻². It travels 350 m while its speed halves. Find the time it takes to do this.

8   A car reduces its speed from 18 m s⁻¹ to 9 m s⁻¹ while travelling 200 m. Assuming the car continues to move with the same uniform acceleration, how much further will it travel before it stops?

9   a   A particle moves in a straight line with constant acceleration $a = -3.4$ m s⁻². At $t = 0$ its velocity is $u = 6$ m s⁻¹. Find its maximum displacement from the starting point.

   b   Explain why this is not the maximum distance from the starting point.

Section 3: Vertical motion under gravity

When an object is thrown in the air, the force of gravity acts on it: if the object is moving upwards the force of gravity slows it down; if it is moving downwards the force of gravity speeds it up.

The force of gravity produces acceleration. This acceleration is the same regardless of the mass of the object, and is called **gravitational acceleration** or **acceleration of freefall**. On or near the surface of Earth, this value is denoted by g and is approximately 9.8 m s⁻². In fact, this value varies slightly with the geographical position and height above sea level, but in this course you can assume that it is constant.

The motion of the object may also be affected by air resistance. However, if the object is modelled as a particle, you can assume that the air resistance is sufficiently small as not to affect the resulting motion significantly. With these modelling assumptions (that any other force can be ignored), an object moving vertically under gravity moves in a straight line with constant acceleration. You can therefore use the equations from Section 2 to calculate its velocity and displacement.

🔍 **Explore**

What relationship did Newton discover between the gravitational force between two objects and the distance between them?

📷 **Focus on ...**

See Focus on ... Modelling 4 if you want to explore the effects of air resistance and variable g.

WORKED EXAMPLE 20.7

A small ball is thrown straight downwards from a window 4.6 m above the ground with an initial velocity of 1.2 m s⁻¹. Air resistance can be ignored.

a   How long does it take for it to reach the ground? Give your answer to 2 s.f.

b   How would your answer change if air resistance were included?

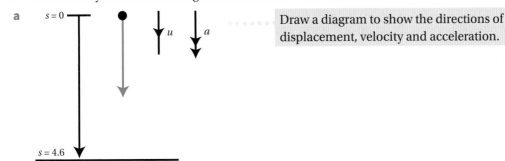

a   Draw a diagram to show the directions of displacement, velocity and acceleration.

Continues on next page ...

463

$s = 4.6$ .... Write down what you are given and what you are trying to find. Since the displacement is measured downwards, the ground is at $s = +4.6$ m.

$u = 1.2$

$a = 9.8$

$t = ?$

$s = ut + \dfrac{1}{2}at^2$ .... Select the equation involving s, u, a and t:

$4.6 = 1.2t + 4.9t^2$ $\qquad s = ut + \dfrac{1}{2}at^2$

$4.9t^2 + 1.2t - 4.6 = 0$

$t = 0.854$ or -1.1

$\therefore t = 0.854$ s .... We want the positive root.

b The time taken would be greater as air resistance would decrease the acceleration.

In Worked example 20.7 we took the positive direction to be downward, so the acceleration, velocity and displacement were all positive. The displacement–time graph is a positive parabola with equation $s = 4.9t^2 + 1.2t$. Only the part of the parabola from $t = 0$ to $t = 0.85$ is relevant in this situation. You can see that the velocity increases as the ball approaches the ground.

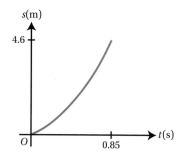

If an object is thrown vertically upwards, it makes more sense to measure displacement in the upward direction. In this case the initial velocity is positive but the acceleration, which always points downwards, is negative: $a = -9.8$ m s^{-2}. The velocity-time graph has equation $v = u - 9.8t$. As can be seen from the graph, if the object is allowed to move freely under gravity, the velocity will eventually become negative, corresponding to the object changing direction and starting to fall.

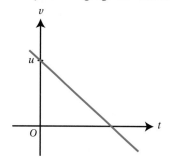

WORKED EXAMPLE 20.8

A stone is thrown upwards with a velocity of 5.6 m s⁻¹ from a platform 1.2 m above ground. Find the velocity of the stone when it hits the ground.

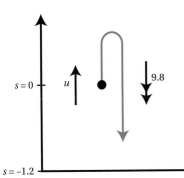

Draw a diagram to show the directions. Since the initial direction of motion is upwards, take this to be the positive direction.

$s = -1.2$

$u = 5.6$

$a = -9.8$

$v = ?$

Write down what you are given and what you are trying to find.

The displacement is measured upwards, so the ground is at $s = -1.2$ m.

Acceleration is downwards so a is negative.

$v^2 = u^2 + 2as$

$v^2 = 5.6^2 + 2(-9.8)(-1.2)$

$v^2 = 54.88$

$v = \pm 7.41$

The final velocity of the stone is -7.41 m s⁻¹.

Select the equation involving s, u, v and a:
$v^2 = u^2 + 2as$

Before hitting the ground the stone is moving downwards, so its velocity is negative.

The displacement–time graph for the motion of the stone is a negative parabola with equation $s = -4.9t^2 + 5.6t$. Its vertex corresponds to the highest point reached by the stone. Note that the value of s at this point is not the maximum height of the stone above ground, because the displacement is measured from the platform.

The part of the graph below the horizontal axis represents the motion of the stone below the platform until it hits the ground.

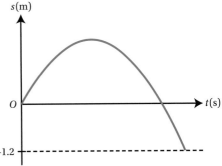

WORKED EXAMPLE 20.9

For the stone from the previous example, find:

a the greatest height above the ground

b how long it takes to reach the highest point

c for how long it is falling.

a $u = 5.6$

$v = 0$

$a = -9.8$

$s = ?$

> Write down what you are given and what you are trying to find.
>
> At the greatest height, $v = 0$.

$v^2 = u^2 + 2as$

$0 = 5.6^2 + 2(-9.8)s$

$19.6s = 31.36$

$s = 1.6$

> You can use the same equation as in Worked example 20.8.

$h = s + 1.2$

$\quad = 2.8 \text{ m}$

> s is the displacement from the starting point, which is itself 1.2 m above the ground.

The maximum height of the stone is 2.8 m.

b $u = 5.6$

$v = 0$

$a = -9.8$

$t = ?$

> You now want to find t rather than s.

$v = u + at$

$0 = 5.6 - 9.8t$

$t = 0.571 \text{ s}$

> Select the equation involving u, v, a and t:
> $v = u + at$
>
> The stone falls from its highest points until it hits the ground.

c $u = 0$

$s = 2.8$

$a = 9.8$

$t = ?$

> When it is at the highest point, the stone is at rest ($u = 0$) and 2.8 m above ground (from part **a**).
>
> The direction of motion is downwards, so take that as the positive direction. This means that both s and a are positive.

Continues on next page ...

$$s = ut + \frac{1}{2}at^2$$

$$2.8 = 0 + \frac{1}{2}(9.8)t^2$$

$$t^2 = 0.571$$

$$t = 0.756$$

The stone spends 0.756 seconds falling.

Select the equation involving u, s, a and t.

You can see all this information on the displacement-time graph.

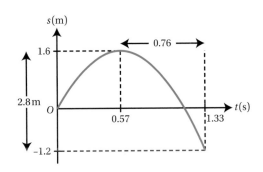

WORK IT OUT 20.1

A stone is thrown vertically upwards from the top of a cliff with speed 10 m s^{-1}. It hits the sea below with speed 33 m s^{-1}. Find the time taken, giving your answer to 2 s.f.

Which is the correct solution? Can you identify the errors made in the incorrect solutions?

Solution 1	Solution 2	Solution 3
$u = 10$	$u = 10$	Highest point when $v = 0$:
$v = 33$	$v = -33$	$u = 10$
$a = 9.8$	$a = -9.8$	$v = 0$
$v = u + at$	$v = u + at$	$a = -9.8$
$33 = 10 + 9.8t$	$-33 = 10 - 9.8t$	$v = u + at$
$23 = 9.8t$	$-43 = -9.8t$	$0 = 10 - 9.8t$
$t = \dfrac{23}{9.8} = 2.4\text{ s}$	$t = \dfrac{43}{9.8} = 4.4\text{ s}$	$-10 = -9.8t$
		$t = \dfrac{10}{9.8} = 1.0\text{ s}$
		Same time to come down:
		$\therefore t = 1.0 \times 2$
		$= 2.0\text{ s}$

WORKED EXAMPLE 20.10

An object is thrown upwards from ground level with initial velocity u.

a Find an expression in terms of u and g for the time it takes to

    i reach the highest point   **ii** return to the ground.

b Find the speed of the object when it hits the ground.

a i At the highest point, $v = 0$:	At the highest point, $v = 0$. You need an equation involving u, v, a and t.
$v = u + at$	
$0 = u + (-g)t$	If the displacement is measured upwards, u is positive and a is negative: $a = -g$.
$\Rightarrow t = \dfrac{u}{g}$	
ii When the object returns to the ground: $s = 0$:	When the object returns to the ground, $s = 0$. You need an equation involving u, a, s and t.
$s = ut + \dfrac{1}{2}at^2$	
$0 = ut - \dfrac{1}{2}gt^2$	
$\Leftrightarrow 0 = t\left(u - \dfrac{1}{2}gt\right)$	The expression on the right can be factorised.
$\Leftrightarrow t = 0 \text{ or } t = \dfrac{2u}{g}$	
$\therefore t = \dfrac{2u}{g}$	$t = 0$ is the starting point, so you need the other value of t.
b $v = u + at$	
$= u + (-g)\left(\dfrac{2u}{g}\right)$	You now know the time when the object hits the ground, so you can use it to find the velocity.
$= u - 2u$	
$= -u$	
$\therefore$ The speed is u.	

You should notice two things here, summarised in Key point 20.5.

Key point 20.5

For an object thrown upwards from ground level:

- the time taken to return to the ground is twice the time to the highest point; the time to go up is the same as the time to come down
- the speed of the object when it hits the ground equals its initial speed.

This can also be seen from the displacement–time graph and the velocity–time graph, which are both symmetrical.

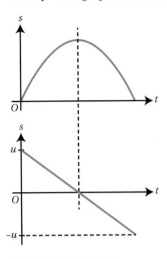

 Tip

'The speed of the particle when it hits the ground' means its speed at the moment of impact. It is not zero!

EXERCISE 20C

1 A ball is thrown vertically downwards with the given initial speed. Assume the air resistance can be ignored, and that the ball does not reach the ground. Find the speed and the distance travelled by the ball at the specified time.

    a **i**   initial speed = 19 m s^{-1}, $t = 0.3$ seconds

        ii initial speed = 23 m s^{-1}, $t = 0.8$ seconds

    b **i**   initial speed = 0 m s^{-1}, $t = 3.1$ seconds

        ii initial speed = 0 m s^{-1}, $t = 6$ seconds

2 A ball is thrown vertically upwards with the given initial speed. Assume that air resistance can be ignored. Find the magnitude and direction of the velocity, and the height above the projection point, at the specified time.

    a **i**   initial speed = 9 m s^{-1}, $t = 2.5$ seconds

        ii initial speed = 12 m s^{-1}, $t = 0.8$ seconds

    b **i**   initial speed = 35 m s^{-1}, $t = 3.1$ seconds

        ii initial speed = 20 m s^{-1}, $t = 1.1$ seconds

3 A stone is dropped from rest from a height of 25 m. Find its velocity when it hits the ground.

4 A ball is thrown vertically upwards from ground level with a speed of 18.5 m s^{-1}. Assuming that air resistance can be ignored, find:

    a how long the ball takes to reach the height of 15 m

    b the speed of the ball at this time.

    c Explain how your answers to parts **a** and **b** would change if air resistance was included?

 Elevate

For more examples of vertical motion see Support sheet 20.

5 An object was projected vertically upwards with velocity $u \text{ m s}^{-1}$. When it has reached the height of 5.6 m its velocity is 3.5 m s^{-1}. Find the value of u.

6 A ball is projected vertically upwards from the top of a 15 m tall cliff with a velocity of 28 m s^{-1}.

    a Find the maximum height of the ball above ground.

    b How long does the ball take to reach the ground and how fast is it going when it hits it?

7 A bunch of flowers is projected vertically upwards towards a window 8.3 m above the point from which it is thrown.

    a Given that the initial speed is 6.5 m s^{-1}, and assuming that air resistance can be ignored, will it reach the window?

    b Find the minimum projection speed required for the flowers to reach the window.

    c How would your answer to part **b** change if the air resistance were included?

8 A ball is thrown vertically upwards from a window 12 m above ground level. The initial velocity of the ball is 16 m s^{-1}.

    a After what time will the ball reach the highest point?

    b How long does the ball take to fall to the ground?

    c Sketch the velocity–time graph for the ball's motion.

9 A particle is projected upwards from ground level with initial speed u. Air resistance can be ignored.

    a Find an expression, in terms of u, for the time it takes the particle to return to ground level.

    b Which of the following graphs shows the distance travelled by the particle as a function of time?

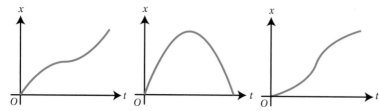

10 A small stone is projected vertically upwards from the top of a cliff, with speed 8 m s^{-1}. It hits the ground with speed 18 m s^{-1}. How high is the cliff?

Section 4: Multi-stage problems

You may have information about two separate stages of the motion, which will often lead to simultaneous equations.

WORKED EXAMPLE 20.11

Three cameras are positioned on a straight road. The distance between the first and the second camera is 50 m and the distance from the second to the third camera is 30 m.

A car passes the first camera with speed u m s^{-1} and immediately starts braking. It passes the second camera 3.1 seconds later and the third camera 2.3 seconds after that. Assuming the deceleration remains constant, find the value of u.

From the first to the second camera:	Write down the information you have for the first stage of motion.
$s = 50$ m	
$t = 3.1$ s	
$u = u$	This is not enough information to find u. However, you also have some information about the second stage of the motion.
$s = ut + \dfrac{1}{2}at^2$	
$50 = 3.1u + \dfrac{1}{2}a(3.1^2)$	You can write down an equation involving s, t and u (for example, the second one from the table), and hope you can use the extra information to find a.
$50 = 3.1u + 4.805a$	
From the first to the third camera:	Now write down the information for both stages together. t and s are still measured from the first camera.
$s = 80$	
$t = 5.4$	
$u = u$	You still can't find u, but you can write another equation.
$s = ut + \dfrac{1}{2}at^2$	
$80 = 5.4u + \dfrac{1}{2}a(5.4^2)$	
$80 = 5.4u + 14.58a$	
$\therefore \begin{cases} 3.1u + 4.805a = 50 \\ 5.4u + 14.58a = 80 \end{cases}$	You now have two simultaneous equations. You can solve them on your calculator, or substitute for a from one equation into the other.
$\Rightarrow u = 17.9$m s^{-1}	

In Worked example 20.11 you were told that the acceleration remains constant throughout the 5.4 seconds. But there are many situations where the acceleration changes part-way through the motion. For example, changing gears while driving a car might change its acceleration. Because the acceleration is not constant, you need to consider the two stages of motion separately.

WORKED EXAMPLE 20.12

A car starts from rest and accelerates at a constant rate of 2.7 m s⁻² for 6 seconds. It then changes to a higher gear and accelerates for 10 seconds, reaching a speed of 28.2 m s⁻¹. Find the acceleration for the second stage of motion.

First stage:

$u = 0$

$a = 2.7$

$t = 6$

$v = u + at$

$\quad = 0 + 2.7 \times 6$

$\quad = 16.2\ \text{m s}^{-1}$

For the second stage, you have the time and the final speed. To work out the acceleration, you need the initial speed. But this is the same as the final speed for the first stage.

Second stage:

$u = 16.2$

$t = 10$

$v = 28.2$

$\quad v = u + at$

$28.2 = 16.2 + 10a$

$\quad a = 1.2\ \text{m s}^{-2}$

Using the value of v from the first part as u in the second, you can find a.

Sometimes it is not possible to find all the information for the first stage before using it in the second stage.

WORKED EXAMPLE 20.13

A dog accelerates uniformly from rest, reaching a speed of V m s⁻¹. It then decelerates back to rest. If the dog ran the total distance of 18 m in 6 seconds, find the value of V.

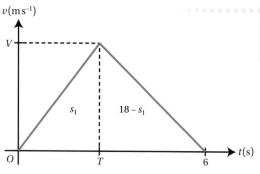

You only know the total distance and total time, but you still need to split the motion into two separate stages as the acceleration changes.

First stage:

$$s_1 = \frac{VT}{2} \qquad\qquad (1)$$

Let the first stage of the motion be from $t = 0$ to $t = T$ and the distance covered be s_1. You can write an equation involving T, V and s_1 by using the area of the triangle on the left.

Continues on next page ...

Second stage:

$$18 - s_1 = \frac{1}{2}(V)(6 - T)$$

$$18 - s_1 = 3V - \frac{VT}{2} \qquad (2)$$

$$18 - \frac{VT}{2} = 3V - \frac{VT}{2}$$

$$18 = 3V$$

$$V = 6$$

The second stage is from $t = T$ to $t = 6$, so the time taken for this stage is $6 - T$. The distance covered is $18 - s_1$. You can use the area of the triangle on the right to write another equation.

Now substitute s_1 from equation (1) into equation (2).

The calculations in Worked example 20.13 are quite involved, and at the beginning it looked as if there wasn't enough information to answer the question. For this example, you can arrive at the answer more quickly if you use the velocity–time graph.

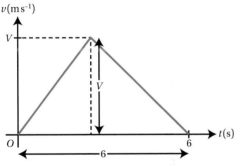

> **Tip**
>
> If the equations look too complicated, you should always try sketching the graph to see if it gives you a simpler method.

Although you don't know T or s_1, you can use the fact that the total distance is the area under the graph:

$$18 = \frac{1}{2} \times 6 \times V$$

$$V = 6$$

Notice that you never found T, so you can't tell when the dog changes from accelerating to decelerating. In fact, there isn't sufficient information in the question to determine this. You can see from the following graph that the dog could accelerate and decelerate for equal amounts of time (red graph), or it could accelerate at a lower rate for longer and then stop suddenly (blue graph). In both cases it covers the same distance (as both triangles have the same area).

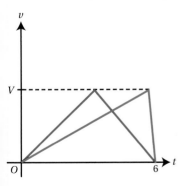

Many two-stage problems involve vertical motion. You need to be very careful about the direction of velocity and acceleration.

473

WORKED EXAMPLE 20.14

A toy rocket with an engine starts from rest at ground level and moves vertically upwards with constant acceleration of 3.6 m s⁻². After three seconds the engine is turned off and the rocket moves freely under gravity. Find:

a the greatest height reached by the rocket

b the total time the rocket spends in the air.

a

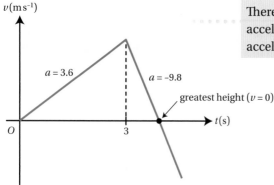

There are two stages: first the rocket has upward acceleration of 3.6 m s⁻² and then downward acceleration of 9.8 m s⁻².

First stage:

$u = 0$

$a = 3.6$

$t = 3$

$v = u + at$

$\quad = 0 + 3.6 \times 3$

$\quad = 10.8 \, \mathrm{m \, s^{-1}}$

The greatest height is when $v = 0$ and is reached during the second stage, so you need to find the initial velocity for that stage, which is the final velocity for the first stage.

$s = ut + \dfrac{1}{2}at^2$

$\quad = 0 + \dfrac{1}{2}(3.6)(3^2)$

$\quad = 16.2 \, \mathrm{m}$

You also need the height reached during the first stage, because the displacement for the second stage is measured from there.

Second stage:

$u = 10.8$

$v = 0$

$a = -9.8$

$v^2 = u^2 + 2as$

$0 = 10.8^2 + 2(-9.8)s$

$s = 5.95 \, \mathrm{m}$

The initial velocity is upwards but the acceleration is now downwards so it is negative.

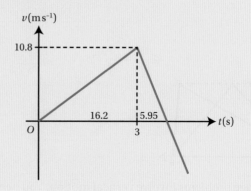

Continues on next page ...

The height is $16.2 + 5.95 = 22.2$ m .... Calculate the total height.

b Second stage:

The total time spent in the air equals 3 seconds from the first stage, plus the time it takes to reach the ground in the second stage. The ground is 16.2 m below the starting point for the second stage.

$u = 10.8$

$a = -9.8$

$s = -16.2$

$s = ut + \dfrac{1}{2}at^2$

$-16.2 = 10.8t - 4.9t^2$

$4.9t^2 - 10.8t - 16.2 = 0$

$t = -1.02$ or 3.23

$\therefore t = 3.23$ s

Total time:

You need to add the time from the first stage.

$3.23 + 3 = 6.23$ s

EXERCISE 20D

1. A car accelerates from rest for 8.3 seconds, reaching a speed of 12.8 m s^{-1}. It then travels for another 12 seconds with deceleration 0.8 m s^{-2}. Find the total distance travelled by the car.

2. A fox is running in a straight line. It passes tree A with a speed of 8.3 m s^{-1} and starts accelerating uniformly. It passes tree B, 120 m away, 13 seconds later. It immediately starts decelerating, coming to rest next to tree C, 250 m from tree B.

   a Find the speed of the fox when it passes tree B.

   b Find the deceleration of the fox.

3. A runner starts with speed u and accelerates uniformly. She covers the first 10 m in 2.1 s and the next 10 m in another 1.1 s. Find the value of u.

4. A cyclist starts at the bottom of a hill moving at a speed of 13.5 m s^{-1}. She moves with a constant deceleration of 0.9 m s^{-1}, reaching the top of the hill 9.2 seconds later. She then accelerates down the hill at 1.6 m s^{-2} for 86 m. Find the speed of the cyclist when she reaches the bottom of the hill.

5. A ball is dropped from a height of 2.6 m above the surface of a water well and falls freely under gravity. After it enters the water, the ball's acceleration decreases to 1.2 m s^{-2}. It reaches the bottom of the well 0.9 seconds later. Assuming the acceleration through the water is constant over a short period of time, find the depth of the water in the well.

6. A rocket is projected vertically upwards with a speed of 260 km h^{-1}. After 6 seconds the engines are switched on and the rocket starts accelerating at 2.8 m s^{-2}. Find the total time from the launch it takes for the rocket to reach a height of 400 m.

7. A car starts from rest at time $t = 0$. It accelerates uniformly until its speed reaches V m s^{-1}. It travels at constant speed for 12 seconds and then decelerates uniformly, coming to rest when $t = 26$. The total distance travelled by the car is 840 m. Find the value of V.

8 A model rocket starts from rest. It has an engine that produces an upward acceleration of 5.2 m s^{-2}. When the rocket has reached the height of 25 m the engine is switched off. Find the maximum height of the rocket and its speed when it returns to the ground.

9 A ball is dropped (with zero initial velocity) from a window 30 m above the ground. Half a second later, another ball is projected vertically upwards from the ground, vertically below the window. The balls collide when they are 15 m above the ground. Find the initial velocity of the second ball.

10 A motorbike is overtaking a lorry on a straight horizontal road. The length of the lorry is 15.2 m and the motorbike is modelled as a particle. Initially the motorbike and the lorry are moving at a constant velocity of 18.6 m s^{-1}. The lorry continues to move with constant velocity. The motorbike starts 35 m behind the lorry, accelerates at a constant rate until it reaches speed V m s^{-1}, then decelerates at a constant rate back to 18.6 m s^{-1}. It ends up 40 m in front of the lorry at the point they again have the same velocity. The overtaking takes 28 seconds.

a How much further does the motorbike travel than the lorry during the 28 seconds?

b On the same axes, sketch the velocity–time graphs for the lorry and the motorbike. Hence find the value of V.

Checklist of learning and understanding

- When an object is moving with constant acceleration you can use the following equations:
  - $v = u + at$
  - $s = ut + \dfrac{1}{2}at^2$
  - $s = vt - \dfrac{1}{2}at^2$
  - $s = \dfrac{1}{2}(u + v)t$
  - $v^2 = u^2 + 2as$

  where a is the acceleration, u is the initial velocity, v is the velocity at time t and s is the displacement from the starting position.
- You can derive these equations using integration or from a straight line velocity–time graph.
- In these equations all the quantities (usually with the exception of t) can be either positive or negative.
  - The object is instantaneously at rest, and may be changing direction, when $v = 0$.
  - The object returns to the starting point when $s = 0$.
- A special case of motion with constant acceleration is vertical motion under gravity. The acceleration is directed downwards and has magnitude $g = 9.8$ m s^{-2}.
  - The object reaches maximum height when $v = 0$.
  - For projection from ground level, time going up equals time going down, and the object hits the ground with the same speed with which it was projected.
  - The constant acceleration model requires two assumptions:
    - air resistance can be ignored (true if the object is modelled as a particle)
    - g is constant (true for small heights).

Mixed practice 20

1 A particle is moving with a speed of $12\ \text{m s}^{-1}$ when it starts to accelerate uniformly at $1.6\ \text{m s}^{-2}$.

  a Find how long it takes for the particle's speed to increase to $26\ \text{m s}^{-1}$.

  b How far does the particle travel in that time?

2 A stone is projected vertically upwards from the ground with a speed of $11\ \text{m s}^{-1}$.

  a Find the speed and the direction of motion of the stone after 2 seconds.

  b Find the height of the stone above ground at this time.

3 A cyclist passes point P with a speed of $6.2\ \text{m s}^{-1}$ and starts to decelerate uniformly at $2.1\ \text{m s}^{-2}$. How fast is she moving after she has travelled 8 m?

4 An object is projected vertically upwards with speed $7\ \text{m s}^{-1}$. Calculate

  i the speed of the object when it is 2.1 m above the point of projection,

  ii the greatest height above the point of projection reached by the object,

  iii the time after projection when the object is travelling downwards with speed $5.7\ \text{m s}^{-1}$.

© OCR, AS GCE Mathematics, Paper 4728, June 2009

5 A car travels on a straight horizontal road. It passes point A with a speed of $32\ \text{km h}^{-1}$ and starts to decelerate uniformly until it reaches speed v km/h. It then accelerates uniformly. When it reaches point B its speed is $32\ \text{km h}^{-1}$ again.

  a Draw the velocity–time graph representing the car's journey.

  b Given that the distance AB is 550 m and the journey takes 1.2 minutes, find the value of v.

  c Find the average speed of the car during its journey from A to B.

6 **a** Use the formulae $v = u + at$ and $s = ut + \frac{1}{2}at^2$ to derive the formula $v^2 = u^2 + 2as$.

  b A ball is projected vertically downwards from the top of a building, with a speed of $8.5\ \text{m s}^{-1}$. It reaches the ground with a speed of $110\ \text{m s}^{-1}$. Find the height of the building.

7 Two particles are projected simultaneously with a speed of 15.4 m s⁻¹. The first particle is projected vertically upwards from ground level. The second particle is projected vertically downwards from a height of 20 m. The two particles move on the same straight line. Find:

a the height above ground where the particles collide

b the speed of each particle at the moment they collide.

8 A particle moves with constant acceleration a. When $t = 0$ it passes point O with velocity u. Let s be the displacement from O at time t.

Use integration to show that $s = ut + \dfrac{1}{2}at^2$.

9 A particle P is projected vertically upwards, from horizontal ground, with speed 8.4 m s⁻¹.

i Show that the greatest height above the ground reached by P is 3.6 m.

A particle Q is projected vertically upwards, from a point 2 m above the ground, with speed u m s⁻¹. The greatest height **above the ground** reached by Q is also 3.6 m.

ii Find the value of u.

It is given that P and Q are projected simultaneously.

iii Show that, at the instant when P and Q are at the same height, the particles have the same speed and are moving in opposite directions.

© OCR, AS GCE Mathematics, Paper 4728, June 2007

10 Two cars start from rest, from the same start line, and accelerate uniformly along a racetrack running perpendicular to the start line. After 5 seconds the first car is 30 m in front of the second car. How far in front is it after another 5 seconds?

11 A ball is projected vertically upwards from ground level with speed u_1. At the moment when this first ball is at its maximum height, a second ball is projected vertically upwards from ground level with speed u_2. The two balls fall back on the ground at the same time without colliding in the air. Find the ratio $u_1 : u_2$.

12 A particle travels in a straight line and decelerates uniformly at 2 m s⁻². When $t = 0$ its velocity is u m s⁻¹ and when $t = 100$ its velocity is $-v$ m s⁻¹ (where $u > v > 0$). The average speed of the particle over the 100 seconds is 62.5 m s⁻¹. Find the values of u and v.

 Elevate

For a selection of more challenging problems using constant acceleration formulae see Extension sheet 20.

21 Force and motion

In this chapter you will learn:

- what causes motion and the concept of a force (Newton's first law)
- how force is related to acceleration (Newton's second law)
- what happens when several forces act on an object
- about different types of forces, including gravity
- how to determine whether a particle is in equilibrium.

Before you start…

Chapter 20	You should know how to use the constant acceleration formulae.	1	A particle accelerates from $3\,\text{m}\,\text{s}^{-1}$ to $8\,\text{m}\,\text{s}^{-1}$ in 12 seconds with constant acceleration. a Find its acceleration. b Find the distance the particle travels in this time.
Chapter 12	You should know how to work with vectors in component form.	2	a Add the vectors $\begin{pmatrix} 1 \\ -3 \end{pmatrix}, \begin{pmatrix} 2 \\ 2 \end{pmatrix}$ and $\begin{pmatrix} -5 \\ 7 \end{pmatrix}$. b Find vector $\mathbf{v}$ so that $3.5\mathbf{v} = -14\mathbf{i} + 7\mathbf{j}$.
Chapter 12	You should know how to find the magnitude and direction of a vector from its components.	3	Find the magnitude of each vector and the angle it makes with the direction of vector $\mathbf{i}$: a $1.2\mathbf{i} + 2.5\mathbf{j}$ b $\begin{pmatrix} 4 \\ -1 \end{pmatrix}$

What causes motion?

In Chapters 19 and 20 you derived formulae to describe how the displacement, velocity and acceleration of a particle vary with time. So far nothing has been said about the causes of motion: Why should a particle start to move, or change its velocity? You probably already know that motion is caused by forces and you are familiar with some types of forces – such as gravitational, electromagnetic and frictional forces. In this chapter you will investigate the relationship between force and acceleration for forces acting in one and two dimensions. You will also see how to work out the combined effect of several forces; this requires the application of vectors from Chapter 12.

Section 1: Newton's laws of motion

Imagine a box lying on a table. If you want the box to move, you need to push or pull it – you need to act on it with a **force**. If you do not apply a force, the box will remain at rest. Once the box is moving, a force is required to change its velocity. For example, a friction force might cause it to slow down, or you may continue to push it to make it accelerate. If there is no force at all, the box will continue to move at a constant speed. This may be difficult to imagine – objects around us are constantly subject to forces like gravity and friction – but it may help to think about, for example, a stone sliding across ice. It takes a very long time to slow down because the forces acting on it are very small.

Any change in velocity of an object is caused by a force. This is one of the most important principles of mechanics.

Key point 21.1

Newton's first law: An object continues to move with constant velocity, or remains at rest, unless acted upon by an external force.

Notice that the law refers to the **velocity**, rather than just the speed of the object. So a force is required to change the **direction** of motion, as well as the speed.

Once you apply the force, the box will start to accelerate. If you want to produce greater acceleration, you need to push or pull harder. But you also know from experience that heavier objects are more difficult to move. So the force required to produce a given acceleration depends on the mass of the object; it is, in fact, directly proportional to it.

Key point 21.2

Newton's second law: The force, F newtons, required to make an object of mass m kg move with acceleration a m s^{-2} is given by the equation $\mathbf{F} = m\mathbf{a}$.

Force and acceleration are both vectors. The direction of the acceleration is the same as the direction of the force. If the direction of the force is the same as the direction of motion, the object will continue to move in the same direction but its speed will change. However, if the force acts in a direction different from the direction of motion, it will also change the direction of the velocity vector.

The magnitude of a force is measured in **newtons** (N). The equation $F = ma$ tells you how the newton is related to the fundamental units of the S.I. system: $1\,\text{N} = 1\,\text{kg m s}^{-2}$.

 Tip

F and a denote the **magnitudes** of the vectors $\mathbf{F}$ and $\mathbf{a}$.

Did you know?

The force you feel when holding an apple is about 1 newton. Sir Isaac Newton (1642–1727) was the English physicist and mathematician whose work laid the foundations for classical mechanics.

WORKED EXAMPLE 21.1

A truck of a mass 3.2 tonnes is moving in a straight line under the action of a constant driving force. Find the magnitude of this force when the truck is:

a   accelerating at a constant rate of 1.6 m s⁻²
b   moving at a constant speed of 58 km h⁻¹.

a $F = ma$	Use Newton's second law in scalar form.
$m = 3.2$ tonnes $= 3200$ kg $F = 3200 \times 1.6 = 5120$ N	To apply the equation, the mass must be in kilograms and the acceleration in m s⁻².
b $Constant\ speed \Rightarrow F = 0$ N	According to Newton's first law, if the velocity is constant, there is no force acing on the object. Notice that this also fits in with Newton's second law: if $v = $ constant then $a = 0$, so $F = m \times 0 = 0$.

WORKED EXAMPLE 21.2

A box of mass 3.5 kg is being acted on by a single force $\mathbf{F} = \begin{pmatrix} 14 \\ -21 \end{pmatrix}$ newtons. Find:

a   the vector acceleration of the box
b   the magnitude of the acceleration.

a $\underline{F} = m\underline{a}$	Use Newton's second law in vector form.

$$\begin{pmatrix} 14 \\ -21 \end{pmatrix} = 3.5\,\underline{a}$$

$$\Rightarrow \underline{a} = \frac{1}{3.5}\begin{pmatrix} 14 \\ -21 \end{pmatrix}$$

$$= \begin{pmatrix} 4 \\ -6 \end{pmatrix} \text{m s}^{-2}$$

b $\left|\underline{a}\right| = \sqrt{4^2 + 6^2} = 7.21 \text{ m s}^{-2}$ (3 s.f.)	Use the components to find the magnitude.

If you know the force acting on an object you can find the equations of motion: use $F = ma$ to find the acceleration, then use integration (or the constant acceleration formulae) to find equations for velocity and displacement.

Fast forward

A In Student Book 2 you will extend constant acceleration formulae to work with two-dimensional vectors.

WORKED EXAMPLE 21.3

A block of mass 1.2 kg slides across the floor with the initial speed of 3.6 m s⁻¹. It slows down due to a constant friction force of magnitude 9 N. How far does the block travel before coming to rest?

> You first need to find the deceleration. You can then use one of the constant acceleration equations to find the distance. Take the direction of the initial motion to be positive.

$F = ma$

$-9 = 1.2a$

> Use Newton's second law, with $F = -9$ as the force is acting against the positive direction.

$\Rightarrow a = -7.5 \text{ m s}^{-2}$

> You now know the acceleration (which is negative!), the initial and final velocities, and want to find the displacement; look for an equation involving u, v, a and s.

$u = 3.6$

$v = 0$

$a = -7.5$

$s = ?$

$v^2 = u^2 + 2as$

$0 = 3.6^2 + 2(-7.5)s$

$\Rightarrow 15s = 12.96$

$s = 0.864 \text{ (3 s.f.)}$

The block travels 0.864 m before coming to rest.

EXERCISE 21A

1   Find the magnitude of the force, in newtons, acting on the object in each case.

a   A crate of mass 53 kg moves with constant acceleration of 2.6 m s⁻².

b   A stone of mass 1.5 kg is pushed across ice and decelerates at a constant rate of 0.3 m s⁻².

c   A truck of mass 6 tonnes accelerates uniformly at 1.2 m s⁻².

d   A toy car of mass 230 g moves with constant acceleration of 3.6 m s⁻².

e   A box of mass 32 kg is dragged across the floor in a straight line, at a constant speed of 5.2 m s⁻¹.

f   A ball of mass 120 g falls with a constant acceleration of 9.8 m s⁻².

g   A book of mass 340 g rests on a horizontal table.

2 Find the acceleration of the object in the following examples:

    a A constant force of magnitude 86 N acts on a box of mass 36 kg.

    b A toy truck of mass 400 g is pushed with the force of 7.3 N.

    c A car of mass 1.5 tonnes moves under the action of a constant force of magnitude 600 N.

    d A ball of mass 120 g is slowed down by a force of magnitude 2.6 N.

3 In each question a particle of mass m moves with constant acceleration **a** under the action of a constant force **F**.

    a i $m = 3\,\text{kg}$, $\mathbf{a} = \begin{pmatrix} 1.6 \\ -2.5 \end{pmatrix}\,\text{m s}^{-2}$, find **F**.   **ii** $m = 5\,\text{kg}$, $\mathbf{a} = \begin{pmatrix} -0.7 \\ 1.3 \end{pmatrix}\,\text{m s}^{-2}$, find **F**.

    b i $m = 0.6\,\text{kg}$, $\mathbf{F} = \begin{pmatrix} 3.6 \\ 1.2 \end{pmatrix}\,\text{N}$, find **a**.   **ii** $m = 6.3\,\text{kg}$, $\mathbf{F} = \begin{pmatrix} -12.6 \\ 9 \end{pmatrix}\,\text{N}$, find **a**.

    c i $\mathbf{a} = \begin{pmatrix} 0.5 \\ -1.5 \end{pmatrix}\,\text{m s}^{-2}$, $\mathbf{F} = \begin{pmatrix} 0.7 \\ -2.1 \end{pmatrix}\,\text{N}$, find m.   **ii** $\mathbf{a} = \begin{pmatrix} 5 \\ 2 \end{pmatrix}\,\text{m s}^{-2}$, $\mathbf{F} = \begin{pmatrix} 2.5 \\ 1 \end{pmatrix}\,\text{N}$, find m.

4 Discuss the following questions in class:

    a Imagine a car driving at a constant speed around a bend. Is there a force acting on the car? What is its direction?

    b Newton's first law states that an object will continue to move with constant velocity if there is no force acting on it. Is this ever the case?

    c In many questions in this and the next chapter you will state that forces like friction or air resistance can be ignored. How realistic are these assumptions?

5 A car of mass 900 kg accelerates from rest to 15 km h^{-1} in 3.5 seconds. Assuming the driving force is constant, find its magnitude.

6 A stone of mass 120 g is pushed across ice with a speed of 3.2 m s^{-1}. It comes to rest 8 seconds later. Find the magnitude of the friction force acting on the stone.

7 A crate of mass 28 kg is pulled across a horizontal floor. The pulling force acting on the crate is 260 N. Assuming that any friction forces can be ignored, how long does it take for the crate to accelerate from rest to 2.5 m s^{-1}?

8 Find, in vector form, the force required to move an object of mass 1.8 kg with acceleration $(0.6\mathbf{i} + 1.1\mathbf{j})\,\text{m s}^{-2}$.

9 A particle of mass 6.5 kg accelerates under the action of force $\mathbf{F} = \begin{pmatrix} -8.5 \\ 6.5 \end{pmatrix}\,\text{N}$. Find:

    a the acceleration in vector form   **b** the magnitude of the acceleration.

10 A van of mass 2.3 tonnes, travelling in a straight line, decelerates under the action of a constant braking force. Its speed decreases from 50 km h^{-1} to 30 km h^{-1} while it covers the distance of 650 m. Find the magnitude of the braking force.

11 A girl pulls a toy truck with a constant horizontal force of 23 N. The truck starts from rest and accelerates uniformly, travelling 16 m in 3 seconds. Find the mass of the truck.

Section 2: Combining forces

In many situations there is more than one force acting on an object. If you are pushing a box across a carpet you are providing a force to accelerate it, but there is also a frictional force slowing it down. A light suspended from a ceiling is being pulled down by the force of gravity but pulled up by the tension in the wire.

When several forces are acting on an object, their combined effect is to produce a certain acceleration. You can find a single force that would produce the same acceleration; this force is called the **resultant force** or **net force**.

 Fast forward

A In Student Book 2 you will learn about geometrical methods of adding forces.

 Key point 21.3

The resultant or net force is a single force that produces the same acceleration as several forces acting together. It is found by adding vectors representing the original forces.

When all forces act along the same straight line it is straightforward to add the vectors: you can treat forces as scalars, except that you use + and – signs to indicate the direction. If you know the direction of motion of the particle, take that as positive; otherwise take the positive direction to be to the right or up.

WORKED EXAMPLE 21.4

Two forces act on a particle P, as shown in the diagram. Find the direction and magnitude of the resultant force.

16 N ←———●———→ 9 N
          P

$|F| = 16 - 9$
$\quad = 7 \text{ N}$

The direction is to the left.

Both forces act along the same line but in opposite directions. So the resultant is in the direction of the larger force.

When forces are acting in two dimensions, the easiest way to add them is using components. You can then use the components to find the magnitude and direction of the resultant force.

 Rewind

You learnt about the magnitude and direction of a vector in Chapter 12, Section 1.

WORKED EXAMPLE 21.5

Three forces act in a vertical plane, with the unit vectors i and j directed to the right and up, respectively. The force F equals $(5i - 8j)$ N. Find the magnitude of the resultant force, and the angle it makes with the horizontal direction.

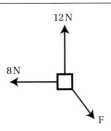

$\underline{F} = (-8\underline{i}) + (12\underline{j}) + (5\underline{i} - 8\underline{j})$

Write all three forces in vector form. Note that the horizontal force is to the left, so it is $-8i$.

$= (-3\underline{i} + 4\underline{j})$ N

Add the i and j components separately.

You can now use the components to find the magnitude and direction. Draw a diagram to help.

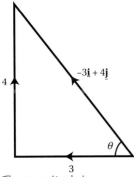

The magnitude is

$|\underline{F}| = \sqrt{3^2 + 4^2} = 5$ N

For the direction:

$\tan \theta = \dfrac{4}{3}$

$\theta = 53.1°$

So the angle from the horizontal is

$180 - 53.1 = 126.9°$

The angle is measured from the *positive* horizontal direction.

Once you have found the resultant force, you can use Newton's second law to find the acceleration.

WORKED EXAMPLE 21.6

Two children are pulling a box of mass 8 kg in opposite directions, as shown in the diagram.

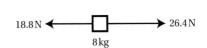

a Find the acceleration of the box.

A third child joins in, pulling with the force F_3.

b The acceleration of the box is now 0.7 m s^{-2} to the right. Find the magnitude and direction of F_3.

a $F = ma$

$26.4 - 18.8 = 8a$

$\Rightarrow a = 0.95$ m s^{-2}

Use $F = ma$ where F is the magnitude of the resultant force. Take the positive direction to be to the right (since that is the direction of the larger force, so you expect the box to move in that direction).

Continues on next page ...

b $F = ma$

$26.4 - 18.8 + F_3 = 8 \times 0.7$ .... Use $F = ma$ again, but now with all three forces. You don't know the direction of the new force, so should you put $+F_3$ or $-F_3$ in the equation?

Let's assume that it's to the right (so use $+F_3$).

$\Rightarrow F_3 = -2$

The magnitude of F_3 is 2 N and its direction is to the left.

The negative sign means that the force is actually to the left.

If the resultant force equals zero, the object will remain at rest or continue to move with constant speed (this is Newton's first law). In case of forces in two dimensions, this means that both components equal zero.

 Fast forward

When the resultant force is zero, you say that the object is in equilibrium. You will see more examples of this in Section 5.

WORKED EXAMPLE 21.7

A particle is subject to three forces, as shown in the diagram. Given that the particle moves with constant speed, find $\mathbf{F}_3$ in vector form.

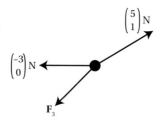

$\begin{pmatrix} -3 \\ 0 \end{pmatrix} + \begin{pmatrix} 5 \\ 1 \end{pmatrix} + F_3 = \begin{pmatrix} 0 \\ 0 \end{pmatrix}$ .... Since the particle does not accelerate, the resultant force must be zero.

$\Rightarrow F_3 = \begin{pmatrix} 3 \\ 0 \end{pmatrix} + \begin{pmatrix} -5 \\ -1 \end{pmatrix}$

$= \begin{pmatrix} -2 \\ -1 \end{pmatrix}$ N

EXERCISE 21B

1 Find the magnitude and direction of the resultant force in each case.

a i 5N ← ● → 3N **ii** 7N ← ● → 12N

b i 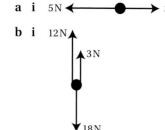 **ii**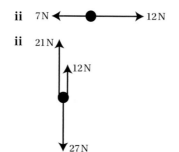

c i

ii

2 Find the resultant force in the form $p\mathbf{i} + q\mathbf{j}$.

a i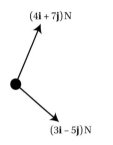

ii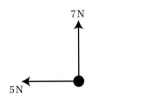

b i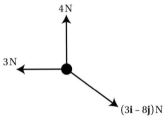

ii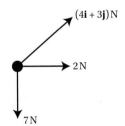

c i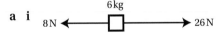

ii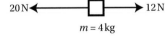

3 Find the magnitude and direction of each resultant force in question 2.

4 For each object shown in the diagram, find the magnitude and direction of acceleration.

a i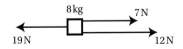

ii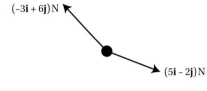

b i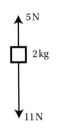

ii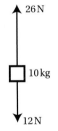

c i

ii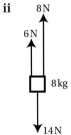

d i

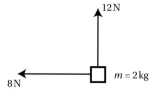

ii

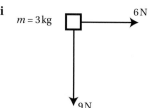

5 Find the acceleration in the form $p\mathbf{i} + q\mathbf{j}$.

a i

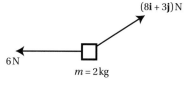

ii

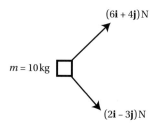

b i

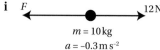

ii

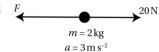

6 In each diagram, the mass of the object and the acceleration are given, with the positive direction to the right or up. Find the magnitude of the force marked F.

a i

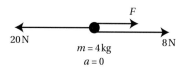

ii

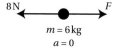

b i

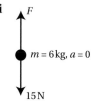

ii

8 N ←——————• ———→ F
$m = 6\,\text{kg}$
$a = 0$

c i

20 N ←——————•———→ 8 N
             F
$m = 4\,\text{kg}$
$a = 0$

ii

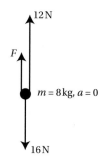

d i

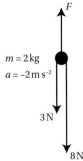

$m = 2\,\text{kg}$
$a = -2\,\text{m s}^{-2}$

F

$3\,\text{N}$

$8\,\text{N}$

ii

F

$10\,\text{N}$

$28\,\text{N}$

$m = 3\,\text{kg}$
$a = 5\,\text{m s}^{-2}$

⬇ Elevate

For more examples like this see Support sheet 21.

7 Two people attempt to push-start a car on a horizontal road. One person pushes with a force of 100 N; the other with a force of 80 N. The car starts to accelerate constantly at 0.15 m s^{-2}. Assuming these are the only horizontal forces acting, find the mass of the car.

8 A sledge of mass m kg is pushed horizontally through the snow by a force of 40 N. There is resistance to its motion of magnitude 10 N as shown in the diagram.

If the sledge is accelerating at 1.5 m s^{-2}, find its mass.

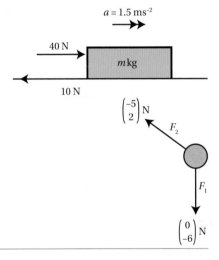

$a = 1.5\,\text{ms}^{-2}$

$40\,\text{N}$

$m\,\text{kg}$

$10\,\text{N}$

9 Two forces F_1 and F_2 act on a particle as shown.

A third force, F_3, is added so that the resultant force on the particle is 2 N to the right.

Find:

a the magnitude of F_3

b the direction F_3 makes with the direction of motion.

$\begin{pmatrix} -5 \\ 2 \end{pmatrix}\,\text{N}$

F_2

F_1

$\begin{pmatrix} 0 \\ -6 \end{pmatrix}\,\text{N}$

Section 3: Types of forces

There are several common examples of forces you should be familiar with. You need to be able to identify all forces acting on an object in a given situation and draw a force diagram, before using techniques from the previous section to do calculations.

Many examples you will meet involve moving vehicles. A **driving force** accelerates the vehicle. A **braking force**, acting in the direction opposite to the velocity, will slow the vehicle down.

When an object is sliding across a surface, there is normally some **friction** (or **frictional force**) resisting the motion. The frictional force always acts in the direction opposite to the velocity of the object. There are other types of forces that resist the motion: for example, **air resistance**. The magnitude of each of these resistance forces depends on many different factors, which are beyond the scope of the AS course. For now, you will usually be told the magnitude of any resistance forces.

Sometimes the frictional force is so small that it can be ignored. This can be the case, for example, when you consider an object sliding on ice. We say that the contact between the object and the ice is **smooth** to indicate that friction can be ignored.

▶▶ Fast forward

🅐 You can learn more about friction in Student Book 2.

WORKED EXAMPLE 21.8

a A car moves under the action of a driving force of 1740 N. The total resistance to motion equals 600 N. Given that the acceleration of the car is 1.2 m s⁻², find its mass.

b The car starts to brake and decelerates at 2.5 m s⁻². Assuming that the total resistance force remains the same, find the magnitude of the braking force.

a 600 N ← □ → 1740 N

Draw a diagram showing all the relevant forces. You don't need to include the car's weight because the question is only about forces and motion in the horizontal direction.

$$1740 - 600 = m \times 1.2$$

Use $F = ma$ with the positive direction to the right.

$$\Rightarrow m = 950 \, kg$$

b 600 N

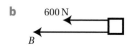

The braking force is in the opposite direction to the driving force.

$$-B - 600 = 950 \times (-2.5)$$

The acceleration is negative.

$$\Rightarrow B = 1775 \, N$$

WORKED EXAMPLE 21.9

A small toy of mass 230 g moves along the floor with an initial speed of speed of 8 m s⁻¹.

a The contact between the toy and the floor is modelled as smooth. Predict the time it would take the toy to travel 6 m.

b The toy actually takes 0.82 seconds to travel 6 m. Find the magnitude of the frictional force, assuming it is constant.

a No force, so constant speed.

$$t = \frac{s}{v} = \frac{6}{8} = 0.75 \, s$$

There are no horizontal forces acting on the toy, so its speed remains constant. This means that you can use $speed = \frac{distance}{time}$.

b $u = 8$

$s = 6$

$t = 0.82$

$a = ?$

You first need to find the acceleration and then use $F = ma$.

$$s = ut + \frac{1}{2}at^2$$

Find the constant acceleration formula involving u, s, t and a.

$$6 = (8 \times 0.82) + \frac{1}{2}a(0.82^2)$$

$$6 = 6.56 + 0.3362a$$

Continues on next page ...

$\Rightarrow a = -1.67 \text{m s}^{-2}$ .... The acceleration is negative because the friction is slowing the toy down.

$F = ma$ .... You can now find the force. Since you only want its magnitude, you can ignore the minus sign (which tells you that the direction is opposite to the direction of motion).

$= 0.23 \times 1.67$

$= 0.383 \text{ N}$

WORKED EXAMPLE 21.10

A box of mass 24 kg moves on a rough horizontal floor under the action of a constant horizontal force $(16\mathbf{i} + 11\mathbf{j})$ N. Find, in vector form, the frictional force acting on the box when its acceleration is $(0.7\mathbf{i} - 1.1\mathbf{j})$ ms^{-2}.

The net force acting on the box is $(16\mathbf{i} + 11\mathbf{j}) + F$, where F is the frictional force.

Identify all the forces acting on the box.

Newton's second law:

Apply Newton's second law in vector form: $m\mathbf{a} = $ net force.

$24(0.7\mathbf{i} - 1.1\mathbf{j}) = (16\mathbf{i} + 11\mathbf{j}) + F$

$F = (16.8\mathbf{i} - 26.4\mathbf{j}) - (16\mathbf{i} + 11\mathbf{j})$

$= (0.8\mathbf{i} - 37.4\mathbf{j})$ N

If you are pulling a box using a rope, you are not acting on the box directly. You are pulling on the rope and the rope pulls the box; the force exerted by the rope on the box is called **tension**, and is directed away from the box (towards you). If you use a stick, a rod or a tow bar instead of a rope, then you could push the box as well as pull. The pushing force provided by the tow bar is called **thrust**, and it is directed towards the box.

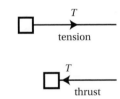

WORKED EXAMPLE 21.11

A boy is using a light horizontal stick to pull a toy box of mass 3.2 kg across rough carpet. The tension in the stick is 18 N and the friction force is 7 N.

a Find the acceleration of the box, and the time it takes for it to accelerate from rest to 2.1 m s^{-1}.
b Assuming that the friction force remains the same, what tension is required for the box to maintain the constant speed of 2.1 m s^{-1}?

The boy now makes the box slow down by applying a different constant force though the stick, and the box comes to rest after travelling 0.8 metres. The friction force is still the same.

c Find the magnitude of the force in the stick, and state whether it is tension or thrust.

Continues on next page ...

a 7N $\longleftarrow$ ☐ $\longrightarrow$ 18N ⋯⋯ Draw a diagram showing all the forces acting on the box.

$18-7=3.2a$ ⋯⋯ $F=ma$. The box is moving to the right, so take that as the positive direction.

$\Rightarrow a = 3.44\,\text{m}\,\text{s}^{-2}$

$u=0$

$v=2.1$

$a=3.44$

$t=?$

$v=u+at$ ⋯⋯ Use a constant acceleration formula involving u, v, a and t.

$2.1=0+3.44t$

$t=0.611\,\text{s}$

b $T-7=0$ ⋯⋯ If the box is moving at constant speed, the acceleration is now zero.

$\Rightarrow T = 7\,\text{N}$

c $u=2.1$

$v=0$

$s=0.8$

$a=?$

$v^2=u^2+2as$ ⋯⋯ To use $F=ma$ you need to find the acceleration. Use a constant acceleration formula.

$\Rightarrow a = -2.76\,\text{m}\,\text{s}^{-2}$

$T-7=3.2\times(-2.76)$ ⋯⋯ Use $F=ma$. The box is still moving to the right, but now the acceleration is negative. You don't know the direction of the force in the stick; try taking it as positive.

$\Rightarrow T = -1.82$

The force in the stick is a thrust of magnitude 1.82 N. ⋯ The negative sign means that the force is in fact to the left. Since this is directed towards the box, it is a thrust rather than tension.

You may wonder whether you should include the mass of the rope or the rod in your calculations. In practice, its mass is almost always a lot smaller than the mass of the object you are trying to move, so you can ignore it. You say that you are modelling the rope (or the rod, tow bar, and so on) as **light**. When you are using a rope or a string, you also need to assume that it does not stretch; otherwise the two ends could move with a different velocity. You say that the string or rope is **inextensible**. You will look at the importance of this assumption further in Chapter 22, Section 4.

EXERCISE 21C

In each question draw a force diagram first.

1 A child pushes a box of mass 8 kg horizontally with a constant force of 28 N. The frictional force between the box and the floor is 12 N. Find the acceleration of the box.

2 A car moves in a straight line on a horizontal road. The driving force has magnitude 1200 N and the total resistance to the motion is 500 N. Given that the acceleration of the car is $2.6\,\mathrm{m\,s^{-2}}$, find its mass.

3 A truck of mass 6.2 tonnes moves in a straight line with a constant acceleration of $1.2\,\mathrm{m\,s^{-2}}$. The driving force is 8200 N.

   a Find the total resistance to the motion.

   Now assume that the resistance can be ignored.

   b How much less time would it take for the truck to accelerate from rest to $40\,\mathrm{km\,h^{-1}}$?

4 A box of mass 8 kg moves on rough horizontal floor under the action of a constant horizontal force $(p\mathbf{i} + q\mathbf{j})$ N. When the acceleration of the box is $(2.5\mathbf{i} + 3.1\mathbf{j})\,\mathrm{m\,s^{-2}}$, the frictional force between the box and floor is $(6.8\mathbf{i} - 5.2\mathbf{j})$ N. Find the values of p and q.

5 A particle rests on a rough horizontal floor. Two perpendicular horizontal forces, shown in the diagram, act on the particle. Given that the particle is in equilibrium, find the magnitude of the frictional force and the angle it makes with the 16 N force.

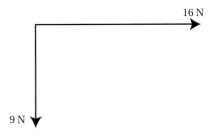

6 A box of mass 45 kg moves on a rough horizontal floor under the action of a constant horizontal force of magnitude 62 N. Find the magnitude of the acceleration of the box when the frictional force has magnitude 18 N and makes a 170° angle with the 62 N force.

7 Two girls are pulling a crate using two horizontal ropes. The mass of the crate is 56 kg. The tension in one of the ropes is 120 N and the friction force is 80 N. Given that the crate moves with constant acceleration of $0.8\,\mathrm{m\,s^{-2}}$ and that the girls are pulling in exactly the same direction find the tension in the other rope.

8 Two men are pushing a car, in a straight line each using an equal force of magnitude FN. The resistance to motion has magnitude 420 N. The mass of the car is 850 kg and it is moving at a constant speed of $6\,\mathrm{km\,h^{-1}}$. Find the value of F.

9 A car of mass 950 kg is moving with a speed of $15.3\,\mathrm{m\,s^{-1}}$ when the driver applies the brakes. The total resistance force, excluding the braking force, is 320 N. The car travels 120 m in a straight line before coming to rest. Find the magnitude of the braking force.

10 A box of mass 45 kg is pulled across a horizontal floor using a light inextensible rope. The rope is horizontal and the tension in the rope is 180 N. The box starts from rest.

   a The contact between the box and the floor is modelled as smooth. According to this model, how long will it take for the box to travel 25 m?

   b The box in fact travels 25 m in 4.2 seconds. Find the magnitude of the friction force between the box and the floor.

11 A car travels along a straight horizontal road. The total resistance to the car's motion is constant and has magnitude 320 N.

   a The driving force is constant at 1200 N. The car passes point A with a speed of 12 m s^{-1} and accelerates to 26 m s^{-1} in 7 seconds. Show that the mass of the car is 440 kg.

   b The driving force is reduced so that the car travels at a constant speed of 26 m s^{-1}. State the magnitude of the driving force.

   c The car travels at the constant speed for 12 seconds. Then the driver turns off the engine and the car stops at point B. Find the distance AB.

12 An object of mass 4.6 kg rests on a horizontal surface. It is acted on by two parallel pulling forces of magnitudes 8 N and 6.5 N, as shown in the diagram, and it starts to accelerate uniformly.

     6.5 N ← ☐ → 8 N
         4.6 kg

After 4 seconds a third pulling force is added, acting parallel to the other two. When the object has moved a further 2 m in the same direction as before, its speed is 1.24 m s^{-1}. Find the magnitude and direction of the third force.

13 In this question vectors $\mathbf{i}$ and $\mathbf{j}$ lie in the horizontal plane and point east and north, respectively.

Two people are pulling a box of weight 1400 N using two ropes. The ropes are modelled as light and inextensible, and the forces in the ropes are $(p\mathbf{i} + q\mathbf{j})$ N and $(p\mathbf{i} - q\mathbf{j})$ N, as shown in the diagram. The friction force of magnitude 180 N is directed west. The box starts from rest.

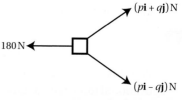

   a Explain why the box moves in a straight line in the east direction.

   b Given that the acceleration of the box is $(0.003p)$ m s^{-2}, find the value of p.

   c The tension in each rope has magnitude 200 N. Find the value of q.

> ⬇ **Elevate**
>
> Extension sheet 21 looks at estimating magnitudes of different types of forces.

Section 4: Gravity and weight

If you pick up a ball and let it go, it falls downwards. This is because the Earth exerts gravitational force on it. The force with which the Earth attracts any object is called the **weight** of the object. You know from Chapter 20 that all objects under the influence of gravity alone move with the same acceleration, $g \approx 9.8$ m s^{-2}.

You should be very careful to use the correct terminology here. In everyday language, you tend to use the word 'weight' to mean 'mass'; so you would say, for example, that the bag of apples weighs 1.2 kg. In mechanics, the 1.2 kg is the mass of the bag; its weight is a **force** with approximate magnitude $1.2 \times 9.8 = 11.76$ N.

Key point 21.4

The magnitude of the weight force on an object of mass m is $W = mg$ where $g \approx 9.8\,\mathrm{m\,s^{-2}}$.

Its direction is towards the centre of the Earth (which is normally described as 'downwards').

The mass is a property of the object itself, independent of where it is. The magnitude of the weight force depends both on the object and on the properties of the Earth. On a different planet the weight would be different: for example, the gravitational acceleration near the surface of Mars is about $3.7\,\mathrm{m\,s^{-2}}$ so the weight of the same bag of apples on Mars would be $1.2 \times 3.7 = 4.44\,\mathrm{N}$.

You should know that gravitational acceleration is not exactly the same everywhere on Earth. It depends on the latitude (this is because the Earth is not perfectly spherical, and also because of its rotation); it also depends on the altitude: it is lower on a mountain than at sea level. The variation is between around $9.76\,\mathrm{m\,s^{-2}}$ and $9.83\,\mathrm{m\,s^{-2}}$, which both round to 9.8. The average is normally quoted as $9.81\,\mathrm{m\,s^{-2}}$. The approximate figure of $9.8\,\mathrm{m\,s^{-2}}$ is appropriate up to the height of about $10\,\mathrm{km}$, so you can use it in all the questions involving balls being thrown in the air or lifts taking you to the top floor of a building.

 Focus on ...

Focus on ... Modelling 4 explores the effect of changing the value of g.

WORKED EXAMPLE 21.12

In his house on Planet X, Zixo has a crystal ball suspended from the ceiling by a light inextensible string. The mass of the ball is $1.6\,\mathrm{kg}$ and the tension in the string is $18.7\,\mathrm{N}$. Find the magnitude of the gravitational acceleration on Planet X.

18.7 N ↑ ↓ W

Always draw a diagram showing all the forces. In this case there are two forces acting on the ball: its weight and the tension in the string.

$W - 18.7 = 0$

Since the ball is not moving, the net force is zero.

$\therefore W = 18.7\,\mathrm{N}$

$W = mg \Rightarrow 1.6g = 18.7$

$\therefore g = 11.7\,\mathrm{m\,s^{-2}}$

Whenever there is a possibility of an object moving in the vertical direction, you should include weight on your force diagram. You need to be very careful about the direction of acceleration.

WORKED EXAMPLE 21.13

A crate of mass 87 kg is being lowered using a light inextensible rope.

a Find the acceleration of the crate when the tension in the rope is 750 N.
b Find the tension in the rope if the crate is being lowered at constant speed.
c Find the tension in the rope required to decelerate the crate from 1.2 m s^{-1} to rest in 3.5 seconds.

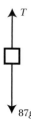

T

$87g$

a $ma = mg - T$

To find acceleration, use $F = ma$.

$87a = 87 \times 9.8 - 750 = 102.6$

$\Rightarrow a = 1.18 \text{ m s}^{-2}$

The crate is being lowered, so take the positive direction to be downwards.

b $0 = 87 \times 9.8 - T$

Constant speed means that $a = 0$.

$\Rightarrow T = 853 \text{ N}$

c $v = u + at$

$0 = 1.2 + 3.5a$

$\Rightarrow a = -0.343 \text{ m s}^{-2}$

You first need to find the acceleration, given that $u = 1.2$, $v = 0$ and $t = 3.5$. We need to pick one of the constant acceleration formulae.

You expect a to be negative because the crate is decelerating.

$ma = mg - T$

$87(-0.343) = 87 \times 9.8 - T$

$\Rightarrow T = 29.8 + 853 = 882 \text{ N}$

You took the positive direction to be downwards, so you should use negative a here.

WORKED EXAMPLE 21.14

A ball falling through the air is subject to a constant resistance force of magnitude 0.3N. The ball starts from rest and takes 1.6 seconds to fall 12 metres. Find the mass of the ball.

Newton's second law for the ball:
$$ma = 9.8m - 0.3$$

The forces acting on the ball are its weight and the air resistance.

To find the acceleration:

$u = 0, t = 1.6, s = 12, a = ?$

Using $s = ut + \dfrac{1}{2}at^2$:

$12 = 0.5a(1.6^2)$

$a = 9.375 \text{ m s}^{-2}$

You can find the acceleration from the information about the time and displacement.

Continues on next page ...

So:

$9.375m = 9.8m - 0.3$ ⋯⋯⋯⋯ Now use this in Newton's second law equation.

$0.425m = 0.3$

$m = 0.706 \text{ kg (3 s.f.)}$

The mass of the ball is about 706 grams.

EXERCISE 21D

1 The diagram shows an object of mass m kg suspended by a light inextensible string. The magnitude of the tension in the string is T N. Find the direction and magnitude of the acceleration.

   a i $m = 3$ kg, $T = 32$ N   **ii** $m = 8$ kg, $T = 92$ N

   b i $m = 0.6$ kg, $T = 4.5$ N   **ii** $m = 3.2$ kg, $T = 27$ N

2 An object of mass m is suspended by a vertical rope. The acceleration of the object is a m s^{-2} in the stated direction. Find the tension in the rope.

   a i $m = 12$ kg, $a = 0.6$ m s^{-2} downwards

     ii $m = 3.2$ kg, $a = 1.2$ m s^{-2} downwards

   b i $m = 8$ kg, $a = 1.4$ m s^{-2} upwards

     ii $m = 3$ kg, $a = 2$ m s^{-2} upwards

3 An object is suspended by a string, with tension T N. The acceleration of the object is a m s^{-2} in the stated direction. Find the mass of the object.

   a i $T = 26$ N, $a = 1.2$ m s^{-2} downwards

     ii $T = 18.6$ N, $a = 0.7$ m s^{-2} downwards

   b i $T = 26$ N, $a = 1.2$ m s^{-2} upwards

     ii $T = 18.6$ N, $a = 0.7$ m s^{-2} upwards

4 A crate of mass 98 kg is being lifted using a rope which can be modelled as light and inextensible. The tension in the rope is 367 N. Find the acceleration of the crate.

5 A ball is at rest, suspended from a ceiling by a light inextensible cable. The tension in the cable is 12 N.

   a Find the mass of the ball.

The tension in the cable is increased to 15 N.

   b Find the magnitude and direction of the acceleration of the ball.

6 A crate is lowered from a window of a space ship on Mars, using a rope. The tension in the rope is 328 N and the crate is descending at a constant speed. Given that the gravitational acceleration on Mars is 3.7 m s^{-2}, find the mass of the crate.

7 A box of mass 1.2 kg falls vertically downwards with a constant acceleration of 8.9 m s^{-2}. Find the magnitude of the air resistance acting on the box.

8 A ball falls vertically downwards, starting from rest, from a height of 24 m. It takes 2.3 seconds to reach the ground. Given that the ball is subject to a constant air resistance of magnitude 0.25 newtons, find the mass of the ball.

9 A stone is dropped vertically from the top of a 25 m tall cliff.

    a A simple model assumes that air resistance can be ignored. According to this model, how long does it take for the stone to reach the ground?

    b The stone actually takes 2.42 seconds to reach the ground. Given that the mass of the stone is 1.2 kg, find the magnitude of the air resistance.

10 A crane is lifting a 350 kg load, which is initially at rest on the ground, using a light inextensible cable. It takes 6 seconds to raise it to the height of 84 m. Find the tension in the cable, assuming it is constant.

11 A crate of mass 124 kg is being lowered using a light inextensible rope. The crate is decelerating at the rate of 1.8 m s^{-2}. Find the tension in the rope.

12 A fisherman is lifting a crate caught on the end of his fishing line. The mass of the crate is 3.5 kg and it is being lifted vertically through the water.

    a While the crate is moving through the water, the water exerts a net force of magnitude 5 N, acting downwards. Given that he is raising the crate at a constant speed, find the tension in the fishing line.

    b The crate breaks the surface of the water and the tension in the string remains unchanged. Air resistance can be ignored. Find the acceleration of the crate at that moment.

13 A horizontal platform of mass 120 kg is supported by a vertical steel rod, as shown in the diagram. The platform is being lowered and decelerating from 3.2 m s^{-1} to rest in 4.5 seconds. Find the thrust in the rod.

Section 5: Forces in equilibrium

You saw in Section 1 that when several forces act on an object, you can find its acceleration by using $\mathbf{F} = m\mathbf{a}$ with $\mathbf{F}$ being the resultant force. A special case of this is when the resultant force is zero: in this case, there is **no** acceleration. According to Newton's first law, the object remains at rest or continues to move with constant velocity. We say that the object is **in equilibrium**.

> ### Key point 21.5
>
> If an object is in equilibrium then the resultant force is zero.

WORKED EXAMPLE 21.15

A large box of mass 80 kg hangs in equilibrium supported by four
cables, as shown in the diagram. The tension in each cable has
magnitude T. Find the value of T.

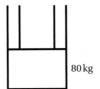

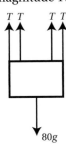

Draw a force diagram. The forces are the four tensions
and the weight of the box.

$80g - 4T = 0$ · · · · · · · · · · Since the box is in equilibrium, the resultant force is zero.
Take positive direction to be downwards.

$$\Rightarrow T = \frac{80g}{4} = 196\,\text{N}$$

If forces are acting in two dimensions, both horizontal and vertical
components need to be zero.

Explore

A falling object can be in equilibrium. Find out about terminal velocity.
Why do astronauts sometimes feel 'weightless'?

WORKED EXAMPLE 21.16

A particle is in equilibrium under the action of three forces: $\mathbf{F}_1 = \begin{pmatrix} 40 \\ 2x \end{pmatrix}$, $\mathbf{F}_2 = \begin{pmatrix} y \\ -32 \end{pmatrix}$ and $\mathbf{F}_3 = \begin{pmatrix} x \\ y \end{pmatrix}$.
Find the values of x and y.

$\mathbf{F}_1 + \mathbf{F}_2 + \mathbf{F}_3 = 0$ · · · · · · · · · Since the particle is in equilibrium, the resultant force is zero.

$$\Rightarrow \begin{cases} 40 + y + x = 0 \\ 2x - 32 + y = 0 \end{cases}$$

You can write separate equations for the horizontal and
vertical components to get two simultaneous equations.

$$\Rightarrow \begin{cases} x + y = -40 \\ 2x + y = 32 \end{cases}$$

$$\Rightarrow x = 72, y = -112$$

Sometimes all forces are either horizontal or vertical. In that case
you don't need to use vector notation; you can simply write separate
equations for horizontal and vertical forces.

WORKED EXAMPLE 21.17

A box of mass 60 kg hangs in equilibrium supported by five light inextensible cables, as shown in the diagram. The tensions in the two vertical cables are T N and $2T$ N and the tensions in the horizontal cables are 160 N, 50 N and P N. Find the values of T and P.

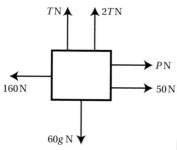

Vertically:

$3T = 60g$

$\Rightarrow T = 196$

Horizontally:

$P + 50 = 160$

$\Rightarrow P = 110$

> You can write separate equilibrium equations for horizontal and vertical directions.

> The equilibrium equation is $3T - 60g = 0$.
> However, sometimes it is easier to think of it as 'forces up = forces down'.

EXERCISE 21E

1   Determine which of these particles are in equilibrium:

a
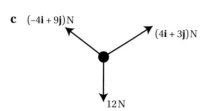

b
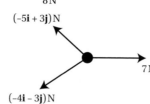

c $(-4\mathbf{i} + 9\mathbf{j})$ N
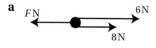
$(4\mathbf{i} + 3\mathbf{j})$ N

12 N

d $(-5\mathbf{i} + 3\mathbf{j})$ N

7 N

$(-4\mathbf{i} - 3\mathbf{j})$ N

2   Each diagram shows a particle in equilibrium. Find the magnitudes of the forces marked with letters. Assume that the unknown forces are vertical or horizontal, as depicted.

a F N ← → 6 N
8 N

b F N ↑
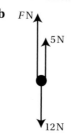
5 N

12 N

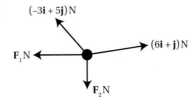

c $(16\mathbf{i} + 9\mathbf{j})\,\mathrm{N}$

d $(-3\mathbf{i} + 5\mathbf{j})\,\mathrm{N}$, $(6\mathbf{i} + \mathbf{j})\,\mathrm{N}$

3 A particle is in equilibrium under the action of the three given forces. Find the values of x and y.

a i $\mathbf{F}_1 = 12\mathbf{i} + 8\mathbf{j}$, $\mathbf{F}_2 = x\mathbf{i} - 15\mathbf{j}$, $\mathbf{F}_3 = 6\mathbf{i} - y\mathbf{j}$
   ii $\mathbf{F}_1 = 25\mathbf{i} + 18\mathbf{j}$, $\mathbf{F}_2 = x\mathbf{i} + 12\mathbf{j}$, $\mathbf{F}_3 = -31\mathbf{i} + y\mathbf{j}$

b i $\mathbf{F}_1 = \begin{pmatrix} 3 \\ 8 \end{pmatrix}$, $\mathbf{F}_2 = \begin{pmatrix} -5 \\ 2 \end{pmatrix}$, $\mathbf{F}_3 = \begin{pmatrix} x \\ y \end{pmatrix}$
   ii $\mathbf{F}_1 = \begin{pmatrix} -2 \\ 1 \end{pmatrix}$, $\mathbf{F}_2 = \begin{pmatrix} 11 \\ 3 \end{pmatrix}$, $\mathbf{F}_3 = \begin{pmatrix} x \\ y \end{pmatrix}$

c i $\mathbf{F}_1 = x\mathbf{i} + y\mathbf{j}$, $\mathbf{F}_2 = -4\mathbf{j}$, $\mathbf{F}_3 = 8\mathbf{i}$
   ii $\mathbf{F}_1 = x\mathbf{i} + y\mathbf{j}$, $\mathbf{F}_2 = 15\mathbf{i}$, $\mathbf{F}_3 = -9\mathbf{j}$

d i $\mathbf{F}_1 = \begin{pmatrix} x \\ -7 \end{pmatrix}$, $\mathbf{F}_2 = \begin{pmatrix} 3y \\ 2x \end{pmatrix}$, $\mathbf{F}_3 = \begin{pmatrix} -11 \\ y \end{pmatrix}$
   ii $\mathbf{F}_1 = \begin{pmatrix} y \\ 5 \end{pmatrix}$, $\mathbf{F}_2 = \begin{pmatrix} 3x \\ 4y \end{pmatrix}$, $\mathbf{F}_3 = \begin{pmatrix} -2 \\ 25x \end{pmatrix}$

4 A particle is in equilibrium under the action of the forces shown in the diagram. Find the magnitudes of $\mathbf{F}_1$ and $\mathbf{F}_2$, which are horizontal and vertical respectively.

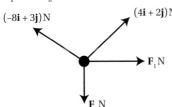

$(-8\mathbf{i} + 3\mathbf{j})\,\mathrm{N}$ $(4\mathbf{i} + 2\mathbf{j})\,\mathrm{N}$ $\mathbf{F}_1\,\mathrm{N}$ $\mathbf{F}_2\,\mathrm{N}$

5 A particle is acted on by three forces, $(3\mathbf{i} - 6\mathbf{j})\,\mathrm{N}$, $(-5\mathbf{i} + 2\mathbf{j})\,\mathrm{N}$ and $(x\mathbf{i} + y\mathbf{j})\,\mathrm{N}$. Given that the particle is in equilibrium, find the values of x and y.

6 The diagram shows a particle in equilibrium under the action of four forces. Find the values of a and b.

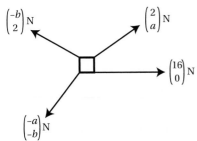

$\begin{pmatrix} -b \\ 2 \end{pmatrix}\mathrm{N}$ $\begin{pmatrix} 2 \\ a \end{pmatrix}\mathrm{N}$ $\begin{pmatrix} 16 \\ 0 \end{pmatrix}\mathrm{N}$ $\begin{pmatrix} -a \\ -b \end{pmatrix}\mathrm{N}$

7 A ball of mass 1.4 kg is attached to the floor and the ceiling by two light inextensible strings, as shown in the diagram.

21 N

$T\,\mathrm{N}$

Given that the ball is in equilibrium, find the value of T.

8 A crate rests on a rough horizontal floor. Two people are pulling the crate in opposite directions using two horizontal ropes. The tensions in the ropes are of 16 N and 28 N. Given that the crate is in equilibrium, find the magnitude of the friction force between the crate and the floor.

9 A particle rests on a smooth horizontal floor between two walls. It is attached to the wall on the right by a light inextensible string and the tension in this string is 63 N. It is attached to the wall on the left by a light inextensible string and a light rod. The tension in the string is 82 N. Both strings and the rod are horizontal.

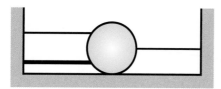

Find the force in the rod and state whether it is a tension or a thrust.

10 A ball of mass m kg is attached to the ceiling by two identical light, inextensible strings. The strings make equal angles with the horizontal. The force on the ceiling from the left string is $\begin{pmatrix} a \\ 7b \end{pmatrix}$ N. The force on the ceiling from the right string is $\begin{pmatrix} a-12 \\ 9b+7 \end{pmatrix}$ N.

Determine the values of a, b and m.

11 Two people are trying to move a heavy box lying at rest on a carpet, using two light inextensible ropes. The tensions in the ropes are $(32\mathbf{i} + 12\mathbf{j})$ N and $(25\mathbf{i} - 18\mathbf{j})$ N, where $\mathbf{i}$ and $\mathbf{j}$ point east and north respectively. The box remains at rest. Find the magnitude of the frictional force.

12 A particle is in equilibrium under the action of three forces shown in the diagram.

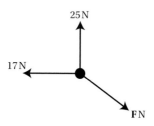

a Find the horizontal and vertical components of $\mathbf{F}$.

b Find the magnitude of $\mathbf{F}$ and the angle it makes with the horizontal.

Checklist of learning and understanding

- A force can start or stop the motion of an object, change the magnitude or the direction of its velocity. Force is a vector and its magnitude is measured in newtons ($1\,\mathrm{N} = 1\mathrm{kg\,m\,s^{-2}}$).
- Newton's first law states that an object remains at rest or continues to move with a constant velocity unless a force acts on it.
- Newton's second law states that the force required to produce a given acceleration is proportional to the acceleration and the mass of the object: $\mathbf{F} = m\mathbf{a}$. The acceleration is in the same direction as the force.
- If several forces are acting on an object, their combined effect is represented by the resultant force. This force is found by adding the vectors corresponding to all the original forces.
- The examples of forces you have met in this chapter are: driving force, braking force, resistance forces (including friction and air resistance), tension, thrust and weight. Whenever you draw a force diagram, you should consider which of these forces need to be included.
- The weight of an object is $W = mg$, where m is the object's mass and g is the gravitational acceleration (on the surface of the Earth $g \approx 9.8\,\mathrm{m\,s^{-2}}$). The mass of an object is fixed but its weight depends on its location in the universe.
- An object is in equilibrium if the resultant force is zero.
- When working with force vectors, you can consider horizontal and vertical components separately.

Mixed practice 21

1 A car moves on a straight horizontal road, under the action of a constant driving force of magnitude 1360 N. It accelerates from rest to the speed of 12.6 m s⁻¹ in 8 seconds.

    a Assuming that any resistance forces can be ignored, find the mass of the car.

    b How would your answer change if a resistance force were included?

2 A box of mass 13 kg slides across a rough horizontal floor with an initial speed of 2.6 m s⁻¹ and moves in a straight line. It comes to rest after it has travelled 3.7 m. Find the magnitude of the frictional force between the box and the floor.

3 A van of mass 1600 kg travels on a straight horizontal road under the action of a constant driving force of magnitude 2170 N. The total resistance force on the van is 865 N.

    a Find the acceleration of the van.

    b Given that the van starts from rest, find the time taken for it to travel 260 m.

4 **a** A box has weight 268 N. Find its mass.

    b The box is being pulled vertically upwards using a light inextensible rope and accelerates uniformly with $a = 0.9$ m s⁻². Find the tension in the rope.

    c The box is now lowered at a constant speed. Find the tension in the rope.

    d Explain how you have used the modelling assumption that the rope is:

       i light   **ii** inextensible.

5 A particle of mass 2.5 kg is in equilibrium under the action of three forces, $\mathbf{F}_1 = (6.3\mathbf{i} + 1.7\mathbf{j})$ N, $\mathbf{F}_2 = (-3.7\mathbf{i} + 2.1\mathbf{j})$ N and $\mathbf{F}_3 = (p\mathbf{i} + q\mathbf{j})$ N.

    a Find the values of p and q.

The force $\mathbf{F}_3$ is now removed.

    b Find, in vector form, the acceleration of the particle.

6 In the sport of curling, a heavy stone is projected in a straight line across a horizontal ice surface. A player projects a stone of mass 21 kg, and it comes to rest 14 s after the instant of projection, having travelled 32 m.

    a Calculate the deceleration of the stone.

    b Find the magnitude of the frictional force acting on the stone.

Elevate

For a reminder and more practice of questions like this that combine Newton's second law with the constant acceleration formulae, see Support sheet 21.

7 A car of mass 750 kg accelerates uniformly from 30 km h⁻¹ to 40 km h⁻¹ while travelling 200 m in a straight line. The resistance to the motion of the car has magnitude 380 N.

    a Find the magnitude of driving force.

The car now starts to brake with a braking force of 620 N. The resistance force remains unchanged.

    b How long does it take for the car to stop?

8 A box rests in equilibrium on a smooth horizontal floor. Four children pull the box using light inextensible ropes, all in the horizontal plane. The tensions in the ropes are shown in the diagram.

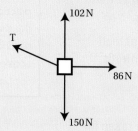

Find the magnitude of the force marked **T** and the angle it makes with the 102 N force.

9 A particle is in equilibrium under the action of the three forces shown in the diagram.

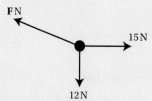

Find the magnitude of **F** and the angle it makes with the direction of the 15 N force.

10 Two horizontal forces **X** and **Y** act at a point O and are at right angles to each other. **X** has magnitude 12 N and acts along a bearing of 090°. **Y** has magnitude 15 N and acts along a bearing of 000°.

    i Calculate the magnitude and bearing of the resultant of **X** and **Y**.

    ii A third force **E** is now applied at O. The three forces **X**, **Y** and **E** are in equilibrium. State the magnitude of **E**, and give the bearing along which it acts.

© **OCR, AS GCE Mathematics, Paper 4728, January 2008**

11 A box of mass 24 kg is held in equilibrium in mid-air. It is supported by three light rigid rods, as shown in the diagram. All forces act in the vertical plane.

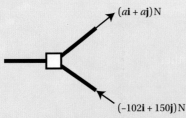

Find the magnitude of the force in the horizontal rod and determine whether it is a tension or a thrust.

12 **a** A particle of mass 4 kg moves on a smooth horizontal surface under the action of the three forces shown in the diagram. All three forces act in the horizontal plane.

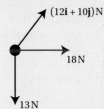

Find, in vector form, the acceleration of the particle.

b A fourth force is added so that now the particle moves with constant velocity. Find the magnitude of the new force and the angle it makes with the 18 N force.

13 A particle of mass 53 kg is attached to three light inextensible strings as shown in the diagram. The particle hangs in equilibrium in the vertical plane.

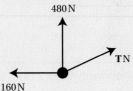

Find the magnitude and direction of **T**.

22 Objects in contact

In this chapter you will learn:

- that two objects always exert equal and opposite forces on each other (Newton's third law)
- how to calculate the contact force between two objects
- how to find the tension in a string or rod connecting two objects
- how to analyse the motion of particles connected by a string passing over a pulley.

Before you start...

Chapter 21	You should know how to find the resultant force and use it in Newton's second law.	1 A particle of mass 2.4 kg is acted upon by two horizontal forces, 25 N to the left and 32 N to the right. Find the acceleration of the particle.
Chapter 21	You should know how to calculate and use the weight of an object.	2 Find the weight of a box with mass 34 kg.
Chapter 21	You should know that if a particle is in equilibrium then the resultant force is zero.	3 The particle in the diagram is in equilibrium. Find the values of x and y.

Chapter 20	You should know how to use the constant acceleration formulae.	4 A particle accelerates uniformly from 2 m s^{-1} to 8 m s^{-1} while travelling 75 m in a straight line. a Find the acceleration. b How long does the journey take?

What is different about objects in contact?

In many situations, two objects are in contact or connected in some way. For example, several boxes stacked on top of each other, or a car pulling a trailer. There are contact forces acting between the objects that need to be taken into account. In this chapter you will meet the normal reaction force and use the tension/thrust force in a connecting string, cable or rod. You will also look at modelling assumptions relating to the type of contact or connection between the objects.

Another important force that exists when two surfaces are in contact is friction. You will learn more about it if you study the full A level course.

Section 1: Newton's third law

If you push against the wall, you can feel the wall 'pushing you back'. If you were standing on ice you would probably slide backwards, although you are pushing towards the wall, not away from it. What is the force that you feel? The answer is given by **Newton's third law**.

Key point 22.1

Newton's third law: If object A exerts a force on object B, then object B exerts a force on object A, with the same magnitude but opposite direction.

This means that whatever force you are exerting on the wall (which is directed towards the wall), the wall exerts a force on you. Since this force is away from the wall, this force stops you moving through the wall.

Newton's third law is commonly stated as: 'Each action has an equal and opposite reaction.' An important point to remember is that the two forces do **not** act on the same object so they do not cancel each other. It is a good idea to draw two separate force diagrams, one for each object.

force on wall　　　　force on man

WORKED EXAMPLE 22.1

Two skaters are standing on ice. They push against each other and start to move away from each other. Skater A, whose mass is 75 kg, moves with acceleration of $3.7\,\mathrm{m\,s^{-2}}$. Skater B's mass is 63 kg. Assuming that any frictional forces can be ignored, find the acceleration of skater B.

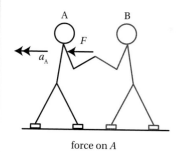

force on A

Draw two separate force diagrams. The force on each skater is away from the other one (i.e. backwards).

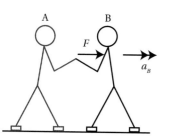

force on B

Continues on next page ...

Skater A:

$$F = m_A a_A$$

$$= 75 \times 3.7 = 277.5 \, \text{N}$$

According to Newton's third law, the two forces have equal magnitude. You can find this using Newton's second law for skater A.

Skater B:

$$277.5 = 63 a_B$$

$$\therefore \, a_B = 4.40 \, \text{m s}^{-2}$$

Now you can use Newton's second law for skater B.

EXERCISE 22A

1. Two bumper cars collide. Their masses are 265 kg and 280 kg. While the cars are in contact, the acceleration of the first car is $5.8 \, \text{m s}^{-2}$. Assuming any resistance forces can be ignored, find the acceleration of the second car.

2. Two skaters stand on ice facing each other. They push off each other and start to accelerate backwards. The mass of the first skater is 78 kg and his acceleration is $3.5 \, \text{m s}^{-2}$. The acceleration of the second skater is $4.2 \, \text{m s}^{-2}$. Find her mass.

3. Two robots with long extendible arms push against each other with a constant force of 215 N. They start next to each other, and slide away from each other in a straight line. The first robot has mass 120 kg and the friction force between its feet and the floor is 96 N. The second robot has mass 90 kg and the friction force between its feet and the floor is 65 N. How far are the robots from each other after 2 seconds?

4. Two skaters, of masses 52 kg and 68 kg, stand on ice facing each other and holding hands with their arms outstretched, 1.2 m apart. They pull towards each other so that the acceleration of the first skater is $0.4 \, \text{m s}^{-2}$.

   a Find the acceleration of the second skater.

   The skaters keep holding hands and pulling with the same force.

   b How long does it take for them to come together?

5. An apple of mass 120 g falls from the third floor window, 10 m above the ground.

   a Find the magnitude of the force with which the Earth attracts the apple.

   b How long does the apple take to fall the 10 metres?

   c State the magnitude of the force with which the apple attracts the Earth.

   d The mass of the Earth is 5.97×10^{24} kg. If no other forces acted on the Earth, how much would it move in the time it takes the apple to fall 10 m?

Section 2: Normal reaction force

Look at this book resting on your desk. You know that there is weight acting on it, so why is it not accelerating downwards? There must be another, upward force to make the net force zero. This force, exerted by the table on the book, is called the **normal reaction force**.

Key point 22.2

Whenever an object is in contact with a surface, the surface exerts a normal reaction force on it. This force acts in the direction perpendicular to the surface and away from it.

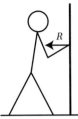 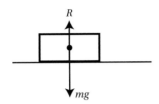 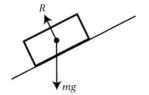 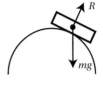

You need to include the normal reaction force, as well as the object's weight, on your force diagram.

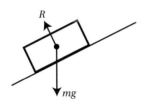

Did you know?

If an object is in contact with a curved surface, you can find the direction of the normal reaction force by calculating the gradient of the normal, as you learnt to do in Chapter 14, Section 1.

WORKED EXAMPLE 22.2

A person of mass 76 kg is standing in a lift. Find the magnitude of the normal reaction force exerted by the floor of the lift on the person when the lift is

a moving upwards with acceleration $2.6 \, \mathrm{m \, s^{-2}}$
b moving downwards with acceleration $2.6 \, \mathrm{m \, s^{-2}}$
c moving downwards with deceleration $2.6 \, \mathrm{m \, s^{-2}}$.

a

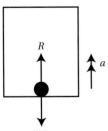

The forces acting on the person are the weight (down) and the normal reaction force (up).

The acceleration of the person is the same as the acceleration of the lift.

Since the lift is moving upwards, take the positive direction to be up.

Continues on next page ...

$F = ma$

$R - mg = ma$

$R - 76 \times 9.8 = 76 \times 2.6$

$\Rightarrow R = 942 \, \text{N}$

b

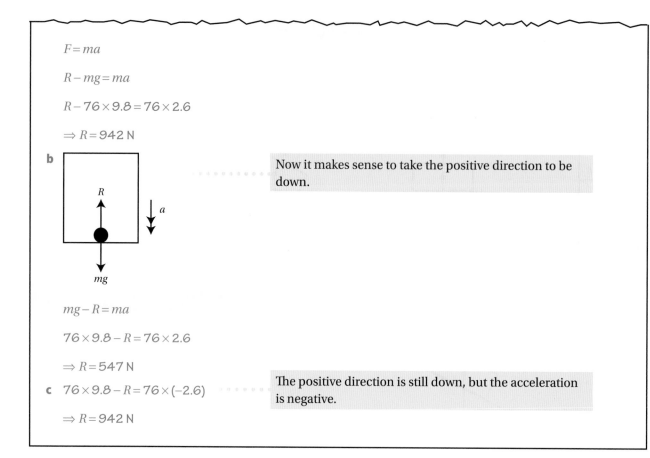

Now it makes sense to take the positive direction to be down.

$mg - R = ma$

$76 \times 9.8 - R = 76 \times 2.6$

$\Rightarrow R = 547 \, \text{N}$

c $76 \times 9.8 - R = 76 \times (-2.6)$

The positive direction is still down, but the acceleration is negative.

$\Rightarrow R = 942 \, \text{N}$

Notice that the normal reaction force is larger when the lift is accelerating upwards or decelerating downwards, than when it is accelerating downwards. Think about what you would feel if you were standing in the lift. If it is accelerating upwards, it feels as if the floor is pushing against your feet. But if it's accelerating downwards you feel as if the floor is moving away from you. This is because the normal reaction force in the two cases is different.

Be careful not to confuse normal reaction force with Newton's third law; a common misconception is that normal reaction is the 'reaction' to the object's weight. However, the weight and the normal reaction are both acting on the object itself, so they are not a Newton's third law pair. In the example of a book on the table, the reaction to the book's weight is the force with which the book acts on the Earth. The reaction to the normal reaction force is the downward force with which the book pushes the table.

WORKED EXAMPLE 22.3

A book of mass 260 g rests on a horizontal table of mass 65 kg. The table has four legs, and the thrust in each leg is the same. Assume that the table legs are light.

a Draw two separate diagrams showing the forces acting on the book and the table top.
b Find the thrust in each leg.
c State the magnitude and direction of the force exerted on the ground by the table top.

Continues on next page ...

a

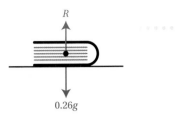

Forces on book

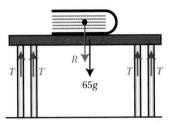

Forces on table top

In the diagrams, the Newton's third law pairs of forces are shown in the same colour.

The forces on the book are its weight and the normal reaction from the table top.

The forces on the table top are the table top's weight, normal reaction from the book and the thrusts in the legs.

b Forces on the book:

$0.26g = R$

Forces on the table top:

$65g + R = 4T$

$\Rightarrow 4T = 65g + 0.26g$

$\Rightarrow T = 160 \text{ N}$

Both the book and the table top are in equilibrium, so the net force on each must be zero. This means that forces up = forces down.

c The force on the ground from the table top equals $4T = 640$ N, directed downwards.

The force exerted on the ground by the table top has the same magnitude as the normal reaction on the table top from the ground.

In Worked example 22.3, the normal reaction force exerted by the table on the ground is equal to the total weight of the book and the table: the ground 'feels' the combined weight of the table and the book. However, this is only the case because all the objects are at rest.

If the table were being lifted using a cable attached to it, the normal reaction forces would change depending on the acceleration. You can write Newton's second law equations for both the book and the table, keeping in mind that they have the same acceleration.

WORKED EXAMPLE 22.4

A book of mass 260 g rests on a horizontal table of mass 65 kg. The table is being lifted by a cable attached to it and accelerates upwards. The tension in the cable is 710 N. Find the normal reaction force between the book and the table.

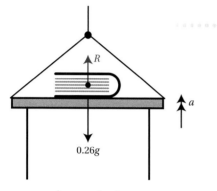

forces on book

Draw separate force diagrams for the book and the table.

Forces on the book are its weight and the normal reaction.

Forces on the table are its weight, normal reaction and the tension in the cable.

The book is not attached to the cable, so the tension does not act on it directly.

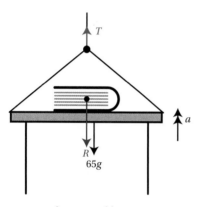

forces on table

Table: $65a = 710 - 65g - R$

Book: $0.26a = R - 0.26g$

$65.26a = 710 - 65g - 0.26g$

$65.26a = 70.452$

$a = 1.08\ \text{m s}^{-2}$

$R = 0.26a + 0.26g$

$R = 2.83\ \text{N}$

Newton's second law for each object: the positive direction is upwards.

You have two simultaneous equations. You may be able to solve them on the calculator. Otherwise it's easiest to find a by adding the two equations and then substitute it back to find R.

Notice that the equation you got for acceleration in Worked example 22.4 can be written as $65.26a = 710 - 65.26g$. This is the same equation you would get if you considered the table and the book as a single object with mass 65.26 kg (which is the combined mass of the table and the book) being pulled up using the tension of 710 N. The normal reaction forces do not appear in this equation.

Key point 22.3

When two objects are in contact and moving with the same acceleration, you can consider them as a single particle. Newton's second law, $\mathbf{F} = m\mathbf{a}$, applies with m being the combined mass of the two objects and $\mathbf{F}$ being the resultant of all the external forces.

Tip

'External force' excludes any forces acting between the two objects. So, for example, the normal reaction forces should not be included in the resultant force.

WORKED EXAMPLE 22.5

A person of mass 72 kg stands in a lift of mass 540 kg. The lift is supported by a cable that can be modelled as light and inextensible.

a Draw two diagrams showing all the forces acting on the person and the lift.

The lift is moving downwards and decelerating at $2.1\,\mathrm{m\,s^{-2}}$.

b Find the tension in the cable.

c Find the magnitude of the normal reaction force exerted on the person by the floor of the lift.

a

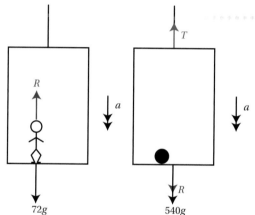

forces on person   forces on the lift

The forces on the person are weight and normal reaction.

The forces on the lift are its weight, tension (T) and normal reaction.

According to Newton's third law, the two normal reactions have equal magnitudes but opposite directions.

b Newton's second law for the two objects together:

$$612 \times (-2.1) = 612g - T$$

$$T = 7280\,\mathrm{N}$$

To find the tension, which is an external force on the system, you can treat the lift and the person as a single object of mass $540 + 72 = 612$ kg.

The two normal reaction forces are not included.

Take the positive direction to be downwards, so the acceleration is negative.

c For the person:

$$72 \times (-2.1) = 72g - R$$

$$R = 857\,\mathrm{N}$$

To find the normal reaction force consider only the forces acting on the person. However, the acceleration is the same as for the whole system.

If you want to find the contact force, you need to consider each object separately.

EXERCISE 22B

1 For each situation draw a separate force diagram for each object.

   a i A book of mass 300 g rests on a table of mass 18 kg. The table is on the floor.

     ii A book of mass 120 g rests on a shelf of mass 25 kg. The shelf is on the floor.

   b i A box of mass 2 kg rests on a table of mass 12 kg. A vertical cable is attached to the table and the tension in the cable is 15 N. The table is not in contact with the floor.

     ii A box of mass 5 kg rests on top of a crate of mass 20 kg. The crate is suspended by a vertical cable. The tension in the cable is T.

   c i A person of mass 65 kg stands in a lift of mass 200 kg. The lift is suspended by a cable and the tension in the cable is T.

     ii A person of mass 80 kg stands in a lift of mass 200 kg. The lift is suspended by a cable and the tension in the cable is 2800 N.

   d i A box of mass 12 kg is suspended by a string from the ceiling of a lift of mass 400 kg. The lift is suspended by a vertical cable.

     ii A box of mass 15 kg is suspended by a string from the ceiling of a lift of mass 350 kg. The lift is suspended by a vertical cable.

2 Each diagram shows an object of mass 10 kg resting on a platform. The platform is moving in the direction shown by a single arrow, with acceleration shown by a double arrow. Find the magnitude of the normal reaction force exerted on the object by the platform.

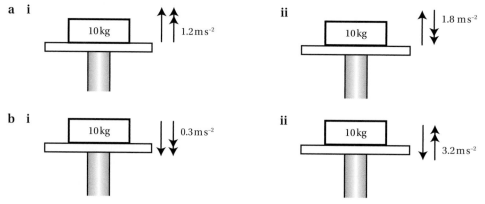

3 A book of mass 0.6 kg rests on a horizontal table. A child pushes down on the book with a force of 12 N. Find the magnitude of the normal reaction force between the book and the table.

4 A box of mass 15 kg rests on horizontal ground. The box is attached to a vertical cable that can be modelled as light and inextensible. The magnitude of the normal reaction force between the box and the ground is 68 N. Find the tension in the cable.

5 A crate of mass 120 kg lies on the horizontal floor of a lift. The lift accelerates upwards at 0.4 m s⁻². Find the magnitude of the normal reaction force between the crate and the floor of the lift.

6 A basket of mass 750 grams is attached to a light inextensible rope and is being lowered at a constant speed. A box of mass 120 grams rests at the bottom of the basket. Find the magnitude of the normal reaction force between the box and the basket.

7 A horizontal plank of mass 27 kg rests on two light vertical supports. A box rests on top of the plank. The thrust in each support is 186 N.

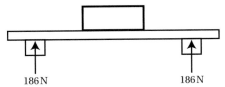

Find the mass of the box.

8 A child of mass 35 kg stands in a lift of mass 500 kg. The lift is suspended by a light inextensible cable and accelerates upwards at 0.6 m s⁻². Find:

  a the tension in the cable

  b the magnitude of the normal reaction force between the child's feet and the floor of the lift.

9 A person of mass 85 kg stands in a lift of mass 360 kg. The lift is suspended by a light inextensible cable. Find the magnitude of the normal reaction force between the person's feet and the floor of the lift when the lift is:

  a moving downwards and decelerating at 4.2 m s⁻²

  b moving upwards at a constant speed.

10 A lift of mass 520 kg is supported by a steel rod attached to its bottom. The rod can withstand the maximum thrust 15 400 N. The lift can accelerate at 2.5 m s⁻² and decelerate at 7.8 m s⁻². Find the maximum allowed load in the lift.

11 A woman of mass 63 kg stands in a lift of mass 486 kg. The lift is supported by a cable and moves with acceleration 2.2 m s⁻². The magnitude of the normal reaction force between the woman's feet and the floor of the lift is 756 N.

  a Is the lift going up or down?

  b Find the tension in the cable.

Section 3: Further equilibrium problems

In Chapter 21 you met the idea of equilibrium, where all the forces on an object balance. When the object is in contact with a surface you need to include a normal reaction force in the calculations.

WORKED EXAMPLE 22.6

A box of mass 16 kg rests on a smooth horizontal table. Four light inextensible strings are attached to the box. The tensions in the string are 12 N, 23 N, 18 N, and T N, as shown in the diagram.

Given that the box is in equilibrium, find:

a the value of T

b the magnitude of the normal reaction force between the box and the table.

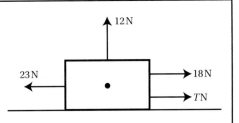

Continues on next page ...

a Horizontal components:

$$18 + T - 23 = 0$$

$$\Rightarrow T = 5$$

> All the horizontal forces add up to zero. The components to the right are taken as positive and those to the left as negative.

b Vertical components:

$$12 + R - 16g = 0$$

$$\Rightarrow R = 16g - 12 = 145\,\text{N}$$

> Forces in the vertical direction are tension, weight and normal reaction.
>
> All the vertical forces add up to zero. The components upwards are taken as positive.

The normal reaction force only acts as long as the object is in contact with the surface. When there is another force pulling the object away from the surface the normal reaction force will decrease. If it reaches zero then the object is no longer in contact with the surface.

WORKED EXAMPLE 22.7

A book of mass 320 g rests on a horizontal table. A girl pushes vertically down on the book with a force of 8.2 N. The book is attached to a light inextensible string, and a boy pulls the string vertically upwards so that the tension in the string is T N.

a Express the normal reaction force in terms of T.
b Find the smallest value of T required to lift the book off the table.
c Find the acceleration of the book when $T = 12$.

a

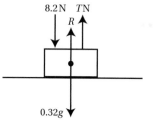

> The forces on the book are: its weight, the normal reaction force, the tension and the pushing force of 8.2 N.

$$mg + 8.2 - R - T = 0$$

$$\therefore R = 3.136 + 8.2 - T$$

$$= 11.336 - T$$

> When the book is equilibrium, the resultant force is zero. Write the equation taking the positive direction to be down.

b $11.336 - T = 0$

$$\Leftrightarrow T = 11.3$$

> The normal reaction force cannot be negative. The book will leave the table when $R = 0$.

Continues on next page ...

c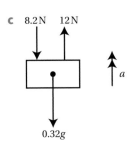

Since $T > 11.3$ the book is no longer in contact with the table so $R = 0$.
The equilibrium is broken and the book has upward acceleration.

$F = ma$ with the positive direction upwards:

$0.32a = 12 - 0.32g - 8.2$

$0.32a = 0.664$

$a = 2.08 \, m \, s^{-2}$

Remember that the normal reaction force does not need to act in a vertical direction. It is always perpendicular to the contact surface, and acting away from it.

WORKED EXAMPLE 22.8

A box of mass 1.2 kg is pushed against a rough vertical wall with a force of 40 N and rests in equilibrium. Find:

a   the normal reaction force between the box and the wall
b   the magnitude and direction of the friction force between the box and the wall.

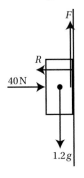

The forces on the box are its weight, the pushing force, the normal reaction force (away from the wall) and the friction force (up along the wall, stopping the box from slipping downwards).

a Horizontally: $R = 40 \, N$

Write equilibrium equations for horizontal and vertical directions separately.

b Vertically: $F = 1.2g$

$= 11.8 \, N \, upwards$

⏭ Fast forward

🅐 In Student Book 2 you will find out how the magnitude of the friction force is related to the normal reaction.

EXERCISE 22C

1. A crate of mass 150 kg rests on a horizontal floor. A vertical cable is attached to the crate and the tension in the cable is 820 N. Find the normal reaction force between the crate and the floor.

2. A box of mass 68 kg rests in equilibrium on a horizontal table under the action of three forces shown in the diagram.

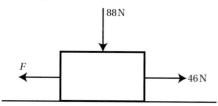

Find the value of F and the magnitude of the normal reaction force.

3. A box rests in equilibrium on a horizontal table. The mass of the box is 16 kg and the mass of the table top is 86 kg. The table is supported by four light legs, as shown in the diagram.

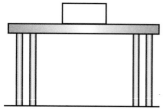

Find the thrust in each leg, assuming they are all the same.

4. A book of mass 320 g rests in equilibrium on a horizontal table. Find the magnitude of the normal reaction force between the book and the table in each situation.

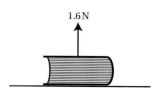

   a A light inextensible string is attached to the book, as shown in the diagram. The string is vertical and the tension in the string is 1.6 N.

   b The string is now removed and a girl pushes vertically down on the book with a force of 8.2 N.

5. A ball of mass 6.5 kg is suspended by a vertical string and is in contact with a horizontal table. The string can be modelled as light and inextensible.

   a Find the magnitude of the normal reaction force between the ball and the table when the tension in the string is 38 N.

   b Find the minimum tension force required to lift the ball off the table.

6. Blocks A, B and C, of masses 13 kg, 21 kg and 18 kg, are stacked on top of each other, as shown in the diagram. A light inextensible string is attached to block C and the system is in equilibrium.

   The magnitude of the normal reaction force between blocks A and B is 260 N. Find the tension in the string and the magnitude of the normal reaction force between blocks B and C.

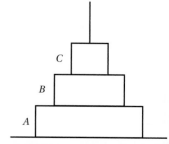

7 A small box of mass 1.2 kg is held in equilibrium between two rough planks. The planks are vertical and the friction forces between the box and the two planks are equal. Each plank is held in position by a horizontal force of magnitude 140 N.

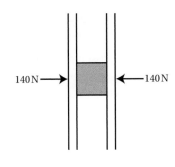

Find:

a the magnitude of friction force between each plank and the box

b the normal reaction force between each plank and the box.

8 A box of mass 34 kg rests in equilibrium on a rough horizontal floor. A light inextensible string is attached to the box as shown in the diagram.

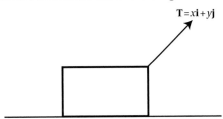

T = xi + yj

The friction force has magnitude 220 N and the magnitude of the normal reaction force is 180 N. Find the magnitude of the tension in the string.

Section 4: Connected particles

In Chapter 21, Section 2, you looked at examples of objects being pulled using a rope or a stick, and you saw that one of the forces acting on the object is tension. When two objects are connected by a taut rope or string then the tension acts on both of them. The magnitude of the tension is the same at both of its ends. However, the directions at the two ends are different, because the tension acts away from the object that is attached to its end.

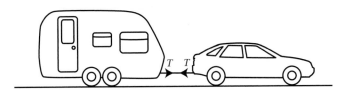

If the rope is inextensible, the connected objects will move with the same speed and the same acceleration. Any external forces, such as driving or resistance forces, can be different for each object. Remember that, to find the acceleration, you can consider them as a single object and not include the connecting tension forces.

Two main modelling assumptions have been made here, and it is important that you know what specific effect each has.

> **Tip**
>
> The term string is used for anything that transmits tension but not compression forces, such as a rope, wire, cable, chain.
>
> The term rod is used for an object that transmits tension and compression forces, such as a tow bar or plank. A rod cannot stretch or compress itself (it is rigid).

🔑 Key point 22.4

Modelling assumptions about a string connecting two particles:

Assumption	What it means	How it is used
Inextensible	The string cannot stretch, e.g. not an elastic band or spring.	The magnitude of the acceleration and velocity of each connected particle is the same (if the string is taut).
Light	The string has a mass that is negligible in the context of the system.	1 When treating the whole system as a single particle the mass of the string is ignored. 2 In vertical systems the tension of the string is the same throughout. This is because lower parts do not 'pull' on upper parts.

WORKED EXAMPLE 22.9

A car of mass 780 kg is pulling a trailer of mass 560 kg using a light, inextensible cable. The driving force on the car is constant and has magnitude 1800 N. The total resistance forces on the car and the trailer are 800 N and 600 N, respectively.

a Find the acceleration of the car.
b Find the tension in the cable.
c Explain how you used the assumption that the cable is:
    i light   **ii** inextensible.

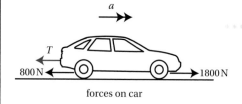

forces on car

Draw separate force diagrams for the car and the trailer. The tension is the same magnitude at both ends of the cable, and both the car and the trailer have the same acceleration.
The driving force acts on the car only.

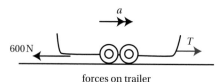

forces on trailer

a For car and trailer together ($m = 1340$ kg):

$$1340a = 1800 - 800 - 600$$

$$a = 0.299 \text{ m s}^{-2}$$

Write $F = ma$ for the combined object, taking into account only the external forces.

b For the trailer:

$$560 \times 0.299 = T - 600$$

$$T = 767 \text{ N}$$

To find the tension you need to consider each object separately. You can choose which equation to use. Here the trailer equation is used, as there are fewer forces to include.

Continues on next page ...

c i The mass of the cable wasn't included in the total mass of the two objects.

'Light' means that you can ignore the mass of the cable.

ii The car and the trailer have the same acceleration.

If the cable could stretch, the two ends could have different accelerations.

What would happen in Worked example 22.9 if the car started to brake? The braking force is acting on the car only, so there is nothing to slow down the trailer. The cable would go slack and the trailer would get closer to the car. This is why for towing we use rigid objects such as a tow bar, which can exert thrust as well as tension.

WORKED EXAMPLE 22.10

A trailer is attached to a car by a light tow bar. The mass of the trailer is 350 kg and the mass of the car is 680 kg. The car starts to brake and decelerates at 4.6 m s^{-2}. Assuming all other resistance forces can be ignored, find the thrust in the tow bar.

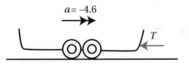

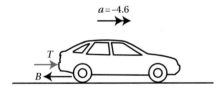

Draw a separate force diagram for each object. The thrust force is directed towards the object. The braking force acts on the car only.

car: $T - B = 680 \times (-4.6)$

trailer: $-T = 350 \times (-4.6)$

Since you want to find the connecting thrust force between the two objects, write separate $F = ma$ equations for each. The acceleration is negative.

$T = 1610 \text{ N}$

You only need the second equation to find T.

WORK IT OUT 22.1

Particles P and Q, of masses 0.6 kg and 0.4 kg, are connected by a light inextensible string. The particles are initially at rest on horizontal ground and the string is taut. A force of magnitude 15 N starts acting on P, in the direction away from Q. The friction force between P and the ground is 2 N and the contact between Q and the ground is smooth. Find the acceleration of the two particles.

Continues on next page ...

Decide whether each solution is correct or not. Can you identify the errors made in the incorrect solutions?

Solution 1	Solution 2	Solution 3
Considering P and Q as a single particle: $m = 1$ kg	Considering P and Q as a single particle: $m = 1$ kg	For P:
		$0.6a = 15 - T - 2$
$1a = 15 - T - 2$	$1a = 15 - 2$	
Forces on Q:	$a = 13 \,\mathrm{m\,s^{-2}}$	For Q:
$0.4a = T$		$0.4a = T$
So: $1a = 15 - 0.4a - 2$		So: $0.6a = 15 - 0.4a - 2$
$1.4a = 13$		$a = 13 \,\mathrm{m\,s^{-2}}$
$a = 9.3 \,\mathrm{m\,s^{-2}}$		

EXERCISE 22D

1 A car of mass 750 kg is towing a trailer of mass 350 kg. The driving force on the car has magnitude 15 kN. The resistance forces on the car and the trailer are 600 N and 400 N, respectively. Find:

   a the acceleration of the car and the trailer

   b the tension in the tow bar.

2 Particle P of mass 4.5 kg is being pulled by a light inextensible string. Another light inextensible string is attached to the other side of P and particle Q, of mass 6 kg, is attached to the other end of this string. The particles move with acceleration 2.1 m s^{-2} in a straight line on a smooth horizontal table.

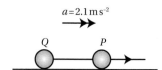

   Find the tension in each string.

3 Two identical boxes, each of mass 10 kg, are connected by a light inextensible cable. One box is pushed away from the other one with a force of 75 N. The boxes move in a straight line at constant velocity on a rough horizontal table. Find the magnitude of the friction force between each box and the table.

4 A car of mass 1200 kg is towing a trailer of mass 400 kg using a light tow bar. The resistance forces acting on the car and the trailer are 500 N and 300 N, respectively. The car starts to brake and decelerates at 1.2 m s^{-2}. Find the magnitude of the braking force.

5 A box of mass 24 kg is pulled across a rough horizontal floor with a force of F N. The friction force between this box and the floor is 80 N. Another box, of mass 15 kg, is attached to the first box by a light inextensible string. The friction force between the second box and the floor is 50 N.

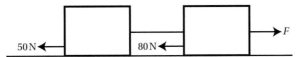

a The string connecting the two boxes will break if the tension exceeds 120 N. Find the largest possible value of F.

b The string breaks when the boxes are moving with a speed of 2.4 m s⁻¹. Assuming the two boxes do not collide, how long does it take for the second box to stop?

6 A crate of mass 35 kg is suspended by a light inextensible cable. Another crate, of mass 50 kg, is attached to the bottom of the first crate by another light inextensible cable. Find the tensions in the two cables when the crates are:

a being raised with acceleration 0.8 m s⁻²

b being lowered at constant speed.

7 A train is made up of a locomotive of mass 4500 kg and two carriages of mass 2500 kg each. The train is accelerating at 0.9 m s⁻². The resistance force acting on the locomotive is 1200 N and the resistance force acting on each carriage is 500 N. Find:

a the driving force on the locomotive

b the tension in each coupling.

8 A train consists of a locomotive of mass 4000 kg and two carriages of mass 2000 kg each. The train is decelerating at 2 m s⁻². The resistance forces are: 9000 N on the locomotive, 6000 N on the first carriage and 3000 N on the second carriage.

a Determine whether the locomotive is driving or braking.

b Find the magnitude of the force in each coupling, stating whether it is a tension or a thrust.

Section 5: Pulleys

A rope or string connecting two objects doesn't need to be straight. For example, you could be using a rope passing over a pulley to lift a crate.

As before, if the string is inextensible then the magnitude of acceleration of both objects will be the same. If the pulley has some mass, or if there is friction between the pulley and the axis it rotates around, then the magnitude of the tension will not be the same at both ends of the string. However, if you make some further modelling assumptions then the tension is the same throughout the string.

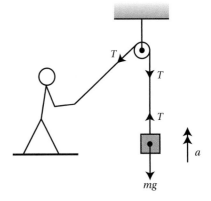

🔑 Key point 22.5

Modelling assumptions for a pulley:

Assumption	What it means	How it is used
Smooth	There is no friction between the pulley and its axis.	The tension in the string is the same on both sides of the pulley.
Light	The mass of the pulley can be ignored.	

💡 Tip

Note that there must be some friction between the pulley and the string – otherwise the string would be slipping over the pulley.

The presence of a smooth, light pulley doesn't alter the method used for connected particles in the previous section.

WORKED EXAMPLE 22.11

A crate of mass 52 kg is attached to a light rope hanging over the edge of a wall and passing over a smooth pulley. A man pulls the other end of the rope, keeping it horizontal. The crate is moving upwards with acceleration 0.3 m s^{-2}. Find the tension in the rope.

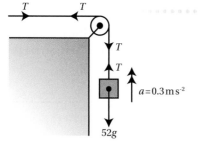

Draw a diagram showing all the forces.

crate: $T - 52g = 52 \times 0.3$

$\Rightarrow T = 525 \text{ N}$

Write the force equation for the crate, taking the positive direction to be up.

A string could also be passed over a fixed peg instead of a pulley. If the peg is smooth (so that the string slides freely over it) the tension on either side of the peg will have the same magnitude.

WORKED EXAMPLE 22.12

A box of mass 12 kg rests on a rough horizontal table. It is attached to one end of a light inextensible string that passes over a smooth peg. The other end of the string is attached to a small object of mass 4.8 kg, as shown in the diagram. Given that the system is in equilibrium, find the magnitude of the frictional force between the box and the table.

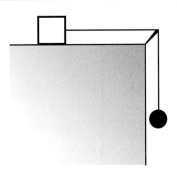

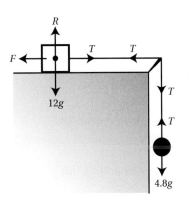

Draw a diagram showing forces acting on each object.

Since the peg is smooth, the tension force is the same on either side.

Ball: $4.8g = T \Rightarrow T = 47.04$ N

Box, horizontally: $F = T$

Because the system is in equilibrium, the net force on each object is zero.

The magnitude of the frictional force is 47.04 N.

You can also say that $R = 12g = 117.6$ N, but this is not required in the question.

You should remember that the tension in a rope or string exists only as long as it is taut. Once a string goes slack the tension force becomes zero.

WORKED EXAMPLE 22.13

Particles P and Q are connected by a light inextensible string passing over a smooth pulley. The mass of P is 2.3 kg and the mass of Q is 3.1 kg. Initially Q is held at rest 80 cm above the floor and P is 0.9 m below the pulley.

The particles are released from rest and the system moves freely under gravity.

a   Find the speed of Q when it reaches the ground.

Once Q reaches the ground, P continues to move upwards.

Continues on next page ...

b Find the time it takes P to reach the pulley from the moment it is first released.

a

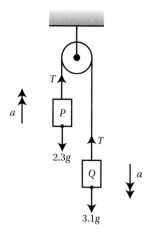

To find the speed of Q you need to know its acceleration. Draw a force diagram for each particle.

$P: T - 2.3g = 2.3a$

$Q: 3.1g - T = 3.1a$

Write an equation for each particle, taking the positive direction to be its direction of motion.

$\quad 0.8g = 5.4a$

$\Rightarrow a = 1.45 \, \text{m s}^{-2}$

You only want to find a, so eliminate T by adding the two equations.

$u = 0$

$a = 1.45$

$s = 0.8$

$v = ?$

You need the final speed given the initial speed, acceleration and distance.

$v^2 = u^2 + 2as$

$\quad = 0 + 2(1.45)(0.8) = 2.32$

$v = \sqrt{2.32} = 1.52 \, \text{m s}^{-1}$

b

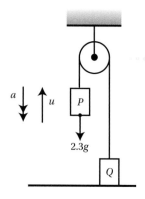

Once Q is on the ground there is no more tension in the string, so the only force acting on P is its weight. This means that its acceleration is g downwards. However, P has an upward speed (equal to the speed Q had when it hit the ground), so it will continue to move upwards for a while. It will reach the pulley before stopping and falling down again.

$u = 1.52$

$s = 0.1$

$a = -9.8$

P has moved 0.8 m from its initial position, so it is now 0.1 m from the pulley. Its speed is 1.52 m s^{-1} upwards.

Continues on next page ...

$t = ?$

$s = ut + \frac{1}{2}at^2$

$0.1 = 1.52t - 4.9t^2$

$4.9t^2 - 1.52t + 0.1 = 0$ ··········· This is a quadratic equation for t.

$t = 0.0947$ or 0.216

P reaches the pulley 0.0947 seconds after Q hits the ground. ···· *P* is moving freely under gravity so it will pass the pulley twice, once on the way up and once on the way down. You want the first of the two times.

Time taken for Q to reach the ground: ···· You need to add the time it took for *Q* to reach the ground. To do this, you need to use the information from part **a**.

$u = 0$

$a = 1.45$

$v = 1.52$

$t = ?$

$v = u + at$

$1.52 = 0 + 1.45t$

$\Rightarrow t = 1.05$

Total time taken for P to reach the pulley:

$t = 1.05 + 0.0947 = 1.14\text{ s}$

EXERCISE 22E

1 A man is holding a crate of mass 76 kg using a light inextensible rope passing over a smooth pulley.

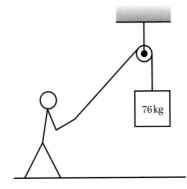

76 kg

Elevate

For more examples and further practice with pulleys see Support sheet 22.

Given that the crate is in equilibrium, find the magnitude of the force exerted by the man on the rope.

2 Two particles of masses 5 kg and 7 kg are connected by a light inextensible string that passes over a fixed smooth pulley. The system is released from rest with both ends of the string vertical and taut. Find the acceleration of each particle and the tension in the string.

3 Box A, of mass 15 kg, rests on a rough horizontal table. It is connected to one end of a light inextensible string which passes over a fixed smooth peg. Box B, of mass 6 kg, is attached to the other end of the string.

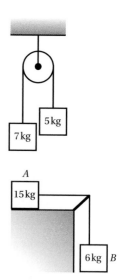

    a Given that the system is in equilibrium, find the magnitude of the frictional force between box A and the table.

    b Given instead that the contact between box A and the table is smooth, find the acceleration of the system and the tension in the string.

4 A box of mass 7 kg lies on a smooth horizontal table. It is attached to one end of a light inextensible string, which passes over a smooth pulley placed at the edge of the table. A ball hangs on the other end of the string. The system is released from rest with the string taut and the ball starts to move downwards. The tension in the string is 18.2 N. Find the mass of the ball.

5 Two particles have masses m and km, with $k > 1$. The particles are connected by a light inextensible string passing over a smooth pulley. The system is released from rest and the particles move with acceleration $\frac{2}{3}g$. Find the value of k.

6 A particle of mass 4 kg is attached by light inextensible strings to two other particles of masses 7 kg and 5 kg. The string connecting the 4 kg particle to the 7 kg particle passes over a smooth pulley, as shown in the diagram.

The particle of mass 7 kg is attached to the floor by another light inextensible string.

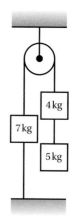

    a Given that the system is in equilibrium, find the tension in the string connecting the 7 kg particle to the floor.

    b This string is now removed. Find the acceleration of the system.

7 A crate is held in equilibrium by a light inextensible rope. The rope passes over a smooth peg. The other end of the rope is attached to a wall, as shown in the diagram. The force exerted by the rope on the wall is $(15\mathbf{i} + 86\mathbf{j})$ N. Find the mass of the crate.

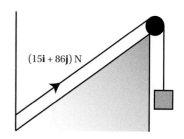

8 Particle P, of mass 8.5 kg, is attached to one end of a light inextensible string and rests on a rough horizontal table. The string passes over a smooth light pulley. Particle Q, of mass m kg, is attached to the other end of the string and hangs with the string vertical. When the system is in equilibrium, the force exerted by the string on particle P is $\mathbf{T} = (15\mathbf{i} + 12\mathbf{j})$ N.

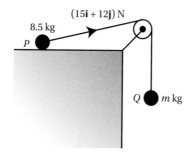

a Find the magnitude of **T**. Hence find the value of m.

b Find the magnitude of:

  i the normal reaction force

  ii the frictional force between P and the table.

9 A small box of mass 6 kg rests on a smooth horizontal table. It is attached to one end of a light inextensible string which passes over a smooth pulley at the edge of the table. The other end of the string is attached to a particle of mass 3.5 kg, which hangs with the string vertical. The system is held in equilibrium by a force $\mathbf{F} = (p\mathbf{i} + q\mathbf{j})$ N, as shown in the diagram.

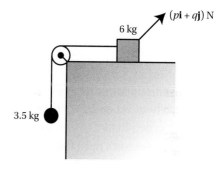

The normal reaction exerted on the box by the table is 28 N. Find the magnitude of **F**.

10 Particles P and Q, of masses 0.8 kg and m_Q kg, are connected by a light inextensible string passing over a smooth pulley. The particles are held at rest, both 2 m above the floor, with the string taut. The particles are more than 2 m below the pulley. When the system is released from rest, it takes the heavier particle 1.6 seconds to reach the floor. Find the two possible values of m_Q.

11 The diagram shows a tape passing over a fixed smooth pulley. One end of the tape is fixed to the ceiling and the other is attached to a box of mass 3 kg. A smooth cylinder of mass 8 kg is placed in a loop formed by the tape.

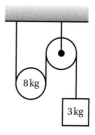

The system is released from rest and the cylinder starts to accelerate downwards.

a The cylinder moves downwards a distance x. How far upwards does the box move in that time?

b The acceleration of the cylinder is a. Write down an expression, in terms of a, for the acceleration of the box.

c Find the tension in the tape.

12 A box of mass 10 kg rests on a rough horizontal table. It is attached to two other boxes, of masses 10 kg and M kg, by two light inextensible strings. Each string passes over a smooth pulley, as shown in the diagram.

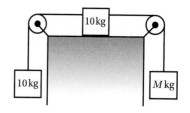

The system is in equilibrium. Given that the maximum possible magnitude of the friction force between the box and the table is 49 N, find the range of possible values of M.

13 Discuss which of the modelling assumptions for connected particles hold in the following situations:

   a   Two cars colliding and one pushing the other a further 5 m.

   b   A steel chain being used to lift a chair.

   c   A steel chain being used to lift a car.

   d   A pendulum hanging on an old clock.

   e   A water-skier being pulled by a boat.

   f   A glass-blower shaping a bottle between two pliers.

   g   A caravan being towed by a car.

   h   A steel cable hanging between supports on a bridge.

Checklist of learning and understanding

- Newton's third law states that if object A exerts a force on object B, then object B exerts a force on object A, with the same magnitude but opposite direction.
- Whenever an object is in contact with a surface, the surface exerts a normal reaction force. This force is perpendicular to the surface and directed away from it.
  - Newton's third law implies that when two objects are in contact, each object exerts a normal reaction force on the other one.
- If two objects are connected by a light taut string then the tension is the same throughout the string.
  - The tension at the point where the string is attached to an object is directed away from the object.
  - If the string is inextensible, the two objects have the same acceleration.
  - If the string passes over a light smooth pulley, or a fixed smooth peg, the tension is the same on either side of the pulley/peg.
- If the string is replaced by a light rod, then the force can be a thrust as well as a tension. The thrust force is directed towards the object.
- Two connected objects move with the same acceleration and same speed.
  - To find the acceleration you can treat them as a single particle, but to find the normal reaction or tension force you need to consider each object separately.

Mixed practice 22

1 Two skaters, of masses 58 kg and M kg, stand facing each other on ice. They push away from each other and move with initial accelerations of 3.6 m s⁻² and 4.1 m s⁻². Find the value of M.

2 A car of mass 850 kg is pulling a trailer of mass 320 kg. The driving force on the car has magnitude 1800 N. The resistance forces acting on the car and the trailer are 450 N and 220 N, respectively. Find:

a the acceleration of the car

b the tension in the tow bar.

3 A crate of mass 80 kg lies on a horizontal platform. The platform is being raised and decelerates at 2.6 m s⁻². Find the magnitude of the normal reaction force between the crate and the platform.

4 A book of mass 310 g lies on a rough horizontal table. A light inextensible string is attached to the book. The string passes over a smooth pulley fixed at the edge of the table. A ball of mass 120 g is attached to the other end of the string.

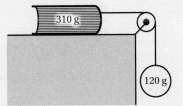

The system is in equilibrium with the string taut. Find the magnitude of the friction force between the book and the table.

5 Two balls are connected and suspended from the ceiling by two light inextensible strings, as shown in the diagram.

Given that both balls have mass 3 kg, find the tension in each string.

6 A man of mass 70 kg stands on the floor of a lift which is moving with an upward acceleration of 0.3 m s⁻². Calculate the magnitude of the force exerted by the floor on the man.

© OCR, AS GCE Mathematics, Paper 4728, January 2008

7 A car is pulling a trailer using a light rigid tow bar. The mass of the car is 1200 kg and the mass of the trailer is 350 kg. Assume that any resistances to motion can be ignored.

  a The car is moving with a speed of 9.2 m s⁻¹ when it starts to accelerate at 1.8 m s⁻². Find the driving force acting on the car.

  b The car continues to accelerate uniformly for 4 seconds. It then starts to brake, with uniform deceleration, until it comes to rest. During the braking phase, it travels 26 m. Find the magnitude of the thrust in the tow bar during the braking phase.

8 A person of mass 75 kg stands in a lift of mass 450 kg. The lift is suspended by a light inextensible cable and moving downwards.

  a The lift is decelerating at 5.2 m s⁻². Find the normal reaction force between the person's feet and the floor of the lift.

  b Given instead that the normal reaction force between the person's feet and the floor of the lift is 577.5 N:

   i find the magnitude and direction of the acceleration of the lift

   ii calculate the tension in the cable.

9 Two skaters stand on ice 5 m from each other, holding onto the ends of a light inextensible rope. They pull at the rope with a constant force and come together in 1.5 seconds. Any friction can be ignored. Given that the mass of the first skater is 62 kg, and that he moves with acceleration 1.8 m s⁻², find the mass of the second skater.

10 In the diagram the three strings can be modelled as light and inextensible and the pulley can be modelled as smooth. The masses of the balls are 5.2 kg, 3.7 kg and m kg. The system hangs in equilibrium in the vertical plane.

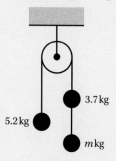

  a Find the value of m.

  b Find the tension in each string.

11 A particle of mass 12 kg rests in equilibrium on a rough horizontal table, under the action of two forces, $\mathbf{F}_1 = (16\mathbf{i} + 7\mathbf{j})$ N and $\mathbf{F}_2$, as shown in the diagram.

The magnitude of the normal reaction force between the particle and the table is 72 N and the magnitude of the friction force is 9 N. Find the two possible values for the magnitude of $\mathbf{F}_2$.

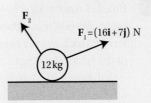

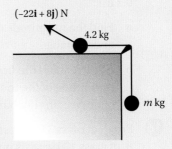

12 A particle of mass 4.2 kg rests on a rough horizontal table. The magnitude of the frictional force between the particle and the table is 4N. The particle is attached to one end of a light inextensible string which passes over a smooth peg at the edge of the table. Another particle, of mass m kg, is attached to the other end of the string. The system is held in equilibrium by a force $(-22\mathbf{i} + 8\mathbf{j})$ N, as shown in the diagram.

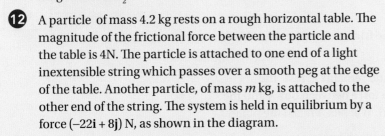

a Find the magnitude of the normal reaction force exerted on the table by the particle.

b Find two possible values for the magnitude of the tension in the string.

c Hence find two possible values of m.

13 A trailer of mass 500 kg is attached to a car of mass 1250 kg by a light rigid horizontal tow-bar. The car and trailer are travelling along a horizontal straight road. The resistance to motion of the trailer is 400 N and the resistance to motion of the car is 900 N. Find both the tension in the tow-bar and the driving force of the car in each of the following cases.

i The car and trailer are travelling at constant speed.

ii The car and trailer have acceleration 0.6 m s^{-2}.

© OCR, AS GCE Mathematics, Paper 4728, January 2009

14 Particles P and Q, of masses 0.45 kg and m kg respectively, are attached to the ends of a light inextensible string which passes over a small smooth pulley. The particles are released from rest with the string taut and both particles 0.36 m above a horizontal surface. Q descends with acceleration 0.98 m s^{-2}. When Q strikes the surface, it remains at rest.

i Calculate the tension in the string while both particles are in motion.

ii Find the value of m.

iii Calculate the speed at which Q strikes the surface.

iv Calculate the greatest height of P above the surface. (You may assume that P does not reach the pulley.)

© OCR, AS GCE Mathematics, Paper 4728, June 2011

15 Box A of mass 6 kg is held at rest at one end of a rough horizontal table. The box is attached to one end of a light inextensible string which passes over a smooth pulley fixed to the other end of the table. The length of that part of the string extending from A to the pulley is 3 m. Box B, of mass 2.5 kg, is attached to the other end of the string and hangs 1.2 m above the ground.

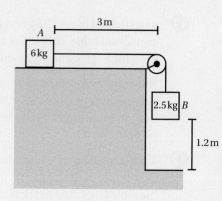

The system is released from rest and moves with acceleration $0.3 \, \text{m s}^{-2}$.

a Find the magnitude of the friction force between box A and the table.

b Box B reaches the floor and remains at rest. The magnitude of the friction force between box A and the table remains unchanged. Will box A reach the pulley?

16 Box A, of mass 34 kg, rests on rough horizontal ground. Box B, of mass 49 kg, rests on top of box A. A string is attached to box B and the tension in the string is $(75\mathbf{i} + 60\mathbf{j})$ N. The system is in equilibrium.

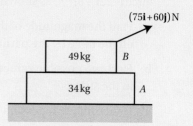

Find:

a the magnitude of the normal reaction force between box A and the ground

b the magnitude of the friction force between box A and the ground.

The tension in the string is now changed to $(75k\mathbf{i} + 60k\mathbf{j})$ N and the value of k is increased from 1. The maximum possible friction force between box A and box B is 120 N and the maximum possible friction force between box A and the ground is 180 N.

c Describe how the equilibrium is broken.

17 Particles P and Q, of masses 3 kg and 5 kg, are connected by a light inextensible string. The string passes over a smooth pulley and the particles hang in the vertical plane with Q 2.5 m above the ground.

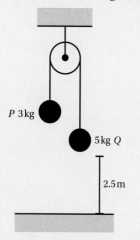

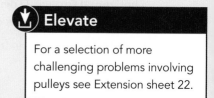

Elevate

For a selection of more challenging problems involving pulleys see Extension sheet 22.

At time $t = 0$ the system is released from rest with the string taut.

a Find the time required for Q to hit the ground.

Once Q is on the ground, P continues to move. Assume that in subsequent motion, neither particle reaches the pulley.

b Find the greatest height of P above its start point.

c Find the time when the string becomes taut again.

Using mechanics to derive proofs

You have often used algebra and calculus to derive formulae in mechanics: for example, various forms of the constant acceleration formulae. But you don't normally think of using mechanics to prove algebraic results. This section looks at two examples of such proofs.

1 Prove that, for any positive real numbers a, b, c and d:

$$\text{If } \frac{a}{b} < \frac{c}{d} \quad \text{then} \quad \frac{a}{b} < \frac{a+c}{b+d} < \frac{c}{d}$$

PROOF 10

Consider a particle moving in a straight line. Suppose it travels at a constant speed v_1 for b seconds covering the distance of a metres, and then at a different constant speed v_2 for d seconds covering the distance of c metres.

Then $v_1 = \dfrac{a}{b}$ and $v_2 = \dfrac{c}{d}$, so the inequality $\dfrac{a}{b} < \dfrac{c}{d}$ says that $v_1 < v_2$.

The expression $\dfrac{a+c}{b+d}$ represents the total distance divided by total time, so this is the average speed for the whole journey. This has to be somewhere between the smaller and the larger speeds, so:

$$v_1 < \frac{a+c}{b+d} < v_2$$

which proves the required inequality.

2 Prove that, for any two positive numbers a and b, $\dfrac{a+b}{2} > \sqrt{ab}$.

PROOF 11

Consider again an object moving in a straight line, and let s be the total distance travelled.

a Suppose the object travels half the time with speed a and then the other half of the time with speed b. Find an expression for the total time travelled in terms of a, b and s.

b A second object travels half the distance with speed a and half the distance with speed b. Find an expression for its total time in terms of a, b and s.

c Draw displacement–time graphs to see which object takes longer to travel the distance s. Make sure you consider both possibilities: $a < b$ and $a > b$. Can you explain this without referring to the graph?

d Use this to complete the proof that $\dfrac{a+b}{2} > \sqrt{ab}$.

🔍 Explore

The result in the second proof is called the AM–GM inequality. There are several similar inequalities, and they are particularly important in probability and statistics. Find out about their applications in probability and statistics.

Alternative representations

It is easy to categorise problems in mathematics by topic, labelling things as a 'mechanics problem' or 'geometry problem'. But sometimes unexpected links provide elegant solutions to otherwise difficult problems.

Consider the following problem:

A farmer wants to build a straight path from his house to the stream and then from the stream to the stables. The positions of the two buildings are shown in the diagram.

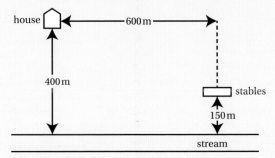

What is the shortest possible length of the path?

This looks like a 'calculus problem' you encountered in Chapter 14. You could set up a coordinate system, write an expression for the total distance in terms of x and use differentiation to find the minimum.

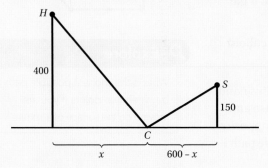

▶▶ Fast forward

A You don't know how to differentiate this expression for d yet, but you will learn how to do so in Student Book 2.

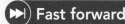
$$d = \sqrt{x^2 + 400^2} + \sqrt{(600-x)^2 + 150^2}$$

However, there is a much simpler solution if you use an idea from geometry: the shortest distance between two points is along a straight line. Of course, the straight line between the house and the stables does not go to the stream. The trick is to find a point on the other side of the stream that is the same distance from the stream as the stables. This is achieved by reflecting the point which represents the stables in the line which represents the stream.

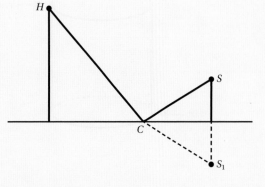

Suppose the path goes from the house to the point C, crosses the stream and then goes in a straight line to point S_1. Then the total length of the path is $d = HC + CS = HC + CS_1$. But the shortest distance between H and S_1 is along a straight line, so C should be the point where the line HS_1 crosses the stream.

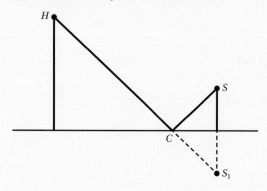

Questions

1 Find the length of the shortest possible path in the above problem.

2 A cube has side of length 1 m. An ant starts at one corner of the cube and crawls to the opposite corner. The ant can only move on the surface of the cube. Find the shortest possible path and calculate its length.

How does this compare to the length of the shortest path if the ant could pass through the cube?

3 Repeat question 2 for an ant moving on the surface of a cuboid with sides of lengths 1 cm, 2 cm and 3 cm.

4 A caterpillar crawls on the surface of a cylinder with radius r and height h. It starts at a point on the edge of the bottom base and crawls to the point on the top base that is diametrically opposite the starting point. Find the length of the shortest possible path it can take.

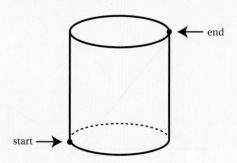

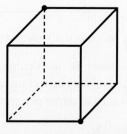

Explore

What is the shortest possible path between two points if you are moving on the surface of a sphere?

Investigating the effect of modelling assumptions

Throughout the mechanics chapters you have made various modelling assumptions that enabled you to write relatively simple equations to describe the motion of an object. You will now look at how changing some of these assumptions affects the results predicted by the model.

Changing the value of g

You usually assume that the value of gravitational acceleration is constant on the surface of the Earth, and take $g = 9.8 \text{ m s}^{-2}$. However, the value of g actually varies with the latitude and height above sea level.

Questions

A student conducts an experiment to measure the height of a building by dropping a small stone from the top and timing how long it takes to hit the ground.

The stone takes 1.6 seconds to fall.

1 Taking $g = 9.8 \text{ m s}^{-2}$, estimate the height of the building. Give your answer to 3 s.f.

2 The building is actually located in Greenland, where $g = 9.825 \text{ m s}^{-2}$. What is the percentage error in the estimate in question 1?

3 If, instead, the building is located in Denver, where $g = 9.796 \text{ m s}^{-2}$, find the percentage error in the estimate of the height.

4 The experiment is repeated with a much taller building, and the stone takes 10.2 seconds to fall. Repeat all the calculations from questions 1, 2 and 3.

Effect of air resistance

Another common modelling assumption is that there is no air resistance. Air resistance depends on many different factors, including the size and shape of the object, the material of which it is made, and on the density of air (which varies with height and temperature). It also varies with the speed of the object. There are two common models for air resistance.

At low speeds, air resistance can be modelled as being proportional to the speed of the object.

Questions

A cyclist starts moving from rest and applies a constant driving force of 180 N. The air resistance has magnitude 40v, where v is the speed. Assume all other forces can be ignored. The cyclist and her bike have a mass of 120 kg.

5 Write the Newton's second law equation for the motion of the cyclist. Verify that $v = 4.5\left(1 - e^{-\frac{t}{3}}\right)$ satisfies this equation.

6 Write down an equation for $v(t)$ if air resistance is ignored.

7 Use each model to predict how long it would take the cyclist to reach the speed of:

    a 0.5 m s^{-1} **b** 2 m s^{-1} **c** 5 m s^{-1}

Would you say that ignoring air resistance is a good modelling assumption in this problem?

At higher speeds, a better model is to assume that air resistance is proportional to the square of the speed. In this model, the constant of proportionality depends on drag coefficient b and the mass of the object. The model leads to the following expression for the velocity:

$$v = A\left(\frac{1 - e^{-kt}}{1 + e^{-kt}}\right)$$

where $A = \sqrt{\dfrac{mg}{b}}$ and $k = \sqrt{\dfrac{4bg}{m}}$.

Questions

For a parachutist of mass 80 kg, $b = 0.27$:

8   **a** For a model without air resistance, what is the velocity of the parachutist after 1 second? How does this compare to the velocity predicted by the given model?

    b How do the velocities after 10 seconds compare in the two models?

For a 2 pence coin of mass 7.2g, $b = 2 \times 10^{-4}$:

9   **a** For a model without air resistance, what is the velocity of the coin after 1 second? How does this compare to the distance predicted by the given model?

    b How do the velocities after 10 seconds compare in the two models?

    c For a model without air resistance, find how long it takes for an object to reach the ground from a height of:

       i 5 m   **ii** 500 m

    d Hence investigate whether ignoring air resistance is a suitable modelling assumption for a parachutist and a coin falling from the height of 5 m and 500 m.

Explore

Models with air resistance predict that the object will reach a **terminal velocity**, as the resistance force increases with speed and eventually balances the weight. How does the weight of an object affect its terminal velocity, and the time it takes to reach it?

CROSS-TOPIC REVIEW EXERCISE 4

1 A particle of mass 3 kg moves under the action of two perpendicular forces, as shown in the diagram.

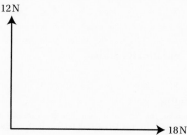

Find, in vector form, the acceleration of the particle.

2 The diagram shows the velocity–time graph for a particle moving in a straight line.

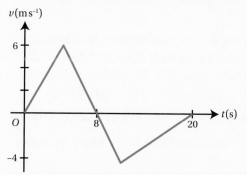

Find the average speed of the particle during the 20 seconds.

3 A particle of mass 4.2 kg starts from rest and accelerates uniformly under the action of a constant force of magnitude 13.6 N. Find the speed of the particle after it has travelled the distance of 6.2 m.

4 Two perpendicular forces have magnitudes x N and $3x$ N (see diagram). Their resultant has magnitude 6 N.

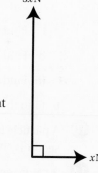

  i Calculate x.

  ii Find the angle the resultant makes with the smaller force.

© OCR, AS GCE Mathematics, Paper 4728, June 2009

5 A particle P is projected vertically upwards and reaches its greatest height 0.5 s after the instant of projection. Calculate

  i the speed of projection of P,

  ii the greatest height of P above the point of projection.

It is given that the point of projection is 0.539 m above the ground.

  iii Find the speed of P immediately before it strikes the ground.

© OCR, AS GCE Mathematics, Paper 4728, June 2013

6 A person of mass 60 kg stands in a moving lift of mass 420 kg. The normal reaction force between the person's feet and the floor of the lift is 312 N.

   a Find the magnitude and direction of the acceleration of the lift.

The lift is suspended by a cable, which can be modelled as light and inextensible.

   b Find the tension in the cable.

   c Explain how you have used the assumption that the cable is light.

7 A car is travelling in a straight line along a horizontal road, with constant acceleration a m s^{-2}. It passes point A with speed u m s^{-1}, reaches point B five seconds later and point C two seconds after that.

   a Given that the distance $AB = 95$ m and $BC = 80$ m, find the values of u and a.

   b The driving force of the car has magnitude 7200 N. The resistance to the motion of the car is 2500 N. Find the mass of the car.

8 A train consists of a locomotive and two carriages. The mass of the locomotive is 5600 kg and the mass of each carriage is 3200 kg. The train is moving with a speed of 40 km h^{-1} when a driver applies the brakes. The train comes to rest after travelling 360 m. The resistance forces throughout this motion are constant, 700 N on the locomotive and 400 N on each carriage.

Find the force in the coupling between the first carriage and the locomotive. Is it a tension or a thrust?

9 A particle P moves in a straight line, passing the point O with speed 35 m s^{-1}. At time t seconds after leaving O the acceleration a m s^{-2} is given by:

$$a = 6t - 22 \qquad 0 \leqslant t \leqslant 5$$

   a i Find an expression for the velocity at time t.

     ii Find the times at which P is at rest.

     iii Find the maximum speed of the particle in its 5-second journey.

   b Find the total distance travelled by P.

10 A particle has velocity given by $v = t^2 + 1$ for $t \geqslant 0$. Velocity is measured in m s^{-1} and time in seconds. The average velocity of the particle from $t = 0$ to $t = T$ is 4 m s^{-1}. Find the value of T.

11 A car is travelling at 13 m s^{-1} along a straight road when it passes a point A at time $t = 0$, where t is in seconds. For $0 \leqslant t \leqslant 6$, the car accelerates at $0.8t$ m s^{-2}.

   i Calculate the speed of the car when $t = 6$.

   ii Calculate the displacement of the car from A when $t = 6$.

   iii Three (t, x) graphs are shown below, for $0 \leqslant t \leqslant 6$.

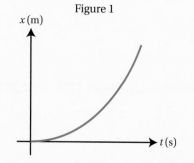

Figure 1

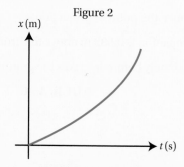

Figure 2

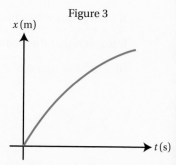

Figure 3

    a State which of these three graphs is most appropriate to represent the motion of the car.

    b For each of the two other graphs give a reason why it is not appropriate to represent the motion of the car.

© OCR, AS GCE Mathematics, Paper 4728, January 2009

12 A particle is projected vertically upwards with velocity 5 m s⁻¹ from a point 2.5 m above the ground.

    i Calculate the speed of the particle when it strikes the ground.

    ii Calculate the time after projection when the particle reaches the ground.

    iii Sketch on separate diagrams

        a the (t, v) graph,   **b** the (t, x) graph,

    representing the motion of the particle.

© OCR, AS GCE Mathematics, Paper 4728, January 2011

13 A swimmer C swims with velocity v m s⁻¹ in a swimming pool. At time t s after starting, $v = 0.006t^2 - 0.18t + k$, where k is a constant. C swims from one end of the pool to the other in 28.4 s.

    i Find the acceleration of C in terms of t.

    ii Given that the minimum speed of C is 0.65 m s⁻¹, show that $k = 2$.

    iii Express the distance travelled by C in terms of t, and calculate the length of the pool.

© OCR, AS GCE Mathematics, Paper 4728, January 2010

14 A particle P is projected from a fixed point O on a straight line. The displacement x m of P from O at time t s after projection is given by $x = 0.1t^3 - 0.3t^2 + 0.2t$.

    i Express the velocity and acceleration of P in terms of t.

    ii Show that when the acceleration of P is zero, P is at O.

    iii Find the values of t when P is stationary.

At the instant when P first leaves O, a particle Q is projected from O. Q moves on the same straight line as P and at time t s after projection the velocity of Q is given by $(0.2t^2 - 0.4)$ m s⁻¹. P and Q collide first when $t = T$.

    iv Show that T satisfies the equation $t^2 - 9t + 18 = 0$, and hence find T.

© OCR, AS GCE Mathematics, Paper 4728, June 2011

Pure mathematics and statistics

90 minutes, 75 marks

Section A: Pure mathematics

1 Find the exact value of $\int_{2}^{3} 2 - \frac{4}{x^2}\, dx$ **[4 marks]**

2 Find the exact solution of the equation $\log_3(2x+1) = \log_3(x-2) + 2$.   **[5 marks]**

3 Points M, N and P have position vectors $\mathbf{m} = 6\mathbf{i} - 3\mathbf{j}$, $\mathbf{n} = 2\mathbf{j}$ and $\mathbf{p} = \mathbf{j} - 5\mathbf{i}$.

   a Point Q is such that $MNQP$ is a parallelogram. Find the position vector of Q.

   b Find the exact magnitude of the vector $\mathbf{v} = \overrightarrow{MN} + \overrightarrow{MP}$.   **[8 marks]**

4 Differentiate $3x^2$ with respect to x from first principles.   **[4 marks]**

5 In the diagram, ABC is a right angle, $AC = 1$ and angle $BAC = \alpha$.
Points D and E are on the line AC such that $CD = CE = CB$.

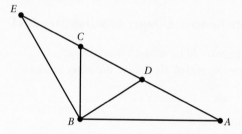

   a Express the lengths AB and BC in terms of α.

   b Hence prove that $\dfrac{1}{AD} + \dfrac{1}{AE} = \dfrac{2}{AB^2}$.   **[8 marks]**

6   **a** Find the coordinates of the intersection points of the graphs of $y = 12x - 2x^2$ and $2y = 6 - x$.

   b Illustrate the region determined by the inequalities $y \leqslant 12x - 2x^2$ and $x + 2y \geqslant 6$ on a graph.
Leave the required region unshaded.

   c The inequality $x^2 + px + q \geqslant 0$ is satisfied for $x \in (-\infty, -3] \cup [5, \infty)$. Find the values of p and q.   **[11 marks]**

7 Points A and C have coordinates $(-8, 0)$ and $(0, 20)$ respectively. Point B lies on the x-axis and CB is perpendicular to AC. Find the equation of the circle that passes through points A, B and C.   **[11 marks]**

Section B: Statistics

8 Elena is sometimes late for school, but never more than three times in a week. For any week, the number of days she is late has the following probability distribution:

Days late	0	1	2	3
Probability	0.50	0.25	0.15	0.10

Find the probability that, in two randomly chosen weeks, Elena is late for school a total of four times.   **[4 marks]**

9 Pre-election polls suggest that 35% of voters in a certain town are undecided about how they are going to vote. Following a televised debate, a survey is carried out to find out whether the proportion of undecided voters has decreased.

    a Describe briefly how to select a simple random sample of 200 registered voters in this town.

In a random sample of 200 voters, 62 are still undecided about how they are going to vote.

    b Test, at a 5% significance level, whether the proportion of undecided voters in this town has decreased. **[9 marks]**

10 The scatter graph shows data about average age and the percentage of people who cycle to work. The information is from a survey done in 2015. Each data point represents one local authority. The data shown is for all the 250 local authorities that provided information.

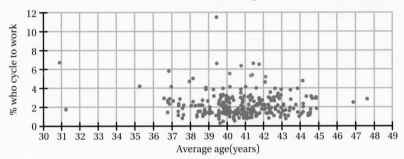

    a Describe the correlation between average age and the percentage of people who cycle to work.

The data for the percentage of people who cycle to work, $p\%$, is summarised as follows:

$$\sum p = 561, \quad \sum p^2 = 1699$$

    b Calculate the mean percentage of people who cycle to work, and show that the standard deviation is 1.33.

    c Hence identify the outliers in the 'percentage who cycle to work' data. Show your method and circle the outliers on the graph. [In this question, outliers are defined as data values that are more than 3 standard deviations from the mean.]

    d One local authority has a particularly high percentage of people who cycle to work. Is this local authority more likely to be in an urban or a rural area? Explain your answer. **[11 marks]**

Pure mathematics and mechanics

90 minutes, 75 marks

Section A: Pure mathematics

1 Find the exact solutions of the equation $2\cos(2x) = 1$ for $x \in [0°, 180°]$. **[3 marks]**

2 The diagram shows the graph of $y = f(x)$.

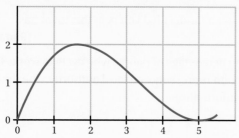

On separate diagrams sketch graphs of:

a $y = f(2x)$

b $y = f'(x)$. **[5 marks]**

3 Solve the equation $3^{2x+1} - 28 \times 3^x + 9 = 0$. **[5 marks]**

4 **a** Find the first four terms, in ascending powers of x, in the expansion of $\left(1 - \frac{1}{2}x\right)^8$.

b Find the coefficient of x^3 in the expansion of $(2-x)\left(1 - \frac{1}{2}x\right)^8$. **[7 marks]**

5 A polynomial is defined by $f(x) = x^3 - x^2 + ax + 12$. It is given that $(x - 2)$ is a factor of $f(x)$.

a Find the value of a and factorise $f(x)$ completely.

b Hence sketch the graph of $y = f(x)$ giving coordinates of any axis intercepts. **[8 marks]**

6 **a** A student says: 'When you square a prime number, the sum of the digits of the answer is either a prime number or a square number.' (For example, $5^2 = 25$ and $2 + 5 = 7$; $13^2 = 169$, $1 + 6 + 9 = 16$.) Give a counter example to disprove the student's statement.

b Prove that the difference of squares of two odd numbers is always a multiple of 4. **[6 marks]**

7 A scientist models a population of insects using the equation $N = Ae^{kt}$ where N thousand is the number of insects t days after the observations started. Initially, there are 30 000 insects and the population is increasing at a rate of 12 000 insects per day.

a Find the values of A and k.

b According to this model, how long will it take for the population to reach 1 million? **[7 marks]**

8 **a** Sketch the graph of $y = \frac{5}{x^2}$.

b Show that the curve with equation $y = x^2 - x + \frac{5}{x}$ has only one stationary point. **[8 marks]**

Section B: Mechanics

9 A particle of mass 5 kg moves in a horizontal plane under the action of forces $\mathbf{F}_1 = (23\mathbf{i} - 16\mathbf{j})$ N, $\mathbf{F}_2 = (7\mathbf{j})$ N and $\mathbf{F}_3 = (11\mathbf{i} + 8\mathbf{j})$ N. Find the acceleration of the particle in the form $(p\mathbf{i} + q\mathbf{j})$ m s^{-2}. **[4 marks]**

10 A ball is projected vertically upwards with a speed of 12.6 m s^{-1}. Assume that the air resistance can be ignored.

   a Find the speed and the direction of motion of the ball 2.1 seconds after projection.

   b How long does the ball take to travel a distance of 15 metres?

   c How would your answer to part **b** change if air resistance was included?
     Give a reason for your answer. **[8 marks]**

11 A box of mass 12 kg is attached to the roof of a lift by a light inextensible string. The mass of the lift is 450 kg and it is supported by a cable that is modelled as light and inextensible. The tension in the cable is 5300 N. Find the tension in the string. **[5 marks]**

12 A particle moves in a straight line. Its velocity, v m s^{-1}, at time t seconds is given by the equation:

$$v(t) = \begin{cases} 9.6 + 4.2t - 0.3t^2 & \text{for} \quad 0 \leqslant t \leqslant 7 \\ 52.65 - 4.05t & \text{for} \quad t > 7 \end{cases}$$

   a Calculate the acceleration of the particle when $t = 9$.

   b At what time does the particle change direction?

   c How long does it take for the particle to travel 190 m? **[9 marks]**

FORMULAE

The following formulae will be given on the AS and A Level assessment papers.

Binomial series

$$(a+b)^n = a^n + {}^nC_1\, a^{n-1}\, b + {}^nC_2\, a^{n-2}\, b^2 + \ldots + {}^nC_r\, a^{n-r}\, b^r + \ldots + b^n \qquad (n \in \mathbb{N}),$$

where ${}^nC_r = \dbinom{n}{r} = \dfrac{n!}{r!(n-r)!}$

Differentiation from first principles

$$f'(x) = \lim_{h \to 0} \frac{f(x+h) - f(x)}{h}$$

Standard deviation

$$\sqrt{\frac{\sum (x - \bar{x})^2}{n}} = \sqrt{\frac{\sum x^2}{n} - \bar{x}^2} \quad \text{or} \quad \sqrt{\frac{\sum f(x - \bar{x})^2}{\sum f}} = \sqrt{\frac{\sum fx^2}{\sum f} - \bar{x}^2}$$

The binomial distribution

If $X \sim B(n,p)$ then $P(X = x) = \dbinom{n}{x} p^x (1-p)^{n-x}$, Mean of X is np, Variance of X is $np(1-p)$

Kinematics

$$v = u + at$$

$$s = ut + \frac{1}{2}at^2$$

$$s = \frac{1}{2}(u+v)t$$

$$v^2 = u^2 + 2as$$

$$s = vt - \frac{1}{2}at^2$$

Answers

Chapter 1

Before you start...

1 3

2 $(2x+1)(2x-1)$

3 a $180°$ **b** $360°$

4 π and $\sqrt{2}$

5 15

Exercise 1A

1 a i 5   **ii** 10
  b i 21   **ii** 16
  c i x^2+1 **ii** y^2+1
  d i $4x^2+1$ **ii** $9y^2+1$
  e i x^2+2x+2 **ii** x^2-4x+5

2 a i $\Leftarrow$ **ii** $\Leftarrow$
  b i $\Rightarrow$ **ii** $\Rightarrow$
  c i $\Leftrightarrow$ **ii** $\Leftrightarrow$
  d i $\Leftarrow$ **ii** $\Leftrightarrow$
  e i $\Leftarrow$ **ii** $\Rightarrow$
  f i $\Leftrightarrow$ **ii** $\Leftarrow$
  g i None   **ii** None

3 $a=2, b=3$

4 $a=2, b=8$

5 Equals sign is used to match up non-equal values

6 Not all lines can be connected with $\Leftrightarrow$

7 a $\sqrt{x^2+9}=3x-7$

$\Rightarrow x^2+9=9x^2-42x+49$

$\Leftrightarrow 0=8x^2-42x+40$

$\Leftrightarrow 0=4x^2-21x+20$

$\Leftrightarrow 0=(4x-5)(x-4)$

$\Leftrightarrow x=\dfrac{5}{4}$ or $x=4$

b $x=\dfrac{5}{4}$ is the solution to $\sqrt{x^2+9}=-(3x-7)$, which gives the same second line of working

8 a $\Rightarrow, \Leftrightarrow, \Leftrightarrow, \Leftrightarrow$
  b Multiplying through by x^2 introduced the false solution $x=0$

9 a $\Leftrightarrow, \Leftarrow$
  b Alternative solution to the second line is $x=-3$

10 In maths, the statement is false; A OR B means A is true or B is true or both are true. In spoken (informal) English, it depends on context.

11 All is fine until cancelling $(a-b)$. Since $a=b$, this is equivalent to dividing both sides by zero.

Exercise 1B

1 a i $\{x:x>7\}$; $(7,\infty)$
    ii $\{x:x<6\}$; $(-\infty,6)$
  b i $\{x:x\leqslant 10\}$; $(-\infty,10]$
    ii $\{x:x\geqslant 5\}$; $[5,\infty)$
  c i $\{x:x>0\}\cap\{x:x\leqslant 1\}$; $(0,1]$
    ii $\{x:x>5\}\cap\{x:x<7\}$; $(5,7)$
  d i $\{x:x>5\}\cup\{x:x\leqslant 0\}$; $(-\infty,0]\cup(5,\infty)$
    ii $\{x:x\geqslant 10\}\cup\{x:x<2\}$; $(-\infty,2)\cup[10,\infty)$

2 a i $1\leqslant x<4$ **ii** $2<x\leqslant 8$
  b i $1\leqslant x\leqslant 3$ **ii** $2<x<4$
  c i $x<5$ **ii** $x\geqslant 12$
  d i $8\leqslant x<10$ **ii** $3\leqslant x<4$

3 a i

ii

b i

ii

c i

ii

d i

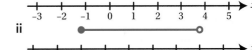

ii

4 a $x\in[1,3]\cap(2,\infty)=(2,3]$
  b $x\in(-\infty,-1]\cap(1,3)=\varnothing$
  c $x\in(-\infty,-2]\cup[2,\infty)$
  d $x\in[1,5)\cup[7,\infty)$

5 a i $[10,\infty)$ **ii** $(6,\infty)$
  b i $[-12,12)$ **ii** $(4,6]$
  c i $(9,\infty)$ **ii** $\left(-\infty,-\dfrac{16}{11}\right]$

Exercise 1C

1 e.g. $x = 4$
2 e.g. $x = 45°$
3 e.g. $x = -1$
4 e.g. 2×3
5 e.g. 4
6 e.g. $-\pi + \pi$
7 e.g. $x = -4$
8 e.g. $n = 41$
9 No – consider skew lines

Exercise 1D

1 Use $n = 2m + 1$
2 Use $a = 2n$ and $b = 2m + 1$
3 Use $n, n + 1, n + 2$
4 a Use $5n, 5(n + 1)$ b Use $5n, 5(n + 1)$
5 Consider areas
6 Either use an argument with exterior angles or divide the hexagon into triangles
7 Use $n = 3m + 2$
8 a $x^2 + 4x + 4$
  b Write as $y = (x + 2)^2 + 6$
9 Label the exterior angle x and use knowledge of angles on a straight line and interior angles of a triangle
10 Factorise to $(n + 1)(n + 2)$
11 a Position value
   b Consider $n - (a + b + c + d)$
   c Consider $n + (a - b + c - d)$
12 Consider rationality of $\sqrt{2}^{\sqrt{2}}$

Exercise 1E

1 Use proof by exhaustion for all possible factors up to square root of 11
2 Use proof by exhaustion for all possible factors up to square root of 83
3 Use proof by exhaustion for all polygons from triangles to hexagons
4 Use proof by exhaustion for squares of single-digit integers
5 Use proof by exhaustion for all single-digit positive integers
6 Use proof by exhaustion for all integers between 1 and 5 inclusive
7 Use proof by exhaustion for even or odd n
8 Use proof by exhaustion for $n = 5m + i$ for $i = 0, 1, 2, 3, 4$
9 Factorise and use proof by exhaustion for $n = 3m + i$ for $i = 0, 1, 2$
10 Consider cases a, b both positive; a, b both negative; a, b different signs

Mixed practice 1

1 Use $a = 2m + 1$, $b = 2n + 1$
2 Use $n = 2m$
3 Use a non-reduced fraction
4 Consider, for example, $3 + (-2)$ and $3 - (-2)$
5 Use definition of rational numbers
6 Subdivide the n-gon as for Exercise 1E question 6
7 $a = 1, b = -1, c = 1$
8 Factorise and use an exhaustive proof
9 Construct further lines to find isosceles triangles; construct a proof using knowledge of angles in triangles
10 Consider n^3 where $n = 3k$ or $n = 3k \pm 1$
11 a This does not work in the forward direction, e.g. $a = 4, b = 0.5$
   b This does not work in either direction, e.g. $a = \sqrt{2}, b = \sqrt{2}$ so $ab = 2$ **or** $ab = \pi$, $a = \pi, b = 1$
12 Use $a = n - 1$, $b = n$ and $c = n + 1$
13 Use $a = 2m + 1$ and $b = 2n + 1$
14 a e.g. $n = 1601$ b factorise $n^2 - 1$
15 Factorise and use an exhaustive proof considering whether $a + b$ is odd or even

Chapter 2

Before you start...

1 24
2 3
3 a $2x^{-3}$ b $x^{-\frac{2}{3}}$
4 $2 - y + 2x - xy$
5 $4a^2 - b^2$

Work it out 2.1

Solution 1 is correct.

Exercise 2A

1 a i 4   ii 3
  b i $\dfrac{1}{8}$ ii $\dfrac{1}{25}$
  c i $\dfrac{9}{4}$ ii 64
  d i 9   ii 27
  e i $\dfrac{1}{25}$ ii $\dfrac{1}{8}$
  f i $\dfrac{27}{8}$ ii $\dfrac{4}{9}$

g i 0.5 **ii** 4

h i 2 **ii** $\dfrac{1}{3}$

2 a i $4^{\frac{1}{2}}$ **ii** $4^{\frac{1}{3}}$

b i 4^2 **ii** 4^0

c i $4^{\frac{1}{2}}$ **ii** $4^{-\frac{1}{2}}$

d i 4^{-1} **ii** $4^{-\frac{1}{2}}$

e i $4^{\frac{3}{2}}$ **ii** $4^{\frac{5}{2}}$

f i $4^{\frac{4}{3}}$ **ii** $4^{\frac{7}{10}}$

g i $4^{\frac{1}{4}}$ **ii** $4^{\frac{3}{4}}$

3 a i x^3 **ii** x^{12}

b i $2x^5$ **ii** $\dfrac{1}{2x^4}$

c i $\dfrac{3x^3}{4}$ **ii** $\dfrac{y^{12}}{x^6}$

4 a i $x=\dfrac{1}{4}$ **ii** $x=\dfrac{4}{9}$

b i $x=2$ **ii** $x=\dfrac{9}{2}$

5 a i $3x^{\frac{1}{2}}$ **ii** $5x^{\frac{1}{3}}$

b i $x^{\frac{4}{3}}$ **ii** $x^{\frac{5}{2}}$

c i $3x^{-\frac{1}{2}}$ **ii** $5x^{-\frac{1}{3}}$

d i $\dfrac{1}{2}x^{-2}$ **ii** $\dfrac{1}{3}x^{-2}$

e i $\dfrac{2}{3}x^{-\frac{1}{2}}$ **ii** $\dfrac{5}{2}x^{-\frac{1}{3}}$

6 a i $3x^{-\frac{1}{2}}+2x^{\frac{1}{2}}$ **ii** $4x^{-1}-3x^{-\frac{1}{2}}$

b i $\dfrac{1}{2}x-\dfrac{3}{2}x^{-1}$ **ii** $2x^{-1}-\dfrac{3}{2}x^{-2}$

c i $\dfrac{1}{2}x^{\frac{3}{2}}+\dfrac{1}{4}x^{-\frac{1}{2}}$ **ii** $\dfrac{2}{3}x^{-1}-3x^{-\frac{1}{2}}$

7 $\dfrac{1}{10x^2}$

8 x

9 $2p^2q^{\frac{1}{3}}$

10 $x^{-\frac{1}{3}}-x^{\frac{8}{3}}$

11 5×10^{-4}

12 a $\dfrac{1}{3}$ **b** $16\,\text{cm}^2$

13 8 cm

14 $\dfrac{2}{3x^3}$

15 $a=0.75b$

16 $a=9,\ b=1,\ c=-6,\ n=1.5$

17 $\dfrac{\ln b}{(2a-3)\ln 2}$

18 1 (accept 'undefined')

19 16

Work it out 2.2

Solution 2 is correct.

Exercise 2B

1 a i $5\sqrt{5}$ **ii** $2\sqrt{5}$

b i $5\sqrt{5}$ **ii** $7\sqrt{5}$

c i $2\sqrt{5}$ **ii** $26\sqrt{5}$

2 a i $\sqrt{32}$ **ii** $\sqrt{300}$

b i $\sqrt{63}$ **ii** $\sqrt{80}$

c i $\sqrt{108}$ **ii** $\sqrt{72}$

3 a i $3+\sqrt{3}$ **ii** $2\sqrt{3}$

b i $-4+3\sqrt{3}$ **ii** $5+3\sqrt{3}$

c i $4+2\sqrt{3}$ **ii** $7-4\sqrt{3}$

4 a i $\sqrt{7}$ **ii** $\dfrac{2\sqrt{5}}{5}$

b i $\dfrac{\sqrt{6}-2}{2}$ **ii** $\dfrac{\sqrt{6}+3\sqrt{2}}{3}$

c i $1+\sqrt{2}$ **ii** $\dfrac{\sqrt{7}-\sqrt{5}+\sqrt{35}-1}{6}$

5 $\dfrac{2}{1-n}$

6 $a=5,\ b=3$

7 $a=19,\ b=13$

8 $\left(3\sqrt{2}\right)^2=18$ and $\left(2\sqrt{3}\right)^2=12$

9 $x=-4$

10 $\dfrac{2\sqrt{n}+3}{4n-9}$

11 $15n^2+5-10n\sqrt{3}$

12 a $-ab+\left(b^2-a^2\right)\sqrt{2}$ **b** $\sqrt{3\left(a^2+b^2\right)}$

13 a $\sqrt{48}$

b $\sqrt{27}-\sqrt{20}>\sqrt{5}-\sqrt{3}$

14 a $a^2+2b^2+2\sqrt{2}ab$

b Proof

15 a Proof **b** $\sqrt[3]{9}+\sqrt[3]{6}+\sqrt[3]{4}$

16 No; not if $x<0$

Mixed practice 2

1 $n^2+5+2n\sqrt{5}$

2 $z=9x^3$

3 $\sqrt{2}+\sqrt{7}$

4 $\dfrac{1}{16}x^2$

5 $x=0.8$

6 a x^2 **b** $1500y^2$

7 a 3^{-2} **b** $3^{\frac{1}{3}}$ **c** 3^{280}

8 $\dfrac{3}{4x^2}$

9 $\dfrac{1+n+2\sqrt{n}}{n-1}$

10 a $a^2+5b^2+2ab\sqrt{5}$

    b Proof

    c Proof

    d i Upper bound because $3-\sqrt{5}>0$ so an odd power is also bigger than zero; worse because $\sqrt{5}$ is closer to 2 than to 3

      ii Because $4-\sqrt{5}>1$, large powers get further away from zero or one

Chapter 3

Before you start...

1 $6x^2-7x-3$

2 a $x=-5, 4$ **b** $x=-8, \dfrac{1}{2}$

    c $x=0, \dfrac{3}{5}$ **d** $x=\pm\dfrac{3}{2}$

3 a $2\pm\sqrt{2}$ **b** $x=\dfrac{5\pm\sqrt{35}}{2}$

4 $x>2$

Exercise 3A

1 a i $2, -\dfrac{3}{2}$ **ii** $5, \dfrac{2}{3}$

    b i $\dfrac{4}{3}$ **ii** $-\dfrac{5}{4}$

    c i $5, -4$ **ii** $\dfrac{5}{2}, -3$

    d i $6, -\dfrac{1}{2}$ **ii** $\dfrac{4}{3}, 1$

2 a i $x=\dfrac{3\pm\sqrt{5}}{2}$ **ii** $x=\dfrac{1\pm\sqrt{5}}{2}$

    b i $x=\dfrac{-3\pm\sqrt{11}}{2}$ **ii** $x=\dfrac{9\pm\sqrt{21}}{10}$

    c i $x=-2\pm\sqrt{6}$ **ii** $x=-1, \dfrac{4}{3}$

    d i $x=\dfrac{3\pm\sqrt{7}}{2}$ **ii** $x=2\pm\sqrt{7}$

3 No real solution

4 $x=\dfrac{4}{3}, -\dfrac{1}{2}$

5 $x=\dfrac{3\pm\sqrt{5}}{2}$

6 $x=2k, 4k$

7 $x=-\dfrac{\sqrt{5}}{2}, \dfrac{\sqrt{5}}{5}$

8 $x=\dfrac{-\sqrt{10}\pm\sqrt{22}}{2}$

9 $x=\dfrac{-b\pm\sqrt{b^2-4a(c-y)}}{2a}$

10 $k=\pm9$

Exercise 3B

1 a i A   **ii** C   **iii** B

    b i C   **ii** A   **iii** B

2 a i 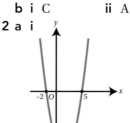   **ii**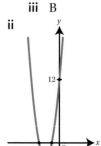

    b i 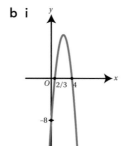   **ii**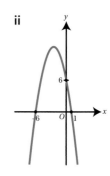

    c i 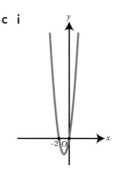   **ii**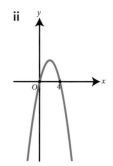

d i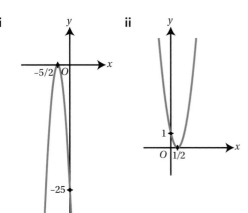

ii

3 a i $y = 3x^2 - 15x + 12$ **ii** $y = 4x^2 + 4x - 8$
b i $y = -2x^2 - 2x + 4$ **ii** $y = -x^2 - 6x - 5$

Work it out 3.1

Solution 2 is correct.

Exercise 3C

1 a i $(3, 4)$ **ii** $(5, 1)$
b i $(7, -1)$ **ii** $(1, -5)$
c i $(-1, 3)$ **ii** $(-7, -3)$
d i $(-2, -4)$ **ii** $(-1, 5)$

2 a i $(x - 3)^2 - 5$ **ii** $(x - 5)^2 - 4$
b i $(x + 2)^2 - 3$ **ii** $(x + 3)^2 - 12$
c i $2(x - 3)^2 - 13$ **ii** $3(x + 1)^2 + 7$
d i $-(x - 1)^2 - 4$ **ii** $-(x + 2)^2 + 5$
e i $(x + 1.5)^2 - 1.25$ **ii** $(x - 2.5)^2 + 3.75$
f i $2(x + 1.5)^2 + 10.5$ **ii** $2(x - 1.25)^2 - 4.125$

3 a i $y = 2(x - 2)^2 + 4$ **ii** $y = 3(x + 1)^2 - 5$
b i $y = -2(x + 1)^2 + 3$ **ii** $y = -5(x - 2)^2 + 1$

4 a $y = (x - 3)^2 + 2$ **b** 2

5 a $b = -3, c = 6$ **b** $a = 2$

6 a $y = -5 - (x - 4)^2$ **b** $(4, -5)$
c $y \leqslant -5$

7 a $2(x + 1)^2 - 3$ **b** $x = -1 \pm \sqrt{1.5}$
c

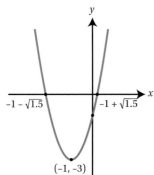

d $x = -1$

8 a $(x + 3)^2 - 9$ **b** $p \geqslant -9$

9 a $3\left(x + \dfrac{1}{3}\right)^2 + \dfrac{2}{3}$ **b** Proof

c $x = -\dfrac{1}{3}$

10 a Proof

Exercise 3D

1 a i $-2\sqrt{2} \leqslant x \leqslant 2\sqrt{2}$ **ii** $-\sqrt{5} < x < \sqrt{5}$
b i $x < -\sqrt{6}$ or $x > \sqrt{6}$
   ii $x \leqslant -2\sqrt{3}$ or $x \geqslant 2\sqrt{3}$
c i $x < -1$ or $x > 4$ **ii** $-\dfrac{2}{3} < x < \dfrac{5}{2}$
d i $x < -1$ or $x > 3$ **ii** $2 < x < 4$
e i $x < 3$ or $x > 12$ **ii** $-2 < x < 2$

2 a i $x \in (2, 3)$ **ii** $x \in (-3, 2)$
b i $x \in (-\infty, -2] \cup [6, \infty)$
   ii $x \in (-\infty, -6] \cup [-1, \infty)$
c i $x \in (-\infty, -2) \cup (1.5, \infty)$
   ii $x \in \left(-\infty, -\dfrac{5}{3}\right) \cup (2, \infty)$
d i $x \in [-2.5, 1]$ **ii** $x \in [-1, -0.2]$

3 $x < -2$ or $x > 1.5$

4 $-\dfrac{5}{3} \leqslant x \leqslant 2$

5 0.904 s

6 a i $x < 2.5$ **ii** $0.5 < x < 5$
b $0.5 < x < 2.5$

7 $x \leqslant -1$ or $1 \leqslant x < 2$ or $x > 3$

8 $-0.4 \leqslant x \leqslant 0$ or $2 \leqslant x \leqslant 3$

9 $5 \leqslant n \leqslant 38$

Exercise 3E

1 a i 36 **ii** 68
b i -47 **ii** -119
c i 0 **ii** 0
d i 49 **ii** 49

2 a Two   **b** None
c One   **d** Two

3 a i $k < \dfrac{1}{24}$ **ii** $k > -\dfrac{25}{12}$

b i $k = \dfrac{3}{5}$ **ii** $k = -\dfrac{17}{24}$

c i $k \geqslant -\dfrac{13}{4}$ **ii** $k \leqslant \dfrac{1}{16}$

d i $k > \dfrac{9}{24}$ **ii** $k < -\dfrac{25}{12}$

e **i** $k = \dfrac{17}{4}$ **ii** $k = \dfrac{55}{32}$

f **i** $k = 1$ **ii** $k = \dfrac{1}{32}$

g **i** $k < 0$ **ii** $k < 0$

4 $m = \pm\sqrt{2}$

5 $k = \dfrac{11 \pm 2\sqrt{30}}{2}$

6 $c \geqslant \dfrac{1}{16}$

7 $0 < k < 6$

8 $-9 < k < -1$

9 $m \leqslant -8$ or $m \geqslant 0$

10 $m < -\dfrac{9}{16}$

Exercise 3F

1 a i $a = \pm\sqrt{3}, \pm\sqrt{7}$ **ii** $x = \pm 2, \pm\sqrt{3}$

  b i $x = -\sqrt[3]{5}, \sqrt[3]{1.5}$ **ii** $a = -2, 1$

  c i $x = \pm\sqrt{2 + \sqrt{6}}$ **ii** $x = \pm\sqrt{6}$

  d i $x = 4, 16$ **ii** $x = 16, 36$

  e i $x = 1, 2$ **ii** $x = 0, 4$

2 $x = 9$

3 $x = \pm 3, \pm 1$

4 $x = 0, -\dfrac{4}{15}$

5 $x = 4, 1$

6 $x = 0, 2$

7 $x = 0, 1$

8 $x = -2, 1.5$

9 a $(x^2 - 2x)^2 - 11x^2$ **b** $x = -2, -1, 3, 4$

10 $x = -1, 3$

11 $x = 16$

Mixed practice 3

1 $x = k + 2$

2 $x = 1, 6$

3 $x = \pm 1, \pm 2$

4 a Minimum   **b** $a = 3, b = 7$

5 $a = -3, b = 2, c = 48$

6 a $p = 1, q = 4$ **b** $x = 1.5$

7 a $16 - 4k^2$ **b** $k = \pm 2$

8 $x \geqslant 3$ or $x < 0$

9 a, c negative, b positive, $b^2 - 4ac = 0$

10 a $(x - 5)^2 + 10$ **b** $\dfrac{1}{1000}$

11 $3 - 2\sqrt{2} < k < 3 + 2\sqrt{2}$

12 $x = 1, 16$

13 $x = 1$

14 a $2\left(x - \dfrac{3}{2}\right)^2 + \dfrac{9}{2}$ **b** $\left(\dfrac{3}{2}, \dfrac{9}{2}\right)$ **c** Zero

15 a $P = 14x + 4$ **b** Proof   **c** $\dfrac{5}{2} \leqslant x < 3$

16 $x = 3, 2$

17 $k = \pm 5$

18 a $k - 1, 1$ **b** $k = -3, 5$

19 Proof

20 a Proof   **b** 6 km

Chapter 4

Before you start...

1 x^6

2 $2x^2 - 5x - 3$

3 $(x - 3)(x - 5)$

4 $x = -2 \pm \sqrt{2}$

Exercise 4A

1 a Degree 3, 3   **b** Degree 5, −1

  c No   **d** No

  e No   **f** No

  g Degree 7, 2   **h** Degree 0, 1

2 a i $6x^3 + 8x^2 - 29x + 14$

    ii $3x^3 + 16x^2 + 23x + 6$

  b i $2x^4 - 15x^3 + 4x^2 + 4x - 1$

    ii $2x^4 - 7x^3 - 30x^2 + 6x + 15$

  c i $b^4 + b^3 - 3b^2 + 14b - 4$

    ii $r^4 - 11r^3 + 33r^2 - 62r + 14$

  d i $-x^6 + 2x^5 + 5x^4 - 10x^3 - x^2 + 5$

    ii $-x^6 + 2x^4 + x^3 - x^2 - x$

3 Discussion

4 a Yes   **b** No

Exercise 4B

1 a i $x^2 - 8x - 3$ **ii** $x^2 - 2x + 3$

  b i $x^2 - 2$ **ii** $x^2 + 3$

  c i $x^2 - 2x + 2$ **ii** $x^2 - 5x + 2$

  d i $x^3 - 5x^2 + 3x - 2$ **ii** $2x^3 + 3x + 5$

2 a i $x - 6$ **ii** $x + 7$

  b ii $x^2 + 4x + 2$ **ii** $x^2 + 7x - 1$

Work it out 4.1

Solution 3 is correct.

Exercise 4C

1 a i No   **ii** Yes
  b i Yes   **ii** No
  c i Yes   **ii** No
  d i Yes   **ii** No
  e i No   **ii** No

2 a i $(x+1)(x-1)(x+2)$
    ii $(x+1)(x-2)(x+2)$
  b i $(x-2)^2(x-3)$ **ii** $(x+2)^3$
  c i $(x-1)(x^2-2x+10)$ **ii** $(x-3)(x^2+x+5)$
  d i $(x-1)(2x-1)(3x-1)$
    ii $(x+2)(4x+3)(3x-5)$

3 a i $x=-3, 1, 4$ **ii** $x=-1, -3, 5$

  b i $x=2, \dfrac{3\pm\sqrt{5}}{2}$ **ii** $x=1, \dfrac{5\pm\sqrt{17}}{2}$

4 a i $x=1, 2, 3$ **ii** $x=-2, 1, 3$
  b i $x=1, -1$ **ii** $x=-3, 2, 4$

5 a $p(2)=0$
  b $(x-2)(x-4)(x+3)$ $x=-3, 2, 4$

6 a $p(3)=0$
  b Proof

7 $c=14, d=8$

8 a $a=2, b=59$ **b** $(x+8)$

9 $x=0, 4$

10 $k=-\dfrac{1}{2}$

11 $a=37, b=-30$

Exercise 4D

1 a i 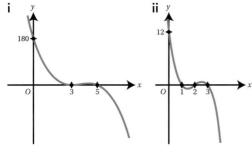   **ii**

  b i 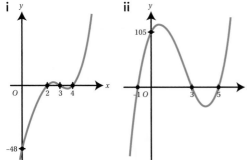   **ii**

c i 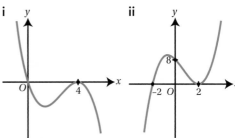   **ii**

d i 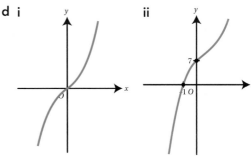   **ii**

e i 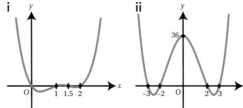   **ii**

2 a i 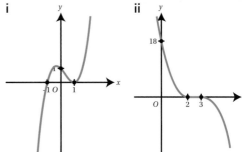   **ii**

  b i 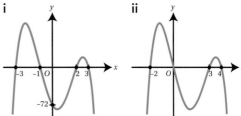   **ii**

  c i 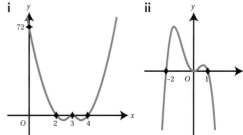   **ii**

d i

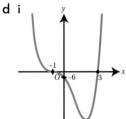

ii

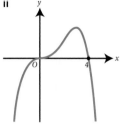

e i

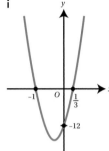

ii

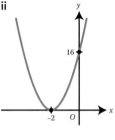

3 a i $y = 2(x-1)(x-4)(x+2)$
  ii $y = 6x(x+2)(x-3)$
 b i $y = -5x(x-1)(x+2)$
  ii $y = -(x-1)(x+2)(x+4)$
 c i $y = -(x+1)(x-2)^2$
  ii $y = (x+1)^2(x-2)$
 d i $y = x(x+2)(x+3)(2x-1)$
  ii $y = -2(x-3)(x-4)(x+1)(x-2)$
 e i $y = -3x^2(x-1)(x-3)$
  ii $y = 5x(x-2)^2(2x+1)$
 f i $y = 2(x-3)^2(x+1)^2$
  ii $y = -(x-3)^2(x-1)^2$

4 a $f(2) = 0$
 b $(x-2)(x-1)(2x+1)$
 c

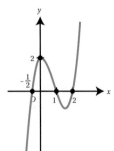

5

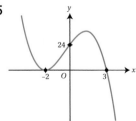

6 a $p = 2, q = -8, r = -6, s = 36$
 b $p = -1, q = 3, r = 0, s = 0$

7 a $(x-q)(x+q)(x^2+q^2)$
 b

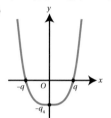

8 a

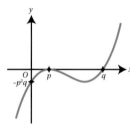

 b One

Mixed practice 4

1 $a = 1, b = 2, c = -12, d = -18, e = 27$

2 $b = 0, c = -3$

3 a $f(2) = 0$
 b $f(x) = (x-2)(x+1)(x-3)$
 c

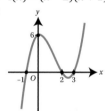

4 a $b = 3$
 b $f(x) = (x-2)(x+3)(x-1)(x+3)$ is also a factor of $g(x)$.

5 a $a = 7, b = -4$
 b

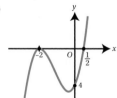

6

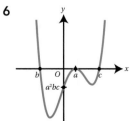

7 a $(x-2)$

8 $a = -10, b = -18$

b $2, \dfrac{-3 \pm \sqrt{29}}{2}$

Chapter 5

Before you start...

1 $x = \dfrac{-1 \pm \sqrt{5}}{2}$

2 One

3 $x = 1, y = 2$

4 $x = 3$

5 $x > 4$

6 $V = \dfrac{48}{r^2}$

Work it out 5.1

Solution 3 is correct.

Exercise 5A

1 a i $(-2, -3), (1, 0)$ **ii** $(3, 0)$
   b i $(-3, -9), (4, 5)$ **ii** No intersection

2 a i $(-2.2, -1.6), (3, 1)$ **ii** $(-3, 3), (5, -1)$
   b i $(1, 3), (3, 1)$ **ii** $(-3, -5), (-5, -3)$
   c i $(-1, 6), (2, 3)$ **ii** $(1, -3), (-1, -5)$

3 $\left(\dfrac{\sqrt{2}}{2}, \sqrt{2} \right), \left(-\dfrac{\sqrt{2}}{2}, -\sqrt{2} \right)$

4 $x = 2$

5 $x = 3, y = 8$

6 a $4x^2 - 32x + 39 = 0$ **b** $1.5, 6.5$

7 $(0, 2), (0, -2) \left(-\sqrt{3}, -1 \right), \left(\sqrt{3}, -1 \right)$

8 $m = 0$

Exercise 5B

1 Proof

2 $-1 \pm 2\sqrt{6}$

3 $\pm 6\sqrt{2}$

4 $a < 0$ or $a > 2$

5 Proof; that $k^2 + 12 > 0$ for all k

Exercise 5C

1 a **i**
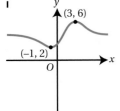

ii
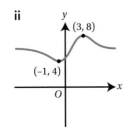

b i
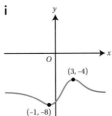

ii
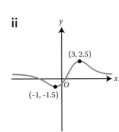

c i
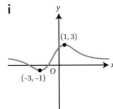

ii
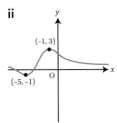

d i
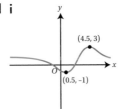

ii
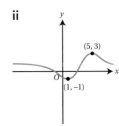

e i
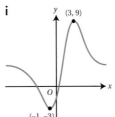

ii
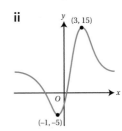

f i
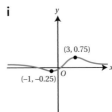

ii
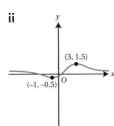

g i
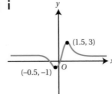

ii
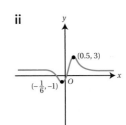

h i

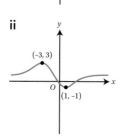
(4.5, 3)
(−1.5, −1)

ii

(3.6, 3)
(−1.2, −1)

i i

(−1, 1)
(3, −3)

ii

(−3, 3)
(1, −1)

2 a i $y = 3x^2 + 3$
    ii $y = 9x^3 - 7$
  b i $y = 7x^3 - 3x + 4$
    ii $y = 8x^2 - 7x + 6$
  c i $y = 4(x - 5)^2$
    ii $y = 7(x + 3)^2$
  d i $y = 3(x + 4)^3 - 5(x + 4)^2 + 4$
    ii $y = (x - 3)^3 + 6(x - 3) + 2$

3 a i Vertically down 5 units
    ii Vertically down 4 units
  b i Left 1 unit
    ii Left 5 units
  c i Left 3 units
    ii Right 2 units

4 a i $y = 21x^2$
    ii $y = 18x^3$
  b i $y = \dfrac{1}{3}(7x^3 - 3x + 6)$

    ii $y = \dfrac{4}{5}(8x^2 - 7x + 1)$
  c i $y = x^2$
    ii $y = 7\left(\dfrac{x}{5}\right)^2$
  d i $y = 3(2x)^3 - 5(2x)^2 + 4$

    ii $y = \left(\dfrac{3x}{2}\right)^3 + 6\left(\dfrac{3x}{2}\right) + 2$

5 a i Vertical stretch, scale factor 4
    ii Vertical stretch, scale factor 6
  b i Horizontal stretch, scale factor $\dfrac{1}{3}$

    ii Horizontal stretch, scale factor $\dfrac{1}{4}$

  c i Horizontal stretch, scale factor $\dfrac{1}{3}$ (or vertical stretch, scale factor $\sqrt{3}$)
    ii Horizontal stretch, scale factor 2

6 a i $y = -3x^2$
    ii $y = -9x^3$
  b i $y = -7x^3 + 3x - 6$
    ii $y = -8x^2 + 7x - 1$
  c i $y = 4x^2$
    ii $y = -7x^3$
  d i $y = -3x^3 - 5x^2 + 4$
    ii $y = -x^3 - 6x + 2$

7 a i Reflection in the x-axis
    ii Reflection in the x-axis
  b i Reflection in the y-axis
    ii Reflection in the y-axis
  c i Reflection in the y-axis
    ii Reflection in the y-axis

Exercise 5D

1 a Translation d to the right
  b $x = d, y = 0$

2 $\sqrt{a}$

3 a $\left(\dfrac{b}{a}, \dfrac{a^2}{b}\right)$
      b Area $= a$

4 $m = -\dfrac{c^2}{4a}$

5

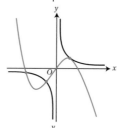

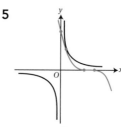

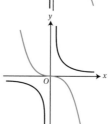

Exercise 5E

1 a 48
    b

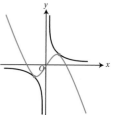

2 a 2
    b

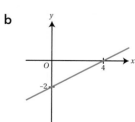

3 a 1.25 **b**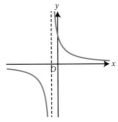

4 a 6 **b**

5 a $y_S = 8p - 80$

  b It is the number of items that would be sold if they were free. It is likely that more would be 'sold' if they were given away for free.

  c £39.87   **d** £25

6 a $C_A = 65 + 0.03m$, $C_B = 0.05m$

  b After 3250 minutes

7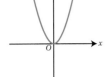

8 17.4%

Exercise 5F

1 a i 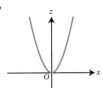   **ii**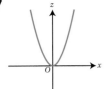

  b i 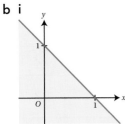   **ii**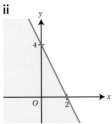

c i 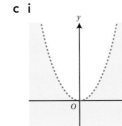   **ii**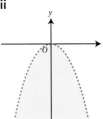

d i 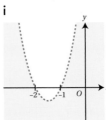   **ii**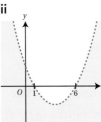

e i   **ii**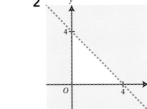

2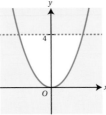

3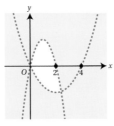

4

5 $y > x$

  $x + y \leqslant 4$

6 $y > (x - 1)(x - 2)$

$y < 2$

7 54

8

Mixed practice 5

1 $(3, 4)$ and $(4, 3)$

2 a

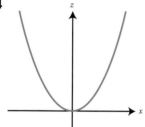

b 2

3 Translation left 3 units

4

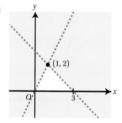

5 3.75 km

6 a

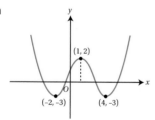

b $(1, 2)$

7

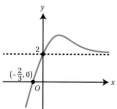

8 a $y = (x - 2)^2$

  b $y = 4 - x^3$

9 a Proof

  b $M = 3.63$ kg represents the weight at birth, 0.233 kg is the weight gain every week

  c Not appropriate (predicts $M = 15.7$ kg)

10 a $x = -\dfrac{1}{2}, y = -3$

  b The line is tangent to the curve.

11

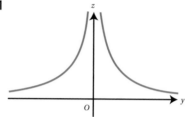

12 a $x = \pm 2, \pm 3$

  b $-3 \leqslant x \leqslant -2$ or $2 \leqslant x \leqslant 3$

Chapter 6

Before you start...

1 a $y = 3x - 1$ **b** $y = -2x + 9$

  c $y = 3x$

2 11

3 $x = \dfrac{45}{11}, y = \dfrac{29}{11}$

4 $(x - 2)^2 - 7$

5 a $(2, 4), (-3, 9)$ **b** Proof

6

	Parallelogram	Rectangle	Rhombus	Square
opposite sides parallel	✓	✓	✓	✓
opposite sides equal	✓	✓	✓	✓
all four sides equal			✓	✓
sides perpendicular		✓		✓
diagonals equal		✓		✓
diagonals perpendicular			✓	✓
diagonals bisect each other	✓	✓	✓	✓

7 a $w = 70°, x = 5, y = 90°, z = 20°$

  b $a = 50°, b = 90°, c = 130°$

  c $d = 4, e = 3$

Exercise 6A

1 a i 13   **ii** 5
   b i $\sqrt{5}$ **ii** $\sqrt{10}$
   c i $2\sqrt{5}$ **ii** $2\sqrt{2}$
   d i $\sqrt{10}$ **ii** $\sqrt{17}$

2 a i $(2.5, 6)$ **ii** $(1.5, 2)$
   b i $(1.5, 5)$ **ii** $(2.5, 3.5)$
   c i $(1, 3)$ **ii** $(-2, 2)$
   d i $(-2.5, -1.5)$ **ii** $(-1.5, -3)$

3 $3a\sqrt{5}$

4 $(2 - a, 2 - b)$

5 a Both are 5
   b It does not lie on the line AB

6 $1 \pm \dfrac{2\sqrt{5}}{5}$

7 $y = \dfrac{x^2 + 1}{2}$

8 Proof

9 a i $2\sqrt{5}\sqrt{a^2 + 1}$ **ii** $(-1 + 2a, 2 + a)$
   b It is 2:1

10 $5\sqrt{5}\,\text{m}$

Exercise 6B

1 a i $y + 1 = 3(x - 4)$ **ii** $y - 2 = 5(x + 3)$
   b i $y - 1 = -\dfrac{1}{2}(x + 3)$ **ii** $y - 3 = \dfrac{4}{3}(x - 1)$
   c i $y - 7 = 4(x - 3)$ **ii** $y - 1 = 3(x - 4)$
   d i $y + 1 = -\dfrac{6}{7}(x - 3)$ **ii** $y + 7 = \dfrac{9}{4}(x + 1)$

2 a i $2x + y - 1 = 0$ **ii** $5x + y - 13 = 0$
   b i $x - 3y - 20 = 0$ **ii** $3x + 2y + 4 = 0$
   c i $5x - 3y + 11 = 0$ **ii** $9x + 2y - 37 = 0$
   d i $6x + 5y - 17 = 0$ **ii** $7x + 4y + 13 = 0$

3 a i $3, \left(-\dfrac{1}{3}, 0\right), (0, 1)$
     ii $-2, (1.5, 0), (0, 3)$
   b i $1.5, \left(-\dfrac{5}{3}, 0\right), (0, 2.5)$
     ii $-0.8, (0.25, 0), (0, 0.2)$
   c i $1, \left(\dfrac{5}{3}, 0\right), \left(0, -\dfrac{5}{3}\right)$
     ii $4, (-1.5, 0), (0, 6)$
   d i $\dfrac{4}{3}, (1.75, 0), \left(0, -\dfrac{7}{3}\right)$
     ii $-2.5, (0.6, 0), (0, 1.5)$

e i $2, (0.5, 0), (0, -1)$
   ii $3, \left(\dfrac{16}{3}, 0\right), (0, -16)$

4 a i $(-8, -7)$ **ii** $(3, 4)$
   b i $\left(\dfrac{7}{3}, -\dfrac{11}{9}\right)$ **ii** $\left(\dfrac{16}{17}, -\dfrac{3}{17}\right)$
   c i $\left(-\dfrac{5}{7}, \dfrac{11}{14}\right)$ **ii** $\left(\dfrac{15}{14}, \dfrac{23}{14}\right)$

5 a $4x + 9y - 11 = 0$ **b** $4x + 9y - 2 = 0$
   c $k = \dfrac{2}{21}$

6 $\dfrac{361}{12}$

7 a $x - y = -2, \; 3x + 2y = -24$
   b $\left(-\dfrac{28}{5}, -\dfrac{18}{5}\right)$
   c $\dfrac{54}{5}$

8 a $k = 3$
   b $2x - 3y = -17$

9 $\dfrac{\sqrt{65}}{4}$

10 area $= \dfrac{4}{3}$

Work it out 6.1

Solution 2 is correct.

Exercise 6C

1 a i $-\dfrac{3}{5}$ **ii** -6
   b i $-\dfrac{1}{2}$ **ii** $-\dfrac{2}{5}$
   c i $\dfrac{1}{2}$ **ii** $\dfrac{1}{3}$
   d i $-\dfrac{7}{3}$ **ii** -5

2 a i Perpendicular   **ii** Parallel
   b i Parallel   **ii** Parallel
   c i Perpendicular   **ii** Neither
   d i Neither   **ii** Neither

3 a Proof
   b $2x + 5y - 22 = 0$

4 Right angle at A, area $= 6.5$

5 a $\left(2, \dfrac{9}{2}\right)$ **b** $y = 1.2x + 2.1$

6 a $2x + 3y = -5$ **b** $\dfrac{11}{2}$

7 $\left(6\pm 2\sqrt{2},0\right)$

8 $18x-4y-1=0$

9 a Proof   **b** $q=\dfrac{14}{3}$, area $=\dfrac{53}{3}$

10 a $y=-2x+4$ **b** $2\sqrt{5}$

11 a Proof   **b** $k=2$

Exercise 6D

1 a i $(x-3)^2+(y-7)^2=16$

   ii $(x-5)^2+(y-1)^2=36$

 b i $(x-3)^2+(y+1)^2=7$

   ii $(x+4)^2+(y-2)^2=5$

2 a i Centre $(2,-3)$, radius $\dfrac{3}{2}$

   ii Centre $(-1,-5)$, radius $\dfrac{2}{5}$

 b i Centre $\left(3,\dfrac{1}{2}\right)$, radius $\sqrt{6}$

   ii Centre $\left(-\dfrac{3}{4},\dfrac{1}{5}\right)$, radius $\sqrt{3}$

3 a i Centre $(-2,3)$, radius 3

   ii Centre $(4,-1)$, radius 3

 b i Centre $(1,-3)$, radius 3

   ii Centre $(5,-2)$, radius $\sqrt{30}$

 c i Centre $\left(-\dfrac{5}{2},\dfrac{1}{2}\right)$, radius $\dfrac{3\sqrt{2}}{2}$

   ii Centre $\left(\dfrac{3}{2},-\dfrac{7}{2}\right)$, radius $\dfrac{\sqrt{70}}{2}$

 d i Centre $\left(0,\dfrac{5}{2}\right)$, radius $\dfrac{\sqrt{73}}{2}$

   ii Centre $\left(-\dfrac{3}{2},0\right)$, radius $\dfrac{7}{2}$

4 a i On circumference

   ii On circumference

 b i Outside circle   **ii** Inside circle

5 a $(x+6)^2+(y-3)^2=117$ **b** $(0,-6),(0,12)$

6 a $\left(\dfrac{5}{2},-\dfrac{1}{2}\right)$, $r=\dfrac{\sqrt{38}}{2}$ **b** Outside

7 $4\sqrt{6}$

8 a Proof   **b** $\sqrt{442}$

 c $\left(x-\dfrac{5}{2}\right)^2+\left(y+\dfrac{3}{2}\right)^2=\dfrac{221}{2}$

9 a $\sqrt{17}$

 b Outside the circle

10 a $90°$ **b** Proof

Exercise 6E

1 a i $y=4$ **ii** $y=\dfrac{3}{5}x+\dfrac{19}{5}$

 b i $y=-\dfrac{2}{3}x+\dfrac{5}{3}$ **ii** $y=\dfrac{2}{3}x-\dfrac{4}{3}$

 c i $y=-2x+9$ **ii** $y=-x+6$

2 a i $\left(\dfrac{-7\pm\sqrt{509}}{10},\dfrac{-2\pm\sqrt{509}}{5}\right)$

   ii $\left(\dfrac{7\pm\sqrt{389}}{10},\dfrac{2\pm\sqrt{389}}{5}\right)$

 b i $(2,7)$ **ii** $(4,4)$

 c i No intersection   **ii** No intersection

3 a i Intersect   **ii** Intersect

 b i Disjoint   **ii** Intersect

 c i Inside   **ii** Tangent

4 $\left(\dfrac{33}{29},-\dfrac{19}{29}\right)$

5 a Proof   **b** $(1,-2)$ **c** $y=x+5$

6 a $y=\dfrac{1}{2}x+1$ **b** $\left(\dfrac{18}{5},\dfrac{14}{5}\right)$ **c** $\dfrac{49}{5}$

7 a $y=8-x$, $y=-\dfrac{1}{6}x+\dfrac{25}{4}$ **b** $(2.1,5.9)$

 c $y=\dfrac{3}{2}x+\dfrac{11}{4}$ **d** $\dfrac{\sqrt{962}}{10}$

8 a $(x-2)^2+(y-5)^2=29$ **b** Proof

 c 7.43

9 a 7 or 21

 b $(-2.39,-1.99)$ and $(-2.39,12.0)$

10 $\dfrac{200}{3}$

11 $1.04, 6.16$

12 4.11

13 a $(2,-1)$

 b Proof

14 a Proof   **b** Proof   **c** $150-25\pi$

15 $a^2+b^2=(1\pm r)^2$

Mixed practice 6

1 13

2 a $k=-\dfrac{5}{2}$ **b** $p=-6$

 c $3x-2y-6=0$ **d** $(2,0)$

3 a $(1,5)$ **b** proof   **c** $(3.4,3.8)$

4 a Centre $(-3,2)$, radius $\sqrt{17}$

 b $\left(\dfrac{1}{5},\dfrac{23}{5}\right)$ and $(-2,-2)$

5 $k = -19$

6 a Proof   **b** $(x-6)^2 + y^2 = 13$

  c $3x + 2y - 5 = 0$

7 $-6 - 5\sqrt{5} < k < -6 + 5\sqrt{5}$

8 a $\dfrac{256}{3}$ **b** $\dfrac{104}{3}$

9 $x^2 - 2x + y^2 - 6y - 22 = 0$

10 $k = \pm\sqrt{\dfrac{1}{8}} = \pm\dfrac{\sqrt{2}}{4}$

11 a $x^2 + y^2 - 4x - 2y - 95 = 0$ **b** $k = 1 + \sqrt{91}$

  c Inside   **d** $y = -\dfrac{3}{4}x + 15$

12 $\dfrac{24\sqrt{13}}{13}$

13 Proof; $\sqrt{80} > 7$

14 a $p = 8; (x-5)^2 + (y-7)^2 = 58$ **b** $21 + 5\sqrt{33}$

Chapter 7

Before you start...

1 a False   **b** False

  c True   **d** False

2 a 81   **b** $\dfrac{1}{27}$

3 a $x^{2.5}$ **b** $x^{-0.5}$

4 $x = \dfrac{7}{3}$

5 a $x = 2, -4$ **b** $x = \pm 1$

Exercise 7A

1 a i 3   **ii** 2

  b i 1   **ii** 1

  c i 0   **ii** 0

  d i -1 **ii** -3

  e i $\dfrac{1}{2}$ **ii** $\dfrac{1}{3}$

  f i $\dfrac{1}{2}$ **ii** $\dfrac{1}{2}$

  g i $\dfrac{2}{3}$ **ii** $\dfrac{3}{4}$

  h i $\dfrac{3}{2}$ **ii** $\dfrac{5}{4}$

  i i $\dfrac{3}{4}$ **ii** $\dfrac{9}{4}$

  j i $-\dfrac{1}{2}$ **ii** $-\dfrac{1}{2}$

2 a i 1.70   **ii** -0.602

  b i -2.30 **ii** 2.30

  c i 1.95   **ii** -0.317

  d i -0.683 **ii** 2.29

3 a i $5 \log x$ **ii** $5 \log x$

  b i $\log x \log y - \log y + 3\log x - 3$

    ii $(\log x)^2 + 4\log x + 4$

  c i $\dfrac{1}{\log b} + \dfrac{1}{\log a}$ **ii** $\log a + 1$

4 a i $x = 3^y$ **ii** $x = 16^y$

  b i $x = a^{y+1}$ **ii** $x = a^{y^2}$

  c i $x = \sqrt[3]{3y}$ **ii** $x = \sqrt{y}$

  d i $x = e^{y-2}$ **ii** $x = e^2 y$

5 a i $x = 32$ **ii** $x = 16$

  b i $x = 0.4$ **ii** $x = 0.25$

  c i $x = 6$ **ii** $x = 100$

6 $x = 111$

7 $x = -3$

8 $x = \dfrac{e^2 + 1}{3}$

9 $x = 10^{1.5} = 31.6$

10 $x = 9, \dfrac{1}{9}$

11 $x = 81, y = 25$

12 It is very close to e.

Work it out 7.1

Solution 2 is correct.

Exercise 7B

1 a i 4   **ii** $\dfrac{1}{2}$

  b i 6   **iv** $\dfrac{3}{2}$

2 a i $7y$ **ii** $2x + y$

  b i $x + 2y - z$ **ii** $2x - y - 3z$

  c i $2 - y - 5z$ **ii** $1 + y + 2z$

  d i $x - 4y$ **ii** $2 + 2x + y + 2z$

3 a i $x = 1$ **ii** $x = 4$

  b i $x = 9$ **ii** $x = 2$

  c i $x = 8$ **ii** $x = 4$

4 $x = 4$

5 $x = 27$

6 $x = 8$

7 a $2x + y$ **b** $2 + x - \dfrac{z}{2}$

8 a $a + 2b$ **b** $2(a - b)$

9 $x = \dfrac{1}{3}e^{\frac{3}{2}}$

10 $x = \dfrac{5}{3}$

11 $x = 2$

12 $x = \dfrac{1}{3}$

Work it out 7.2

Solution 1 is correct.

Work it out 7.3

Solution 2 is correct.

Exercise 7C

1 a i $x = 2.45$ **ii** $x = 116$

  b i $x = -1.83$ **ii** $x = 4.62$

  c i $x = -1.71$ **ii** 9.83

  d i $x = 1.11$ **ii** $x = -2.98$

2 a i $x = \dfrac{\ln 5 - \ln 2}{\ln 3}$ **ii** $x = \dfrac{\ln 3 - \ln 5}{\ln 7}$

  b i $x = -\ln 4$ **ii** $x = -\ln 3$

  c i $x = \dfrac{\ln 5}{2\ln 2}$ **ii** $x = \dfrac{\ln 7}{2\ln 10}$

  d i $x = \dfrac{1}{3}\left(\dfrac{\ln 10}{\ln 2} - 1\right)$ **ii** $x = \dfrac{1}{2}\left(\dfrac{\ln 4}{\ln 5} + 3\right)$

  e i $x = \dfrac{\ln 2}{\ln\left(\frac{5}{2}\right)}$ **ii** $x = \dfrac{2\ln 5}{\ln\left(\frac{5}{3}\right)}$

  f i $x = \dfrac{\ln 3}{3\ln 2 - 1}$ **ii** $x = \dfrac{\ln 5}{2 - \ln 2}$

  g i $x = \dfrac{\ln\left(\frac{5}{64}\right)}{\ln\left(\frac{8}{3}\right)}$ **ii** $x = \dfrac{\ln\left(\frac{7}{12}\right)}{\ln\left(\frac{9}{2}\right)}$

  h i $x = \dfrac{\ln\left(\frac{27}{7}\right)}{\ln\left(\frac{27}{8}\right)}$ **ii** $x = \dfrac{\ln\left(\frac{1}{30}\right)}{\ln\left(\frac{25}{8}\right)}$

3 $x = -0.232$

4 $x = 5 - \log_3 4 \left(\text{or } 5 - \dfrac{\ln 4}{\ln 3}\right)$

5 $x = \dfrac{(3 - \ln 10)}{2}$

6 $x = \dfrac{\log_{10} 5}{1 - \log_{10} 8}$

7 Proof

Exercise 7D

1 a i $x = 1, \log_2 3$ or $\dfrac{\log 3}{\log 2}$ **ii** $x = \log_3 2, \log_3 4$

  b i $x = 2$ **ii** $x = \log_5 3$

  c i $x = \ln 4$ **ii** $x = \ln 4, \ln 5$

  d i $x = 1, \dfrac{1}{\log 5}$ **ii** $x = 2, \dfrac{\log 3}{\log 2}$

  e i $x = 1, \sqrt{2}$ **ii** $x = 3, 9$

2 a Proof   **b** $1.26, 1.46$

3 $x = 1, 3$

4 $x = 2\ln 2, -\ln 2$

5 $x = \log_5 3$

6 $x = \ln 3, \ln 5$

Mixed practice 7

1 $x = \pm 24$

2 d

3 a $2a + \dfrac{b}{2} - c$ **b** $\dfrac{a-1}{2}$ **c** $\dfrac{b-c}{2}$

4 $x = 0.367$

5 $x = 3$

6 $x = 1.17$

7 $y = \dfrac{a^4}{7}$

8 $x = \dfrac{\log_3 4 + 1}{2}$

9 $x = e^{\frac{4}{3}} = 3.79, y = e^{\frac{10}{3}} = 28.0$

10 $b = \dfrac{x^2}{3}$

11 11

12 $x = 1 \pm \sqrt{1 - e^y}$

13 $x = 1.46$

14 $x = \dfrac{1}{3}$

15 $x = 146$

16 a i $p + q$ **ii** $2 + 3p - q$

  b i $\log_{10}\left(\dfrac{x^2 - 10}{x}\right)$ **ii** $x = 10$

17 $x = \dfrac{\ln 3}{\ln 2}$

18 $x = \dfrac{\ln\left(\frac{4}{5}\right)}{\ln 36}$

19 $x = \ln\left(2 \pm \sqrt{3}\right)$

20 $x = 3, 9$

Chapter 8

Before you start...

1 a $2 + \ln 5$ **b** $5e$

2 $2 + 3\log x$

3 Horizontal stretch, scale factor $\dfrac{1}{2}$

4 $-\dfrac{2}{3}$

5 $y = 3 - \dfrac{2}{3}x$

Exercise 8A

1 a i C   **ii** B   **iii** A
  b i C   **ii** B   **iii** A
  c i A   **ii** B

2 a i $3.2e^{3.2x}$ **ii** $0.6e^{0.6x}$
  b i $-1.3e^{-1.3x}$ **ii** $-e^{-x}$

3 a 57.6   **b** 0.0893
  c -0.0160 **d** -0.784

4 a 25.5   **b** 2.4
  c -2.1 **d** -0.5

5 a 0.0643   **b** 18

6 a -1.15 **b** $x = -0.0363$

7 a $k = 3.25$ **b** 0.126

8 $x = -11.3$

9 a $k = \ln 8$ **b** 0.735

10 a $p = \ln 0.3$ **b** -0.0783

Exercise 8B

1 a

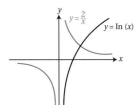

  b One

2

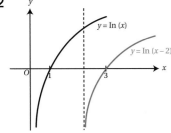

3 Proof

4 translation by $\begin{pmatrix} 0 \\ \ln 3 \end{pmatrix}$ or horizontal stretch with scale factor $\dfrac{1}{3}$

5 a

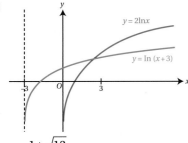

  b $x = \dfrac{1 + \sqrt{13}}{2}$

6 a Proof
  b Vertical stretch with scale factor $\dfrac{1}{\ln 10}$

Work it out 8.1

Solution 2 is correct.

Exercise 8C

1 a i $C\left(1 + \dfrac{p}{100}\right)$ **ii** $C\left(1 + \dfrac{p}{200}\right)^2$

    iii $C\left(1 + \dfrac{p}{400}\right)^4$

  b Proof

  c It tends to (or approaches) e.

  d $V = Ce^x$

2 a 100   **b** 48 300
  c 2.24 h   **d** 1030 cells per hour

3 13.31 m^2

4 a 3 billion   **b** 6.44 billion

5 a

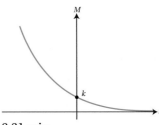

  b 2.31 min

6 a $N_0 = 450$, $a = 4.8$ **b** 3600 per day
  c 7.46 hours

7 $N = 500e^{-0.4t}$

8 a $V = 6800e^{-0.223t}$ **b** £730

9 a $P = 70\,000\,000 \times 1.02^n$
  b e.g. Population growth rate might change due to changing economic conditions. Immigration is not being taken into account.

10 a 21.2°C above room temperature
  b i No change
    ii a would get larger, but not above 1

11 a 0 m s^{-1} **b** 40 m s^{-1}

12 a e^{-2} **b** Proof

Exercise 8D

1 a $A = 2.01$, $b = 3.32$
  b $A = 22.2$, $b = 0.549$
  c $A = 0.0183$, $b = 9.97$

2 a $C = 3.32$, $n = 0.7$ **b** $C = 0.00910$, $n = 2.1$
  c $C = 7.39$, $n = -0.9$

3 a B   **b** $A = 150$ **c** $k = 0.165$
  d Not suitable, as it predicts indefinite growth.

4 a The initial number of bacteria

  b $b = \dfrac{1}{3}$

  c 19.5 hours

5 a $\ln(M) = -0.16t + 2.0$ **b** $K = 7.4, c = 0.85$
  c 13 seconds

6 a $y = 1.2x + 2$ **b** $C = 7.4, n = 1.2$
  c 15.6 years

7 a $N = 330e^{0.16t}$
  b 190 mice per week

8 a $\ln\left(\dfrac{1 - N}{N}\right)$ against t will have gradient $-b$ and
    intercept $\ln J$.
  b The logistic function predicts that the
    population will level off (to one unit),
    which is more realistic than the exponential
    model, which predicts unlimited population
    growth.

Mixed practice 8

1 a

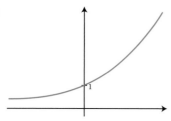

  b 8.82   **c** One

2 a 32 g   **b** $-2.94\,\text{g s}^{-1}$ **c** 4.95 s

3 One

4 a $0.4\,\text{cm}^3$ **b** 10 weeks
  c Model is for algae in a jar, which limits volume;
    extrapolation beyond model's validity

5 a $A = 18, k = 0.0141$ **b** 64
  c 1.58 p.m.

6 a $12\,\mu\text{U/ml}$
  b No – long-term level is $2\,\mu\text{U/ml}$

7 a i Proof
    ii $k = 37\,000, a = 0.949$
  b 2700   **c** 2039

8 a $\ln(N) = kt + \ln(A)$ **b** 4.13
  c $\ln(N) = 0.0137t + 3.56; N = 35.2e^{0.0137t}$
  d 1240
  e Size of the lake limits indefinite growth;
    seasonal variation

9 $p = -2.5, a = 10^{10}$

10 a 17.3 years   **b** 38.0 years

11 a i 40, 320   **ii** $k = 0.0330$
  b $2.64\,\text{g h}^{-1}$

12 0.002 67

13 a $0\,\text{m s}^{-1}$ **b** $42\,\text{m s}^{-1}$ **c** 3.71 s

14 a $C = 76, k = 0.027$ **b** 11.3 min

Chapter 9

Before you start...

1 18

2 a $16x^{12}$ **b** x^{11} **c** x^9

3 $4x^2 + 12x + 9$

4 $x = -4, -1$

Work it out 9.1

Solution 1 is correct.

Exercise 9A

1 a i 35   **ii** 36
  b i 1   **ii** 1
  c i 8   **ii** 45

2 a i $32 - 80x + 80x^2 - 40x^3 + 10x^4 - x^5$
    ii $729 + 1458x + 1215x^2 + 540x^3 + 135x^4 +$
        $18x^5 + x^6$
  b i $16 - 96x + 216x_2 - 216x^3 + 81x^4$
    ii $8x^3 - 84x^2 + 294x - 343$
  c i $243x^5 + 405x^4 y + 270x^3 y^2$
    ii $16c^4 - 32c^3 d + 24c^2 d^2$
  d i $8x^6 - 36x^5 + 54x^4 - 27x^3$
    ii $\dfrac{8}{x^3} + \dfrac{60y}{x^2} + \dfrac{150y^2}{x} + 125y^3$
  e i $8x^3 + 12x + \dfrac{6}{x} + \dfrac{1}{x^3}$
    ii $x^4 - 12x^2 + 54 - \dfrac{108}{x^2} + \dfrac{81}{x^4}$

3 a 4   **b** 35
  c 7   **d** 56

4 a i -216 **ii** 20
  b i $560x^3 y^4$ **ii** $-280x^3 y^4$
  c i -5 **ii** 78 030

5 $27 + 27x + 9x^2 + x^3$

6 a $80y^4$ **b** $-80y^3$

7 $-10\,500$

8 $20\,412x^2$

9 $y^6 + 18y^7 + 135y^8 + 540y^9$

10 a $1+8x+24x^2+32x^3+16x^4$

b $1+\dfrac{8}{x}+\dfrac{24}{x^2}+\dfrac{32}{x^3}+\dfrac{16}{x^4}$

11 56

12 a $n=6$ **b** $a=\pm 2$

13 $16z^8+96z^5+216z^2+216z^{-1}+81z^{-4}$

14 a $n=3$

b $27x^6y^3+135x^5y+225x^4y^{-1}+125x^3y^{-3}$

15 -672

16 $-945x^5$

17 $792\,00\,000$

Exercise 9B

1 a i 21   **ii** 10
  b i 120   **ii** 220
  c i 8   **ii** 15
  d i 1   **ii** 1
  e i 1   **ii** 1
  f i 7   **ii** 12

2 a i $n=10$ **ii** $n=13$
  b i $n=10$ **ii** $n=12$

3 a $n=5$ **b** $a=80$

4 a $n=10$ **b** $a=180$

5 a $n=12$ **b** $a=6$

6 $n=2k+1$

7 a, b Student's own (reasonable) answers.

Exercise 9C

1 a $1+10x+40x^2+80x^3+80x^4+32x^5$

b $3+29x+110x^2+200x^3+160x^4+16x^5-32x^6$

2 a $128-2240x+16\,800x^2-70\,000x^3$

b $-36\,400$

3 a $81-540x+1350x^2$ **b** 80.461

4 a $32\,768+40\,960x+20\,480x^2$ **b** 33 179.648

5 a $128+1344x+6048x^2$

b i 322.88   **ii** 142.0448

c ii Smaller value of x means higher order terms much smaller and therefore less important, so the error is less for 2.03^7.

6 $16384-28672x+21504x^2$; $-30\,720$

7 a $e^5+10e^3+40e+\dfrac{80}{e}+\dfrac{80}{e^3}+\dfrac{32}{e^5}$

b $2e^5+80e+\dfrac{160}{e^3}$

8 a $\left(1-x^2\right)^n$ **b** $1-10x^2+45x^4$

9 126

Mixed practice 9

1 $n=8$

2 $-101\,376$

3 $8x^{-3}+60x^{-2}y+150x^{-1}y^2+125y^3$

4 720

5 $232-164\sqrt{2}$

6 -32

7 $x^8-8x^5+24x^2-32x^{-1}+16x^{-4}$

8 $-\dfrac{1}{3}$

9 5733

10 -5

11 a $16x^4+160x^3+600x^2+1000x+625$
  b $k=2000$ **c** $x=0.5,-2.5$

12 a $n=5$ **b** $a=0.5$
  c $32x^5+40x^4y+20x^3y^2+5x^2y^3$ **d** $3\,240\,200$

13 80

14 $a=2, n=5$

15 a

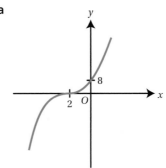

b $x^3+6x^2+12x+8$ **c** 8.120601
d $x=-4$

16 a proof   **b** $k=4, a=\dfrac{1}{2}$ **c** 2

Focus on ... 1

Focus on ... Proof 1

1 Discussion

2 $f\dfrac{a}{b}$

3 Proof

4 a Proof   **b** No

Focus on ... Problem solving 1

1 a, b $4\sqrt{6}$ Accept student's own (reasonable) answers.

2 $f\dfrac{a}{b}$

3 a, b $k=\pm\dfrac{\sqrt{2}}{4}$

c Discussion

4 $r=4$ or 6

Focus on ... Modelling 1

1 a, b, d, e Student's own (reasonable) answers

  c $k \approx 0.24$, $A \approx 10.5$

2 a A

  b Discussion

  c $k \approx 0.27$, $A \approx 10$, $C \approx 460$

3 a, b Discussion

4 a A

  b, c Discussion

5 a $A = 7\,430\,000$, $k = 0.005\,59$

  b 10.3 per 1000 people

  c i About 40 250

    ii They have the same difference between the birth and death rate as the indigenous population.

Cross-topic review exercise 1

1 a 2   **b** $z + 2y - 2x$ **c** $K = \dfrac{e^2}{c}$

2 a i $(x-3)^2 - 4$

    ii Translation by $\begin{pmatrix} 3 \\ -4 \end{pmatrix}$

    iii

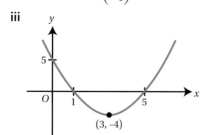

  b i

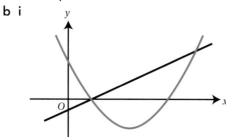

    ii $x = 1, 6$

    iii

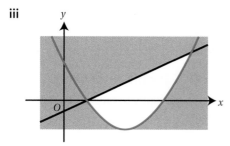

3 a $p(3) = 0$

  b $(x-3)(2x+3)(x-1)$

c

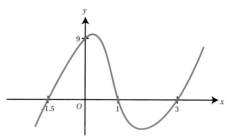

d

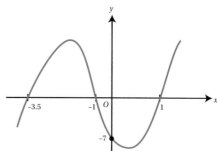

4 84

5 $x = -\ln 3, \ln 2$

6 a $A = 5$, $C = 2$ **b** $k = \dfrac{\ln 5}{2}$

7 a $2 + 12x^2 + 2x^4$ **b** 34

8 a Proof

  b i $x^2 + 2 + \dfrac{1}{x^2}$, $x^3 + 3x + \dfrac{3}{x} + \dfrac{1}{x^3}$

    ii 7, 18

9 a $\dfrac{1}{k}$ **b** $\begin{pmatrix} 0 \\ \ln k \end{pmatrix}$

10 $n = \dfrac{1 + \sqrt{1 + 8k}}{2}$

11 a $A = 42$, $k = \dfrac{1}{9}$, $m = 0.0770$ **b** 11.3

  c 47.9 plants per year

12 Proof

13 a $x = \ln\left(\dfrac{y \pm \sqrt{y^2 - 4}}{2} \right)$

  b i $y \geqslant 2$

    ii Proof that the sum of the two values of x is zero

14 a

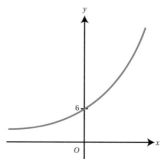

  b Proof

Chapter 10

Before you start...

1 3.86 cm

2 21.8°

3 13

4 $x = 1$

5 $x = \dfrac{1}{e}$ or e_3

Exercise 10A

1 a i 0.669   **ii** −0.978
   b i −0.766   **ii** −0.682

2 a i 1   **ii** 0
   b i 1   **ii** −1
   c i −1   **ii** 0

3 a 0.766   **b** 0.766
   c −0.766   **d** −0.766

4 a 0.766   **b** 0.766
   c −0.766   **d** −0.766

5 a i

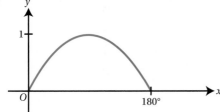

     ii

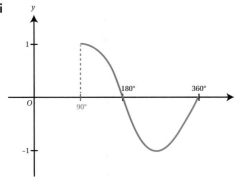

   b i

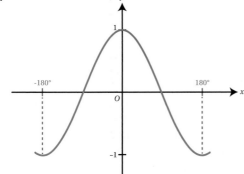

ii

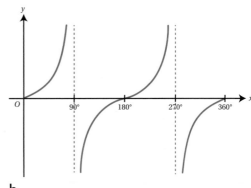

6 0

7 $k = -2$

8 $k = -1$

9 $\sin x$

10 $90 - \ln 3$, $\ln 3 - 90$
    $-270 - \ln 3$, $270 + \ln 3$

Exercise 10B

1 a

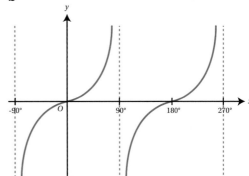

   b

2 a i 0.625   **ii** −0.213
   b i 0   **ii** 1.28

3 a 0.364   **b** 0.364
   c −0.364   **d** −0.364

4 a $\dfrac{1}{\tan x}$ **b** $-\dfrac{1}{\tan x}$
   c $\dfrac{1}{\tan x}$ **d** $-\tan x$

5 $2\tan x$

6 $e, e-180$

7 $-t^2$

Exercise 10C

1 a $\dfrac{\sqrt{2}}{2}$ **b** $\dfrac{\sqrt{2}}{2}$

  c $-\dfrac{\sqrt{2}}{2}$ **d** 1

  e -0.5 **f** $-\dfrac{\sqrt{3}}{2}$

  g $\dfrac{1}{\sqrt{3}}$ **h** $\dfrac{-\sqrt{3}}{3}$

2 a 0.75 **b** $\dfrac{4}{3}$

  c $\dfrac{\sqrt{2}+\sqrt{3}}{2}$ **d** $\dfrac{1-\sqrt{3}}{2}$

3 a Proof   **b** Proof   **c** Proof   **d** Proof

4 a Proof   **b** $120°$

5 a $\dfrac{1-\sqrt{3}}{2}$ **b** $A=B=0°$

6 $a=2, b=-2$

Exercise 10D

1 a i $\cos x=\dfrac{2\sqrt{2}}{3}, \tan x=\dfrac{\sqrt{2}}{4}$

   ii $\cos x=0.6, \tan x=\dfrac{4}{3}$

  b i $\sin\theta=-\dfrac{\sqrt{8}}{3}, \tan\theta=2\sqrt{2}$

   ii $\cos\theta=-\dfrac{\sqrt{7}}{4}, \tan\theta=\dfrac{3\sqrt{7}}{7}$

  c i $\cos x=-\dfrac{2\sqrt{6}}{5}$ **ii** $\cos x=\dfrac{\sqrt{3}}{2}$

  d i $\tan x=\dfrac{4}{3}$ **ii** $\tan x=0$

  e i $\pm\dfrac{3\sqrt{13}}{13}$ **ii** $\pm\dfrac{\sqrt{5}}{5}$

2 a 3 **b** 1

  c -2 **d** $\dfrac{3}{2}$

3 a $4-\sin^2 x$ **b** $2\cos^2 x-1$

4 a i Proof   **ii** Proof

  b i Proof   **ii** Proof

5 a $-\dfrac{\sqrt{5}}{3}$ **b** $-\dfrac{\sqrt{5}}{2}$

6 $\pm\dfrac{3\sqrt{10}}{10}$

7 $-\sqrt{1-s^2}$

8 a $5-\dfrac{2}{\cos^2 x}$ **b** $\cos^2 x$

9 1

10 $k=-2$

11 a $\dfrac{1}{1+t^2}$ **b** $\dfrac{t^2}{1+t^2}$

  c $\dfrac{1-t^2}{1+t^2}$ **d** $\dfrac{2+3t^2}{t^2}$

12 a Proof   **b** Proof

13 Proof

Exercise 10E

1 a i $44.4°$ **ii** $17.5°$

  b i $128.3°$ **ii** $138.6°$

  c i $81.1°$ **ii** $-82.0°$

2 a i $x=30°, 150°$ **ii** $x=45°, 135°$

  b i $x=60°, 300°$ **ii** $x=30°, 330°$

  c i $x=45°, 225°$ **ii** $x=60°, 240°$

  d i $x=240°, 300°$ **ii** $x=210°, 330°$

  e i $x=135°, 225°$ **ii** $x=180°$

  f i $x=150°, 330°$ **ii** $x=135, 315°$

3 a i $x=26.7°, 153.3°$ **ii** $x=44.4°, 135.6°$

  b i $x=-138.6°, 138.6°$ **ii** $x=101.5°, -101.5°$

  c i $\theta=18.4°, 198.4°, 378.4°, 558.4°$

   ii $\theta=53.1°, 233.1°, 413.1°, 593.1°$

  d i $t=-138.2°, -41.8°, 221.8°, 318.2°$

   ii $t=-165.5°, -14.5°, 194.5°, 345.5°$

4 a i $\theta=5.74°, 174°$ **ii** $\theta=-14.5°, 194°$

  b i $x=63.6°, 296°$ **ii** $x=57.3°, 303°$

  c i $t=-121°, 59.0°$ **ii** $t=65.6°, 246°$

5 $x=-150°, -30°$

6 $x=121°, 301°$

7 $x=\pm30°, \pm330°$

8 $\theta=0°, 48.2°, 180°, 312°, 360°$

9 $23.6°, 135°, 156°, 315°$

10 e.g. $x=1$

11 e.g. $x=180°$

Work it out 10.1

Solution 3 is correct.

Exercise 10F

1 a i $x=22.2°, 67.8°, 202°, 248°$

   ii $x=63.8°, 116°, 184°, 236°, 304°, 356°$

  b i $x=37.9°, 82.1°, 158°, 202°, 278°, 322°$

   ii $x=0°, 90°, 180°, 270°, 360°$

  c i $x=14.1°, 59.1°, 104°, 149°, 194°, 239°,$
       $284°, 329°$

   ii $x=58.3°, 148°, 238°, 328°$

2 a i $\theta = -25.5°, 126°$ **ii** $\theta = -106°, -23.6°$
  b i $\theta = -156°, -104°$ **ii** $\theta = 7.46$ to
                                three s.f°, $153°$
  c i $\theta = -71.6°, 108°$ **ii** $\theta = -132°, 48.4°$

3 $x = 20°, 80°, 140°$

4 $x = -120°, -60°, 60°, 120°$

5 $x = -276°, -83.6°$

6 $\theta = 205°$

7 $x = -255°, -225°, -75°, -45°, 105°, 135°, 285°, 315°$

8 $x = -88.3°, 1.67°, 31.7°$

9 $x = \pm30°, \pm150°$

10 $x = \pm5.48°, \pm12.2°$

Exercise 10G

1 a i $x = 54.7°, 125°, 235°, 305°$
    ii $x = 52.2°, 128°, 232°, 308°$
  b i $x = 71.6°, 117°, 252°, 297°$
    ii $x = 48.2°, 180°, 312°$
  c i $x = 41.4°, 319°$ **ii** $x = 53.1°, 127°$
  d i $x = 0°, 180°, 199°, 341°, 360°$
    ii $x = 0°, 129°, 180°, 309°, 360°$

2 a i $\theta = \pm180°, \pm66.4°, 0°$
    ii $\theta = -127°, -90°, -53.1°, 90°$
  b i $\theta = -90°, 14.5°, 90°, 166°$
    ii $\theta = \pm180°, \pm53.1°, 0°$

3 $x = -330°, -270°, -210°, -90°, 30°, 90°, 150°, 270°$

4 a -0.5 **b** $x = 210°, 330°$

5 $x = -104.0°, -71.6°, 76.0°, 108.4°$

6 $\theta = 90°, 180°, 270°$

7 $36.5°, 83.5°, 156°$

Work it out 10.2

Solution 2 is correct.

Exercise 10H

1 a i $x = 33.7°$ **ii** $x = 59.0°$
  b i $x = 66.8°$ **ii** $x = 78.7°$

2 a i $x = 45°, 135°, 225°, 315°$
    ii $x = 54.7°, 125°, 235°, 305°$
  b i $x = 45°, 135°, 225°, 315°$
    ii $x = 0°, 180°, 360°$

3 $x = 67.5°, 158°, 248°, 338°$

4 $\theta = 26.6°, -153°$

5 $x = 0°, 135°, 180°, 315°, 360°$

6 $x = 0°, \pm180°$

7 $\theta = \pm41.8°, \pm138.2°$

8 $\theta = 30°, 150°, 270°$

9 $-14.5°, -90°, -166°$

10 a $\dfrac{1}{3}$
   b $t = 70.5°, 289°$

11 a $\dfrac{2}{3}, -\dfrac{1}{2}$
   b $x = 48.2°, 120°, 240°, 312°$

12 a Proof
    b $x = -153°, -135°, 26.6°, 45°$

Mixed practice 10

1 $-a$

2 $x = -31.8°, 148.2°$

3 $\theta = -135°, -45°, 225°, 315°$

4 $x = 570°, 690°$

5 $\theta = \pm48.6°, \pm131°$

6 a Proof   **b** $60°, 300°$

7 a Proof
   b $\theta = 90°, 120°, 240°, 270°$

8 Eight

9 $a = 5, b = 45°$

10 $x = 48.2°, 120°, 240°, 312°$

11 Proof

12 a Proof
    b $x = 48.2°, 120°, 240°, 312°$

13 Proof

14 a Proof
    b $x = 63.4°, 108°, 243°, 288°$

15 Proof

16 $x = -69.1°, -20.9°, 15°, 75°$

17 a $k = \pm4$
    b Proof
    c i One   **ii** $\theta = \pm60°, \pm300°$
      iii $k = 5$ **iv** Seven

Chapter 11

Before you start...

1 $41.8°$

2 $110°$

3 $x = -1, -4$

4 $8.63°, 171°$

Work it out 11.1

Solution 1 is correct.

Exercise 11A

1 a i $x = 6.04$ **ii** $y = 14.4$
  b i $a = 10.6$ cm   **ii** $b = 23.3$ cm

2 a i $x = 49.7°$ **ii** $y = 59.2°$
  b i $z = 74.6°$ or $105°$ **ii** $u = 62.0°$ or $118°$
  c i $a = 50.9°$ **ii** $b = 54.4°$

3 $21.0°, 29.0°, 8.09$ cm

4 10.4 cm, $49.9°, 95.1°$ or 2.69 cm, $130°, 14.9°$

5 9.94

6 23.3 m

7 Proof

Exercise 11B

1 a i $x = 5.37$ **ii** $y = 3.44$
  b i $z = 8.00$ **ii** $u = 11.3$

2 a i $A = 60.6°$ **ii** $B = 120°$
  b i $C = 81.5°$ **ii** $D = 99.9°$

3 a $106°$ **b** $36.2°$

4 7.08 km

5 25.6 km

6 $x = 7.95$ cm

7 $x = 4.4$

8 $x = 8$

9 $2\sqrt{2} + \sqrt{41}$

Exercise 11C

1 a i 10.7 cm^2 **ii** 23.8 cm^2
  b i 27.6 cm^2 **ii** 26.2 cm^2

2 a $x = 81.7°, 98.3°$
  b $y = 60.9°, 119°$

3 17.7 cm, 29.7 cm^2

4 10 cm

5 $x = 5$

6 $x = 8$

7 $4\sqrt{3}$ cm^2

Mixed practice 11

1 $58.7°, 121°$

2 a 8.09 m   **b** 6.58 m

3 a 11.6 cm   **b** 49.2 cm^2 **c** 6.49 cm

4 a $115°$ **b** 20.3 cm^2

5 $2\sqrt{43}$ cm

6 7.23 cm^2

7 a $\dfrac{23}{32}$ **b** $\dfrac{3\sqrt{55}}{32}$ **c** $\dfrac{15\sqrt{55}}{4}$

8 a $\dfrac{x^2}{4} + 25 - 5x\cos\theta$ **b** Proof
  c $\theta = 41.4°$

9 a $009°$ or $071°$ **b** 15.5 km

10 10.8 cm

11 a Proof
  b $\left[-1, -\dfrac{\sqrt{3}}{2}\right] \cup \left[\dfrac{\sqrt{3}}{2}, 1\right]$ **c** $0° < \theta \leqslant 30°$

Chapter 12

Before you start…

1 $\begin{pmatrix} 3 \\ -1 \end{pmatrix}$

2 $5.39, 21.8°$

3 Two

Work it out 12.1

Solution 2 is correct.

Exercise 12A

1 $\mathbf{a} = 2\mathbf{i} + \mathbf{j}, \mathbf{b} = -3\mathbf{j}, \mathbf{c} = -2\mathbf{i} + \mathbf{j}, \mathbf{d} = \mathbf{i} - \mathbf{j}$

2

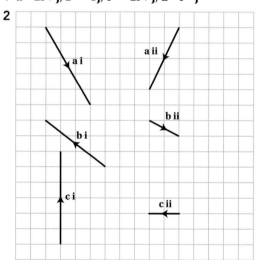

3 A a i 5.83 **ii** 4.47
   b i 5 **ii** 2.24
   c i 6 **ii** 2

  B a i $-59.0°$ **ii** $-117°$
   b i $143°$ **ii** $-26.6°$
   c i $90°$ **ii** $180°$

  C a i $-149°$ **ii** $153°$
   b i $53.1°$ **ii** $117°$
   c i $0°$ **ii** $90°$

4 a No, magnitude $= \dfrac{\sqrt{13}}{6}$ **b** Yes

   c Yes

   d No, magnitude $= 3$

5 $\pm\dfrac{1}{\sqrt{29}}$

6 $\pm\dfrac{1}{\sqrt{13}}$

7 $t = -1$ or -3

8 a $63°$ **b** $5.45\mathbf{i} + 10.7\mathbf{j}$

9 $\begin{pmatrix} -3 \\ \sqrt{3} \end{pmatrix}$

Exercise 12B

1 a

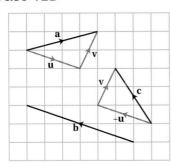

b

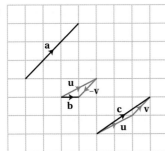

2 a i $\begin{pmatrix} 21 \\ 3 \end{pmatrix}$ **ii** $\begin{pmatrix} 20 \\ -8 \end{pmatrix}$

   b i $\begin{pmatrix} 2 \\ 3 \end{pmatrix}$ **ii** $\begin{pmatrix} 6 \\ -1 \end{pmatrix}$

   c i $\begin{pmatrix} 11 \\ -3 \end{pmatrix}$ **ii** $\begin{pmatrix} -3 \\ 5 \end{pmatrix}$

   d i $\begin{pmatrix} 10 \\ -3 \end{pmatrix}$ **ii** $\begin{pmatrix} 17 \\ 6 \end{pmatrix}$

3 a i $-6\mathbf{i}$ **ii** $4\mathbf{i} + 8\mathbf{j}$

   b i $\mathbf{i} - 3\mathbf{j}$ **ii** $2\mathbf{j}$

   c i $4\mathbf{i}$ **ii** $5\mathbf{i} - 4\mathbf{j}$

4 a $-4\mathbf{i} + 2\mathbf{j}$ **b** $-\dfrac{8}{3}\mathbf{i} + \dfrac{4}{3}\mathbf{j}$

   c $4\mathbf{i} - 3\mathbf{j}$ **d** $-\dfrac{1}{2}\mathbf{i} + \mathbf{j}$

5 a i Parallel   **ii** Parallel

   b i Not parallel   **ii** Not parallel

   c i Parallel   **ii** Not parallel

6 $\begin{pmatrix} 2 \\ 0 \end{pmatrix}$

7 $t = -2$

8 $p = -\dfrac{4}{3}$

9 $\lambda = -2$

10 $q = \dfrac{1}{2} - p$

11 $\dfrac{11}{7}$

12 $\pm\begin{pmatrix} 12 \\ -16 \end{pmatrix}$

13 $\pm\begin{pmatrix} \frac{6}{\sqrt{5}} \\ \frac{3}{\sqrt{5}} \end{pmatrix}$

14 $\pm\begin{pmatrix} \frac{-2}{\sqrt{5}} \\ \frac{1}{\sqrt{5}} \end{pmatrix}$

15 a Proof   **b** $t = 0$

Work it out 12.2

Solution 1 is correct.

Exercise 12C

1 a i $\begin{pmatrix} 4 \\ 2 \end{pmatrix}$ **ii** $\begin{pmatrix} -3 \\ 2 \end{pmatrix}$

     iii $\begin{pmatrix} 3 \\ -2 \end{pmatrix}$ **iv** $\begin{pmatrix} -6 \\ -5 \end{pmatrix}$

   b i, ii, iii On grid diagram

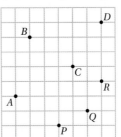

2 a i $\begin{pmatrix} -1 \\ 3 \end{pmatrix}$ **ii** $\begin{pmatrix} 3 \\ -3 \end{pmatrix}$

   b i $\begin{pmatrix} -6 \\ 1 \end{pmatrix}$ **ii** $\begin{pmatrix} 3 \\ 2 \end{pmatrix}$

   c i $\begin{pmatrix} 4 \\ -6 \end{pmatrix}$ **ii** $\begin{pmatrix} 2 \\ 5 \end{pmatrix}$

3 a i $(2, 1)$ **ii** $(-4, -4)$
b i $(1, -2)$ **ii** $(2, 0)$
c i $(11, -15)$ **ii** $(-9, -1)$
d i $(-8, 7)$ **ii** $(1, -34)$

4 a i $\sqrt{205}$ **ii** $\sqrt{2}$
b i $3\sqrt{2}$ **ii** $\sqrt{137}$

5 a $\overrightarrow{PR} = 5\mathbf{i} - \mathbf{j}$ **b** $\overrightarrow{SP} = -7\mathbf{i} - 4\mathbf{j}$

6 a $\overrightarrow{AC} = \begin{pmatrix} -2 \\ -3 \end{pmatrix} \overrightarrow{DB} = \begin{pmatrix} -4 \\ -6 \end{pmatrix}$ **b** $(0, 3)$

7 $(3, -19)$

8 a $\overrightarrow{AC} = \begin{pmatrix} 8 \\ -4 \end{pmatrix}$

b $\overrightarrow{BP} = \begin{pmatrix} r-6 \\ q+3 \end{pmatrix} \overrightarrow{CP} = \begin{pmatrix} r-8 \\ q+4 \end{pmatrix}$ **c** $CP = 2\sqrt{5}$

Exercise 12D

1 a i $\mathbf{b}$ **ii** $\mathbf{a}+\mathbf{b}$
b i $-\mathbf{a}$ **ii** $-\dfrac{1}{2}\mathbf{a}$
c i $\mathbf{a}+\dfrac{1}{2}\mathbf{b}$ **ii** $\dfrac{1}{2}\mathbf{b}-\dfrac{1}{2}\mathbf{a}$

2 a i $\mathbf{a}+\dfrac{4}{3}\mathbf{b}$ **ii** $\mathbf{a}+\dfrac{1}{2}\mathbf{b}$
b i $-\dfrac{3}{2}\mathbf{a}+\mathbf{b}$ **ii** $-\dfrac{1}{2}\mathbf{b}+\dfrac{1}{2}\mathbf{a}$
c i $\dfrac{3}{2}\mathbf{a}-\mathbf{b}$ **ii** $-\dfrac{4}{3}\mathbf{b}+\dfrac{1}{2}\mathbf{a}$

3 a i Collinear; $AB:BC = 1:13$
ii Collinear; $AB:BC = 2:5$
b i Not collinear
ii Not collinear
c i Not collinear
ii Collinear; $AB:BC = 1:2$
d i Collinear; $AB:BC = 1:1-2a$
ii Not collinear

4 $2\mathbf{i} + 12\mathbf{j}$

5 $AB:BC = 1:2$

6 a $\begin{pmatrix} 8 \\ -4 \end{pmatrix}$ **b** No

7 a $\begin{pmatrix} 6 \\ 4 \end{pmatrix}$ **b** $\overrightarrow{AB} = \overrightarrow{DE} = \begin{pmatrix} 2 \\ 1 \end{pmatrix}$

8 Proof

9 $\begin{pmatrix} 0.8 \\ 1.8 \end{pmatrix}$

10 $\overrightarrow{MN} = \overrightarrow{QP} = \dfrac{1}{2}(\mathbf{c}-\mathbf{a})$

11 a $C(10 - 8x, 1 + 6x)$ **b** $x = \dfrac{6}{25}$

12 a $\dfrac{1}{2}(\mathbf{p}+\mathbf{q})$ **b** Proof

13 a Proof **b** Proof

Mixed practice 12

1 $3\sqrt{2}$

2 a $6\mathbf{i} - 5\mathbf{j}$ **b** $(0, 1)$

3 a $\begin{pmatrix} 4.5 \\ -1 \end{pmatrix}$ **b** $\dfrac{3}{2}\sqrt{41}$

4 $6\mathbf{i} - 2\mathbf{j}$

5 $\overrightarrow{MN} = \mathbf{b} - \dfrac{1}{3}\mathbf{a}$

6 Proof

7 $\sqrt{9 + 16\cos^2\theta}$

8 $\pm\left(\dfrac{9}{\sqrt{97}}\mathbf{i} + \dfrac{4}{\sqrt{97}}\mathbf{j}\right)$

9 a $(4, -6)$
b $\overrightarrow{OP} = \sqrt{65}, \overrightarrow{ON} = 2\sqrt{13}, \overrightarrow{PN} = \sqrt{13}$

10 a $\overrightarrow{MN} = \dfrac{1}{2}(\mathbf{c}-\mathbf{a}), \overrightarrow{PQ} = \dfrac{1}{2}(\mathbf{a}-\mathbf{c})$
b Parallelogram

11 a $\mathbf{a}+\mathbf{b}$ **b** $\mathbf{a}+\dfrac{1}{2}\mathbf{b}$
c $t\mathbf{a}+(t-1)\mathbf{b}; t = \dfrac{2}{3}$

12 a $\begin{pmatrix} 5-3t \\ 2+t \end{pmatrix}; \sqrt{10t^2 - 26t + 29}$ **b** $\dfrac{11\sqrt{10}}{10}$

13 a $1:1$
b Diagonals bisect each other

Chapter 13

Before you start...

1 a $x^{\frac{2}{3}} - \dfrac{5}{2}x^{-1}$ **b** $2x^{-\frac{1}{2}} + x^{\frac{1}{2}}$

2 a $x \leqslant -3$ **b** $x \leqslant -2, x \geqslant 6$

3 $-\dfrac{3}{4}$

4 $x^3 + 6x^2 + 12x + 8$

Exercise 13A

1 a i 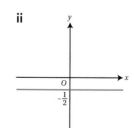 **ii**

b i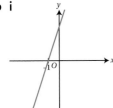

ii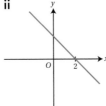

c i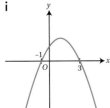

ii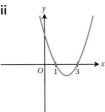

d i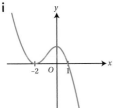

ii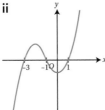

e i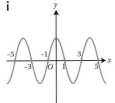

ii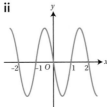

f i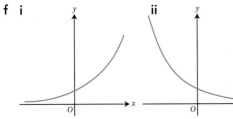

2 a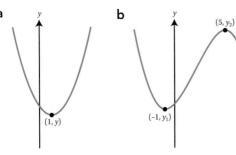

b

c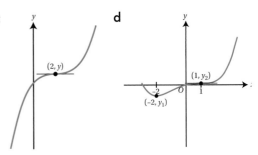

d

3 a False $y = 3x$ at $(-1, -3)$
  b False $y = 3x$ at $(-1, -3)$
  c Always true
  d False $y = x^3$
  e False $y = -e^{-x}$
  f False $y = x^3$

Exercise 13B

1 Proof

2 -4

3 $6x$

4 Proof

5 $2x - 6$

6 $2x - 3$

7 a $x^3 + 3x^2h + 3xh^2 + h^3$ **b** $3x^2$

8 $9x^2$

9 a $x^4 + 4x^3h + 6x^2h^2 + 4xh^3 + h^4$
  b Proof

10 a $12a^2 + 12ah + 4h^2$

  b $12a^2$

  c It is the gradient of the tangent to the curve at A.

11 Proof

12 Proof

Exercise 13C

1 a i $y' = 4x^3$ **ii** $y' = 6x^5$
  b i $y' = 21x^6$ **ii** $y' = -20x^4$
  c i $y' = -1$ **ii** $y' = 3$
  d i $y' = 0$ **ii** $y' = 0$

  e i $y' = 2x^5$ **ii** $y' = -\dfrac{3}{2}x$

  f i $y' = 12x^2 - 10x + 2$ **ii** $y' = 8x^3 + 9x^2 - 1$

  g i $y' = 7 - \dfrac{3}{2}x^2$ **ii** $y' = -20x^3 + x^4$

2 a i $f'(x) = \dfrac{3}{2}x^{\frac{1}{2}}$ **ii** $f'(x) = \dfrac{2}{3}x^{-\frac{1}{3}}$

  b i $f'(x) = 4x^{-\frac{1}{2}}$ **ii** $f'(x) = 8x^{\frac{1}{3}}$

c **i** $f'(x) = \frac{1}{3}x^{-\frac{1}{4}}$ **ii** $f'(x) = \frac{1}{2}x^{-\frac{1}{6}}$

d **i** $f'(x) = 12x^3 - 6x^{-\frac{3}{5}}$

   ii $f'(x) = 3x^2 - x^{\frac{2}{3}} + \frac{2}{3}x^{-\frac{1}{2}}$

e **i** $f'(x) = -x^{-2}$ **ii** $f'(x) = -3x^{-4}$

f **i** $f'(x) = -\frac{1}{2}x^{-\frac{3}{2}}$ **ii** $f'(x) = -\frac{2}{3}x^{-\frac{5}{3}}$

g **i** $f'(x) = 8x^{-\frac{7}{3}}$ **ii** $f'(x) = 6x^{-\frac{7}{4}}$

h **i** $f'(x) = 5 + \frac{4}{3}x^{-\frac{7}{2}}$ **ii** $f'(x) = x^{-\frac{10}{7}} - 8x^{-7}$

3 a i $10.8x^{1.7}$ **ii** $10.5x^{2.5}$
b i $3x^{-0.4}$ **ii** $-1.2x^{-0.6}$
c i $1.4x^{-1.7}$ **ii** $-6x^{-2.5}$

4 $\frac{dy}{dx} = 2x - \frac{3}{2}x^{-\frac{1}{2}}$

5 $f'(x) = 12x^2 - 6x - 3x^{-\frac{5}{2}}$

6 $f'(x) = -4x^{-\frac{4}{3}} + \frac{1}{3}x^{-\frac{3}{5}}$

Work it out 13.1
Solution 2 is correct.

Exercise 13D

1 a i $y' = \frac{1}{3}x^{-\frac{2}{3}}$ **ii** $y' = \frac{1}{5}x^{-\frac{4}{5}}$

b i $y' = 2x^{-\frac{3}{4}}$ **ii** $y' = \frac{1}{6}x^{-\frac{1}{2}}$

c i $y' = x^{-2}$ **ii** $y' = -4x^{-5}$

d i $y' = -6x^{-3}$ **ii** $y' = 4x^{-11}$

e i $y' = -\frac{1}{2}x^{-\frac{3}{2}}$ **ii** $y' = -\frac{4}{3}x^{-\frac{4}{3}}$

f i $y' = 2x^{-\frac{6}{5}}$ **ii** $y' = -\frac{2}{3}x^{-\frac{5}{4}}$

2 a i $f'(x) = 4x + 5$ **ii** $f'(x) = 6x - 15$

b i $f'(x) = 6x^{\frac{1}{2}} + \frac{3}{2}x^{-\frac{1}{2}}$ **ii** $f'(x) = \frac{4}{3}x^{\frac{1}{3}} - \frac{1}{3}x^{-\frac{2}{3}}$

c i $f'(x) = 1 + 8x + 6x^{\frac{1}{2}}$ **ii** $f'(x) = \frac{1}{2}x^{-\frac{1}{2}} - 2x^{-\frac{3}{4}}$

d i $f'(x) = 2x - 2x^{-3}$ **ii** $f'(x) = 2x + 8x^{-3}$

3 a i $f'(x) = 2x^{-2}$ **ii** $f'(x) = -\frac{1}{2}x^{-2} + 2$

b i $f'(x) = -\frac{3}{2}x^{-\frac{5}{2}} + 6x^{-3}$ **ii** $f'(x) = \frac{3}{2}x^{\frac{1}{2}} - 2x^{-\frac{3}{2}}$

4 $y' = 9x^2 - 8x$

5 $y' = 7x^{\frac{5}{2}} + 4x^{-\frac{1}{2}}$

6 $\frac{dy}{dx} = \frac{4}{5}x^{-\frac{1}{5}}$

7 $f'(x) = -2x^{-\frac{7}{4}}$

8 a $y = 3x^3 - 2x^{-1}$ **b** $y' = 9x^2 + 2x^{-2}$

9 Proof

10 $f'(x) = \frac{15}{2}x^{\frac{2}{3}} - \frac{1}{2}x^{-\frac{4}{3}}$

11 $y' = -2x^{-\frac{3}{2}} + 12x^{-2} - \frac{27}{2}x^{-\frac{5}{2}}$

Work it out 13.2
Solution 2 is correct.

Exercise 13E

1 a $\dfrac{dz}{dt}$ **b** $\dfrac{dQ}{dP}$ **c** $\dfrac{dR}{dm}$

   d $\dfrac{dV}{dt}$ **e** $\dfrac{dy}{dx}$ **f** $\dfrac{d^2z}{dy^2}$

   g $\dfrac{d^2H}{dm^2}$

2 a i $\frac{5}{3}x^{-\frac{2}{3}}$ **ii** $15q^4$

   b i $3 - 7t^{-2}$ **ii** $1 - c^{-2}$

   c i $18 + 6x$ **ii** $6t^{-3}$

3 a i 30 **ii** $\dfrac{227}{36}$

   b i 7 **ii** $-29\,999.8$

   c i 12 **ii** -10

   d i 24 **ii** 32

   e i 6 **ii** $\dfrac{7}{2\sqrt{6}}$

4 a i $2ax + 1 - a$ **ii** $3x^2$

   b i $\frac{1}{2}\sqrt{\dfrac{b}{a}}$ **ii** $6a^2v$

5 a i 54 **ii** 384

   b i 8 **ii** $\dfrac{1}{108}$

   c i 0 **ii** 42

6 a i $x = \pm 2$ **ii** $x = 1$

   b i $y = \pm 17$ **ii** $y = 6$

   c i $x = -3$ **ii** $x = 2$

7 a i $x > \dfrac{1}{2}$ **ii** $x < -1$

   b i $x < -1$ or $x > 1$ **ii** $-\dfrac{4}{3} < x < 0$

   c i $x < 0$ **ii** $x > \dfrac{1}{6}$

8 a $-\dfrac{1}{18}$ **b** Increasing

9 $\dfrac{3}{16}$

10 $-\dfrac{2}{3} < x < \dfrac{2}{3}$

11 $x = \dfrac{-3}{5}$

12 $x = \pm\sqrt{2}$

13 Proof

14 $(1, 0)$ and $(3, 4)$

15 $x < 0$ or $x > 4$

16 $a = -6,\ b = 2$

17 $x > -\dfrac{1}{3}$

18 $-1 - \dfrac{2\sqrt{3}}{3} < x < -1 + \dfrac{2\sqrt{3}}{3}$

19 $2 < x < 3$

20 $n!$

Mixed practice 13

1 $\dfrac{3}{2}x^{-\frac{1}{2}} + x^{-\frac{3}{2}}$

2 $\dfrac{dy}{dx} = -12x^2 + 24x + 1$

3 $-\dfrac{1}{2}$

4 a $f'(x) = \dfrac{3}{2}x^{-\frac{1}{2}} + x^{-\frac{3}{2}}$ **b** $\dfrac{7}{8}$

5 $b = 8,\ c = -7$

6 a $\dfrac{9}{4}$

b Positive gradient; increasing

7 $x > \dfrac{2}{3}$

8 $\dfrac{109}{54}$

9 a $-\dfrac{10}{x^3} + \dfrac{1}{4x^2} + 1$ **b** $\dfrac{30}{x^4} - \dfrac{1}{2x^3}$

10 $a = -10$

11 11

12 D

13 a 2 **b** 1.3

c Anything between 2 and 2.3

14 $3x^2 - 5$

15 a 0 **b** Increasing

c

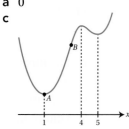

16 $\left(\dfrac{1}{16}, \dfrac{7}{16}\right)$

17 -54

18 $a = 4.8,\ b = -1.8$

19 $x = 1,\ 25$

20 $\dfrac{-1}{\sqrt{3}} < x < \dfrac{1}{\sqrt{3}}$

Chapter 14

Before you start...

1 a $\dfrac{6x}{5} + \dfrac{4x^{-3}}{5}$ **b** $-\dfrac{3}{4}x^{-\frac{3}{2}}$

2 $\dfrac{9}{16}$

3 $y = 3x + 7$

4 $y = -\dfrac{4}{3}x - \dfrac{1}{3}$

Work it out 14.1

Solution 2 is correct.

Exercise 14A

1 a i Tangent $y + 2 = 0$, normal $x - 1 = 0$
   ii Tangent $4x + y - 28 = 0$, normal $x - 4y + 95 = 0$
  b i Tangent $x + 3y + 6 = 0$, normal $3x - y + 8 = 0$
   ii Tangent $3x - 2y - 9 = 0$, normal $4x + 6y + 1 = 0$
  c i Tangent $x - 4y + 36 = 0$, normal $4x + y - 26 = 0$
   ii Tangent $x + 6y - 32 = 0$, normal $6x - y - 44 = 0$

2 $11x - 4y - 4 = 0$

3 $32x + 70y - 583 = 0$

4 $(162, 0)$

5 $\dfrac{9}{4}$

6 $y = 5,\ y = 6$

7 1.55 or -0.215

8 $a = -6,\ b = 8$

9 $p = -1,\ q = -\dfrac{1}{6}$

10 $\left(\dfrac{1}{4}, \dfrac{7}{2}\right)$

11 $(-1, -4)$

12 $(0.410, 0.348)$

13 $c = -2$

14 Proof; area $= 2k$

15 Proof

Exercise 14B

1 a i $(0, 0)$ local maximum; $\left(\dfrac{10}{3}, -\dfrac{500}{27}\right)$ local minimum

   ii $(0, 1)$ local minimum; $(16, 2049)$ local maximum

 b i $(0, 0)$ local maximum; $(\pm 2, -16)$ local minima

   ii $(0, 3)$ local maximum; $(\pm 1, 2)$ local minima

 c i No stationary points

   ii $(1.14, 11.8)$ local minimum

 d i $\left(\dfrac{1}{9}, \dfrac{1}{3}\right)$ local maximum

   ii $(0.303, 2.73)$ local minimum

2 $(-4, 92)$ local maximum; $(2, -16)$ local minimum

3 Consider discriminant of the derivative expression

4 a $x = \pm\dfrac{1}{3}$

 b $\left(\dfrac{1}{3}, 6\right)$ local minimum; $\left(-\dfrac{1}{3}, -6\right)$ local maximum

5 $\left(\dfrac{1}{4}, -\dfrac{1}{4}\right)$ local minimum

6 a $(0, 0)$ and $(1, -1)$

 b $(0, 0)$ local maximum; $(1, -1)$ local minimum

7 a $x = \dfrac{4}{3}$

 b Local maximum at $x = -8$

   Local minimum at $x = \dfrac{4}{3}$

8 $a = 3, b = 12$

9 $0 \leqslant f(x) \leqslant 54$

10 Proof

11 a $(0, 6), (1, 11), (3, -21)$ **b** $6 < c < 11$

12 $(0, 0)$ local minimum; $\left(-\dfrac{4}{k}, \dfrac{32}{k^2}\right)$ local maximum if $k \neq 0$

Exercise 14C

1 a i 2 **ii** $\dfrac{49}{12}$

 b i $2\sqrt{3}$ **ii** $4\sqrt{2}$

 c i $4\sqrt{2}$ **ii** $\dfrac{8}{3}$

2 a $225\,\text{m}^2$ **b** $60\,\text{m}$

3 a Proof

 b i $r = 10\,\text{cm}$

   ii Proof

4 a Proof   **b** $x = 2$

5 Proof

6 a $V = 225r - \pi r^3$ **b** $733\,\text{cm}^3 \left(\dfrac{d^2 y}{dx^2} < 0\right)$

7 a $V = \dfrac{(243 - x^2)x}{2}$ **b** $729\,\text{cm}^3 \left(\dfrac{d^2 y}{dx^2} < 0\right)$

8 a Proof   **b** $166\,\text{cm}^2$

 c Proof

9 a Proof   **b** $r = 5.56, h = 7.86$

10 a 3 and 3 **b** 0 and 6

11 Maximum time 4 min; minimum time 2 min

12 a Proof

 b Proof

13 Proof

14 $\left(\sqrt{\dfrac{7}{2}}, \dfrac{7}{2}\right)$

15 a Proof

 b $V = \pi(6 + x)^2 \left(\dfrac{12}{x} + 2\right)$

 c 486π

Mixed practice 14

1 C

2 $19x - 4y = 28$

3 $x = 2$

4 $x = 2 + \sqrt{2}$ local minimum; $x = 2 - \sqrt{2}$ local maximum

5 a $(0, -1)\,(2, 3)\,(4, -1)$

 b $(0, -1)$ local minimum $(2, 3)$ local maximum $(4, -1)$ local minimum

6 $\left(\dfrac{2\sqrt{3}}{3}, 0\right)$

7 a Proof   **b** $50\,\text{m}^2$

8 $a = 3$

9 $a = 2, b = -13$

10 $(1, -2)$ local maximum

    $(4, -3)$ local minimum

11 a $\left(-\sqrt{3}, 6\sqrt{3}\right)$ and $\left(\sqrt{3}, -6\sqrt{3}\right)$

 b Minimum: $-6\sqrt{3}$; maximum: 80

12 $\dfrac{3}{4}$

13 a 4 litres   **b** 41.5 litres

 c 20 seconds

14 a Proof   **b** $40\sqrt{2}\,\text{m}$

15 a $(-1, 7)$ **b** Minimum

16 a Proof

  c $a = 1, b = 3$

b $3a + b = 6$

d $(-7, -192)$

17 $a = 3^{-\frac{1}{4}}$

18 $a = 1.5$

Chapter 15

Before you start...

1 a $x = 0, \dfrac{4}{3}$

  c $x = 0, \pm\sqrt{5}$

b $x = 0, 4$

2 a $\dfrac{dy}{dx} = 6x - 1$

  b $\dfrac{dy}{dx} = \dfrac{1}{2}x^{-\frac{1}{2}} + 2x^{-\frac{5}{3}}$

3 a $\dfrac{dy}{dx} = -3x^{-3}$

  b $\dfrac{dy}{dx} = \dfrac{9}{2}x^{\frac{1}{2}}$

Exercise 15A

1 a i $y = \dfrac{1}{6}x^6 + c$ **ii** $y = \dfrac{1}{7}x^7 + c$

  b i $y = x^3 + c$ **ii** $y = -x^5 + c$

  c i $y = \dfrac{1}{2}x^4 + c$ **ii** $y = -\dfrac{3}{8}x^8 + c$

  d i $y = \dfrac{1}{2}x^2 + c$ **ii** $y = -2x^2 + c$

  e i $y = c$ **ii** $y = x + c$

  f i $y = -\dfrac{1}{6}x + c$ **ii** $y = \dfrac{1}{27}x^9 + c$

  g i $y = \dfrac{2x^7}{5} + c$ **ii** $y = \dfrac{5x^2}{7} + c$

  h i $y = \dfrac{1}{2}x^6 - \dfrac{1}{2}x^2 + 4x + c$

    ii $y = \dfrac{2}{5}x^5 + x^4 - 4x^2 - x + c$

  i i $y = \dfrac{x^3}{6} + x^2 - \dfrac{3x}{4} + c$ **ii** $y = \dfrac{x^3}{3} - \dfrac{x^6}{16} + c$

2 a i $\dfrac{3}{5}x^{\frac{5}{3}} + c$ **ii** $\dfrac{3}{4}x^{\frac{4}{3}} + c$

  b i $3x^{\frac{5}{3}} + c$ **ii** $8x^{\frac{7}{4}} + c$

  c i $x^{\frac{5}{4}} + c$ **ii** $-x^{\frac{3}{2}} + c$

  d i $-\dfrac{x^{\frac{7}{3}}}{2} + c$ **ii** $\dfrac{2x^{\frac{7}{5}}}{3} + c$

  e i $\dfrac{5}{2}x^2 - 2x^{\frac{7}{2}} + c$ **ii** $6x + \dfrac{x^2}{6} - 8x^{\frac{3}{2}}$

f i $-x^{-1} + c$ **ii** $-\dfrac{1}{2}x^{-2} + c$

g i $\dfrac{3}{2}x^{\frac{2}{3}} + c$ **ii** $\dfrac{4}{3}x^{\frac{3}{4}} + c$

h i $-12x^{\frac{1}{3}} + c$ **ii** $10x^{-\frac{1}{2}} + c$

i i $2x^{\frac{1}{2}} + \dfrac{2x^{-3}}{5} + c$ **ii** $-\dfrac{3x^{-4}}{4} + \dfrac{42x^{\frac{5}{6}}}{5} + c$

3 a i $3t + c$ **ii** $7z + c$

  b i $\dfrac{q^6}{6} + c$ **ii** $\dfrac{r^{11}}{11} + c$

  c i $\dfrac{15}{2}g^{\frac{8}{5}} + c$ **ii** $\dfrac{4}{3}y^{\frac{9}{2}} + c$

  d i $20a^{\frac{1}{4}} + c$ **ii** $-21p^{-\frac{1}{3}} + c$

4 $f(x) = \dfrac{1}{8}x^4 + 9x^{-\frac{2}{3}} + 2x + c$

5 $\dfrac{2}{5}x^{\frac{5}{2}} + 2x^{-\frac{1}{2}} + c$

6 $\dfrac{1}{12}x^6 + \dfrac{3}{4}x^{-2} + \dfrac{1}{4}x^2 + c$

Work it out 15.1

Solution 1 is correct.

Exercise 15B

1 a i $\dfrac{2}{3}x^{\frac{3}{2}} + c$ **ii** $\dfrac{4}{5}x^{\frac{5}{4}} + c$

  b i $5x^{\frac{6}{5}} + c$ **ii** $\dfrac{1}{8}x^{\frac{4}{3}} + c$

  c i $-\dfrac{1}{2}x^{-2} + c$ **ii** $\dfrac{1}{6}x^{-6} + c$

  d i $2x^{-4} + c$ **ii** $-\dfrac{2}{3}x^{-5} + c$

  e i $2x^{\frac{1}{2}} + c$ **ii** $\dfrac{3}{2}x^{\frac{2}{3}} + c$

  f i $-18x^{\frac{5}{6}} + c$ **ii** $\dfrac{3}{2}x^{\frac{3}{4}} + c$

2 a i $\dfrac{2}{3}x^3 + \dfrac{5}{2}x^2 + 3x + c$ **ii** $\dfrac{3}{4}x^4 - 2x^3 + c$

  b i $2x^{\frac{5}{2}} + \dfrac{8}{3}x^{\frac{3}{2}} + c$ **ii** $\dfrac{3}{5}x^{\frac{10}{3}} + \dfrac{9}{4}x^{\frac{4}{3}} + c$

  c i $\dfrac{2}{3}x^{\frac{3}{2}} + 3x^3 + \dfrac{8}{3}x^{\frac{9}{4}} + c$

    ii $\dfrac{1}{2}x^2 + \dfrac{1}{5}x^5 - \dfrac{4}{7}x^{\frac{7}{2}} + c$

  d i $\dfrac{1}{3}x^3 - x^{-1} - 2x + c$ **ii** $\dfrac{4}{3}x^3 + \dfrac{1}{3}x^{-3} + c$

3 a i $-7x^{-1}+x^{-2}+c$ **ii** $-\dfrac{1}{4}x^{-2}-\dfrac{5}{4}x^{-1}+c$

b i $-2x^{-\frac{1}{2}}+3x^{-1}+c$ **ii** $\dfrac{2}{5}x^{\frac{5}{2}}-4x^{\frac{3}{2}}+c$

4 $4x^{\frac{5}{2}}+c$

5 $\dfrac{3}{10}x^{\frac{10}{3}}-4x^3+c$

6 $4x^{\frac{9}{4}}+c$

7 $x^{\frac{1}{3}}+c$

8 $2x^{\frac{1}{2}}-x+c$

9 $-\dfrac{1}{6}x^{-2}-\dfrac{1}{12}x^{-3}+c$

10 a $f(x)=6x^{-\frac{1}{3}}+x^{\frac{2}{3}}$ **b** $9x^{\frac{2}{3}}+\dfrac{3}{5}x^{\frac{5}{3}}+c$

11 a $a=\dfrac{1}{2}, b=-2$ **b** $\dfrac{1}{5}x^{\frac{5}{2}}-4x^{\frac{1}{2}}+c$

12 Proof

13 $\dfrac{1}{12}x^{\frac{3}{2}}+2x^{\frac{1}{2}}-4x^{-\frac{1}{2}}+c$

Work it out 15.2

Solution 3 is correct.

Exercise 15C

1 a i $y=\dfrac{x^2}{2}+5$ **ii** $y=2x^3+5$

b i $y=\dfrac{-1}{x}$ **ii** $y=-\dfrac{1}{x}+4$

c i $y=\dfrac{3}{2}x^2-5x+10$ **ii** $y=3x-\dfrac{1}{2}x^4+\dfrac{5}{2}$

d i $y=2x^{\frac{3}{2}}-56$ **ii** $y=2\sqrt{x}+4$

2 a i $y=x^3-x+5$ **ii** $y=3x^{-1}+2x-2$

b i $f(x)=\dfrac{1}{2}x^2-\dfrac{1}{3}x^3+3x-\dfrac{19}{3}$

   ii $f(x)=\dfrac{1}{4}x^4-\dfrac{1}{6}x^3+\dfrac{5}{2}x+\dfrac{89}{12}$

3 $y=\dfrac{x^2}{2}+\dfrac{1}{x}+\dfrac{3}{2}$

4 $f(x)=\dfrac{4}{3}x^{\frac{3}{2}}-2x^{\frac{1}{2}}-\dfrac{14}{3}$

5 $\dfrac{149}{3}$

6 $y=2x^2-16$

7 a $x=-2$ **b** Proof

8 $y=x^2-\dfrac{x^4}{12}+\dfrac{10x}{3}-\dfrac{5}{4}$

9 858

10 $y=\dfrac{1}{x}+\dfrac{5}{2}$

Exercise 15D

1 a i 320   **ii** 420.2

b i 0   **ii** 36

c i 46   **ii** 48

d i 28.5   **ii** $\dfrac{33}{2}$

e i $\dfrac{76}{3}$ **ii** $\dfrac{585}{2}$

f i 36   **ii** 2

g i $\dfrac{5}{2}$ **ii** $-\dfrac{26}{3}$

2 $-60+28\sqrt{2}$

3 $a=2,\ b=10$

4 $2k+\dfrac{1}{k}-3$

5 $8-a^4-a^3$

6 $a=16$

7 $p=-\dfrac{10}{3}$ or $p=-1$

8 20

9 $\dfrac{15}{2}$

10 a i 16   **ii** -16

b i a^2-b^2 **ii** b^2-a^2

c $\displaystyle\int_b^a f(x)dx = -\int_a^b f(x)dx$

11 a $\dfrac{a^3}{3}-\dfrac{1}{3}$ **b** a^2

c i $f'(a)=a^2$

   ii $f'(a)=a^2$ the same

d i $4a^3-2a$ **ii** $\dfrac{3}{a^2}$

   iii $1-3a^2$

Work it out 15.3

Solution 3 is correct.

Exercise 15E

1 a i $\dfrac{7}{3}$ **ii** $\dfrac{1}{4}$

b i $\dfrac{2}{3}$ **ii** $\dfrac{22}{3}$

c i $\dfrac{11}{4}$ **ii** $\dfrac{79}{6}$

2 a i 45   **ii** $\dfrac{17}{3}$

  b i $\dfrac{32}{3}$ **ii** $\dfrac{4}{3}$

  c i $\dfrac{243}{2}$ **ii** $\dfrac{1}{2}$

3 2

4 $k = 9$

5 a 6

  b $\dfrac{22}{3}$

6 a $(x-2)(x-5)$

  b $\dfrac{9}{2}$

7 a $(0, 0)\,(k, 0)$

  b $k = 2$

8 a 15   **b** 18

9 96

10 108

11 $\dfrac{1}{6}p\sqrt{p}$

12 $\dfrac{a^3}{48}$

> **Tip**
>
> (Question 7) Instead of evaluating both areas, you could simply write $\int_0^3 y\,dx = 0$

Mixed practice 15

1 $y = \dfrac{3}{2}x^2 - \dfrac{2}{3}x^{\frac{3}{2}} - \dfrac{59}{3}$

2 $-\dfrac{1}{x} + 2\sqrt{x} + c$

3 $\dfrac{2}{3}x^{\frac{3}{2}} - \dfrac{2}{5}x^{\frac{5}{2}} + 2x - x^2 + \dfrac{26}{15}$

4 a $-12 + 8\sqrt{3}$ **b** $12 - 4\sqrt{3}$

5 a $\dfrac{1}{3}x^3 - x^2 + 5x + c$ **b** $\dfrac{1}{3}x^3 - x^2 + 5x - 4$

6 $4x + 5$

7 a $\dfrac{1}{4}x^4 - 2x^3 + 2x^2 - 24x + c$

  b $\dfrac{28}{5}$

8 26

9 $a = 4$

10 a $a = \sqrt{2}$

  b $\dfrac{1}{2}$

11 $\dfrac{4k^3}{3}$

12 a i $(x-2)(2x-1)(x+1)$

  ii

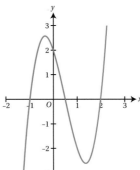

  b $\dfrac{81}{16}$

13 a i a^{n+1} **ii** $\dfrac{b^{n+1} - a^{n+1}}{n+1}$

  b $n = 3$

14 a i $A(-a, 0),\, B(a, 0),\, C(0, a^2)$

  ii $\dfrac{1}{3}a^3$

  b $\dfrac{1}{3}a^3$

15 Proof

16 a A (local) minimum

  b $x^3 + 3x^2 - 45x + 100$

17 $\dfrac{27}{2}$

Focus on ... 2

Focus on ... Proof 2

1 Proof

2 Discussion

3 Proof

Focus on ... Problem solving 2

1 1200 kg

2 20 kg

3 a $\sqrt{65}$

  b 29.7°

Focus on ... Modelling 2

1 a 7:11 am

  b 3:44 am

2 5 h 36 min after local noon

3 a 12 h 29 min

  b 11 h 8 min

4 23.44; 13 h 56 min

5 Proof

6 No sunrise or sunset on those days ($L > 66.5$ corresponds to places north of the Arctic Circle)

7 a

b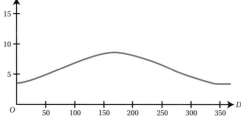

8 a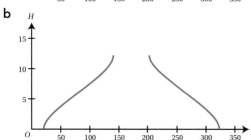

b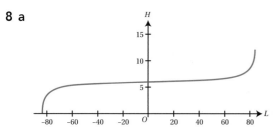

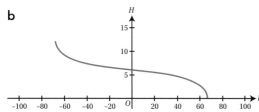

9 Discussion (D could be 59, 59.5 or 60)

10 Discussion

11 Division by 15 rescales the answer from $[0, 180]$ to $[0, 12]$; 23.44 is the inclination of the Earth's axis; 284 makes January Day 1 (it is 284 days after the Spring Equinox); $\dfrac{360}{365}$ rescales from $[0, 365]$ to $[0, 360]$ so that the value is in degrees.

12 Discussion (for example: the Earth is spherical; the Sun is modelled as a point)

Cross-topic review exercise 2

1 $a = 2, b = -7$

2 $180°$

3 a $\overrightarrow{MP} = \dfrac{1}{3}a + \dfrac{3}{4}b, \overrightarrow{QN} = \dfrac{1}{2}b + \dfrac{2}{9}a$

   b Proof

4 $\theta = 30°, 120°$

5 a $(x + 1)(x - 1)(x - 5)$ **b** $\dfrac{148}{3}$

6 a $a = \dfrac{3}{2}, b = \dfrac{1}{2}, c = -\dfrac{1}{2}$

   b $y = -4x + 14$

   c i $P\left(\dfrac{7}{2}, 0\right), Q(0, 14)$ **ii** $\dfrac{49}{2}$

7 a Proof

   b i Proof

     ii $225°$

8 $\dfrac{20}{3}$

9 $4 + 2\sqrt{7} = 9.29$

10 a $4x^3h + 6x^2h^2 + 4xh^3 + h^4$

   b Proof

11 a $f(x) = x^2 - 6x + 8$ **b** $y = \dfrac{x}{2} - 1$

   c $\left(\dfrac{9}{2}, \dfrac{5}{4}\right)$

12 a $a = \dfrac{1}{4}, p = 4, q = 5$

   b $M(0, 9), N\left(\dfrac{16}{3}, \dfrac{49}{9}\right)$

   c $\dfrac{16}{3}$

13 $\left(\dfrac{3}{8}, \dfrac{631}{64}\right)$

14 a $x = 1, \pm\sqrt{3}$ **b** $x = 45°, 60°, 120°$

15 $\dfrac{2\sqrt{2}}{3}$

16 a Proof

   b $r \leqslant \dfrac{1}{2a}$

17 a $a^4 + b^4$

   b Proof

18 a

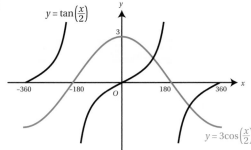

$y = \tan\left(\frac{x}{2}\right)$

$y = 3\cos\left(\frac{x}{2}\right)$

b 116° or 244°

Chapter 16

Before you start...

1 20%

2 Mean: 5, median: 4.5, mode: 1

3 Range: 8 IQR: 5.5

Exercise 16A

1 A a

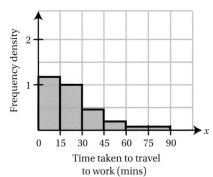

b

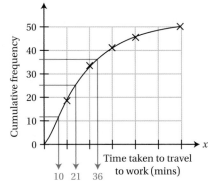

c Median = 21 s, IQR ≈ 26 s

d

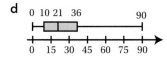

B a

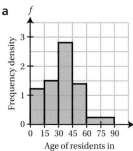

b

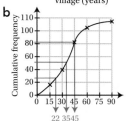

c Median = 35 years, IQR ≈ 23 years

d

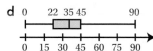

2 a i 0.3   **ii** $\frac{4}{15}$

  b i 0.4   **ii** 0.25

  c i $\frac{2}{15}$ **ii** 0.25

3 Median = 12, IQR = 9

4 a 197s   **b** $c = 191, d = 203$

  c 12s

5 a 53%   **b** 28 minutes

6 a Results in English were generally lower but more consistent.

  b 75%

  c For example, if the results were for the same group of pupils

  d The number of pupils sitting each test

7 a 15 minutes

  b Alpha Commerce, 25%

  c Beta Bank, 50%

8 a 0.10   **b** A

9 a Median = 23.5 seconds, IQR = 12.5 seconds

  b 25.2 seconds

  c Group 2 has a symmetrical distribution, Group 1 doesn't. The range is the same.

10 A3, B2, C1

11 $\frac{2bh}{3}$

Work it out 16.1

Solution 1 is correct.

Exercise 16B

1 a i $\sigma = 7.23$, IQR $= 12.6$
  ii $\sigma = 6.57$, IQR $= 13.5$
  b i $\sigma = 11.1$, IQR $= 3$
  ii $\sigma = 35.3$, IQR $= 72$
  c i $\sigma = 1.50$, IQR $= 3$
  ii $\sigma = 2.75$, IQR $= 6$

2 a i 2.07 **ii** 0.943
  b i 2.20 **ii** 32.8
  c i 8.78 **ii** 21.4

3 a $x = 12$ **b** 2.92

4 a 46.8 **b** 527

5 a 124.5 mph **b** 11.8 mph **c** Andy

6 a 15.2
  b The Physics result is skewed by one very low score. We do not know the total mark available in the two subjects so the values might not be comparable.

7 18

8 101 or 141

9 a Proof
  b Proof

Exercise 16C

1 a i $\bar{x} = 1$, $\sigma = 0.894$, $q_2 = 1$
  ii $\bar{x} = 0$, $\sigma = 1.06$, $q_2 = 0$
  b i $\bar{x} = 12.1$, $\sigma = 1.90$, $q_2 = 12$
  ii $\bar{x} = 0.263$, $\sigma = 0.137$, $q_2 = 0.2$

2 a i $\bar{x} = 26.1$ s, $\sigma = 20.4$ s
  ii $\bar{x} = 253$ g, $\sigma = 151$ g
  b i $\bar{x} = 6.38$ cm, $\sigma = 5.23$ cm
  ii $\bar{x} = 102$ W, $\sigma = 5.78$ W
  c i $\bar{x} = 6.58$ years, $\sigma = 5.11$ years
  ii $\bar{x} = £15.30$, $\sigma = £9.85$

3 a 17, 21 **b** 17, 20
  c 16.5, 20.5 **d** 16.01, 20

> **Tip**
>
> The first group starts at 0, not −0.5

4 a 64, 15, 5 **b** $\bar{x} = 1.68$, $\sigma = 0.875$
  c Households in Mediton tend to have more cars but there is greater variation.

5 a $\bar{x} = 3.82$ kg, $\sigma = 1.67$ kg
  b Use more groups; measure more accurately.

> **Tip**
>
> You might be tempted to say measure more than 50 dogs. This answers a different question – it would give you a better estimate of the mean of **all** dogs.

6 a 1.5 **b** 1.84 **c** 3.01
  d i The variance is lower so the process is more consistent.
  ii There were more broken eggs on average.
  iii The sample size is too small for small differences to be significant – they may be due to chance.

7 a $\bar{x} = 9.88$, $\sigma = 7.42$
  b Data is at the centre of each group
  c The mean is skewed to a higher value by a small number of very large values.

8 a Proof
  b $1 \pm 2k$ **c** 3

9 $p = 45$, $q = 5$ and $p = 10$, $q = 40$

10 Proof

Exercise 16D

1 a Strong positive **b** No correlation
  c Strong positive **d** Perfect positive
  e Strong negative **f** Strong positive
  g Weak negative

2 a Strong positive **b** Strong negative
  c Weak positive **d** Weak negative
  e No linear correlation
  f Non-linear correlation
  g Perfect negative
  h Two separate groups, each with strong positive correlation

3 a Strong positive linear relationship – faster processors tend to last longer
  b No – both may be due to improvements in technology

4 a Strong positive linear relationship – older cars have a longer braking distance
  b Yes – the correlation coefficient is positive

5 a Strong positive linear relationship – as the age of the babies increases, the mass increases

b i This is the amount of mass typically gained each month.

ii This is the predicted birth mass of a baby.

c 14 years is a large extrapolation from the data. It does not take into account gender which might be an important factor.

6 a i 24.8 s is the predicted 100 m time of students when they start school

ii 0.609 s is the typical improvement in 100 m time each year

b The low correlation coefficient suggests that a straight line model is not appropriate. Even if it were appropriate, 60 years is a large extrapolation from the data.

7 a A   **b** D   **c** B   **d** C

8 a i 1.5 m   **ii** 3 m

b i Is valid as the correlation coefficient is large, but

ii Is problematic as it is extrapolating from the data.

9 a i 5 Hz   **ii** Impossible to say

b The points are not in order, so there is no sense in using a line to interpolate between points.

c if the points were ordered in time – for example, vertical and horizontal displacement of a ball over time.

10 a false   **b** false

c true   **d** false

Exercise 16E

1 a i No   **ii** No

b i Yes   **ii** Yes

2 a i No   **ii** No

b i Yes: −3   **ii** Yes: 64 and 0

3 There appear to be two distinct groups – he should find the correlation coefficient for each group separately.

4 a 5   **b** Proof

5 Proof

6 a underestimate   **b** close   **c** overestimate

7 46.5, 48.7

8 a 21°C

b i Decrease   **ii** Decrease

9 a $t = 62.9$ min, $\sigma = 7.40$ min   **b** Thursday

c $\bar{x} = 63$ min, $\sigma = 7.98$ min   **d** 0.314 km/min

e No – it is extrapolating from the data

10 a Proof   **b** $\bar{x} = 11.6$, $\sigma = 2.58$

11 a 1458, 11826,   **b** 4.24, 17.0

12 a Proof   **b** Proof

c $q = 3$, $p = 27$ **d** Such as $p = 9$, $q = 32$

Mixed practice 16

1 a 24   **b** 125   **c** 124

2 2

3 a 4.08 minutes   **b** 8.80 minutes^2

4 $x > 140$ or $x < -20$

5 a e.g. 1, 0   **b** 0, e.g. 1, 1

6 a i Mean = 17.7, SD = 3.84

ii Exact data values unknown

b 4   **c** 16–20

d i Increase   **ii** Decrease

7 a $\bar{t} = 10.0$ min, $\sigma = 6.71$ min   **b** 0.323

8 a 84%   **b** 79%   **c** 14.0%

9 a 66 mph   **b** 9

c $a = 61$ mph, $b = 71$ mph

d 24, 9, 4, 2   **e** $\bar{x} = 67$ mph, $\sigma = 10.8$ mph

f Do not remove – they are extreme but no reason to believe they are incorrect

10 a Shows relationships

b Strong positive

c 200 km^2

d It will go down because the city deleted had above average population.

e the increase in population for each area increase of 1 km^2

f Extrapolating from the data

11 a 23   **b** $x = w = 0$

c 38, 39   **d** Shows all data

e Easier to find median and quartiles

12 a α:D, β:B, γ:C

b i B   **ii** A   **iii** C

13 150

14 118 888.2

Chapter 17

Before you start...

1 $\dfrac{1}{20}$

2 $\dfrac{7}{24}$

3 a 5040   **b** 840   **c** 35

   d 1   **e** 1

Exercise 17A

1 a i Mutually exclusive $\dfrac{1}{2}$

    ii Mutually exclusive $\dfrac{2}{3}$

   b i Not mutually exclusive

    ii Not mutually exclusive

   c i Mutually exclusive $\dfrac{1}{3}$

    ii Not mutually exclusive

   d i Mutually exclusive $\dfrac{13}{25}$

    ii Not mutually exclusive

   e i Not mutually exclusive

    ii Mutually exclusive $\dfrac{7}{15}$

2 a i Not independent

    ii Not independent

   b i Independent $\dfrac{1}{26}$

    ii Independent $\dfrac{1}{52}$

   c i Not independent

    ii Not independent

   d i Not independent

    ii Independent $\dfrac{4}{25}$

   e i Not independent

    ii Not independent

3 a i pq **ii** 0

   b Only if the probability of at least one of them is zero

4 a $\dfrac{1}{16}$ **b** $\dfrac{7}{16}$

5 $\dfrac{1}{9}$

6 a ACT, ATC, CAT, CTA, TAC, TCA

   b $\dfrac{1}{3}$

7 a $\dfrac{1}{6}$ **b** Not independent

8 a i $\dfrac{19}{60}$ **ii** $\dfrac{61}{300}$

   b Not independent

9 $\dfrac{1}{32}$

10 a $\dfrac{1}{8}$ **b** $\dfrac{7}{8}$

11 a 0.858

   b Not reasonable; group behaviour, common experiences and external events

Exercise 17B

1 a

t	0	1	2	3
$P(T=t)$	$\dfrac{1}{8}$	$\dfrac{3}{8}$	$\dfrac{3}{8}$	$\dfrac{1}{8}$

   b

d	0	1	2	3	4	5
$P(D=d)$	$\dfrac{6}{36}$	$\dfrac{10}{36}$	$\dfrac{8}{36}$	$\dfrac{6}{36}$	$\dfrac{4}{36}$	$\dfrac{2}{36}$

   c

x	1	2	3	4	6
$P(X=x)$	$\dfrac{1}{6}$	$\dfrac{2}{6}$	$\dfrac{1}{6}$	$\dfrac{1}{6}$	$\dfrac{1}{6}$

   d

g	1	2	3
$P(G=g)$	$\dfrac{6}{72}$	$\dfrac{36}{72}$	$\dfrac{30}{72}$

   e

c	1	2	3	4
$P(C=c)$	$\dfrac{1}{4}$	$\dfrac{3}{16}$	$\dfrac{9}{64}$	$\dfrac{27}{64}$

   f

x	1	2	3	4	6	8	9	12	16
$P(X=x)$	$\dfrac{1}{16}$	$\dfrac{2}{16}$	$\dfrac{2}{16}$	$\dfrac{3}{16}$	$\dfrac{2}{16}$	$\dfrac{2}{16}$	$\dfrac{1}{16}$	$\dfrac{2}{16}$	$\dfrac{1}{16}$

2 a i $k=\dfrac{1}{8}$ **ii** $k=\dfrac{1}{8}$

   b i $\dfrac{1}{8}$ **ii** $k=\dfrac{3}{7}$

   c i $k=\dfrac{1}{10}$ **ii** $k=\dfrac{12}{25}$

3 a $k=\dfrac{1}{12}$ **b** $\dfrac{5}{12}$

4 a $k=0.19$ **b** 0.55

5 a 0.8   **b** 0.01

6 a

X	2	3	4	5	6	7	8
$P(X=x)$	$\dfrac{1}{16}$	$\dfrac{2}{16}$	$\dfrac{3}{16}$	$\dfrac{4}{16}$	$\dfrac{3}{16}$	$\dfrac{2}{16}$	$\dfrac{1}{16}$

  b $\dfrac{3}{8}$

7 $a = 0.1$, $b = 0.2$

8 a Proof **b** 0.72

9 a $\dfrac{13}{60}$ **b** 0.207

10 a 0.11 **b** 0.97

11 a $\dfrac{1}{9}$

  b

x	1	2	3
$P(X \leqslant x)$	$\dfrac{1}{9}$	$\dfrac{4}{9}$	$\dfrac{9}{9}$
$P(X = x)$	$\dfrac{1}{9}$	$\dfrac{3}{9}$	$\dfrac{5}{9}$

12 a 4

  b

y	0	1	4	9	16
$P(Y = y)$	$\dfrac{1}{9}$	$\dfrac{2}{9}$	$\dfrac{2}{9}$	$\dfrac{2}{9}$	$\dfrac{2}{9}$

Work it out 17.1

Solution 1 is correct.

Work it out 17.2

Solution 4 is correct.

Exercise 17C

1 a $X \sim B(20, 0.5)$; $P(X = 15)$

  b Not binomial, the probability may not be the same for each question (e.g. if the questions get harder)

  c Not binomial, there are three possible outcomes

  d Not binomial – trials are not independent

  e Approximately binomial: $X \sim B(100, 0.02)$; $P(X \geqslant 1)$

2 a i 0.147 **ii** 0.0459

  b i 0.944 **ii** 0.797

  c i 0.0563 **ii** 0.0104

  d i 0.990 **ii** 0.797

  e i 0.203 **ii** 0.832

  f i 0.0562 **ii** 0.822

  g i 0.486 **ii** 0.203

  h i 0.203 **ii** 0.495

3 a $X \sim B(20, 0.7)$; $P(X \geqslant 16) = 0.238$

  b $X \sim B(5, 0.35)$; $P(X = 3) = 0.181$

  c $X \sim B(5, 0.5)$; $P(X \geqslant 3) = 0.5$

4 a i $\dfrac{5}{32}$ **ii** $\dfrac{1}{32}$

  b i $\dfrac{31}{32}$ **ii** $\dfrac{6}{32}$

  c i $\dfrac{1}{32}$ **ii** $\dfrac{26}{32}$

5 a Drawing from a finite population without replacement so probability is only approximately constant

  b 0.103

6 a 0.0231 **b** 0.0273

7 a 0.108 **b** 0.0267

  c The probability that a person going to the doctor has the virus is the same as for the whole country.

8 The second one (0.0165 > 0.0154)

9 a i 0.6 **ii** 0.6 **iii** $\dfrac{1}{3}$ **iv** 0.3; 0.288

  b i 0.6 **ii** 0.6 **iii** 0.36 **iv** 0.288

10 a Not independent, but constant probability

  b Independent and constant probability

  c Independent, but different probabilities

11 0.377

12 a 0.630

  b His guesses are independent of each other

13 a Both genders are equally likely. Genders of different babies are independent of each other.

  b 0.00591

14 a No. The probability of being late depends on, for example, the distance they live from school.

  b One student being late is independent of other students. This is not a reasonable assumption; for example, friends from the same class may be travelling together.

15 $p = \dfrac{2}{3}$

16 $p = 0.6$ or 0.4

17 a Proof   **b** $n = 10$

18 $n = 3$

19 $n = \dfrac{5 - p}{p}$

Mixed practice 17

1 0.261

2 a $k = 0.16$ **b** 0.72   **c** 3

3

x	0	1	2	3	4	5	6
$P(X = x)$	$\frac{1}{4}$	$\frac{1}{8}$	$\frac{1}{8}$	$\frac{1}{8}$	$\frac{1}{8}$	$\frac{1}{8}$	$\frac{1}{8}$

4 a 0.142   **b** 0.335

5 a 0.2   **b** $p = 0.05$, $q = 0.15$

6 a 0.572   **b** 0.0319   **c** 0.537

7 a 0.232   **b** 0.894

   c That the attempts are independent of each other

8 a 16%   **b** 52%

9 0.653

10 0.36

11 a

x	−5	−4	−3	−2	−1	0	1	2	3	4	5
$P(X = x)$	$\frac{1}{36}$	$\frac{2}{36}$	$\frac{3}{36}$	$\frac{4}{36}$	$\frac{5}{36}$	$\frac{6}{36}$	$\frac{5}{36}$	$\frac{4}{36}$	$\frac{3}{36}$	$\frac{2}{36}$	$\frac{1}{36}$

   b $\dfrac{5}{12}$

12 a 0.64

   b $p = 0.3$ or 0.7

13 a 0.0296   **b** 2.44×10^{-4}

14 a 0.031 25   **b** 0.015 625

15 a 0.460   **b** $1 - (0.95)^n$

   c 32

16 a

x	0	1	2	3	4	5
$P(X = x)$	$\frac{6}{36}$	$\frac{10}{36}$	$\frac{8}{36}$	$\frac{6}{36}$	$\frac{4}{36}$	$\frac{2}{16}$

   b 0.0697

17 a Proof

   b

1	4	5
$\frac{1}{1296}$	$\frac{175}{1296}$	$\frac{369}{1296}$

18 a 0.0781   **b** 0.0130

Chapter 18

Before you start...

1 a 0.575   **b** 0.274

2 $X \sim B(12, 0.7)$

Exercise 18A

1 a Sixth form students may be more likely to progress to university and so be more worried about fees than people who are not affected.

   b People in supermarkets are more likely to be knowledgeable about food prices.

   c School children will be shorter than average.

   d This is a real-life example. Mostly richer people had telephones, so the poll predicted the wrong winner.

2 a Quota sampling

   b Stratified sampling

   c Cluster sampling

   d Simple random sampling

   e Systematic sampling

   f Opportunity sampling

3 a 2.55

   b Probably larger

   c It is likely to be better, but with random fluctuations it is possible to be worse.

4 a This would require a complete list of all fish in the North Sea and the ability to get measure any fish required.

   b Quota sampling

   c It will be more representative.

5 Obtain a numbered list of all the students; use a random number generator to generate 70 different random numbers; select students with those numbers.

6 a Opportunity sampling

   b Students who eat burgers may not be interested in healthy eating.

7 16, 762, 537, 722, 152

8 a

	Female	Male
Under 42	16	24
42 or over	16	24

b It is random therefore less biased or more generalisable.

c It is cheaper. It does not require all selected people to participate. It does not require a list of all people in the city.

9 a A – cluster, B – simple random, C – quota, D – stratified

b D

c Less time-consuming – no need to travel as far; cheaper

10 Not everybody will return the questionnaire so not all possible samples are equally likely.

11 a 9.33×10^{-4}

    b i 0.0441   ii 0.00996

c 4.65%

d Increase – genders may cluster together

Work it out 18.1

1 should state that there is evidence of a decrease in the proportion of red flowers.

2 should include some reference to the context.

3 should state that there is insufficient evidence that the proportion of girls differs from 45%.

5 should state that there is insufficient evidence of bias in the dice.

Work it out 18.2

Solution 3 is correct.

Exercise 18B

1 a i $H_0: p = 0.6\ H_1: p > 0.6$; p is the proportion of children who like football

    ii $H_0: p = \dfrac{1}{3}\ H_1: p > \dfrac{1}{3}$; p is the proportion of households with a pet

b i $H_0: p = 0.06\ H_1: p < 0.06$; p is the proportion of faulty components produced

    ii $H_0: p = 0.5\ H_1: p < 0.5$; p is the proportion of children who eat 5 or more pieces of fruit a day.

c i $H_0: p = 0.5\ H_1: p \neq 0.5$; p is the probability that the coin shows heads

    ii $H_0: p = 0.26\ H_1: p \neq 0.26$; p is the proportion of entries in AS level Psychology graded 'A'

2 a i p-value 19.3% > 5%, insufficient evidence

    ii p-value 91.4% > 10%, insufficient evidence

b i p-value 31.8% > 10%, insufficient evidence

    ii p-value 18.2% > 3%, insufficient evidence

c i p-value 17.9% > 4%, insufficient evidence

    ii p-value 41.1% > 2.5%, insufficient evidence

3 a $H_0: p = 0.63\ H_1: p < 0.63$

b Cannot reject H_0, no evidence of lower car ownership in David's neighbourhood

4 Insufficient evidence of an increase

5 Insufficient evidence of a probability less than $\dfrac{1}{6}$

6 Insufficient evidence that a higher proportion of teachers drive to work

7 Insufficient evidence that the new treatment is better

8 Insufficient evidence that the proportion with a younger sibling at the same school is different

9 There is evidence that a six has a probability significantly less than $\dfrac{1}{6}$

10 Insufficient evidence that the proportion able to run 100 metres in under 12 seconds has changed

11 14

12 It was greater than 4.45%

13 $q < 0.0247$

Exercise 18C

1 a i $X \leqslant 23$ ii $X \leqslant 4$

b i $X \leqslant 51$ ii $X \leqslant 51$

c i $X \geqslant 37$ ii $X \geqslant 12$

d i $X \geqslant 69$ ii $X \geqslant 69$

2 a i 0.0314   ii 0.0759

b i 0.0602   ii 0.009 60

c i 0.0280   ii 0.0875

d i 0.0602   ii 0.00 388

3 $X \leqslant 10$

4 a $H_0: p = 0.85\ H_1: p > 0.85$ where p is the proportion of patients the drug cures

b $X \geqslant 162$

5 a $H_0: p = 0.12\ H_1: p > 0.12$ where p is the proportion of the population who have purchased the manufacturer's products

b Cannot reject H_0; no significant rise in product purchase history among the population

c 0.0556

6 a acceptance region **b** 0.0600

7 a $H_0: p = 0.3$ $H_1: p > 0.3$ where p is the proportion of children who walk to school

b $X \geqslant 62$

c Reject H_0: significant evidence that the proportion of children who walk to school is greater than 30%

8 a $H_0: p = 0.72$ $H_1: p \neq 0.72$ where p is the proportion of students passing the test on their first attempt

b $X \leqslant 30$ or $X \geqslant 42$

c 0.0814; $SL \geqslant 8.14\%$

Mixed practice 18

1 Quota sampling

2 a Cluster sampling

b Students from the same tutor group are likely to go or not go together

c Obtain a list of all students, number sequentially, use a random number generator to generate 50 numbers, select students with those numbers (ignore repeats and numbers larger than the number of students)

3 a $H_0 : p = \frac{1}{6}$ $H_1 : p > \frac{1}{6}$ where p is the underlying probability of rolling a 5

b There is insufficient evidence that the probability of rolling a 5 is greater than $\frac{1}{6}$

4 $H_0 : p = \frac{1}{8}$ $H_1 : p < \frac{1}{8}$ where p is the underlying proportion of days that Lisa is late. There is insufficient evidence that Lisa's probability of being late has decreased from 1 in 8

5 a $\frac{5}{6}$

b Not correct; this sample has the same probability as any other sample

6 a Pupils who are interested in politic are more likely to volunteer.

b simple random sample – obtain a list of all pupils, number sequentially, use a random number generator to generate 50 numbers,

select pupils with those numbers (ignore repeats and numbers larger than the number of pupils)

7 2

8 $p = 0.00523 < 0.025$, sufficient evidence to reject H_0, there is evidence to conclude that home ownership in Germany is lower than 64%

9 a Each possible group of a given size has an equal probability to be included within the sample.

b i Stratified sample

ii Attitudes to sport may differ between boys and girls.

c $X \geqslant 34$

d 0.0906

e There is insufficient evidence that the proportion of students who play in a school sports team is greater than 40%.

10 a $H_0: p = 0.19$, $H_1: p > 0.4$. Reject H_0 at 10%, $p = 0.0841$

b Letters are not distributed independently.

11 a No **b** No **c** Yes **d** No

Focus on ... 3

Focus on ... Proof 3

1 Discussion

2 Proof

3 Proof

Focus on ... Problem solving 3

1 a 22.4% **b** Still an underestimate

2 a 100 million

b assuming no fish have entered or left the North Sea and that the fish have thoroughly mixed up

Focus on ... Modelling 3

1 $\frac{\pi}{4}$

2 About 8

3 Investigation

Cross-topic review exercise 3

1 $\frac{5}{36}$

2 $\sqrt[4]{\dfrac{e}{24}}$

3 a 0.31   **b** 0.303

4 a i Quota sampling

  ii In a stratified sample, the 20 men and 20 women would be selected using random sampling.

 b $p = 0.274$; insufficient evidence that the proportion is greater

5 a i 256

  ii The population of Year 13 is not known.

 b i Box-and-whisker plots do not indicate population size at all.

  ii The females scored more highly on average, but the males' marks were more spread out.

  iii Box-and-whisker plots provide a more immediate comparison between the quartiles of the two sets. However, histograms show more clearly the distribution of <u>all</u> the data.

 c 52.625

6 a 6, 10, 16, 7

 b Mean = 21.3 minutes, variance = 82.8 minutes^2

 c Actual data values are not given.

7 $\dfrac{11}{12}$

8 $\dfrac{8}{3}$

9 a A survey may have only used a sample. The population of the city may have increased.

 b $p = 0.044$; insufficient evidence that the proportion has changed

10 a $P(A \text{ and } B) \neq P(A) \times P(B)$

 b i 0.0199

  ii Same probability for each building; completion of different buildings independent of the others

 c Evidence of increase ($p = 0.0294$)

11 a Proof   **b**

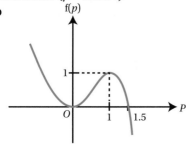

 c Proof, no other solutions.

12 New mean = 34.9, new variance = 6.32

13 £518

14 a $\ln 5$ **b** 0.001 62

15 a Binomial, $n = 12$, $p = 0.1$, assume faults are independent.

 b i 0.0852   **ii** 0.718

 c 0.317

16 a $p = \dfrac{4}{5}$ **b** $p = 0.634$

17 $x = 3, 11$

18 a Selections are not independent. The probabilities with replacement are very close to the probabilities without replacement.

 b 0.0240

 c The statement is incorrect; all samples are equally likely.

Chapter 19

Before you start...

1 a $-\dfrac{7}{5}$ **b** $\dfrac{2}{3}$

2 a i $\dfrac{dy}{dx} = 6x - 4 - 5x^{-2}$ **ii** -15 **b** $(2, 21)$

3 $S = 24$, $T = 42$

4 4

5 $y = 5x - 2x^3 - 1$

6 a $2\,\text{m s}^{-2}$ **b** 40 m

Exercise 19A

1 a Yes   **b** No

 c No   **d** No

2 These are some suggestions for discussion:

 a Shape and size of box, which affects air resistance; change in g at different heights

 b Size of each ball; where it was hit; friction

 c The actual shape of the road; mass of passengers inside the bus; resistance forces (may depend on weather conditions)

 d Take-off and landing times; changes in height and related changes in g; weather conditions, turbulence; the path is circular, not straight

Exercise 19B

1 a i -410 m   **ii** -290 m

   b i 290 m   **ii** 210 m

   c i -120 m   **ii** -210 m

2 a i $7.32\,\mathrm{m\,s^{-1}}, 2.93\,\mathrm{m\,s^{-1}}$

     ii $8.64\,\mathrm{m\,s^{-1}}, -1.48\,\mathrm{m\,s^{-1}}$

   b i $15.3\,\mathrm{m\,s^{-1}}, 0\,\mathrm{m\,s^{-1}}$

     ii $9.55\,\mathrm{m\,s^{-1}}, 0\,\mathrm{m\,s^{-1}}$

3 a i $1.00\,\mathrm{m\,s^{-1}}$ **ii** $17.2\,\mathrm{m\,s^{-1}}$

   b i $18.7\,\mathrm{km\,h^{-1}}$ **ii** $0.936\,\mathrm{km\,h^{-1}}$

   c i $0.00926\,\mathrm{m\,s^{-2}}$ **ii** $0.0347\,\mathrm{m\,s^{-2}}$

   d i $10\,600\,\mathrm{km\,h^{-2}}$ **ii** $35\,000\,\mathrm{km\,h^{-2}}$

4 Any of them

Exercise 19C

1 a i $v = 9t^2 - 4,\ a = 18t$

     ii $v = 4t^3 - 6t + 4,\ a = 12t^2 - 6$

   b i $v = \dfrac{2t}{5} - 4.2,\ a = \dfrac{2}{5}$

     ii $v = -1.5t^2 + \dfrac{2t}{3},\ a = -3t + \dfrac{2}{3}$

2

	$x(0)$	$x(3)$	$v(0)$	$v(3)$	$a(0)$	$a(3)$
a i	2	71	-4	77	0	54
ii	0	66	4	94	-6	102
b i	0	-10.8	-4.2	-3	$\dfrac{2}{5}$	$\dfrac{2}{5}$
ii	0	-10.5	0	-11.5	$\dfrac{2}{3}$	-8.33

3 a i $x = \dfrac{3}{2}t^2 - 4t + 2$ **ii** $x = t - t^2 + 1$

   b i $x = 5t - t^3$ **ii** $x = \dfrac{1}{3}t^3 - t^2$

4 a i 19.5 **ii** -19

   b i -100 **ii** 16.7

5 a i $v = t - t^2 + 3,\ x = \dfrac{1}{2}t^2 - \dfrac{1}{3}t^3 + 3t$

     ii $v = 2t^2 + 2t - 2,\ x = \dfrac{2}{3}t^3 + t^2 - 2t$

   b i $v = -5t + 3,\ x = -\dfrac{5}{2}t^2 + 3t + 5$

     ii $v = 3t - 2,\ x = \dfrac{3}{2}t^2 - 2t + 7$

6 a $-3.6\,\mathrm{m\,s^{-2}}$ **b** $0.96\,\mathrm{m\,s^{-1}}$

   c $x = 1.2t^2 - 0.5t^3$

7 a $0.1\,\mathrm{m\,s^{-1}}, 1.2\,\mathrm{m\,s^{-2}}$ **b** $1\,\mathrm{m\,s^{-1}}$

   c 1.92 s, 3.00 m

8 a $v = 0.04t^3 - 0.72t^2 + 4.32t,$

     $x = 0.01t^4 - 0.24t^3 + 2.16t^2$

   b $v = 8.64\,\mathrm{m\,s^{-1}}, x = 38.9$ m

9 a $v = 7.5 + t - 0.3t^2,$ **b** $x = 50$ m

   c $x = 62.5$ m

10 $-116\,\mathrm{m\,s^{-1}}$

Exercise 19D

1 i a $0.65\,\mathrm{m\,s^{-2}}, -0.52\,\mathrm{m\,s^{-2}}$ **b** 1950 m

   ii a $1\,\mathrm{m\,s^{-2}}, -3\,\mathrm{m\,s^{-2}}$ **b** 888 m

   iii a $-1.39\,\mathrm{m\,s^{-2}}, 1.25\,\mathrm{m\,s^{-2}}$ **b** 398 m

2 a $d = 1350$ m

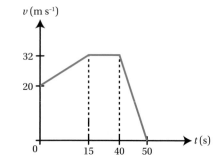

   b $d = 495$ m

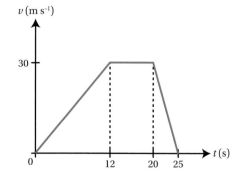

   c $d = 863$ m

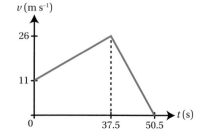

3 a 50 metres   **b** away

  c Particle changes direction

  d The particle stops moving (it is stationary), 30 m from P

  e When $t = 50$

  f Decreasing

  g Speed is decreasing, velocity is increasing

  h 200 m

4 a v (m s^{-1})

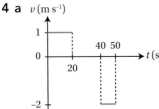

  b v (m s^{-1})

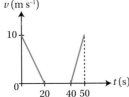

  c v (m s^{-1})

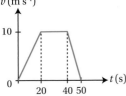

  d v (m s^{-1})

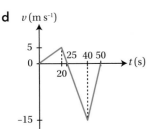

5 a v (m s^{-1})

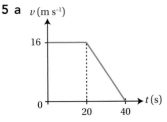

  b 480 m

6 a 2 m s^{-2} **b** 25 s

  c -7.5 m s^{-1} **d** 175 m (to the right)

7 a v (m s^{-1})

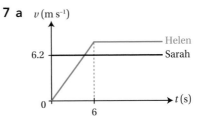

  b 14.6 s

8 a 8   **b** 0.8 m s^{-2} **c** C

9 $x = 5$

10 a 45   **b** 115 s

  c s (m)

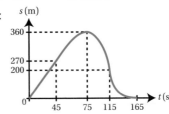

Exercise 19E

1 i a 16.25 m s^{-1} **b** 16.25 m s^{-1}

  ii a 20.2 m s^{-1} **b** 20.2 m s^{-1}

  iii a 6.31 m s^{-1} **b** 3.69 m s^{-1}

2 2.45 m s^{-1}

3 a v (m s^{-1})

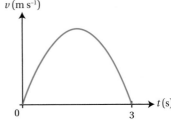

  b 9 m s^{-1}

4 a Stationary   **b** 200 m, 6.67 m s^{-1}

  c 20 m s^{-1}

5 a $t = 4, 7$ **b** 85.75 m

  c 12.3 m s^{-1}, 33.5 m s^{-1}

6 a v (m s^{-1})

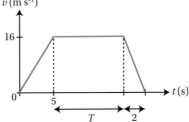

  b 7

7 a When $t=0$, $v=0$; 8 s, 12 s

  b $v=3.6\,\mathrm{m\,s^{-1}}$, $x=30.6\,\mathrm{m}$

  c $3.29\,\mathrm{m\,s^{-1}}$

8 $28.9\,\mathrm{m\,s^{-1}}$

9 $1.82\,\mathrm{s}$

10 $10.2\,\mathrm{m\,s^{-1}}$

Exercise 19F

1 $1.5\,\mathrm{s}$

2 a when $t=0$, $v=0$ **b** $5.4\,\mathrm{m\,s^{-1}}$

3 $34.0\,\mathrm{m}$; $5.76\,\mathrm{m\,s^{-2}}$

4 $5.6\,\mathrm{s}$

5 a $-2.4\,\mathrm{m\,s^{-2}}$

  b i $13.5\,\mathrm{m}$ **ii** $40.5\,\mathrm{m}$

6 a 3.7 **b** $1.43\,\mathrm{m\,s^{-1}}$

  c $37.8\,\mathrm{m}$ **d** $7.13\,\mathrm{s}$

7 a $v=6.5t-0.65t^2$ **b** $v=31.85-2.6t$

8 a Positive acceleration throughout, starting from rest

  b $3.125\,\mathrm{m\,s^{-1}}$

  c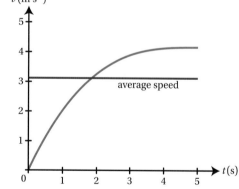

9 a $v=t^3-7t^2+10t$

  b i $4.06\,\mathrm{m\,s^{-1}}$ **ii** $8.21\,\mathrm{m\,s^{-1}}$

10 a $15\,\mathrm{m}$ **b** $11.4\,\mathrm{s}$

11 13.3

12 $34.7\,\mathrm{m}$

Mixed practice 19

1 a $4\,\mathrm{m\,s^{-2}}$ **b** $x=t^3-4t^2$

2 a $11.2\,\mathrm{m}$ **b** $2.8\,\mathrm{m\,s^{-1}}$

3 a $1.4\,\mathrm{m\,s^{-2}}$ **b** 0, 12, 15 s

  c $3\,\mathrm{m\,s^{-1}}$

4 a $30\,\mathrm{m}$ **b** $76\,\mathrm{s}$

  c $-0.667\,\mathrm{m\,s^{-2}}$

5 $-15\,\mathrm{m\,s^{-2}}$

6 a $v=\dfrac{100}{9}+\dfrac{25}{9}t-\dfrac{5}{36}t^2$

  b $a=\dfrac{25}{9}-\dfrac{5}{18}t$; $t=10$

  c $253\,\mathrm{m}$

  d i No   **ii** Yes

7 4.25

8 a $v=0.04t^3-0.48t^2+1.44t$

  b $a=0.12t^2-0.96t+1.44$

  c $0\,\mathrm{m\,s^{-1}}$

  d Forwards (away from A)

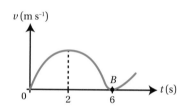

  e $4.32\,\mathrm{m}$

9 $9.93\,\mathrm{s}$, $30.1\,\mathrm{s}$

10 a $8.73\,\mathrm{s}$ **b** Proof   **c** $0\,\mathrm{s}$

11 $17.3\,\mathrm{m\,s^{-1}}$

Chapter 20

Before you start...

1 a $v=2t-t^3+4.2$

  b $x=t^2-\dfrac{1}{4}t^4+4.2t+14$

2 a $t=0.249$, 2.49 **b** $t=0.563$, 1.89

3 a $(0.169, 1.03)$ **b** $(1.5, 2.28)$

Exercise 20A

1 Proof

2 a Proof   **b** Proof

3 a Proof   **b** $49.9\,\mathrm{m\,s^{-1}}$

4 a $v\,(\mathrm{m\,s^{-1}})$

  b Proof

5 a $v = u + 0.5kt^2$

b Proof

6 Proof

7 a $v = u + aT$

b At the start and after 1 second

c $T = 0$ or 1.5 s

8 Proof

Exercise 20B

1 a i $u = 3.6\,\mathrm{m\,s^{-1}}, s = 64.8\,\mathrm{m}$

   ii $u = -23.1\mathrm{m\,s^{-1}}, s = -77.2\,\mathrm{m}$

   b i $v = 5\,\mathrm{m\,s^{-1}}, t = 6.67\,\mathrm{s}$ or $v = -5\,\mathrm{m\,s^{-1}}, t = 15\,\mathrm{s}$

   ii $v = 12.6\,\mathrm{m\,s^{-1}}, t = 2.45\,\mathrm{s}$ or $v = -12.6\,\mathrm{m\,s^{-1}}, t = 10.9\,\mathrm{s}$

   c i $a = -0.45\,\mathrm{m\,s^{-2}}, t = 13.3\,\mathrm{s}$

   ii $a = 1.03\,\mathrm{m\,s^{-2}}, t = 18.5\,\mathrm{s}$

   d i $a = -1.83\,\mathrm{m\,s^{-2}}, s = -3\,\mathrm{m}$

   ii $a = -1.3\,\mathrm{m\,s^{-2}}, s = 15\,\mathrm{m}$

2 a $1.92\,\mathrm{m\,s^{-2}}$ **b** 40.5 m

3 a $6.3\,\mathrm{m\,s^{-2}}$ **b** 36.8 m

4 a $-0.873\,\mathrm{m\,s^{-2}}$ **b** 26.6 m

5 14.1 s

6 4.43 s

7 8.05 s

8 66.7 m

9 a 5.29 m

   b It will go an unlimited distance in the negative direction.

Work it out 20.1

Solution 2 is correct.

Exercise 20C

1 a i $21.9\,\mathrm{m\,s^{-1}}, 6.14\,\mathrm{m}$ **ii** $30.8\,\mathrm{m\,s^{-1}}, 21.5\,\mathrm{m}$

   b i $30.4\,\mathrm{m\,s^{-1}}, 47.1\,\mathrm{m}$ **ii** $58.8\,\mathrm{m\,s^{-1}}, 176\,\mathrm{m}$

2 a i $15.5\,\mathrm{m\,s^{-1}}$ downward, $-8.13\,\mathrm{m}$

   ii $4.16\,\mathrm{m\,s^{-1}}$ upward, 6.46 m

   b i $4.62\,\mathrm{m\,s^{-1}}$ upward, 61.4 m

   ii $9.22\,\mathrm{m\,s^{-1}}$ upward, 16.1 m

3 $22.1\,\mathrm{m\,s^{-1}}$

4 a 1.18 s   **b** $6.95\,\mathrm{m\,s^{-1}}$

   c i Increase   **ii** Decrease

5 $11.0\,\mathrm{m\,s^{-1}}$

6 a 55 m   **b** 6.21 s; $32.8\,\mathrm{m\,s^{-1}}$

7 a No   **b** $12.8\,\mathrm{m\,s^{-1}}$

   c Increase

8 a 1.63 s   **b** 3.89 s

   c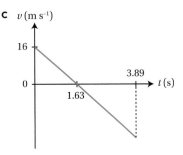

9 a $\dfrac{u}{4.9}\mathrm{s}$

   b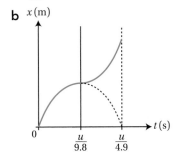

10 13.3 m

Exercise 20D

1 149 m

2 a $10.2\,\mathrm{m\,s^{-1}}$ **b** $0.207\,\mathrm{m\,s^{-2}}$

3 $1.92\,\mathrm{m\,s^{-1}}$

4 $17.4\,\mathrm{m\,s^{-1}}$

5 6.91 m

6 12.4 s

7 44.2

8 Maximum height 38.3 m, speed as it hits the ground $27.4\,\mathrm{m\,s^{-1}}$

9 $18.1\,\mathrm{m\,s^{-1}}$

10 a 90.2 m

b 25.0 m s^{-1}

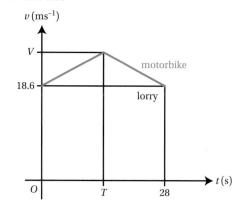

Mixed practice 20

1 a 8.75 s　　　　　**b** 166 m

2 a 8.6 m s^{-1}, downwards

b 2.4 m

3 2.2 m s^{-1}

4 a 2.8 m s^{-1}　　**b** 2.5 m　　**c** 1.30 s

5 a v (km h^{-1})

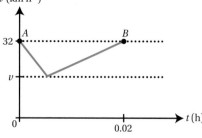

b 23 km h^{-1}　　　　**c** 27.5 km h^{-1}

6 a Proof　　**b** 614 m

7 a 7.93 m

b 9.04 m s^{-1}, 21.8 m s^{-1}

8 Proof

9 a Proof　　**b** 5.6　　　**c** Proof

10 120 m

11 2 : 1

12 $u = 163$, $v = 37.5$

Chapter 21

Before you start...

1 a 0.417 m s^{-2}　　　　**b** 66 m

2 a $\begin{pmatrix} -2 \\ 6 \end{pmatrix}$　　　　　**b** $-4\mathbf{i} + 2\mathbf{j}$

3 a Magnitude 2.77, 64.4° above horizontal

b Magnitude 4.12, 14.0° below horizontal

Exercise 21A

1 a 138 N　　　　　　**b** 0.45 N

c 7200 N　　　　　**d** 0.828 N

e 0 N　　　　　　**f** 1.18 N

g 0 N

2 a 2.39 m s^{-2}　　　　**b** 18.3 m s^{-2}

c 0.4 m s^{-2}　　　　**d** 21.7 m s^{-2}

3 a i $\begin{pmatrix} 4.8 \\ -7.5 \end{pmatrix}$ N　　**ii** $\begin{pmatrix} -3.5 \\ 6.5 \end{pmatrix}$ N

b i $\begin{pmatrix} 6 \\ 2 \end{pmatrix}$ m s^{-2}　　**ii** $\begin{pmatrix} -2 \\ 1.43 \end{pmatrix}$ m s^{-2}

c i 1.4 kg　　　　**ii** 0.5 kg

4 a Towards the centre　**b** Deep space

c Depends on the object

5 1070 N

6 0.048 N

7 0.269 s

8 $\begin{pmatrix} 1.08 \\ 1.98 \end{pmatrix}$ N

9 a $\begin{pmatrix} -1.31 \\ 1 \end{pmatrix}$ m s^{-2}　　**b** 1.65 m s^{-2}

10 218 N

11 6.47 kg

Exercise 21B

1 a i 2 N left　　　　**ii** 5 N right

b i 3 N down　　　**ii** 6 N up

c i 7 N right　　　**ii** 4 N right

2 a i $(13\mathbf{i} + 8\mathbf{j})$N　　**ii** $(-5\mathbf{i} + 7\mathbf{j})$N

b i $(7\mathbf{i} + 2\mathbf{j})$N　　**ii** $(2\mathbf{i} + 4\mathbf{j})$N

c i $(-4\mathbf{j})$N　　　**ii** $(6\mathbf{i} - 4\mathbf{j})$N

3 a i 15.3 N, 31.6°　　**ii** 8.60 N, 126°

b i 7.28 N, 15.9°　　**ii** 4.47 N, 63.4°

c i 4 N, −90°　　　**ii** 7.21 N, −33.7°

4 a i 3 m s^{-2} right　　**ii** 2 m s^{-2} left

b i 3 m s^{-2} down　　**ii** 0.8 m s^{-2} up

c i 0 m s^{-2}　　　**ii** 0 m s^{-2}

d i 6 m s^{-2} left　　**ii** 2 m s^{-2} down

5 a i $(-4\mathbf{i} + 6\mathbf{j})$ m s^{-2}　　**ii** $(2\mathbf{i} - 3\mathbf{j})$ m s^{-2}

b i $(\mathbf{i} + 1.5\mathbf{j})$ m s^{-2}　　**ii** $(0.8\mathbf{i} + 0.1\mathbf{j})$ m s^{-2}

6 a i 15 N   **ii** 14 N
  b i 15 N   **ii** 8 N
  c i 12 N   **ii** 4 N
  d i 7 N   **ii** 3 N

7 1200 kg

8 20 kg

9 a 8.06 N   **b** 29.7°

Exercise 21C

1 2 m s^{-2}

2 269 kg

3 a 760 N
  b 0.86 s less (8.40 compared to 9.26)

4 $p = 13.2, q = 30$

5 18.4 N, 151°

6 0.986 ms^{-2}

7 4.8 N

8 210 N

9 607 N

10 a 3.54 seconds   **b** 52.4 N

11 a proof   **b** 320 N   **c** 910 m

12 1.69 N against the direction of travel

13 a Proof
  b 115   **c** 164

Exercise 21D

1 a i 0.867 m s^{-2} upwards
    ii 1.7 m s^{-2} upwards
  b i 2.3 m s^{-2} downwards
    ii 1.36 m s^{-2} downwards

2 a i 110 N   **ii** 27.5 N
  b i 89.6 N   **ii** 35.4 N

3 a i 3.02 kg   **ii** 2.04 kg
  b i 2.36 kg   **ii** 1.77 kg

4 6.06 m s^{-2} downwards

5 a 1.22 kg
  b 2.45 m s^{-2} upwards

6 88.6 kg

7 1.08 N

8 0.344 kg

9 a 2.26 s   **b** 1.51 N

10 5060 N

11 1440 N

12 a 39.3 N   **b** 1.43 m s^{-2}

13 1260 N

Exercise 21E

1 a No   **b** Yes
  c Yes   **d** No

2 a 14 N   **b** 7 N
  c 16 N, 9 N   **d** 3 N, 6 N

3 a i $x = -18, y = -7$ **ii** $x = 6, y = -30$
  b i $x = 2, y = -10$ **ii** $x = -9, y = -4$
  c i $x = -8, y = 4$ **ii** $x = -15, y = 9$
  d i $x = 2, y = 3$ **ii** $x = -1, y = 5$

4 4 N, 5 N

5 $x = 2, y = 4$

6 $a = 8, b = 10$

7 7.28

8 12 N

9 19 N thrust

10 $a = 6, b = -3.5, m = 5$

11 57.3 N, because $\mathbf{F} = (-57\mathbf{i} + 6\mathbf{j})$ N

12 a $\mathbf{F} = \begin{pmatrix} 17 \\ -25 \end{pmatrix}$ **b** 30.2 N, $\theta = 55.8°$

Mixed practice 21

1 a 863 kg   **b** Lower mass

2 11.9

3 a 0.816 m s^{-2} **b** 25.2 s

4 a 27.3 kg   **b** 293 N
  c 268 N
  d i Does not contribute to system mass
    ii Constant tension throughout, perfectly transmits tension forces

5 a $p = -2.6, q = -3.8$ **b** $\begin{pmatrix} 1.04 \\ 1.52 \end{pmatrix}$ m s^{-2}

6 a 0.327 m s^{-2} **b** 6.86 N

7 a 481 N   **b** 8.33 s

8 98.5 N, 60.8°

9 19.2 N, 141°

10 a 19.2 N, 038.7°   **b** 19.2 N, 219°

11 16.8 N, thrust

12 a $(7.5\mathbf{i} - 0.75\mathbf{j})$ m s^{-2} **b** 30.1 N, 174°

13 165 N, 13.8° above horizontal

Chapter 22

Before you start...

1 2.92 m s^{-2} to the right.

2 333 N

3 $x = 2, y = 6$

4 a 0.4 m s^{-2} **b** 15 seconds

Exercise 22A

1 5.49 m s^{-2}

2 65 kg

3 5.32 m

4 a 0.306 m s^{-2} **b** 1.84 s

5 a 1.18 N   **b** 1.43 s

   c 1.18 N   **d** 2.01×10^{-25} m

Exercise 22B

1 a i

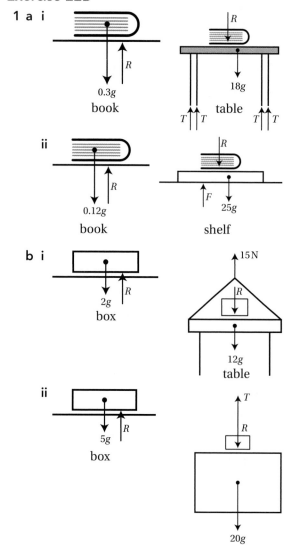

b i

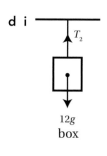

c i

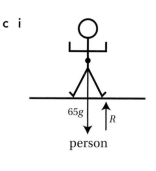

ii

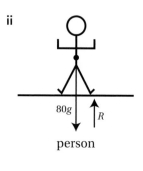

d i

ii

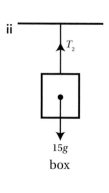

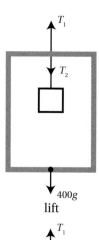

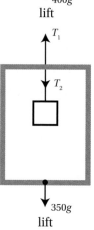

2 a i 110 N   **ii** 80 N

  b i 95 N   **ii** 130 N

3 17.9 N

4 79 N

5 1220 N

6 1.18 N

7 11.0 kg

8 a 5560 N   **b** 364 N

9 a 1190 N   **b** 833 N

10 355 kg

11 a Up   **b** 6590 N

Exercise 22C

1 650 N

2 $F = 46$ N, $R = 754$ N

3 250 N

4 a 1.54 N   **b** 11.3 N

5 a 25.7 N   **b** 63.7 N

6 122 N, 54.2 N

7 a 5.88 N   **b** 140 N

8 268 N

Work it out 22.1

Solutions 2 and 3 are both correct.

Exercise 22D

1 a 12.7 m s^{-2} **b** 4850 N

2 12.6 N, 22.1 N

3 37.5 N

4 1120 N

5 a 312 N   **b** 0.720 s

6 a 901 N, 530 N   **b** 833 N, 490 N

7 a 10.8 kN   **b** 5.5 kN, 2.75 kN

8 a Driving (driving force = 2000 N)

   b Tension of 1000 N between the locomotive and the first carriage, thrust of 1000 N between the two carriages

Exercise 22E

1 745 N

2 1.63 m s^{-2}, 57.2 N

3 a 58.8 N   **b** 2.8 m s^{-2}, 42 N

4 2.53 kg

5 $k = 5$

6 a 19.6 N   **b** 1.23 m s^{-2}

7 8.91 kg

8 a 19.2 N, 1.96 kg

   b i 71.3 N   **ii** 15 N

9 46.1 N

10 0.58, 1.10

11 a $2x$ **b** $2a$

   c 35.3 N

12 $5 \leqslant M \leqslant 15$

13 Discussion

Mixed practice 22

1 50.9 kg

2 a 0.966 m s^{-2} **b** 529 N

3 576 N

4 1.18 N

5 29.4 N, 58.8 N

6 707 N

7 a 2790 N   **b** 1810 N

8 a 1130 N

   b i 2.1 m s^{-2} downwards   **ii** 4040 N

9 42.2 kg

10 a 1.5   **b** 51.0 N, 14.7 N

11 39.2 N, 46.0 N

12 a 33.2 N   **b** 18 N or 26 N

   c 1.84 kg or 2.65 kg

13 a 400 N, 1300 N   **b** 700 N, 2350 N

14 a 4.85 N   **b** 0.55

   c 0.84 m s^{-1} **d** 0.756 m

15 a 22.0 N

   b No (stops after total distance of 1.30 m)

16 a 753 N   **b** 75 N

   c Box B moves on top of box A.

17 a 1.43 s   **b** 3.13 m

   c 2.14 s

Focus on ... 4

Focus on ... Proof 4

1 proof

2 a $\dfrac{2s}{a+b}$ **b** $\dfrac{s(a+b)}{2ab}$

c, d Proof

Focus on ... Problem solving 4

1 814 m

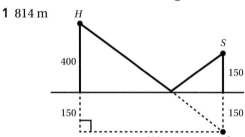

2 $\sqrt{5}$ m; $\sqrt{3}$ through cube

3 $3\sqrt{2}$; $\sqrt{14}$ through cuboid

4 $\sqrt{h^2+\pi^2 r^2}$

Focus on ... Modelling 4

1 12.5 m

2 0.25%

3 0.04%

4 i 510 m   **ii** 0.25%   **iii** 0.04%

5 $120a = 180 - 40v$; remember that $a = \dfrac{\mathrm{d}v}{\mathrm{d}t}$

6 $v = 1.5t$

7 Note that when there is air resistance, the cyclist can never exceed the speed of 4.5 m s^{-1} (this is called **terminal velocity**).

	a 0.5 m s^{-1}	**b** 2 m s^{-1}	**c** 5 m s^{-1}
without air resistance	0.333 s	1.33 s	3.33 s
with air resistance	0.353 s	1.76 s	–
% difference	5.7%	24%	–

Ignoring air resistance is only reasonable in the initial stages of the motion.

8 a, b and **9 a, b**

	a Speed after 1 second (m s^{-1})		**b** Speed after 10 seconds (m s^{-1})	
	air resistance ignored	with air resistance	air resistance ignored	with air resistance
parachutist	9.8	9.69	98	51.1
coin	9.8	9.00	98	18.8

9 c i 1 s   **ii** 10 s

d The model is suitable for short distances (a few metres), although there is already a noticeable difference for coin (but not for the parachutist). It is not suitable over distances as long as 10 m; the discrepancy is much larger for the coin.

Cross-topic review exercise 4

1 $(6\mathbf{i} + 4\mathbf{j})$ m s^{-2}

2 2.4 m s^{-1}

3 6.34 m s^{-1}

4 a 1.90   **b** 71.6°

5 a 4.9 m s^{-1} **b** 1.23 m
   c 5.88 m s^{-1}

6 a 4.6 m s^{-2} downwards   **b** 2500 N
   c mass of the cable was not included in the calculation

7 a $u = 4$, $a = 6$ **b** 783 kg

8 297 N, thrust

9 a i $v = 3t^2 - 22t + 35$
     ii $\dfrac{7}{3}$ and 5 s
     iii 35 m s^{-1}
   b 44.0 m

10 3

11 a 27.4 m s^{-1} **b** 107 m
   c i Figure 2
     ii Figure 1 has zero initial velocity; figure 3 has decreasing velocity.

12 a 8.60 m s^{-1} **b** 1.39 s

   c

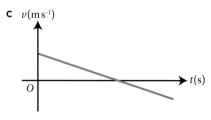

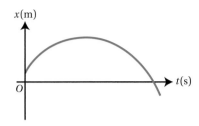

13 a $a = 0.012t - 0.18$ **b** Proof   **c** 30 m

14 a $v = 0.3t^2 - 0.6t + 0.2$, $a = 0.6t - 0.6$

  b Proof   **c** 0.423 s, 1.58 s   **d** 3 s

AS Practice paper 1

1 $\dfrac{4}{3}$

2 $\dfrac{19}{7}$

3 a $-11\mathbf{i} + 6\mathbf{j}$ **b** $\sqrt{370}$

4 $f'(x) = 6x$

5 a $AB = \cos\alpha$, $BC = \sin\alpha$ **b** Proof

6 a $\left(\dfrac{1}{4}, \dfrac{23}{8}\right)$ and $(6, 0)$

  b

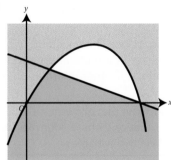

  c $p = -2$, $q = -15$

7 $(x - 21)^2 + y^2 = 841$

8 0.0725

9 a Obtain a list of all registered voters, numbered sequentially. Use a random number generator to select 200 numbers from the list, ignoring repeats. The sample is made up of voters with those numbers.

  b $p = 0.133 > 0.05$, insufficient evidence that the proportion of undecided voters has decreased

10 a No correlation   **b** 2.24

  c 6 outliers above 6.23   **d** Urban

AS Practice paper 2

1 30°, 150°

2 a

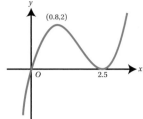

  b

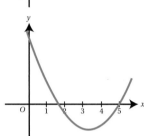

3 $-1, 2$

4 a $1 - 4x + 7x^2 - 7x^2 + \ldots$ **b** -21

5 a $a = -8$, $f(x) = (x - 2)^2(x + 3)$

  b

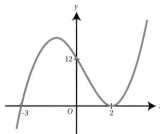

6 a e.g. 19   **b** Proof

7 a $A = 30\,000$, $k = 0.4$ **b** 8.77 days

8 a

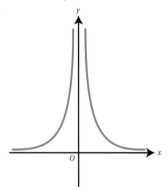

  b Proof

9 $(6.8\mathbf{i} - 0.2\mathbf{j})\,\mathrm{m\,s}^{-2}$

10 a $7.98\,\mathrm{m\,s}^{-1}$ downwards   **b** 2.47 seconds

  c t would increase because air resistance would make the ball travel more slowly.

11 138 N

12 a $a = -4.05\,\mathrm{m\,s}^{-2}$ **b** $t = 13$

  c 9.96 s

Glossary

Acceleration: The rate of change of velocity.

Acceleration of freefall: Acceleration caused by the force of gravity. (See also **gravitational acceleration**.)

Acceptance region: The set of values of the test statistic which do not provide sufficient evidence to reject the null hypothesis.

Air resistance: The force opposing the motion of an object whilst travelling through air.

Alternative hypothesis: In hypothesis testing, specifies how you think the proportion may have changed. It is denoted H_1.

Amplitude: The maximum 'height' of a periodic function, i.e. half of the distance from the minimum value of y to the maximum value of y.

Asymptote: A line that a function gets increasingly close to (but never meets).

Average speed: Total distance divided by the time taken.

Average velocity: Change in displacement divided by time taken.

Base vectors: Vectors **i** and **j** which can be used to express other vectors.

Biased: 1. A sample that is not a good representation of a population. 2. An unfair dice or a coin.

Binomial coefficients: The constants in the expansions of expressions of the form $(a + b)^n$.

Binomial distribution: Probability distribution of the number of 'successes' out of a fixed number of independent trials.

Binomial expression: An expression that contains two terms.

Binomial theorem: A 'pattern' for quickly evaluating expansions of expressions of the form $(a + b)^n$.

Bivariate: Data in pairs coming from the same source (for example, a person's height and weight).

Box-and-whisker plot: A statistical diagram showing the range, quartiles and median of a set of data.

Braking force: A force that causes an object to slow down.

Census: Collection of data from the whole of a population.

Chord: The line segment between two points on a curve.

Cluster sampling: The population is split into groups (clusters) based on convenience; a simple random sample of clusters is then chosen to study further.

Coefficient: A constant in front of (multiplying) a variable.

Collinear: Points that lie along the same straight line.

Complement: Everything except a given event. The sum of the probabilities of an event and its complement is one.

Component form: A vector written in a way that shows its components (i.e. either as a column vector or using **i**, **j** base vectors).

Components (of a vector): The values pertaining to the x and y directions.

Component vector: A component of a vector in the direction of one of the base vectors. For example, the component vectors of 2**i** + 3**j** are 2**i** and 3**j**.

Conditional probability: A probability that depends on the result of a preceding event.

Congruent (expressions): Expressions connected by the identity symbol; they are equal for all values of the variable(s).

Constant of integration: The constant introduced whenever indefinite integration takes place. It can be found if other information is provided.

Constraint: A condition that allows a variable to be eliminated in situations where a function would normally depend on two variables.

Continuous (data): Data that can take any value within a range, e.g. height.

Correlation: A relationship between two variables where, as one variable increases, the other either increases or decreases.

Correlation coefficient: A number measuring the 'strength' of correlation between two variables.

Counter example: An example used to prove that some proposition is not always true.

Critical region: The set of values of the test statistic that provide sufficient evidence to reject the null hypothesis. (See also **rejection region**.)

Critical value: The value at the edge of the critical region.

Cumulative frequency: The total number of things less than or equal to a particular value.

Cumulative frequency diagram: A curve showing the values of the variable on the horizontal axis and cumulative frequency on the vertical axis.

Cumulative probability: The sum of the probabilities up to and including a specified value of the variable.

Deceleration: Negative acceleration. The rate of change of velocity as an object slows down.

Decreasing: A function whose values decrease as the value of the input increases.

Definite integration: The evaluation of an integral between two points (this eliminates the need for the constant of integration and gives a numerical answer).

Degree (of a polynomial): The highest power of x occurring in a polynomial function.

Derivative: A function which gives the gradient of $y = f(x)$ at any point. (Also sometimes called the 'gradient function'.)

Differentiation: The process of finding a 'gradient function' of a given function.

Differentiation from first principles: The process of finding the derivative by considering the limit of the gradient of a chord.

Direct proportion: A relationship between two variables in which their quotient is constant.

Direction (of a vector): The angle the vector makes with the horizontal

Discrete (data): Data that can only take certain specific values (for example, the scores when rolling a dice).

Discrete (probability distribution): A probability distribution with a finite, specific list of outcomes (for example, the scores when rolling a dice).

Discriminant: In the quadratic formula, the expression $b^2 - 4ac$ (within the square root) which determines how many roots a quadratic equation has.

Displacement (mechanics): The vector from the initial position to the current position of a particle.

Displacement vector: The vector representing the 'translation' from one point to another.

Driving force: A force provided by, for example, the engine of a car, that causes an object to accelerate in the direction of motion.

Equation: A mathematical statement involving an '=' sign.

Equation of motion: An equation for displacement, velocity or acceleration in terms of time.

Equilibrium: A state where the resultant of the forces on an object is zero.

Exponential decay: A relationship of the form $y = a^x$, where $0 < a < 1$. As x increases, y decreases.

Exponential equation: An equation with the 'unknown' variable in the power.

Exponential function: A function with the variable in the power.

Exponential growth: A relationship of the form $y = a^x$, where $a > 1$. As x increases, so does y.

Extrapolation: Predicting results beyond the limits of the collected data.

Factor theorem: A theorem relating to polynomials, $p(x)$: if $p(a) = 0$ then $(x - a)$ is a factor of $p(x)$.

Factorial: The product of integers from 1 to n. Denoted $n!$

Force: An interaction that acts to change the velocity of an object.

Frequency density: In a histogram, equals class frequency ÷ class width.

Friction: A force (between surfaces) that acts to resist motion. Always acts parallel to the surface.

Function: A number machine that changes an input into an output following a particular rule.

Gradient: A number measuring the steepness of a line or curve.

Gradient function: See '**Derivative**'.

Gravitational acceleration: Acceleration caused by the force of gravity. (See also **acceleration of freefall**.)

Gravity: The force of attraction of a massive object (for example, the Earth) on all objects around it.

Histogram: A chart that resembles a bar chart but where the area is used to represent the frequency. The vertical scale is the frequency density.

Hypothesis test: A procedure for determining whether a given sample provides significant evidence that a population parameter (mean/spread/proportion) has changed from a previously known or assumed value.

Identity: A relation which is true for all values of the unknown. It is given the '≡' symbol.

In equilibrium: See **equilibrium**.

Increasing: A function whose values increase as the value of the input increases.

Indefinite integration: Integration without limits. There will always be a constant of integration here.

Independent (events): Two (or more) events where the probability of the second (subsequent) events does not depend on the outcome of the first.

Inextensible: Does not stretch. (In Mechanics, relating to string, rope, etc.)

Instantaneous acceleration: Acceleration at a specific point in time; it equals the derivative of the velocity function (and the gradient of the velocity – time graph).

Instantaneous velocity: Velocity at a specific point in time; on a displacement–time graph, it is given by the gradient of a tangent to the graph.

Instantaneously at rest: An object is instantaneously at rest when $v = 0$. The object may change direction at this point.

Integer: Whole number.

Integration: The process of 'reversing' differentiation.

Interquartile range: A measure of spread. The difference between the lower and upper quartile of a data set.

Interval notation: A form of notation to represent all numbers in a range . This uses the end points of the range in ( ) brackets if the end points are not included, and [ ] brackets if the end points are included.

Inverse proportion: A relationship between two variables in which their product is constant.

Lead coefficient: The coefficient of the highest degree term in a polynomial.

Leading order term: The term of a polynomial with the highest degree.

Light: In Mechanics, when an object's weight is small enough to be negligible and so can be ignored in calculations.

Limits of integration: The lower and upper values used for a definite integral.

Linear function: A function of the form $y = mx + c$, whose graph is a straight line.

Local maximum: A turning point whose value is higher than the values to either side of it. (This may not be the largest value of the function overall.)

Local minimum: A turning point whose value is lower than the values to either side of it. (This may not be the smallest value of the function overall.)

Logarithm: The power to which a base needs to be raised to produce a given value.

Magnitude (modulus): The 'size' of a vector. (See also **modulus**.)

Mathematical model: A 'simplification' of a real world situation into mathematical equations.

Mean: A measure of average; it equals the sum of all the data divided by the number of data values.

Median: The middle value when the data are arranged in order.

Mid-interval value: For grouped data, the centre value of a group.

Modulus: 1. The magnitude of a vector. 2. The distance of the number from the origin: for example, the modulus of −3 is 3.

Mutually exclusive: Events that cannot occur at the same time.

Natural logarithm: The logarithm to base e.

Net force: The resultant force when more than one force acts on an object. (See also **resultant force**.)

Newton: The unit of the magnitude of a force. (Named after Sir Isaac Newton.)

Newton's third law: If object A exerts a force on object B, then object B exerts a force on object A, with the same magnitude but opposite direction.

Normal: A line perpendicular to a tangent at its point of contact to a curve.

Normal reaction force: The force exerted by a surface on any object in contact with that surface. It acts in the direction perpendicular to the surface and away from it.

Null hypothesis: In hypothesis testing, specifies the previous or assumed population proportion. Denoted H_0.

One-tail test: A hypothesis test where the alternative hypothesis takes the form $p < \alpha$ or $p > \alpha$.

Opportunity sampling: Choosing respondents based upon their availability and convenience.

Origin: The point with coordinates (0, 0).

Outliers: Values that do not appear to fit the 'trend' of a data set.

Parabola: The curve in the shape of a quadratic graph.

Parallel (vector): A vector that is a scalar multiple of another vector.

Parameter (of a statistical distribution): A numerical characteristic of the population, such as its mean or variance.

Particle: An object that has mass but no size: it occupies a single point in space.

Particle model: A mathematical model which assumes that an object occupies a single point in space.

Percentiles: The data value a given percentage of the way through the data when it is put in order.

Period (of a function): A value p such that $f(x + p) = f(x)$ for all x.

Periodic: A function that repeats after a certain period.

Perpendicular bisector: A line through the midpoint of a line segment between two points, and at right angles to it.

Polynomial: A function that is a sum of terms containing non-negative (positive or zero) integer powers of x.

Population: All the individuals of interest for collection of data.

Population parameter: See 'parameter'.

Position vector: The vector connecting a point to a fixed origin.

Probability distribution: The list of all possible outcomes together with their probabilities.

Proof by exhaustion: Checking that all possibilities are true.

p-value: The probability of the observed or a more extreme sample value occurring if H_0 is correct.

Quartile: The value of the data item $\frac{1}{4}$ and $\frac{3}{4}$ of the way through the data (when put in order)

Quota sampling: The proportion of members of the sample with certain characteristics is fixed to be the same as in the whole population; the individuals for each group are then selected by opportunity sampling.

Random variable: A variable whose value is subject to variations due to chance.

Range: A measure of spread. The difference of the largest and smallest values in a data set.

Rate of change: The rate at which one variable changes in relation to another variable.

Rationalising the denominator: The process of removing surds from a denominator.

Regression line: A line of best fit to bivariate data.

Rejection region: The set of values of the test statistic that provide sufficient evidence to reject the null hypothesis. (See also **critical region**.)

Representative: A sample that is a good representation of a population.

Resultant force: A single force producing the same effect as several forces acting together. (See also **net force**.)

Resultant vector: The result of the sum of two (or more) vectors.

Sample: A part of a population.

Scalar: A quantity that has magnitude but no direction (for example, mass).

Scalar multiplication: The operation of multiplying a vector by a scalar.

Second derivative: The result of differentiating a function twice.

Set notation: Notation used to describe sets.

Significance level: In a hypothesis test, a number that specifies the probability which is sufficiently small to be accepted as evidence against the null hypothesis.

Simple random sampling: A method of sampling where every sample (of a given size) has an equal chance of being selected.

Smooth: A surface for which the frictional force is so small it can be ignored.

Standard deviation: A measure of spread. This uses all the data in the data set.

Stationary point: A point on a curve where the tangent is horizontal and so the gradient is zero. (See also **turning point**.)

Stem-and-leaf diagram: A way or recording data by sorting it in rows according to the first digit.

Stratified sampling: The proportion of members of the sample with certain characteristics is fixed to be the same as in the whole population; the individuals for each group are then selected randomly.

Substitution: The replacement of every occurrence of one variable in one equation by its expression from another equation.

Surd: Any number that needs to be expressed using roots.

Systematic sampling: Participants are taken at regular intervals from a list of the population.

Tangent: 1. A straight line which touches the curve at a point but does not intersect it again (near the given point). 2. The trigonometric function, $\tan x$.

Tension: The force exerted by a rope (rod, stick, etc.) when it is pulling an object.

Test statistic: In hypothesis testing, a value determined from the sample to be compared to what is expected under the null hypothesis.

Thrust: A pushing force.

Trigonometric functions: Sine, cosine and tangent.

Turning point: A local maximum or minimum point on a curve (See also **stationary point** and **vertex**.)

Two-tail test: A hypothesis test where the alternative hypothesis takes the form $p \neq \alpha$.

Unit vector: A vector with magnitude one.

Variance: The square of the standard deviation.

Vector: A quantity that has both size (magnitude) and direction. (For example, velocity.)

Velocity: Speed in a certain direction.

Vertex: For a parabola, the maximum or minimum point. (See also **turning point**.)

Weight: The force with which the Earth attracts an object.

y-intercept: The point(s) where a line or curve crosses the y-axis.

Index

Acknowledgements

The authors and publishers acknowledge the following sources of copyright material and are grateful for the permissions granted. While every effort has been made, it has not always been possible to identify the sources of all the material used, or to trace all copyright holders. If any omissions are brought to our notice, we will be happy to include the appropriate acknowledgements on reprinting.

Thanks to the following for permission to reproduce images:

Cover image: Radius Images/Getty Images

Back cover: Fabian Oefner www.fabianoefner.com

zhudifeng/Getty Images; Lev Savitskiy/Getty Images; Tara Moore/Getty Images; Tinyevilhog/Getty Images; pexels.com; De Agostini Picture Library/Getty Images; Tetra Images/Getty Images; from2015/Getty Images; Jason Edwards/Getty Images; baona/Getty Images; Celso Da Silva/EyeEm/Getty Images; Marco Simoni/Getty Images; Raimund Linke/Getty Images; Oli Kellett/Getty Images; Jeremy Horner/Getty Images; zodebala/Getty Images; Huw Jones/Getty Images; hakkiarslan/Getty Images; UniversalImagesGroup/Getty Images; SCIEPRO/Getty Images; Laguna Design/Getty Images; Culture Club/Getty Images; Willie Schumann/EyeEm/Getty Images; Lee Beach/EyeEm/Getty Images; Michael Reinhard/Getty Images; Kent Miles/Getty Images; Marcin Bulinski/EyeEm/Getty Images; UniversalImagesGroup/Getty Images; allanswart/Getty Images